WATCH IT MADE
IN THE U.S.A.

*A Visitor's Guide to the Best
Factory Tours and Company Museums*

Karen Axelrod & Bruce Brumberg

AVALON
TRAVEL

Dedications

To the American workers, engineers, and managers who strive to make the best quality products in the world.

To our marriage and the love and times we share together.

To Hilary Dana and Gregory Seth, the best products we've made.

Hilary and Gregory Brumberg inspecting bears they just stuffed at the Basic Brown Bear Factory in San Francisco, CA.

Preface

When you were younger, you probably read *Charlie and the Chocolate Factory* or watched the movie version, *Willy Wonka and the Chocolate Factory*. As you may remember, Charlie won the opportunity to visit a chocolate factory by finding a special golden ticket in his Wonka Bar. His luck led to a fascinating journey.

This book is like that golden ticket in Charlie's chocolate bar. With this guide you can visit factory tours and company museums throughout the U.S.A. Whether you're with your family, traveling alone, or on a field or business trip, you'll have fun, discover how well-known products are made, and learn what these companies did to grow and prosper. Along the way, you will receive plenty of free samples and tastes.

Ours is a harried society that just wants to plug it in, mix it with milk, turn the ignition, or open the box. We want you to experience the excitement of watching people and machines make the food we eat, the cars we drive, the musical instruments we play, and the sporting goods we use.

After visiting (by foot or armchair) the more than 300 companies featured in this book, you'll marvel at the behind-the-scenes processes involved in producing the products we take for granted. You'll be proud of the hardworking American people and companies that make it all possible. We like to say that this book gives you the opportunity to go out and "kick the tires" of the American economy.

To compile the list of companies that offer tours, museums, and visitor centers, we followed many paths and traveled thousands of miles. The book focuses on recognized national or regional companies that make familiar products, whether chocolates, cars, clothes, toys, or beer. Each tour or museum either has regular hours or is open to the general public by reservation.

The fourth edition includes hundreds of factory tours, company museums, and visitor centers to enjoy. We've completely updated all the existing write-ups and added 60 new sites! We have branched out to include NASA tours and the U.S. Olympic Training Center. (Unfortunately, we had to drop some sites from the book because facilities closed or moved, tours were discontinued, or companies didn't want the continued publicity. September 11, 2001, with its heightened physical security concerns, had an impact.)

In addition to the new write-ups, this edition has several new features. It is organized geographically, with more maps, to make it easier for you to plan trips. The new "For Kids by Kids" section, written by our daughter Hilary, highlights some of the coolest aspects of her favorite tours.

We hope you will take the opportunity to use this book to visit the companies that make your favorite products and keep our economy strong. Even if you cannot physically visit a company, our narrative description gives you a vicarious feel for the experience. In addition, companies may have virtual tours on their websites. However, nothing matches the true sights and sounds of actually visiting. Plus, because most of the tours in this book are free, and many give free samples, factory tours and company museums remain the best vacation value in America.

We sincerely hope that your adventures bring you as much enjoyment and wonder as we have experienced! Enjoy the tours. But don't stuff yourself with the free samples as the guests did on the tour of Willy Wonka's chocolate factory!

Watch It Made in the U.S.A. Regions

C A N A D A

WASHINGTON

PACIFIC NORTHWEST
page 335

OREGON

MONTANA

ROCKY MOUNTAINS
page 321

IDAHO

WYOMING

NORTH DAKOTA

SOUTH DAKOTA

NEBRASKA

NEVADA

UTAH

H E A R T

CALIFORNIA
page 355

SOUTHWEST
page 311

COLORADO

KANSAS

PACIFIC OCEAN

ARIZONA

NEW MEXICO

OKLAHOMA

TEXAS
page 297

HAWAII
page 391

PACIFIC OCEAN

M E X I C O

RUSSIA

CANADA

ALASKA
page 391

PACIFIC OCEAN

D A

MAINE

MINNESOTA

Lake
Superior

M I C H I G A N

Lake
Huron

VT

NH

NEW
ENGLAND
page 57

MA

NEW YORK

CT RI

WISCONSIN

Lake
Michigan

NJ

GREAT LAKES
page 147

Erie
Lake

PENNSYLVANIA

IOWA

ILLINOIS

INDIANA

OHIO

DE

MID-ATLANTIC
page 93

L A N D
page 277

WEST
VIRGINIA

VIRGINIA

MISSOURI

KENTUCKY

NORTH
CAROLINA

TENNESSEE

ARKANSAS

SOUTH
page 221

SOUTH
CAROLINA

GEORGIA

OCEAN

MISSISSIPPI

ALABAMA

LOUISIANA

ATLANTIC

FLORIDA

Gulf   of   Mexico

CAYMAN
ISLANDS

CUBA

JAMAICA

HAITI

PUERTO
RICO

CARIBBEAN
page 391

DOMINICAN
REPUBLIC

U.S. VIRGIN
ISLANDS

Contents

Introduction

Featured Tours

Regions

How to Use This Book

Watch It Made in the U.S.A. is much more than just a directory. Therefore, we did not write it by sending surveys to companies and then publishing a compilation of the responses. We visited most of the companies included here. We took periodic breaks from our regular jobs to travel the U.S.A. in search of its economic soul. For those companies that time did not permit us to visit, we either hired writers to do so or conducted in-depth phone interviews that required companies to send us videos, articles, and tour scripts in addition to reviewing their websites. After we wrote each feature, we verified its accuracy with the company.

Each feature includes a narrative description and a practical information section on the company tour or museum. This book is organized regionally from east to west across the United States. Each state is listed alphabetically within its region (see map on pages IV–V) and write-ups appear in alphabetical order within each state unless positioning of photographs necessitated slight alterations.

Narrative Description

Some people are awed by fast-moving bottling machines and fascinated by robotic welders or giant presses, while others appreciate the artisanship of a glassblower, woodworker, or potter. The narrative description will help you determine which tours you and your family will enjoy.

Each feature has a three- to five-paragraph write-up that captures the highlights of the tour and some background on the company. The write-ups also provide a basic understanding of how different products are made. We try to give you a sense of being there: what you might see, hear, smell, taste, or even touch; whether a company is big or small; and whether you actually visit the factory floor or watch production through glass windows. We wrote this part in a conversational tone so that even the armchair traveler would be able to vicariously experience the tour or museum.

Practical Information Section

The second part of the feature provides basic practical information on location, hours, admission charge, freebies, age and group requirements, disabled access, gift shop and outlet stores, and nearby attractions. The category titles in this section are self-explanatory. The following are special notes on the different categories in this section:

Cost: Many company tours, visitor centers, and museums are free or have a nominal charge, which makes them a great vacation value. However, charges may change after this book's printing, so call ahead.

Freebies: Many tours give samples, ranging from beer and ice cream to miniature baseball bats. Remember: these companies are proud of their products, and your appreciative acceptance of free samples is a compliment to their work.

Video/DVD Shown: These are often interesting, informative, and even humorous. They provide a close-up view inside machines and show production steps not seen on the tour. If videos are optional, we suggest you view them before going on the tour. They help you understand what you will see.

Reservations Needed: If a company requires reservations, it is crucial to do so. Do not just show up—you will not get a tour. Make reservations as far in advance as possible. Some companies require individuals and families to join a scheduled group tour that has not reached its maximum size, which this section will note. For these companies, you need to be more flexible in scheduling your visit. Many companies produce a range of products; if you have certain favorites, call ahead to find out what will be in production on the day of your visit.

Days and Hours: These are the hours for the tour or museum, not for the gift shop or outlet store. Hours are subject to change, and factories may shut down (hopefully for expansion construction), so call before your visit to avoid disappointment. Automobile

SAFETY GUIDELINES

Lawsuits are a product we make too many of in the U.S.A. During our research we discovered many companies that have discontinued their tours because of fears of lawsuits from injured guests and increases in liability insurance rates for allowing public visitors. Follow basic safety rules and your common sense to avoid injury.

The authors and publisher of *Watch It Made in the U.S.A.* make no warranty, expressed or implied, regarding the safety of any of the tours in this book and assume no liability with respect to the consequences of using the information contained herein. If you have any special safety concerns, contact the companies directly before you decide to visit.

The factories in this book are all working facilities, not full-time tourist attractions. While many of them provide the kind of space-age excitement you normally see only in the movies, these factories are the real thing, with potentially dangerous machines.

If you are injured, it is likely that the company will completely discontinue its public tours. Please listen to your tour guide and read any safety warnings. Remember the following rules:

1. Do not wander away from your tour guide or away from any specified tour path. Many factory tours have lines painted on the floor. You must stay between them.

2. Parents and adult group leaders should keep a close watch on children. Kids will be very curious about the sights, sounds, and smells, and may be tempted to wander off and touch things that could be dangerous.

3. Wear any protective equipment that you are provided with on your tour. This may include eyeglasses, earplugs, hard hats, or hairnets. If you have trouble wearing any of these items, tell your tour guide immediately.

4. Do not touch anything, including machines, products, parts, or boxes, unless your tour guide specifically hands something to you.

5. Wear closed-toe shoes with rubber soles that have good traction. Do not wear sandals or high heels (many companies will not allow you to go on the tour). Wear shoes that will provide protection against sharp objects and that are comfortable for walking. Floors can be slippery. For safety reasons, it is best not to wear shorts.

plants, for example, often temporarily discontinue their tours so assembly lines can be reconfigured for major model changes. Many of the companies with regular tour schedules have tour hotlines and websites that answer common questions on schedule changes and directions. The hours listed in the book are the range during which tours are given, unless a frequency is specified. Holiday schedules vary by company. For example, some companies view the day after Thanksgiving as a holiday.

Plan to Stay: We included the amount of time needed for the basic visit, plus extra time for additions such as the gift shop. The length of time spent on self-guided tours depends on the level of your interest. A short recommended time provides an indication of the company size or the amount you'll see.

Minimum Age: Tours have minimum age restrictions because of safety and insurance requirements. Companies strictly enforce these limits.

Disabled Access: Almost all of the tours in this book are working factories first and not full-time visitor attractions. They try to accommodate people with disabilities while focusing on the safety concerns of both visitors and workers. Few companies told us absolutely "no" for disabled access. Almost all plants, however, have some limited-access areas, which we tried to note, and some may require advance notice. We are not commenting on the restrooms or compliance with the Americans with Disabilities Act standards, only the ease with which people with disabilities can visit these companies.

Group Requirements: Reservations are almost always required for groups, and some companies have maximum group sizes. This section is useful for group tour planners.

Special Information: Re-read the safety guidelines (page XII), since we do not repeat them in this section. For worker safety, security, and proprietary reasons, many tours do not allow photography (which includes snapshot and video cameras). "No photography" refers to factory production areas, not gift shops, museums, and display areas. If you or a family member are sensitive to noise, smells, or temperature changes, be aware of these conditions when selecting a tour. However, these shocks to the senses are part of the exciting realism of factory tours.

Gift Shop/Outlet Store: Most gift shops sell logoed items and company products. The real factory outlet stores offer great bargains. Hours are often longer than the tour hours.

Directions: While we have made our best efforts to give you accurate narrative directions (double-checked with the companies and often given from two possible directions), call the company for directions or check its website. At the top of each write-up is the street address of the factory or museum.

Nearby Attractions: To round out your day, we list nearby parks, museums, and other activities. We also draw your attention to other nearby factory tours and company museums. These factory tours and museums, which are listed first, are within a larger radius from the plant than the other nearby attractions. In addition to the more than 300 full-page company features in the book, we list more than 150 additional factory tours in this section (phone numbers included). For reasons of variety, quality, tour restrictions, or time, we decided not to write full features on these other tours.

Trademarks

We have used the commonly known company name rather than the longer corporate name. To the best of our knowledge, all of the product names in this book are trademarks. Throughout the text, we capitalized the first letter of all words that are trademarks. When companies provided us with their logos, we included them at no charge. The logos in no way imply that a company is a sponsor of the book. These logos are also trademarks that cannot be reproduced without a company's express consent.

In accordance with standard practice in publishing, we do not use symbols denoting registered trademarks with every registered tradename, as this would visually clutter the text. Such symbols appear only where the relevant company strongly required their inclusion for legal reasons. At the special request of The Walt Disney Company, we specifically state that this book refers to various trademarks, marks, and registered marks owned by The Walt Disney Company and Disney Enterprises, Inc., though we have not used trademark symbols with these names.

How Companies Were Selected

Our search for companies to include in *Watch It Made in the U.S.A.* began in stores where their products are sold. We went through supermarkets, department stores, car dealerships, and sporting goods stores, searching for the names of companies that make popular products in the U.S.A. Sometimes store owners thought we were competitors, as we would pick up a box, turn it over to see who made the product, and scribble down the company's address and phone number.

We also searched through directories and magazine ads, hunting down more manufacturers of U.S.A.—made products. We contacted state travel offices, local convention and visitors bureaus, and chambers of commerce looking for names of companies in their areas that gave tours. For the fourth edition, we did numerous Internet searches. Readers of the book and companies that had started tours also contacted us with suggested additions. These lists, which we continued making and updating throughout our writing and traveling, were only the start of our research.

Then we called... and called... and visited most of the sites in the book. We spoke with companies throughout the U.S.A., asking whether they give tours or have a museum (often called a "visitors center"). We didn't hide the fact that we were writing a book. We wanted to include only those companies that accept public visitors and would talk with us about their history, tours, and products.

No company pays for its written feature in *Watch It Made in the U.S.A.* We give the companies the opportunity to review their write-ups; however, we accept only factual changes from the companies. Each write-up is in our words, not theirs. The companies had to meet the following criteria:

1.   Tours open to the general public. Throughout our research we found companies that give tours only to buyers, to technical organizations, or upon special request. We did not include these companies or others that had too many requirements for visitors.

2.   Tours available to individuals and families. Some companies will give tours only to local school groups, senior citizen clubs, Boy and Girl Scout troops, or bus tour companies. To be included in *Watch It Made in the U.S.A.*, a company had to at least allow individuals and families not affiliated with a group tour to visit. You may need to join a scheduled group tour (or the company may combine individual requests to form a group) and make reservations far in advance, but every facility in this book should be open to you.

3.   Products of general interest that are worth traveling to see made. Unless you have a technical background or are in a specific industry, we thought that seeing how your favorite everyday products are made would hold the most fascination. In addition to tours of the icons of American business, we sought small companies that have good products and interesting tours. Most of the companies in the book make consumer-related or widely recognized products. We also selected companies where you could watch the completion of the final product; therefore we excluded parts manufacturers.

4.   Company did not object to being featured in this book. Companies generally do not make money from their tours. They give tours as a public and community service, often pulling employees from their regular jobs to conduct the tours. We excluded companies that did not want the calls and tour requests that this widely distributed book would generate, if the tour was not already mentioned in other public sources. A small number of companies asked not to be included after we had visited them and written our extensive features. In most cases we were able to retain their features after modifying the tour information to meet the companies' concerns. We italicized the qualifying language to alert you to the irregularities of tour availability. In a few instances we had to drop tours of well-known companies.

We will occasionally retain a write-up—even if

a tour has been temporarily discontinued—if we've learned that the tour may restart at some point in the future; an italicized note of explanation is included in the write-up. Given the enduring shelf-life of the book, we feel this long perspective is helpful to readers who will keep their copy for many years.

We strove to select companies from diverse industries and all areas of the country. We wanted to capture the industries for which different regions are known, such as cheese in Wisconsin, glass in West Virginia, movies in Southern California, bourbon in Kentucky, RVs in northern Indiana, Cajun hot sauces in Louisiana, and wood products in the Pacific Northwest. Certain high-tech industries, such as computer manufacturing and biotechnology, do not give regular public tours for proprietary reasons, so they are excluded by their choice. In other industries, such as beer brewing and newspaper publishing, tours are a standard practice; from this group we selected the most high-profile companies or those with interesting processes or histories.

We were surprised that companies in certain states, even though very industrial, do not seem interested in giving public tours. For example, while manufacturing-intensive states such as Pennsylvania, Wisconsin, and Ohio offer a variety of captivating tours, most New Jersey and Connecticut companies remain closed to the public. In contrast, companies in less industrial states such as Kentucky and Vermont have exhibited great pride in opening themselves to the public.

In addition to factory tours, we also included company museums or visitors centers. Some companies have actually replaced their public factory tours with educational and entertaining museums that explain how they started, succeeded, and make their products. These museums preserve the company's heritage and tell its story to the public, new employees, and customers. The Crayola FACTORY at Two Rivers Landing in downtown Easton, Pennsylvania, is an example. As Jelly Belly Candy Co.'s factory tours in Fairfield, California, have become so popular, the company opened Jelly Belly Center in Pleasant Prairie, Wisconsin. (Conversely, sometimes museums lead to tours. The Henry Ford, a nonprofit group unaffiliated with the Ford Motor Company, has added a tour of the nearby Ford Rouge factory to its attractions at the Henry Ford Museum and Greenfield Village in Dearborn, Michigan.) We did not include company museums that are like art exhibits. The museums we selected, like the tours, give you a sense of what the companies are all about.

Going Beyond This Book

We excluded wineries, power plants, chemical factories, meat processors, most service industries, and tobacco manufacturers. The company tours in this book are the easiest ones to join—you either just show up or call in advance to reserve a space. If you are interested in visiting a company not featured here, contact the public affairs or human resources department at the corporate headquarters or local plant. With persistence, you can tour many firms if you're not a direct competitor. Explain your individual request and also ask if the company offers tours for specialized business and technical groups (often for a fee).

No book like this has ever been published before. Since we will update this book again, we would like your comments on the sites you visit from this guide and on tours we should consider for the next edition. Please write us at Watch It Made in the U.S.A., c/o Avalon Travel Publishing, 1400 65th Street, Suite 250, Emeryville, CA 94608 and visit our website at www.factorytour.com. We hope this book's success will lead more companies to open their doors to the general public.

Advice for Business Travelers

These tours are not merely a new way to grab a free beer during a business trip to Milwaukee or St. Louis. At its core, *Watch It Made in the U.S.A.* is a travel guide to American business. Our business backgrounds led us to write this book. When we took a factory tour or visited a company museum, we discovered how that company makes and markets its products, how the company started and grew, and even whether it's a good stock investment.

From our visits, we developed ideas that we couldn't get from any newspaper, magazine, or business book. Sure, you can read a book about Ted Turner, Andy Grove, Mary Kay Ash, or Bill Gates—but *Watch It Made in the U.S.A.* tells you how to visit CNN, Intel, Mary Kay Cosmetics, or Microsoft to see the companies they founded in action. Visiting the sites in this book will spice up a business trip with new experiences that may help you in your own work.

Improve Your Understanding of Business News and Trends

The tours offer a new perspective on our economy, workplace productivity, and job creation. After visiting a few of the companies profiled, whether *Fortune* 500 corporations or typical small businesses making a quality product, you'll have a better filter for understanding business and economic news. The concepts of total quality management, re-engineering, just-in-time inventory, or *kaizen* (constant improvement), for example, which many companies in this book use in some form, have new meaning when you see how they are adapted to the production of baseball bats, cars, and chocolate. You'll also notice production and product trends before they are reported in the media and appear on store shelves.

Sources of Useful New Ideas

By visiting these companies, you will not only experience firsthand how they operate but also expose yourself to new business techniques. You

may even discover a company whose stock you want to own, as you have a chance to go beyond its financials, press releases, and annual report.

Don't think that these tours appeal only to people in manufacturing-related jobs. Many of the tours and museums show you much more than just how the company makes its products; they also reveal its marketing, management, and new-product development approach. To get the most from your visit, make it a point to look for and ask about innovative approaches and solutions that the company has developed, then think about how your business could adopt them. Try to discover what really makes the company successful and admired, then ponder how your firm can emulate it.

The companies' public relations departments may at times shape the tour scripts, but what you see, hear, sense, and ask cannot be totally controlled. The tour guides, especially those who are company retirees or volunteer line employees, can provide great insights and amusing anecdotes. However, while you want to be inquisitive, be careful not to sound like an industrial spy. Companies are very concerned about protecting what they view as proprietary technology, processes, or information, and, after September 11, 2001, their physical security.

These are not new worries. Kellogg's, for example, ended its cereal-factory tours in 1986 because of suspected spying by competitors. Because of these anxieties, some businesses have limited their tours, replaced them with museums or visitors centers (such as Kellogg's Cereal City USA in Battle Creek, Michigan), or asked us not to include them in the book.

Don't confine yourself to visiting firms that make products similar to your company's. Trips outside your own industry can provide stimulus, inspiration, and new techniques. The cross-fertilization of ideas from other industries helps develop business creativity. To have a "Learning Organization," one of the training buzzwords popularized by Peter Senge in *The Fifth Discipline*, you need to seek new experiences. In *A Whack on the Side of the Head,* author Roger von Oech writes "many good ideas have been discovered because someone poked around in an outside industry or discipline, and applied what he found to his own field." Follow von Oech's advice—be a business "explorer" and search for insights from companies outside your own industry.

In two of Tom Peters' best-selling business books, *In Search of Excellence* and *A Passion for Excellence,* he explains how the best managers practice a form of "management by walking around." Go out and walk around someone else's company—you'll be surprised at what you learn.

Business-Only Tours

The public tours in *Watch It Made in the U.S.A.* are suitable for both family and business travelers. They are either free or inexpensive. However, we have discovered higher-priced, in-depth tours and seminars for people who want to learn how a particular company manages workers and operations. For example, Disney Institute (www.disneyinstitute.com) offers a field seminar that uses the Walt Disney World Resort as a "living laboratory" to educate guests in the company's business and management practices. Meanwhile, some companies offer business-to-business tours that are more pragmatic than educational. These may include sales-oriented tours for prospective customers of big items (such as helicopters or boats), or business-related tours for vendors, suppliers, and VIPs.

Our Hope

Touring factories anywhere in the country is a fun experience for children. It can also be highly educational. Children will remember the smell of crayons, the taste of breads right off the production line, the sight of car- and paper-making machinery. And because they are kids, they'll be curious about how it all works.

One of our hopes in writing this book is that more children will visit production facilities and company museums in the U.S.A. and be inspired to build things or go into business themselves. America needs entrepreneurs, factory workers, engineers, and business managers to keep its industries strong. By taking these tours, kids can develop a sense of pride in "Made in the U.S.A." products. They will see that we make many things in the U.S.A., and we make them well.

Before Your Visit

Whether you're a parent, trip leader, or teacher, there are a number of things you can do with your children to maximize the learning experience while still having fun. The more kids learn before they go on the tour, the more they will get out of it. For teachers, field trips can be an exciting part of an integrated unit.

Before you go, talk about the products you are about to see made. Examine your crayons, teddy bears, or the family car or piano. Ask your kids how they think those products are made. In the kitchen or classroom, try making your own batch of bread, fudge, or pretzels. This will give children a frame of reference for how the factory makes the same thing on a much larger scale.

Do a little background research with your children. Read about the tour or company museum in this book. If you are going on a local outing or a family trip, let the kids have some input as to which places you visit. Check the library for books telling the history of the baseball, or how

corn flakes were invented. Some books include great drawings illustrating production of all sorts of products. Visit the company's website. (For easy reference, companies' websites are listed in this book.) Teenagers might be interested in looking at a company's investor relations information on the Web or in calling for its annual report.

Talk with your children about the things they want to learn on the field trip. What questions do they want answered? Think about the product and the people, facilities, and materials that go into making it. Write down questions and bring them with you. Kids can make their own clipboards by stapling their questions onto a piece of cardboard and tying on a pencil. With questions in hand, the junior reporters are ready for the tour.

During the Tour

Tour guides are a great source for answers to your children's questions. But first, kids should try observing their surroundings. What happens first? Second? Third? How does the toothpaste get into the tube? What puts the windshield on the car? Watch the workers closely. Are they working together as a team to produce something, or are they working independently? Do they use machines or small hand tools? Why are the workers wearing aprons, hard hats, or goggles? Do you think the workers are proud of the products they make? Similar questions delving into the history of the company, its products, and its culture can be developed for company museums.

The most important thing to remember on the tour is to **follow the safety guidelines** we list in this book, as well as any special instructions the company gives you. Children must understand that factories can be dangerous places. Be sure to tell them that when they are on a tour, they must listen to the tour guide, wear any protective gear the guide gives them, and walk only where they are allowed.

After the Tour

After the tour or visit to a company museum, talk about which parts were most interesting, a great topic for long car rides during driving vacations. What did each person learn? Younger children can draw pictures of how products are made or of workers doing their jobs. They can discuss what they found "cool" and share their experiences with their classes at school.

Parents and teachers might also encourage teenagers to imagine being an integral part of a company. Companies need all sorts of people, the innovators and creators, the builders and writers, the people selling on the front line and the ones doing the work behind the scenes. Perhaps they will leave with a new job or career idea. (That goes for adults, too!)

INTRODUCTION

By Kids For Kids

As our daughter, Hilary has gone on factory tours her whole life. She earned her first frequent-flier points when she was three months old, traveling to The Creegan Company's "Animation Factory" in Ohio— her first official factory tour. We have led factory tour field trips for her elementary school classes and we visit factory tours during family vacations, so she is almost as expert as we are. And she certainly knows a lot, from a kid's point of view.

Below, Hilary has written a brief introduction with descriptions about some of the more recent cool factory tours she has been on. So let your kids read and enjoy this section for themselves.

Hi, my name is Hilary and I am eleven years old. Because my parents have written this book, I have gone on over 50 factory tours in 22 states. Some factory tours I found more interesting than others. Below I describe the coolest parts of some of my favorite tours. Hope you get to go. Have fun!

Fortune Cookies

Have you ever wondered how the fortunes get into the fortune cookies, but all the explanations you have heard are too complicated? In order to know the answer to this simple question, you'll have to listen to the whole process of how fortune cookies are made in a simple manner. Fortune cookies start

out looking like pancakes. The only difference is that the pancakes are much smaller (only about three inches) and sweeter. Before the workers fold up the fortune cookies, they gently place a fortune on the pancake and then fold it up. If you want to see this procedure in action, before your very eyes, then you should go to Golden Gate Fortune Cookie and Fortune Cookie Factory (see pages 364 and 363).

Jelly Beans

Have you ever wondered how jelly beans get their color? The question is quite simple, but in order to know you must be willing to dedicate this moment to pure reading and learning about something that everybody loves to eat. Jelly beans start out as jelly-feeling mixtures called "slurry," made of water, corn starch, corn syrup, sugar, flavoring, and color syrups. After the "slurry" settles overnight, the jelly beans are ready for a "steam bath and a sugar shower." The jelly bean centers settle overnight for a second time, after these procedures. Then, when the "slurry" is finished resting, the jelly bean centers are ready to have their colored shells put on. They are thrown into spinning, open drums, where the beans get tossed about. An expert candy maker pours freshly made color and flavor syrups onto the jelly beans. If you want to see this in action, you should go to Jelly Belly (see page 369).

Stickers

Have you ever wondered how stickers are made? Not the simple dogs and hearts, but the detailed Golden Gate bridges and landscapes? These stickers are laser cut. Each one starts out as a big rectangular sticker with random splotches of color all over the place. Then they are laser cut. A 10,000°F laser carefully skims the top of the sticker many times, creating a unique lacy effect. The awesome thing is that this is the only laser web in the world that cuts stickers. If you want to see how stickers are made and watch a video of this procedure while standing next to the laser, you should go to Mrs. Grossman's Stickers (see page 376).

Teddy Bears

Have you ever wondered how teddy bears get stuffed with just the right amount of stuffing? Do they just come like that? Is there a special monitor that beeps when the teddy bear is stuffed just the right amount? No, no, and no. Each teddy bear is hand stuffed by a teddy bear expert. Each piece of a teddy bear is cut separately before all the pieces are sewn together. The teddy bear is filled by the "stuffer," a machine filled with stuffing, with a tube on the end where the stuffing comes out. When a bear is ready to be stuffed, the worker slides the tube into each part of the bear. If you want to see bears being stuffed, you should go to Basic Brown Bear Factory (see page 357).

Itinerary Planners and Vacation Ideas

Factory tours and company visitors centers/ museums are free or inexpensive highlights you can add to a family vacation or business trip. This section helps you plan trips based on your favorite products and regions of the U.S.A. Factory tours allow you to watch workers and machines in action, so you'll see most production Monday through Friday during normal business hours (some companies' tours are offered only on specified days or at certain times of year). Company visitors centers/museums usually also have weekend and holiday hours. Most of the trips listed in this section require minimal planning; however, many tours require reservations, so plan accordingly.

Please refer to the full write-ups in the book for more information.

MULTIPLE-DAY TRIPS

Auto Factory Adventure (2–4 days)

Day 1: Toyota in Georgetown, Kentucky, page 253; see color photos, page 50.
Ford in Louisville, Kentucky, page 245.

Day 2: Corvette Assembly Plant (cars) and National Corvette Museum (cars) in Bowling Green, Kentucky, pages 244 and 249.

or

Day 2: International (trucks) in Springfield, Ohio, page 197.

Day 3: Nissan in Smyrna, Tennessee, page 275.

Saturn tour and visitor center in Spring Hill, Tennessee, page 272.

Day 4: BMW in Greer, South Carolina, page 270.

or

Day 4: Mercedes-Benz in Vance, Alabama, page 224.

and/or

Day 4: Hyundai in Montgomery, Alabama, page 222; see color photos, page 266.

Boston and Beyond (2–4 days)

Day 1: Boston Beer (Samuel Adams beer), page 66.

National Braille Press (Braille publications), page 74.

The Boston Globe (newspaper publishing), page 67.

Day 2: Cape Cod Potato Chips (potato chips) in Hyannis, Massachusetts, page 68.

Pairpoint Crystal (glass) in Sagamore, Massachusetts, page 75.

or

Day 2: American Textile History Museum (cloth) in Lowell, Massachusetts, page 65.

Stonyfield Farm (yogurt) in Londonderry, New Hampshire, page 80.

Day 3: Anheuser-Busch (beer) in Merrimack, New Hampshire, page 77; see color photos, page 4.

Hampshire Pewter (pewter tableware, ornaments, and gifts) in Wolfeboro, New Hampshire, page 78.

Day 4: Magic Wings Butterfly Conservatory (live butterflies) in South Deerfield, Massachusetts, page 73.

Yankee Candle (candles) in South Deerfield, Massachusetts, page 76.

Bourbon Bounty in Kentucky (2 days)

Day 1: Old Kentucky Candies (bourbon candy) in Lexington, page 250.

Rebecca-Ruth Candies (chocolates and Bourbon Balls) in Frankfort, page 251; see color photos, page 46.

Buffalo Trace Distillery (bourbon) in Frankfort, page 240.

Day 2: Maker's Mark (bourbon) in Loretto, page 248; see color photos page 38.

Additional places of interest for bourbon lovers:

Wild Turkey in Lawrenceburg, see page 254, Heaven Hill Distillery; Oscar Getz Museum of Whiskey History; Jim Beam's American Outpost; Annual Bardstown September Bourbon Festival. (See Nearby Bourbon-Related Attractions under Maker's Mark.)

China, Glass, and Pottery in Eastern Ohio Area (2 days)

Day 1:   Senator Heinz History Center in Pittsburgh, Pennsylvania, page 130.

Homer Laughlin China in Newell, West Virginia, page 145.

Side trip to Creegan (animated characters) in Steubenville, Ohio, page 194.

Day 2:   Mosser Glass in Cambridge, Ohio, page 202.

Roseville-Crooksville pottery communities' attractions and annual July pottery festival featuring tours of other pottery factories. (See Nearby Attractions under Robinson Ransbottom.)

Side trip to Longaberger (baskets) in Frazeysburg, Ohio, page 200.

Disney World and Beyond (3 days)

Day 1:   The Magic of Disney Animation (animated features) in Lake Buena Vista, page 227.

Day 2:   E-One (fire trucks) in Ocala, page 228.

Day 3:   Sally Corporation (animatronic dark rides) in Jacksonville, page 233.

Food and Festivity in Louisiana (2 days)

Day 1:   New Orleans area

Blaine Kern's Mardi Gras World (parade floats and props) in New Orleans, page 255.

Day 2:   Cajun Country

Konriko (rice and Cajun seasonings) in New Iberia, page 257.

McIlhenny Company (Tabasco brand pepper sauce) on Avery Island, page 258.

Tony Chachere's (Creole seasonings and rice mixes) in Opelousas, page 261.

Gastronomic Tours in Texas (4 days)

Day 1:   Collin Street Bakery (fruitcake) in Corsicana, page 302.

Day 2:   Blue Bell Creameries (ice cream) in Brenham, page 300.

Day 3:   Jardine's Foods (Texas-style foods) in Buda, near Austin, page 304.

Day 4:   Dublin Dr. Pepper Bottling (soda), bottling on Tuesdays, in Dublin, page 303.

Dr. Pepper Museum in Waco (see Special Information under Dr. Pepper).

Mrs. Baird's Bakery (bread) in Fort Worth, page 308.

Glassblowing in West Virginia (2 days)

Day 1:   Fenton Art Glass in Williamstown, page 144; see color photos, page 12.

Side trip to Lee Middleton Original Dolls in Belpre, Ohio, page 199.

Day 2:   Blenko Glass in Milton, page 143.

Gibson Glass factory (see Nearby Attractions under Blenko Glass).

Hawaii—Off the Beaches (2 days)

Day 1:   Oahu

Maui Divers of Hawaii (jewelry) in Honolulu, page 400.

Day 2:   Hawaii (the Big Island)

Big Island Candies (chocolate-covered macadamia nuts and cookies) in Hilo, page 396.

Mauna Loa (macadamia nuts and candy) in Hilo, page 401.

Holualoa Kona Coffee (Kona coffee) in Holualoa, page 399.

Ueshima Coffee (Kona coffee) in Captain Cook, page 402.

Maine Coast (3 days)

Day 1:   Stonewall Kitchens (specialty foods) in York, page 62.

Tom's of Maine (natural toothpaste) in Sanford, page 64.

Day 2:   Sabre Yachts (yachts) in South Casco, page 61.

Day 3:   Poland Spring (water) in Poland Spring, page 60.

Milwaukee—Beer and Beyond (4 days)

Day 1:   Harley-Davidson (motorcycles) in Wauwatosa, page 208; see color photos, pages 18–21.

Miller Brewing (beer), page 213; see color photo, page 40.

Quality Candy/Buddy Squirrel (chocolates and popcorn) in St. Francis, page 215.

Day 2:   Allen-Edmonds (shoes) in Port Washington, page 205.

Kohler (bathtubs, whirlpools, toilets, and sinks) in Kohler, page 212.

Day 3:   SC Johnson Wax (specialty home-cleaning products) in Racine, page 216.

Day 4:   Natural Ovens (breads and cereals) in Manitowoc, page 214.

or

Day 4:   General Motors (sport-utility vehicles and pickups) in Janesville, page 207.

Trek (bicycles) in Waterloo, page 218.

Musical Mystery Tour (4 days)

Day 1:   Radio City Music Hall (live entertainment) in New York City, page 114.

Day 2:   Steinway & Sons (pianos) in Long Island City, New York, page 116.

Day 3:   Martin Guitar (guitars) in Nazareth, Pennsylvania, page 128.

Day 4:   Kazoo Boutique (kazoos) in Eden, New York, page 110.

QRS Music (player-piano rolls) in Buffalo, New York, page 113.

Pretzels and Potato Chips in Pennsylvania (2–3 days)

Day 1:   Herr's Snack Factory Tour in Nottingham, page 124; see color photos, page 22.

Sturgis Pretzel House in Lititz, page 113.

Day 2:   Snyder's of Hanover in Hanover, page 132.

Utz Quality Foods in Hanover, page 135.

(On the way to Utz and Snyder's, visit Harley-Davidson Motor Company in York, page 123.)

or

Day 2:   Chocolate Diversion

Asher's Chocolates in Souderton, page 117.

Hershey's Chocolate World in Hershey, page 125.

Day 3:   Utz Quality Foods in Hanover, page 123.

St. Louis and Kansas City— Bud and Beyond (3 days)

Day 1:   Anheuser-Busch (beer) in St. Louis, page 284; see color photos, page 2.

Boeing (airplanes, missiles, and spacecraft) in St. Louis, page 346.

Day 2:   Purina Farms (pets and farm animals) in Gray Summit, page 288.

Day 3:   Hallmark Visitors Center (greeting cards) in Kansas City, page 286; see color photos, page 14.

Harley-Davidson Motor Company (motorcycles) in Kansas City, page 287; see color photos, page 18.

San Francisco with Kids— Fun for Adults, Too! (3 days)

Day 1:   Basic Brown Bear Factory (teddy bears) in San Francisco, page 357; see color photos, page 6.

Golden Gate Fortune Cookies in San Francisco or Fortune Cookie Factory (fortune cookies) in Oakland, pages 364 and 363.

(Consider side trip to Intel in Santa Clara for science-oriented children, page 368; see color photos, page 28.)

Day 2:   Guide Dogs for the Blind (guide dogs and instruction) in San Rafael, page 366.

or

Day 2:   Jelly Belly Candy Co. (jelly beans, chocolates, and Gummi candies) in Fairfield, page 369.

MULTIPLE-DAY TRIPS (continued)

Day 3: Hershey's Visitors Center (chocolate) in Oakdale, page 367.

Studios of Southern California (2–3 days)

Day 1: Paramount Pictures in Hollywood, page 379.

Day 2: NBC Studios in Burbank, page 377.

Warner Bros. Studios in Burbank, page 388.

Day 3: Universal Studios Hollywood in Universal City, page 387.

Sony Pictures Studios in Culver City, page 383.

Sweet Tooth Tour—East Coast (3 days)

Day 1: Moore's Candies in Baltimore, Maryland, page 91.

Day 2: Hershey's Chocolate World in Hershey, Pennsylvania, page 125.

Day 3: Asher's Chocolates in Souderton, Pennsylvania, page 117.

or

Day 3: Sherm Edwards in Trafford, Pennsylvania, page 131.

Sweet Tooth Tour—West Coast (3 days)

Day 1: Phoenix

Cerreta's Candy in Glendale, Arizona, page 312.

Day 2: Las Vegas

Ethel M Chocolates in Henderson, Nevada, page 315.

Day 3: San Francisco Area (fly to San Francisco) Choose one:

Jelly Belly Candy Co. in Fairfield, California, page 369.

Hershey's Visitors Center in Oakdale, California, page 367.

or

Day 3: Seattle Area (fly to Seattle)

Boehms Chocolates in Issaquah, Washington, page 345.

Vermont—Beyond Ben & Jerry's (3 days)

from the South:

Day 1: Simon Pearce (glass and pottery) in Windsor and Quechee, page 90.

Grafton Village Cheese (cheese) in Grafton, page 85.

Crowley Cheese (cheese) in Healdville, page 84.

Day 2: Rock of Ages (granite quarry, memorials, and sculptures) in Graniteville, page 89.

Maple Grove Farms (maple syrup and salad dressing) in St. Johnsbury, page 87.

Cabot Creamery (cheese) in Cabot, page 83.

Day 3: Vermont Teddy Bear (teddy bears) in Shelburne, page 92.

Ben & Jerry's (ice cream and frozen yogurt) in Waterbury, page 82.

York, Pennsylvania— "Factory Tour Capital" (2 days)

Day 1: Harley-Davidson Motor Company (motorcycles) in York, page 123; see color photos, page 18.

Wolfgang Candy (candy) in York, page 137.

Day 2: Herr's Snack Factory Tour (snack food) in Nottingham, page 124; see color photos, page 22.

Snyder's of Hanover (pretzels and potato chips) in Hanover, page 132.

See the Day-Trip Itinerary Planner in the Resources section for more ideas.

WATCH IT MADE
IN THE U.S.A.

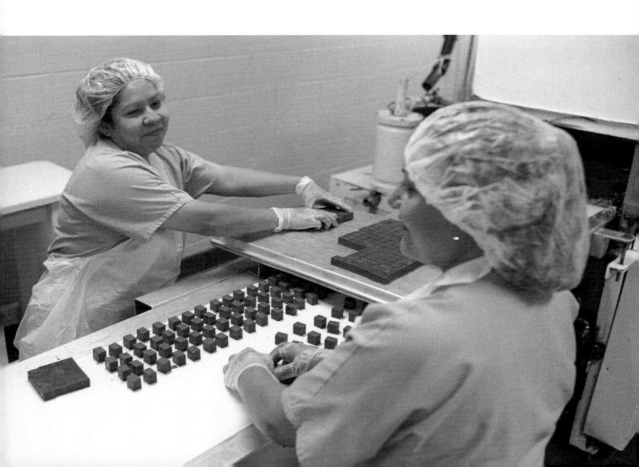

Anheuser-Busch

12th and Lynch Streets, St. Louis, MO 63118   (314) 577-2626   www.budweisertours.com

FEATURED TOURS

The tour of the St. Louis brewery (founded 1852), ocated next to the Anheuser-Busch World Headquarters, puts a face on the world's largest brewer. As the tour guide leads you from the tour center to the Budweiser Clydesdale paddock ard stable, lager cellar, Brew House, Lyon's Schoolhouse, and Bevo packaging plant, a sense of history and the smell of hops surround you.

The Budweiser Clydesdales tradition began in 1933 when August A. Busch Jr. presented his father with the first team of Clydesdales to celebrate the repeal cf Prohibition. Today the gentle giants make more than 500 appearances annually with their bright red beer wagon. See where the beer is actually made in the historic six-story Brew House. Built in 1891, the Brew House is a tour favorite with its clock tower, ornate wrought-iron railings, and hop vine chandeliers from the 1904 World's Fair. The Lyon School House, built in 1868, is the oldest structure in the Anheuser-Busch complex. It served as the company's headquarters from 1907 until 1981.

Visit the beechwood aging and fermentation cellars and Bevo Packaging Plant. Anheuser-Busch is the only major brewer that still uses the famous beechwood aging process to age and naturally carbonate its beers. In the lager cellar, stainless-steel lager tanks are lined with a layer of beechwood chips, providing additional surface area to attract and retain yeast. Beechwood aging is part of the secondary fermentation. Each of the lager tanks holds enough beer to fill approximately 200,000 six-packs.

The Bevo Packaging Plant was constructed in 1917 and stands eight stories tall and houses 27 acres of floor space and over 25 miles of conveyor belts. You will see fast-paced action as bottles and cans are filled. Whimsical fox sculptures are perched on each corner of the building, all munching on chicken legs and holding a mug of Bevo, a nonalcohol cereal-based beverage that Anheuser-Busch produced during the Prohibition era.

During the brewing process, wort is transferred into the brew kettles and hops are added for flavor, aroma, and character.

Cost: Free

Freebies: For guests 21 or older, beer samples, soda, and snacks.

Videos/DVDs Shown: Brew House: multimedia presentation tells story of brewing process. Bevo Packaging Plant: 3-minute video tells how bottles and cans are filled with the world's favorite brews.

Reservations Needed: No, except for groups of 15 or more.

Days and Hours: March–May, Sept–Oct: Mon–Sat 9:00 AM–4:00 PM, Sun 11:30 AM–4:00 PM. June–Aug: Mon–Sat 9:00 AM–5:00 PM, Sun 11:30 AM–5:00 PM. Nov–Feb: Mon–Sat 10:00 AM–4:00 PM, Sun 11:30 AM–4:00 PM. Schedules change; visit website for up-to-date schedules. Call for holiday hours.

Plan to Stay: 1.25 hours for tour, plus additional time for gift shop.

Minimum Age: Under age 18 must be accompanied by adult.

Disabled Access: Yes

Group Requirements: Groups larger than 15 should call 1 week ahead.

Special Information: Anheuser-Busch also gives tours in Merrimack, NH; Jacksonville, FL; Fort Collins, CO; and Fairfield, CA. For general information on all tours, see above website. See page 284 for feature on Merrimack, NH, tour.

Gift Shop: The Anheuser-Busch Gift Shop sells clothing, hats, glassware, beach gear, framed pictures, and Anheuser-Busch logoed items. Gift shop closes 90 minutes after last tour.

Directions: Take I-55 to Arsenal St. exit. Follow signs to Tour Center (on 12th and Lynch Sts.).

Nearby Attractions: St. Louis area attractions include Boeing Museum (see page 285), Grant's Farm, St. Louis Zoo, Gateway Arch, Union Station and Science City, Missouri Botanical Garden, St. Louis Science Center, and International Bowling Museum & Hall of Fame. Tour Center front desk has information sheet with directions and hours for nearby attractions.

Built in 1891, the St. Louis Brew House is one of several national historic landmarks on the property.

One of every two beers consumed in America is made by Anheuser-Busch, with this brewery serving all of New England. Of Anheuser-Busch's 12 U.S. breweries, this brewery is in the prettiest setting, located in the picturesque Merrimack Valley. It can package 8 million 12-ounce servings in 24 hours.

Your tour guide will lead you to the brewery, built in 1970, past a life-size replica of a Clydesdale horse. In the brewhouse, a mixture of water and rice or corn fills three stainless-steel mash tanks. Malt enzymes break the starch in the corn or rice into fermentable sugars. Once strained, the remaining liquid ("wort") is boiled and hops are added. After cooling, the liquid is pumped into 45°F fermentation cellars. On the ground floor of this four-story cellar, you may see a worker place a layer of beechwood chips in the stainless-steel tanks. These chips provide a surface area on which yeast settles during secondary fermentation.

On your way to the packaging area, notice the eight-foot carved mahogany mural of the Anheuser-Busch corporate trademark. Through glass windows, watch the tightly woven maze of filling lines. Once rinsed, bottles proceed to the rotating bottle-filler. They then speed through capping and labeling to packaging. After the brewery tour, don't miss the Old World–style Clydesdale Hamlet, modeled after an 18th-century German Bauernhof. This stable and courtyard are home base for the traveling East Coast Clydesdale eight-horse show hitch. This close-up look at the Budweiser Clydesdales (special photo opportunities first Saturday of each month) is a highlight of the tour.

Cost: Free

Freebies: Beer, soda, and snacks.

Video/DVD Shown: If packaging line isn't operating, 2 6-minute films show packaging and brewing processes.

Reservations Needed: No, except for groups larger than 15.

The entrance to the Merrimack Tour Center is surrounded by New England charm and award-winning landscape.

Days and Hours: January–April: Thur–Mon 10:00 AM–4:00 PM; May, September–December: Mon–Sun 10:00 AM–4:00 PM; June–August: Mon–Sun 9:30 AM–5:00 PM. Call to see if bottling on weekends or holidays. Generally closed day before and day of Thanksgiving, Christmas, and New Year's.

Plan to Stay: 1.5 hours for tour, hospitality room, and Clydesdale Hamlet, plus time for shopping and tour assembly room displays.

Minimum Age: Under age 18 must be accompanied by adult.

Disabled Access: Yes

Group Requirements: Groups larger than 15 should call 1 day in advance. Groups of more than 35 people will be split into smaller groups. No maximum group size.

Special Information: No photography inside brewery. First Saturday of each month is Budweiser Clydesdale Camera Day (1:00–3:00 PM), when you can pose with one of the Clydesdale horses. Tour includes indoor and outdoor walking and some stairs. See page 284 for St. Louis, MO, feature and information about other Anheuser-Busch brewery tours.

Gift Shop: Tour Center Store sells logoed items, including T-shirts, bathing suits, steins, and jackets. Closes 1 hour later than tours.

Directions: From Boston, take I-93 North to I-495 South to Rt. 3 North. In New Hampshire, Rt. 3 becomes Everett Tnpk. Get off at Exit 10. At end of ramp, go right. At the next set of lights, turn left onto Daniel Webster Hwy. At the next traffic light, turn right into the brewery. Park in second lot on right. From Rt. 101, take Everett Tnpk. South to Exit 10 in Merrimack. At end of ramp, turn left. At the second set of lights, turn left onto Daniel Webster Hwy. Follow to next traffic light and turn right into brewery.

Nearby Attractions: Stonyfield Farm Yogurt tour (see page 80); American Textile History Museum (see page 65); Currier Gallery of Art (call 603-669-6144); New England Quilt Museum (call 978-452-4207).

FEATURED TOURS

A symbol of Anheuser-Busch tradition since 1933, this Budweiser Clydesdale welcomes guests to the Merrimack Brewery.

2801 Leavenworth St., San Francisco, CA 94133   (866) 5BB-BEAR   www.basicbrownbear.com

You'll enjoy playing teddy bear obstetrician on this tour. At this factory, discover how teddy bears are born and participate in their delivery. One of the few U.S. manufacturers of stuffed bears, Basic Brown Bear (BBB) lets you watch them handmake the cuddly creatures from start to finish.

In the cutting and sewing area, often the owner proudly explains her process. First, she draws each pattern on paper and makes a sample animal from the pattern. Workers use bandsaws to slice 24 layers of plush fabric into pattern pieces. Seamstresses sew together individual bear parts and outfits, stitching the sections inside out, then reaching inside to push out the bear legs, ears, and noses. Each seamstress can make about 35 baby bears or 10 grandparent bears a day, plus their clothes.

You learn that the first stuffed bears had shoe buttons for eyes. Now, grommets snap mushroom-shaped plastic eyes into place. A tour highlight is stuffing bears with polyester from a bright yellow machine used to fill life jackets during World War II. Now you can bring a bear to life by inflating it like a balloon. Wait on a line of yellow paw prints to push the filler's foot pedal. Out shoots a mixture of air and polyester. Another machine injects beans into bears. Once a bear is cuddly enough, its back is hand sewn shut.

At the beauty parlor, workers smooth out bear seams with an electric wire brush. A pressurized-air "bear bath" or "bear shower" (depending on the critter's size) removes fur "fuzzies." Children (and adults) giggle when they too receive a "bear shower" or give a bear a "bath." Bears are dressed in their outfits, including company-made wire-rim glasses. Visitors leave with a special affection for the bears they brought to life.

Cost: Free tour. Prices for stuffing your own animal run from $14 to $300.

Freebies: No

Kids observe as an energetic tour guide demonstrates how the plush fabric is cut for each bear's parts.

Video/DVD Shown: 20-minute Emmy award–winning video, "The Teddy Bear Factory," with its catchy tune, tells how teddy bears are made.

Reservations Needed: No, except for groups of 8 or more people.

Days and Hours: Mon–Sat 10:00 AM–6:00 PM, Sun 11:00 AM–6:00 PM, on the hour. Last tour at 4:00 PM. Closed holidays.

Plan to Stay: 30 minutes, plus time for stuffing and showering your own bear, and the gift shop.

Minimum Age: 3

Disabled Access: Yes

Group Requirements: Groups of 8 or more people should call 2 weeks in advance. Maximum group size is 40.

Special Information: Can also stuff your own animals at BBB's other stores in Old Town San Diego (call 877-234-2327) and in the Mall of America in Bloomington, MN (call 800-396-2327).

Gift Shop: More than 30 styles of stuffed bears (and other animals) and bear clothes, all handmade by BBB, are sold exclusively at this location.

Directions: Westbound from the Bay Bridge, take the Fremont St. exit. Turn left onto Fremont St. Fremont become Front St. Turn left onto Pine St. Turn Right onto Sansome St. Turn left onto Washington St. Make a slight right onto Columbus Ave. and another slight right onto Leavenworth St. From the South Bay, take U.S. 101 North, then merge onto I-280 North toward the Port of SF. Take the exit on the left, then merge onto King St. (becomes The Embarcadero). Turn left onto Bay St. Make a slight right onto Columbus Ave. Make another slight right onto Leavenworth St. Parking is available at the Anchorage Parking Garage located between Jones and Leavenworth Sts.

Nearby Attractions: Scharffen Berger chocolate tour, Boudin's Bakery tour, Golden Gate Fortune Cookies, and Wells Fargo Bank Museum (see pages 381, 360, 364, and 389). Fisherman's Wharf; Ghiradelli Square.

FEATURED TOURS

Sewing together the parts and outfits, each seamstress can produce up to 35 bears in one day.

The Crayola FACTORY

Two Rivers Landing, 30 Centre Square,
Easton, PA 18042

(610) 515-8000   www.crayola.com

You can't help feeling like a kid again when you visit The Crayola FACTORY at Two Rivers Landing, the discovery center built in 1996 by Binney & Smith, makers of Crayola products. In fact, don't be surprised if the experience raises many childhood memories. You may remember when the now-classic 64-crayon box with built-in sharpener was introduced in 1958; or you may remember your 10th birthday, by which time you, like the average American child, had probably worn down 730 crayons.

The "Factory Floor" level of the discovery center features crayon manufacturing and marker assem-bly, using machinery transferred from the nearby production plant. Behind a glass wall is the flat-bed molder that makes a small percentage of the company's crayons. Watch a worker pour a mixture containing melted paraffin wax and powdered pig-ment from a bucket onto a long table with thou-sands of small holes. Bright yellow wax seeps into the holes. After four to seven minutes of cool-ing, 1,200 crayons magically appear as they are pushed up and out of the molds! The worker also demonstrates and explains the labeling and pack-aging machines.

In the marker assembly area, the marker machine has actually been slowed down so you can follow the process of mating the barrels, cylinders, and marker caps. At normal speed, this machine can make 42,000 markers in one eight-hour shift.

Follow the ramp down to the "Creative Studio," which begins the playful, interactive portion of your visit. Draw on clear glass walls with spe-cial glass-writer markers. Step into "Cool Moves," where a computer captures your image on a huge video screen.

In the "Easton Press and Bindery," you can prac-tice printmaking. At the end of your colorful experi-

hands-on fun at The Crayola FACTORY

ence, you can use Crayola Model Magic to create three-dimensional art.

Cost: Adults and children, $9; seniors 55+, $8.50; 2 and younger, free. Includes admission to National Canal Museum, located in same building. Check website for updated pricing.

Freebies: Box of 4 crayons and a marker from the assembly lines, and art projects you create while there.

Videos/DVDs Shown: A 10-minute video covers products made by the company, including Silly Putty, chalk, paint, and crayon production. Another video shows TV clips.

Reservations Needed: No, with walk-ins accommodated on a first-come, first-served basis until day is sold out, however advanced reservations are accepted. Groups over 10 people, see below.

Days and Hours: Schedule variable. Check calendar on website.

Plan to Stay: 1.5–2.5 hours, plus time in gift shops.

Minimum Age: None

Disabled Access: Yes

Group Requirements: Groups over 10 people should call 2 weeks in advance.

Gift Shops: Museum Shop sells logoed clothing, candy, and toys. Open same hours as Crayola Factory. The 7,200-square-foot Crayola Store, next door, sells a range of Binney & Smith products, from mini to large boxes of crayons, and from posters to teddy bears wearing logoed sweatshirts. Call toll-free for hours (888) 827-2966. Closed holidays.

Directions: From Philadelphia, take Northeast Extension of Pennsylvania Tnpk. to Allentown Exit onto Rt. 22 East. Get off at the 4th St. exit (last exit in PA). At traffic light, turn left on Buskill St. Turn right onto N. 3rd St. Follow signs to "The Crayola FACTORY."

Nearby Attractions: Martin Guitar and Mack Trucks tours (see pages 128 and 127); Allen Organ Company tour (call 610-966-2202); canal boat ride and walking tour of Easton; Lehigh Valley attractions, including Dorney Park and Wildwater Kingdom.

Crayola crayons being made at The Crayola FACTORY

6701 West Forest Preserve Drive, Chicago, IL 60634   (773) 736-3417
(800) 999-8300   www.elicheesecake.com

After its public debut at the Taste of Chicago in 1980, Eli's Cheesecake has become a sweet symbol of success for the Windy City. Eli Schulman, a guy from the "West Side of Chicago," created a special dessert for his restaurant, Eli's The Place for Steak. His son Marc continues Eli's level of dedication and commitment to making the best quality cheesecake.

Before starting your tour, notice the mural highlighting Eli's Cheesecake's history. In the back of this bright, atrium café, look through the glass window into the research and development department. This 62,000-square-foot bakery, built in 1996, uses more than 4 million pounds of cream cheese, 500,000 pounds of eggs, 250,000 pounds of butter, and 13,000 pounds of Bourbon vanilla annually.

After donning your hair net, walk through the double doors. Racks filled with all-butter cookie crusts baked twice the previous night await today's production. In the mixing area, a crane system lifts up and tilts the mixing bowl, which contains 500 pounds of batter for each batch of cheesecake. A big spatula with a black plastic paddle fills each crust. Up to 18,000 cheesecakes march along the conveyor through the 70-foot tunnel oven. Stand on the royal blue nonskid path observing rows 10 cheesecakes wide emerge.

After baking, the cheesecakes take a leisurely two-hour journey spiraling up and back down a two-story cylindrical cooling tower. This densely coiled spiral cooler slowly cools more than 2,000 cheesecakes at one time. Cheesecakes travel single-file down the conveyor belt and are depanned individually by hand.

In the blast freezer, cakes freeze solid in eight to ten hours. More than 30 trained pastry chefs and cake decorators hand-decorate some two-thirds of Eli's cheesecakes. Decorating a cheesecake involves great teamwork, taking up to three different steps. After decorating, cheesecakes are sliced, packaged, and shipped.

All of Eli's Cheesecakes are decorated by hand by trained pastry artists.

Cost: Adults, $3; children under 12, $2 (costs go to Eli's Charitable Fund to support the community).

Freebies: Cheesecake slice.

Video/DVD Shown: Slide show on Eli's history and the baking process.

Reservations Needed: No, for the 1:00 PM "Sneak Peek" tour. Yes, for groups over 10 people and for "quiet tours" (no production) on weekends.

Days and Hours: Mon–Fri 8:00 AM–6:00 PM Tour packages available for groups of 10 or more. Call ahead to confirm the bakery is in production, otherwise Eli's offers a modified tour.

Plan to Stay: 25 minutes for tour, plus additional time in the retail store.

Minimum Age: 3

Disabled Access: Modified tour available.

Group Requirements: Groups over 10 people should schedule at least 2 weeks in advance, with contract and payment. Enjoy tour packages such as "Lunch & Munch," "The Ultimate Eli's Experience" (participate in "Quality Star" taste test and decorate your own cheesecake), and "Sail and Dine" (includes sightseeing cruise plus lunch). Group discount in café. Maximum group size is 45.

Special Information: No photography or strollers. Must wear rubber-soled, low-heeled shoes, otherwise receive modified tour. The Cheesecake Festival is in September.

Retail Store: Café sells many of Eli's 100 cheesecake varieties and logoed merchandise including hats, T-shirts, and polo shirts. Selection ranges from Original Plain (for the "cheesecake purist") to indulgent Belgian Chocolate Hazelnut, plus holiday specials like Egg Nog. Open Mon–Fri 8:00 AM–6:00 PM, Sat 9:00 AM–5:00 PM, Sun 11:00 AM–5:00 PM. Order Eli's C-Cake from website, picking from some 600 combinations of decorations and toppings.

Directions: From I-90/94 West, take Montrose St. Turn left. At light, turn left just before factory onto Forest Preserve Dr. Turn right into parking lot.

Nearby Attractions: Chicago Board of Trade and Chicago Mercantile Exchange tours (see page 149 and 150); Chicago's attractions include Sears Tower, Shedd Aquarium, and Lincoln Park Zoo.

Eli's Cheesecakes are slowly baked to a golden brown in a 70-foot-long and 12-foot-wide tunnel oven.

420 Caroline Avenue, Williamstown, WV 26187 | (304) 375-7772 (800) 319-7793 | www.fentonartglass.com

Handcrafted American Glass Artistry

In western West Virginia—rich in mountains, sand, and natural gas—the art and traditions of glassmaking are kept alive by a handful of artisans and factories. Fenton Art Glass began in 1905, when two Fenton brothers pooled $284 to start their business. Now in its fourth generation of family ownership and management, Fenton Art Glass continues this art in the U.S.A. The tour takes you from the extreme heat and speed of the glassmaking shops to the decorating area's exacting calm.

After a brief chemistry lesson (sand is the main ingredient in glass), follow your guide onto the glassmaking shop floor. Gatherers and carriers can be seen with gobs of red-hot glass, handles, and newly blown or pressed pieces. Each worker, trained by apprenticeship, has a specific function in the team effort of creating each item. To produce a bowl, the "gatherer" rolls the long pole (punty) inside the 2,200°F furnace to gather a gob of glass, which is dropped into a bowl-shaped mold. The presser, one of the most experienced craftsmen in the shop, lowers a lever with exacting pressure, forcing molten glass into a decorative bowl.

Downstairs in the decorating area, fresh-air-masked artisans paint crushed 22-karat gold onto glass items of all kinds. Elsewhere in the decorating area, artists paint designs on glass using crushed-glass pigments. When applying floral designs, an artist first paints the blossoms on a dozen pieces, returning later to add leaves and stems. You gain an appreciation for the steps involved in producing tomorrow's heirlooms.

Cost: Free

Freebies: Brochure on glassmaking.

Video/DVD Shown: "Experience Fenton," 22-minute video in Museum Theater, covers the basics of glass production, company history, and hand carving of cast-iron molds.

Handpainting and ringing are two signature skills Fenton has developed since 1905.

Reservations Needed: No, except for groups larger than 20 people.

Days and Hours: Mon–Fri starting at 8:15 AM. Approximately nine 35–40 minute tours offered, except on major holidays. Limited factory tours for two weeks starting late June or early July. Call (800) 319-7793 or visit www.fentongiftshop.com for exact tour times.

Plan to Stay: 2 hours, including tour, video, and museum, plus time for gift shop. Museum emphasizes a century of Fenton Glass (1905–2005) and historic Ohio Valley glass. Museum has same hours as gift shop.

Minimum Age: 2. Supervise children carefully, since you get very close to the hot glass.

Disabled Access: Blowing/pressing area, gift shop, and museum are accessible. Stairs to decorating department.

Group Requirements: Groups of 20 or more need advance reservations.

Special Information: Wear closed-toe, thick-soled shoes. Glassblowing area is well ventilated but hot during summer. Watch where you walk.

Gift Shop and Factory Outlet: Sells Fenton's first-quality line at suggested retail, as well as retired, first-quality, and preferred seconds at reduced prices. Also carries other fine gift and home décor items. Museum sells glassmaking history books. Annual February Gift Shop Sale and Summer Tent Sale. Open Mon–Sat 8:00 AM– 5:00 PM, Sun 12:00 PM–5:00 PM. Additional hours April– December: Mon–Fri open until 8:00 PM. Closed New Year's, Easter, Thanksgiving, and Christmas. Catalog available through telephone or website.

Directions: From I-77, take Exit 185; follow black-and-white signs to gift shop. From Rt. 50, take I-77 North. Follow directions above.

Nearby Attractions: Lee Middleton Original Doll factory tour (see page 199); Blennerhassett Island; Historic Marietta, OH, across Ohio River.

Fenton factory tours take you where the action is, close to glassblowers like Mike Sine, Jr.

Crown Center Complex, 2501 McGee,
Kansas City, MO 64141

(816) 274-3613

www.hallmark
visitorscenter.com

VISITORS CENTER

Hallmark's slogan, "When You Care Enough to Send the Very Best," applies to its visitors center. You will walk through 14 exhibits that tell the story of the world's largest greeting-card company. See a 40-foot historical timeline and learn how Hallmark started when a man named Joyce C. Hall began selling picture postcards from his fourth-floor room at the Kansas City YMCA. The timeline has memorabilia from Hallmark's history intertwined with world events.

During the six-minute multimedia film presentation on the essence of creativity, listen and watch Hallmark artists explain how the creative process works. Did you know that Winston Churchill was an artist? One of his paintings hangs in the visitors center along with other originals by Norman Rockwell, Grandma Moses, and Saul Steinberg.

Another area is devoted to the craft and technology of card production. You can watch a technician make engraving dies—the metal plates that raise the three-dimensional designs on paper—or cutting dies, which work like steel cookie cutters to make unusually shaped cards. Two presses churn out the cards you might purchase 10 months from now. At the touch of a button, you can watch a machine turn ribbon into a miniature star bow and take one home with you.

View clips from Hallmark commercials and Hallmark Hall of Fame television dramas. Costumes, props, and a real Emmy award are on display. Hallmark employees' affection for company founder Hall shows in a display of Christmas trees that employees gave Hall from 1966 to 1982. Each tree's decorations reflect a theme of importance to the company during that year. To experience Hallmark's international appeal (cards sell in more than 100 countries), rub the sheep dog's nose on the handrail of one of the cards to hear birthday greetings in 12 languages. One of the newest exhibits features the Hallmark Keepsake Ornament collection. You can see some of the most popular Keepsake Ornaments, like the Starship Enterprise, the 1957 Corvette, Peanuts characters, and sports heroes.

Cost: Free

Freebies: Postcard and a bow.

Videos/DVDs Shown: Short videos on topics related to the exhibits are shown throughout the visitors center.

Reservations Needed: No, except for guided tours for groups of 10 or more.

Days and Hours: Tue–Fri 9:00 AM–5:00 PM and Sat 9:30 AM–4:30 PM. Closed holidays and most holiday weekends. Also usually closed the first 2–3 weeks in January for yearly renovations.

Plan to Stay: About 1 hour, but can spend any amount of time for self-guided tour.

Minimum Age: None

Disabled Access: Yes. Call (816) 274-3613 for information or visit website.

Group Requirements: Escorted tours available for groups of 10 or more. Groups should make reservations 2–4 weeks in advance. School/youth groups need 1 adult for every 7 children. Call (816) 274-3613 or visit website.

Special Information: Hallmark Cards tour in Topeka, KS (see page 282). Some Hallmark Production Centers in other cities conduct tours by advance reservation; check with visitors center for information.

Gift Shop: Not in visitors center. The closest of the 47,000 independent retail outlets is in Crown Center.

Directions: Located in Crown Center Complex, about 1 mile south of downtown Kansas City. Take Grand Ave. to 25th St. and park in the Crown Center Parking Garage. Proceed to third level of Crown Center shops. The visitors center is located outside Halls department store.

Nearby Attractions: Liberty Memorial World War I Museum (call 816-784-1918); Kaleidoscope children's interactive exhibit (call 816-274-8301); Science City at Union Station (call 816-460-2020).

Push a button at the Hallmark Visitors Center to watch robotic twists and turns transform 42 inches of ribbon into a souvenir bow for you to keep!

5735 North Washington Street, Denver, CO 80216   (888) CANDY-99   www.hammonds candies.com

FEATURED TOURS

Ever wonder how candy canes or other hard candies get their stripes? At Hammond's, you'll see how hard candy has been made by hand since the 1920s.

First, step into the packing room, where workers pack lollipops or candy canes. Next, through a wall of windows in the kitchen, you'll see large copper kettles. Inside, 50 pounds of sugar, water, and corn syrup heats to over 300°F. Two men lift and carry a huge kettle and pour the bubbling, amber-colored liquid onto a metal table. Next you may see the candy maker adding different colors to areas of this sheet of candy: for a candy cane, he scoops out some red paste with a spatula and mixes it into one section, then adds green in another corner. Another section remains clear. Finally, the "scrap"—the crushed beginnings and ends of other candy—is melted into another section: this will become the candy canes' center.

Once the sheet has cooled, the candy maker cuts the color sections with giant scissors—these will become the candy canes' stripes. A clear section is placed on a taffy-puller-like machine. As the machine pulls, it adds air, turning the candy white. Next the red, white, and green sections are laid out on a heated table in a long, flat "blanket."

The cooks then place the center piece on the puller, to add air (so it will melt faster in your mouth) and flavoring, like cherry. Next this centerpiece, which is shaped like a big duffel bag, is placed on the blanket of stripes, and the blanket is wrapped around it. The candy makers put this roll on a heated canvas mat. The mat is on a machine that rotates the bundle. When the bundle is hot enough, a cook takes one end in his hands and pulls it to the width of a candy cane. As the cook pulls, the machine rolls the bundle. This motion creates the twist in the candy cane stripes. As the cook cuts the strip into pieces, a worker takes each

handmade ribbon candy products in Hammond's Denver factory

piece and puts a crook in it. Other workers place the canes on trays to cool, and then they roll the finished candy canes into the packaging room.

Cost: Free

Freebies: Candy samples.

Video/DVD Shown: 10-minute segment about the tour, from a Food Network program.

Reservations Needed: No, except for groups over 10 people or special needs groups.

Days and Hours: Mon–Fri 9:00 AM–3:00 PM, Sat 10:00 AM–3:00 PM, every 20 minutes. Closed Easter, Memorial Day, July 4th, Labor Day, Thanksgiving, Christmas, and New Year's.

Plan to Stay: 30 minutes for tour and video, plus time for gift shop.

Minimum Age: None

Disabled Access: Yes, call a day ahead for reservations.

Group Requirements: Groups of 10 or more should call in advance.

Special Information: Must wear hairnets. Very small children may wear a hat. Strollers do not fit in factory. Tour can be hot in the summer in the cooking area. Candy Cane Festival held in December; call for dates.

Gift Shop: Sells factory seconds, a range of handmade candies, Christmas decorations, books on candy making, and T-shirts. Mon–Fri 9:00 AM–4:30 PM.

Directions: From I-25, take 58th Ave. east. Turn right onto Washington St. Take the first right into Mapelton Distribution Center and look for the Hammonds sign.

Nearby Attractions: U.S. Mint tour (see page 326); Denver Zoo; Denver Museum of Natural History; Denver Museum of Miniature Dolls & Toys; City Park and Botanical Garden.

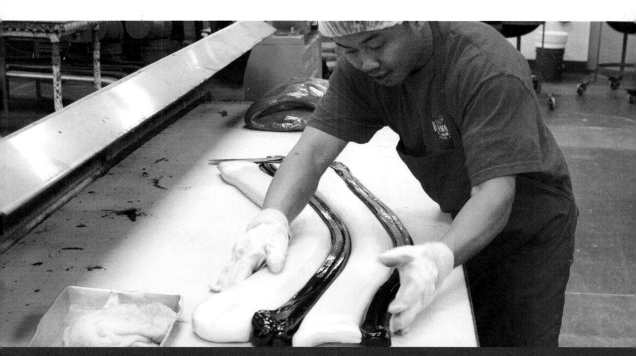

handmade candy canes being constructed in Hammond's Denver factory

York, PA (see p. 123),
Kansas City, MO (see p. 208)
Wauwatosa, WI (see p. 287)

(877) 883-1450   www.harley-davidson.com

The company that William Harley and the Davidson brothers started in 1903 now produces one of the most recognized and admired products in the world. There is nothing quite like riding a Harley-Davidson® motorcycle. As H.O.G.® (Harley Owners Group) members and motorcycling enthusiasts worldwide can attest, the brand has come to represent a lifestyle of individuality, freedom, and adventure.

The company has come a long way from the 10-by-15-foot shed where the founders handcrafted their first motorcycle. The Harley-Davidson Motor Company now produces hundreds of vehicles each day at several facilities in the United States. You can learn more about these world-famous motorcycles by seeing firsthand how they are made at one or all three of the plants offering factory tours: Powertrain Operations in Wauwatosa, Wisconsin; Vehicle Operations in York, Pennsylvania; or Vehicle & Powertrain Operations in Kansas City, Missouri.

At the Wauwatosa plant, you witness the assembly of the powertrain (the combined engine and transmission) for the company's Sportster® and Buell® models. You'll also see the manufacturing processes for Genuine Harley-Davidson Motor Parts and Screamin' Eagle® Performance Parts. Different engine components are available to touch and examine more closely. The tour also shows how Evolution® and Twin Cam 88® engines get a new lease on life through the Remanufacturing program.

The prospect of seeing the final assembly of a Harley-Davidson motorcycle draws visitors to the York and Kansas City sites. Here you will see how the passion of Harley-Davidson employees joins technology to create legendary American motorcycles. Observe hydraulic presses as they transform sheets of metal into fenders, fuel tanks, and tailpipes. The unmistakable Harley-Davidson look begins to take shape as fenders are trimmed, tanks are polished, and steel

tubes are melded together to create the frames. Watch the motorcycles travel by conveyor to various work stations for attachment of parts and assembly.

Following the assembly process, bikes cruise into the roll-test booth, where they are placed on rollers and "driven" at speeds up to 60 miles per hour. Finally, the motorcycle is wrapped in plastic and crated by a robot.

All three of Harley-Davidson's manufacturing facilities have Tour Centers, which feature exhibits highlighting manufacturing and assembly, a video, and "sit-on" motorcycles. Each Tour Center also features a gift shop which includes a large selection of authentic branded merchandise.

Cost: Free

Freebies: Collectible badge and *The Enthusiast* magazine; product catalogs may also be available.

Video/DVD Shown: Yes

Reservations Needed: See the specific page of the site you plan to tour.

Days and Hours: See the specific page of the site you plan to tour.

Plan to Stay: Allow 90 minutes to 2 hours for the factory tour, exhibits, and gift shop.

Minimum Age: 12

Disabled Access: Yes (call ahead).

Group Requirements: Groups of 10 or more must arrange tours in advance.

Special Information: Closed-toe shoes are required; additional shoe requirements, listed by facility, are available at www.harley-davidson.com. Photography is permitted in Tour Centers but not in the factory. For site-specific requirements, see the page of the plant you want to tour. Due to manufacturing requirements and model year changeover, tours may be modified throughout the year. Please call ahead for specific information.

Gift Shop: Yes; hours are listed on the specific page of the site you plan to tour.

Directions: See the specific page of the site you plan to tour.

Nearby Attractions: See the specific page of the site you plan to tour.

an operator works on a powertrain in Wauwatosa, WI

Harley-Davidson Motor Company

The Vaughn L. Beals Tour Center in York, PA, features exhibits detailing the manufacturing and assembly processes.

a bird's-eye view of the VRSC assembly line at Harley-Davidson's Vehicle & Powertrain Operations in Kansas City, MO

An employee polishes a Softail® oil tank in York, PA.

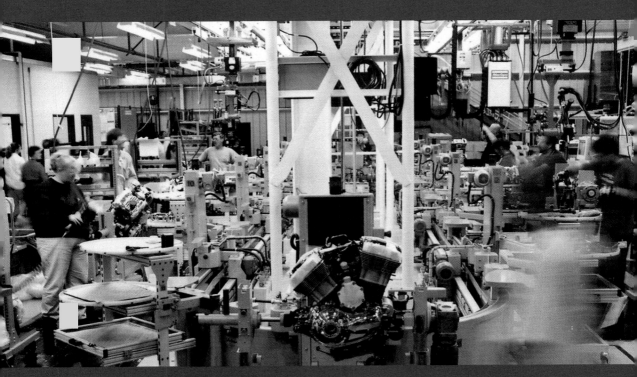
Harley-Davidson employees use state-of-the-art technology and ergonomically designed equipment to assemble the powertrain (engine + transmission) for the company's VRSC motorcycles.

Visitors Center, Rts 1 and 272, Nottingham, PA 19362 | (800) 63-SNACK (800) 637-6225 | www.herrs.com

Herr's snack food production has come a long way from when the company used a small, old-fashioned cooker in a barn. It now has an advanced and highly automated plant that makes tens of thousands of potato chips, corn chips, tortilla chips, popcorn batches, cheese curls, and pretzels every day. The comfortable, specially designed visitors center and café, creative video, and extensive guided tour provide a tasty education in how Herr's makes its products.

While watching the action through glass walls, you'll "ooh" and "aah" at the panoramic views. In the pretzel area, gaze at a 100-yard stretch of pretzel twists, in rows of 20 to 24 across, marching to massive ovens. In the corn chip, cheese curl, potato chip, and popcorn production sections, your vista overlooks the entire process. Follow the raw ingredients—either corn or potatoes—as they tumble in by the truckload at the beginning of the production line; travel along a conveyor belt through a series of machines that wash, slice, cook, or season them; then head out on bucket lifts to a sorting and bagging area. Other memorable images include machines and workers bagging and boxing together in almost symphonic unison, and the cavernous warehouse filled with snack-food boxes.

Except for the boxing of bags, machines do most of the work. Notice how only a few people oversee production in most areas. Smart machines can even sense discolored potato chips and use air jets to blow these rebels off the line. The guides salt and pepper the tour with interesting facts and figures about the company, including Herr's recycling efforts. But the best thing the guides do is grab samples of warm potato chips directly from the quickly moving conveyer belt. Bagged chips will never again taste the same!

Visitors at Herr's enjoy a close-up tour, a café for lunch or parties, and a gift shop.

Cost: Free

Freebies: Warm potato chips during the tour; small sample bag at end of tour.

Videos/DVDs Shown: 10-minute video on company history, narrated by Herr family members; short videos throughout tour show unique views of snacks being made.

Reservations Needed: Yes, but can take walk-ins if space permits.

Days and Hours: Mon–Thur 9:00 AM–3:00 PM on the hour; Fri 9:00 AM, 10:00 AM, and 11:00 AM. Closed holidays.

Plan to Stay: 1.5 hours, including video, tour, gift shop, and café.

Minimum Age: None

Disabled Access: Yes

Group Requirements: With advance notice, can handle any size group, which will split into smaller ones for tour. Video shown in 140-seat auditorium.

Special Information: If you are interested in particular products, such as tortilla chips or cheese curls, call ahead for production schedule on day of your visit.

Gift Shop: Sells Herr's food products; logoed clothing items; Nottingham, PA, T-shirts; scale model of Herr's delivery truck; and Chipper the Chipmunk doll. Open Mon–Fri 8:00 AM–5:00 PM. Call for extended holiday hours. Catalog available from above number.

Directions: From Philadelphia, take I-95 South to Rt. 322 West exit. From Rt. 322, turn left onto Rt. 1 South. Turn left onto Rt. 272 South and right at light onto Herr Dr. Factory and Visitors Center at end of road. From Baltimore, take I-95 North to Exit 100. Take Rt. 272 North. Turn left at light onto Herr Dr.

Nearby Attractions: Hagley Museum tour (see page 94), about 1 hour away; Longwood Gardens; Plumpton Park Zoo; Franklin Mint Museum; Brandywine River Museum; Lancaster County attractions about 30 miles away.

freshly baked Special Pretzels at the exit end of an 80-foot pretzel oven

Herr's Snack Factory Tour

It's a free, fun-filled morning or afternoon of educational tidbits, technological wizardry, and tasty little morsels.

Visitors to Herr's snack factory tour taste warm, freshly cooked potato chips straight from the production line.

Unseasoned potato chips are transported by stainless steel vibrating conveyors to seasoning applicators and packaging stations.

700 Hyundai Boulevard, Montgomery, AL 36105 | (334) 387-8019 | www.hmmausa.com

This tour is not just for car buffs but for anybody interested in modern manufacturing methods. Robots and people work together in futuristic harmony, and the atmosphere is friendly rather than forbidding. People wave a lot. During the tour, your guide may point out a (human) Team Member and encourage you to raise a cheer of support.

Guests gather in the visitor center and start the tour in the auditorium with an overview of Hyundai and a video about the manufacturing operation. Donning headsets for hearing your guide's commentary, you put on safety glasses and board the tour's electric tram, which your guide drives into the plant.

In the stamping shop, rolls of coiled steel are cut and then stamped under great pressure into 17 different vehicle body parts. Here you meet your first Hyundai robots, which collect the parts and store them. More robots (over 250) await you in the corridors of the weld shop. They weld together, with precision and a lot of flying sparks, the stamped metal parts into the recognizable body of a car. These skeletal cars proceed by overhead trestle to the paint shop, where they turn 11 somersaults in a preparatory bath before robots spray on their coats of color and glossy finish.

Your tour moves to the next area for general assembly. Through modern ventilation and conveyance, this zone is surprisingly clean, cool, and quiet. Humans join robots here: over a thousand Team Members install the parts and pieces of each vehicle, including wiring, brake controls, engine, drive train, tires, battery, doors, seats, and glass. However, robots play an important role even here. One of the most striking sights of the tour is the snakelike robot that places the windshields; when the glass is perfectly poised and ready, it lunges forward like a Hollywood dinosaur and sets the windshield in place.

The tour guide uses a wireless microphone/headset system to explain how a car is made as guests ride, look, and listen in the plant.

After receiving oil, coolant, gasoline, and other fluids, the car undergoes rigorous quality tests. Your tour follows this process outside to a two-mile test track, where the examinations include a check of the brakes and a ride along a rough road to listen for rattles and loose parts.

The Montgomery facility has its own shop for making V6 engines, and this is the last stop on your tour. Having seen the installation of the engines back in general assembly, here you can learn about their construction. Feel free to browse through the visitor center and gift shop after the tour.

Cost: Free

Freebies: No

Video/DVD Shown: An 8-minute overview before the tour explains the process of making vehicles.

Reservations Needed: Yes. Visit www.hmmausa.com/tours.cfm and click on the "Book a Tour Today" link, or call the reservation line (334-387-8019), Mon–Fri 9:00 AM–4:00 PM.

Days and Hours: Tours: Mon, Wed, and Fri at 9:30 AM, 12:30 PM, and 2:00 PM. Visitor center: Mon–Fri 9:00 AM–4:00 PM. Closed holidays.

Plan to Stay: 1.5 hours.

Minimum Age: First-graders with parent or guardian; third-graders for school groups.

Disabled Access: Yes, please call ahead to make arrangements.

Group Requirements: The tour permits a maximum of 32 people. Larger groups must schedule more than one tour.

Gift Shop: The shop sells Hyundai promotional merchandise. Open Mon–Fri 9:30 AM–5:30 PM (closed 12:45–1:15 PM). Closed holidays.

Directions: From I-65, take Hope Hull/Hyundai Blvd. exit, travel west about 0.7 mile, merge on Hyundai Blvd., and drive east for 1.3 miles. Plant is on left. Look for Visitor Entrance and Visitor Parking. Tell security you are there for tour.

Nearby Attractions: Rosa Parks Library and Museum; Civil Rights Memorial; Hank Williams Museum.

Weld-shop robots apply approximately 2000 welds to the car body. The finished body moves from here to the paint shop.

Corporate Museum, Robert N. Noyce Building,
2200 Mission College Blvd, Santa Clara, CA 95052

(408) 765-0503

www.intel.com

Few U.S. companies embody the computer revolution as well as Intel Corporation. Its 10,000-square-foot museum contains interactive displays that demonstrate how silicon chips are made, how they work, their effects on our lives, and their evolution. You'll also learn about Intel, the world's largest maker of silicon chips that power computers, cell phones, and thousands of other digital products.

Located at Intel's Santa Clara, California, campus in the heart of Silicon Valley, the museum offers a rare, inside look at a high-tech world where distance is measured in billionths of meters, and time in billionths of seconds. The Intel Museum is a self-guided experience that mixes Intel history, technology explanations, demonstrations, and popular culture in more than 30 exhibits.

The most recent additions chronicle the fascinating life of high-tech inventor and Intel cofounder Robert Noyce and show how digital technology has transformed how we record sounds, take pictures, and communicate. In the Intel Timeline, the history of Intel and the evolution of its products are depicted through artifacts and stories that entertain, whether or not you have technical insight.

Silicon chip manufacturing processes are shown in the "Intel Fab" exhibit area, where museum visitors, over closed-circuit flat-screen TV, watch Intel employees inside ultraclean "Fabs" (silicon chip factories) as they work wearing "bunny suits." No, these workers aren't dressed in costumes with floppy ears. The process used to manufacture silicon chips requires air many times cleaner than is found inside hospital operating rooms, so workers wear special white coveralls and head gear designed to prevent impurities from destroying sensitive silicon chips. You can even try on a bunny suit yourself and walk around on perforated flooring just like that through which purified air circulates in a real fab. A dazzling, 12-inch-diameter silver ingot of silicon on display may be the purest thing you'll ever touch.

How silicon chips are produced, assembled, and tested, are among many interactive demonstrations inside the Intel Museum in Santa Clara, CA.

The Intel Museum's exhibits appeal to all levels of technical knowledge and interest. Many exhibits are hands-on, like one that allows you to "spell" your name in the two-digit "binary" language of computers. Another exhibit allows you to place templates over a touch screen to replicate the steps taken to etch intricate circuitry onto silicon wafers. All the exhibits are informative and fascinating.

Cost: Free

Freebies: Occasionally for prescheduled tour groups.

Video/DVD Shown: Various video interviews with Intel engineers, scientists, and other employees, live video from an Intel factory, and more.

Reservations Needed: No, except for scheduled guided group tours.

Days and Hours: Mon–Fri 9:00 AM–6:00 PM, Sat 10:00 AM–5:00 PM. Closed holidays.

Plan to Stay: About 1–2 hours.

Minimum Age: None, but 8 is the recommended minimum. Displays have interactive components that are enjoyed most by children interested in computers or science.

Disabled Access: Yes

Group Requirements: Maximum group size is 20 people or 35 students. Minimum 8 people to be considered a group. Call (408) 765-0503 at least 6 weeks in advance to schedule a group tour.

Special Information: Bags and backpacks not permitted. No coat check. Cameras and handheld video cameras are allowed. Drop-in guided tours are available at preset times. Tours last approximately 1 hour. Please call for current tour times.

Intel Museum Store: Sells Intel branded merchandise, including apparel, pens, gifts, computer devices, toys, and other items. Open same hours as museum.

Directions: Take U.S. 101 to the Montague Expwy. East. Turn left onto Mission College Blvd. The Robert N. Noyce Building is on left. Museum is to the left of the lobby and can be entered through a plaza directly in front of the building.

Nearby Attractions: Stanford Linear Accelerator Center tour (call 650-926-2204); Tech Museum of Innovation (call 408-294-8324); San Jose Children's Discovery Museum (call 408-298-5437); Great America Theme Park (call 408-988-1776).

Children visiting the Intel Museum try on "bunny suits." Workers wear the suits in the ultra-clean factories where computer chips are made. The suits keep hairs and skin flakes from contaminating the microscopic circuitry on the chips.

(574) 825-5861 | www.jayco.com

AMERICA'S MOST **LIVEABLE** RVS

Since the mid-1960s, when Jayco founder Lloyd Bontrager first built his pop-up camper prototypes in a converted chicken coop, family members and friends have been an integral part of Jayco's success. Watching the construction of Travel Trailers and Fifth Wheels, both towable RVs, you still sense that family feeling, even though Jayco is the largest privately held RV manufacturer in the country. About 70 percent of Jayco's 1,500 workers are Amish or Mennonite, and their dedication to quality is evident as you travel through the factory.

Every Jayco trailer begins with a tubular steel frame built by a firm that specializes in RV frames. Workers lay tongue-and-groove plywood floor, insulate with fiberglass, and use Polyflex fabric on the bottom. Following these steps, you'll see the entire trailer flipped upside-down, like an immense turtle on its back. Workers attach axles and wheels to the underbelly and install a fresh-water tank. The unit is turned back over and placed on dollies that run down a track to various workstations in the plant.

Next, they lay the carpeting and linoleum. Workers then attach white-pine sidewalls, which have the interior paneling fastened with glue and brand nails. Look up, and you'll see the cabinet shops above the plant floor. Wood from the mill room is assembled into cabinets. Each production line, for the Jay Flight, Jay Feather, Eagle, and top-of-the-line Designer Fifth Wheels, has its own cabinet shop. Carpenters slide the finished cabinets down a ramp to the production area.

Toward the end of the RV's construction, workers attach the roof. They screw on tapered trusses or two-by-fours for the rafters, then stretch a rubber or aluminum roof over them. The area resounds with noises of drills, routers, and sanders. The RV's "skin" of .024-gauge aluminum or fiberglass is then secured onto the units. Once the RV's body is complete, appliances, drawer and cabinet fronts,

The "Griner House," an old farmhouse built in 1880, has been restored and renovated to house the Jayco Visitor Center.

windows, and custom-made upholstery are added. Afterward, at your leisure, you can view completed trailers displayed in a campground setting.

Cost: Free

Freebies: Product brochures.

Video/DVD Shown: 15-minute video on the company's history and production methods.

Reservations Needed: No, except for groups larger than 15 people.

Days and Hours: Tours Mon–Fri 12:00 PM; June–August a second tour is added at 9:30 AM. Display area and Visitors Center open Mon–Fri 8:00 AM–5:00 PM. Closed holidays. No production July 4th week and week between Christmas and New Year's.

Plan to Stay: 1.5 hours for video and tour, plus time for gift area, display area, and Visitors Center.

Minimum Age: None

Disabled Access: Limited, although must be careful of tools and wires on factory tour. No wheelchairs; call for more information.

Group Requirements: Groups larger than 15 people need to make reservations 10 days in advance. Maximum group size is 50.

Special Information: No photography or video equipment of any kind allowed on tours. Upon request, tours are available of the mini–motor home production buildings. Visitors Center displays Jayco memorabilia, including brochures from 1968.

Gift Area: Sells logoed items, including mugs, apparel, and miscellaneous gifts. Open same hours as Visitors Center. Closed holidays.

Directions: From I-80/90 (Indiana Toll Rd.), take Exit 107 for SR 13 South to Middlebury. Located on right, just south of the intersection with U.S. Rt. 20.

Nearby Attractions: Monaco and Coachmen tours (see pages 167 and 164). Elkhart County is the RV manufacturing capital of the world. For a list of tours, call (800) 262-8161. The RV/MH Heritage Foundation (call 574-293-2344) features museum, library, exhibition hall, and Hall of Fame dedicated to recreational vehicle and manufactured housing industries.

When you visit and tour Jayco, Inc. in Middlebury, IN, you will see many local Amish workers among the 1500 employees.

John Deere Pavilion

AGRICULTURAL EQUIPMENT

1400 River Drive, Moline, IL 61265

(309) 765-1000
(800) 765-9588

www.johndeere
pavilion.com

The John Deere Pavilion, the world's largest agriculture museum, celebrates the past, present, and future of agriculture, as well as the history of the company. The 14,000-square-foot Pavilion is like one you'd see at a fairground, except the walls are made almost entirely of glass. Inside, stop at reception to request your own personal tour guide, likely a Deere retiree, who will happily customize your visit any way you like.

If you've never been on a farm, this is your chance to climb aboard a brand-new, shiny green tractor or combine that sits on the Pavilion floor. How has equipment like the tractor changed over the years, since Deere made the 1918 Water oo Boy model? To find out, compare the new machines to their antique counterparts, also on display at the Pavilion (but don't climb on the antiques—they're too fragile). To see a tractor or combine in action, take a virtual tour at one of the touch-screen displays. "Tour" the combine factory and watch employees assemble this boxy piece of machinery, then see the machine harvest wheat, soy, and corn. At another station the "tour" shows workers assembling tractors. Notice all the different attachments—each attachment performs a different task on the field.

"Cornucopia" is a touch-screen exhibit that takes you from the beginning of a product's life until it gets to market. Learn the life story of apples, pork, or cotton. Another interactive exhibit called "The Past" walks you through the history of agriculture, while "The Future" educates guests about how the world will feed its booming population, which may double in the next 40 years. Like many guests, you may find yourself returning to the Pavilion again and again simply to reminisce and share experiences of life on the farm.

The John Deere Pavilion is a 14,000-square-foot glass-enclosed structure located in downtown Moline, IL. It is the world's most comprehensive agricultural exhibit.

Cost: Free

Freebies: No

Video/DVD Shown: 14-minute film shown on a new high-definition screen system, "Anthem," about global farming practices.

Reservations Needed: No

Days and Hours: Mon–Fri 9:00 AM–5:00 PM, Sat 10:00 AM–5:00 PM, Sun 12:00 PM–4:00 PM. Closed Easter, Thanksgiving, Christmas, and New Year's.

Plan to Stay: 1 hour for tour and "Anthem," plus time to visit the John Deere Store and John Deere Collectors Center, just a few steps away.

Minimum Age: None

Disabled Access: Yes

Group Requirements: Groups of 30 or more should call in advance if possible.

Special Information: No videotaping of "Anthem." Visit John Deere factory tours in East Moline, IL (see page 155) and Waterloo, IA (see page 279).

Gift Shop: John Deere Store sells a variety of items emblazoned with the company logo, from baseball caps and towels to fishing lures and mailboxes. January–February: Mon–Sat 10:00 AM–5:00 PM, Sun 12:00 PM– 4:00 PM. March–December: Mon–Fri 10:00 AM–6:00 PM, Sat 10:00 AM–5:00 PM, Sun 12:00 PM–4:00 PM. Closed same days as the Pavilion.

Directions: From the east, take I-74 West into Moline. Take the 7th Ave. exit (last Illinois exit). Turn left on 7th Ave. Go 4 blocks and turn right on 15th St. Go 4 blocks. From the west, take I-80 to I-74 East. Follow I-74 East across the Mississippi River to Illinois. Take the River Dr. exit (the first exit). Turn left on River Dr. and go 4.5 blocks. John Deere Pavilion is on the corner of River Dr. and 15th St.

Nearby Attractions: John Deere Harvester Works tour (see page 155); John Deere Collectors Center half block away on John Deere Commons (call 800-240-5265); Mississippi River; Historic Deere family homes; Deere & Company World Headquarters; Tournament Players Club at Deere Run.

New products and fully restored antique equipment are featured on the floor of the John Deere Pavilion.

Long Grove Confectionery Company

333 Lexington Drive, Buffalo Grove, IL 60089 (888) 459-3100 www.longgrove.com

Tours of Long Grove Confectionery Company start in the shadow of a nine-foot-high Statue of Liberty, sculpted in solid chocolate with elaborate detail, that weighs over a ton. A 500-pound chocolate Santa Claus greets visitors throughout the year, and chocolate reproductions of paintings by Monet and Seurat adorn the walls elsewhere. These works are a fitting introduction to Long Grove, which has been combining art and chocolate in a big way since 1975.

However, as a tour of the chocolate factory reveals, much of the company's work occurs on a miniature rather than a colossal scale. After seeing a brief video on how chocolate is made from the seed of the tropical cacao tree, visitors embark on a tour of the factory and view production areas through windows. The strong, sweet smell of chocolate pervades every corner of this immense facility, which sprawls over 85,000 square feet.

The first stop is the kitchen area. Depending on the schedule, visitors may see homemade caramel as it cooks in copper kettles, English toffee on hot and cold tables, or caramel apples, which workers roll in pecans and drizzle with milk chocolate. You may also see how Long Grove makes its own cream and peanut-butter fillings in a huge mixer—a giant version of a kitchen blender.

The two vital zones for handmade chocolate are the molding and unmolding areas. The decorative use of colored chocolate is a signature of Long Grove. Staff paint colored elements by hand in the molds before chocolate is poured. The results, after over an hour in the cooling chamber, are intricately colored sculptures. The workers in the unmolding area then trim excess chocolate by hand with a small knife. Why doesn't the chocolate melt in their fingers? Depending on its chemistry, chocolate melts between 86°F and 90°F; the unmolding area

A family watches Long Grove Confectionery's expert "painters" hand decorating various unique chocolate molds.

FEATURED TOURS

is maintained at 60°F, and the bundled-up workers wear cotton gloves. After trimming, each piece is ready for wrapping.

Other chocolates are made for boxed collections in the enrobing area, where a machine coats each filling center with chocolate and sends it on a belt to the cooling tunnel. (Although visitors cannot see this area, a video shows the process.) After cooling, the chocolates ride into the packaging area, a large space where staff box them. Molded chocolates also end up here. Elegant decorations are another signature of Long Grove: workers dress each handmade piece in a careful raiment of cellophane, bows, and sometimes seasonal ornaments. A tasting of fresh chocolate ends the tour.

Cost: $2 per person.

Freebies: Free tasting of chocolate.

Video/DVD Shown: Various videos (total: 20 minutes) on manufacturing and on company background.

Reservations Needed: Yes

Days and Hours: Daily by appointment. Closed holidays.

Plan to Stay: 1.5 hours.

Minimum Age: None

Disabled Access: Yes

Group Requirements: No

Gift Shop: The shop sells the full range of chocolates. Open Mon–Sat 9:30 AM–5:30 PM, Sun 11:00 AM–4:00 PM. Closed holidays.

Directions: From I-94 East, take exit for Lake Cook Rd., turn right at end of ramp, drive 4 miles, and turn right on Lexington Dr. From I-94 West, take Lake Cook Rd. exit, turn left at end of ramp, drive 3 miles, and turn right on Lexington Dr.

Nearby Attractions: Haeger Potteries (see page 154); in Chicago (45 minutes away), Chicago Mercantile Exchange, Chicago Board of Trade, McDonald's Museum, and USPS mail-distribution center (see pages 150, 149, 158, 160).

FEATURED TOURS

candy corn whiskers being placed on Long Grove Confectionery Halloween Pops

Hillerich & Bradsby Co., 800 West Main Street, Louisville, KY 40202

(502) 588-7228
(877) 7-SLUGGER

www.sluggermuseum.org

FEATURED TOURS

The Louisville Slugger bat, created by Bud Hillerich in 1884, has been called "one of the greatest original American products ever made." In 1996, Hillerich & Bradsby Co. opened the Louisville Slugger Museum, a tribute to baseball's greatest hits and hitters. You'll see actual bats swung by such legendary sluggers as Ty Cobb, Lou Gehrig, and Joe DiMaggio, plus the bat Babe Ruth used during his 1927 record-setting 60-home-run season. Listen to Hall of Fame broadcasters call baseball's greatest moments. Take the field in a replica of Camden Yards. Choose a famous pitcher to throw the ball in your direction at 90 miles per hour, crawl through a giant ball and glove sculpture, or step into a batting cage and take a few swings of your own.

After walking through the museum and a replica of a Northern white ash forest, take a guided tour of the plant. With the ever-present smell of wood in the air, H&B turns the Northern white ash and maple billets into bats. Most of the bats are made on automatic lathes.

It takes about 40 seconds to make a bat on the tracer lathes. Workers use a metal pattern of the exact bat shape and guide the machine to trace this pattern, a process similar to copying a key at the hardware store. All of the Major League bats are made on a special CNC lathe, the only one of its kind in the world.

With sizzle and smoke, the famous oval trademark, bat model number, and the player's autograph are still seared into the "flat of the grain" on some bats. Bats can also be foil-branded with either gold or silver. Behind the branders are large cabinets holding more than 8,500 professional baseball players' autograph brands. You'll leave the museum and tour having witnessed a part of true Americana.

The world's biggest baseball bat marks the entrance to Louisville Slugger Museum & Factory. The bat is 120 feet tall, made of steel, and hand-painted to look like wood.

Cost: Adults, $9; seniors 60+, $8; children 6–12, $4; children 5 and under, free.

Freebies: 18-inch miniature wood bat.

Video/DVD Shown: 13-minute film, "Heart of the Game," relives some of the greatest hits in baseball. Overhead flat screen monitors show close-up production at various stops.

Reservations Needed: No, except for groups larger than 20 people.

Days and Hours: Mon–Sat 9:00 AM–5:00 PM, year-round; open until 6:00 PM in July; also open Sun 12:00 PM–5:00 PM, April 1–November 30, but no bat production. Production at other times varies based on factory needs. Closed holidays.

Plan to Stay: 1.5 hours for tour and museum, plus time for gift shop.

Minimum Age: Discourages children under age 5.

Disabled Access: Yes

Group Requirements: Reservations needed for groups over 20 people. At least 1-month advance notice suggested for summer tours. Call (502) 588-7227.

Special Information: No photography in plant.

Gift Shop: Sells Louisville Slugger logoed items, including T-shirts, hats, towels, gym bags, and pen bats. Personalized bats are also available. Open same hours as tour.

Directions: From Indianapolis, take I-65 South to I-64 West. Exit on 3rd St. Turn right onto River Rd. Turn left onto 8th St. You can't miss the Louisville Slugger Museum—just look for the world's tallest bat. From Cincinnati, take I-71 South to I-64 West and follow above directions.

Nearby Attractions: Colonel Harland Sanders (KFC) Museum, Ford, Louisville Stoneware, and American Printing House for the Blind tours (see pages 239, 245, 247, and 238); Louisville Science Center (across the street from the Louisville Slugger Museum); Frazier Historical Arms Museum; Muhammad Ali Center, Kentucky Derby Museum; Churchill Downs.

The bats sizzle and smoke when the world-famous Louisville Slugger trademark is branded onto the wood. The burn-branding station is one of several stops on the factory tour.

3350 Burks Spring Road, Loretto, KY 40037   (270) 865-2099   www.makersmark.com

FEATURED TOURS

Maker's Mark ®

An illustration of the Maker's Mark distillery appears on its bottles; the label invites you to visit "any time you're in the neighborhood," so you know the place must be special. Just as Bill Samuels Sr. wanted to create his own distinctive bourbon by using gentle winter wheat instead of rye, he wanted to restore a historic distillery complex into the home of Maker's Mark.

Your tour of this National Historic Landmark distillery begins near the stonewalled creek that runs through the peaceful, landscaped grounds, where you'll hear a brief history of the distillery. Its black buildings feature bright red shutters with a Maker's Mark bottle cutout. Unlike larger distilleries' 600-barrel-per-day production, Maker's Mark crafts its bourbon in 19 barrel batches.

In the still house you'll smell corn, wheat, and malted barley cooking. The bubbling yellow mash ferments in century-old cypress vats. Vaporization of the mash in the shiny copper still separates out the whiskey, which is placed in charred oak casks for aging. When you enter the aging warehouse's ground floor, the aromas alone tell you what's in the barrels. Barrels reach maturity only after completing a rotation system in which the newest barrels are placed on the warehouse's hot upper floors and are rotated to the cooler lower levels after about three years.

Only in the bottling house does the production pace quicken. Near the end of the line, each bottle's glass neck is hand-dipped into red sealing wax and then twisted to allow the excess to drip off and run down the neck. Notice each worker's distinctive dipping and twisting technique.

Cost: Free

Freebies: Water and lemonade; bourbon ball sample; great smells.

Video/DVD Shown: No

Reservations Needed: No, except for groups larger than 25 people.

Every bottle of Maker's Mark is hand-dipped in the signature red wax.

Days and Hours: Mon–Sat 10:30 AM, 11:30 AM, 12:30 PM, 1:30 PM, 2:30 PM, and 3:30 PM, Sun 1:30 PM, 2:30 PM, and 3:30 PM. Closed on Sundays in January and February. No production from mid-August–mid-September, but tour still runs. Limited weekend production. Closed Thanksgiving, Christmas Eve, Christmas Day, New Year's Day, and Easter Sunday.

Plan to Stay: 45 minutes to an hour for the tour, plus time for visitors center and Quart House. Once a pre–Civil War distiller's home, the visitor's center has pieces from the Samuels' collection of early-1800s furniture and other historical and craft items. The Quart House, oldest standing package liquor store in America, is a restored pre-Prohibition retail store.

Minimum Age: Recommends that children under 10 be accompanied by an adult. You must be 21 to purchase and dip your own bottle of Maker's Mark.

Disabled Access: Yes. Paved walking paths between buildings.

Group Requirements: Requests prior notice for groups of 25 people or more.

Special Information: The Bottling line does not run every day, but visitors can purchase souvenir bottles to dip in the signature red wax every day except Sunday.

Gift Shop: The Gift Gallery in the visitor center sells logoed and craft items, including shirts, sweaters, jackets, key chains, and shot glasses. Also, gourmet sauces and candies made with Maker's Mark. Open Mon–Sat 10:00 AM–4:30 PM, Sun 1:00–4:30 PM.

Directions: From Bardstown, take KY 49 South and follow signs to distillery. You're there when you see the sign that says, "You've Just Found the Home of Maker's Mark."

Nearby Bourbon-Related Attractions: Heaven Hill Distillery tour (call 502-348-3921); Oscar Getz Museum of Whiskey History (call 502-348-2999); Jim Beam's American Outpost (call 502-543-9877); Annual September Kentucky Bourbon Festival in Bardstown.

In the still house you will have the opportunity to see how Maker's Mark is crafted.

Visitor Center, 4251 West State Street, Milwaukee, WI 53208

(414) 931-BEER
(414) 931-2337

www.millerbrewing.com

MILLER BREWING C°

SINCE 1855

MILWAUKEE, WIS. USA

In 1855, German immigrant Fredrick Miller purchased the Plank Road Brewery. Surrounded by woods, the small brewing operation was no bigger than a Victorian house. Today, a replica of the Plank Road Brewery is just one of the historic highlights in Milwaukee's Miller Valley—the home of the nation's second largest brewer, Miller Brewing Company.

Walk outdoors and upstairs to Miller's packaging-center balcony. A blur of cans roars along conveyor belts that wind through wet machinery, packing up to 200,000 cases of beer daily.

The next stop is Miller's mammoth distribution center that covers the equivalent of five football fields. Typically, you can see half a million cases of beer.

In the brew house, Miller makes its beer, up to 8.5 million barrels annually in Milwaukee alone. Climb 56 stairs to look down on a row of towering, shiny brew kettles where "wort," a grain extract, is boiled and combined with hops. Stroll through Miller's historic Caves, a restored portion of the original brewery where beer was stored before the invention of mechanical refrigeration.

Finish your tour at the Bavarian-style Miller Inn and sample a Miller beer or soft drink. Be sure also to take a few minutes to inspect the impressive collection of antique steins. In the summer, you can enjoy your beverage in an adjoining beer garden enlivened by music.

Cost: Free

Freebies: Beer (for those 21 years of age and older with proper ID), soda, peanuts, and postcards (Miller will cover postage to any world destination).

Video/DVD Shown: 15-minute video shows brewing process and overview of Miller's history, information about their present operation, and the future of the company.

Reservations Needed: No, but recommended for groups of 15 or more.

Days and Hours: Mon–Sat 10:30 AM–3:30 PM. Closed holidays and week between Christmas and New Year's.

Plan to Stay: 1 hour for video and tour, plus time for product sampling and gift shop.

Minimum Age: No

Disabled Access: Plant tour: no. Visitor Center (includes video), Miller Inn, and Caves: yes.

Group Requirements: Groups of 15 or more should call at least 1 day ahead for reservations. Maximum group size is 105. Limited reservations on Saturdays.

Special Information: Best time to see production is weekdays. Miller Brewing Company also gives tours and has a gift shop in Tumwater, WA (call 360-754-5217), and the Miller Marketplace and Brew Kettle Museum in Ft. Worth, TX (call 817-568-BEER).

Gift Shop: Girl in the Moon Brewery Shop sells clothing, caps, glassware, steins, mirrors, tap handles, and other Miller-logoed items. Open Mon–Sat: summer 10:00 AM– 5:30 PM; winter 10:00 AM–5:00 PM.

Directions: From Chicago, take I-94 West to 35th St. Turn right (north) on 35th St. Turn left (west) onto State St. Pass through "Miller Valley" (well marked) to last building on left, Miller Visitor Center and Gift Shop. From Madison, take I-94 East to Hwy. 41 North to the State St. exit. Follow signs to right, down hill to traffic light. Turn left onto State St. Visitor Center is 1 block ahead on right.

Nearby Attractions: Quality Candy/Buddy Squirrel factory tour (see page 215); Miller Park (home of Milwaukee Brewers); Milwaukee County Zoo; Mitchell Park Horticulture ("The Domes"); Milwaukee County Museum; Milwaukee Art Museum; Boerner Botanical Gardens; Cedar Creek Winery. Miller Visitor Center front desk has information on and directions to many local attractions.

FEATURED TOURS

NO 3 BREW KETTLE CAP. 590 BBLS.

NO 2 BREW KETTLE CAP. 590 BBLS.

NO 1 BREW KETTLE CAP. 590 BBLS.

Miller's brewhouse in Milwaukee

Miller Brewing

Welcome to Miller Valley, the home of Miller Brewing Company.

Guests can take a stroll through the historic Miller High Life Cruiser.

Guests can sample a variety of Miller products at the historic Miller Inn.

The Milwaukee campus includes 82 acres of land and 76 buildings.

New Orleans GlassWorks
& PrintMaking

722 Magazine Street, New Orleans, LA 70130   (504) 529-7277   www.neworleans
glassworks.com

The New Orleans Arts District was unaffected by Hurricane Katrina, and it offers visitors plenty to do. Located in a restored 19th-century brick building, the New Orleans School of GlassWorks & Printmaking Studio lets you watch artisans use their skills in glassblowing, printmaking, bookbinding, and related crafts in jewelry, metal sculpture, and papermaking.

The heart of this facility is the two continuous-melt furnaces, encircled by three fully equipped traditional European glassblowing benches. After you walk through the store and enter the studios, you'll immediately notice the teams of glassblowers as they jump, jive, and wail in the glassblowing arena to the sounds of New Orleans music. They like to say their maneuverings are similar to the choreography of swing danc-ers, as they "swing out" their vessels to lengthen them and skillfully balance the glowing, honeylike molten glass on the end of their blowpipes.

Faculty members occasionally narrate for the crowd as they instruct students making Venetian-inspired blown- and cast-glass creations. You may be invited to take part in the final step, known as the "fiber optic pull." Notice the special skills involved in "torch working" glass objects into such shapes as sea creatures or beads. These are made from rods and tubes of colored glass (called cane) that become soft and malleable when heated by the flame of a tabletop torch. The techniques used by flame-working artists often resemble those used in glassblowing, but are just much smaller in scale. Gravity, heat, and simple steel hand tools are the basic provisions they need to shape glass into sculptural designs.

You're encouraged to stroll through each studio to discuss the processes with the artists at work in the open studios. Papermaking equipment fills the back area of this studio, a 25,000-square-foot space with skylights. You see an etching press, automated letterpress, and other machines used to hand-make

glassweaving being torched in New Orleans GlassWorks & PrintMaking Studio

and marble paper and to bind books. Note how printmakers use acid to etch copper plates, set lead type for hand-bound books, and make custom wedding invitations and "shoot screens" for hand-printed fabric designs.

Cost: Free

Freebies: None

Video/DVD Shown: No

Reservations Needed: Reservations are required for groups of more than 10 people and for hands-on participatory events to accompany demonstrations.

Days and Hours: Mon–Sat 10:00 AM–5:00 PM (September–May); Mon–Fri 10:00 AM–5:00 PM (June–August). Closed major holidays. Production varies. Call for details.

Plan to Stay: 30 minutes for a self-guided tour, plus time for gift shop/crafts store in front area.

Disabled Access: Yes

Group Requirements: Groups of 10 or more should contact GlassWorks to reserve guided tours.

Special Information: During summer, local culinary artists create chocolate and sugar sculptures. If you call at least 2 days in advance, you can design a colorful ornament, have a glass impression of your hand cast in solid glass, create a glass bead, or make your own prints on the star wheels press. Regularly scheduled classes, workshops, and private lessons are available (call 504-529-7277).

Gift Shop: Gallery store sells glass, metal, marble, and print creations made in studios.

Directions: From I-10 (toward Mississippi Bridge), take St. Charles Ave. exit. Continue on Calliope (under interstate) for 3 lights, until Camp St. Turn left on Camp St. Continue on Camp St. and turn right on Girod. Take another right on Magazine. GlassWorks is on Magazine, between Girod and Julia.

Nearby Attractions: The Ogden Museum of Southern Art; Contemporary Arts Center; various art galleries; D-Day Museum; RiverWalk; Convention Center. French Quarter is a 30-minute walk away.

Head Gaffer in front of Glory Hole spinning out incomo plate

Rebecca-Ruth Candies

CHOCOLATES AND BOURBON BALLS

112 East 2nd Street, Frankfort, KY 40601

(502) 223-7475
(800) 444-3766

www.rebeccaruth.com

Kentucky's famous 100-proof bourbon whiskeys—and a lot of local pride—are key ingredients in this family-owned company's world-renowned chocolates. These chocolates are as rich as the history surrounding the Rebecca-Ruth name itself. Founded in 1919 by two uncommonly courageous schoolteachers, Rebecca Gooch and Ruth Booe, the company's popularity grew as a result of the women's highly acclaimed chocolates and was aided by their creative sales techniques—which included loudly plugging their products on street corners. Ruth Booe originated the "Bourbon Ball." Made with real Kentucky bourbon and crowned with a Southern pecan, this confection has become the treat of the South.

The bright red awning shading this small, house-like store and factory creates an unpretentious atmosphere. The 10 to 15 employees (some of whom have been here for over 30 years) make about 100,000 pounds of confections a year.

In the cream-candy room are articles about Rebecca-Ruth from national magazines such as *Southern Living* and *Gourmet*. Workers pull candy cream on a hook by hand and then use a taffy-pull machine. When it's "just right," the rope of candy is cut into pieces and left to sit. It becomes very creamy, rich, and flaky. Peanut brittle and toffee are also made in this room.

In the kitchen, the cast-iron candy furnace and copper kettles emit the sweet scent of hand-stirred, melting sugars. In the production area, large mixers prepare rich fillings for their assembly-line journey down the enrobing line. First the candy dough is extruded onto a belt, and then it goes through a "chocolate waterfall." Two workers personally apply the finishing touches: a luscious southern pecan, sprinkles, or a swirled flourish on top.

A tour highlight is seeing "Edna's table." For close to 70 years, Edna Robbins handmade delicacies on

Owner Charles Booe enjoys a piece of Rebecca-Ruth Candies, based in Frankfort, Kentucky.

FEATURED TOURS

the same marble table used by Rebecca and Ruth. (Ruth bought "Edna's table" for $10 in 1917.)

Cost: 75 cents per person.

Freebies: Samples of the original Bourbon Balls and other chocolates (children receive liquor-free samples only).

Video/DVD Shown: 8-minute video on candy production.

Reservations Needed: No, except for bus groups.

Days and Hours: January–November Mon–Sat 9:00 AM–12:00 PM and 1:00–4:30 PM. No tours 4 days before Valentine's Day, Mother's Day, and Easter.

Plan to Stay: 45 minutes, plus time in retail store.

Minimum Age: Young children should be accompanied by an adult.

Disabled Access: No

Group Requirements: Bus operators should call (800) 444-3766, or visit the website, to make reservations or obtain additional information, or send email to tours@rebeccaruth.com.

Special Information: Video cameras not allowed. Production more likely in mornings.

Retail Store: Sells a wide variety of liquor-cream chocolates (including Bourbon Balls, Kentucky Irish Coffees, and Kentucky Mint Juleps), and liquor-free chocolates, including nut clusters, butter creams, and Kentucky Creamed Pull Candy. Open year-round Mon–Sat 9:00 AM–5:30 PM. Closed Thanksgiving, Christmas, and New Year's Day. Catalog available from 800 number above.

Directions: From Lexington, take I-64 West to Frankfort Exit 58, then take U.S. 60 West. Turn left onto Second St. Rebecca Ruth is on left. From Louisville, take I-64 East to Frankfort Exit 53. Take Rt. 127 North to U.S. 60 East, which becomes Second St. Stay on Second St. Cross over Capital Ave. Rebecca-Ruth is on left.

Nearby Attractions: Three Chimneys horse farm, Toyota, and Buffalo Trace Distillery tours (see pages 252, 253, and 240–241).

At the decorating station, workers hand-place pecans on Rebecca-Ruth chocolates.

Sutter Gold Mine

13660 Highway 49, Sutter Creek, CA 95685

(209) 736-2708
(800) 225-3764

www.caverntours.com

If your only mining experience is watching the Seven Dwarves in *Snow White,* it might be time for you to witness the real thing. The Sutter Gold Mine tour focuses on educating people about life inside a mine, the safety issues involved, and what the earth looks like so far underground.

Safety is a priority right from the beginning. The guide counts everyone and "tags them in" by placing a metal tag over a number so everyone will be accounted for at the end of the tour. Then everyone is fitted with hard hats, an accessory you must wear throughout the tour.

A bus buggy shuttle, used in real mines, carries you to the entrance of the mine. The entrance is cut into the rocky hillside, framed by a metal gate and metal pipes. You'll hear a loud noise, which is the ventilation fan. Beyond the first 30 feet, the mine is pitch black.

As you tunnel down the mineshaft, you'll stop four times to view mining equipment exhibits. After traveling 1,850 feet down, you'll enter the safety chamber. The guide will tell you how the safety chamber works and will explain the map of the Motherlode. Next, you'll walk through the "comet zone," where gold-bearing quartz was extracted. Up some stairs and through a tunnel you'll see more mining displays depicting mining activity and see the drills that are used to extract ore. There are still places where gold can be seen in the walls of the mine, and you'll learn how to distinguish real gold from fool's gold.

You'll board the bus buggy shuttle to come back out of the mine, where you'll turn in your hard hat and be tagged out before going back above ground.

Be sure to save some time after the tour to pan for gold and do some gemstone mining.

Cost: Adults, $14.95; children, $9.95. Gold panning, $5 each; gemstone mining, $4.50 small bag, $6.95 large bag.

Freebies: No

Video/DVD Shown: Free movies about gold mining shown in the Gold Theater.

Reservations Needed: No, but groups of 10 or more should call ahead to make sure there will be space on a tour for them. School groups should also call ahead.

Days and Hours: Mid-May–mid-September: daily 9:00 AM–5:00 PM. Mid-September–mid-May: weekdays 10:00 AM–4:00 PM, weekends and holidays 10:00 AM–5:00 PM.

Plan to Stay: One hour for walking tour; up to all day for above-ground activities.

Minimum Age: 3 for underground tour, but recommended for 4 or older. No minimum age for above-ground activities.

Disabled Access: Yes, with advance notice.

Group Requirements: School groups and groups of 10 or more should call ahead. Group discounts available. Maximum of 23 persons on each tour, although larger groups can be accommodated; no minimum.

Special Information: Hard hats must be worn underground. Tour not recommended for people who are claustrophobic or have serious heart or lung problems.

Gold Store: Sells handmade gold nugget jewelry, books about the gold rush and gold mining, science activities, and lots of rocks. Open same hours as mine.

Directions: From Sacramento, take Hwy. 16 East to Hwy. 49 South. Look for entrance on the left approx. half a mile south of Amador City, just north of Sutter Creek. From the Bay Area, take U.S. 50 East to I-205 to Hwy. 120 East to Hwy. 99 North. Take Hwy. 88 East to Hwy. 49 North. Look for entrance on the right approximately 1 mile north of Sutter Creek.

Nearby Attractions: Black Chasm Cavern National Natural Landmark, California Cavern State Historic Landmark, Moaning Cavern, Kennedy Gold Mine, Indian Grinding Rock State Historic Park, The Miners Pick Antques & Western Hardrock Mining Museum.

Two brothers enjoy their Sutter Gold Mine tour through the drifts of the "comet zone."

1001 Cherry Blossom Way,
Georgetown, KY 40324

(502) 868-3027
(800) 866-4485

www.toyota
georgetown.com

Toyota's largest vehicle manufacturing plant outside of Japan is located in this growing community in Kentucky's Bluegrass Region. Toyota Motor Manufacturing, Kentucky (TMMK), covers 7.5 million square feet of floor space, the equivalent of 156 football fields. But don't worry about your legs getting tired on the plant tour, because you'll be riding comfortably in one of their trams.

TMMK employs about 7,000 team members who build nearly 2,000 quality vehicles each day. A "takt time" of 55 seconds on both of the vehicle assembly lines means that two new Toyota vehicles are built in Georgetown every 55 seconds!

TMMK began production in 1988 with the popular Toyota Camry sedan. The Avalon sedan was added in 1994, while the Sienna minivan was produced from 1997 to 2002. Production of the Camry Solara coupe began in 2003.

Toyota vehicles get their start in Stamping, taking shape from huge coils of cold-rolled steel. The steel is cleaned, straightened, and stamped into sheet-metal components that make up the vehicle bodies. With hundreds of tons of force, the automatic presses shape the steel into doors, hoods, roofs, and many other parts.

The sheet-metal components then move to Body Weld, where team members and computer-controlled robots perform the welding that results in a completed body shell. The new vehicle bodies then travel by overhead conveyors to Paint before moving on to the Trim, Chassis, and Final lines in Assembly.

As you tour TMMK, your guide points out the foundations of the world-renowned Toyota Production System. These will include examples of *kaizen,* or continuous improvement; just-in-time parts delivery; and the *andon* system, where team members can stop the line at any time to address quality concerns or any problems.

In the TMMK Visitor Center, you will see current models of the vehicles and engines built in Georgetown, plus the very first Camry produced by team members in May 1988. The Visitor Center also includes interactive video displays and exhibits on Quality, Teamwork, the Toyota Production System, and hybrid technology.

Cost: Free

Freebies: Toyota vehicle (in the form of a refrigerator magnet!).

Video Shown: 10-minute video provides a brief plant overview, including sections not included on the tour.

Reservations Needed: Yes, but walk-ins will be accommodated as space permits.

Days and Hours: Plant tour: Mon–Fri 10:00 AM, 12:00 PM, and 2:00 PM, Thur also 6:00 PM. Closed holidays. Visitor Center: Mon–Fri 9:00 AM–4:00 PM, Thur until 7:00 PM. *Toyota reserves the right to cancel or reschedule tours at any time.*

Plan to Stay: 1.5–2 hours for plant tour, video, and exhibits.

Minimum Age: Plant tour: 1st grade for public tours and 4th grade for school tours. Visitor Center: no minimum age.

Disabled Access: Yes

Group Requirements: Maximum group size is 64 adults. Large groups must call several months in advance.

Special Information: Photographs and video and mechanical recordings are allowed in the Visitor Center but not during the plant tour.

Gift Shop: Sells logoed golf shirts, T-shirts, caps, etc. Open same hours as Visitor Center.

Directions: From Lexington, take I-75 North to Exit 126 (Georgetown/Cynthiana). Turn right onto U.S. 62 (Cherry Blossom Way). Drive exactly 2.5 miles and turn left at Visitor Entrance sign.

Nearby Attractions: Three Chimneys horse farm, Rebecca-Ruth Candies, Buffalo Trace Distillery, and Old Kentucky Candies tours (see pages 252, 251, 240–241, and 250); Kentucky Horse Park; Keeneland Racecourse; Calumet horse farm; Georgetown College.

Each vehicle produced at TMMK receives over 4,400 welds; 97 percent are performed by robots.

Toyota

Many team members at the Toyota-Kentucky plant utilize special robotic arms that help them get inside and up close to the cars to install parts in the vehicle.

Inspection team members at TMMK give a brand-new Avalon the white-glove treatment.

TMMK also builds V-6 and 4-cylinder engines at its production facility in Kentucky.

Solaras, Camrys, and Avalons are produced at Toyota's Georgetown, Kentucky plant. TMMK builds about 500,000 vehicles each year.

1316 South 4th Street, Forest City, IA 50436 | (641) 585-6936 | www.winnebagoind.com

Winnebago Industries was born in 1958, when a group of local businesses, worried about Iowa's depressed farm economy, persuaded Modernistic Industries of California to build a travel-trailer factory in Forest City. Local businessmen soon bought the factory and, in 1960, named it Winnebago Industries, after the county in which it was located. Since 1966, when the company started making motor homes, the name Winnebago has become synonymous with "motor home."

You will not doubt Winnebago's self-proclaimed position as an industry leader after touring the world's largest RV production plant. The company prides itself on its interlocking joint construction and on the fact that it produces the majority of parts in-house, including fabric covers for its seats and sofas. The 200-acre factory includes the main assembly areas (which you'll see on the tour), metal stamping division, plastics facility, sawmill and cabinet shop, and sewing and design departments.

In the chassis prep building (not on tour), parts of the all-steel frame are stamped out. Sparks fly as workers weld floor joints and storage compartments to the chassis. The completed RV (including windshield) will be set into this steel frame. The front end drops from a mezzanine onto the chassis and is aligned by laser beams.

The motor-home production lines are in a building employees affectionately call "Big Bertha." From your vantage point on the catwalk, you'll see the developing motor homes creep down three 1,032-foot-long assembly lines at 21 inches per minute. First, workers install a heat-resistant laminated floor. Next, they install the bathroom fixtures, then screw the Thermo-Panel sidewalls (made of block foam embedded with an aluminum frame and steel supports, interior paneling, and an exterior fiberglass skin) onto steel outriggers extending from the floor of the motor home. Farther down the line, cabinets are installed.

Finally, the entire unit receives a one-piece, fiber-

Automotive-styled assembly lines are used to manufacture Winnebago Industries motor homes. Decorative striping is applied by hand by the company's skilled employees.

glass-covered, laminated roof. The motor home is then driven to the company's Stitchcraft building to receive its furniture and window coverings. The completed motor home is rigorously inspected in the test chambers, where it experiences severe "rainstorms." Select units also travel through a test track of road hazards.

Cost: Free

Freebies: Product brochures.

Video/DVD Shown: 22-minute "Winnebago Industries—A Closer Look" video takes you through a detailed view of the world's largest motor-home factory. When no factory tours, visitors can watch this video as well as informative videos on individual Winnebago and Itasca motor homes.

Reservations Needed: No, except for groups larger than 6 people.

Days and Hours: April–October: Mon–Fri 9:00 AM and 1:00 PM; November–mid-December: Mon–Fri 1:00 PM. No tours mid-December–March 31. Closed holidays and 1 week in July.

Plan to Stay: 1.5 hours for video and tour, plus time for Visitors Center motor-home exhibits and wall displays.

Minimum Age: No, but small children must be accompanied by an adult.

Disabled Access: Yes, for Visitors Center. Factory tour includes 3 staircases.

Group Requirements: Groups larger than 6 people should make reservations 2 weeks in advance.

Special Information: Photography allowed in Visitors Center but not in plant.

Gift Shop: Winnebago-Itasca Travelers Club gift shop sells logoed items, including jackets, shirts, and caps. Open 8:30 AM–4:00 PM year-round. Closed holidays.

Directions: From I-35, exit at Hwy. 9 West. At junction of Hwy. 9 and Hwy. 69, take Hwy. 69 South. Turn right on B14 and immediately turn right on 4th St. in Forest City. Visitors Center is on right.

Nearby Attractions: Pammel RV Park; Pilot Knob State Park; Mansion Museum; Waldorf College; Heritage Park.

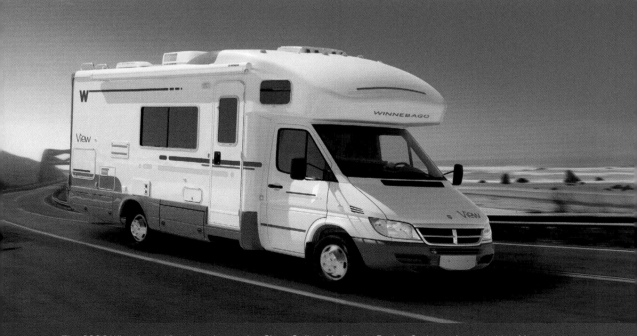

The 2006 Winnebago View is an innovative Class C diesel built on a Dodge Sprinter chassis with a Mercedes Benz diesel engine, and achieves fuel economy of 17–19 miles per gallon.

New England

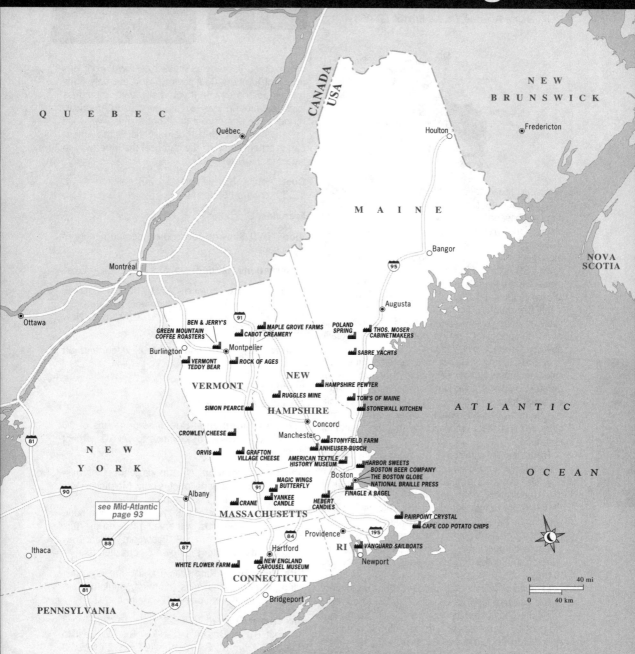

QUEBEC

Québec

Ottawa

Montréal

CANADA
USA

NEW
BRUNSWICK

Fredericton

Houlton

MAINE

Bangor

NOVA
SCOTIA

Augusta

91

BEN & JERRY'S
GREEN MOUNTAIN
COFFEE ROASTERS

MAPLE GROVE FARMS
CABOT CREAMERY

POLAND
SPRING

THOS. MOSER
CABINETMAKERS

Montpelier

Burlington

VERMONT
TEDDY BEAR

ROCK OF AGES

SABRE YACHTS

VERMONT

RUGGLES MINE

NEW

HAMPSHIRE PEWTER

SIMON PEARCE

HAMPSHIRE

TOM'S OF MAINE

STONEWALL KITCHEN

ATLANTIC

CROWLEY CHEESE

Concord

STONYFIELD FARM

Manchester

ANHEUSER-BUSCH

ORVIS

GRAFTON
VILLAGE CHEESE

AMERICAN TEXTILE
HISTORY MUSEUM

HARBOR SWEETS
BOSTON BEER COMPANY
THE BOSTON GLOBE
NATIONAL BRAILLE PRESS

OCEAN

81

NEW
YORK

MAGIC WINGS
BUTTERFLY

Boston

FINAGLE A BAGEL

90

Albany

91

CRANE

YANKEE
CANDLE

HEBERT
CANDIES

see Mid-Atlantic
page 93

PAIRPOINT CRYSTAL
CAPE COD POTATO CHIPS

88

Ithaca

87

MASSACHUSETTS

Providence

RI

84

Hartford

195

VANGUARD SAILBOATS

WHITE FLOWER FARM

NEW ENGLAND
CAROUSEL MUSEUM

Newport

81

CONNECTICUT

84

Bridgeport

PENNSYLVANIA

0   40 mi

0   40 km

Walk into the rustic, Victorian building and find a magical carousel land, filled with horses and other carousel essentials in every stage of restoration and production. Inside the 33,000-square-foot renovated hosiery factory, the pieces range from horses, menagerie figures, and carousel pieces from the early 1800s to contemporary pieces by Juan Andreu, the museum's master carver. Andreu's creations include a UConn Husky carousel dog and a full-size dolphin. Few antique menagerie pieces, such as lions, tigers, swans, and frogs, have survived the popularity of the horse, so they usually have tremendous value today.

In the carving shop, horses become time capsules once their hollow bellies are opened for restoration. Onlookers have seen beehives, ride tickets, personal letters, and even Irish Sweepstakes tickets. Some horses have been restored to their former glory, while others appear only in primer coat or bare wood.

Try to tell the difference between Coney Island, Philadelphia, and Country Fair carving styles. Coney Island horses probably look the most familiar with their glitzy gold and jeweled exteriors, but Philadelphia horses are so realistically carved that you might be tempted to feed them an apple or two. Most of the Country Fair horses represent the portable carousel era. They had parallel legs, and were often smaller and less detailed since they had to travel.

Exhibits of private collections recount the history of the carousel and its carvers. The band organ—originally considered an annoying idea because it blasted its theme song with no volume control—ended up the defining attractor of ride-goers. Trim pieces, like chariots, were introduced to accommodate the fashionable wide skirts of the 1800s, and the mirrors, lights, and paintings on rounding boards and valences were designed to hide the ride's mechanism.

The next time you go to a fair or amusement park, find yourself expertly identifying standers (three legs down, one up), prancers (back legs down, front legs up), and jumpers (four legs up and the only ones that go up and down). If you really want to impress everyone around you, explain the reason American rounding boards do not spell out a message while they twirl like the British carousels do—the American mechanism spins the carousel the other way to sidestep the British patent.

Cost: Adults, $5; seniors, $4.50; children 4–14, $2.50; children under 4, free.

Freebies: Brochures

Video/DVD Shown: 40-minute video on history of carousel.

Reservations Needed: No, except for bus groups.

Days and Hours: Mon–Sat 10:00 AM–5:00 PM, Sun 12:00 PM–5:00 PM. December 1–March 31: closed Mon–Wed. Closed Easter, Christmas, New Year's.

Plan to Stay: 1.5–2 hours for tour, video, and gift shop.

Minimum Age: None

Disabled Access: Yes, in the back.

Group Requirements: Bus tours or groups of 30 or more call 1 week in advance to get 10 percent discount.

Special Information: No tripods without permission in writing. Personal photos only. Meeting rooms available by calling main number. Museum of Fire History and working artists studio on second floor. Children under 45 lbs. will enjoy a ride on the Tots Carousel and the Carousel Classroom, where they can cut out and color their own carousel crafts.

Gift Shop: Brass Ring sells jewelry, music boxes, wind chimes, brass rings, clothing, miniature ceramic carousels, and carousel novelty items.

Directions: From Rt. 84 East, take Rt. 229 West St., Exit 31, to Bristol and follow Rt. 72 West to museum. From Rt. 84 West, take Exit 33 to Rt. 72 West (Bristol-Plainville). At end of expwy., take right onto Rt. 72 West.

Nearby Attractions: ESPN tour (call 860-766-2000); Bushnell Park Carousel; American Clock and Watch Museum; American Lock Museum; Lake Compound's Festival Park.

White Flower Farm

PLANTSMEN SINCE 1950

American industry is more than just big factories, labs, and technology. In 1939, William Harris and his wife, Jane Grant, two successful writers from New York, converted a barn in Litchfield, Connecticut, into what would sprout into one of America's best-known mail-order nurseries. Their gardening avocation evolved into an obsession and then a local nursery. Their focus changed in 1950, when the first issue of *The White Flower Farm Garden Book* was mailed to a list of nursery (now called garden center) visitors. Today, gardeners from every state have ordered from this exquisitely written and photographed catalog.

On this self-guided tour of the retail garden center grounds (not of the mail-order business), you learn more about the company's products and history, plus enjoy walking around the beautiful settings. Depending on the season of your visit, you will see examples everywhere of what appears in the various catalogs. In the Display Gardens, for instance, you find a broad sampling of the colorful perennials that have made White Flower Farm famous. In early spring, you enjoy the bulbs and by the fall, its asters and mums. Throughout the grounds, most plants are labeled with their botanical names.

Other tour favorites include the "Tree Peony Grove," the 280-foot "Long Border," and the stunning "Blackmore & Langdon" tuberous begonia greenhouse. The Long Border serves as a showcase for roughly 200 types of bulbs, perennials, shrubs, trees, and annuals.

Company historical sites also include the barn that the company founders purchased and first turned into their country residence. Notice the all-white perennial border around part of the house, now called the Moon Garden because the white flowers gleam even by moonlight. White Flower Farm takes its name from this border garden.

Cost: Free, possible fee in future.

Freebies: Current catalogs.

Video/DVD Shown: No

Reservations Needed: Reservations required for groups over 20 people.

Days and Hours: April–October: Mon–Sun 9:00 AM–5:30 PM.

Plan to Stay: At least 1 hour, if you want to go through all areas of the grounds and gardens, plus additional time for the retail store.

Minimum Age: None

Disabled Access: Most of the grounds are not wheelchair accessible because of steps and stone walkways in parts.

Group Requirements: Reservations required for groups over 20 and bus tours.

Special Information: Pick up self-guided tour map in the retail store or at the Visitor Information Center (when open).

Gift Shop: The Store at White Flower Farm sells a broad range of indoor and outdoor plants, plus gardening tools, books, pots, and gifts. The store does not duplicate all the catalog offerings. Depending on the growing season, varieties, sizes, and prices vary. Not an outlet store for catalog, although will have some specials at end of growing season for certain plants. Open same schedule as above. Catalog available at (800) 503-9624.

Directions: From I-84, take exit for Rt. 8 North, then eventually turn onto Hwy. 118 West. Turn left onto Rt. 63 South. Located 3.5 miles south of Litchfield Center.

Nearby Attractions: Litchfield History Museum; Topsmead State Forest; Housatonic Meadows State Park; Wisdom House Retreat and Conference Center; White Memorial Conservation Center; Hartford's attractions about 1 hour away.

NEW ENGLAND

Poland Spring

115 Preservation Way, Poland Spring, ME 04274 | (207) 998-7143 | www.polandspring.com

The Poland Spring Company is very proud of its location and past. Its extensive history begins deep in the woods of Maine. When first bottled in 1845 by the Ricker family, Poland Spring water was drawn from only one source; today the water is drawn from several. You can visit "The Source" inside the elaborate 1906 Spring House, built of Italian Pavanazzo marble. Enter between two tall white marble columns and take a few steps down onto the mosaic floor, where you will find the Ricker family crest. Notice the stained-glass skylights atop this two-story atrium space. The spring itself is enclosed by glass walls and a bronze grill to keep water free of dust and impurities. Guests of the resort were served freshly dispensed spring water in glass tumblers. This silent space was also known as a prayer room.

The 1906 bottling factory, then considered at the state of the art, is now a museum. Upstairs in a corner room of the museum, you can sit on black pew benches to watch a 10-minute virtual tour. In the same room, there are seven white doors. Peek behind one of them to discover a shower stall used by 25 men to take showers before entering the bottling plant; they wore clean white linen uniforms before starting work in the filling area. Also peer inside the replica quality lab of Dr. Whitaker, the first scientist to do an analysis of Poland Spring water. View many historical photos of the original bottling plant, built in 1845.

On the first floor, in the corner of the museum closest to the Spring House, water bubbles up into a gray granite basin. Glass pipes shipped from Italy carried the water under ground from the spring to the bottling factory. One display covers the groundwater's journey. In the middle of the room is a Poland Spring timeline from 1790–2000. The top of the timeline covers world history while the bottom shows company history. Learn that in 1985, Poland Spring water became the most popular brand of bottled water in the U.S., even though it is primarily sold in the Northeast.

Cost: Free

Freebies: Poland Spring water.

Video/DVD Shown: 10-minute video which covers environmental stewardship, The Source, water processing, molded bottles, production, quality, warehouse.

Reservations Needed: No

Days and Hours: Tues–Sun 8:00 AM–4:00 PM.

Plan to Stay: 45 minutes.

Minimum Age: None

Disabled Access: Yes, for Source and bottom floor of museum only. No, for gift shop, café, and video.

Group Requirements: Groups over 10 people should call 1 week in advance.

Special Information: Main sponsor for Project Wet, a water education program for teachers.

Gift Shop: Sells logoed T-shirts and sweatshirts, canvas bags, picnic umbrellas, white towels with forest green Poland Spring letters. Assortment includes Maine-made products and trail map. Open same hours as museum. Sadie's Place Café serves breakfast Tue–Sun 8:00 AM–11:00 AM, and lunch Tue–Sun 11:00 AM–3:00 PM. The café's perimeter walls are lined with historic photographs and letters, one from Calvin Coolidge ordering Poland Spring from original owner Hiram Ricker. Call (207) 998-7146.

Directions: From Portland, take I-95 North to Rte. 26 North. Turn right on Ricker Rd. and onto the Poland Spring grounds. Turn right, following signs for Preservation Park. Turn left on Preservation Way.

Nearby Attractions: On-site attractions include nature trails, golf course (first golf course built in the U.S. for a resort), Maine State Building (served originally as the state pavilion for the Columbian Exposition at the Chicago World's Fair in 1893), All Soul's Chapel, and Poland Spring Inn & Resort. Nearby are Thomas Moser (see page 63), Shaker Village, Maine lakes region.

SABRE

Did you know that building a yacht is more complicated than building a house? A yacht includes the same elements as a modern house, such as central air-conditioning, plumbing, electrical wiring, and heating, but it all needs to fit neatly into 42 feet that can ride ocean waves. Did you know a yacht qualifies as a second home as long as it has a bedroom and a bathroom? These are some of the interesting facts you can learn on a tour of Sabre Yachts.

The Sabre story began in 1970, when the company's founder, Roger Hewson, set out to build the finest possible 28-foot sailing yacht. He introduced the first Sabre 28 at the 1971 Newport Boat Show. Now the company produces three sailboat models and six powerboat models. What started in a small 4,000-square-foot building, with a handful of employees, has grown into a 83,750-square-foot facility with 175 associates assembling sail and powerboat models.

The company makes 80 boats a year. Taking approximately eight weeks to build, 20 to 25 boats are in production at one time. You will see boats at many stages of construction. In the fiberglass bay, you may observe the process of building a fiberglass hull, from the layers of the fiberglass cloth to the lamination process. Face-masked workers lay up the hull by laying out structural fabric precut to pattern, brushing on liquid red resin and hardener, and creating a fiberglass sandwich. Once dry, this hull shell will be peeled out of its mold. Notice signature navy-blue fiberglass hull shells with white waterline stripes leaning sideways against the wall, almost reaching the ceiling of the bay.

In assembly area, workers install the engine in the bare hull. Walk up a few steps to come alongside a hull. Notice the complex wiring. As you walk along other boats, you will see the woodworking being installed, and you can begin to visualize where the refrigerator, stove, and head will go. The deck, with assembled hardware, will meet the hull in eight days.

Since each yacht is custom built and as complicated as building a house, you will notice architectural renderings next to each boat. A "Boat Parent," an office associate who follows each boat through the production process, acts as the eyes of the consumer. Many of these boats are destined for the waters of Long Island, New Jersey, or even the British isles. You will see finished boats standing two stories tall from the bottom of the prop to the top of the fly bridge. The mast will be installed once the boat is put in the water.

Cost: Free

Freebies: No

Video/DVD Shown: No

Reservations Needed: Yes

Days and Hours: By appointment only Mon–Fri 2:00 PM.

Plan to Stay: 30 minutes.

Minimum Age: 12

Disabled Access: Limited

Group Requirements: Large groups should make arrangements in advance.

Special Information: The strong smell of styrene may be uncomfortable for some people.

Gift Shop: No

Directions: From I-95/Maine Turnpike, take Rte. 302 West to Raymond. Turn left on Hawthorne Rd. Your nose will know you are close. Turn left into Sabre Yachts driveway. From Portland, take Rt. 302 West and follow above directions.

Nearby Attractions: Portland's attractions include Green Furniture and Portland Museum of Art.

NEW ENGLAND

Stonewall Lane, York, ME 03909

(800) 207-JAMS
(800) 207 (5267)

www.stonewall
kitchen.com

Stonewall Kitchen offers a small-business success story, a wonderful flagship store with plentiful samples, and a glimpse through big glass windows at part of its production process. Founders Jonathan King and Jim Stott started by selling their jams and other homemade products at farmers' markets in 1991. They built their business into one of the most awarded and recognized specialty-food manufacturers in the U.S.A.

As you drive into the company's facility, you see relaxing gardens, comfortable outdoor chairs, a building with a sign that says Company Store, and, during summer, an ice-cream cart. You'll be tempted to head first inside the store or go to the bistro-style café, perhaps forgetting about the tour. Instead, walk to the building marked Viewing Gallery. Inside, you can see the main machines that jar and package specialty foods, along with display cases with artifacts highlighting their corporate history, including their first income statement, and an interactive kiosk.

Each of the production areas has an overhead sign identifying what the machine does, and you can read more about the process on the posters near the viewing windows. Watch the tube that runs down from the ceiling and follow the manufacturing process. When in full production, you can observe filling, capping, cooling, labeling, testing, and quality control.

The filling machine handles 55 jars a minute, and over 20,000 units can be made daily. The kitchen, which you can look up at from a side window, is on the second floor. It houses five steam-jacketed kettles that can cook up to 150 gallons individually. The product is fed by gravity through the overhead tube, not pumped, allowing the fruit in the jams and marmalade to pass through without breaking up.

The capping machine automatically screws lids on the filled jars of jam and mustard. Peer to the left of the wheel: you will see the caps fall through one by one. This custom-made machine has a maximum speed of 150 caps per minute.

Cost: Free

Freebies: Samples of specialty foods in the Company Store and at a demonstration kitchen.

Video/DVD Shown: A 20-minute video in the Viewing Gallery.

Reservations Needed: No

Days and Hours: The Viewing Gallery is open daily 9:00 AM–5:00 PM. Production stops at 4:00 PM on weekdays, and no production occurs on weekends and legal holidays.

Plan to Stay: 1 hour for Viewing Gallery, display cases, and Company Store.

Minimum Age: None

Disabled Access: Yes. Everything is on ground level, and the facility is new.

Group Requirements: Group tours are given only for local schools and other educational entities, such as culinary schools.

Gift Shop: The Company Store sells all of Stonewall Kitchen's products, such as blueberry jam and flavored mustards, plus kitchenware and other home/garden items. Although this is not an outlet store, a small area has discounted items. Open daily 8:00 AM–6:00 PM, with some seasonal changes (call 207-351-2712). Café stops sit-down service at 3:00 PM.

Directions: Located on Rt. 1 in York. From I-95 North, take York exit and bear right at end of ramp (left from I-95 South). Company is straight ahead at lights.

Nearby Attractions: Tom's of Maine tour (see page 64); York Beach, Nubble Lighthouse, York's Wild Kingdom.

72 Wright's Landing, Auburn, ME 04210   (207) 784-3332   www.thomasmoser.com
(800) 708-9703

THOS. MOSER
CABINETMAKERS

Woodworking tours can provide a feast for all your senses with the sound of the saws, the smell of the wood and the finishes, and the touch of the wood grains at different stages of production. The Thos. Moser workshop tour lets you see everything involved in making their natural-finished heirloom furniture, including laminating, rasping, machining, sanding, routing, milling, planing, dovetailing, making mortises and tenons, and assembling. This tour also provides a bountiful lesson in wood selection and its role in furniture making. While we all enjoy the beauty of natural solid wood, we may not realize how it expands and contracts, playing a key part in its design. As you walk on the factory floor, the guide explains all of this and more.

The process begins with rough mill panel making, where they make the tabletops and panels that become parts of their furniture. You see many different size saws, jointers, and panel glue racks. With the table saws buzzing in the background, observe how carefully the craftspeople marry the American black cherry woods by grain and color to create the panels. Throughout the process, notice the unique techniques to join pieces where grains do not match completely and to allow movement.

Chair making involves lots of wedging, fitting, and grinding to create their signature Thos. Moser Continuous Arm Chair. To form the gently curving back brace and arms, 11 knife-cut slices of the same tree, each one-tenth -of -an inch thick (called a flitch), are laminated together and held in tension for superior strength. Notice how each "continuous arm" is carefully rasped, filed, and sanded to perfect smoothness. The natural tension in the wood ensures it will keep its shape for generations, and the flexibility of the northern ash spindles bend and conform to your back.

You will be delighted by the aromatic finishing area. Here the boiled linseed oil is sprayed onto the furniture, then wiped in; afterward, the furniture is sanded and given a hand-rubbed wax finish. You leave the tour appreciating what it takes to custom-build furniture of truly lasting value.

Cost: Free

Freebies: Beautiful catalog upon request, which includes production and product pictures.

Video/DVD Shown: No

Reservations Needed: Yes

Days and Hours: Fri 1:00 PM, except for holidays.

Plan to Stay: 1.5 hours or longer, depending on your interest in woodworking.

Minimum Age: 10

Disabled Access: Yes

Group Requirements: Groups over 20 should call 1 month in advance; will be split into smaller groups.

Special Information: Must wear closed-toe shoes. Wear your eyeglasses, or company will provide protective eyewear.

Gift Shop: Does not directly sell the furniture, although if you ask after tour, you can meet with a customer service representative to place an order. May have limited items in inventory at the workshop, but most of their products are made-to-order. Showroom in Freeport, ME, at 149 Main St. (207-865-4519) about 30 minutes away, does have some special-priced items (seconds, consignment items, returns) in the "Must-Be-Seen Room." Catalog available by calling (877) 708-1973 or on website. Also showrooms in Chicago, Boston, New York, and San Francisco.

Directions: From Maine Tnpk. (I-495), take Exit 12. Turn right from the exit ramp. At the first light, take right onto Kitty Hawk Ave. (follow airport sign), continue straight through blinking red light. Shop is on the right.

Nearby Attractions: Tom's of Maine tour (see page 64); Bates College and Lost Valley Ski Area; Shaker Village; The Center for Furniture Craftsmanship about 1 hour away; Freeport's outlet stores and Portland about 30 minutes away in different directions. Maine Wood Product Assoc. brochure lists woodshop tours (call 207-767-0188).

Tom's of Maine
NATURAL PERSONAL CARE PRODUCTS

27 Community Drive, Sanford, ME 04073

(207) 985-2944
(800) FOR-TOMS

www.tomsofmaine.com

In 1970, Kate and Tom Chappell moved to Maine to live a simpler life and to create a company committed to developing all-natural personal hygiene products, such as toothpaste, mouthwash, soap, and deodorant. While we don't know if they found a simpler life, they have created a successful, socially conscious, environmentally committed company. In fact, their tasty toothpaste—made without artificial preservatives, sweeteners, or coloring—is the top-selling brand in many major stores.

Almost all Tom's of Maine products are made in a green (meaning environmentally sensitive) manufacturing facility. Toothpaste ingredients are mixed in a 3,000-pound vat. Ingredients for liquid products such as mouthwash or shampoo have a second mixing area.

As you walk upstairs to the second floor, you'll know what products the toothpaste and liquid lines are packaging. If you smell cinnamon, they're packaging that flavor toothpaste or mouthwash. An intense coriander smell usually means deodorant. You cannot miss the machine that pumps the still-warm toothpaste into recyclable tubes and clamps the backs closed. Notice how the company tries to reduce the amount of product packaging. For the mouthwash, the outer paper carton has been replaced with a thin leaflet that folds into the back of the recyclable plastic container.

What's most interesting about this tour isn't so much the production process, but the sense that the workers enjoy their jobs and take seriously their responsibility for quality control. The smiles you see aren't just to show off good teeth. Every hour, most workers on the packaging line switch positions. A worker who just put the tubes into the filler machine now boxes toothpaste. While you may be bored brushing your teeth, the people who make your toothpaste aren't!

Cost: Free

Freebies: Just-finished product sample.

Video/DVD Shown: No

Reservations Needed: Yes

Days and Hours: Tours given in the summer only. Call for hours and availability.

Plan to Stay: 1 hour for the tour and a talk about the company and its philosophy.

Minimum Age: 5

Disabled Access: No

Group Requirements: Groups larger than 8 people should call 1 month ahead. Groups larger than 15 people may be split into smaller ones.

Special Information: No photography.

Outlet Store: Located in Kennebunk, about 15 minutes away (call 207-985-3874). Sells all Tom's natural personal-hygiene products, including discounted factory seconds. Open Mon–Sat 9:30 AM–5:00 PM. Closed holidays.

Directions: Tours meet at the Tom's of Maine factory. From I-95, take Exit 19 (Wells). Turn right onto Rt. 109 toward Sanford. Follow Rt. 109 for about 7.4 miles until you reach Sanford Industrial Estate/Eagle Dr. and turn right. When that road ends, you'll make a right onto Community Dr. The factory is on the right.

Nearby Attractions: Thos. Moser Cabinetmakers tour (see page 63); Kennebunkport Brewing Co. tour (call 207-967-4311; larger plant gives tours in Portland, call 207-761-0807); Wedding Cake House; Brick Store Museum; Kennebunkport resort area, beaches, and former President George H.W. Bush's residence.

AMERICAN TEXTILE HISTORY MUSEUM

In 1814, Lowell became America's first factory town when Frances Cabot Lowell, a Boston merchant, learned the secrets of the power loom from England. Thanks to nature's abundance and this early act of espionage, textile production in America grew swiftly from a necessary domestic craft into one of the country's primary industries. The American Textile History Museum traces this technological revolution and its effect on the lives of American people.

The American Textile History Museum is housed in a redesigned 1850s mill. Two floors are dedicated to the museum's permanent exhibit, "Textiles in America." The display features re-created scenes from 200 years of textile production, beginning with an 18th-century farmhouse kitchen, where a spinning wheel takes pride of place, and ends at a working 1940s weave room.

In the weave shed, watch cloth being woven. The museum manufactures new cloth using vintage looms and the classic overshot design and patterns. The antique looms, some of the oldest power looms still in operation, re-create the rich beauty of traditional fabrics made in America during the 18th and 19th centuries. The finished products include coverlets, runners, decorative pillows, and throws.

The first floor offers changing exhibits. As you walk up the ramp to the second floor, look at spinning wheels through floor-to-ceiling glass windows. There are around 250 spinning wheels among the exhibits! Behind a flax processing window exhibit, hear recorded sounds of flax breaking, wooden knives beating flax, and stems breaking apart. Ask a guide to point out tools such as swifts, niddy-noddies, teasels, and spinning jennies. A range of fabrics is also on display, from hand-woven bedcovers to the upholstery of the 1926 Ford; there is machinery from an 1870s woolen factory and period clothing.

Cost: Adults, $8; children under 17, seniors, and students with ID, $6; children under 6 and museum members, free.

Freebies: No

Video/DVD Shown: 5-minute video covering flax making.

Reservations Needed: No, for self-guided tours. Yes, for all programs, guided tours, and groups of 15 or more people.

Days and Hours: Thur–Fri 9:00 AM–4:00 PM, Sat–Sun 10:00 AM–5:00 PM. Closed holidays.

Plan to Stay: 2 hours.

Minimum Age: None, but 6 is recommended minimum.

Disabled Access: Yes

Group Requirements: Groups of 15 or more, call (978) 441-0400, ext. 244, for reservations and group discounts. Fee of $6 for guided and self-guided tours. Reservations required for guided tours only.

Special Information: Museum features Osborne Textile Research Library, Webster Education Center, and Gazebo Café. For information on their changing calendar of public programs and special events, visit website. School programs available.

The Museum Store: Temporarily closed.

Directions: From I-495, take the Lowell Connector to Thorndike St. After the 4th traffic light, bear right onto Dutton St. and the Museum's red brick building with green and yellow banners will be on the left. Museum is adjacent to Lowell's National Historic Park.

Nearby Attractions: Harbor Sweets tour (see page 71); Lowell's National Historic Park Service offers many guided tours, walks, exhibits, mill and canal tours, etc. (call 978-970-5000); New England Quilt Museum (call 978-452-4207); Boott Cotton Mills Museum (call 978-970-5000); Whistler House Museum of Art; Brush Art Gallery and Studios; Tsongas Industrial History Center; New England Sports Museum; July Lowell Folk Festival (largest free folk festival in U.S.).

NEW ENGLAND

In 1984, Jim Koch revived his great-great-grandfather's beer recipe and launched the Boston Beer Company. Almost immediately, the company's full-bodied Samuel Adams beers started winning awards.

While Samuel Adams brews most of its beers at regional breweries so that they are fresh when they reach area retailers, it develops new beers at its facility in the Jamaica Plain district of Boston. It's part of an urban development park that once housed the Haffenreffer Brewery. Lining the walls of the beer museum are lithographs tracing the site's history, plaques describing the history of beer, and beer memorabilia.

Your tour guide, often a brewer, begins by handing out tastes of barley malt and hops. As you chew on barley malt, which tastes like Grape Nuts cereal, your guide explains that the use of only these ingredients (plus yeast and water) makes Samuel Adams one of the few beers to pass the strict German laws on purity, allowing Sam Adams beer to be brewed and sold in Germany.

All the shiny tubs, vats, and kettles of the brewhouse are in one small area, providing a good introduction to the steps involved in brewing beer. Each vessel is labeled so that you can identify the mash tub, the copper brew kettle, and the glass-lined stainless-steel aging tank. The custom-made "Jules Verne Tank" resembles a submarine standing on end, complete with portholes and interior lights. If fermentation is beginning, you can see the sudsy froth from the top porthole. Although Samuel Adams makes only a small percentage of its output at this Boston site, you'll leave with the full story of the company and its beer.

Cost: $2, which is donated to Youth Enrichment Services and the restoration of Granary Graveyard, final resting place of Samuel Adams.

Freebies: 7-oz. logoed tasting glass for visitors who are at least 21 years old. Free postage for Samuel Adams postcards. In the tap room, glasses of beer and perhaps a taste of seasonal ale, brewed only at this location.

Video/DVD Shown: In the tasting room, a short video tells why Jim Koch, a 6th-generation brewer, started the company and how it operates.

Reservations Needed: No, except for groups of more than 25 people.

Days and Hours: Thu and Fri 2:00 PM, Fri also 5:30 PM, Sat 11:00 AM–2:00 PM. Tours depart according to attendance. May–August: also Wed 2:00 PM. Call above number for schedule changes. No beer production during Saturday tours. Closed holidays.

Plan to Stay: 1 hour for tour and tasting, plus time for gift shop and beer museum.

Minimum Age: None. Children are welcome. Root beer is available for minors.

Disabled Access: Yes

Group Requirements: Groups larger than 25 people should call 2 weeks in advance for reservations (call 617-368-5000).

Gift Shop: Sells logoed mirrors, glasses, hats, T-shirts, bottle openers, and sweatshirts. Open during tour.

Directions: Take I-93 North to Massachusetts Ave./Roxbury exit. Go straight down Melnea Cass Blvd. toward Roxbury through 7 lights. At 8th light, turn left on Tremont St., which eventually becomes Columbus Ave. Continue straight on Tremont through 7 lights, then right on Amory St. (at Muffler Mart). Follow Amory St. through 2 lights. After the 2nd light, turn left on Porter St. At end of Porter St., Samuel Adams Brewery is on right.

Nearby Attractions: Doyle's, a nearby pub full of Irish family history, has many Samuel Adams beers on tap. *Boston Globe* tour and National Braille Press (see pages 67 and 74); Franklin Park Zoo; Arnold Arboretum.

The Boston Globe

Founded in 1872, *The Boston Globe* has the largest circulation of any newspaper in New England. It is now a wholly owned subsidiary of The New York Times Company. Your tour through its main facility provides insight into the process of news-gathering, reporting, printing, and distribution (and the online edition at www.boston.com).

The tour provides a close look at the massive three-level presses that spin out hundreds of thousands of papers a day. Rolls of paper, each weighing up to 1,800 pounds, feed the presses from different directions. When you stand on the ground level with the presses, notice the robots that deliver these rolls automatically to the presses so that they can keep running. This high-speed process produces one newspaper every two minutes. In another area, you'll see where the printing plates are produced with specialized laser machines that engrave the images of each page.

If writing interests you more than big machines, you can walk by respected journalists in various departments as they research and write about news. They work in large open rooms with interconnected desks. Each appears to be diligently typing, concentrating on a computer screen, or chatting with a colleague. The staff in the art department seem to have the most fun. On their desks, creative knick-knacks such as miniature hula dancers, lava lamps, and stuffed animals encourage their creativity.

Cost: Free

Freebies: Sometimes daily papers in lobby.

Video/DVD Shown: Either a short presentation by your guide on the history of paper and the printing process, or a video (depending on when video is updated).

Reservations Needed: Yes

Days and Hours: Mon and Thu 10:00 AM, 11:15 AM, 1:15 PM. One Wednesday evening per month at 6:30 PM and 7:45 PM (call for schedule).

Plan to Stay: 1 hour.

Minimum Age: 9

Disabled Access: Yes

Group Requirements: Maximum size in range of 30–35 people. Tour guide can focus the tour and the discussion on any special interests of a group.

Special Information: Presses usually run from 11:30 PM, and editions are finalized through the early morning, so you are unlikely to see the big presses in action unless special printings or inserts are in progress. Usually only pre-press operations are under way during your visit.

Gift Shop: Hours vary at the store on the premises. The telephone/online store (888-665-2667, http://services.bostonglobe.com/globestore/) sells reprints of photographs and newspaper front pages, including from the date of your birth. It also offers commemorative posters based on pages in the newspaper, such as those in the sports section during the 2004 World Series (when the Boston Red Sox won).

Directions: From the subway, take the Red Line to JFK/UMASS. Turn right after leaving station. *The Globe* is a short walk down Morrissey Blvd. From I-93 South, take Columbia Road/JFK Library exit. At end of ramp, turn left. Take first right on Morrissey Blvd. Stay to right and then turn right into *The Globe*. From I-93 North, take Morrissey Blvd/JFK Library exit. Make a U-turn at Day Blvd. to go in the other direction on Morrissey Blvd. *The Globe* is on your right, a short way down the road. Limited parking is available in front of the building. Enter through the front door and check in with security at the front desk.

Nearby Attractions: Tours in Boston include Samuel Adams and National Braille Press (see pages 66 and 74); also, Fenway Park (call 617-226-6666); near *The Globe* is Castle Island (an old fort with tours, a park, and playgrounds).

NEW ENGLAND

100 Breed's Hill Road, Hyannis, MA 02601 (508) 775-3358 www.capecodchips.com

Cape Cod Potato Chips still follows the company's original intent—"to make the best potato chip possible." Just as when Steve Bernard founded it in 1980, the company still kettle-cooks its potato chips one batch at a time. Cape Cod's production, which started in 1980 at 200 bags per day, is now 150,000 to 200,000 bags a day, using 28 million pounds of potatoes each year.

From the plaques in the entranceway, you'll learn that four pounds of potatoes yield one pound of potato chips and that, depending on the month, the potatoes come from different Eastern Seaboard states. Each truckload of 45,000 to 50,000 pounds of potatoes is unloaded into its own silo, since the potatoes must be inspected for solid mass (or "gravity"), external defects, size, and color before farmers receive payment. Different rollers and brushes, depending on the skins' thickness, wash and peel the inspected spuds, which then tumble down to the trim table for further inspection and halving of large potatoes.

Through glass windows, you watch sliced potatoes feed into one of the three production lines, each with six gas-fired cooking kettles. Raw potatoes sizzle in hot oil, creating clouds of steam. In the midst of this steam, workers rake raw potato slices into the kettles. The steam subsides as the cooking cycle ends. An automated rake mechanism pushes finished chips out of the kettle and onto a belt conveyor that takes them to a nearby centrifuge, a very large spinner basket with holes. The centrifuge spins the potato chips at high speed and high temperature for several minutes to drain off excess oil, returning it to the oil recycling system. When the chips are dry, they automatically fall onto a cooling conveyor belt.

As you walk along the production line, read the plaques that describe potato-chip making. Along the opposite wall of the corridor, a schematic diagram explains how popcorn is produced. Farther down the corridor, workers inspect the cooled chips along a vibrating table that moves them forward without breaking them. The chips pass under the salter box and are transported by "bucket elevator" to the next room for packaging. On each packaging line, a carousel of 14 hoppers weighs and releases the correct amount of chips into the bagging machine. Workers hand-pack bags into cardboard boxes, which are shrink-wrapped for shipment or storage in the warehouse.

Cost: Free

Freebies: Sample bag of potato chips.

Video/DVD Shown: No

Reservations Needed: No, except for groups over 25 people.

Days and Hours: Mon–Fri 9:00 AM–5:00 PM. Closed holidays.

Plan to Stay: 15 minutes for self-guided tour, plus time in gift shop.

Minimum Age: None, except small children will need to be picked up to see activity beyond cooling chip conveyor.

Disabled Access: Yes

Group Requirements: Groups over 25 people should call in advance.

Special Information: No photography. On rainy summer days, allow for waiting time to enter the tour.

Gift Shop: Sells all Cape Cod potato chips, popcorn, logoed caps, golf balls, and T-shirts. Open same hours as tours. Closed holidays.

Directions: From Rt. 6, take Exit 6 for Rt. 132 South. At 4th traffic light, turn left into Independence Park. Take 2nd right onto Breed's Hill Rd. Factory is on the left.

Nearby Attractions: Pairpoint Crystal tour (see page 75); Cape Cod Mall; JFK Hyannis Museum; Hyannis waterfront and beaches; Thornton W. Burgess Museum.

NEW ENGLAND

Crane's fine papers are used worldwide for stationery and by the Bureau of Engraving and Printing for currency (see page xx). Since 1801, Crane has produced 100 percent cotton paper that offers strength, durability, and surface texture unsurpassed by paper made from wood. The company uses denim scraps from Levi Strauss jeans and worn dollar bills to make recycled paper. This family-owned company's mills are in Dalton, in western Massachusetts. The Crane Museum, housed in the company's Old Stone Mill (built in 1844), has welcomed visitors since 1930.

The museum sits on the banks of the Housatonic River, which supplied water to wash the rags and drive the machines of the early Crane paper mills. This ivy-covered stone building has a completely different feel from the modern, multimedia-filled company museums built recently. The museum's interior resembles the Old Ship Church in Hingham, Massachusetts, with rough-hewn oak beams, colonial chandeliers, many-paned windows, and wide oak floorboards. The ceiling looks like an upside-down ship's hull.

After you watch the video on Crane's modern paper-production techniques, walk through exhibits on the history of the company and of papermaking since the Revolutionary War. A scale model of the vat house in the original Crane mill shows the laborious process of hand-making paper one sheet at a time. This process, used by company founder Zenas Crane, contrasts with the modern method of making long continuous rolls of paper.

Among the many different kinds of paper displayed in glass cases are those used for currency, American Express checks, stock certificates, and the stationery of presidents and movie stars. One exhibit of corporate innovation features Crane's paper collars, which the company made after the Civil War. Although they are rarely seen today, at the time these disposable collars were fashionable and very profitable.

Cost: Free

Freebies: Crane writing pad.

Video/DVD Shown: 20-minute video on company's history and papermaking methods.

Reservations Needed: No, except for groups.

Days and Hours: Open June–mid-October only: Mon–Fri 1:00–5:00 PM. Closed holidays.

Plan to Stay: 30 minutes for exhibits, plus time for video.

Minimum Age: None

Disabled Access: Museum is all on one ground-level floor. However, there are a couple of steps to reach it.

Group Requirements: With 1 week's notice, Crane can handle groups up to 50 people.

Special Information: Company retirees run museum; they answer questions and offer interesting anecdotes.

Gift Shop: No

Directions: From I-90 (MA Trnpk.), take the Lee Exit. Follow Rts. 7 and 20 North through Pittsfield. Take Rts. 8 and 9 East about 5 miles. Turn right onto Housatonic St. At bottom is Pioneer Mill. Museum is on the right at the end of Mill.

Nearby Attractions: Berkshire attractions include Clark Art Museum, Mt. Greylock, Berkshire Museum, and Tanglewood.

NEW ENGLAND

Finagle a Bagel

77 Rowe Street, Newton, MA 02466

(617) 213-8428
(617) 213-8400

www.finagleabagel.com

Americans love their bagels, and this company gives you a view of large-scale bagel making, producing over 100,000 bagels and 2,000 pounds of cream cheese daily. The walls of the factory also present a colorful museum of bagel and company history.

Bagel making arrived in the U.S. in the 1880s with immigrants from Eastern Europe. It was considered such a special craft that Bagel Bakers' Local #338 started in 1907 to preserve the tradition. Bagels became widespread after the Thompson Bagel Machine was invented in 1961 to automate the forming and shaping of bagels. Finagle a Bagel started in 1982 and has grown to having 20 stores plus wholesale business throughout New England.

After you walk through the bagel outlet store to the hall running along the production area, you look through big glass windows at all the major stages of bagel production: making and forming the fresh dough, proofing, boiling, baking, and cooling. The trademark bagel character of a crusty outside and soft inside requires them to be both boiled and then baked. Although some windows on this self-guided tour are much closer to production than others, each gives a good view, and signs describe the process.

You get the best views in the baking and cooling areas. Depending on what's in production when you visit, bakers quickly remove boiled bagels from the cool-down tables, sprinkle on any toppings (e.g., sesame, poppy), and place them on thin burlap-covered boards known as "sticks." These are loaded onto rotating shelves in the 500°F oven. Bakers then carefully remove or "peel" the bagels from the oven and place them on the cooling conveyer belt, where they travel to the giant beehive-shaped spiral bagel-cooler.

Here you'll see one of the most fascinating machines of any factory. This 15-foot-wide and 10-foot-high machine has a series of metal conveyor belts that spiral from top to bottom, filled with bagels that are being cooled on the way down by blown air. It looks like a gigantic marble track. The bagels take about an hour to cool.

Cost: No

Freebies: No

Video/DVD Shown: No. Company and bagel history is displayed on walls.

Reservations Needed: No, except for groups of over 20 people who request a guided tour.

Days and Hours: The walk-in tour is self-guided. Production runs Sun–Fri 11:00 AM–3:00 PM. Closed major holidays.

Plan to Stay: 30 minutes (longer if you want to read all the displays) plus time for a nosh in the Outlet Store.

Minimum Age: None

Disabled Access: Yes. Factory is on one level.

Group Requirements: To schedule a guided tour, call a week beforehand. Catered meals are available with tour.

Outlet Store: Sells all bagels at lower prices than its other stores (about 20 stores in Boston area). Also serves breakfast and lunch every day, including soups, salads, and sandwiches. Open 7:00 AM–3:00 PM daily.

Directions: From I-90 West (MA Trnpk.), take exit 16. Turn right at end of ramp. Turn right at next light on Rte. 16 West and proceed to Commonwealth Ave. (Rte. 30). Turn right on Commonwealth Ave. and travel over I-90. Take next right across traffic island to Rowe St. Company is ahead on right after stop sign. From I-90 East, exit at I-95. After tolls, take I-95 North and follow signs to turn right on Rte. 30/Commonwealth Ave. Continuing on Commonwealth, just past the Auberndale Shopping Plaza on your right, take the next left on Rowe St.

Nearby Attractions: In Boston, Samuel Adams and National Braille Press (page 66 and 74); in Lincoln, Walden Pond State Reservation.

Palmer Cove, 85 Leavitt Street,
Salem, MA 01970

(978) 745-7648
(800) 234-4860

www.harborsweets.com

Harbor Sweets
HANDMADE CHOCOLATES

While Salem is known for its witches' potions, Harbor Sweets brews only the sweet variety. The company's key players are its 100 part-time/flex-time employees (many disabled, elderly, or foreign-born).

The company has expanded into three connected brick buildings. From the slightly raised gift-shop platform, you can observe the labor-intensive production of Sweet Sloops, one of Harbor Sweets' most popular nautical New England–theme candies; you can also see molded candies at the far end. Workers will gladly answer your questions. The air smells of caramel, toffee, and chocolate.

Notice the home-style, four-burner gas stove in the back. Leaning over copper cauldrons, workers stir batches of almond butter crunch and caramel with wooden paddles. The butter crunch is poured onto a cooling table and then smoothed. With a bladed metal rolling pin, a worker scores the crunch into squares and then triangles. A helper breaks the triangles apart. The triangles proceed through the enrober for a coating of white chocolate. With a long metal ice-cream spoon, a worker draws lines representing the mast and jib. After the cooling tunnel, workers hand-dip the Sweet Sloops into melted chocolate and chopped pecans, often a tough job—they must eat their mistakes.

All other candies are molded. Depending on the candies being made, melters contain milk or dark chocolate, some with crushed orange or peppermint crunch. A worker holds a 16-cavity plastic mold, while the "depositor" drops a specially timed amount of chocolate into each cavity. Another worker inserts dollops of raspberry/cranberry ganache and white chocolate from a hand-held funnel. After they have been chilled, the candies are individually foil-wrapped before being beautifully gift-boxed.

Cost: Free

Freebies: Chocolate sample from a silver serving platter.

Video/DVD Shown: No

Reservations Needed: No, except for groups over 10 people.

Days and Hours: Mon–Fri 8:30 AM–4:30 PM. Call about Saturday hours before candy-giving holidays. Closed holidays and 2 weeks in July. Limited production May–August.

Plan to Stay: 10–15 minutes for self-guided viewing, plus time in gift shop.

Minimum Age: None

Disabled Access: Yes

Group Requirements: Groups larger than 10 should call 1 week in advance to arrange a tour guide. Groups over 12 will be split into smaller groups. No maximum group size.

Special Information: Best time to see production is September–Easter.

Gift Shop: Sells Harbor Sweets' themed candies in a variety of gift box sizes. Themes include Nautical, New England, Equestrian, Garden, and others. Sugar-free chocolates also available. Open Mon–Fri 8:30 AM–5:00 PM, Sat 9:00 AM–3:00 PM, with extended hours before holidays and shorter hours in summer. Catalog available from (800) 243-2115.

Directions: From Rt. 128, take Rt. 114 East to Salem. Turn left onto Leavitt St. Harbor Sweets is the last building on the left. From 1A North (follow Rt. 1A as it meanders to Salem), turn right onto Leavitt St.

Nearby Attractions: American Textile History Museum tour (see page 65); Saugus Iron Works, first integrated ironworks in North America, with reconstructed blast furnace, 17th-century iron mill, and working waterwheel (call 781-233-0050); Salem's attractions include Pickering Wharf, Salem Witch Museum, The House of the Seven Gables, and Peabody Essex Museum.

Other Eastern Massachusetts Candy Tours: Stowaway Sweets candy tour in Marblehead (call 800-432-0304).

With events such as weekly summer "Thursday Night Cruising" charity family fun nights, "Chick Cliques" birthday parties with ice-cream sundaes, and special school vacation-week tours and activities, you know this fifth-generation candy company (started in 1917) prides itself on giving back to the local community. So now that we know this place is fun, let's find out how they make chocolate.

First don a hair net before your tour guide takes you into the Geneva room. Geneva candies, their signature candies, start with chocolate from 10-pound blocks of solid chocolate, broken with a hammer. A worker tosses pieces of white, dark, milk, or dietetic chocolate into corresponding 110°F vats. The Geneva chocolate machine dispenses liquid chocolate into clear plastic trays containing 50 squares. If needed, a worker hand-places almonds individually in each of the 10 rows of five squares. The chocolate hardens in the 55°F cold room.

In another area, a few workers may hand-place white cardboard sticks at an angle into chocolate lollipops. To make hollow molded chocolates, such as soldiers, a workers pours just the right amount of liquid chocolate up to the soldier's belly button, then clamps the clear plastic molds shut with heavy-duty paper clamps. The worker rolls the mold to distribute the chocolate inside. After letting the chocolate stand to stiffen, the worker turns it again to coat the mold.

Walk downstairs to the kitchen. The Dayton ball beater turns in circles making cream centers. The extruder squeezes out rows of nine centers, such as peanut butter, which march side by side along the big white enrober. Once coated in chocolate, they receive a swirl design on top designating the type of center, perhaps peppermint.

In the packing area, rubber-gloved employees put individual chocolates into paper cups and fill boxes as they move along the conveyor belt. The last worker brushes the candies to maintain their sheen and weighs the candy boxes. Next pass through the warehouse adjacent to the huge overhanging funnel full of Styrofoam packing pieces.

Walk down the ramp to the noisy candy-bar department. In this mazelike three-stage process, liquid chocolate flows into empty clear plastic molds. The resulting chocolate shells wind their way around the bend. Spigots pour fillings such as peanut butter into shells. Chocolate covers them and the bars drop out when flipped over. Daily two machines can make 130,000 candy bars—most become fundraiser candies, a mainstay of Hebert's business.

Cost: Free

Freebies: Chocolate samples during the tour.

Video/DVD Shown: Plans for 25-minute video.

Reservations Needed: No, except for groups over 10 people.

Days and Hours: Tue–Thur 10:30 AM–2:30 PM.

Plan to Stay: 45 minutes, plus additional time for video and candy store.

Minimum Age: None

Disabled Access: Yes, tour route altered slightly.

Group Requirements: Groups over 10 people should call 1 week in advance. Groups enjoy special discounts. Maximum group size is 20.

Special Information: Hebert Candies was America's First Roadside Candy Store. Mascot is Geneva man.

The Hebert Candy Mansion: Sells Geneva candies and assorted boxes such as Mansion Fancy. Sells kosher candies and ice cream. Open Mon–Fri 9:00 AM–8:00 PM (9:00 AM–9:00 PM during the holidays), Sun 10:00 AM–8:00 PM.

Directions: From I-90 East, take Rt. 20 West. On your left in 2.5 miles, drive between the stone fence to Hebert Candies stone Tudor-style mansion. From I-90 West, take Exit 11. At light, make left onto Grafton St. Take Rt. 20 East. Drive 5 minutes. Hebert's will be on your right.

Nearby Attractions: Green Hill Farm maple sugaring in March (call 508-842-2588); National Plastics Center & Museum (call 978-537-9529); EcoTarium; Higgins Armory Museum; Worcester Art Museum; Old Sturbridge Village 30 minutes away.

NEW ENGLAND

Magic Wings Butterfly Conservatory & Gardens

LIVE BUTTERFLIES

281 Greenfield Road (Routes 5 & 10),
South Deerfield, MA 01373

(413) 665-2805   www.magicwings.com

Everybody loves butterflies, but many species occur in remote tropical rainforests that most of us never have a chance to visit. Hence the concept of the butterfly conservatory: these places let you see living insects rather than mounted specimens in museums. Located in the countryside of western Massachusetts, Magic Wings is the offshoot of a garden center that still operates on the premises. In its large conservatory, which covers 8,000 square feet, you can roam paths through dense rows of tropical plants and enjoy thousands of vivid butterflies that flutter wherever you look.

When you buy your ticket for admission, be sure to purchase a one-page guide to the species in the living collection. You enter through heavy double doors; a rush of forced air from above, directed inwards, helps to keep stray butterflies from escaping while you enter and exit. As you step into the conservatory, you enter a world of luxuriant greenery, tropical flowers, and gurgling streams. Immediately you notice the colorful movement of butterflies, both small and large, in every direction. Maintained at a humid 80°F throughout the year, the warmth of the environment envelops you (be sure to check coats at reception).

Most of the butterflies at Magic Wings are from tropical regions, and some species are extraordinarily large. Electric blue, bright scarlet, golden yellow, and many other colors play in your vision as the insects flap their broad wings. If you remain still long enough, some may even land on you. (Tip: Wearing a bright Hawaiian shirt with flowers in the pattern increases your chances of attracting butterflies to you.) Your guide sheet can tell you the common and scientific names of the species you spot; a world map in one area of the conservatory shows where each species comes from. Watch also for birds in the undergrowth: Australian finches, African parrots, and Chinese quails. Gentle background music, benches for taking breaks, and a helpful information desk round out the experience.

The average life of a butterfly in the conservatory is five weeks. How does Magic Wings maintain its collection? The staff raise their own caterpillars, which hatch from eggs the adult insects lay. After feeding, these larvae pupate to metamorphose into the next generation of butterflies. A glass case in one area of the greenhouse displays the pupae from which the butterflies eventually emerge—some may come out during your visit.

Cost: For general admission, adults, $8; seniors, $7; children aged 3–17, $5 (up to age 22 with valid student ID); children under 3, free.

Freebies: No

Video/DVD Shown: Yes

Reservations Needed: Not for general admission. Tours must be arranged in advance.

Days and Hours: Daily 9:00 AM–5:00 PM (summer till 6:00 PM). Closed Thanksgiving and Christmas.

Plan to Stay: At least 1 hour.

Minimum Age: None (but strollers are not allowed in the butterfly conservatory).

Disabled Access: Yes

Group Requirements: Groups of 20 or more receive special discounted rates.

Special Information: Weddings can be held in the butterfly conservatory (call for information).

Gift Shop: The gift shop sells butterfly-related items. The garden shop sells plants and decorative items. Meals are available in the food court. All open daily 9:00 AM–5:00 PM (summer till 6:00 PM). Closed Thanksgiving and Christmas.

Directions: From I-91, take the exit for Routes 5 & 10. Drive 3 miles on Routes 5 & 10 North. Magic Wings is on the left.

Nearby Attractions: Yankee Candle (see page 76); Historic Deerfield; North River Glass Studio/Gallery, Shelburne Falls (413-625-6422).

NEW ENGLAND

88 Saint Stephen Street, Boston, MA 02115

(617) 266-6160
(888) 965-8965

www.nbp.org

NATIONAL BRAILLE PRESS

National Braille Press, a nonprofit organization founded in 1927, is one of only five companies in the U.S.A. that mass-produce braille materials, and the only one that publishes original books for the blind. The company prides itself on fund-raising to provide affordable books and on hiring people with disabilities (about one-third of its 50-person in-house staff).

The company produces approximately 14 million braille pages per year from this four-story converted piano factory on a tree-lined street in the Northeastern University area. Specialized translation software helps workers transcribe the written word into braille pages. To find any errors in the transcription, blind proofreaders listen to an audiotape of what should be written while following the braille version with their hands. The proofreading room chatters with the sound of the braille typewriters that proofreaders use to note mistakes.

Once the pages are corrected, a software version of the publication to be printed directs the computerized plate-embossing machines, which punch the raised braille onto zinc printing plates. Then in the busy printing area, you'll watch and hear modified Heidelberg cylinder presses spin out up to 8,000 Braille pages per hour. Workers then hand-collate braille versions of original publications, computer manuals, or popular children's books such as the *Harry Potter* series, before stitch-binding completes the production process.

Cost: Free, but donation appreciated.

Freebies: Samples of braille materials and braille alphabet cards.

Video/DVD Shown: Yes

Reservations Needed: Yes, call 1 week in advance.

Days and Hours: Mon–Thur 10:30 AM and 2:30 PM. Closed holidays.

Plan to Stay: 1 hour.

Minimum Age: While there is no official minimum age, children should be at least 6 to appreciate the tour. The company tries to make the tour more interactive for children and offers a chance for children to meet blind and visually impaired employees.

Disabled Access: Yes; enter from bottom floor.

Group Requirements: Can handle groups up to 8 people with 5 days' advance notice.

Special Information: Supervise children around the printing presses. Tours also available at the American Printing House for the Blind in Louisville, KY, the largest and oldest (1859) publishing house for the blind (see page 238).

Gift Shop: No

Directions: By subway, take the "E" train on the Green Line to the Northeastern University stop on Huntington Ave. Cross Huntington onto Opera Pl. and turn right onto St. Stephen St. The building is 1 block ahead on your right. By car, take the Massachusetts Ave. exit on I-93 (Southeast Expwy.). Turn right on Massachusetts Ave. and go straight until you cross Huntington Ave. At Symphony Hall (on your left), turn left on St. Stephen St. National Braille Press is ahead on your left. Construction changes are ongoing, so for up-to-date directions, please see our website. There is metered parking in the area and some limited private parking at the facility.

Nearby Attractions: Boston Beer (Samuel Adams) and *Boston Globe* newspaper tours (see page 66 and 67); Fenway Park tour (call 617-226-6666); Boston's museums and attractions include Symphony Hall, Christian Science Center, Museum of Science, Back Bay.

851 Sandwich Road, Sagamore, MA 02561   (508) 888-2344   www.pairpoint.com
                                              (800) 899-0953

Pairpoint CRYSTAL COMPANY

Since Pairpoint's philosophy is "made in America the old-fashioned way," it utilizes the same hand tools and processes as when Deming Jarves founded the company in 1837. Pairpoint makes cup plates (many are collectors' items), limited editions, and other fine pieces for such museums as New York City's Metropolitan Museum of Art and Boston's Museum of Fine Arts.

Though the observation window shields you from the furnaces' 2,500°F heat, you know the factory below is hot—the artisans wear shorts year-round. Watch a gaffer, the most experienced glassblower on the five-person team, fill his cheeks with air and blow into the blowpipe. Once the glass at the other end of the pipe reaches the desired size, he twirls the rod like a baton to elongate the glass.

Using another rod, a team member gathers glass from the furnaces and brings it to the gaffer, who attaches it to the original piece, snips it with shears, then shapes the piece with wooden and metal hand tools. Eventually the piece is transferred to the pontil rod and cracked off from its original blowpipe. The gaffer inserts the work, perhaps a vase or a flask, into a reheating furnace called a "glory hole" and then shapes its opening.

Cup plates, widely used in the mid-1800s as plates for handle-less cups of hot tea, have increased in popularity since Pairpoint started pressing them in the early 1970s. A gob of 34 percent lead crystal glass is placed in a mold, and an artisan pulls on a lever to exert just the right amount of pressure. While the standard patterns on these 3.5-inch-diameter cup plates include endangered species, birds, and geometric shapes, you will also want to see the gift-shop display of collector's cup plates commissioned by companies, clubs, and towns.

Cost: Free

Freebies: Product brochures.

Video Shown: No

Reservations Needed: No

Days and Hours: May–December: Mon–Fri 9:00 AM–12:00 PM and 12:30 PM–4:00 PM. February–April: Mon–Fri 10:00 AM–5:00 PM with limited production. Closed holidays. No weekend glassblowing.

Plan to Stay: 20 minutes for self-guided tour, plus time for gift shop.

Minimum Age: None

Disabled Access: Yes

Group Requirements: Maximum group size is 40.

Special Information: Call to find out about production January–April.

Retail Store: Sells works by the artists, including museum reproductions, vases, candlesticks, and cup plates. Open May– December: Mon–Fri 9:00 AM–6:00 PM, Sat 10:00 AM–6:00 PM, Sun 11:00 AM–6:00 PM. Open January–April: Mon–Sat 10:00 AM–5:00 PM and Sun 11:00 AM–5:00 PM. Closed holidays. Catalog available from (800) 899-0953.

Directions: From Boston, take I-93 South to Rt. 3 South to Sagamore Bridge. After bridge, take first exit onto Rt. 6A. Pairpoint is on your left. From Hyannis, take Rt. 6 West. Take last exit before bridge. Turn left onto Adams St. and left onto 6A. Pairpoint is on your right.

Nearby Attractions: Sandwich Glass Museum; Thornton Burgess Museum; Sandwich Boardwalk (look for nearby plaque designating site of original Boston and Sandwich Glass Co., also founded by Jarves); Yesteryears Museum; Old Grist Mill.

NEW ENGLAND

Route 5, South Deerfield, MA 01373   (413) 665-2929   www.yankeecandle.com

YANKEE CANDLE®

a passion for fragrance™

If you've ever made candles by melting wax and crayons, you have something in common with Mike Kittredge, founder of Yankee Candle. While you can no longer tour the factory, you can see historical storyboards depicting the beginning of Yankee Candle, and the original Queen Atlantic gas stove Mike used to melt wax in his parents' cellar at age 17 in 1969. Adjacent to the candle museum, where you see candle-making demonstrations, the walls display a pictorial history of the company's development from Mike's parents' house to a renovated paper mill in 1974 to the current Yankee Candle Complex.

Watch videos at four different locations in the Candle Emporium to discover all the steps performed at the nearby factory to make taper, jar, pillar, and sampler candles. Yankee Candle's workers describe the factory, which has piped-in music, as a huge craft studio that smells like a spice rack. The automatic taper-candle-dipping machine, resembling a chandelier with wicks instead of light bulbs, dips up to two miles of wicks per day. To create the standard seven-eighths-inch taper candle, the machine dips braided cotton wicks into liquid wax as many as 30 times, alternating with dips into a cooling water bath. Workers then hand-dip the final, harder wax layers to create smooth, dripless candles.

Textured pillar candles start as colorful solid-wax cylinders. Workers place four smooth pillar candles on pedestals to begin their transformation. The candles, pushed up through 300°F grooved rings, emerge from the top of the press as ionic (vertically grooved) or twist (spirally grooved) pillars. The making of jar candles will remind you of Jell-O molding—a machine fills eight glass containers at a time with hot, colorful, fragrant wax.

The Candlemaking Museum is designed as an 1810 chandler's workshop. Workers dressed in period garb give continuous live demonstrations, hand-dipping bayberry and beeswax candles. After you watch the candle making, you'll want to dip your own candles and test sniff some of the 175 fragrances of Sampler's votive candles in the Candle Emporium. Fragrances include the traditional (vanilla), the unexpected (cottage breeze), the delicious (chocolate chip cookie), and the inspirational (sweet honeysuckle).

Cost: Free

Freebies: No

Video/DVD Shown: Continuously running video provides close-up shots of the production processes.

Reservations Needed: No, except for bus tours.

Days and Hours: Mon–Sun 9:30 AM–6:00 PM. Extended hours from November–Christmas. Closed Thanksgiving and Christmas.

Plan to Stay: 20 minutes for video and Candlemaking Museum, plus 1–2 hours for retail stores and any special events on the grounds.

Minimum Age: None

Disabled Access: Yes

Special Information: Chandler's restaurant has fine dining (call 413-665-1277 for reservations); Candlewick Café and Coffee Haus offer casual dining.

Group Requirements: Bus tours call (413) 665-2929 for special parking and to reserve space in museum for 20-minute demonstration.

Retail Store: Sells thousands of different styles, varieties, and fragrances of candles, including Country Kitchen, Housewarmer jar candles, and aromatic samplers. Seconds Room has overruns and flawed candles at marked-down prices. Open Mon–Sun 9:30 AM–6:00 PM; extended hours during holiday season. Catalog available from (800) 243-1776. Entire 80,000-square-foot Yankee Candle Village complex includes Candle Shop, Bavarian Christmas Village, Kringle Market, Candle Emporium, the Black Forest, Enchanted Castle, and Santa's Workshop.

Directions: Take I-90 (MA Trnpk.) to I-91 North to Exit 24. Turn right on Rtes. 5 and 10. Yankee Candle will be on the left.

Nearby Attractions: Mt. Sugarloaf State Reservation; Historic Deerfield; Mohawk Trail Autoroad; Magic Wings Butterfly Conservatory (see page 73).

One of every two beers consumed in America is made by Anheuser-Busch, with this brewery serving all of New England. Of Anheuser-Busch's 12 U.S. breweries, this brewery is in the prettiest setting, located in the picturesque Merrimack Valley. It can package 8 million 12-ounce servings in 24 hours.

Your tour guide will lead you to the brewery, built in 1970, past a life-size replica of a Clydesdale horse. In the brewhouse, a mixture of water and rice or corn fills three stainless-steel mash tanks. Malt enzymes break the starch in the corn or rice into fermentable sugars. Once strained, the remaining liquid ("wort") is boiled and hops are added. After cooling, the liquid is pumped into 45°F fermentation cellars. On the ground floor of this four-story cellar, you may see a worker place a layer of beechwood chips in the stainless-steel tanks. These chips provide a surface area on which yeast settles during secondary fermentation.

On your way to the packaging area, notice the eight-foot carved mahogany mural of the Anheuser-Busch corporate trademark. Through glass windows, watch the tightly woven maze of filling lines. Once rinsed, bottles proceed to the rotating bottle-filler. They then speed through capping and labeling to packaging. After the brewery tour, don't miss the Old World–style Clydesdale Hamlet, modeled after an 18th-century German Bauernhof. This stable and courtyard are home base for the traveling East Coast Clydesdale eight-horse show hitch. This close-up look at the Budweiser Clydesdales (special photo opportunities first Saturday of each month) is a highlight of the tour.

Cost: Free

Freebies: Beer, soda, and snacks.

Video/DVD Shown: If packaging line isn't operating, 2 6-minute films show packaging and brewing processes.

Reservations Needed: No, except for groups larger than 15.

Days and Hours: January–April: Thur–Mon 10:00 AM–4:00 PM; May, September–December: Mon–Sun 10:00 AM–4:00 PM; June–August: Mon–Sun 9:30 AM–5:00 PM. Call to see if bottling on weekends or holidays. Generally closed day before and day of Thanksgiving, Christmas, and New Year's.

Plan to Stay: 1.5 hours for tour, hospitality room, and Clydesdale Hamlet, plus time for shopping and tour assembly room displays.

Minimum Age: Under age 18 must be accompanied by adult.

Disabled Access: Yes

Group Requirements: Groups larger than 15 should call 1 day in advance. Groups of more than 35 people will be split into smaller groups. No maximum group size.

Special Information: No photography inside brewery. First Saturday of each month is Budweiser Clydesdale Camera Day (1:00–3:00 PM), when you can pose with one of the Clydesdale horses. Tour includes indoor and outdoor walking and some stairs. See page xxx for St. Louis, MO, feature and information about other Anheuser-Busch brewery tours.

Gift Shop: Tour Center Store sells logoed items, including T-shirts, bathing suits, steins, and jackets. Closes 1 hour later than tours.

Directions: From Boston, take I-93 North to I-495 South to Rt. 3 North. In New Hampshire, Rt. 3 becomes Everett Tnpk. Get off at Exit 10. At end of ramp, go right. At the next set of lights, turn left onto Daniel Webster Hwy. At the next traffic light, turn right into the brewery. Park in second lot on right. From Rt. 101, take Everett Tnpk. South to Exit 10 in Merrimack. At end of ramp, turn left. At the second set of lights, turn left onto Daniel Webster Hwy. Follow to next traffic light and turn right into brewery.

Nearby Attractions: Stonyfield Farm Yogurt tour (see page 80); American Textile History Museum (see page 65); Currier Gallery of Art (call 603-669-6144); New England Quilt Museum (call 978-452-4207).

NEW ENGLAND

See color photos, page 4.

43 Mill Street, Wolfeboro, NH 03894

(603) 569-4944

www.hampshire
pewter.com

hampshire pewter company

Wolfeboro is the oldest summer resort in the U.S.A., making it a fitting home for Hampshire Pewter. In fact, new owners Harold and Kathy Guptill and Abe and Wendy Neudorf left their computer-industry jobs for this distinctly small-town setting. Using skilled craftspeople and modern machines, the company has revived the craft of colonial pewter making. As high-tech manufacturers strive to develop lighter, stronger, and more durable metals, it's good to know that pewter is still valued.

On your guided tour, watch through glass windows as craftspeople mix pure tin with other fine metals to create Queens Metal Pewter. Hampshire Pewter is the only U.S. company to use this special alloy, which consists mostly of tin. Unless you remember your high-school chemistry, you probably don't think of metal as a liquid. But to combine the metals, a worker liquefies them at over 1,900°F in a big pot in the back of the small foundry, "cools" the mixture to 600°F, then carefully pours it into specially designed, heavy bronze molds to form shapes.

When the temperature cools to 450°F, the liquid becomes a solid. The crafter judges when the pewter has solidified enough to be carefully knocked from the mold. The different castings that make up an item, such as the stem and bowl of a goblet, must be soldered together quickly—otherwise the flame's heat may melt or scorch the joined pieces.

In the workshop area, craftspeople called finishers then turn the pewter piece on a lathe, using chisels to chip away all the rough, gray metal. As a piece spins, the finishers artfully and gently carve the fine details of traditional designs. Delicately holding the pewter pieces, a crafter buffs them on cotton wheels to obtain the soft pewter luster. When you see workers finish the process by stamping each piece with the distinctive "touchmark" that identifies a Hampshire Pewter original, you know that the trademark is well deserved.

Cost: Free

Freebies: No

Video/DVD Shown: 8-minute video on history of pewter and close-up views of the Hampshire Pewter production process.

Reservations Needed: No reservations needed June–mid-October, except for groups of 15 or more. Reservations are needed mid-October–May.

Days and Hours: Memorial Day–Columbus Day: Mon–Fri 10:00 AM, 11:00 AM, 1:00 PM, 2:00 PM, and 3:00 PM. Labor Day–Columbus Day: same schedule except no 1:00 PM tour. Call for hours and reservations mid-October–May. Closed holidays.

Plan to Stay: 20 minutes for tour and video, plus time for gift shop.

Minimum Age: None, but viewing windows start 4 feet up from the ground.

Disabled Access: Yes, but viewing windows start 4 feet up from the ground.

Group Requirements: 10 days' advance notice for groups of 15 or more.

Special Information: No photography.

Retail Store: Tabletop Shop sells full selection of 200 hand-cast pewter items, ranging from teddy bear birthday-candle holders to flower vases and classic goblets. Personal engraving available. Open Mon–Sat 9:00 AM–5:00 PM. Closed Memorial Day, Thanksgiving, Christmas, and New Year's. Downtown store nearby on Main St. is open Mon–Sat 9:30 AM–5:30 PM. Catalog available from (800) 639-7704.

Directions: From Boston and southern New Hampshire, take I-95 North. Exit at Rt. 16 North. From Rt. 16, exit at Rt. 11 North. At the traffic circle, take Rt. 28 North. Stay on this road into Wolfeboro. Soon after the center of town, turn right on Mill St. Hampshire Pewter is in a red barnlike building on your right.

Nearby Attractions: Pepi Herrman Crystal tour (call 603-528-1020); Annalee Dolls Museum (call 800-43-DOLLS); Lake Winnipesaukee; Libby Museum.

The mountains and valleys of New Hampshire are rich in mineral formations. The Ruggles Mine is part of what geologists call the Littleton Formation. It has a proud, long history as an active, productive mine dating to 1803, when farmer Sam Ruggles went into the mica-mining business. The end of mica mining in 1969 closed an important chapter in the history of New Hampshire. For over 40 years, visitors enjoyed a geological and mining experience, exploring the open pit mine's caverns and tunnels, and hammering away at the rocks in search of minerals.

Drive right to the top of Isinglass Mountain over an access road off Route 4 and park on the summit plateau. You can see a panoramic view of valleys, forests, and surrounding mountains, including Cardigan, Kearsage, and Ragged. After a short walk from your car past a museum of old mining equipment, you are in Pit A, a man-made canyon with walls of white quartz and feldspar which gleam like alabaster in the sun.

Over 150 minerals occur here, including feldspar, beryl, mica, amethyst, rose and smoky quartz, and garnet. You can rent hammers and buckets at the mine entrance, keeping whatever minerals you collect. The mine's uranium minerals such as gummite and autunite are prized by collectors and museums throughout the world.

Cost: $20 adults; $10 children (ages 4–11).

Freebies: Mineral-identification sheets and brochures on the mine. You can take with you any minerals you find.

Video/DVD Shown: The small museum near the entrance shows a 6-minute video on the history of the mine.

Reservations Needed: No. Groups of over 30 should make reservations two weeks in advance. School groups should have 1 adult for every 5 children.

Days and Hours: Open daily 9:00 AM–5:00 PM, mid-June–mid-October (open weekends mid-May–mid-June).

Plan to Stay: At least 2 hours for mining and gift shop.

Minimum Age: None, though the mine has steep and slippery areas.

Disabled Access: Gift shop and museum area are accessible. Mine is not suitable for wheelchairs, especially older types.

Group Requirements: Groups of 30 or more get a discount of $1 per person.

Special Information: Although this is no longer a working mine with big machines, you need to take precautions, including wearing protective clothing and safety glasses, when chiseling at the rocks. You can rent hammers.

Gift Shop: Wide collection of minerals, gems, rocks, fossils, jewelry, local crafts, and souvenirs. Special children's section has educational items, including geodes you can crack and fluorescent-mineral kits. Small snack bar open during busy season.

Directions: From Concord or Manchester, take I-93 North to Rt. 4. In Grafton, follow signs. From New London, take Rt. 11 East to Rt. 4 West. From Lebanon, take I-89 to Rt. 4. From the north country, take I-93 South to Rt. 4.

Nearby Attractions: Polar Caves Park, White Mountains, Crystal Lake.

NEW ENGLAND

As the name suggests, Stonyfield Farm began on a farm. But meteoric growth forced this award-winning company to its present location in Londonderry. Developed in 1983 by two environmentalists, the all-natural yogurt can now be found in grocery stores nationwide. Their original mission hasn't changed—to demonstrate that a company can do good for the world and still be profitable. The tour shows you how they work their "magic" and live their corporate mission, despite selling 85 percent ownership to the French corporation *Groupe DANONE.*

Your tour begins in a mini-theater, where you see a lively video about the company's beginnings at the Wilton, New Hampshire, farm. Pass Stonyfield's Memory Lane, which chronicles many of the company's memorable "mooments." These notable milestones highlight the successes and failures of Stonyfield innovations—such as the short-lived Garden Salad Yogurt.

The windowed viewing area reveals different sections of the bustling Yogurt Works. Look into the research and development lab, where new ideas for flavors and products take form. Peek inside quality control and discover a science lab with petri dishes, test tubes, and the quality control team checking the incoming ingredients and the yogurt as it is being made. You may catch a glimpse of one of the shiny tanker trucks delivering a load of fresh farm milk as you pass the receiving bay. Your tour guide will explain the yogurt-making process: how Stonyfield mixes its special concoction of healthy yogurt bacteria (or "culture") into the milk and then provides the right environment for this "good bacteria" to turn the milk into yogurt (via the "magic of science").

Watch through large windows as empty cups are stacked in the filler, then drop onto the conveyer belt. First, a dollop of fruit goes into the bottom of each cup, then yogurt sprays out of spouts that look like showerheads, filling the containers. Next a suction cup reaches up, gets a foil seal and flips it onto the top of the cup. Finally the cups travel beneath the heat sealer, which secures the tops, and off they go, down to the packing machine, at the rate of 240 cups per minute. Once the cups are sealed in cases,

the yogurt elevator takes the cases up to the overhead tracks that carry them to the incubator. The containers may appear ready to ship to the stores, but the "magic" yogurt process has just begun.

Cost: $1.50; children 4 and under, free.

Freebies: Various yogurt samples.

Video/DVD Shown: 10-minute video covers company history and close-up views of production process.

Reservations Needed: No, except for groups larger than 10 people.

Days and Hours: Mon–Fri 10:00 AM–4:00 PM on the hour. Closed holidays and special Stonyfield days. For current schedule, check website or call (603) 437-4040 ext. 3270.

Plan to Stay: 1 hour for tour, video, and sampling, plus time for gift shop.

Minimum Age: Recommended minimum age is 4; however, strollers welcome.

Disabled Access: Yes

Group Requirements: Groups of more than 10 people should call in advance. Maximum group size is 40 people. Group rate is $1 per person.

Special Information: No production on Saturdays; video shown.

Gift Shop: Logoed and cow-motif products, country gifts, books, and kids' stuff; all Stonyfield Yogurt flavors and types at factory price. Open Mon–Sat 9:30 AM–5:00 PM.

Directions: From Boston, take I-93 North to North Londonderry (Exit 5). Turn left onto Rt. 28 North. After 2 miles, turn left onto Page Rd. At traffic light, turn left onto Webster Rd. At stop sign, turn left onto Harvey Rd. In 0.8 mile, turn left (which keeps you on Harvey Rd.) and in about a half mile. turn right onto Burton Dr. Stonyfield is on right side of road. From Nashua, take Everett Tnpk. North. Take Rt. 101 East to S. Willow St. Turn right onto Rt. 28 South. Bear left at the 4th set of lights. Turn right onto Harvey (follow as it turns right in 1 mile). Turn right onto Burton Dr.

Nearby Attractions: Anheuser-Busch Brewery tour (see page 77); Redhook Brewery tour in Portsmouth (call 603-430-8600); Currier Museum of Art in Manchester; Canobie Lake Park in Salem; The Met, a children's museum in Derry.

NEW ENGLAND

Vanguard Sailboats is the largest U.S. supplier and leading world manufacturer of recreational and high performance small sailboats. So that no sailor has an advantage, precision manufacturing drives Vanguard's boat-building process to ensure that the boats are identical. If you can tolerate the strong glue smell, you can walk along the plant floor, stand next to the workers, and observe all the stages in making the different Vanguard models.

Fiberglass boats are built from the outside in, starting from separate molds of the hull and deck. The molds are mirror images of these boat body parts. The precision begins in the room where a band saw cuts stacks of fiberglass sheets according to an exacting pattern. In the spray booth, the bright gel coat that's sprayed into the mold provides the boat's color.

In a process called "laying up fiberglass," workers use paint rollers to glue the strips down into the molds. You'll see them hand-lay the resin-soaked fiberglass sheets, reminding you of making papier-mâché dolls. To ensure that each boat weighs the same, the resin and fiberglass are carefully weighed before being laid into each boat; the hulls are specially measured against a template. The separately made hull and deck are also cored with PVC foam and vacuum-bagged.

In a nearby area, workers add hardware such as the cleats and mast step. Hanging from the ceiling

are decks and hulls joined by glue and married together with huge pterodactyl clamps. Even if you're only an occasional sailor, you'll appreciate what's involved in building a small sailboat.

Cost: Free

Freebies: Stickers

Video/DVD Shown: No

Reservations Needed: Yes

Days and Hours: Mon–Fri 9:00 AM–2:30 PM. Closed holidays.

Plan to Stay: 1 hour for tour.

Minimum Age: 10

Disabled Access: Yes

Group Requirements: No maximum group size as long as 5 days' advance notice is given.

Special Information: As with any fiberglass-boat manufacturing plant, there is a strong glue smell.

Gift Shop: No

Directions: From Rt. 114 North, turn right into Portsmouth Business Park (Hedly St.) and follow signs to production offices. From Rt. 114 South, turn left into Portsmouth Business Park and follow signs.

Nearby Attractions: Thames Glass tour in Newport is less than 1 hour away (call 401-846-0576); Herreshoff Marine Museum in Bristol; Colt State Park; Haffenreffer Museum of Anthropology; Newport's beaches, mansions, Naval War College Museum, Museum of Yachting at Fort Adams State Park, International Tennis Hall of Fame, and other attractions are 20 minutes away. (This area of Rhode Island has many sailboat manufacturers, but very few give public tours. However, if you own a boat made by a company in this region, or are considering the purchase of one, a tour probably could be arranged by calling the company or your local dealer directly.)

NEW ENGLAND

Ben & Jerry's

ICE CREAM AND FROZEN YOGURT

Route 100 North, Waterbury, VT 05676

(802) 882-1240
(866) BJTOURS

www.benjerry.com

Nestled in the heart of the Green Mountains, the Ben & Jerry's ice-cream factory sits on a rolling pasture. The grounds are filled with whimsical interactive displays and games, like the interactive timeline, to ease the waiting time for this popular tour. Given Ben & Jerry's down-home image, you'd expect to see hundreds of workers using individual churns to make its ice creams and yogurts. Instead, from a glass-enclosed, temperature-controlled mezzanine area, you look down at a state-of-the-art ice-cream factory that can turn out 250,000 pints per day.

The tour starts in the Cow over the Moon Theater. In the movie, you'll find out how two childhood friends, Ben Cohen and Jerry Greenfield, turned a five-dollar correspondence course on ice-cream making into a business that shares its success with its employees and the community—and has fun while doing it!

Afterwards, follow the enthusiastic tour guide up to the mezzanine. Ice cream and frozen yogurt begin as an unflavored base mix stored in the 36°F tank room. The mix travels to the flavor vat, to the freezer (where it gets the consistency of soft-serve), into the fruit and chunk feeder, to the automatic pint-filler that handles "chunk intensive" flavors, and finally to the spiral hardener. In this last step, the ice cream freezes solid at a temperature of -40°F. When in production, watch live-feed, real-time videos showing ice-cream pints emerging from the spiral hardener, then groups of eight are shrink-wrapped or "bundled."

Then it's off to the Flavoroom for the sample of the day. After you've had a taste, make sure you peek into the Quality Assurance Lab. Every hour a quality control worker grabs pints off the production line, freezes them, and slices them open, inspecting the ice cream for the proper amount of chunks and swirls.

After passing by the QA Lab, enter the Ben & Jerry's Hall of Fame, full of pictures, posters, and paraphernalia that humorously document the company's proud, offbeat history.

Cost: Adults, $3; senior citizens, $2; children 12 and under, free.

Freebies: An ice-cream sample and a souvenir factory tour ticket.

Video/DVD Shown: 7-minute movie about founders. A video of the production process is shown on the mezzanine portion of the tour to help visitors see the process in action.

Reservations Needed: No, except for groups of 10 or more. Reservations not accepted for July, August, and holidays.

Days and Hours: November–May: Sat–Sun 10:00 AM–5:00 PM. June: 9:00 AM–6:00 PM. July–August: 9:00 AM–8:00 PM. Late August–October: 9:00 AM–6:00 PM. Tours leave at least every 30 minutes, with tickets sold on a first-come, first-served basis. No ice-cream production on Sat, Sun, holidays, or company celebration days, although tours are still offered. Call for up-to-date schedules. Closed on New Year's Day, Thanksgiving, and Christmas.

Plan to Stay: 30 minutes for tour and movie, plus time for grounds, displays, and gift shop. Grounds are a low-key family activity park.

Minimum Age: None

Disabled Access: Yes

Group Requirements: Groups of 10 or more call (802) 882-1240, ext. 2289.

Special Information: Afternoon tours fill quickly, particularly in summer.

Gift Shop: Scoop Shop features variety of Ben & Jerry's flavors. Gift shop offers Vermont gifts, logoed clothes, memorabilia, and other fun stuff. Gift and scoop shops remain open for 1 hour after the last tour of the day has left.

Directions: Take I-89 to Exit 10. Go north on Rt. 100 toward Stowe. Factory is about 1 mile ahead on left.

Nearby Attractions: Rock of Ages, Vermont Teddy Bear, and Cabot Creamery tours (see pages 89, 92, and 83); Cabot Creamery Annex Store; Stowe and Sugarbush ski areas; Cold Hollow Cider Mill; Mt. Mansfield.

**Owned by Dairy Farmers
Since 1919**

On a hillside in Vermont, sparkling white 130,000-gallon milk silos emblazoned with the red-and-green Cabot Creamery logo overlook the entrance to the visitors center and plant, where the world's best cheddar cheese is made (as judged at the 22nd Biennial World Championship Contest in Green Bay, Wisconsin). This guided tour shows you how the cooperative creamery, dating back to 1893 and owned since 1919 by the dairy farmers that ship their high-quality milk here, converts milk from local farms into award-winning Vermont cheddar cheeses, and also how it packages its yogurts, cottage cheese, and sour cream.

You'll peer through glass windows into the packaging and processing rooms, where workers fill large cooking vats with quality-tested, heat-treated milk and a starter culture. The curd that forms is cut with stainless-steel knives that help separate the curd from the whey. Once the whey is separated and drained off, workers vigorously mix the curd on huge metal finishing tables to "cheddar" it until the correct pH level is reached.

In overhead towers, the curd is then pressed into 42-pound blocks or round stainless-steel frames to create cheese wheels. Every 90 seconds another block emerges from a tower and enters an airtight cellophane bag for natural aging. With the cheese-making process in various stages of production, your 10-minute walk captures the five hours needed for every vat of milk to become cheese (33,000 pounds of whole milk in each vat yields approximately 3,500 pounds of cheese).

Cost: $2; children under 12, free.

Freebies: Cabot cheese samples, dips, and other VT specialty food samples under the "Grazing Encouraged" sign in gift shop. Cabot Activity Book, 1 per child.

Video/DVD Shown: 10-minute video on the history of Cabot, including the town, the farmers, and the creamery, development of Cabot Cooperative Creamery in 1919, and highlights of processes used to make different Cabot products.

Reservations Needed: No, except for groups larger than 20 people.

Days and Hours: June–October: Mon–Sun 9:00 AM–5:00 PM; November–May: Mon–Sat 9:00 AM–4:00 PM; January: Mon–Sat 10:00 AM–4:00 PM. Tours run every 30 minutes. Last tour 30 minutes before closing. Call ahead for cheese-making days.

Plan to Stay: 30 minutes for tour and video, plus time to nibble in the gift shop.

Minimum Age: None

Disabled Access: Yes

Group Requirements: Groups larger than 20 should call in advance.

Special Information: Cabot Creamery Annex store (near Ben & Jerry's factory on Rt. 100) shows cheese-making video, sells Cabot products, Vermont specialty foods, beer, and wine, and houses Lake Champlain chocolates, VT Teddy Bear, and Snow Farm Vineyards under the same copper roof.

Gift Shop: Sells all Cabot products, including such specialty cheddars as Reduced Fat or Flavored Cheddars. Offers selected weekly specials and other Vermont-made food products and gifts. Open same hours as tour. Cheese catalog available from (800) 639-3198.

Directions: From I-89, take Exit 8 for Montpelier. Head east on Rt. 2 and turn left onto Rt. 215 East in Marshfield Village. Cabot Creamery is 5 miles ahead on right. From I-91, take St. Johnsbury exit. Head west on Rt. 2 and turn right on Rt. 215 to Creamery.

Nearby Attractions: Maple Grove Farms, Ben & Jerry's, and Rock of Ages tours (see pages 87, 82, and 89); Goodrich's Sugarhouse (call 800-639-1854); contact Vermont Cheese Council (www.vtcheese.com) for other Vermont cheese tours.

NEW ENGLAND

Healdville Road, Healdville, VT 05758

(802) 259-2340
(802) 259-2210

www.crowley
cheese.com

When most cheese factories call their cheese "handmade," they usually mean that machines did the processing with a little human involvement. At the U.S.'s oldest still-operating cheese factory (established 1882), "handmade" means what it says. Except for modern sanitation and refrigeration techniques, Crowley's cheese-making tools are from the 1800s.

The outside of this three-story brown clapboard building, a National Historic Place, looks more like a house than a cheese "factory." But inside, the solo cheese-maker proudly enjoys showing visitors how to make old-style Colby cheddar using 19th-century techniques. You can stand near the 1,000-gallon sterile vat that looks like a large bathtub filled with milk. Steam flows through the hollow walls to heat the milk.

The cheese maker adds the culture and, later, rennet (a milk-coagulating enzyme). Once the mixture has a yogurt texture, it is "cut" into small cubes, which separate from the whey and become the curd. Watch how the cheese maker uses the cheese rake to gently stir the curd. This keeps curd particles separate and helps them cook evenly.

Once the whey is drained, the curds look like mounds of popcorn. The cheese maker works the curds by hand, rinsing them with fresh spring water before placing them into cheesecloth-lined metal hoops. Overnight, old crank presses remove excess whey. Then the cheese wheels age at least two months for mild and over a year for extra-sharp. After looking at the pictures on the walls, listening to the cheese maker's explanation, and watching traditional cheese-making techniques, you leave saying the Little Miss Muffet nursery rhyme.

Cost: Free

Freebies: Cheese

Video/DVD Shown: 9-minute video on history of company and cheese-making process, usually shown when not in production.

Reservations Needed: No, except for groups over 25 people.

Days and Hours: Mon–Fri 8:00 AM–4:00 PM. Closed holidays. Since small operation, call ahead about cheese production schedule.

Plan to Stay: 15 minutes for tour, plus time for gift shop and duck pond.

Minimum Age: None. Tour is very popular with young children; *Sesame Street* filmed feature on cheese making at Crowley.

Disabled Access: Yes

Group Requirements: Groups larger than 25 should call a few days ahead.

Special Information: Best time to see production and talk to cheese maker is 11:00 AM–midafternoon. When no one is in factory, calls to above number may not always be answered. Don't despair, just call back or try contacting gift shop at (800) 683-2606.

Retail Store: Located 1.5 miles away on main Rt. 103; sells mild, medium, and sharp Crowley Cheese in 8-oz. bars, 2.5- and 5-pound wheels, smoked bars, and spiced (caraway, dill, garlic, hot pepper, onion, and sage) bars; Vermont specialty foods and gifts. Open Mon–Sat 10:30 AM–5:30 PM, Sun 11:00 AM–5:30 PM (suggest calling to check if open). Closed Christmas and New Year's. Call above number for order form.

Directions: From I-91, take Rt. 103 North. At split with Rt. 100, stay on Rt. 103 for 3 miles. Pass Crowley Cheese Shop, turn left onto Healdville Rd. for factory. From Rutland, take Rt. 7 South to Rt. 103 South. Then go approx. 10 miles to flashing yellow light at Belmont Rd. in Mt. Holly. Continue on Rt. 103 South for about 3 miles and turn right onto Healdville Rd.

Nearby Attractions: Vermont Marble Exhibit (call 802-459-3311 ext. 436); Weston (a lovely small New England village); Coolidge Family Homestead; Okemo ski area.

533 Townshend Road, Grafton, VT 05146   (802) 843-2221   www.graftonvillage
                                      (800) 472-3866   cheese.com

Premium Vermont Cheddar

Cheese making has long been a part of Vermont life, with grazing dairy cows a familiar sight. The state has cheese factories of all sizes, from the large Cabot Creamery (see page 83) to the very small Crowley Cheese (see page 85). They often sit in picturesque locations, and you discover them just when you're hungry for a small snack.

Grafton, Vermont, is likely the prettiest home of any of the state's cheese factories. Cheese-making traditions in this historic village date from the 19th century (started in 1892), when dairy farmers gathered together in a cooperative to make their surplus milk into cheese. The town's preservation has retained much of the character from that century.

Grafton Village Cheese, now owned by the nonprofit Windham Foundation, has won numerous awards, especially for its Classic Reserve and Premium cheddars. It owes much of its fame to Scott Fletcher, Grafton's master cheese maker, who has been with the company for more than 30 years. He is one of the deans of Vermont cheese making and gives his personal touch to each step of the process. As with most cheese factories, you can watch production through big glass windows. You see long metal tables and vats, with cheese in various stages of its creation.

The process, almost eight hours long, requires close monitoring. It begins with fresh Vermont Jersey cow milk that is pumped into the cheese vats. Depending on the time of day and Grafton's production schedule, you will gather glimpses of cheese makers adding rennet to separate the milk solids from the whey, stirring the heated milk, testing the mixture for flavor and acidity, squeezing whey from the coagulated curd, and then packing the curd into hoop molds for aging. Look for the critical step called "cheddaring," when the curd is cut into slabs, then stacked and pressed together several times until most of the whey is drained off. Grafton naturally ages its cheeses: one year for a sharp cheddar

and up to six years for a mature Vermont cheddar. In another area, big blocks of properly aged cheddar are cut into different sizes, before waxing and perhaps smoking.

Cost: Free

Freebies: Plentiful samples in the retail store.

Video/DVD Shown: 9-minute video that shows close-ups of the production process and history of the company. Video continually shows even when not in production.

Reservations Needed: No

Days and Hours: Mon–Fri 8:00 AM–4:00 PM, Sat and Sun 10:00 AM–4:00 PM. Closed Thanksgiving, Christmas, and New Year's. Most production occurs Mon–Fri 8:00 AM–1:00 PM, depending on the season and demand. Call for current production schedule.

Plan to Stay: 15 minutes, plus time for gift shop.

Minimum Age: None

Disabled Access: Yes

Group Requirements: Large bus groups call ahead to break into groups of 15–20 people. Guide available.

Special Information: In summer, see, pet, and feed Vermont Jersey cows, next to the covered bridge.

Gift Shop: Sells all of the company's cheeses, including the Classic Reserve, Premium, Yankee Thrift, and flavored cheddars in bricks, blocks, and wheels of different sizes. Offers other Vermont-made specialty foods, including jellies and mustards, and crafts. Catalog available from above number. Open same hours.

Directions: From I-91, take Exit 5. Take Rt. 121/U.S. 5 West. Turn left at the Old Tavern onto Townshend Rd.

Nearby Attractions: Grafton Pond's cross-country skiing, snowshoeing, ice-skating, and mountain biking; The Nature Museum at Grafton; The Old Tavern; Okemo and Stratton Ski Mountains about 1 hour away; contact Vermont Cheese Council (www.vtcheese.com) for other Vermont cheese tours.

One Rotarian Place, Waterbury, VT 05676

(802) 882-2700
(800) 545-2326

www.greenmountain
coffee.com

The Green Mountain Coffee Roasters Visitor Center and Café are housed in Waterbury Railroad Station, a historic and newly renovated working Amtrak station (built in 1867) adjacent to the company's headquarters. You will learn how the company began in 1981 with a modest café in nearby Waitsfield and grew into one of the nation's leading specialty-coffee companies. Green Mountain now sells its coffee to cafés, markets, and offices throughout the country, and through its catalog and website.

When you enter the restored railroad station, you'll see an area with information about Waterbury, trains, and regional history. Travelers can learn much about the "Crossroads of Vermont" and its environs—from Mount Mansfield and Stowe to the Mad River Valley. Next, you enter the Green Mountain Coffee Roasters exhibition space. Here you learn all about coffee and what makes specialty coffee "special." Bringing education, storytelling, and entertainment technology together in a fun and innovative way, the Visitor Center invites, guides, and shares Green Mountain's passion for coffee.

Green Mountain Coffee Roasters travels the world, from Central America to Africa to Indonesia, to purchase the finest coffee beans. The company brings them to Waterbury, roasts them to peak flavor, and packages them. The exhibit area includes informative displays about fair trade and organic coffees. These show how buying coffee with the Green Mountain Fair Trade label helps bring beneficial change to developing countries. You'll learn how fair trade guarantees coffee farmers a decent price, which means they can afford to feed their families, keep their kids in school, and invest in the quality of the land and their coffee. You will also see displays about Green Mountain's approach to the art and craft of roasting, flavoring,

and blending coffee, and their commitment to ensuring quality.

In addition, you will learn about the company's inspiring corporate philosophy and commitment to employee ownership. The company takes pride in its social mission, which many of the displays emphasize. In fact, 5 percent of its pretax profit goes directly to social-responsibility initiatives. All the displays emphasize how the company celebrates and supports the power of businesses and individuals to bring about good change, locally and globally. After the self-guided tour in the exhibition space, enter the Green Mountain Coffee Roasters Café, where you can enjoy a cup of fresh-brewed coffee, a cappuccino, or a latte with a new appreciation of what goes into that perfect cup of coffee.

Cost: Free

Freebies: Occasional sampling of fresh-brewed coffees and seasonal blends.

Video/DVD Shown: Yes

Reservations Needed: Encouraged for groups of 10 or more.

Days and Hours: Visitors Center is open 9:00 AM–5:00 PM. Closed Thanksgiving, Christmas, and New Year's Day. The Railroad Station is open with extended hours to accommodate the Amtrak schedule.

Plan to Stay: 30–45 minutes.

Minimum Age: None

Disabled Access: Yes

Group Requirements: Bus tours and school groups are encouraged and welcome.

Gift Shop: Coffee and coffee-related items are available for purchase in the Visitor Center and in the Café. Café is open Mon–Sun 7:00 AM–5:00 PM.

Directions: From I-89, take the exit for Rte. 100. Take Rte. 100 South and turn left into downtown Waterbury. At the second traffic light, turn left. The Train Station is on the right behind the park.

Nearby Attractions: Ben & Jerry's and Vermont Teddy Bear (see pages 82 and 92); Cold Hollow Cider Mill (call 802-244-8771 or 800-327-7537); Stowe and Sugarbush (skiing); Mt Mansfield.

Maple Grove Farms

1052 Portland Street, St. Johnsbury, VT 05819

(802) 748-5141
(800) 525-2540

www.maplegrove.com

The company that two women started in 1915 is now one of the world's largest packagers of maple syrup and manufacturers of maple products. Maple Grove Farms has also developed a full line of natural fruit syrups and gourmet salad dressings, with its four fat-free salad dressings having become some of the top-selling gourmet dressings in the U.S.A.

This guided factory floor tour has a small-town feeling. You'll watch bottles of pure maple syrup or salad dressing filled, labeled, and packed on the assembly line. Downstairs in the "kitchen," workers heat and mix maple syrup for making candy. The sights, sounds, and sweet smells delight visitors.

A vintage 1930s candy depositor pours the maple candy mix into rubber sheet molds. The mixture cools for about an hour before the "ladies," as the tour guide calls them, shake the candy out onto padded mats. The candies are placed into metal baskets for an overnight bath in a crystallizing mixture of sugar and syrup, a natural preservative. Look through the glass window at carts filled with candy air-drying on metal trays, and at the quick-moving hands that individually pack the maple candies into boxes (3,000 to 4,000 pounds per day).

Cost: $1; children under 12, free.

Freebies: Small sample bag of maple candies. Gift shop offers free tastes of different maple syrups and the salad dressing of the day.

Video/DVD Shown: Tour begins with 8-minute video highlighting maple syrup–making process, company history, and manufacturing. When factory tour not operating, this video plays in Cabin Store.

Reservations Needed: No, except for groups of more than 40 people.

Days and Hours: Mon–Fri 8:00 AM–2:00 PM, year-round. Tour runs about every 12 minutes. Closed holidays.

Plan to Stay: 45 minutes, including tour, video, Maple Museum, and gift shop. Maple Museum is an authentic sugarhouse with all tools and equipment used by Vermont sugar makers and complete explanation of evaporation process.

Minimum Age: None

Disabled Access: Only on bottom floor of factory, but company does not encourage it because floor can be slippery.

Group Requirements: Tours for groups of more than 40 people require reservations.

Special Information: Production stops around 1:00 PM (subject to change). Winter is off-peak season, so please call ahead to check on production for tours.

Gift Shop: Cabin Store sells many maple products, such as maple butter, maple crunch, and maple drops. Also offers company's gourmet dressings and fruit-flavored syrups, along with standard Vermont tourist items. Look for factory seconds in seconds area. Cabin Store and Maple Museum open Mon–Sun 8:00 AM–5:00 PM, from beginning of May until late October. During winter, store is open Mon–Fri 8:00 AM–5:00 PM.

Directions: From I-91, take Exit 20 for Rt. 5 North. Take Rt. 2 East. Factory is about 1 mile from center of town. From I-93, take Exit 1 in Vermont, turn onto Rt. 18 toward St. Johnsbury, then turn left onto Rt. 2 West. Factory is a few miles ahead on left.

Nearby Attractions: Cabot Creamery tour (see page 83); Goodrich's Sugarhouse (call 800-639-1854); Fairbanks Museum and Planetarium; New England Maple Museum, about 1.5 hours away in Pittsford.

NEW ENGLAND

The Orvis Company proudly traces its start to 1856, when it manufactured and sold rods and flies to affluent sportsmen. It continues that practice today, making both traditional bamboo rods and modern carbon-fiber fly rods that are the industry standard. The product line has also greatly expanded since the 1800s. It now includes men's and women's casual attire, gear and clothing for fly-fishing and hunting, products for pets, and various other items, sold through more than 30 of its own stores and outlets, at 500 retailers, by catalog, and on its website. Orvis also fields an active travel business and fly-fishing school.

The tour of Orvis's rod factory in Vermont shows all the steps involved in making fly-fishing rods. You begin the tour by walking through hallways that display pictures of fly-fishing manufacturing over the past century, while your guide talks about the history and craft of this profession.

Most of the rods they sell are made of various graphite composites, using materials and technology pioneered by the aerospace and defense industries. These techniques yield a powerful rod with the sensitivity to enhance line control and casting accuracy. Only a few of the rods they make now are bamboo, so you may not see the methods used to make these classic items, which gave the company its start.

The graphite needs to be stored in freezers in flat sheets. These are then turned into blanks that are cut into shapes, molded, and baked for almost two hours at 250°F. After sanding, the high-end rods get three coats of finish, finely polished with a final layer that blocks ultraviolet light. In the assembly area, 10 to 20 people put on the butts, cork grips, and guides.

You also see craftsmen fixing rods. Although Or-vis rods rarely need repair and come with a 25-year guarantee, freak damage occasionally occurs in the field (such as when a rod must be deployed to fight off a bear). In these cases, owners can send their rods to the factory for repair.

With a new appreciation for the labor-intensive process of making fly rods, afterwards you can take a lesson in casting at the edge of the nearby pond (stocked with trout) outside the factory.

Cost: Free

Freebies: Lessons in casting with state-of-the-art rods in the pond next to the factory and store; learn fly-fishing tips.

Video/DVD Shown: No

Reservations Needed: No, except for groups of 10 or more.

Days and Hours: Tour runs Mon–Fri at 10:00 AM. Closed major holidays and first week of July.

Plan to Stay: 45 minutes for tour, plus time for store.

Minimum Age: None

Disabled Access: Limited (call ahead).

Group Requirements: Groups of 10 or more should reserve in advance.

Special Information: No cameras.

Gift Shop: The flagship store across the street stands on the site of Charles Orvis's very first fly-rod shop in 1856. This store sells all the company's products; call (802) 362-3750. The full product line is also available at Orvis.com.

Directions: From Rtes. 11 and 30, turn left on Rte. 7A. Complex with flagship store is on left. Tour groups assemble at front office of rod factory.

Nearby Attractions: American Museum of Fly Fishing (call 802-362-3300) includes a historical collection of 1,000 rods, 400 reels, thousands of flies, and other items; Simon Pearce (page 90–91); Southern Vermont Arts Center; Hildene (summer family home built by Robert Todd Lincoln).

Rock of Ages Corporation was founded in 1885 by native Yankees and immigrants looking for a better life. The company has grown to become the largest quarrier, manufacturer, retailer of finished granite memorials, and wholesaler of granite blocks for memorial use in North America, with 13 active quarry properties and 10 manufacturing and sawing facilities. Rock of Ages has conducted narrated tours of its quarrying operations since 1924, currently letting you experience the world's largest-dimension granite quarry located in Graniteville, part of Barre, Vermont, the self-proclaimed "Granite Center of the World."

The narrated shuttle bus tour of the E. L. Smith Quarry offers expansive views of the 50-acre, 600-foot-deep active quarry. From behind a wire fence at the edge of the quarry, look down at the process of mining granite by man and machine. The walls form deep canyons of Barre gray granite. Slot-drilling machines cut huge blocks of granite off the walls (you may also hear controlled explosions that split the bottom of the block). Notice the powerful, tall derricks towering above the quarry that lift the blocks. At the nearby saw plant, these blocks are sliced into slabs.

After the outdoor tour, with its views of Vermont's Green Mountains in the background, journey inside the dramatic new Visitors Center for a self-guided tour of the manufacturing plant that spans two football fields. From one end of the cavernous plant, look over a wood railing from an observation deck as granite artisans labor to make enduring tombstones and other memorials and sculptures. The process of cutting, polishing, and sculpting involves both craftsmanship and the latest technology to produce precision surface plates and machine bases accurate to 25,000,000th of an inch. Interact with computer-based exhibits, view historic photos, and roll a ball down the granite bowling lane.

Cost: Visitors Center and Memorial Design Studio: Free. Quarry tour: Adults, $4; seniors 62+, $3.50; children 6–12, $1.50.

Freebies: Small samples of granite in bins behind Visitors Center.

Video/DVD Shown: 18-minute video in the Visitors Center theater on geology and history of the quarry and modern granite quarry methods.

Reservations Needed: Groups over 20 people that want step-on guide should book tour 1 week in advance, longer in advance in fall.

Days and Hours: Visitors Center and Memorial Design Studio: May 1–October 31: Mon–Sat 8:30 AM–5:00 PM, Sun 10:00 AM–5:00 PM (Fall: Sun 8:30 AM–5:30 PM). Closed July 4th. Quarry tour: June–mid-October: Mon–Fri 9:15 AM–3:35 PM approx. every 45 minutes or more frequently in the fall. Closed July 4th. Manufacturing: all year, Mon–Fri 8:00 AM–3:30 PM. Closed major holidays and usually the first 2 weeks of January.

Plan to Stay: 1.5 hours for all tours and visitor center, plus time for gift shop.

Minimum Age: None

Disabled Access: Yes

Group Requirements: Special rate of $2.75 per person for adults. Step-on guides available for bus groups.

Special Information: Noisy tour for young children. The Visitors Center houses geological displays and exhibits, manufacturing displays, sculpture, and memorials outside.

Gift Shop: Features fine-quality granite gifts, including penholders and clocks. Also carries stone-related gifts from all over the world. Open same months and hours as Visitors Center.

Directions: From I-89, take Exit 6. Follow Rt. 63 to bottom of hill. Go straight through light. Follow signs. From Rt. 302 West, in East Barre turn left onto Rt. 110. Follow signs to "quarries/Graniteville."

Nearby Attractions: Ben & Jerry's and Cabot Creamery tours (see pages 82 and 83); Porter Music Box Museum; Bragg Farm Sugarhouse (call 800-376-5757); Morse Farm Maple Sugarworks (call 800-242-2740); Vermont Marble Exhibit (call 802-459-3311) in Procter, VT, about 70 miles away.

NEW ENGLAND

Route 5 North, Windsor, VT 05089
The Mill, 1760 Main St., Quechee, VT 05059

(802) 674-6280
(802) 295-2711

www.simonpearce.com

SIMON PEARCE

Simon Pearce, originally trained as a potter, apprenticed in Sweden before opening a glassblowing factory in Ireland in 1971. Because of high energy costs, Simon moved his business to the U.S. in 1981. Simon housed his first U.S. factory in a historic, 200-year-old red brick woolen mill next to the Ottauquechee River in Quechee, Vermont. In 1993, Simon designed a brand-new manufacturing facility nine miles away in Windsor, Vermont.

Both facilities offer self-guided tours. From Windsor's raised catwalk viewing gallery, you can observe the entire glassblowing process. The doors of the large furnace in the room's center open automatically when a worker steps on a floor mat to gather glass from the furnace. Workers may appear to be wandering around, but each has a specific mission as part of a two- or three-person team.

The glassblower chooses a blowpipe from the warmer, gathers the appropriate amount of glass from the center furnace, and blows it into a wooden mold. The apprentice opens the mold and gathers glass onto a pontil iron, which holds the piece during hand-finishing of the rim. The cross underneath each piece, made by this pontil iron, has become the Simon Pearce trademark.

In Quechee, you can watch glass and pottery production. Stairs at the back of the extensive, well-displayed showrooms lead you down to a smaller, more intimate operation. From behind a wooden railing, you observe a glassblowing team only a few feet in front of you.

Feel free to ask about the processes as a potter hand-throws pottery on a wheel. Both facilities will impress you with the skill and craftsmanship involved in handmade pottery and glass.

Information below applies to both facilities unless otherwise noted.

Cost: Free

Freebies: No

Video/DVD Shown: No

Reservations Needed: No, except for groups.

Days and Hours: Windsor: Mon–Sun 9:00 AM–5:00 PM. Quechee: Mon–Sun 9:00 AM–9:00 PM. Both closed Thanksgiving and Christmas.

Plan to Stay: 30 minutes each, plus time in gift shops and Simon Pearce Restaurant in Quechee (call 802-295-1470 for reservations).

Minimum Age: None

Disabled Access: Yes, at Windsor. No wheelchair access to production in Quechee, but gift shop and restaurant are accessible.

Group Requirements: Windsor easily accommodates buses. Groups larger than 50 should call 1 month in advance.

Special Information: Facilities can get warm because of furnaces. Similar to the Quechee facility, Simon Pearce on the Brandywine in West Chester, PA, includes gourmet restaurant and glassblowing (call 610-793-0949). At former Bausch & Lomb facility in Mountain Lake Park, MD, can watch glassblowing from catwalk (call 301-334-5277).

Retail Shops: Sell first- and second-quality Simon Pearce pottery and glass. Windsor open Mon–Sun 9:00 AM–5:00 PM. Quechee open Mon–Sun 9:00 AM–9:00 PM. Catalog available from (800) 774-5277. Retail shops at all four facilities as well as stand-alone stores throughout New England.

Directions: To Windsor: from western Massachusetts, take I-91 North to Exit 9, bear right onto Rt. 5. Simon Pearce is 1 mile ahead on left. From New Hampshire, take I-89 to I-91 South. Follow above directions.

To Quechee: From western Massachusetts, take I-91 North to I-89 North to Exit 1. Take Rt. 4 West. Turn right at first blinker after Quechee Gorge. Follow signs. From New Hampshire, take I-89 North to Exit 1 in Vermont. Follow above directions.

Nearby Attractions: For Windsor: Harpoon Brewery (call 802-674-5491); American Precision Museum (call 802-674-5781); Vermont State Craft Center; Constitution House. For Quechee: quaint town of Woodstock; Billings Farm; Killington Ski Resort.

NEW ENGLAND

the Simon Pearce Mill in Quechee, Vermont

Simon Pearce glassblower shaping the blown glass

6655 Shelburne Road, Shelburne, VT 05482

(802) 985-3001
(800) 829-BEAR

www.vermont
teddybear.com

A plain little teddy belonging to a boy named Graham was the inspiration for Vermont Teddy Bears. When Graham's father discovered that none of Graham's stuffed animals—not even that most American of toys, the teddy bear—were made in the U.S.A., he decided to make an American teddy bear. Since the company is located on a 57-pastoral-acre site, you'll drive down its long, winding drive toward the airport hangar–shaped shipping building, the hexagonal retail store (each panel a different color), and the multicolored barn silo topped with a beanie—complete with propeller.

After visiting the company museum in the lobby, you head for the workshop, a magical place that enchants young and old. Moving through the brightly painted workshop, you'll expect Santa's elves to appear at any moment. The enthusiastic tour guides ("Bear Ambassadors"), workers, and bears do everything in their power to make sure you have fun.

Stand behind a railing as your guide uses props to theatrically explain the processes you see. At the cutting area, watch a hydraulic press, with cookie-cutter dies, stamp out bear parts from 12 to 14 layers of soft fur. Workers at several stations sew together bear limbs, torsos, and heads, inside-out so seams are hidden. Bears are then turned right side out and pumped full of stuffing with 130 pounds of air pressure. Limbs are joined to torsos, and eyes are placed.

Bears are dressed as everything from artists to veterinarians and carefully packed in a box with an air hole to make sure the bear will not have to hold his breath the whole trip. Each bear has a board game (so he won't be bored while traveling), some bear food (so he doesn't get hungry), and a personalized message.

After the tour, you'll want to go back to the Make a Friend for Life cub house to help stuff your own teddy bear. Select your fat-free (that is, unstuffed) bear. Spin the dial to choose the bear's filling—dreams, happiness, love, giggles. After the teddy is stitched up, you'll receive its birth certificate.

Cost: Tour: Adults, $2; children under 12, free. Make a Friend for Life (stuff your own bear): $19.95–24.50.

Freebies: Fuzzy little "Button Bear" that fits over tour button.

Video/DVD Shown: Yes, at parts of tour route.

Reservations Needed: No, except for groups of 10 or more.

Days and Hours: Mon–Sun 9:00 AM–5:00 PM. Limited weekend production; however, tours are still fun. Closed holidays. Call 800 number for extended summer hours.

Plan to Stay: 25 minutes for tour, plus time for Bear Shop and Make a Friend for Life cub house.

Minimum Age: None (but must bring the kid inside you).

Disabled Access: Yes

Group Requirements: Groups over 10 should call (802) 985-3001 in advance, if possible. Maximum group size is 50 people.

Gift Shop: Bear Shop is stocked with bears waiting to go home with you. All are handcrafted and guaranteed for life. Carries logoed T-shirts, fleece pullovers, and sweatshirts. Open Mon–Sat 9:00 AM–6:00 PM, Sun 10:00 AM–5:00 PM. For more information on Bear-Grams and catalog, call (800) 829-BEAR.

Special Information: National American Teddy Bear Day celebrated on November 14, the day the American Teddy Bear was born.

Directions: From I-89, take Exit 13 onto I-189 West. When I-189 ends, turn left onto Rt. 7 South through town of Shelburne. Factory located 0.5 mile past Shelburne Museum.

Nearby Attractions: Ben & Jerry's ice-cream tour (see page 82); Lake Champlain Chocolates (call 802-864-1808); Shelburne Farms (call 802-985-8686); Shelburne Museum.

Mid-Atlantic

Augusta

MAINE

VERMONT

NEW HAMPSHIRE

Montpelier

Concord

CANADA

Ottawa

NEW YORK

MASSACHUSETTS

Albany

Boston

RI

see New England
page 57

CT

Hartford

Toronto

Lake Ontario

Rochester

GEORGE EASTMAN HOUSE

PERRY'S ICE CREAM

JELL-O GALLERY

BREWERY OMMEGANG

Lake Huron

Buffalo

QRS MUSIC

BABCOCK

KAZOO BOUTIQUE

CORNING MUSEUM OF GLASS

GILLINDER GLASS

MICHIGAN

Lansing

Detroit

Lake Erie

ZIPPO/CASE VISITOR CENTER

PENNSYLVANIA

STERLING HILL MINING MUSEUM

EDISON NATIONAL HISTORIC SITE

NJ

CNN
NBC STUDIOS
RADIO CITY MUSIC HALL
SONY WONDER TECHNOLOGY LAB
STEINWAY & SONS

New York City

MARTIN GUITAR

THE CRAYOLA FACTORY

Cleveland

YUENGLING

STURGIS PRETZEL HOUSE

HERSHEY'S CHOCOLATE WORLD

MACK TRUCKS

Trenton

ASHER'S CHOCOLATES

BYER'S CHOICE LTD

WENDELL AUGUST FORGE

SENATOR JOHN HEINZ PITTSBURGH
REGIONAL HISTORY CENTER

BENZEL'S BRETZEL BAKERY

Harrisburg

QVC

US MINT

Philadelphia

HOMER LAUGHLIN CHINA

Pittsburgh

SHERM EDWARDS

WOLFGANG CANDY

HARLEY-DAVIDSON MOTOR COMPANY

HOPE ACRES

HAGLEY MUSEUM

HERR'S SNACK FACTORY

WHEATON VILLAGE

OHIO

CANNONDALE

SNYDER'S OF HANOVER

UTZ QUALITY FOOD

Baltimore

Dover

ATLANTIC

see Great Lakes
page 147

MOORE'S CANDIES

BALTIMORE MUSEUM OF INDUSTRY

DE

Columbus

WASHINGTON D.C.

MARYLAND

BARTLEY COLLECTION

FENTON ART GLASS

BUREAU OF ENGRAVING
AND PRINTING

SALISBURY PEWTER

WEST VIRGINIA

OCEAN

BLENKO GLASS

Charleston

Richmond

Frankfort

WILLIAMSBURG POTTERY FACTORY

WILLIAMSBURG DOLL FACTORY

VIRGINIA

ROWENA'S

KENTUCKY

0   80 mi

0   80 km

NORTH CAROLINA

see South
page 221

TN

Raleigh

A mix of breathtaking landscaping and industrial ruins, a visit to Hagley's 235-acre museum shows every facet of life in an industrial river community. The largest powder yard in America, the DuPont community spreads two miles down the Brandywine River. Eleuthère Irénée du Pont came to America from France in 1800. He chose the banks of the Brandywine River as the site for his black powder mills because of the natural water energy, the available timber and granite, and the ease of river transportation for the black powder ingredients.

Of the original 200 buildings, 45 remain as functioning relics of the DuPont black powder reign. In the powder yard, waterwheels and water turbines channel water to operate machinery. Pairs of roll mills with a waterwheel between them produce enough energy to spin two eight-ton iron wheels inside a massive wooden bowl, used for mixing black powder ingredients. Now a scenic, botanical masterpiece, the powder yard used to be smelly, noisy, dirty, and dangerous, with 288 unplanned explosions and 228 deaths during the 19th century. The architecture reflects the risks—building walls are three-foot-thick stone with "flyaway" roofs angled toward the river.

Eleutherian Mills, the first du Pont family home, sits atop a hill overlooking the factory and workers' community. Tour the Georgian-style home where five generations of du Ponts lived, and visit the first company office next door. Auto lovers should also check out the 1928 DuPont Motors car in the barn.

At the 1875 Machine Shop, ask volunteers to demonstrate and explain how leather belts transfer from one pulley to another, animating heavy drilling equipment. The shuttle bus will stop at the Engine House, where the red and green wheel turns under steam power, whistling as it works. On Blacksmith Hill, volunteers in period dress relate life in the late 19th century in the Gibbons House, where powder yard foremen and their families once lived.

Cost: Self-guided tour: Adults, $11; students and senior citizens, $9; children 6–14, $4; children under 6, free. Call for group rates.

Freebies: Brochures and Hagley Visitor's Guide.

Video/DVD Shown: 5-minute orientation video.

Reservations Needed: No, for self-guided tours. Yes, for group tours.

Days and Hours: Mid-March–mid-December daily 9:30 AM–4:30 PM. January–mid-March weekends 9:30 AM–4:30 PM, guided group tour only at 1:30 PM (tickets on sale at 1:00 PM). School tours: mid-September–mid-June. Closed Thanksgiving and Christmas.

Plan to Stay: 4 hours for self-guided tour and gift shop. Guided tours vary.

Minimum Age: None

Disabled Access: Yes, but all areas may not be accessible. Call ahead to check.

Group Requirements: Groups of 15 or more must make reservations at least 2 weeks in advance for guided tour. Guided tours can be conducted for groups under 15 people if visitors pay for 15. Maximum group size is 70 people.

Special Information: Wear comfortable walking shoes. No photography of furniture. Offers variety of specialized tours to groups; call or visit website.

Gift Shop: Sells books, miniature working cannons, cards, T-shirts, stuffed animals, thimbles, and prints.

Directions: From the south, take I-95 North to the Newport Exit. Follow Rt. 141 North for 7 miles. Pass Rt. 100 and look for Hagley on the left. From the north, take I-95 South to I-495 South. Take Rt. 141 North and follow above directions.

Nearby Attractions: Herr's tours (see page 124); Winterthur Museum; Longwood Gardens; Natural History Museum; Delaware Art Museum.

14th and C Streets, S.W., Washington, D.C. 20228   (202) 874-2330
(866) 894-2330   www.moneyfactory.gov

After entering the mammoth gray federal building that houses this bureau, you'll be showered with a wealth of information in display cases and videos about our nation's paper currency. From a narrow, glass-walled, overhead walkway, the guided tour allows you to watch several steps in paper currency production. In the first step, not included on the tour, engravers hand-cut the currency design into soft steel. This engraving, used to create the master die and plate, begins the unique intaglio printing process that deters counterfeiting.

The printing itself is mesmerizing. Sheets of money, each with 32 bills in a four-by-eight pattern, rhythmically spin off the press at 8,000 sheets per hour. Stacks of money, called "skids," are everywhere. You'll wonder how the workers appear to treat their jobs with such detached calm. After inspections, overprinting of the serial number and Treasury seal, and cutting, the final product is a "brick" of 4,000 notes sent to the Federal Reserve Districts for local distribution.

Cost: Free

Freebies: Unfortunately, no money! Informational brochures from the visitor center.

Videos/DVDs Shown: A short video, "The Buck Starts Here," explains the history of paper currency in the U.S.

Reservations Needed: No, however during peak season, tickets may be gone by 9:00 AM. Advanced reservations required for congressional and school groups over 10 people.

Days and Hours: During peak season (March–August): Mon–Fri 9:00–10:45 AM; 12:15–2:00 PM. May–August: evening tours, Mon–Fri 5:00–7:00 PM. Tours every 15 minutes. Tickets marked with a des-

ignated time must be obtained at the booth on Raoul Wallenberg Pl. (formerly 15th St.). Tickets may be gone by 9:00 AM, so get in line early (booth opens at 8:00 AM). During nonpeak season (September–February): 9:00–10:45 AM; 12:15–2:00 PM. Line forms on the 14th St. side of the building for the tour. Congressional VIP tours Mon–Fri. 8:15 AM and 8:45 AM only. Ask your congressperson about tickets for this tour. Closed federal holidays and week between Christmas and New Year's.

Plan to Stay: 45 minutes, including displays, videos, and tour, plus time for the visitor center gift shop, and waiting time.

Minimum Age: None

Disabled Access: Yes. Upon request, accommodations for the hearing-, sight-, and physically impaired.

Group Requirements: Maximum group size is 50 people.

Special Information: Upon request, group tours in French, German, Japanese, Spanish, and Hebrew. Security is very tight. Thorough search performed on everyone entering the building. For information about Bureau of Printing and Engraving tour in Fort Worth, TX, see page 301.

Gift Shop: Sells a variety of items relating to paper money, including uncut sheets of new money and bags of shredded currency. There are videos on engraving, stamp production, and the identification of mutilated currency. Open Mon–Fri 8:30 AM–3:30 PM. Enter at the Tour Entrance, 14th and C Sts.

Directions: Located immediately southwest of the Washington Monument grounds and west of Jefferson Memorial. Parking is nearly impossible to find in this area. Take the Metro (subway) blue line/orange line to the Smithsonian stop and walk out the Independence Ave. exit. Turn left on 14th St. or Raoul Wallenberg Pl., depending on where you need to obtain tickets.

Nearby Attractions: United States Holocaust Memorial Museum; Washington Monument; Jefferson Memorial; Smithsonian Institute.

MID-ATLANTIC

Baltimore Museum of Industry

1415 Key Highway, Baltimore, MD 21230 — (410) 727-4808 — www.thebmi.org

Every American student learns about how industrialization changed our society. The Baltimore Museum of Industry takes you back in time, letting you stroll down the streets of Baltimore during the city's 19th-century industrial dominance. Formerly the Platt & Company Oyster Cannery (circa 1865), the museum now houses hands-on canning, garment, machine shop, and printing exhibits.

Drive onto the museum's six-acre campus. You immediately see an enormous red crane, donated by Bethlehem Steel, that stands twice as high as the museum's main building. Directly ahead of you is the Port of Baltimore, home to the only remaining steam tug on the east coast, the 1906 S.T. *Baltimore*. Enter the main green brick building and walk down the street passing a turn-of-the-century-style bank, bakery, and pharmacy. Your first major stop is at the "Shucking Shed," where workers of all ages and races filled their buckets with oysters in exchange for tokens. Next, learn about the canning process. As you walk past the wall of familiar labels and conveyer belts, look toward the middle of the room and focus on the enormous circular pot. The Steam Retort Closed Cutter Steamer, invented in 1874, holds four rusted baskets of 1,150 cans and steams cut the bacteria in all of the oysters.

Your next stop is a typical machine shop of the early 1900s. Tools hang on the walls. Walk on the warped 1865 wood floor. First, imagine all of the belts and pulleys moving around the cast-iron pipes and metal machines. Then see the mechanisms come alive as your tour guide revs up the steam engine.

Moving from metal machines to garment machines, enter the world of quality clothing. Fabric patterns are strewn across two long wooden tables. Huge shelves stand in the middle of the exhibit, while sewing machines and irons line the sides. See the difference between cutting patterns with heavy iron shears versus an electric silver cutting machine. If scheduled in advance, groups can participate in a pocket-making production line.

Next, journey through the evolution of printing. Tour guides explain how tedious the original typesetting process was until the invention of the Linotype by Baltimore's Ottmar Mergenthaler. Witness printing move through the Portable Wheel Press, Proof Press, and Platen Press all the way through current-day computers. Samples are given out along the way.

Cost: Adults, $10; seniors/students, $6; children under 4, free.

Freebies: Printing samples.

Video: 11-minute video, "Maryland Manufacturing," in an art deco movie theater.

Reservations: No, except for groups of 10 or more.

Days and Hours: Mon–Sat 10:00 AM–4:00 PM; Sun 11:00 AM–4:00 PM. Closed Thanksgiving, Christmas Eve, and Christmas Day.

Plan to stay: 1.5 hours.

Minimum Age: None

Disabled Access: Yes

Group Requirements: Groups of 10 or more should book 10 days in advance, all adults, $6. No maximum size.

Special Information: Birthday parties and school groups can make cardboard moving vans down an assembly line or sew pockets in the garment factory.

Gift Shop: The Emporium offers unique gifts that promote learning for kids, as well as books for adults, T-shirts, and handicrafts made by Museum volunteers. Open same hours as museum.

Directions: From I-83 South, take Lombard St. West. Turn left on Light St. Continue south past Inner Harbor. Turn left on Key Hwy. The Museum is on the left. From Baltimore Bltwy., I-695, take I-95 North. Take Key Hwy, Exit 55. Turn at light, go under overpass, turn left onto Key Hwy. Museum is on your right.

Nearby Attractions: Moore's Candies tours (see page 98); Baltimore Inner Harbor; Fort McHenry.

Bartley Collection

WOODEN FURNITURE REPRODUCTIONS

65 Engerman Avenue, Denton, MD 21629

(800) 787-2800

www.bartley
collection.com

Have you ever yearned for a magnificent Queen Anne sideboard or an 18th-century Chippendale night stand? If you are at all handy with woodworking, you can use Bartley antique reproduction kits to make your own highboys, four-poster beds, dining tables, chairside tables, jewelry boxes, and more. With the plant manager as your guide, you can tour the one-acre factory where these antique reproductions are designed, created, and packed.

Pass the hardware department, where you may see a worker assemble each kit's perfectly reproduced brass fittings. When Bartley designers find desirable antiques to reproduce, they make rubberized castings of the original hardware and intricate moldings. These castings become the foundations for brass pourings and guide workers in reconfiguring their machines.

As you enter the rough mill, the scent of lumber and sound of ripsaws prevail. Bundles of 8- to 16-foot-long rough-cut boards crowd the aisle. Workers plane the rough-cut lumber, revealing the grain and color. Different saws cut the boards to the proper dimensions. Despite a dust collection system, a faint film of sawdust clings to everything in the plant, an unavoidable mark of the woodworker's craft.

The wide sections of wood are matched by grain and color; edges are aligned (or recut) and glued. Notice the radio-frequency gluer: it sends energy through the wood, activating a catalyst in the glue that cures it. The wide belt sander's five sanding heads, with progressively finer grades of sandpaper, then smooth the surfaces.

Amid conventional routers, band saws, drill presses, and shapers are two computerized routers. A vacuum sucks air through holes in the tabletop, holding the board in place. The router's patterns are programmed by a designer in the main office, and it runs automatically, without a worker's intervention. The table moves forward and back as the six router heads spin. Before seeing the showroom, watch the cabinetmakers in the sample shop create prototypes, following the designers' sketches and building reproductions from scratch.

Cost: Free

Freebies: No

Video/DVD Shown: No

Reservations Needed: Yes, since tours not often given.

Days and Hours: Tours *only* given during spring and fall sales. Call for details and dates.

Plan to Stay: 20 minutes for tour, plus additional time in showroom.

Minimum Age: 12

Disabled Access: Limited aisle space and sawdust on floors makes it unsuitable for wheelchairs and walkers.

Group Requirements: Groups should call 1 week in advance. No more than 6 people can be accommodated at a time.

Special Information: Wear sneakers and clothing that will not be harmed by sawdust. Parts of plant can be noisy.

Showroom: Most reproductions are on display. Kits can be purchased or ordered. Open Mon–Fri 9:00 AM–5:00 PM, Sat 10:00 AM–3:00 PM. Catalog available from above number.

Directions: From Annapolis, MD, and points west, cross the Bay Bridge and take Rt. 50 South to Easton. Turn left on Rt. 404 East. In Denton, turn left into the Denton Industrial Park. The Bartley Collection is the second factory on the left. From Norfolk, VA, take Rt. 13 North toward Salisbury. Continue on Rt. 13 to Bridgeville, DE. In Bridgeville, take Rt. 404 West toward Denton. Turn right into industrial park.

Nearby Attractions: St. Michaels and Oxford, old ship-building towns with antique shops, restored buildings, and boat-builders; Black Water Wildlife Refuge, Wild Goose Brewery tour (call 410-221-1121), and Brooks Barrel Company tour (410-228-0790) in Cambridge 20 minutes away; Atlantic Ocean beaches 1 hour away.

MID-ATLANTIC

3004 Pinewood Avenue, Baltimore, MD 21214 (410) 426-2705 www.moores candies.com

Since 1919

How often have you been on a tour where the company owner accompanies you, introduces you to the employees (many of whom are immediate family members), and lets you make your own candy? Here's the place! Don't look for a factory or industrial park—this plant is in the 1,500-square-foot basement of the family residence. The company has produced treats from this same space since 1929. In fact, one employee has been dipping Moore's chocolates since the 1920s.

Owner Jim Heyl grew up in the house's upper level. When young Jim needed to raise money for his Cub Scout pack, his parents worked for and eventually bought Moore's Candies, known for helping groups with fund-raising. These fund-raising sales are still important to Moore's Candies' business. Recently Jim's son, Dana, came into the business to take it into the third generation. In August 2000, the Food Network picked Moore's as one of America's best chocolate makers.

The tour is an informal look at this small, hands-on candy-making operation. Tour guide Jim enthusiastically describes the chocolate "waterfall," the home nut-roaster, and the fillings prepared by all of the candy makers. Rich aromas draw you from one table to the next, where caramel or vanilla buttercream fillings are prepared for their chocolate bath, or special-order chocolate swans are filled with home-dry-roasted cashews.

Watch one worker hand-dip chocolates while another uses a wooden paddle to stir bubbling caramel in a copper cauldron. Cherries roll around in rotating kettles, getting a sugar coating before their journey through the enrober, which workers call the "I Love Lucy" machine, for a chocolate cover. This chocolate coating seals in the cherries, whose natural acid reacts with the coating to form the liquid inside a chocolate-coated cherry. Before you leave, be sure to run your own pretzel through the enrobing machine and eat the rewards of your efforts.

Cost: Adults, $5; children under 4, free.

Freebies: Sample chocolate right off the packing line; Official Candymaker Certificate

Video/DVD Shown: 2-minute video of production process.

Reservations Needed: Suggested for individuals. Required for groups over 10 people. Call ahead to see if in production.

Days and Hours: June 1–September 30: Mon–Thur 10:00 AM and 1:00 PM. Closed holidays and between Christmas and New Year's. No tours 6 weeks before major candy holidays.

Plan to Stay: 20 minutes, plus time in gift area.

Minimum Age: 10; 6 for school groups.

Disabled Access: Yes

Group Requirements: Minimum group size is 10, maximum is 40; 3–5 days' notice required. Special tours may be arranged. For groups larger than 15, with 5 days' advance request, 10-minute slide presentation covers origins of the cocoa bean, harvesting, roasting, and how chocolate is made.

Special Information: Most production in fall through early spring. No photography.

Gift Area: Assorted candies include Maryland chocolate and confection specialties (Crabs by the Bushel, Crab Pop, Chesapeake Chocolates, and Maryland honey caramel). Open Mon–Fri 9:00 AM–4:00 PM and Sat 10:00 AM–3:00 PM. Closed holidays and Saturdays in August. Mail-order price list available.

Directions: From Baltimore Bltwy (I-695), take Exit 31A. Take Rt. 147 South for 2 miles. Turn left onto Pinewood Ave. Factory is the first building on the left, a brick house that looks like a residence. Park in rear and use building's rear entrance.

Nearby Attractions: Baltimore Museum of Industry tours (see page 96); White Marsh Shopping Mall; Fire Museum; Baltimore's attractions include Fort McHenry, Inner Harbor Area, Lexington Market, and National Aquarium.

2611 North Salisbury Blvd, Salisbury, MD 21801   (410) 546-1188   www.salisbury pewter.com

SALISBURY PEWTER

Although Salisbury Pewter was founded in 1979, its craftspeople follow the same production process used 200 years ago. Pewter spinning is one of the oldest crafts in American history. During your guided tour of Salisbury Pewter, you'll learn the components of their lead-free, non-tarnishing pewter and the history of pewter (did you know that during the Civil War, pewter tableware was melted down for bullets?), and observe pewter-smithing from behind Plexiglas walls.

In the spinning department, watch an apprentice or master spinner, trained for up to 10 years, clamp a flat disk (or "blank") onto a lathe. As the disk spins on the lathe, the craftsman sways back and forth. Using a steel rod—which each spinner designs personally—the spinner gently urges the pewter into shape around the brass mold (or "chuck") to form a bowl, coffeepot, or serving tray. During detailing (or "kurling"), a worker uses a tool resembling an architect's compass to add lips and curved bases. The pewter shavings flying into the air are later re-melted to avoid waste.

As you walk down the hall, notice raw materials, tools, and pewter cups in various stages of production. In the back, craftspeople wearing white gloves sit in front of rapidly spinning polishing wheels. To polish a large serving tray, a worker must always keep it moving against the cotton-compound spinning wheel. With the tray on their knees, they rock their bodies from side to side and swing their arms back and forth—it's a rigorous workout. During the three-step polishing process, different grades of compound polish the pewter to high-bright or satin finishes. A worker proudly stamps the trademark on the bottom of the finished piece.

Cost: Free

Freebies: No

Video/DVD Shown: 6-minute optional video covers the history of pewter and Salisbury Pewter's production process.

Reservations Needed: No, except for groups over 20 people.

Days and Hours: Mon–Fri 9:30 AM–4:00 PM. No production week between Christmas and New Year's, and July 4th week, but can watch video and view equipment and display cases. Closed holidays.

Plan to Stay: 15 minutes for tour, plus time for the video and showroom.

Minimum Age: None

Disabled Access: Yes

Group Requirements: Groups over 15 people should call 2 days in advance.

Special Information: This new Salisbury location was built with tours in mind. Other outlet store in Easton has limited tour opportunities (call 410-820-5202).

Showroom: This 3,000-square-foot store sells Salisbury Pewter's 600 items, including jewelry and jewelry boxes, wedding and decorative gifts, picture frames, and Maryland crab gift items. First-quality items sold at outlet prices (20 percent off) and factory seconds discounted up to 75 percent. Open Mon–Fri 9:00 AM–5:30 PM and Sat 10:00 AM–5:00 PM. Closed holidays. Catalog available from above number.

Directions: From Ocean City, take Rt. 50 West. Take Rt. 13 North. Salisbury Pewter will be on your right in approximately 0.5 mile. You'll be greeted by the "Watch Our Craftsmen Work" sign. From Washington/Baltimore area, take Rt. 50 East. Take Rt. 13 North. Follow directions above. (Alternately, from Rt. 50 East, turn left onto Naylor Mill Rd. Turn left onto Rt. 13 North. Salisbury Pewter will be immediately on your right.)

Nearby Attractions: Salisbury Zoo; Ward Museum of Wildfowl Art; Ocean City beaches 30 miles away; Chincoteague and Assateague Islands, VA, are 1 hour away.

MID-ATLANTIC

Most people think of Thomas Edison as the inventor of the light bulb, but after touring his laboratory, you'll realize that the simple bulb was only one of hundreds of inventions. Edison developed the disc phonograph, the motion picture system, and improved electrical generators and meters here.

The laboratory is a quad of brick buildings resembling a campus. Entering it you feel as if you've stepped into the early 20th century—it's full of objects actually used by Edison and his colleagues. Enter Edison's office and library, where you can learn about the laboratory's history from the audio tour.

In the stockroom, you'll find tools and natural materials—like elephant hide and tortoiseshell—that were used in the development of Edison's inventions. In searching for filament materials for the light bulb, Edison experimented with both human hair and coconut hair. In the heavy machine shop, Edison's "muckers" (his nickname for the people who worked for him) built prototypes that were sent to the patent office.

Edison's first love was chemistry, and in the chemistry lab, you'll examine remnants of the work he was doing when he died. Searching for a domestic source of rubber for his friend Henry Ford, Edison grew and made rubber from 14-foot goldenrod plants. Unfortunately, the resulting material was coarse and didn't last long.

You'll also spy the Black Maria, a replica of the first structure built as a motion-picture studio, to see what filming was like in Edison's day. The Black Maria predates electric lighting of film sets—all light had to be obtained from the sun. The roof opens up to let the sun in, and the building itself is built on a track so it can move to follow the sun around. After touring Edison's workplace, you can visit Glenmont, the Victorian mansion where this ingenious man lived with his family.

Cost: Adults, $3; children 17 and under, free.

Freebies: No

Video/DVD Shown: "The Invention Factory," an 18-minute video about the site, and *The Great Train Robbery*, a 10-minute Edison film. (Videos could change at any time.)

Reservations Needed: Yes, for school programs and groups. Special tickets are required for Glenmont tour.

Days and Hours: While the Laboratory and Glenmont undergo renovation, visitors should call ahead to find out what is open. Shorter winter hours. Closed Thanksgiving, Christmas, and New Year's.

Plan to Stay: 2 hours for both tours, plus time for store.

Minimum Age: None

Disabled Access: Laboratory: yes. Glenmont: no.

Group Requirements: Call ahead for reservations.

Special Information: Hot days are not a good time to visit; there is no air conditioning. Tours are abbreviated on hot days. Special tickets required for Glenmont tour.

Bookstore: Sells items such as books, sound recordings, posters, and postcards related to Thomas Edison. Mon–Sun 9:00 AM–5:00 PM.

Directions: From the east, take the New Jersey Tnpk. Take Exit 15-W onto I-280 westbound. Follow I-280 to the West Orange/South Orange/Montclair exit. Make right at end of exit ramp. Go to end of street and make a left onto Main St. Follow Main St. for about 0.75 mile. Parking is on left. From the west, take I-280 eastbound to the Mount Pleasant Avenue/West Orange/Montclair exit. Make a left at end of ramp. At the second traffic light, make a left onto Main St. Follow Main St. for 0.5 mile. Parking is on left.

Nearby Attractions: Turtleback Zoo; Newark Museum; Montclair Art Museum.

30 Plant Street, Ogdensburg, NJ 07439   (973) 209-7212   www.sterlinghill.org

Not many people know that mining once thrived just an hour west of Manhattan. Located in the rural Skylands country of northwestern New Jersey, the Franklin–Sterling Hill mining district was for two centuries a source of over 340 zinc-based minerals—a record concentration of different minerals in one locality. Although underground mining no longer occurs in New Jersey, the Sterling Hill Mining Museum records the scientific and industrial history of mining in the district with a vast collection and an actual mine that visitors may tour.

Tours begin with a 30-minute introduction in the exhibit hall, formerly the changing area where miners suited up before their shifts and showered afterwards. Amid 20,000 pieces of mining equipment and other memorabilia, your guide explains the history of the Sterling Mine. After early efforts to smelt the local ores during the 18th century, improvements in knowledge and technology in the 19th century made mining the deposits economically viable. Until the Sterling Mine closed in 1986, it extracted mainly zinc ores, which included a number of rare minerals.

Your tour then plunges into the mine. The segment you see is 1,300 feet long and extends horizontally (not vertically) 150 feet into the hill adjacent to the museum. (The horizontal orientation and hard-packed gravel floor make the going fairly easy, but appropriate footwear is still required.) In a constant temperature of 56°F, you walk along a series of lit tunnels with solid marble walls. The tour ultimately arrives at one of the ore bodies.

Many of the minerals in this district fluoresce brilliantly in ultraviolet (black) light. This light, which is not visible to our eyes, is absorbed by the minerals, which then emit visible light that we perceive in various colors. Under the ultraviolet lights that the museum has installed in the mineshaft, the zinc ores glow red, blue, violet, yellow, and green—a remarkable sight.

After emerging from the mine, you enter the Thomas S. Warren Museum of Fluorescence. In three galleries with plenty of ultraviolet light, 16 exhibits let you continue to explore the weird world of mineralogical fluorescence.

Cost: Adults, $10; senior citizens, $9; children under 12, $7.50.

Freebies: No

Video/DVD Shown: No

Reservations Needed: No

Days and Hours: Tours run April 1–November 30 daily at 1:00 PM or by appointment. In December and March, tours are available only by appointment. Closed January–February and on Christmas, New Year's Day, Easter, and Thanksgiving.

Plan to Stay: 2 hours plus time for gift shop.

Minimum Age: None

Disabled Access: Yes

Group Requirements: A minimum of 10 people and a maximum of 175.

Special Information: The year-round temperature in the mine is 56°F, so a sweater or a light jacket is recommended. Visitors must have appropriate sturdy footwear to enter the mine.

Gift Shop: The shop sells mineral samples, jewelry, mining memorabilia, and miscellaneous souvenirs. Open daily 10:00 AM–3:00 PM, April 1–November 30. Closed January–February and on Christmas, New Year's Day, Easter, and Thanksgiving.

Directions: From I-95, take I-280 West to I-80 West and exit at Rt. 15 North. Take second Sparta exit (Franklin-Sparta) for Rt. 517 North. Follow Rt. 517 North to Brooks Flat Rd. in Ogdensburg and turn left. Turn right on Plant St. Turn left at stop sign, then left into museum entrance. From I-84, take Rt. 23 South for 21 miles to Rt. 517 and follow above directions.

Nearby Attractions: Snowmobile Barn Museum (call 973-383-1708); Long Pond Ironworks State Park; Oxford Furnace/Shippen Manor.

MID-ATLANTIC

1501 Glasstown Rd., Rt. 55,
Millville, NJ 08332-1566

(856) 825-6800
(800) 998-4552

www.wheatonvillage.org

In 1888, Dr. T. C. Wheaton, interested in making medicine bottles, purchased a Millville glass factory, which burned down in 1889. A working replica of this original factory is the centerpiece of Wheaton Village. Established in 1968, Wheaton Village focuses on the art and heritage of American glassmaking, regional craft, and folk life.

At set times, workers demonstrate traditional glassblowing. One worker narrates as another gathers molten glass onto a long rod (a "punty"). To make a paperweight, the gaffer inverts the gob of glass onto a mold, perhaps flower-shaped. The gob absorbs colored powdered glass from inside the mold. At other times, you can also observe these workers without narration.

Sharing the floor are glassworkers on fellowship from all over the world, making contemporary sculptures. While casting, workers wear protective outfits and face protection. With a saucepan-size ladle, a worker pours 30 to 50 pounds of molten glass into a sandcasting (made in sand) mold.

Elsewhere in the village, the Museum of American Glass houses the largest collection of entirely American-made glass. Its 6,500-plus objects include paperweights, chandeliers, prisms, and the nearly nine-foot-tall, 193-gallon, *Guinness Book of World Records'* largest bottle. The museum covers the glass industry from the first factory (1739), through the 1800s, when South Jersey was a major glassmaking center, to today. The glass whimsy exhibit contains objects such as walking canes that workers made from leftover glass.

The Crafts studios include ceramics, woodworking, and flameworking. Potters transform clay into pots as pottery wheels spin. Over a torch, a lampworker manipulates glass rods of various colors and diameters to create marbles. Each colored swirl requires a separate rod. You may see a worker forming miniature animals or people at a tiny tea table. Af-

terwards, enjoy the peaceful, 60-plus-acre grounds' picnic tables, shrubs, shady pine trees, scampering squirrels, and flocks of birds and Canada geese—or browse the unique museum stores.

Cost: Adults, $10; seniors, $9; students, $7; under 5, free. Reduced admission in winter months.

Freebies: No

Video/DVD Shown: No

Reservations Needed: No. Groups see below.

Days and Hours: Village hours: January–March: Fri–Sun 10:00 AM–5:00 PM (Crafts studios closed); April– December: Tue–Sun 10:00 AM–5:00 PM. Glass demonstrations: 11:00 AM, 1:30 PM, and 3:30 PM, when village is open. Closed Easter, Thanksgiving, Christmas, and New Year's.

Plan to Stay: 3.5 hours, plus time in stores.

Minimum Age: None

Disabled Access: Yes

Group Requirements: Groups of more than 25 adults or 10 schoolchildren need reservations 1 month in advance. Craft Sampler Days (provide hands-on crafts participation for school groups) must be arranged only on the first Monday in November for March programs. Other hands-on programs available year-round.

Special Information: "Make Your Own" Programs (paperweight or vessel) available to individuals over age 18 with 1 week's advance notice. Call (800) 998-4552 for more information.

Museum Stores: Stores sell works made at Wheaton Village and those by other American artists; largest selection of Fenton Art Glass in New Jersey; also, crafts, books, and penny candy. Open same hours as Village.

Directions: From Philadelphia, take Walt Whitman Bridge (follow signs to Atlantic City) to Rt. 42 South. Take Rt. 55 South to Exit 26. Signs lead to main entrance. From Atlantic City, take Atlantic City Expwy. West to Exit 12. Take Rt. 40 West. Turn left onto Rt. 552 West. At first traffic light in Millville, turn right onto Wade Blvd. Follow the signs.

Nearby Attractions: Glasstown Arts District; Parvin State Park; Atlantic City's beaches and casinos 35 miles away; Cape May's beaches and Victorian homes 40 miles away.

36 Delaware Avenue, Bath, NY 14810

(607) 776-334
(800) 840-9705

Babcock presents a nice American small-business, small-town (population 6,000) story of struggle and success in making and marketing a core product found in every home and business in this country. The business started in 1905 and positions itself as one of the country's premier manufacturers of wooden step and extension ladders. It has innovatively developed a new business line in producing gift crates, planters, and other special-purpose boxes from the scrap wood leftover from making ladders. It has many old-time employees, sometimes with fathers, sons, and grandsons from the same family involved in the woodworking.

It takes different types of wood to make a ladder: southern yellow pine, basswood, hemlock, and ash. You will see all the steps involved in turning these into wooden ladders of all sizes from 2 to 30 feet high, recognized as the "World's Tallest Ladder." You experience production from the time wood arrives to when the finished product is shipped out the door. You're surrounded by air tools and riveting guns, plenty of saws, and other woodworking machines for cutting, mooring, and milling.

Walk through a few of the 10 gray sheds. The first one you walk by has stacks of "profiled" wood that has already been planed. Slide the door open to go into the next shed. The royal blue drill presses designed by the company have 15 motors. The Rabbiter makes grooves in the wood at 69° angles, which are a feature of the ladder's steps. Shrill sounds fill the air. You may even want to cover your ears as you walk by the new assembly line

where air guns shoot in solid steel rivets. You'll walk through the warehouse next to ladders of all different heights, closed and standing tall, and even see them laid flat being wrapped in large cardboard sheets for shipping. The next time your feet touch the rungs of an extension ladder or the steps of a stepladder, they will have new appreciation for all the work involved in making it.

Cost: Free

Freebies: No

Video/DVD Shown: No

Reservations Needed: Yes

Days and Hours: *Based on schedule and staff availability.* Closed major holidays and week between Christmas and New Year's.

Plan to Stay: 45 minutes.

Minimum Age: No

Disabled Access: Yes

Group Requirements: No minimum or maximum.

Special Information: Must wear safety glasses that they provide. No sandals. Can be loud. There are plans to turn small white house next to parking lot into a museum.

Gift Shop: Located in the office. Sells full line of products at 50 percent off list price, including wooden ladders, fiberglass ladders, wooden crates, hanging planters, and CD boxes. Open Mon–Fri 8:00 AM–4:30 PM.

Directions: From Corning, take I-86 West or Rt. 17 West. Take Bath Exit 39. Turn right on Rt. 415 North. When in Village of Bath, make left on East Morris St., and then turn left on Delaware Ave. Located at end of street in the dead end. Look for the round blue and yellow logo on the side of the building.

Nearby Attractions: Corning Museum of Glass (see page 106); historic downtown Bath; Keuka Lake Wine Trail (call 800-440-4898 for brochure), with tours of 8 wineries in the area; Glenn Curtiss Museum.

Don't worry about the name. What the mouth can't pronounce the palate can appreciate in the unique Belgian ales of Brewery Ommegang (OH-ma-gang). Founded in 1997, it uses traditional techniques from Belgium to brew fine ales on a former hops farm in the countryside of upstate New York.

The setting alone makes Ommegang a lovely day out. Tucked in pastoral grounds of 136 acres, the barnlike microbrewery, with white walls and sloping roofs, resembles a Belgian farmhouse. The large open interior, crammed with brewing tanks and machinery, houses the entire operation under a high ceiling. Tours begin in a small decorated vestibule before moving into the spacious working area.

Although Ommegang brews beer with the organic chemistry of the old Belgian masters, it makes good use of modern technology. After letting you taste the anise, coriander, ginger, and other spices that flavor the ale, the tour shows you the giant fermenting vats and machinery of brewing. Unusually, Ommegang employs two fermenting processes: the first creates alcohol; the second sets up the natural carbonation that develops during the cellaring period. (In mass-produced beer, carbon dioxide is injected artificially after one fermentation.) Once the ale is filtered, automated machinery bottles it in a mesmerizing conveyor-belt process. Not yet carbonated, the dark liquor flows neatly into bottles that are sealed for the final stage of brewing.

The last step is crucial for the unique flavor and texture of Belgian ales: cellaring. After it is bottled, the beer ages for two weeks in a dark and relatively warm environment. The ingredients meld to create a complex taste and aroma, enhanced by the organic carbonation that develops during this period. While this "warm cellar" is less spectacular than the vats

and machinery elsewhere, the quiet chemistry that occurs here is the key to the Ommegang brew. You can taste the results after the tour in free samples of all the ales.

Cost: Free

Freebies: Tastings of all ales.

Video/DVD Shown: No

Reservations Needed: No. Tours begin on a rolling basis when enough visitors have assembled.

Days and Hours: Memorial Day–Labor Day: daily 11:00 AM–6:00 PM; Labor Day–Memorial Day: daily 12:00 PM–5:00 PM. Closed Thanksgiving, Christmas, and New Year's.

Plan to Stay: At least 1 hour: time before the tour, 30 minutes for the tour, and time to enjoy grounds.

Minimum Age: None for the tour; 21 for tasting.

Disabled Access: Yes

Group Requirements: None. Groups of any size may schedule a private tour for $5 a person (includes a free bottle of ale).

Special Information: Bring lunch; the splendid meadow behind the brewery has picnic tables. (Ommegang plans to add a restaurant and beer garden.) Special events throughout the year include family-oriented festivals and a fine-dining series.

Gift Shop: The Belgian Shop sells bottled Belgian ales, glassware, bottle openers, shirts, caps, books, comics, posters, and food (including Belgian cheese and chocolate). Open Mon–Fri 9:00 AM–closing; Sat–Sun 11:00 AM–closing. Closed Thanksgiving, Christmas, and New Year's.

Directions: From I-90 West, follow I-88 West for 56 miles. Take NY Rt. 28 North toward Cooperstown. Turn right on NY 28, right at NY 166, and left on County Rd. 33. The brewery is on the right. From I-90 East, follow NY Rt. 28 to County Rd. 26. Turn right on NY 28. Turn left on County Rd. 11c. Turn right on County Rd. 33. The brewery is on the left.

Nearby Attractions: National Baseball Hall of Fame and Museum (call 888-HALL-OF-FAME); Fly Creek Cider Mill and Orchard (summer only); Glimmerglass Opera (summer only).

Time Warner Ctr., 10 Columbus Circle, 3rd Flr., New York, NY 10019

(866) 426-6692

www.cnn.com/ insidecnn/

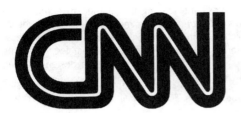

Since Ted Turner introduced 24-hour television news with CNN in the 1980s, the network has become one of the major news providers in the United States. Like its counterpart at CNN's headquarters in Atlanta (see page 235), the tour of CNN's bureau in New York shows visitors how the network produces programs and reports news every day.

It's a busy tour. You start with a film that shows how journalists and producers turn raw information from the field into clear and concise reporting. Then you go up to the eighth floor of the Time Warner Center for a "studio overlook": you gaze through windows at actual broadcasting studios while your guide explains technical aspects of putting programs on the air. Next is an area called Birth of CNN, featuring artifacts from the early days of the network and a one-minute video of clips from its first day of broadcasting.

A popular part of the tour is the interactive special-effects area. Here you experience technology that plays an important role in news broadcasts. A visitor in your group who isn't shy can volunteer to demonstrate the use of a teleprompter. This device feeds lines of text to anchors as they gaze at the camera, letting them talk directly to viewers while they read out news. (This isn't as easy as it seems.) You can also try the chromakey, which is used for reporting weather forecasts. Standing in front of a blank screen, you watch yourself on a monitor as a weather map or other backdrop is projected behind your image. The trick is accurately indicating features behind you that you can see only on the monitor.

Next you look at a control room, visit the studio floors of popular shows, and see the computer hub that manages CNN's flow of information. Through windows, you view the business-news floor for a look at a typical working day in a newsroom. A short video illustrates the chaos that can erupt in a newsroom when big stories break—most vivid is a clip of the frenzied scene in CNN's Atlanta newsroom on September 11, 2001.

Your tour ends with noteworthy artifacts journalists have donated for display, and a video in which CNN anchors explain why they became journalists and what fires them up to report news every day.

Cost: Adults, $15; seniors (65 and over), $13; children (ages 4–12), $11. Groups of 14 or more adults qualify for a special rate of $13 per person.

Freebies: No

Video/DVD Shown: Several short videos throughout the tour give insight into various aspects of CNN's operations.

Reservations Needed: No, but recommended. Visitors may reserve by calling (866) 426-6692 Mon–Fri 8:30 AM–5:00 PM. Same-day reservations are accepted.

Days and Hours: Daily 9:30 AM–5:00 PM. Closed Thanksgiving and Christmas.

Plan to Stay: Tour is 50 minutes.

Minimum Age: No

Disabled Access: The tour involves three flights of stairs. Wheelchair-accessible tours are available by reservation.

Group Requirements: The tour accommodates a maximum of 28 people, but larger groups can be divided into consecutive tours.

Gift Shop: The Inside CNN Store is open Mon–Sat 9:00 AM–9:00 PM and Sun 9:00 AM–6:00 PM. Closed Thanksgiving and Christmas.

Directions: Time Warner Ctr. (10 Columbus Cir.) is located between W. 58th St. and W. 60th St., near the SW corner of Central Park. Take subway train A, B, C, D, or 1 to the stop 59th St./Columbus Cir.

Nearby Attractions: Other workplace tours in Manhattan include NBC Studios, Radio City Music Hall, and Sony Wonder Technology Lab (pages 111, 114, and 115).

MID-ATLANTIC

One Museum Way, Corning, NY 14830

(607) 937-5371
(800) 732-6845

www.cmog.org

Like a glass prism, a visit to the Corning Museum of Glass is multifaceted. The experience of the Glass Innovation Center, the Art and History Galleries, the Sculpture Gallery, the Steuben Factory, and the Hot Glass Show illuminates the history of glass, optical fiber communications, and glassmaking. The Museum's world-famous collection of more than 45,000 glass objects traces 35 centuries of human experience with glass, starting in ancient Egypt's 18th Dynasty, when the search for perfectly clear crystal began.

Learn how light transmits information through optical fibers in the Glass Innovation Center's interactive educational exhibits. The spherical mirror alters your perception. The float glass exhibit explains the production process of large panes of glass. An overhead monitor lets the audience look through the flameworker's lens as he melts glass rods over a single gas-flamed jet and forms tiny glass animals in an on-the-spot demonstration.

The real fascination is watching the Hot Glass Show. Walk along a frosted glass bridge and around to the Hot Glass Stage. In this intimate setting, with the Steuben Factory as a backdrop, you feel the heat from the furnace. Gaffers, whose cheeks as they blow into the long blowpipes resemble Louis Armstrong's when he's playing the trumpet, collect gobs of red-hot glass from a furnace containing molten glass. A narrator and master glassblower explain and demonstrate glassmaking before a walk downstairs offers a look into the working Steuben factory, the only place in the world where Steuben glass is made.

During this walk, look through the glass windows to see the engraving process that makes Steuben glass so unique and valuable. The engraver first coats the glass with protective shellac, then transfers an image onto its surface with India ink. To cut the design, the engraver presses the glass upward against as many as 50 different fine copper wheels on a rotating lathe. Intricate designs may take 300 hours to engrave.

Across the parking lot, at the Museum's Walk-in Workshop, you can make a glass flower, bead, picture frame, or magnet using a variety of glass-working techniques, for a nominal fee. Even the youngest visitors can sandblast a design on their own drinking glass.

Cost: Adults, $12.50; children (17 and under) and members, free.

Freebies: No

Video/DVD Shown: 13-minute award-winning "Glass into Dreams" film and a variety throughout the galleries.

Reservations Needed: No, but recommended for groups larger than 20 people.

Days and Hours: Open Mon–Sun 9:00 AM–5:00 PM, Memorial Day weekend–Labor Day: Mon–Sun 9:00 AM–8:00 PM. Closed Thanksgiving, Christmas Eve, Christmas, New Year's Eve, and New Year's. Best time to see Steuben factory production is Mon–Fri 9:00 AM–5:00 PM. Hot Glass Shows all day, every day. Outdoor stage in summer.

Plan to Stay: 3 hours minimum.

Minimum Age: None

Disabled Access: Yes

Group Requirements: Groups of 20 or more should call 2 weeks in advance for special group rates and reservations (call 607-974-2000). No maximum group size.

Special Information: No photography in Steuben factory visitor's gallery.

Gift Shop: Sells Steuben and other glass objects from around the world, glass-related books, souvenirs, and a variety of housewares. Open same hours as Museum.

Directions: From New York City, take Rt. 17 West. Take Corning exit and follow signs. From Rochester, take I-390 South to I-86/Rt. 17 East. Follow above directions.

Nearby Attractions: Corning Historic Market Street shopping district; Finger Lakes Wine Country Visitor Center in CMoG Lobby; Babcock ladder tour (see page 103); Watkins Glen International Race Track; various wine trails; Rockwell Museum of Western Art; Benjamin Patterson Inn Museum; National Soaring Museum.

In the 1980s, Eastman-Kodak stopped giving public plant tours. While we wouldn't normally include a company founder's home, the exhibits and videos on George Eastman and Kodak provide a personal look at the company's roots. America's great companies begin and grow with individuals, and Kodak owes its existence to this hardworking inventor and businessman. (He probably would also have loved this book.)

George Eastman lived in this house from 1905 to 1932. The 50-room mansion and grounds have been authentically restored. Your guide's amusing gossip and anecdotes give you a sense of this great American entrepreneur, inventor, and marketer. In the conservatory, stand under a huge replica of an elephant's head and tusks while you listen to the story about why Eastman stood his ground to take a photo of an onrushing rhino. It provides a lesson on how he built his successful business.

Colorful displays in three second-floor rooms capture his personality, lifestyle, philanthropy, management techniques, and marketing strategy. Kodak's early history is intertwined with George Eastman's life, so the displays also show the company's development. You'll learn many tidbits, including why Eastman named his company "Kodak," why he gave away 500,000 "Brownie" cameras—one to every child who turned 12 in 1930—and see early Kodak advertising campaigns featuring themes still used today. You'll leave with a taste of how Eastman turned new scientific inventions into enormously popular products—a trait American companies have relearned.

Cost: Adults, $8; seniors, $6; students, $5; children 5–12, $3; children under 4, free.

Freebies: No

Videos/DVDs Shown: A second-floor room continuously screens videos about George Eastman and Kodak. The Kodak video shows manufacturing process and overviews company's new products and direction.

Reservations Needed: No, except for groups larger than 20 people.

Days and Hours: Museum: Tue–Sat 10:00 AM–5:00 PM, Sun 1:00–5:00 PM, Thur open until 8:00 PM. Closed holidays (except Mondays). During May (Lilac Festival in Rochester), open Mon–Sun 10:00 AM–5:00 PM. Tours: Tue–Sat 10:30 AM and 2:00 PM, Sun at 2:00 PM.

Plan to Stay: 2 hours for house and gardens tour (which can be self-guided), watching most of both videos, visiting second-floor exhibits. You'll even have time for the excellent International Museum of Photography and Film attached to the house (one of the world's greatest collections of photography, film, technology, and literature). All are included in the admission fee above.

Minimum Age: None

Disabled Access: Yes

Group Requirements: Groups larger than 20 people must schedule tours in advance by calling (585) 271-3361, ext. 238. Group rates available.

Gift Shop: Books, posters, collectors' items, and other photography-related gifts available in museum's gift shop. Open same hours as museum.

Special Information: Devices available to assist hearing-impaired.

Directions: Take New York State Thrwy. to Exit 45. Take Rt. 490 North toward Rochester. At Exit 19, go north on Culver Rd., then left on East Ave. The museum is on the right.

Nearby Attractions: Jell-O Gallery (see page 109); Memorial Art Gallery; Strong Museum; Rochester Museum and Science Center; Highland Park (annual May Lilac Festival); Seneca Park Zoo; Susan B. Anthony House.

MID-ATLANTIC

Corner of Erie and Liberty Streets,
Port Jervis, NY 12771

(845) 856-5375

www.gillinder
glassstore.com

Gillinder Glass makes half the airport runway lights in the United States. Many works of glass its factory created in the early 1900s are on display in museums, including the Smithsonian. Yet this venerable company is still owned and operated by the family that founded it in 1861. A tour of the friendly and hospitable factory gives visitors an intimate look at the process of making hand-pressed glass products.

Gillinder is located in Port Jervis, New York, right where that state meets New Jersey and Pennsylvania. Tours begin in the store at the front of the building, where your guide presents a brief history of the company and shows examples of its signature pieces. Classic glass-making molds from Gillinder's long history are also on display. You learn how glass is made from sand, soda ash, and limestone, and how chemical recipes create the desired colors. The factory also recycles its own glass; imperfect pieces are ground down (into what is called cullet) to provide further raw material.

You then move to the factory itself. Though items of fine household glass are available in the store, Gillinder prides itself on being a manufacturer of industrial and commercial glass. From a safe but close distance, visitors watch molten glass emerge from the furnace. Using a rod with a clay head, the gatherer pulls out a hot glowing ball of liquid glass into midair and swings around to drip it into a mold. Once the item has been pressed into form, workers remove it from the mold and place it in a "cooling oven" known in glassmaking as an annealing lehr (sometimes leer). Here the glass object cools in a controlled manner that prevents it from shattering at too rapid a change of temperature.

The tour ends back in the store, where visitors may peruse and buy glass items from the factory and from glassmakers throughout the world.

Cost: Adults, $4; seniors (over 55) and children (under 16), $3.50. Groups of 20 or more, $3 per person.

Freebies: No

Video/DVD Shown: No

Reservations Needed: Not for individuals and small groups. Groups of 10 or more must reserve a few weeks in advance.

Days and Hours: Tours run Mon–Fri at 10:15 AM, 12:30 PM, and 1:30 PM. Closed holidays.

Plan to Stay: 30–40 minutes for the tour plus time for the store.

Minimum Age: The tour is not recommended for small children, but they will be admitted if supervision is appropriate.

Disabled Access: Yes

Group Requirements: Groups of 10 or more need reservations. Large groups (40–60 people) may be divided into 2 or 3 separate tours.

Special Information: This is a genuine working factory, and it can be dusty. People with respiratory conditions may want to take precautions.

Gift Shop: The shop sells glass items from the factory plus glass objects from over 80 artists throughout the world. Open Mon–Fri 9:30 AM–5:30 PM, Sat 9:30 AM–4:00 PM, Sun 12:00 PM–4:00 PM. Closed holidays.

Directions: From Connecticut and New York City, take I-84 West to Port Jervis exit and turn left at end of ramp. At traffic light, bear right on E. Main St. (changes to W. Main St.) and follow it until Liberty St. Turn right; factory is one block down. From Pennsylvania, take I-84 East to Port Jervis exit. Turn right at end of ramp and follow directions above. From New Jersey, take Rt. 23 North to Port Jervis. Turn left at light and follow directions above.

Nearby Attractions: Sterling Hill Mining Museum (see page 101).

The famous American dessert was born in this small town in upstate New York. While the Jell-O Gallery is not a factory tour or a company-owned museum, it's around the corner from the original factory site. Fans of U.S.A.–made products, their quirky early history, merchandising, and advertising will pay homage here to "America's Most Famous Dessert."

LeRoy, New York, has a long history with Jell-O, although production stopped here in 1964. The Genesee Pure Food Company purchased the rights to produce it for $450 in 1899. Renamed the Jell-O Company in 1925, the company eventually merged into what was known as the General Foods Company. Today it is part of the even bigger Kraft Foods Company. As the largest selling prepared dessert in the U.S.A., approximately 13 boxes of Jell-O are bought every second (strawberry is the overall best seller). Salt Lake City, Des Moines, and Milwaukee rank as the top cities in per capita Jell-O consumption.

It's not just these fun facts that make the Gallery worth visiting, it's the cute displays, many of which showcase collectibles. The Gallery, run by the local nonprofit historical society, regularly acquires collectibles over eBay and or by donation. Notice the display of gelatin boxes from around the world, the Jell-O molds in various shapes, such as a NASCAR set, and the recipe book covers. Gracing the walls are 19 original oil paintings used in advertising in the 1920s, created by famous illustrators of the era.

In the late 1990s, over 3,000 spoons appeared on a Jell-O billboard on Times Square, with 100 of them now found at the Gallery. Examine the Geleometer, the machine that tests the jiggleness of the gelatin. Before you leave, be sure to have your picture taken as the Jell-O girl from the early advertising or in the Jell-O delivery truck.

Cost: Adults, $3; children ages 6–11, $1.50.

Freebies: No. Occasionally free boxes of Jell-O.

Video/DVD Shown: 5-minute video on Jell-O advertising.

Reservations Needed: No, except for groups.

Days and Hours: Open all year Mon–Fri 10:00 AM–4:00 PM. May–October: also Sat 10:00 AM–4:00 PM, Sun 1:00–4:00 PM.

Plan to Stay: 45 minutes.

Minimum Age: No

Disabled Access: Stairs to get into building.

Group Requirements: Recommend groups of 12 or more people call at least 2 days ahead. Cost is $2.50 per person for groups.

Special Information: Gallery has kids' play area.

Gift Shop: Sells Jell-O items, including shirts, golf balls, magnets, recipe books. Open same hours as Gallery.

Directions: From New York State Thrwy. (I-90), take Exit 47 (Rt. 19). Turn left on Rt. 5 (Main St.). Gallery is a few blocks ahead on the left.

Nearby Attractions: George Eastman House (see page 107); Historic LeRoy House; Underground Railroad driving tour (leaflet available from Historical Society).

8703 South Main Street, Eden, NY 14057   (716) 992-3960   www.edenkazoo.com

"If you can hum . . . you can play the kazoo" is the motto of the Original American Kazoo Company, the only metal-kazoo factory in the world. The kazoo is truly an American instrument, invented in the U.S.A. in the 1840s. Since kazoos are made the same way today as when the company started in 1916, we can say some things never change.

Pass through the toy and gift shop into the museum and factory. Wander around the small museum area looking at exhibits of kazoo trivia, history, and memorabilia. Learn that "Kazoo" was once a brand name for underwear and that the U.S. Navy ship U.S.S. *Kalamazoo* was nicknamed "the Kazoo"—its sailors owned kazoos printed with the ship's real name. Display cases show a variety of creative kazoos. Look for the liquor bottle–shaped kazoo (made in 1934 to "Kazelebrate" the end of Prohibition) and even a Woody Woodpecker model.

An 18-step process transforms sheets of metal into the classic submarine-shaped kazoo, without soldering, welding, or gluing. Pieces are joined by shaping and crimping metal. From behind a railing, you watch as workers operate individual presses (built in 1907) that flange edges, curve bottoms and tops, and stamp out the air hole. Parts are "seamed" together over a sword-shaped mold, then workers hand-insert the resonator and screw on the cap. Notice the single 10-horsepower motor that drives all of the presses, as you listen to the rhythmic thump of the metal blanks being transformed into kazoos.

Don't blow off this place because the manufacturing steps sound confusing—posters describe how the company makes kazoos to the tune of about 35,000 per week. In fact, you'll probably leave playing your favorite song on a kazoo.

Cost: Free

Freebies: No

Video/DVD Shown: 10-minute video in the museum shows news clips about the company.

Reservations Needed: No, except for groups larger than 15 people.

Days and Hours: Mon–Sat 10:00 AM–5:00 PM, Sun 12:00 PM–5:00 PM. Production takes place Tue and Fri 10:00 AM–5:00 PM. Call ahead to check days and times. No tour on weekends, video only. Closed holidays, week between Christmas and New Year's, and inventory days.

Plan to Stay: 20 minutes for self-guided tour, video, and the museum displays, plus time for gift shop.

Minimum Age: None, for families; 6, for school groups.

Disabled Access: Yes

Group Requirements: Reservations required 2 days in advance for group tours given Mon–Fri 10:15 AM–2:30 PM. Minimum group size is 20. Groups larger than 35 people are split into shifts. Minimum age is 6 for school groups. Groups receive a discount on one kazoo per customer.

Special Information: The tour does not take you onto factory floor. As you stand behind the viewing area railing, a worker describes the manufacturing process and answers questions. You can make your own metal kazoo during tour.

Gift Store: Sells kazoos of all kinds, toys, wind chimes, cards, hand-crafted instruments, and children's books. Also sells jewelry, glassware, and other gift items. Open Mon–Sat 10:00 AM–5:00 PM, Sun 12:00 PM–5:00 PM. Closed holidays.

Directions: Take New York State Thrwy. to Exit 57A. Turn left onto Eden-Evans Center Rd. When you reach the first traffic light, turn right onto Main St. (Rt. 62). The company is 2 blocks ahead on the left.

Nearby Attractions: Leon, NY, an Amish community, is 20 minutes away. Perry's Ice Cream (see page 112) and Buffalo's attractions, including QRS Music tour (see page 113), are about 45 minutes away.

30 Rockefeller Plaza, New York, NY 10112

(212) 664-3700

www.nbcuniversal
store.com

**NBC
Experience
STORE**
Rockefeller Plaza™

NBC prides itself on being the first radio network (1926), the first coast-to-coast television network (1951), and the first to broadcast a series in color (1953, *Kukla, Fran & Ollie*). This tour of the network headquarters (NBC employees call it 30 Rock) reflects that spirit. After seeing the behind-the-scenes hardware that helps edit, select, and broadcast shows to millions of homes, you appreciate what's involved when you flick on your TV.

While you will see neat technical TV hardware, the tour's highlight is visiting the sets of well-known shows or possibly meeting a TV star in hallways lined with NBC promotional posters and interactive exhibits. With your guide, you may explore the versatile Studio 3K, used for several NBC sports and entertainment programs. Examine the imitation wood, plants, and other background materials that look so realistic on television.

Up to 12 different sets appear simultaneously in *Saturday Night Live* Studio 8H, with the band and monologue sets the only two "permanents." During the show, actors jump between stages, and workers move walls and props preparing for upcoming skits. If you're here the week a new *SNL* is taped, you can briefly watch a rehearsal through glass walls, with the casually clothed director, guest host, camera operators, and production assistants going over segments. But don't let the relaxed dress fool you. As employees walk briskly by, you can feel the pressures and deadlines of live television. You'll also have a hands-on experience with the news and weather in the mini control studio near the end of the tour. The last stop is the NBC Sharp HD Theater, where visitors can enjoy the splendor of high-definition television.

Cost: Adults, $18.50; children 6–12, seniors, and groups of 10 or more, $15.50 per person.

Freebies: No

Video/DVD Shown: 10-minute video explains NBC history and the television production process. During the introductory time period, you can also participate in an old-time radio show. In the NBC Experience Store, the globe-shaped, high-definition theater shows an 8-minute video that focuses on

the history of NBC programming and the latest NBC Universal HD content.

Reservations Needed: No, but recommended for groups larger than 10.

Days and Hours: Mon–Sat 8:30 AM–5:30 PM, Sun 9:30 AM–4:30 PM, every 30 minutes. Call about extended hours during busy December and summer seasons. Closed Christmas. Purchase tickets early in the day; they can sell out by mid-morning.

Plan to Stay: 1 hour for video and tour, plus time for NBC Experience Store.

Minimum Age: 6

Disabled Access: Yes

Group Requirements: Groups larger than 10 people need at least 1 week's advance reservations (call 212-664-7174). Each tour time slot can accommodate up to 30 people; larger groups will need to divide into smaller parties and leave on a staggered schedule. Group rates available.

Special Information: No photography. Tour varies with fast-breaking news or broadcast schedule changes. For show tickets, write NBC Tickets at the address above. At corner of 49th St. and Rockefeller Plaza, look through the glass walls at the street-level *Today Show* studio. NBC Burbank, CA (see page 377), also gives tours.

NBC Page Program: Tour guides are part of the NBC Page Program that gives people an opportunity to break into broadcasting. For more information, contact NBC Page Program, Employee Relations, at above address.

NBC Experience Store: Sells clothing, CDs, videos, caps, mugs, and other novelty items, many with logos of your favorite shows and NBC Sports. Sweet Shop sells chocolates and bulk bin candy. Open Mon–Fri 8:00 AM–7:00 PM, Sat 9:00 AM–6:00 PM. Extended hours in summer.

Directions: Located on corner of 49th St. between 5th and 6th Aves. Take B, D, or V subway to 47–50th St./Rockefeller Plaza. Walk up a few flights to building lobby.

Nearby Attractions: Radio City Music Hall, Sony Wonder Technology Lab, CNN tour (see pages 114, 115, and 105); Rockefeller Center; Madison Square Garden tour (call 212-465-5800); Museum of Television and Radio; Top of the Rock Observation Deck.

Perry's Ice Cream

One Ice Cream Plaza, Akron, NY 14001

(716) 542-5492
(800) 8-PERRYS

www.perrys
icecream.com

When H. Morton Perry started his business in 1918, he bottled milk for dairy farmers in the Akron area. Every so often, he made small batches of ice cream for his family and friends—to rave reviews. By 1932, he began selling his ice cream to the public, and Perry's Ice Cream Company was born. H. Morton's grandchildren now run the business. You'll see that modern freezers have taken the place of ice-cooled storerooms, and a fleet of trucks has replaced horse-drawn wagons. You'll view an impressive manufacturing facility that makes millions of gallons of ice cream and related frozen treats every year.

After watching a video that covers Perry's proud history and the production of its quality ice cream, you'll walk up to a mezzanine area and peer through glass walls that survey the production floor. To your right are vats that hold the base mixes for ice cream and yogurt. In the center are the ever-moving machines that make ice cream and "novelty items," what they call treats like ice-cream sandwiches and cones. In this area, up to eight movable production lines may be in action. To the left are freezers for the finished products. While you're taking in the view, you'll munch on a delicious novelty item.

The various ice-cream flavors start as base mixes and then journey through enclosed machines and pipes that add goodies like pecan halves, caramel sauce, chocolate chips, or strawberries. Look for the line that makes ice-cream sandwiches. The vanilla ice cream is piped in and squirted between two traveling chocolate wafers. The ice cream and wafers come together in a continuous stream that makes and packages 120 sandwiches per minute.

Perry's can make cones a lot faster than your local ice-cream parlor. The cones are loaded into one end of the production line. Ice cream is shot inside, then chocolate sauce and nuts drop on top. Quicker then you can say "another scoop, please," the cones are packaged and off to the massive freezer.

Cost: $1; children under 3, free. *Subject to change when and if tours resume.*

Freebies: Ice-cream novelty item of your choice.

Video/DVD Shown: 10-minute video on Perry's history and production process.

Reservations Needed: Yes

Days and Hours: *Regular tour program has been discontinued. Call for information about whether tours have resumed.*

Plan to Stay: 30 minutes for video and tour.

Minimum Age: No

Disabled Access: Yes

Group Requirements: Maximum group size is 40 people. Should call 1 month in advance.

Special Information: No photography of production floor.

Directions: From the east, take I-90 West to Exit 48A (Pembroke). Take Rt. 77 South. Turn right onto Rt. 5 West, then right onto Rt. 93 North. Follow Rt. 93 as it turns and curves through Akron. Turn right at Ice Cream Plaza. From the west, take I-90 East to Exit 49 (Depew). Turn left on Rt. 78, then right on Rt. 5 East. Turn left on Rt. 93 North to Ice Cream Plaza.

Nearby Attractions: Kazoo Boutique (see page 110); Erie County Park; Octagon House; Niagara Falls is 35 miles away.

1026 Niagara Street, Buffalo, NY 14213-2099   (716) 885-4600   www.qrsmusic.com

At the world's oldest and largest mass manufacturer of player-piano rolls, you see how computer technology now makes a product whose prime was in the Roaring Twenties. You've gotta love a tour that begins by letting a nostalgic visitor play a popular tune on a player piano. Next to this old-fashioned roll-playing piano sits a baby grand equipped with Pianomation, a contemporary piano-playing system run from CDs.

Enter the memorabilia-filled waiting area, where old ads and letters from Jackie Gleason and Princess Grace of Monaco adorn the walls. In the corner sits a 1912 QRS "marking piano," which produces master rolls by recording an actual performer. The modified piano keys are pneumatically connected to a stylus that makes small markings on a roll of paper in the recorder.

Upstairs, look through glass windows at the predecessor of today's high-tech recording studio. To make the master roll, the "arranger" played a song beat by beat on a "recording piano" that put holes directly on a master sheet. With this time-consuming process (eight hours to make a three-minute song), the roll could not be played back until the recording was finished. Now, a computerized process produces the master roll. Watch the arranger enter keystrokes on the computer and instantly play them back for accuracy. The floppy disk, not holes in paper, creates the master.

In the manufacturing area, a worker feeds the disk into a perforator machine that cuts a pattern on sheets of paper according to computer code. Nearby, another worker handles the printer that puts song lyrics and other information onto the rolls. Look for the device that slurps up the sheets into finished piano rolls. As the tour ends, you're happy

that our world of CD players and digital audiotapes still has room for player-piano music.

Cost: Adults, $2; children under 11, $1.

Freebies: No

Video/DVD Shown: 12-minute historical slide show on company history and how player-piano music is created. Tour guide explains more recent developments.

Reservations Needed: No, except for groups larger than 8 people.

Days and Hours: Mon–Fri 10:00 AM and 2:00 PM (2 tours daily). Closed holidays.

Plan to Stay: 1 hour for slide show and tour, plus time to look at items in waiting area and seconds area.

Minimum Age: None

Disabled Access: Small flight of stairs to the exhibits in the waiting area. However, most of tour is not wheelchair accessible.

Group Requirements: Groups larger than 8 people should call 2 weeks in advance. Maximum group size is 12.

Special Information: The tour is a mecca for people with player pianos and will be most interesting for those with some player-piano experience.

Sales Desk: Sells 3,500 QRS rolls in stock, including children's music, Broadway and movie musicals, country and western hits, and rock 'n' roll hits. Seconds are half-price, but you must sift through individual boxed and unboxed rolls for the song titles. Also sells audiocassettes and CDs of player-piano music. Tour admission is redeemable toward purchase. Open Mon–Fri 8:00 AM–4:00 PM. Catalog available from above number.

Directions: From Rt. 33, take Rt. 198 West to Rt. 266. Turn left on Rt. 266, which is Niagara St. QRS 1 mile ahead on the right.

Nearby Attractions: Original American Kazoo museum and factory (see page 110); Rich Products History Exhibit in Rich Renaissance Niagara building (call 716-878-8422); Buffalo area attractions include Buffalo Museum of Science and Albright-Knox Art Gallery. Niagara Falls is about 20 miles away.

MID-ATLANTIC

1260 Ave. of the Americas, Rockefeller Center, New York, NY 10020

(212) 307-7171

www.radiocity.com

No, this isn't a factory. But they do create the Radio City Rockettes here and produce some of America's best-loved entertainment, such as the Radio City Christmas Spectacular. This behind-the-scenes tour of a New York landmark, built in 1932, combines architecture with a glimpse of what it takes to put together a U.S.–made show that's famous worldwide.

While standing in the art deco Grand Foyer, your theatrical tour guide expounds on the history of Radio City Music Hall, which gained National Historic Landmark status in 1978. Many of its original features have been restored, including a mural so large it had to be painted over a tennis court and shipped to the Music Hall by truck. In the Grand Auditorium, become captivated by the sunrise-inspired design with rays of yellow, red, and orange theatrical lights that can shine down over an ocean of nearly 6,000 red velvet seats from the coves between the Auditorium's 60-foot-high arches. Four 70-foot-wide hydraulic elevators divide the stage's floor into sections that allow for many special effects. For example, the front "pit" elevator can descend 27 feet for loading an ice-skating rink.

Walk through the private apartment built for Roxy, Radio City's famed impresario. Some of today's most famous celebrities and influential dignitaries are entertained in this very suite.

While you may not see a Radio City Rockette practice her legendary "eye high" kicks, you will meet a member of the world's most famous precision dance troupe. Wearing a custom costume, she talks about the history of the Rockettes.

Cost: Adults, $17; seniors (62+), $14; children under 12, $10.

Freebies: Tour button, opportunity to take a photo with a Radio City Rockette.

Video/DVD Shown: No

Reservations Needed: No, however tickets sold on first-come, first-served basis in the Radio City Avenue Store. Tour content and prices may change. Groups, see below.

Days and Hours: Mon–Sun 11:00 AM–3:00 PM. Open 365 days a year. Tours depart approximately every 30 minutes.

Plan to Stay: 1–1.25 hours for tour, plus time in Radio City Avenue Store.

Minimum Age: None

Disabled Access: Yes

Group Requirements: Groups of 20 or more people should call (212) 465-6100 for reservations and discount information. Advance reservations for groups required.

Special Information: Photography allowed, except during rehearsals. No video cameras.

Gift Shop: Radio City Avenue Store sells the popular Radio City Rockette doll, coffee mugs, postcards, and magnets featuring the colorful Radio City marquee and other New York scenes. Open Mon–Sun 10:30 AM–4:00 PM.

Directions: Accessible by 5th and 6th Ave. bus lines. Subway stops below building, so take B, D, Q, or F subway to 47–50th St./Rockefeller Plaza station. When you walk upstairs, you'll see the bright marquee lights. Buy tickets at the Radio City Avenue Store.

Nearby Attractions: NBC Studios, CNN tours, and Sony Wonder Technology Lab (see pages 111, 105 and 115); Top Of The Rock (call 877-692-7625); Madison Square Garden tour (call 212-465-5800); NASDAQ Stock Market in Times Square.

SONY PICTURES STUDIOS

After your high-tech greeting by b.b.wonderbot, Sony Wonder's telepresence robot, you ride up an elevator to a black room dotted with tiny, starlike lights. You hear computer screens beckon "Come here!" "Over here!" You approach a screen where your photo is taken, and you type in your name and record your voice—this information is all stored on your new Sony Wonder Card, which you use to interact with the exhibits.

On your way to the Technology Workshop, read, watch, and listen to the history of communication technology, from early phonographs to the 21st century's newest gadgets. Curious about how digital sound is stored? Have you ever seen the inside of a Sony video camera? Swipe your card at one of the Signal Viewer stations—here, CD players, video cameras, and other everyday Sony devices that record and project signals, images, and audio are explained. Learn how a TV screen works—and that the average American watches 1,825 hours of TV a year!

At the Processing Signals station, you can add an echo to your own voice, or play your voice backward. In the Audio Lab, produce a jazzy tune using a baby's wail, a cow's moo, and other odd sounds in place of instruments—the computer mixes the sounds for you and plays back your composition. In the Image Lab, "point" a laser tracking device at an electronic canvas several feet away to create a silly "painting"—you can even paste in your own face. There are plenty of hands-on exhibits where you can learn how technology is used in industries like TV production, medicine, and meteorology. You

may want to be an ultrasound trainee, performing a simulated ultrasound on a pregnant woman. At another station, search for a "leak" in the area by manipulating an infrared camera on the end of a huge red robotic arm in the center of the room. You may leave Sony Wonder wanting to become a television producer, an imaging specialist, or a computer artist.

Cost: Free

Freebies: Certificate of Achievement with your name and photo.

Videos/DVDs Shown: Several 15-minute videos demonstrating high-definition technology. Videos range in theme from animation to natural wonders.

Reservations Needed: Recommended for guaranteed admission. Same-day tickets are available on a first-come, first-served basis.

Days and Hours: Tue–Sat 10:00 AM–5:00 PM, Sun 12:00 PM–5:00 PM. Closed Mondays and major holidays.

Plan to Stay: 1–2 hours.

Minimum Age: None. Children under 8 may need adult assistance at some exhibits, and youth under 18 must be accompanied by an adult on school days before 3 PM.

Disabled Access: Yes

Group Requirements: Groups of 8–35 people can reserve space 1 week–3 months in advance.

Special Information: Last admission 30 minutes before closing.

Gift Shop: None

Directions: Located in Sony Plaza on 56th St. between Madison and 5th Aves. Take E or V subway to 5th Ave. and walk up 3 blocks to 56th St.; take F subway to 57th St., or take the 4, 5, or 6 train to 59th St.

Nearby Attractions: NBC Studios, Inside CNN, and Radio City Music Hall tours (see pages 111, 105 and 114); Madison Square Garden tour (call 212-465-5800); NASDAQ Stock Market in Times Square; Museum of Modern Art; St. Patrick's Cathedral; Central Park; Rockefeller Center; Museum of Television & Radio.

MID-ATLANTIC

STEINWAY & SONS

A piano mecca exists inside a four-story building in urban Queens, New York. Part lumberyard, woodshop, fine-cabinet studio, music-playing room, and back-office operation, Steinway & Sons is a world microcosm, with 33 different nationalities of workers. More than 500 craftspeople, trained by apprenticeship, hand-build 2,800 pianos each year. Since it takes one year and approximately 12,000 parts to make a Steinway piano, you will be amazed by the number of pianos in progress.

One tour highlight is the rim bending. Six men carry a laminated, rock-maple board (often with 18 layers) to one of the piano-shaped presses, the same ones invented 100 years ago by the founder's son. They wrestle the wood, bending it around the press, then hammer, screw, and clamp the wood into place. Each rim stays one day on the press. Once removed, rims rest calmly for at least six weeks in a sauna-hot, dark room. Here you appreciate the range of piano sizes, as the rims stand from five to nine feet tall.

The belly department is rumored to be named after the original German-American beer-drinking craftsmen whose bellies hung over the pianos as they worked here. Soundboards are custom-fit into each piano. Workers hammer in the bridge to which strings will be attached. Saws hiss and the floors vibrate with the rhythmic banging and drilling. Cast-iron plates suspended in air wait for installation into rims. In the stringing department, you'll watch with fascination as a worker attaches each metal string to the plate (or "harp"), loops it tightly around the bridge, and then clamps it around the tuning pin. This process is skillfully repeated until all strings are installed.

The final stage is tuning. Master voicers in soundproof rooms regulate the "action," which is how piano-makers refer to the key-and-hammer mechanism. To ensure that all hammers rise to the same height, voicers hit each key and watch the corresponding hammer bob like a woodpecker's head. Once the action is regulated, the voicer inserts it into the front of the piano and tests its musical quality, adjusting its tuning and brightness before the piano's first performance in Carnegie Hall, or your living room.

Cost: Free

Freebies: No

Video/DVD Shown: No, but can purchase 15-minute video that alternates between factory and pianists' performances.

Reservations Needed: Yes

Days and Hours: Alternating Mon or Thur 9:00 AM. No tours July and August. Closed holidays and week between Christmas and New Year's.

Plan to Stay: 2.5 hours.

Minimum Age: 16

Disabled Access: Yes, via freight elevators.

Group Requirements: Maximum group size is 15 people. Call several weeks in advance for reservations.

Gift Area: Can order books, videos, posters, and logoed items including mugs, T-shirts, and pens, with delivery in 7–10 days. Product listing available at above number.

Special Information: Since factory covers 450,000 square feet and 4 floors that may have sawdust, wear comfortable walking shoes.

Directions: From LaGuardia airport, take Grand Central Pkwy. West. Take first exit and turn right onto Steinway St. to 19th Ave. Steinway & Sons is on your left. From Manhattan, take Triboro Bridge toward Queens. Take first exit in Queens. Stay in right lane to get onto Astoria Blvd. Turn left onto Steinway St. Follow above directions. Call for subway directions (N train to Ditmars Blvd.).

Nearby Attractions: Shea Stadium; Manhattan's music attractions include Radio City Music Hall "Stage Door Tour" (see page 114), Lincoln Center, Carnegie Hall, Steinway Hall (company's piano showroom and museum—call 212-246-1100).

Approaching Asher's 125,000-square-foot state-of-the-art facility, the aroma of chocolate greets you. Enticed to come inside, you pass through the entranceway, turn left, and proceed up a ramp. Shortly, you enter a 168-foot corridor, not more than four feet from the factory floor.

To the right, a colorful, oil-painted mural extends the length of the corridor. It includes a depiction of Asher's original store window in Center City Philadelphia, as well as painted plaques exhibiting facts about Asher's. One plaque tells you that Asher's is the oldest continuously family-owned and -operated candy manufacturer in the U.S., dating back to 1892, and is currently run by the third and fourth generations. At four stations along the corridor, a video explains in detail what you see through windows to the left, as the machines and employees work in unison during your self-guided tour.

Crispy buttercrunch toffee asserts its beginning in a large copper kettle sitting atop a gas fire. The cook, wearing a shower cap and elbow-length black rubber gloves, pours thick corn syrup into the mixture of sugar and butter. In a circular motion, with much effort and speed, he mixes the ingredients. Lifting the kettle from the fire, he pours the gooey substance onto a cool metal table and spreads it one-quarter-inch thick.

Before it cools, he uses a hand-operated rotary knife, which looks like a rolling pin fit with 12 pizza cutter blades, and scores the toffee to make a square pattern. He then breaks the toffee along the scores and places it on a traveling wire-mesh bed. Liquid chocolate falls from above and rises from below to enrobe the toffee in chocolate majesty. For the crowning final touch, nuts pass through a chute, scatter, and cover the toffee waiting below.

Nearby, the depositor machine drops measured amounts of tempered chocolate onto a bed of yellow, pink, blue, and white sugar beads, which stick to the surface of the chocolate. Pretty nonpareils are in the making.

After your tour, browse the old-fashioned Victorian candy store, with a cobblestone road beneath your feet. Admire the ticket booth and the charming trolley. Sample a chocolate-covered pretzel, for which Asher's is famous, or try a sugar-free, low-sodium chocolate. Take home a box of Rocky Road Fudge or French Mint Truffles, and each time you take a bite into one of these delectable confections, remember your trip to Asher's.

Cost: Free

Freebies: Chocolate samples.

Videos/DVDs Shown: 5-minute videos shown at each station explain in detail the candy-making process.

Reservations Needed: No, except for groups of 10 or more.

Days and Hours: Mon–Fri 10:00 AM–3:30 PM; Sat 10:00 AM–4:00 PM. Closed holidays.

Plan to Stay: 30 minutes, plus time for candy store.

Minimum Age: None

Disabled Access: Yes

Group Requirements: Groups of 10 or more, call (215) 721-3276 to make reservations.

Special Information: Tours also in Lewiston, PA, about 2–3 hours away. Call (717) 248-8613.

Gift Shop: Candy Store offers a variety of candy, stuffed animals, baskets, and seasonal items. Open Mon–Fri 9:30 AM–5:00 PM; Labor Day–Memorial Day, also open Sat 10:00 AM–4:00 PM. Closed holidays.

Directions: From Philadelphia, take Rt. 76 West to I-476 North to Rt. 63 (Lansdale Exit) on the Pennsylvania Tnpk. Turn right at Rt. 63 (Sumneytown Pike). Turn right onto Wambold Rd. Asher's is on the left. From points west, take I-276 East to I-476 North. Proceed as above.

Nearby Attractions: Byers' Choice tour (see pages 120–121); Philadelphia attractions, including the Philadelphia U.S. Mint tour (see page 134), are 15 miles away; Mennonite historical area; King of Prussia Mall (largest mall on the East Coast); Skippack Village; Valley Forge.

MID-ATLANTIC

5200 6th Avenue, Altoona, PA 16602   (814) 942-5062
(800) 344-4438   www.benzels.com

Whether you love trains, pretzels, or factory outlet shopping, Benzel's Bretzel Bakery offers all of the above, plus a bit of nostalgia. In 1911, Adolf Benzel stepped off a boxcar at the Altoona, Pennsylvania, train station with his family and all his worldly belongings and started the Benzel tradition of baking pretzels. Railroad buffs will enjoy the caboose parked on the grounds and the massive train mural along the Outlet Store's back wall. The mural depicts the railroad's influence on the Altoona area, including an unusual look at the Horseshoe Curve.

An in-store video captures the history of Adolph Benzel's arrival in Altoona and the beginnings of Benzel's Bretzel Bakery. The video, a visual factory tour, walks you step by step through the baking process that now generates 80 million pretzels daily. Benzel's is one of the few companies in the U.S.A. that still produces pretzels from the flour, malt, yeast, and salt concoction first used by Catholic monks. You will come to understand what is involved in mixing the dough, shaping it into various pretzel forms from extruders, and baking and bagging the finished pretzels.

At a rapid rate, pretzels travel the conveyor belts, where they rise, steam, and are salted before they reach the 100-foot ovens. You can almost feel the heat as the pretzels are baked by intense flames from the gas-fired ovens. While Grandpa Benzel didn't make his "bretzels" like this in 1911, his grandchildren's products and factory still utilize his basic recipe, continuing the family's traditions and heritage.

Cost: Free

Freebies: Fresh pretzels hot off the line and 1-ounce sample bag.

Video/DVD Shown: 25-minute video explains Benzel family's pretzel-making history and process.

Reservations Needed: No, except for groups larger than 40 people.

Days and Hours: Mon–Fri 10:00 AM–5:00 PM, Sat 10:00 AM–1:00 PM. Holiday hours vary; call above number.

Plan to Stay: 25 minutes for video, plus time in factory store.

Minimum Age: None

Disabled Access: Yes

Group Requirements: Groups larger than 40 should call a few days ahead. No maximum group size.

Special Information: Benzel's has seasonal activities and promotional giveaways throughout the year.

Factory Outlet: Sells all Benzel's and Pennsylvania Brand pretzel products as well as decorated gift tins, gift baskets, candies, nuts, and various snack food items at discounted prices. Open same hours as above. Pretzel catalog available from above number.

Directions: From Pennsylvania Tnpk., exit at Rt. 220 North. Follow Rt. 220 North to Altoona, then take Rt. 764 North. Benzel's is one-quarter mile past 58th St., on the left across from 52nd St. Look for old train caboose in front. From I-80, exit at Milesburg. Follow Rt. 220 South to Altoona, then to 17th St. bypass in Altoona. Turn right onto 17th St. Turn left onto 7th Ave., which joins 6th Ave. Continue on 6th Ave. Benzel's is on the right across from 52nd St., 1 block past traffic light at the corner of 51st St.

Nearby Attractions: Horseshoe Curve National Historic Landmark; Altoona Railroaders Memorial Museum (call 888-425-8666); Mishler Theatre (call 814-944-9434); Baker Mansion Museum (call 814-942-3916); Boyer's Candy Outlet; Lakemont Park.

Cannondale

172 Friendship Village Road, Bedford, PA 15522

(814) 623-9073
(800) 245-3872

www.cannondale.com

cannondale *feel it* ™

Cannondale started in a crowded loft above a pickle factory in 1971, building the industry's first bicycle trailer. It later added cycle apparel and accessory lines, then made its first bicycle in 1983. Its lighter aluminum bicycle revolutionized the industry at a time when steel models dominated. Widely regarded as the bike industry's leading innovator, Cannondale is the leading manufacturer of aluminum bicycles, selling more than 80 models in over 60 countries worldwide.

Headquartered in Connecticut, Cannondale manufactures virtually all of its products at a factory in Bedford, Pennsylvania. This tour of its bicycle plant gives you an opportunity to observe parts of a patented, state-of-the-art production system. You may have glimpses of the welding, decaling, and painting areas, along with the wheel-building room. Look at posters on a bulletin board that illustrate how the paint line runs. In the assembly room, parts such as cranks, derailleurs, and handlebars are attached onto the frame.

When Cannondale decided to become a major player in the worldwide bicycle business in 1988, it wanted to prove that it could economically produce a large number of award-winning bikes in the U.S.A.—not overseas. To do this, it had to convert its factory, change production methods, and maintain less inventory. Computer-instructed laser cutters and electric arc plasma cutters precisely miter each frame tube, and cut water-bottle holes and seat slots at the same time. Other efficient methods include those used for heat-treating the rack of frames and quenching them in their own bath, as well as for frame align-

ment, painting, and quality testing. Whether you are a bike rider or factory tour enthusiast, you will enjoy the combination of sights and processes.

Cost: Free

Freebies: No

Video/DVD Shown: No

Reservations Needed: Yes

Days and Hours: Tues–Thur 8:30 AM–1:30 PM. Closed major holidays.

Plan to Stay: 30–45 minutes.

Minimum Age: 11

Disabled Access: Yes; however, tour is on factory floor.

Group Requirements: Maximum group size is 10 people.

Special Information: No photography. Safety glasses provided.

Gift Shop: No. Products sold only through authorized dealers.

Directions: From the Pennsylvania Tnpk. (I-76), take Exit 146 (Bedford). Turn left at the light, then left at the next light onto Rt. 220/199 South to the Greensburg/Rt. 30 West exit. Drive a short distance on Rt. 30 West and make a right onto Friendship Village Rd. The Cannondale facility is the first on the right side of Friendship Village Road.

Nearby Attractions: Benzel's tour (see page 118); Friendship Village Campground; Shawnee State Park; Old Bedford Village; Fort Bedford Museum; Espy House National Historic Landmark; Bedford Fall Foliage Festival (occurs usually the first 2 weekends in October); Bedford Springs; Bison Corral (call 814-733-4908); Gravity Hill; Blue Knob Four Seasons Resort; Lake Raystown Resort and Lodge; Bedford County's 14 covered bridges.

MID-ATLANTIC

As you step onto the cobblestone floor entranceway of family-oriented Byers' Choice, you are transported back in time to the streets of Victorian England. Tall, blazing street lamps and quaint Victorian storefronts line the walls, beckoning you onward.

You first stop at the St. James Theatre, where you watch a short video that explains the history of family-run Byers' Choice and previews the production of its handcrafted Christmas Carolers figurines. The video details how Joyce Byers' simple hobby of creating cheerful clay and fabric figurines of Christmas carolers, whose heads are uplifted and mouths are open wide as if in song, grew to a nationwide business. Compliments from friends and family encouraged Joyce to sell her homemade figurines at local women's exchanges. The Victorian carolers, representing a simpler time and way of life, were a hit when introduced at the New York Gift Show in 1978.

Upon returning to the Victorian street, peer into life-size versions of Victorian storefronts. View a dining room with decorations that change with the seasons, and walk into a dressmaking and tailoring shop to have a picture taken in Victorian attire.

Then, turn a corner into Ye Olde Curiosity Shoppe—everything is changed! Suddenly, you are like giant Gulliver in the land of the Lilliputians. The life-size Victorian street scenes that you previously viewed are meticulously reproduced to the 13-inch scale of the Carolers figurines. Other nearby rooms contain miniature, picturesque tableaus of Victorian England heavily populated by joyful, singing Byers' Choice Carolers figurines. All of the heartwarming Carolers vignettes were created by owner Joyce Byers. You will also see a unique international collection of over 150 nativities, always on view.

Finally, wind your way to the factory workshop. Through a wall of one-way glass, view the complete production of the Byers' Choice Carolers, from body building to dressing. The 80,000-square-foot workshop appears remarkably calm. Artisans wearing headsets listen to books on tape provided by Byers' Choice, as they handcraft Carolers figurines at wooden tables. Some artisans shape clay heads and paint candid faces on them; others create wire body frames wrapped in tissue paper. A few craftswomen skillfully stitch the delicate fabrics and fur that will become the Carolers' clothing, which other craftswomen painstakingly pin on the figurines.

For most styles, only 100 figurines of each design are produced, thereby creating an endless selection of figurines. An opportunity to purchase a Byers' Choice Carolers figurine, including one available only there, awaits you in the gift shop at the conclusion of the tour.

Cost: Free

Freebies: Christmas Gallery and Byers' Choice sculpture garden brochures.

Video/DVD Shown: 10-minute video of company history and figurine-making process.

Reservations Needed: No, except for groups over 20 people.

Days and Hours: Mon–Sat 10:00 AM–5:00 PM, Sun 12:00 PM–5:00 PM. Closed Easter, Thanksgiving, Christmas, and New Year's.

Plan to Stay: 1 hour for video and self-guided tour, plus time for gift shop, outdoor sculpture garden, and international crêche collection.

Minimum Age: None

Disabled Access: Yes

Group Requirements: Reservations for groups over 20 people.

Special Information: No photography of figurine workshop.

Gift Shop: Primarily sells vast array of Byers' Choice Carolers. Open same hours as tour.

Directions: From Philadelphia, take I-76 West to Pennsylvania Tnpk. East. Get off at Fort Washington (Exit 339). Take Rt. 309 North toward Montgomeryville. Pass Montgomeryville Mall on left. Turn right onto Rt. 202 North. Continue to second traffic light. Turn left onto County Line Rd. Byers' Choice is one-half mile on your right.

Nearby Attractions: Asher's Chocolates tour (see page 117); Moravian Pottery and Tile Works Museum tour (call 215-345-6722); Mercer Museum; James A. Michener Art Museum.

MID-ATLANTIC

The Byers' Choice Ltd. Carolers Figurines are a handcrafted Christmas Tradition.

Travel back to a simpler time at the Byers' Choice Christmas Museum by strolling a life-size Victorian London street where homes are festively decorated for the holidays.

Two Rivers Landing, 30 Centre Square, Easton, PA 18042-7744

(610) 515-8000   www.crayola.com

You can't help feeling like a kid again when you visit The Crayola FACTORY at Two Rivers Landing, the discovery center built in 1996 by Binney & Smith, makers of Crayola products. In fact, don't be surprised if the experience raises many childhood memories. You may remember when the now-classic 64-crayon box with built-in sharpener was introduced in 1958; or you may remember your 10th birthday, by which time you, like the average American child, had probably worn down 730 crayons.

The "Factory Floor" level of the discovery center features crayon manufacturing and marker assembly, using machinery transferred from the nearby production plant. Behind a glass wall is the flat-bed molder that makes a small percentage of the company's crayons. Watch a worker pour a mixture containing melted paraffin wax and powdered pigment from a bucket onto a long table with thousands of small holes. Bright yellow wax seeps into the holes. After four to seven minutes of cooling, 1,200 crayons magically appear as they are pushed up and out of the molds! The worker also demonstrates and explains the labeling and packaging machines.

In the marker assembly area, the marker machine has actually been slowed down so you can follow the process of mating the barrels, cylinders, and marker caps. At normal speed, this machine can make 42,000 markers in one eight-hour shift.

Follow the ramp down to the "Creative Studio," which begins the playful, interactive portion of your visit. Draw on clear glass walls with special glasswriter markers. Step into "Cool Moves," where a computer captures your image on a huge video screen.

In the "Easton Press and Bindery," you can prac-

tice printmaking. At the end of your colorful experience, you can use Crayola Model Magic to create three-dimensional art.

Cost: Adults and children, $9; seniors 55+, $8.50; 2 and younger, free. Includes admission to National Canal Museum, located in same building. Check website for updated pricing.

Freebies: Box of 4 crayons and a marker from the assembly lines, and art projects you create while there.

Videos/DVDs Shown: A 10-minute video covers products made by the company, including Silly Putty, chalk, paint, and crayon production. Another video shows TV clips.

Reservations Needed: No, with walk-ins accommodated on a first-come, first-served basis until day is sold out, however advanced reservations are accepted. Groups over 10 people, see below.

Days and Hours: Schedule variable. Check calendar on website.

Plan to Stay: 1.5–2.5 hours, plus time in gift shops.

Minimum Age: None

Disabled Access: Yes

Group Requirements: Groups over 10 people should call 2 weeks in advance.

Gift Shops: Museum Shop sells logoed clothing, candy, and toys. Open same hours as Crayola Factory. The 7,200-square-foot Crayola Store, next door, sells a range of Binney & Smith products, from mini to large boxes of crayons, and from posters to teddy bears wearing logoed sweatshirts. Call toll-free for hours (888) 827-2966. Closed holidays.

Directions: From Philadelphia, take Northeast Extension of Pennsylvania Tnpk. to Allentown Exit onto Rt. 22 East. Get off at the 4th St. exit (last exit in PA). At traffic light, turn left on Buskill St. Turn right onto N. 3rd St. Follow signs to "The Crayola FACTORY."

Nearby Attractions: Martin Guitar and Mack Trucks tours (see pages 128 and 127); Allen Organ Company tour (call 610-966-2202); canal boat ride and walking tour of Easton; Lehigh Valley attractions, including Dorney Park and Wildwater Kingdom.

See color photos, page 8.

1425 Eden Road, York, PA 17402

(717) 852-6590
(877) 883-1450

www.harley-davidson.com

Among America's most recognized and respected products, Harley-Davidson motorcycles inspire passion in riders, dealers, and employees alike. See firsthand what sparks this enthusiasm by visiting the company's Vehicle Operations in York, Pennsylvania. The facility produces Touring, Softail®, and factory custom motorcycles as well as current and noncurrent replacement parts.

The factory tour takes visitors past many stages of fabrication and motorcycle assembly. You can see firsthand how fenders, fuel tanks, and exhaust pipes are transformed out of sheet metal. Later, fenders are trimmed by lasers, and fuel tanks are polished by robots. Walk by colorful painted parts and various subassembly processes.

As motorcycles are assembled, they journey by overhead conveyor down an assembly line to stations where employees work to secure the different parts to the frame. Following the assembly process, the bike cruises into the roll-test booth, where it is placed on rollers and ridden at speeds up to 60 mph while technicians check various aspects of the bike's performance.

After the tour, you can view exhibits featuring the manufacturing and assembly processes and sit on the latest models displayed in the Tour Center.

Cost: Free

Freebies: Collectible badge and *The Enthusiast* magazine; product catalogs may also be available.

Video/DVD Shown: Yes

Reservations Needed: No, except for groups of 10

or more. Calling ahead is recommended, since plant tour times and availability may change.

Days and Hours: Tours available Mon–Fri 9:00 AM–2:00 PM on a first-come, first-served basis. Open Sat during summer, 9:30 AM–1:00 PM. Closed on major holidays and for year-end maintenance. Tours may be modified at any time due to manufacturing requirements and during model year changeover. Please call ahead for complete details.

Plan to Stay: Allow 1.5–2 hours for the factory tour, exhibits, and gift shop.

Minimum Age: 12

Disabled Access: Yes (call ahead).

Group Requirements: Groups of 10 or more must make reservations in advance.

Special Information: Closed-toe shoes are required. Photography is permitted in the Tour Center but not in the factory. Tour participants aged 18 and over must present a valid government-issued photo ID and complete a registration card. Visitors must pass through a metal detector before entering the plant. Annual 3-day open house at end of September. Tours are also available at the company's plants in Kansas City, MO (see page 287), and Wauwatosa, WI (see page 208).

Gift Shop: Offers a selection of Harley-Davidson souvenir merchandise and features a penny press machine. Open Mon–Fri 8:00 AM–4:00 PM; during summer also open Sat 9:30 AM–2:00 PM.

Directions: From I-83, take Exit 21 or 21A (Arsenal Rd./Rt. 30 East). Turn left on Eden Rd. at factory entrance from Rt. 30. Follow signs to Visitor Parking.

Nearby Attractions: Wolfgang Candy tours (see page 137); Weightlifting Hall of Fame (call 717-767-6481); Industrial and Agricultural Museum (call 717-846-6452); York County Historical Museum; Gates House and Plough Tavern; outlet stores and antique shops; Gettysburg, Hershey, and Lancaster nearby. Conveniently located one hour from Baltimore and two hours from Philadelphia.

MID-ATLANTIC

See color photos, page 18.

Visitors Center, Routes 1 and 272,
Nottingham, PA 19362

(800) 63-SNACK
(800) 637-6225

www.herrs.com

Herr's snack food production has come a long way from when the company used a small, old-fashioned cooker in a barn. It now has an advanced and highly automated plant that makes tens of thousands of potato chips, corn chips, tortilla chips, popcorn batches, cheese curls, and pretzels every day. The comfortable, specially designed visitors center and café, creative video, and extensive guided tour provide a tasty education in how Herr's makes its products.

While watching the action through glass walls, you'll "ooh" and "aah" at the panoramic views. In the pretzel area, gaze at a 100-yard stretch of pretzel twists, in rows of 20 to 24 across, marching to massive ovens. In the corn chip, cheese curl, potato chip, and popcorn production sections, your vista overlooks the entire process. Follow the raw ingredients—either corn or potatoes—as they tumble in by the truckload at the beginning of the production line; travel along a conveyor belt through a series of machines that wash, slice, cook, or season them; then head out on bucket lifts to a sorting and bagging area. Other memorable images include machines and workers bagging and boxing together in almost symphonic unison, and the cavernous warehouse filled with snack-food boxes.

Except for the boxing of bags, machines do most of the work. Notice how only a few people oversee production in most areas. Smart machines can even sense discolored potato chips and use air jets to blow these rebels off the line. The guides salt and pepper the tour with interesting facts and figures about the company, including Herr's recycling efforts. But the best thing the guides do is grab samples of warm potato chips directly from the quickly moving conveyer belt. Bagged chips will never again taste the same!

Cost: Free

Freebies: Warm potato chips during the tour; small sample bag at end of tour.

Videos/DVDs Shown: 10-minute video on company history, narrated by Herr family members; short videos throughout tour show unique views of snacks being made.

Reservations Needed: Yes, but can take walk-ins if space permits.

Days and Hours: Mon–Thur 9:00 AM–3:00 PM on the hour; Fri 9:00 AM, 10:00 AM, and 11:00 AM. Closed holidays.

Plan to Stay: 1.5 hours, including video, tour, gift shop, and café.

Minimum Age: None

Disabled Access: Yes

Group Requirements: With advance notice, can handle any size group, which will split into smaller ones for tour. Video shown in 140-seat auditorium.

Special Information: If you are interested in particular products, such as tortilla chips or cheese curls, call ahead for production schedule on day of your visit.

Gift Shop: Sells Herr's food products; logoed clothing items; Nottingham, PA, T-shirts; scale model of Herr's delivery truck; and Chipper the Chipmunk doll. Open Mon–Fri 8:00 AM–5:00 PM. Call for extended holiday hours. Catalog available from above number.

Directions: From Philadelphia, take I-95 South to Rt. 322 West exit. From Rt. 322, turn left onto Rt. 1 South. Turn left onto Rt. 272 South and right at light onto Herr Dr. Factory and Visitors Center at end of road. From Baltimore, take I-95 North to Exit 100. Take Rt. 272 North. Turn left at light onto Herr Dr.

Nearby Attractions: Hagley Museum tour (see page 94), about 1 hour away; Longwood Gardens; Plumpton Park Zoo; Franklin Mint Museum; Brandywine River Museum; Lancaster County attractions about 30 miles away.

MID-ATLANTIC

See color photos, page 22.

Visitors Center, Park Boulevard,
Hershey, PA 17033

(717) 520-8981

www.hersheys
chocolateworld.com

This visitors center dedicated to chocolate features a wall display of the Hershey's chocolate story and a 12-minute journey through a simulated chocolate factory. The entire chocolate-making process, from harvesting the bean to packaging the bar, will be revealed to you with true-to-life machines, overhead speakers, and videos. You will find new respect for "The Great American Chocolate Bar."

As you stand in line for the ride, take some time to read the company history displayed on the wall; watch the video describing how cocoa beans are cultivated and harvested in South America and Africa before their trek to Hershey, Pennsylvania. Enjoy the indoor tropical garden at the center of Chocolate World. The exotic plants and palm trees displayed here come from regions of the world where cocoa beans are harvested.

Riding inside a cocoa bean–shaped cart, you pass scenes depicting the chocolate-making process. Glance at the initial process of cleaning and sorting the beans. You'll understand the true cocoa-bean experience as you enter the roaster and feel the air temperature suddenly rise. Ride past the extractor, which removes the center "nibs" from the bean. Smell the luscious aroma of liquid chocolate as it flows by to be mixed with milk and sugar. Toward the end of your ride, an impressive display of Hershey's products will confront you, as recorded children's voices sing "It's a Hershey's Chocolate World!" You'll see how Hershey packages and ships its products worldwide and know why, at Chocolate World, they say, "Wherever you go, no matter how far, you'll always be near a Hershey bar."

In Hershey's Factory Works area, you can sign up to become an "Official Hershey's Factory Worker," complete with an "employee" photo ID, authentic factory worker hat, and the opportunity to be part of an interactive chocolate factory.

Cost: Free

Freebies: Samples of Hershey's Miniatures, Hershey's Kisses, or other chocolate products.

Videos/DVDs Shown: Continually running video in waiting area explains cocoa-bean harvesting and initial processing. Videos throughout ride provide close-up views of the real production process.

Reservations Needed: No

Days and Hours: Mon–Sun 9:00 AM–5:00 PM; some extended hours—best to call in advance. Closed Christmas.

Plan to Stay: 12-minute ride, plus time for displays, gift shops, Hershey's Really Big 3-D Show (call for cost), Hershey's Factory Works Experience, and restaurants.

Minimum Age: None

Disabled Access: Yes

Group Requirements: None

Special Information: Expect long lines during summertime, although they tend to move quickly. During the 1970s, the company had to close well-known tour of Hershey plant because of overwhelming crowds and safety concerns. Visitors center in Oakdale, CA (see page 367).

Gift Shops: Gift shops and food court sell Hershey's products, from apparel to souvenirs to chocolatier items. Open same hours as ride. Catalog available from www.hersheysgift.com.

Directions: From the west, take I-83 to Rt. 322 East. Exit at Rt. 39 West to Hersheypark Dr. Chocolate World is the first "Hershey Attraction" on the right. From the east, take Pennsylvania Tnpk. to Exit 20. Follow Rt. 72 North to Rt. 322 West, then follow above directions. From Lancaster, take Rt. 283 West to Rt. 743 North and follow signs to Hershey. Call (800) HERSHEY for recorded directions.

Nearby Attractions: HERSHEYPARK entertainment complex (87-acre amusement park); ZooAmerica North American Wildlife Park; Hershey Gardens; Hershey Museum; the Hotel Hershey; HERSHEYPARK Arena, with concerts, sports, and special events year-round.

MID-ATLANTIC

Cows with a high quality of life produce a lot of high-quality milk. Hope Acres is one of only a few robotic dairy farms in the United States and, thanks to technology, its cows live in the lap of bovine luxury. A tour of the barn shows the comfortable conditions that produce great milk.

Visitors assemble at the Brown Cow Country Market on the farm's edge, overlooking the rural country of the Susquehanna River Valley. Whether you bring your own vehicle or arrive on a bus tour, you drive with your guide to the giant barn that houses the farm's milking cows. (A bus may drive into the barn, providing an elevated view of the livestock; other visitors park their cars outside and walk in.)

In the barn, you stand in an aisle with many cows on both sides amid the wholesome organic smell of manure, which is useful as an agricultural fertilizer. An automatic scraper, the width of the walking area, periodically scoops the cows' manure and dumps it into a holding tank, where it awaits distribution in the fields.

The cows live in stress-free comfort that promotes the copious production of good milk. They stand or recline on thin waterbeds that cover the floor under a layer of sawdust. This forgiving surface helps to protect the cows' joints, which (like yours) would become sore after hours of lying on a hard floor. If a cow has an itchy spot, it can saunter to an automated backscratcher. The cows have learned that this rotating stiff-bristle brush can scratch hard-to-reach places.

Whenever a cow feels the discomfort of a full udder, it can wander into a room in which robots perform milking duties 24 hours a day, with minimal human involvement. Laser-guided technology attaches the milkers to the teats, and the robots

gently extract milk without causing the stress that human intervention can. Your guide will show you the "cow cookies" that help train the animals to seek the robots when their udders need to relieve the pressure of milk.

Next you visit the barn that houses new-born calves. After the tour, you can enjoy a free scoop of Hope Acres ice cream in the store. Choose from dozens of flavors, including "God Save the Queen" and "Brown Cow."

Cost: Adults, $6; seniors, $5; students and children, $4.

Freebies: Ice cream after tour.

Video/DVD Shown: No

Reservations Needed: Yes. Reserving at least 2 weeks in advance is best.

Days and Hours: Tours available Tue–Sat 10:00 AM–3:00 PM except major holidays.

Plan to Stay: 75 minutes for tour plus time for store.

Minimum Age: No

Disabled Access: Nonmotorized wheelchairs can get through milking tour but not into calving area.

Group Requirements: One busload at a time or a maximum of 30 people (but several tours can run in sequence).

Special Information: As the farm grows, so does the tour. Guests will visit a new milk-processing plant after it starts operating.

Gift Shop: The Brown Cow Country Market sells fresh dairy products and other foods. Open Mon–Sat 8:00 AM–6:00 PM (Fri until 8:00 PM). Closed Sun and major holidays.

Directions: From York, take Rt. 74 South. From Lancaster, take Rt. 272 South to Rt. 372 West and turn right on Rt. 74 North. From I-76, take Rt. 202 South to Rt. 30 West. Turn left on Rt. 41 South, right on Rt. 372 West, left on Rt. 896, right on Rt. 372 West, and right on Rt. 74 North.

Nearby Attractions: Harley-Davidson, Herr's Snack Factory, Wolfgang Candy tours (see pages 123, 124, and 137).

Macungie Assembly Operations,
7000 Alburtis Road, Macungie, PA 18062

(610) 709-3566   www.macktrucks.com

Many Americans use the term "Mack truck" for any big truck on the highway, and the phrase "built like a Mack truck" when they mean solid and sturdy. But Mack is actually the brand name for one of the largest U.S. producers of trucks, founded by the Mack brothers in 1900. This plant makes all but four of the company's heavy-duty truck models.

The cavernous plant (just under 1 million square feet) is filled with all the sights, sounds, and smells that make factory tours fascinating. The tour guide, often a Mack retiree, enjoys explaining how the manufacturing process is constantly going through extensive quality improvements. Every step you see, from workers bolting on side-view mirrors to their guiding an 80-pound fuel tank into place, has been videotaped and studied with the scrutiny given to an Olympic athlete.

From the cab assembly line, you stroll through the warehouse and the chassis prep area, walk down the final assembly lines, and peek into the painting booths. Everywhere you look, it seems that air hoses and drills hang from the rafters. Different things may catch your attention. It could be the huge steel-frame rails that form the chassis of each truck, the moving assembly line that workers stand beside to build the cab, the massive engines, or the process used to lower and bolt the engine or the cab to the chassis.

The dynamometer is every visitor's favorite when it is in operation. To simulate road conditions, the trucks are placed on rollers that spin around at 65 miles per hour. A worker sitting in this moving-but-stationary truck tests the drive train, gauges, and electrical systems. Meanwhile, workers at another station inspect the truck's brakes, lights, and other systems.

The process for putting the tires on the rims demonstrates how truck-building has changed. In earlier times, workers used a sledge hammer to pound the tire onto the rim. Today, a worker guides the tire while a machine lifts, stretches, and rolls it snugly onto the rim. Remember to ask how Mack got the nickname "Bulldog."

Cost: Free

Freebies: No

Video/DVD Shown: Yes, videos running in gathering area prior to tour.

Reservations Needed: Yes. Need to form or join a group of at least 5 people.

Days and Hours: Tue and Fri 8:30 AM–1:00 PM. Closed holidays, last week of July, first week of August, week after Thanksgiving, and 2-week period including Christmas and New Year's. Tours are also suspended for a period of time due to the needs of the factory—which is why reservations are essential.

Plan to Stay: 1.5–2 hours.

Minimum Age: 7; specific ratios of adults to children required.

Disabled Access: Tight spaces on factory floor and in museum.

Group Requirements: 5-person minimum, with no maximum. Appreciates 3 weeks' advance notice for large groups.

Special Information: Plant can be warm during summer months. No open-toed shoes.

Gift Shop: Macungie Mack Shop sells hats, toy trucks, T-shirts, belts, pins, and more, all with the famous Mack Bulldog logo (stuffed bulldogs, too). Open Mon–Fri 8:00 AM–4:00 PM. Usually also open after tour. Mack Shop also in company's headquarters in Allentown; open Mon–Fri 10:00 AM–4:00 PM. Call (610) 709-3459 for more information.

Directions: From I-78, take Rt. 100 South. After Laidlaw school-bus parking facility on right, turn right at next traffic light, which is Alburtis Rd. Factory is ahead on left.

Nearby Attractions: Mack Museum, featuring 14 antique trucks and 80,000 photographs (call 610-266-6767); Allen Organ Company tour, almost next door (call 610-966-2202); Martin Guitar tour and Crayola FACTORY visitor center (see pages 128 and 122).

510 Sycamore Street, Nazareth, PA 18064

(610) 759-2837
(800) 345-3103

www.martinguitar.com

Ever since C. F. Martin Sr. started making guitars in 1833, Martins have been widely recognized as one of the top U.S.–made products. The company has received highest accolades from the Buy America and Made in the USA foundations. Many popular musicians use Martins, including Paul McCartney, Willie Nelson, Eric Clapton, and John Mayer. The craftsmanship you'll see on this tour demonstrates why these famous musicians are among more than 1 million satisfied Martin owners.

The guitar-making area resembles a large woodshop. Only recently have computer-operated machines (CNC) carving guitar necks in three dimension appeared, although most of the approximately 300 separate steps that go into making a Martin are done by hand. With so many things to see, the guided tour moves quickly.

Stand beside workers as they diligently bend, trim, shape, cut, glue, fit, drill, finish, sand, stain, lacquer, buff, and inspect the different woods that will become Martins. Look for the station where a craftsman uses ordinary clothespins as clamps. These distinctly low-tech devices help secure serrated strips of cedar wood along the interior edge of the guitar's curvaceous sides during the glue-drying process. This lining provides additional surface area for attaching the front and back of the body to the sides.

Craftsmen use a variety of files, carving knives, and rasps to shape, finish, and attach the neck. Notice how the dovetail neck joint is meticulously trimmed and then checked to ensure a proper fit with the body. When you view a historic Martin or play a current model in the Pickin' Parlor after the tour, you'll really appreciate the three to six months of craftsmanship required to convert rough lumber into a Martin acoustic guitar—a true American classic.

Cost: Free. Group tours, nominal charge.

Freebies: Sound-hole cut-outs; product literature.

Videos/DVDs Shown: Videos show production processes, including interviews with C. F. (Chris) Martin IV, the 6th-generation family member who oversees the company.

Reservations Needed: No, except for groups.

Days and Hours: Mon–Fri 9:00 AM–2:00 PM, best to arrive early. Closed holidays, week between Christmas and New Year's. Museum and 1833 Shop open Mon–Fri 8:30 AM–5:00 PM.

Plan to Stay: 2–3 hours, including tour, gift shop, and museum.

Minimum Age: None, for families; 12, for groups.

Disabled Access: Yes

Group Requirements: Group tours must be arranged in advance. Will split larger groups into groups of 10.

Special Information: Photography permitted without flash. No video cameras.

Gift Shops: 1833 Shop sells guitar accessories, strings, supplies, books, clothing, and other memorabilia. Nearby in the old Martin factory (10 W. North St.) is Guitarmaker's Connection (GMC), which sells acoustic guitar tone woods, kits, parts, instrument-making supplies, and construction/repair books. 1833 Shop open Mon–Fri 8:30 AM–5:00 PM. GMC open Mon–Fri 9:00 AM–4:30 PM. Combined catalog available from (610) 759-2837.

Directions: We suggest contacting Martin Guitar or visiting their website for directions from New York City and other points, and for their detailed map, "Martin Guitar Factory Tour." From Northeast Extension of Pennsylvania Tnpk., take Exit 33 to Rt. 22 East. Exit onto Rt. 191 North. In Nazareth, Rt. 191 turns left onto Broad St. Stay on Broad St. even though Rt. 191 turns right. Pass the Nazareth Boro Park, turn right onto Beil Ave., then right onto Sycamore St.

Nearby Attractions: Crayola FACTORY and Mack Trucks tour (see pages 128 and 127); Old Martin Homestead (call 610-759-9174); Allen Organ Company tour (call 610-966-2202); Moravian historical sites, including the Whitefield House in Nazareth; Lehigh Valley's attractions include Bushkill Falls, Dorney Park, and Wildwater Kingdom.

MID-ATLANTIC

Studio Park, 1200 Wilson Drive,
West Chester, PA 19380

(800) 600-9900   www.qvctours.com

While QVC (Quality, Value, Convenience) does not manufacture products, QVC is all about products—in fact, it sells them via live television, 24 hours a day, seven days a week, including some products made by companies featured in this book. The largest electronic retailer in the world, QVC welcomes you to its headquarters at Studio Park, a state-of-the-art broadcast facility on 80 wooded acres.

You'll enter a lobby that includes the 3,000-square-foot Studio Store. A tour guide will give you a brief history of this multibillion-dollar company, including the fact that it was founded in 1986 by Joseph Segel, also founder of the Franklin Mint. As you follow the tour guide, you learn that QVC is really two businesses: QVC the merchandiser, that searches for, tests, and prepares thousands of different products each year for the other business, and QVC the Network, a round-the-clock live television production.

Follow your tour guide on a route above and around the main studio, designed to demonstrate products in their natural habitats. The 20,000-square-foot studio includes the Home set, made up of a living room, a sun room, a kitchen, a garage, bedrooms, a home office, and a working fireplace. Along the way, the guide will show and tell you about some of the various areas you will see, including Sets and Props, a Quality Assurance lab, backstage areas, and the live control room. You will also see an interactive display showing how orders are taken, processed, and shipped right to you in just a few days. The product Hall of Records includes some of the best-sellers and company favorites.

The climax is the Observation Deck that juts out into the studio. Here you can watch the live show in progress and check out some up-to-date statistics on incoming calls and product sales.

By the end of the tour, you'll understand how the whole thing works, from product selection and testing to on-the-air sales, order processing, and shipping. Millions of calls come in, and millions of products are shipped out each year. You will learn about shopping on the Internet via QVC Online and about the company's ventures around the world, including Germany, the U.K., Mexico, and Japan. You might even spot one of QVC's hosts or guests, or have a chance to be part of a studio audience.

Cost: Adults, $7.50; children 6–12, $5.

Freebies: No

Videos/DVDs Shown: 3-minute video covers what QVC is, and 5-minute video shows how a product gets on the air.

Reservations Needed: No, except for groups of 10 or more. Yes, for participation in studio audiences.

Days and Hours: Mon–Sun 10:00 AM–4:00 PM, every hour on the hour.

Plan to Stay: 2 hours.

Minimum Age: Not recommended for children under 6, but they are welcome.

Disabled Access: Yes

Group Requirements: Groups of 10 or more should call for discounts.

Studio Store: Sells logoed products and a sampling of on-air merchandise, including jewelry, furniture, cosmetics, kitchen products, gourmet food, toys, and more. Open Mon–Sun 9:30 AM–6:00 PM.

Directions: From Philadelphia, take I-76 West to Rt. 202 South. Exit at Boot Rd. Turn left at light onto Boot Rd. At third light, turn right onto Wilson Dr. Go straight, cross Airport Rd., and follow the signs to the QVC Studio Tour entrance.

Nearby Attractions: Herr's Snack Factory and Sturgis Pretzel tours (see pages 124 and 133); Simon Pearce on the Brandywine restaurant and glassblowing (call 610-793-0948); American Helicopter Museum; Longwood Gardens; Brandywine River Museum; Lancaster, Philadelphia, and Wilmington attractions are about 20 miles away.

MID-ATLANTIC

1212 Smallman Street, Pittsburgh, PA 15222   (412) 454-6000   www.pghhistory.org

Vaulted ceilings, red brick walls, steel posts connected by iron braces, a 1949 trolley, an intricate mural of Pittsburgh life—this and plenty more greet you as you walk into the Great Hall of the 200,000-square-foot Smithsonian-affiliated Senator John Heinz Pittsburgh Regional History Center, the largest history museum in Pennsylvania, located in Pittsburgh's historic Strip District. Home of the Chautauqua Lake Ice Company a century ago, where a piece of track remains on which a railroad car brought ice into the building, the Center houses multiple attractions on six floors, including the five-story Smithsonian wing, opened in 2004.

Learn all about Henry J. Heinz and his company, business philosophy, and marketing genius in the "Heinz 57" exhibit, dating back to the company's beginning in 1869. See the original jars that contained horseradish—the company's first product. Note that the bottles are clear. Henry purposely packaged his products in transparent bottles so customers could witness the ingredients' purity. Competitors were using sawdust and other filler items, disguised in green bottles. Henry was determined to show that he was committed to quality.

View silver chafing dishes and cardboard spoons that well-groomed employees used to offer product samples to customers at the markets. Read an 1888 entry from Henry's diary: "Very busy—we are boiling at the rate of 1,000 bushels tomatoes for catsup daily and 300 bushels of apples for apple butter." Put on an apron and race to pack pickles into a jar, imitating the workers in the early factories.

Next, enter the "Glass: Shattering Notions" exhibit and be intrigued by what appears to be a cracked wall of glass facing you. Discover how glass is formed and the pivotal role that Western Pennsylvania played in the nation's glass industry. Enjoy countless varieties—creamers, vases, cake plates, glass doorknobs—and colors—ruby red, yellow, light blue, dark purple—of glass items surrounding you. Guess whether four particular items are glass, then flip up plastic panels to uncover the answers and a description of each product.

A sports museum-within-a-museum presents the region's remarkable sports story through hundreds of artifacts and interactive exhibits. The Special Collections gallery in the Smithsonian wing brings together a rich collection of artifacts that reflect the region's heritage, including the famous sweater, worn by the beloved Fred Rogers on *Mister Rogers' Neighborhood.*

Before you leave the Strip District, visit the unique shops and try the ethnic foods. Stop at a club and dance for a few hours. Above all, look north over the Allegheny River. Sight the friendly neon Heinz Ketchup bottle pouring its glory over the city.

Cost: Adults, $7.50; senior citizens 62+, $6, students with ID, $5; children 6–18, $3.50; children 5 and under, free; special group rates.

Freebies: No

Videos/DVDs Shown: 13-minute video introduces the 2nd-floor "Points in Time" exhibit. Additional video showing old Heinz commercials will bring back memories.

Reservations Needed: No, except for guided tours.

Days and Hours: Daily 10:00 AM–5:00 PM. Closed Easter, Thanksgiving, Christmas, New Year's.

Plan to Stay: 2.5–3 hours for self-guided tour, plus time for Museum Shop.

Minimum Age: None

Disabled Access: Yes

Group Requirements: Make reservations 2–3 weeks in advance; call (412) 454-6304.

Special Information: Self-guided or guided tours. Variety of guided tours, plus classes and teacher programs; call (412) 454-6000 for information.

Gift Shop: Museum Shop sells books, toys, jewelry, and glassware. Open same hours as Museum.

Directions: From north, take I-79 South to I-279 South to I-579. Cross Veterans Bridge. Follow signs for 7th Ave. Turn right on Grant St., left on 11th St., right on Smallman. From east (Pennsylvania Tnpk.), take Pittsburgh/Monroeville exit. Follow signs to Pittsburgh via I-376. Take Grant St. exit. After 7th Ave., turn left on 11th St., right on Smallman.

Nearby Attractions: Creegan and Homer Laughlin China tours (see pages 194 and 145); Carnegie Museums.

509 Cavitt Avenue, Trafford, PA 15085-1060

(412) 372-4331
(800) 436-5424

www.shermedwards
candies.com

Sherm Edwards
CANDIES

"Good Chocolate Is Not Cheap. Cheap Chocolate Is Not Good." The sign greets you as you embark on your tour of this 50-plus-year-old, family-owned candy manufacturer. The inescapable aroma of rich chocolate fills your nostrils as you witness Sherm Edwards's very own special blend of chocolate being mixed in 500-pound melters on the factory floor. Dark, milk, and white chocolate blends are then pumped into molds of everything from gourmet chocolate spoons (that really enhance a cup of coffee!) to three-foot-tall Easter bunnies.

As you progress through the 3,600-square-foot plant whose walls are stacked high with huge bars of raw chocolate, you notice workers, hands awash in chocolate, coating the bottoms of fruit-and-nut eggs. Conveyer belts then transport the eggs through enrobers, where chocolate cascades envelop each egg before it travels into the cooling tunnel to solidify the coating. You may even see sweet baby gherkins being dipped in mild chocolate—yes, chocolate covered pickles, a Heinz family favorite!

Another corner of the factory is the candy kitchen, packed with equipment such as 80-quart mixers, enormous copper pots for caramel making, and marble slabs for cooling fudge and jellies. Award-winning Sherm Edwards's Pecan Crisp is created here, with lots of real butter and pecans and just enough crunchy-sweet brittle to hold all the pecans together. You'll discover just how they make chocolate-covered cherries and strawberries. The liquid filling around the fruit of these cordials is produced in the panner, a machine resembling a miniature cement mixer, which spins the fruit to coat it with sugar. The fruit is then dipped in chocolate and the sugar coating liquefies, producing the syrup inside the chocolate cordials.

Cost: Free

Freebies: Various candy samples.

Video Shown: No

Reservations Needed: Yes

Days and Hours: Mon–Fri 9:00 AM–3:30 PM. Closed major holidays. Easter–mid-September, production slows to 1 or 2 days per week.

Plan to Stay: 30 minutes for tour, plus time for retail outlet store.

Minimum Age: None

Disabled Access: Retail store is accessible. Stairs lead from retail store down to factory floor.

Group Requirements: Can handle groups up to 45 people with 1 day's advance notice. Local Radisson Hotels arrange bus tours for groups staying at hotels. Group discounts on purchases.

Special Information: Candy production depends on holidays; for example, chocolate hearts produced before Valentine's Day and molded chocolate bunnies and eggs before Easter.

Retail Store: Sells chocolates, fudges, and nut brittles made on the premises, over 300 varieties of molded chocolate novelties, and hard candies and jelly beans. Open Mon–Sat 9:00 AM–5:00 PM. Call about holiday hours. Price list available.

Directions: Take I-376 East to Exit 16A. Take Rt. 48 South to Rt. 130 South to Trafford. Cross over bridge into Trafford. Take first left, then immediate right, then another right onto Cavitt Ave. Sherm Edwards Candies is on the right. From Pennsylvania Tnpk., take Exit 57 to Business Rt. 22 West to Rt. 48 South, then follow above directions.

Nearby Attractions: George Westinghouse Museum (call 412-823-0500); Pittsburgh's attractions about 30 minutes away.

MID-ATLANTIC

America's Pretzel Bakery Since 1909™

Pennsylvania is the snack-food capital of the U.S.A. Small family businesses that hand-twist pretzels and mega-companies that churn out over 400,000 pounds of pretzels and potato chips a day cover the state, particularly in the area surrounding York and Lancaster Counties.

In 1909, Gramp Harry began hand-delivering his pretzels locally. Since then, the company has grown tremendously and now supplies pretzels and other products to 43 different countries.

When you tour Snyder's state-of-the-art facility, your tour guide gives a brief introduction full of interesting facts—but can't divulge top-secret baking times, oven speeds, and formulas. Since this is a reverse-chronology tour, first follow your guide down the corridor overlooking the shipping warehouse. At the palletizer, pretzel boxes travel down the conveyor single-file and line up to make rows of three boxes, with four of these rows (12 boxes) filling each case.

Farther down the corridor, look through windows at what is probably the most automated packaging system in the snack-food industry. Machines build boxes from flat cardboard cutouts, machines fill the bags, and more machines close the boxes. Notice the two new auto case-packers in the far corner. These machines perform all the packaging steps, except for sealing the cartons.

To your left, pretzels shake along conveyor belts on their way to the form- and fill-machines. To your right, potato chips vibrate along a conveyor highway to their own set of form- and fill-machines. These stainless steel, circular machines each consist of 14 buckets that weigh and release the appropriate amount into bags that are just being formed below.

The most impressive sight on the tour is the oven room, with seven of the largest ovens in the world. As you keep walking down the hall, it seems like you'll never reach the end of these 150-foot-long, massive gray ovens. Silver exhaust stacks rise through the ceiling. Feel the heat through the windows. Pretzels travel through the upper half of each oven for baking, slide down to reverse direction, and dry or become hard and deliciously crunchy during their journey in the lower half of the oven.

Cost: Free

Freebies: Product samples.

Video/DVD Shown: No

Reservations Needed: Yes

Days and Hours: Tue–Thur 10:00 AM, 11:00 AM, and 1:00 PM.

Plan to Stay: 1 hour, plus time in outlet store.

Minimum Age: None

Disabled Access: No, for factory tour. Yes, for outlet store.

Group Requirements: Groups of 15 or more should call 1 day in advance.

Special Information: No photography.

Outlet Store: Sells 1-oz. vending machine bags to bulk 6-lb. cartons of pretzels, potato chips, and tortilla chips. Also sells decorative gift tins and logoed clothing. Open Mon–Sat 9:00 AM–6:00 PM and Sun 12:00 PM–5:00 PM. Closed holidays. Catalog available by calling (800) 233-7125, ext. 1410.

Directions: From Pennsylvania Tnpk., take I-83 South to Rt. 30 West. Take Rt. 116 West. Snyder's will be on your left. Check in for tour at outlet store counter.

Nearby Attractions: Utz Quality Foods potato chip tour in Hanover (see page 135); Harley-Davidson motorcycle and Wolfgang Candy tours (see pages 123 and 137) in York, about 1 hour away. Lancaster and Pennsylvania Dutch attractions about 1–1.5 hours away.

219 East Main Street, Lititz, PA 17543   (717) 626-4354   www.sturgispretzel.com

Pennsylvania has many large pretzel manufacturers whose tours will "wow" you with massive machines, fast-moving conveyor belts, and mind-boggling production numbers. At Sturgis Pretzel House, though, pretzel-making is more of a participatory art. The workers proudly explain that Sturgis is the first commercial pretzel bakery in the U.S.A. (opened in 1861). Housed in a restored 200-year-old building, with displays of old pretzel-making equipment and brick ovens, the company makes the tour an integral part of its business.

Playing pretzel-maker is the most fun on the tour. As you stand in front of a rolling table, your tour guide will give you a small ball of dough. You'll roll the dough into a thin pencil, pick it up from both ends, cross it to form rabbit ears, then twist the ends and pull them back to rest on the loop. As you twist your pretzel, the guide explains that the monk who invented the pretzel in AD 610 wanted to make from dough the sign of prayer, which involved crossing both arms with hands on the opposite shoulders. The three holes in a pretzel represent the Father, Son, and Holy Ghost.

You won't get rich after you receive an "Official Pretzel Twister" certificate. In the days before automation, founder Julius Sturgis paid twisters about 25 cents per thousand pretzels. Now the company manufactures most of its hard pretzels by machine. While contemporary pretzel-making seems so easy, it doesn't compare to the dexterity shown by professional pretzel twisters who hand-twist all of the soft pretzels at the end of the tour.

Cost: Adults and children 13 and older, $4; children under 3, free.

Freebies: Paper baker's hat for kids to wear during the tour and well-earned "Official Pretzel Twister" certificate.

Video/DVD Shown: No

Reservations Needed: No, except for groups of 20 or more.

Days and Hours: Open January–March: Sat only 9:30 AM–4:30 PM; April–December: Mon–Sat 9:30 AM–4:30 PM. Closed Thanksgiving, Christmas, and New Year's.

Plan to Stay: 20 minutes for tour, plus time for gift shop.

Minimum Age: None

Disabled Access: Yes

Group Requirements: Groups of 20 or more should call ahead.

Special Information: It can be hot standing near the pretzel-baking machine.

Gift Shop: Tour ends at small gift shop. You enter the pretzel house through larger store that sells gift items and pretzels, including their unique horse-and-buggy-shaped pretzels. Open January–March: Tue–Sat 9:00 AM–5:00 PM; April–December Mon–Sat 9:00 AM–5:00 PM. Closed Sunday.

Directions: From Lancaster, take Rt. 501 North to Lititz. Turn right on Main St. (Rt. 772). Sturgis Pretzel House is on the left, with big pretzel in front. From the east, take Pennsylvania Tnpk. (I-76) to Exit 21. Go south on Rt. 222 and turn right onto Rt. 772 into Lititz. Follow above directions.

Nearby Attractions: Wilbur Chocolate Candy Americana Museum (interesting exhibits, including handmade candy demonstrations and video on chocolate making, plus factory outlet; call 717-626-3249); Johannes Mueller House; Lititz Springs Park; Pennsylvania Dutch sites and Lancaster attractions all within short drive.

5th and Arch Streets,
Philadelphia, PA 19106-1886

(215) 408-0114

www.usmint.gov

We all know that money doesn't grow on trees, but do you know where 50 percent of U.S. coins come from? A tour of the Philadelphia U.S. Mint, which currently strikes approximately 8 million quarters, 4 million dimes, 1.5 million nickels, and 16 million pennies each weekday, will show you just that. Encompassing an entire city block, the world's largest mint also houses a museum of rare coins, historic medals, and antique mint machinery.

In the lobby area, see all commemorative coin designs issued since 1892 and notice the 1901 Tiffany mosaics on the walls. Press on past the displays to the glass-enclosed observation gallery above the mint factory floor. From this 300-foot-long vantage point, you witness mere strips of metal and blanks being turned into money. An awesome array of machines heats, washes, dries, sorts, edges, stamps, inspects, counts, and bags the coins that are punched out of the metal strips.

You will better understand what you see on this self-guided tour if you press the buttons to hear the taped explanations. A new video system gives visitors a close-up view of coinage production, of the designing and engraving processes, and of a special ceremony held in the mint's vault. From another area, you can see medals and special collectors' coins produced by a process similar to that used for regular coins.

In the mezzanine area, additional displays of coins and artifacts include the original coining press used at the first mint in 1792. These displays appear more interesting than the earlier ones, probably because you just saw how such coins are made. Then hurry down to the gift shop to purchase your own coins and begin your collection. Or, of course, you can just admire your spare change with your newfound knowledge.

Cost: Free

Freebies: Brochure

Videos/DVDs Shown: 7 videos show close-ups at each production stage.

Reservations Needed: No, self-guided tours available on a first-come, first-served basis.

Days and Hours: Mon–Fri 9:00 AM–3:00 PM. Closed on federal holidays. For security reasons, public tours can be suspended if there is a serious change in the national security alert status. Please check their website, as it is kept very current regarding changes in policy.

Plan to Stay: 45 minutes for self-guided tour and coin gallery, plus time for gift shop.

Minimum Age: None, but smaller children may not be able to see or understand all the displays.

Disabled Access: Yes

Group Requirements: None

Special Information: Security is very tight and visitors must pass through a metal detector. Photo IDs required for admittance. Photography, cameras, packages, strollers, umbrellas, weapons, smoking, and eating are prohibited. Check the website for a complete list of prohibited items.

Gift Shop: Sells commemorative coins and medals, as well as books on money, American history, and U.S. presidents. Mint your own souvenir medal in gift shop for $2. Open same days and hours as tour. For catalog information, call (800) USA-MINT.

Directions: From Pennsylvania, take Schuylkill Expwy. (Rt. 76 East) to Vine St. Expwy., exit right at 6th St. Go south 2 blocks and turn left onto Market St. Go 1 block and turn left onto 5th St. Go 1 block north to Arch St. Mint imposingly occupies entire right side of 5th and Arch Sts. From New Jersey, take Benjamin Franklin Bridge to Philadelphia. Take 6th St./Independence Hall exit on right, follow signs to 6th St. Turn left onto Market St. and follow above directions.

Nearby Attractions: Asher's Chocolates and Byers' Choice tours (see pages 117 and 120–121); downtown Philadelphia attractions include Independence Hall, Liberty Bell, Betsy Ross's House, Christ Church, and Benjamin Franklin's grave.

MID-ATLANTIC

900 High Street, Hanover, PA 17331

(717) 637-6644
(800) 367-7629

www.utzsnacks.com

The Hanover Home brand potato chips made by Salie and Bill Utz in 1921 at a rate of 50 pounds of chips per hour has evolved into a large regional snack-food company that produces up to 14,000 pounds of award-winning chips per hour. This self-guided tour allows you to view the entire 30-minute process that transforms a raw spud into a crunchy chip. An overhead observation gallery equipped with push-button audio and video stations lets you view the entire factory floor.

Potatoes roll and tumble like marbles past you into the peeling machine, which tosses them until the skin is removed. Peeled whole potatoes move along to the slicer, which is programmed to chop them into slices 55-1,000ths of an inch thick. The slices are bathed in 340°F cooking oil, showered with salt, and dried on long conveyors while being inspected for discoloring. Flavorings (such as barbecue or sour cream and onion) are added just before packaging.

Notice the pipes running throughout the factory, along walls and over workers' heads. These pipes carry water and oil to and from the production floor. Utz's innovative in-house recycling program uses water to eliminate most of the discarded product waste, such as unused potatoes, skins, and damaged returns. The "waste" is then sold to local farmers for animal feed, while the oil is used to make soap.

As you walk through the observation gallery, you see several Utz products traveling in different directions until they reach the packaging area. Chips are poured into giant funnels, which dump precisely measured amounts into bags of all sizes. Workers pack the bags into boxes, and Utz's almost 300 trucks transport them all over the eastern U.S. Although your potato chip trip ends above the loading area, don't forget to grab a "souvenir" bag on your way out.

Cost: Free

Freebies: Snack-size bag of potato chips.

Video/DVD Shown: 2 stations on tour show live camera shots; also a newly added theatre room runs large screen presentation of "The Story of Utz."

Reservations Needed: No, except for groups larger than 10 people.

Days and Hours: Mon–Thur 8:30 AM–4:30 PM. Call in advance for Fri schedule. Closed holidays.

Plan to Stay: 45 minutes for video and self-guided tour, plus time for nearby outlet store.

Minimum Age: None

Disabled Access: Flight of steps to observation gallery; however, all visitors are accommodated, so call ahead for assistance.

Group Requirements: Groups of 10 or more should call 2 days in advance to schedule tour guide.

Special Information: Brochure available on recycling program.

Outlet Store: Located just 2 blocks east of tour location on the corner of Carlisle St. (Rt. 94) and Clearview Rd. Find chips, pretzels, and other tasty snacks available in bags, barrels, and even decorated holiday, everyday, and popular sports tins. Look for new Gourmet All Natural kettle-cooked line of chips, chocolate-covered pretzels, and "America's best kept secret," chocolate-covered potato chips. Open Mon–Sat 8:00 AM–7:00 PM, Sun 11:00 AM–6:00 PM. Call (888) SHIP-UTZ for a free catalog.

Directions: From Harrisburg, take I-15 South to PA 94 South into Hanover. Turn right onto Clearview Rd. (outlet store is on corner). Utz potato-chip factory is straight ahead at intersection of Clearview Rd. and High St. Tour entrance is on left side of building. From Maryland, take MD 30 North (becomes PA 94) to Hanover. Turn left onto Clearview Rd. and follow directions above.

Nearby Attractions: Snyder's of Hanover tour (see page 132); Martin's Potato Chips tour (call 717-792-3565); Gettysburg about 20 minutes away.

MID-ATLANTIC

Wendell August Forge

METAL AND CRYSTAL GIFTWARE

620 Madison Avenue, Grove City, PA 16127-0109

(724) 458-8360
(800) 923-4438

www.wendell
august.com

Wendell August Forge is the oldest and largest hand forge in the country. The company that Wendell August started in 1923 with making hand-forged architectural pieces (such as railings and gates) now makes beautiful metal giftware. This self-guided tour shows you the steps in producing their individually handcrafted products, from the cutting of sheet metal to the final hammering and polishing of finished pieces.

Die engraving is the most intricate and time-consuming step. Master die engravers use only a hammer, chisels, and their own creative talents to engrave designs into steel slabs. The carved die design, sometimes taking eight weeks to complete, is the reverse of the actual image. Try to find the engraver's initials on the die; they're cleverly hidden in the design.

Your ears alert you to the hammering area. Watch craftspeople carefully clamp down a blank piece of aluminum or bronze over the design. They use specially designed hammers to force the metal into the die's carved-out portions, creating a raised image on the other side. One moment it's a flat piece of metal, and the next you see the detailed image of an eagle soaring gracefully over a rocky canyon.

After this initial hammering, the piece moves to an anvil to be flattened, anviled, and edged before the remarkable "coloring" process occurs. Each metal piece is placed face down onto a specially grated screen and held over an open fire in an early-1930s forge. The fire's black smoke bakes onto the piece. After cooling, special polishing removes 97 percent of the baked-on smoke, leaving just enough color to highlight the design. Although Wendell August artisans never produce two identical pieces of giftware, their hallmark and company logo on the back of each item attest to its quality.

Cost: Free

Freebies: Brochure and map; catalog available upon request.

Video/DVD Shown: 7-minute video provides close-up view of production steps.

Reservations Needed: No, but recommended for groups of 15 or more.

Days and Hours: November–January: Mon–Fri 9:00 AM–8:00 PM, Sat 9:00 AM–5:00 PM, Sun 11:00 AM–5:00 PM; January–November: Mon–Fri 9:00 AM–2:30 PM. When not in production, see manufacturing process video in gift shop; may be able to view work area.

Plan to Stay: 20 minutes for self-guided tour, plus time for video and gift shop.

Minimum Age: None for families, above elementary-school age for groups.

Disabled Access: Yes

Group Requirements: Welcomes any size group. Recommends 1 week's advance notice for groups larger than 15.

Special Information: You may talk with the craftspeople but, for your own safety, do not touch any metal in production. In heart of Amish Country, Berlin, OH, plant tour (call 330-893-3713) features production tours, museum, and theater.

Gift Shop: Store and showroom display all Wendell August handmade items, including intricately designed coasters, plates, serving pieces, trays, and Christmas ornaments, plus other unique gift items. Open same hours as above except January–November: Mon–Thur 9:00 AM–6:00 PM, Fri 9:00 AM–8:00 PM. Catalog available from numbers above. Gift shop also has LGB model train suspended overhead on 200 feet of track and authentic nickelodeon.

Directions: From I-79, take Exit 113. Follow blue and white signs. From I-80, take Exit 24. Follow signs.

Nearby Attractions: Daffin's Chocolate Factory tour (call 724-342-2892 or 877-323-3465); Troyer Farms Potato Chips tour (call 800-458-0485).

Wolfgang Candy

50 East 4th Avenue, York, PA 17404

(717) 843-5536
(800) 248-4273

www.wolfgang
candy.com

The English Tudor Das Sweeten Haus Center provides your first flavor of Wolfgang Candies. Inside, you get a true sense of family history and involvement in the business. Started in 1921, this fourth-generation family business makes most of its candies for fundraisers. The brown 1926 Model T parked inside the Tudor structure runs on chocolate instead of gas. Notice old company invoices as well as a soda fountain.

Walk on a quiet residential street past R. Wolfgang's house. You enter Building 3 and don a hair net to watch their popular peanut butter marshmallow candies being made. Mixers swirl and stir peanut butter or marshmallow. First, marshmallow drops into molds made from cornstarch. Next the peanut butter drops over the marshmallow. Chocolate coats the whole delicacy. Walk by the taffy pull machine. Four rollers twist peanut butter swirls into peanut butter kisses. Walk downstairs and next to the long white enrober machine that covers fillings with a chocolate waterfall followed by a 10 to 15 minute journey through the 55 to 65°F cooling tunnel.

In the kitchen, two workers pour boiling peanut brittle mixture from a big copper kettle onto a cooling table. The workers, using bendable spatulas, spread the peanut brittle mixture across the table. One of the workers runs a sword underneath the mixture to prevent it from sticking to the table. Water running inside this metal table cools the mixture. Another worker rolls a metal rolling pin with blades to score the candy so that it will break into even pieces.

Corn syrup is stored in tanks above Building 3. Inside, a 40,000-gallon tank stores chocolate at 110 to 115°F. Much of the candy is hand packed. Along the assorted line, candies are placed in proper order on a grid. Computer sorting provides efficiencies for fundraiser candies. Before Easter, you may see them making their famous chocolate-covered peanut butter eggs.

Cost: Free

Freebies: Small bag of chocolates and hard candies.

Video/DVD Shown: 25-minute video covers candy production.

Reservations Needed: No, except groups larger than 10.

Days and Hours: Visitor Center: Mon–Fri 8:00 AM–5:00 PM, Sat 9:00 AM–4:00 PM. Factory tours: Mon–Fri 10:00 AM. Sat tours by appointment. Closed some holidays.

Plan to Stay: 40 minutes, plus additional time for Das Sweeten Haus and Wolfgang Sweet Shoppe.

Minimum Age: None, but must have 1 adult for each child under 6.

Disabled Access: Yes for Das Sweeten Haus Center and Building 2's first floor, 16 steps for Building 3.

Group Requirements: Groups over 10 people should schedule appointment 2 weeks in advance by calling (800) 248-4273 ext.112. Maximum group size is 50 people.

Special Information: Full production September–Easter. June Manufacturers' Day offers the opportunity to tour many York-area factories.

Gift Shop: Wolfgang Sweet Shoppe sells hand-dipped raisin clusters (watch as they are made Mon–Fri 7:00 AM–3:30 PM), peanut butter petals, chocolate-covered pretzelettes, nonpareils, and more. Open same hours as the Visitor Center.

Directions: From I-83, take North George St. exit. Turn right onto North George St. Turn left onto 4th Ave. From I-30 West, turn left onto North George St. Turn left on 4th Ave.

Nearby Attractions: As "factory tour capital of the world," many York-area factories offer tours or museums including Harley-Davidson motorcycles (see page 123); York Barbell Museum (call 717-767-6481), Martin's Potato Chips tour (call 717-792-3565), and Naylor Wines tour (call 800-292-3370); Industrial and Agricultural Museum (call 717-846-6452); Central Market House.

America's Oldest Brewery

Since 1829

Yuengling is the oldest brewery in the United States. Its heritage is even older, drawing on centuries of German beer-making traditions. David Yuengling, one of many German immigrants who shaped Pennsylvania during the 19th century, founded his brewery in 1829. Although fire destroyed it only two years later, he constructed a new brewery in 1831. The historic brick building still stands near downtown Pottsville in the heart of the state's coal region.

Visitors gather in the bar area for a tour, which starts with an account of the brewery's history and the beer-making process. The next step takes you into the brewing plant itself alongside the workers. (The tour involves climbing 170 stairs, so be prepared for a workout.)

The tour focuses on the four giant metal tanks, called kettles, in which the brewers create all the Yuengling beers. The cereal cooker combines water, corn, and malt. In the vat called the mash tun, the brewers add more malt. The lauter separates the grain from the liquid, which by now is known as wort, the base of all beer. Hops join the wort in the brew kettle. Throughout, the aroma of cooking grain fills the nostrils.

The brew cools and then moves to the fermentation stage. Yeast, the universal catalyst of beer making, enters the process. Over time, it eats sugars in the mixture to produce alcohol and carbon dioxide. After the brewers filter the liquor to give it a crisp and clear appearance, it goes to the bottling line. You go with it to watch the machinery fill the bottles with bright fresh beer.

Before the tour ends with a well-earned free tasting, you visit the historic "cave" underneath the building. Lined by stone walls that workers built by hand in 1831, this perpetually cool cellar served the purposes of fermenting and aging beer before modern climate controls.

Cost: Free, except groups of 15 or more. Groups up to 25 people pay $25; groups over 25 pay $1 per person on weekdays and $2 per person on weekends.

Freebies: Tastings after the tour. For visitors under 21, birch beer is available.

Video/DVD Shown: No

Reservations Needed: No, except groups of 15 or more.

Days and Hours: Mon–Fri 10:00 AM and 1:30 PM; Sat (Apr–Dec only) 11:00 AM, 12:00 PM, and 1:00 PM. Closed New Year's, Memorial Day weekend, July 4th, Labor Day weekend, Thanksgiving, Christmas.

Plan to Stay: At least 1.5 hours (tour is 75 minutes).

Minimum Age: None for the tour; 21 to taste.

Disabled Access: No

Group Requirements: Groups of 15 or more need special arrangements.

Special Information: A smaller location in Tampa, FL (call 813-972-8529), offers tours Mon–Fri 10:00 AM and 1:00 PM.

Gift Shop: The Yuengling Gift Shop sells glassware, bar accessories, apparel, books, and signs. The shop also features a museum of historical items from the early years of the brewery. Open Mon–Fri 9:00 AM–4:00 PM; Sat 10:00 AM–3:00 PM. Closed New Year's, Memorial Day weekend, July 4th, Labor Day weekend, Thanksgiving, Christmas.

Directions: From Philadelphia, take I-476 to I-78/Rt. 22 West and then Rt. 61 North. In Pottsville, turn left at Mauch Chunk St., right on South Centre, left on Mahantongo. Brewery is on left. From Harrisburg, take I-81 to Rt. 125 East and then Rt. 209 East, which becomes West Market St. Turn right on Fifth. Brewery is on right.

Nearby Attractions: Jerry's Classic Cars & Collectibles Museum; Jewish Museum of Eastern Pennsylvania; Schuylkill County Historical Society Museum.

Zippo/Case Visitors Center
LIGHTERS AND KNIVES

1932 Zippo Drive, Bradford, PA 16701

(814) 368-1932
(888) 442-1932

www.zippo.com

Located in the wooded hills of northwestern Pennsylvania, the Zippo/Case Visitors Center commands attention from the moment you enter the curving drive flanked by 14 custom made Zippo street lighters. Your eye is drawn first to an enormous three-bladed Case Canoe pocketknife topping the entrance of the building, and then upward to an imposing 40-foot Zippo lighter with a flickering neon flame.

The doors open directly into the Zippo/Case store. Straight across the store, two massive reproductions of chrome Zippo lighters beckon you into the museum, with its open ceiling and colorful exhibits. Take a few minutes to study the time line on the wall to your left, which contains photographs, video clips, and interesting factoids about Zippo, Case, Bradford, and the world. Next to the time line, you'll see the famous Zippo lighter American flag, consisting of 3,393 red, white, and blue Zippo lighters.

Begin your self-guided tour by watching the introductory video in the theater on your right. The maze of exhibits leads through an interactive station full of information about U.S. and Canadian geography as shown on the surface of Zippo lighters. A WWII exhibit features a tableau of a military foxhole and a wall display of letters to George Blaisdell, the founder of Zippo, from commanders including Eisenhower and MacArthur. "Zippo in the Movies" highlights more than 1,000 documented appearances of Zippo lighters on the big screen. The largest exhibit is framed by a huge glass wall, where you can observe the Zippo Repair Clinic in operation. Zippo technicians repair approximately 1,000 lighters per day; follow the process of these repairs, and you will truly appreciate Zippo's legendary guarantee: "It works, or we fix it free."

Continue through striking displays of rare historic Case knives, including a mesmerizing "knife in motion" hologram. The grand finale of the tour is ZAC ("Zippo And Case"), a seven-foot-high audio kinetic sculpture. Colorful, pool-size balls plop, ting, bang,

and ring their way through a dynamic obstacle course, delighting adults and children alike.

Cost: Free

Freebies: No

Video/DVD Shown: 9-minute video on Zippo/Case history and products, and shorter clips at exhibits.

Reservations Needed: No, except for groups over 12 people.

Days and Hours: Visitors Center: Mon–Sat 9:00 AM–5:00 PM, Thur until 7:00 PM; June–December also Sun 11:00 AM–4:00 PM. Repair Center: Mon–Fri 9:00 AM–3:30 PM. Closed major holidays.

Plan to Stay: 1–2 hours for video and guided tour, museum, and Repair Center, plus time for gift shop.

Minimum Age: None, for families; 5th grade, for groups.

Disabled Access: Yes

Group Requirements: Groups of 12 or more should call 1 week in advance (call 814-368-2700). Maximum group size is 65. Groups receive gift bags. Free bus parking.

Special Information: The 1947 Zippo Car "lives" at the Visitors Center when it's not traveling; its travel schedule is accessible via the website. 20 percent discount offered to members of the Zippo Click Collectors Club. Zippo/Case International Swap Meet is held every other July (even numbered years) on the grounds of the Center.

Gift Shop: The Zippo/Case Store carries the full line of Zippo and Case products, including sunglasses and watches, as well as T-shirts, hats, and special Italian leather products unavailable anywhere else in the U.S. Open same hours as Visitors Center.

Directions: Take I-86 to U.S. 219 South, follow to Bradford. When U.S. 219 South ends, turn right. Proceed to intersection (4-way stop). Yield to right. After a quarter mile, bear right at fork. Follow the signs to the Visitors Center.

Nearby Attractions: Northern Lights Candles Factory tour (call 800-836-8797); Allegheny National Forest; Kinzua Bridge State Park; Knox Kane Railroad; Allegheny Arms and Armor Museum; Penn-Brad Oil Museum; Eldred WWII Museum; Holiday Valley Ski Resort; Seneca Allegany Casino.

MID-ATLANTIC

For a taste of Southern hospitality and mouth-watering pound cake, stop by Rowena's in Norfolk. Rowena's began in 1983, when friends and family urged Rowena Fullinwider to sell her jams and cakes, which were already favorite gifts and charity bake-sale items. Today, Rowena's is a million-dollar business that ships its foods nationwide and overseas.

Your tour begins in Rowena's retail store. Within the maze of its compact operation, you'll see every stage of production. As you enter the kitchen, enjoy the sweet smell of Carrot Jam (a Rowena's specialty) or the zesty scent of Heavenly Curry Sauce. Watch a cook drain jam from the mixing bowl by turning a faucet at the bottom or stir up a Lemon Curd Sauce with a three-foot whisk.

Your appetite will be further whetted in the next room, where cakes are made. Most of the equipment will be familiar to anyone who cooks, but on a grander scale. You could curl up in one of the two extra-large mixers (originally they belonged to the sailing vessel U.S.S. *United States*), and you could make a meal licking one of their huge beaters. Rowena's cooks are especially proud of the two enormous six-shelved rotating ovens. Look inside the window and watch 25 large cakes or 250 small loaf cakes take an hour's ride on the Ferris-wheel racks.

After baking and cooling, the cakes are hand-wrapped and decorated with ribbon. Workers also label all sauce and jam jars with flowery stick-on labels. While this room may be quiet when you visit, it's a scene of round-the-clock action during the busy holiday season. Finally you'll be able to taste any of Rowena's foods available. As you savor pound cake with Raspberry Curd or sample Peach Orange Clove Jam, you will appreciate the TLC that goes into Rowena's products.

Cost: Free

Freebies: "I toured Rowena's" paper hat and lots of samples.

Video/DVD Shown: No

Reservations Needed: Yes

Days and Hours: January–September only: Mon–Wed 9:00 AM–3:00 PM. Closed holidays.

Plan to Stay: 30 minutes, plus time in gift shop and tearoom.

Minimum Age: No

Disabled Access: Yes

Group Requirements: Maximum group size is 25 people. Call 1 week in advance.

Special Information: Factory gets hot during warm months.

Gift Shop: Sells Rowena's entire line, including Almond, Lemon, and Coconut Pound Cakes, Lemon Curd Sauce, and Heavenly Curry Sauce. Look for seasonally updated recipe leaflets and two children's story cookbooks, *The Adventures of Rowena and the Wonderful Jam and Jelly Factory* and *The Adventures of Rowena and Carrot Jam the Rabbit,* and her new book *Celebrate Virginia,* 400 years of Virginia history and recipes from the entire state. Open year-round Mon–Fri 8:30 AM–5:00 PM. Catalog and information available at above number.

Tearoom: Charming English tearoom serves Rowena's treats on silver-tiered trays with perfectly brewed tea. Open Mon–Fri 11:00 AM–4:00 PM, Sat 11:00 AM–3:00 PM.

Directions: Since street names change frequently, please pay close attention to directions. From Virginia Beach Expwy., take I-64 or I-264 to Waterside Dr. (becomes Boush St.). Turn left on 22nd St. Rowena's is on right at the end of the street. From Richmond, take Granby St. exit. Pass the Virginia Zoological Park on the left and follow Granby St. when it veers to the right. Take a right on 22nd St. Rowena's is at the end of 22nd St. on right.

Nearby Attractions: Chrysler Museum of Art; Waterside; Nauticus Maritime Museum; Norfolk Botanical Garden; Virginia Zoological Park; Hunter House Victorian Museum; Hermitage Foundation Museum; Virginia Beach and Colonial Williamsburg are less than 45 minutes away.

Williamsburg Doll Factory's showroom instantly transports you to a fanciful world of Victorian weddings and Civil War–era Southern teas. This is the world of Margaret Anne Rothwell and her Lady Anne porcelain dolls.

Margaret Anne's mother taught her to make doll clothing as a child in Belfast, Ireland. When she moved to the U.S., she made dolls for her own daughters. Friends and family urged her to go into business and, in 1977, she began making dolls in her home. Her first business milestone came when her dolls were accepted by theme parks such as Busch Gardens and Walt Disney World. In 1980, she began making porcelain dolls that became very popular; to meet the demand, she moved to her present location. A deal with the QVC shopping network has led to even more success.

Margaret Anne designs each doll's concept. The dress is most important because it determines the doll's complexion, hair color, and style. In the porcelain department, Margaret Anne's son David and other artists create molds, mix porcelain slip, paint, and kiln-fire heads and body parts. Through an observation window, you'll watch them carefully paint doll faces. Completed doll parts are strung with elastic to allow jointlike movement.

Some dolls have porcelain bodies as well as heads and limbs, while others have a "composite" body of latex and clay (a modern version of the glue-and-papier-mâché composite of antique dolls). Every material used in Lady Anne dolls, except some wigs and eyes, is made in the U.S.A.

You can also observe the finishing department operations. Watch a craftsperson glue individual eyelashes onto a doll's face, fit a doll's dress, or crown a doll with a wig of golden curls. After being dressed and inspected, these enchanting dolls are matched with a certificate of authenticity and shipped to a collector who will treasure their quality and beauty.

Cost: Free

Freebies: No

Video/DVD Shown: No

Reservations Needed: No, unless groups larger than 30 people want guided tour.

Days and Hours: Mon–Fri 9:00 AM–5:30 PM, except during 12:00 PM–1:00 PM lunch. Factory does no weekend production; however, you can view workstations. Closed Thanksgiving, Christmas, and New Year's.

Plan to Stay: 20 minutes for self-guided tour through observation windows, plus time in retail store.

Minimum Age: None, but children must be kept off doll displays.

Disabled Access: Yes

Group Requirements: Groups larger than 30 should call 1 week in advance to arrange for tour guide, maybe even Margaret Anne herself.

Special Information: No photography.

Retail Store: Sells limited edition Lady Anne and other collectible dolls, and doll parts for hobbyists. Open Mon–Fri 9:00 AM–5:30 PM (6:00 PM in summer), Sat 9:00 AM–6:00 PM, Sun 10:00 AM–5:00 PM. Closed Thanksgiving, Christmas, and New Year's.

Directions: From I-64, take Exit 231A (Norge exit). Take Hwy. 607 in the direction that exit lets you off. Turn left onto Richmond Rd. (Rt. 60). Doll Factory is on right. From I-95, take I-295 South to I-64 East. Follow above directions.

Nearby Attractions: Williamsburg Pottery (see page 142); Colonial Williamsburg; Busch Gardens; James River Plantations; Richmond Road, "the Discount Boulevard of Virginia."

MID-ATLANTIC

Route 60, Lightfoot, VA 23090

(757) 564-3326

www.williamsburg
pottery.com

Williamsburg Pottery Factory is a sprawling, 200-acre monument to America's love of discount shopping, annually attracting over 3.5 million visitors—more than Colonial Williamsburg and Busch Gardens combined. Within the 32 buildings and outlet stores, you'll find everything and anything: jewelry, gourmet foods, Oriental rugs, furniture, shoes, plants, imports from around the world, lawn Madonnas, cookware, and pottery. You can also tour the main factories—pottery/ceramics and floral design.

The Pottery's nearly 2 million square feet of factory and retail space took nearly 60 years to complete—and it's still growing. It all began in 1938 when James E. Maloney bought the first half acre of land, dug a well, built his kiln and a one-room shack for his young wife and himself, and set up his roadside pottery stand. "Jimmy," as he's always been known in these parts, is first, last, and always a potter. He worked closely with Colonial Williamsburg's archeologists and ceramics experts during that colonial capital's restoration by John D. Rockefeller. In 1952, The Pottery became licensed to make and sell replicas of Colonial Williamsburg's 18th-century salt-glaze and redware. This helped The Pottery grow.

In the pottery/ceramics factory, potters create thousands of pots and decorative home accessories by hand and with molds. Eighteenth-century-style salt-glaze and slipware is made, glazed, and fired here in the giant kiln. Highlights include seeing old-fashioned clay tavern pipes and the famous Williamsburg "Bird Bottle" birdhouses being made. Although signs posted in the workshop provide the basics, the craftspeople are happy to explain their work.

While The Pottery was once known mostly for its pottery, many other things are now made here. In floral design production, designers create arrangements of native Williamsburg dried flowers and plants grown right at The Pottery. Among the numerous retail stores are greenhouse, cactus, silk-flower arranging, and lamp production areas. You leave feeling that you've had a potpourri of experiences.

Cost: Free

Freebies: No

Video/DVD Shown: No

Reservations Needed: No

Days and Hours: Pottery/ceramics factory: Mon–Fri 9:00 AM–4:30 PM, with short breaks at 10:00 AM, 12:00 PM, and 2:00 PM. Grounds: Mon–Sun sunup to sundown. Closed Christmas.

Plan to Stay: 1 hour for self-guided tours, plus hours for shopping.

Minimum Age: None

Disabled Access: Yes

Group Requirements: Group tours available by advance arrangement with Marketing Department.

Special Information: Wear comfortable walking shoes and watch where you walk.

Outlet Shops: Pottery's shops sell nearly everything. Shops are rustic, but prices are great. Open Sun–Fri 9:00 AM–6:30 PM, Sat 9:00 AM–7:00 PM. Shorter hours January–April. Closed Christmas.

Directions: From I-64, take Exit 234A for Lightfoot. Turn right on Hwy. 199. Turn right at first traffic light. After first stop sign, go through back entrance to grounds. Follow driveway around. After second stop sign, ceramic factory will be on your right. From I-95 South, take I-64 East; follow above directions.

Nearby Attractions: Williamsburg Doll Factory tour (see page 141); Colonial Williamsburg; Busch Gardens; James River Plantations.

Fair Grounds Road, Milton, WV 25541

(304) 743-9081
(800) 4BLENKO

www.blenkoglass.com

BLENKO GLASS COMPANY, INC.

At Blenko Glass, you will see a three- to four-inch diameter "gob" of molten glass transformed into a foot-high water vase or pitcher right before your eyes. This self-guided tour allows you to stand behind a wooden railing and observe glassmaking for as long as you want. Only a few yards away, workers hold yard-long blowpipes, or "punties," with red-hot glass at the end. You'll feel the heat gushing out of the furnaces. Although there are no signs to explain the glassblowing process, you will quickly figure out the steps by their artful repetition.

It takes six people and about five minutes to initially shape each item. A "gatherer" delivers a glass gob to a blower seated at a workbench. The blower, who has at least eight years of experience, rolls the punty along the arms of his workbench with his left hand and cups the glass into a wooden scoop-shaped block held in his right. The blower constantly twirls the punty to keep the glass from sagging. Then he lowers it into a hand-carved cherry wood mold and blows air into the punty's opposite end so the glass fills up the mold. Another craftsperson then gently kicks the mold's clamps open and, with a two-pronged pitchfork, carries the translucent object to the finisher. After several more steps, which require reheating, the finished piece is allowed to cool.

Walk through the museum on the second floor as you make your way to the observation area, and learn about Blenko's history. The company started in 1893 to manufacture stained glass for windows but has since diversified. Exhibits include some of Blenko's custom products, such as green and crystal glass buttons made for Miss West Virginia in the 1960s, a paperweight commemorating George Bush's inauguration, and the Country Music Award Trophy. In the Designer's Corner, stained-glass windows made by nine leading American studios glow in the sunlight.

Outside, the "Garden of Glass" affords a relaxing stroll along a gravel walkway lined with stone benches and a menagerie of glass animals. Walk over the wooden footbridge, alongside a fountain, to a peaceful three-acre lake. You'll want to end your tour at the adjacent outlet store, which offers great values on Blenko glass.

Cost: Free

Freebies: No

Video/DVD Shown: No

Reservations Needed: No, except for groups larger than 50 people.

Days and Hours: Mon–Fri 8:00 AM–12:00 PM and 12:30 PM–3:00 PM to watch craftspeople. Days and times vary. Please call number above to confirm. Plant is closed for 2 weeks beginning around July 1 and week between Christmas and New Year's.

Plan to Stay: 30 minutes for self-guided tour and museum, plus time for outlet store.

Minimum Age: None, but children must be supervised.

Disabled Access: Yes, for outlet store and "Garden of Glass." However, flight of stairs leads to museum and observation gallery.

Group Requirements: Groups larger than 50 should call ahead to avoid time conflicts with other groups.

Special Information: Due to furnaces, observation deck is hot in summer.

Factory Outlet/Museum: Store's tables are crammed with various colored vases, seconds, discontinued items, and bargains. Store and museum hours: Mon–Sat 8:00 AM–4:00 PM and Sun 12:00 PM–4:00 PM. Days and times vary. Please call number above to confirm. Catalog also available at above number.

Directions: Take I-64 to Exit 28, then Rt. 60 West. Turn left at traffic light onto Fair Grounds Rd. Follow signs to Blenko Glass Visitor Center.

Nearby Attractions: Gibson Glass, makers of multicolored paperweights, offers self-guided tour (call 304-743-5232); October West Virginia Pumpkin Festival; Camden Park; Berryhill House and Gardens & Craft Center.

MID-ATLANTIC

420 Caroline Avenue, Williamstown, WV 26187 | (304) 375-7772 (800) 319-7793 | www.fenton artglass.com

F E N T O N

Handcrafted American Glass Artistry

In western West Virginia—rich in mountains, sand, and natural gas—the art and traditions of glassmaking are kept alive by a handful of artisans and factories. Fenton Art Glass began in 1905, when two Fenton brothers pooled $284 to start their business. Now in its fourth generation of family ownership and management, Fenton Art Glass continues this art in the U.S.A. The tour takes you from the extreme heat and speed of the glassmaking shops to the decorating area's exacting calm.

After a brief chemistry lesson (sand is the main ingredient in glass), follow your guide onto the glassmaking shop floor. Gatherers and carriers can be seen with gobs of red-hot glass, handles, and newly blown or pressed pieces. Each worker, trained by apprenticeship, has a specific function in the team effort of creating each item. To produce a bowl, the "gatherer" rolls the long pole (punty) inside the 2,200°F furnace to gather a gob of glass, which is dropped into a bowl-shaped mold. The presser, one of the most experienced craftsmen in the shop, lowers a lever with exacting pressure, forcing molten glass into a decorative bowl.

Downstairs in the decorating area, fresh-air-masked artisans paint crushed 22-karat gold onto glass items of all kinds. Elsewhere in the decorating area, artists paint designs on glass using crushed-glass pigments. When applying floral designs, an artist first paints the blossoms on a dozen pieces, returning later to add leaves and stems. You gain an appreciation for the steps involved in producing tomorrow's heirlooms.

Cost: Free

Freebies: Brochure on glassmaking.

Video/DVD Shown: "Experience Fenton," 22-minute video in Museum Theater, covers the basics of glass production, company history, and hand carving of cast-iron molds.

Reservations Needed: No, except for groups larger than 20 people.

Days and Hours: Mon–Fri starting at 8:15 AM. Approximately nine 35–40 minute tours offered, except on major holidays. Limited factory tours for two weeks starting late June or early July. Call (800) 319-7793 or visit www.fentongiftshop.com for exact tour times.

Plan to Stay: 2 hours, including tour, video, and museum, plus time for gift shop. Museum emphasizes a century of Fenton Glass (1905–2005) and historic Ohio Valley glass. Museum has same hours as gift shop.

Minimum Age: 2. Supervise children carefully, since you get very close to the hot glass.

Disabled Access: Blowing/pressing area, gift shop, and museum are accessible. Stairs to decorating department.

Group Requirements: Groups of 20 or more need advance reservations.

Special Information: Wear closed-toe, thick-soled shoes. Glassblowing area is well ventilated but hot during summer. Watch where you walk.

Gift Shop and Factory Outlet: Sells Fenton's first-quality line at suggested retail, as well as retired, first-quality, and preferred seconds at reduced prices. Also carries other fine gift and home décor items. Museum sells glassmaking history books. Annual February Gift Shop Sale and Summer Tent Sale. Open Mon–Sat 8:00 AM– 5:00 PM, Sun 12:00 PM–5:00 PM. Additional hours April–December: Mon–Fri open until 8:00 PM. Closed New Year's, Easter, Thanksgiving, and Christmas. Catalog available through telephone or website.

Directions: From I-77, take Exit 185; follow black-and-white signs to gift shop. From Rt. 50, take I-77 North. Follow directions above.

Nearby Attractions: Lee Middleton Original Doll factory tour (see page 199); Blennerhassett Island; Historic Marietta, OH, across Ohio River.

See color photos, page 12.

6th and Harrison Streets, Newell, WV 26050

(304) 387-1300
(800) 452-4462

www.hlchina.com

Since its beginnings in 1871, Homer Laughlin has grown into the nation's largest manufacturer of restaurant china. Its bright-colored Fiesta tableware, introduced in 1936, is the most collected china pattern in the world. On this tour of one of the most automated pottery factories in the U.S.A., you observe three ways of shaping clay, plus the glazing, firing, and decorating processes.

Your tour starts with a talk in the museum room. Glance at the displays on the walls showing discontinued patterns, including Virginia Rose scalloped-edge plates.

As you walk through this mile-long factory, notice the maze of pipes along the ceiling, the tracks along the floor on which the kiln cars travel, and the row upon row of gray stacked plates, cups, and bowls waiting to enter the kiln. Hear the sounds of dishes rattling together. Watch as automatic jiggers form round plates at a rate of 400 to 500 dozen per day. Ram presses squeeze slabs of clay between two plaster dies to create such irregular shapes as slanted sides, squared corners, and ovals. The top die is pressed into the bottom die under 2,200 pounds per square inch of pressure. In the casting process, liquid clay, known as slip, is poured into plaster molds. The slip dries in the shape of the mold. Cup handles are formed in tree molds of six to eight handles. A machine trims and prepares them for individual hand attachment to each cup.

A spray machine showers liquid glaze onto the dry pottery called greenware. Once glazed, each piece is loaded by hand onto the shelves of a kiln car. Robotics is used to stack a filled kiln car automatically into the largest fast-fire kiln in the industry.

After the short 11-hour journey (it used to take 48 hours) through this 2,400°F, 350-foot-long tunnel kiln, the computer directs each kiln car back to its initial workstation. Presses stamp the Homer Laughlin trademark onto the bottom of each piece. In the decorating department, pattern decals are hand-applied. Workers slide the water-soaked decals onto individual cups and plates and push out air bubbles with small hard-rubber squeegees. Decorative lines are painted on by hand or machine, using a silk-screen pattern, before another firing in the decorating kiln, this time for only 59 minutes. Pieces are shipped out as soon as they're finished, to the tune of 500,000 pieces of china per week.

Cost: Free

Freebies: Souvenir ceramic plate.

Video/DVD Shown: Yes

Reservations Needed: Yes

Days and Hours: Mon–Fri 10:30 AM and 12:30 PM. Closed holidays.

Plan to Stay: 1 hour, plus time in outlet store.

Minimum Age: 10

Disabled Access: No

Group Requirements: No

Special Information: Photography allowed in museum only. Areas near kilns are quite warm in summer.

Outlet Store: Sells first- and second-quality of entire product line, including Fiesta dinnerware. Open Mon–Sat 9:30 AM–5:00 PM, Sun 12:00 PM–5:00 PM. Closed major holidays.

Directions: From Pittsburgh, take Rt. 30 West to Chester, WV. Turn left at end of exit ramp and then left onto Rt. 2 South for 2 miles; factory is on right. From Youngstown, take Rt. 11 South to East Liverpool. Follow signs to Newell Toll Bridge. Once on bridge, follow signs to Homer Laughlin.

Nearby Attractions: Creegan Company and Senator John Heinz Pittsburgh Regional History Center tours (see pages 194 and 130); East Liverpool Museum of Ceramics; Mountaineer Race Track and Gaming Resort.

MID-ATLANTIC

Great Lakes

CANADA

MINNESOTA

POLARIS
CHRISTIAN BROTHERS

ARCTIC CAT

3M BIRTHPLACE MUSEUM
Duluth
STORA ENSO

Lake Superior

M I C H I G A N

HILLESTAD
PHARMACEUTICALS

HOEGH INDUSTRIES

KILWIN'S
CHOCOLATES

Lake Huron

WISCONSIN

ANDERSEN WINDOWS

Minneapolis

WISCONSIN DAIRY
STORA ENSO

Green Bay

AMON ORCHARDS

Toronto

FARIBAULT WOOLEN MILLS

NATURAL OVENS

KOHLER

Lake Michigan

SPAM MUSEUM

CARR VALLEY
CHEESE

ALLEN-EDMONDS

ALTICOR

NY

TREK BICYCLES
Madison

Milwaukee
MILLER BREWING

QUALITY CANDY/BUDDY SQUIRREL
HARLEY-DAVIDSON

Lansing
WALTER P CHRYSLER MUSEUM
LIONEL

GENERAL MOTORS

HONEY
ACRES

Detroit
FORD ROUGE FACTORY TOUR
HENRY FORD MUSEUM

GREAT AMERICAN POPCORN COMPANY

HAEGER POTTERIES
LONG GROVE CONFECTIONERY

DEKLOMP
VELDHEER

KELLOGG'S
CEREAL CITY USA

CHELSEA
MILLING

MALLEY'S
CHOCOLATES

SCHWEBEL BAKING
COMPANY

IOWA

SC JOHNSON
JELLY BELLY CENTER

Chicago

SIMPLICITY
PATTERN

Toledo
Cleveland

PA

CHICAGO MERCANTILE EXCHANGE
CHICAGO BOARD OF TRADE
CHICAGO TRIBUNE
ELI'S CHEESECAKE WORLD
US POST OFFICE
MCDONALD'S #1 STORE

WALTER PIANO

JAYCO
COACHMEN
AMISH HERITAGE FURNITURE

CAROUSEL
MAGIC!

HOOVER HISTORICAL CENTER
HARRY LONDON CANDIES

Des Moines

JOHN DEERE PAVILION
JOHN DEERE

MONACO COACH
CORPORATION

SECHLER'S

LONGABERGER

CREEGAN

Omaha

CATERPILLAR

BERNE FURNITURE

AIRSTREAM

MOSSER
GLASS

Lincoln

MITSUBISHI MOTORS
NORTH AMERICA

KOKOMO OPALESCENT GLASS

AUNT MILLIE'S BAKERIES

KITCHENAID

Columbus
VELVET ICE CREAM
AMERICAN WHISTLE
ANTHONY-THOMAS

ILLINOIS

INDIANA

INTERNATIONAL

LEE MIDDLETON
ORIGINAL DOLLS

NEBRASKA

*see Heartland
page 277*

Springfield

Indianapolis

Dayton

OHIO

VIRGINIA

Bloomington

Charleston

KANSAS

Jefferson City

St Louis

Frankfort

Lexington

*see Mid-Atlantic
page 93*

MISSOURI

KENTUCKY

Wichita

Springfield

Bowling Green

*see South
page 221*

TENNESSEE

NC

0   80 mi
0   80 km

Although this tour has become very difficult for the general public to go on, we decided to include it in the book because the company's construction equipment represents some of the finest American-engineered and -made products. The company is the world's largest manufacturer of construction and mining equipment, natural gas engines and industrial gas turbines, and diesel engines. Caterpillar is one of a few American companies that leads its industry worldwide while principally making its products in the U.S.A.

The tours to prospects, end users, and dealers have become a major selling tool for the company and are customized to the interests of the visitors. You see most of the main assembly steps from start to finish, with the subassembly stations off to the side in this massive facility (6.5 acres under one roof).

Each part of the process seems closely choreographed. The Cat slowly paws down the main assembly line, starting with the frame rails. Air pallets move the heavy frame from position to position. The tractor-to-be seems to move like a hovercraft down the line. Overhead hoists and cranes lower the pieces into place. Workers bolt down the cab, transmission, engine, and other parts. Midway through, the bulldozer goes through quality control computer tests, then on to the paint booth. The sounds of hammer and bolt guns fill the air and hydraulic lines hang from above.

Near the end, you see them start up the king of tractors, with the worker riding on what looks like a giant elephant in a parade, and watch them even apply the decals. Look for the heavily customized versions, usually modified for the project or part of the world the Cat will travel to from the factory. In the display room, you can sit on some of the models and even honk the horn. Visitors leave with the fascination they had as children watching this monster-sized earth-moving equipment build roads and buildings, having now learned what it takes to make these giant yellow machines themselves.

Cost: Free

Freebies: Limited to customers.

Video: 10-minute video welcomes visitors to the factory and supporting facilities.

Reservations Needed: Yes. Limited space for non-customer tours. Must make reservations 3–6 weeks in advance. Subject to availability.

Days and Hours: Mon–Fri by appointment only. Closed major holidays, last two full weeks of July, week between Christmas and New Year's.

Plan to Stay: 1.5 hours.

Minimum Age: 12

Disabled Access: Explain special needs when making reservations.

Group Requirements: See Reservations Needed above. Company will want to know background of people in group.

Special Information: No cameras. Very serious about no shorts or open-toed shoes. You walk on factory floor, so wear comfortable shoes. Customers are able to go on more specialized tours of the foundry and other plants.

Gift Shop: Cat Merchandise Center in downtown Peoria sells wide range of logoed Caterpillar items. Open Mon–Fri 10:00 AM–6:00 PM, Sat 10:00 AM–2:00 PM. Call (309) 676-7990 for holiday hours.

Directions: Tour begins at World Headquarters in downtown Peoria. Directions given out when reservations made.

Nearby Attractions: Wildlife Prairie State Park; Glen Oak Zoo; McGlothin Farm Park; Tower Park Observatory; African-American Hall of Fame; Lakeview Museum; Peoria Mineral Springs.

141 West Jackson Boulevard, Chicago, IL 60604

(312) 435-3590
(312) 435-3625

www.cbot.com

◉ Chicago Board of Trade

Major futures markets at work combine Super Bowl competitiveness, Rose Bowl Parade colors, and Mardi Gras pandemonium. From large, glass-walled observation galleries above the Chicago Board of Trade (CBOT) trading floors, you'll see throngs of traders feverishly shouting, waving their arms, using hand signals, and throwing pieces of paper.

A 60,000-square-foot addition, completed in 1997, gives the CBOT the world's largest contiguous trading hall at 92,000 square feet. The trading floor is bigger than the combined playing fields of the Chicago Cubs and the White Sox. The trading hall has 876 booths located among and around its eight trading pits.

In the various pits, traders use a variation of the centuries-old auction system—appropriately called the "open outcry method"—for buying and selling. With all the skill of a third-base coach, they also use hand signals to cut through the noise. The sea of colors comes from ID badges and lightweight jackets worn by floor personnel. At the tops of the side and far walls are boards with numbers that show futures prices.

Adjacent to the agricultural gallery, a mini-museum houses artifacts and photos tracing the early days of commodity trading. Look at century-old grain measuring and grinding devices. View a visual history of the exchange, including photographs, drawings, documents, and architecture from its beginnings (opened in 1848) to the present day. After examining the mechanics of floor trading and the mini-museum, you'll be even more interested in the financial section of your newspaper.

Cost: Free

Freebies: English and foreign-language brochure.

Video/DVD Shown: 15-minute video, "Link to the Future."

Reservations Needed: Yes. *While Visitor Gallery used to be open to general public, now it's only open to groups sponsored by CBOT member or CBDT management, or industry or education groups.*

Days and Hours: Mon–Fri with educational presentations and video at 9:00 AM, then every half hour until 12:30 PM. Closed national holidays.

Plan to Stay: 30 minutes, plus time for videos and displays.

Minimum Age: 16

Disabled Access: Yes

Group Requirements: Require reservations at least 2 weeks in advance for groups of 10 or more, with customized presentations available. Minimum age for groups is 16 years old.

Special Information: In addition to presentations in English, audio and video explanations are available in 12 languages: Japanese, Chinese, Korean, French, German, Spanish, Portuguese, Italian, Russian, Greek, Danish, and Polish.

Gift Shop: Gift counter sells logoed items, including pens, caps, T-shirts, mugs, golf tees, and teddy bears. CBOT catalog available at number above.

Directions: The landmark art deco CBOT building, topped by a 31-foot statue of Ceres (Roman goddess of grain and harvest), is at the intersection of LaSalle and Jackson.

Nearby Attractions: Chicago Mercantile Exchange, Eli's Cheesecake World, and U.S. Post Office tours (see pages 150, 152, and 160); *Chicago Tribune* tour under construction (see page 151); Chicago Board Option Exchange Observation Gallery (call 312-786-5600); Federal Reserve Bank Visitors Center and tour (call 312-322-5111); Quaker Oats Lobby Exhibit (call 312-222-6887).

Chicago Mercantile Exchange

GREAT LAKES

Established in 1898 as the Chicago Butter & Egg Board, the Chicago Mercantile Exchange (CME) is today the largest and most diverse financial exchange in the world for trading futures and options. It handles more than a billion contracts, worth over $700 trillion, in a single year. You can find out more in the new CME Visitors Center, which tells the history of the exchange. You learn that financial futures are a form of risk management. Artifacts blend with interactive kiosks and videos to help you understand the origins of the futures industry and how CME influences the world's economy. You also learn of CME's electronic trading platform, which lets customers around the planet access CME from a single trading platform virtually 24 hours a day.

Your best chance of seeing the action on the trading floor is by reserving a guided group tour. Traders shout bids and offers in the pit. Clerks at their trading desks take phone orders, review charts, or hand-signal desired deals. Clerks and runners dressed in gold coats constantly signal prices. The goal is to be seen and heard. There may be as many as 4,000 traders on the floor at any one time and, as a trader, you want your bid to get attention. In order to stand out from this colorful sea of people, an independent trader may wear an American flag jacket, or one with hogs, pigs, or cattle on it. Your guide answers questions and explains what the hand signals mean.

A second gallery overlooking the upper trading floor, not necessarily included in the tour, handles currency futures and interest rate futures. The design of the pits is different: each product trades in its own pit. The right side of the gallery faces the Eurodollar pit, home of one of "the world's most actively traded futures contracts." Here traders take positions in contracts that will trade up to 10 years in the future.

Cost: Free

Freebies: Map of trading floor or brief description of products traded.

Videos/DVDs Shown: Interactive videos explain the trading process and CME history.

Reservations Needed: For security reasons, the viewing gallery overlooking the CME trading floor is closed to the public until further notice. Market presentations can be arranged for groups of 10 or more. Participants in such prearranged visits are escorted to the viewing gallery during their tour. No reservations needed for lobby-level Visitors Center.

Days and Hours: Mon–Fri 8:00 AM–4:30 PM with prearranged presentations provided at 9:00 AM, 10:00 AM, and 11:00 AM. Closed financial holidays. On the day before holidays, trading floors close at 12:00 PM.

Plan to Stay: 30 minutes, plus time for videos and displays.

Minimum Age: 7th grade for groups.

Disabled Access: Yes

Group Requirements: Reservations required at least 2 weeks in advance for groups of 10 or more. Maximum is 75 people. Registration form is on website.

Special Information: No photography. No cell-phone use allowed in gallery.

Gift Shop: Sells logoed items, including pens, caps, adult and children's T-shirts, mugs, puzzles, office accessories, and sports bags. Open Mon–Fri 8:00 AM–4:30 PM.

Directions: Visitors Center entrance is on Wacker Dr. near Monroe, 1 block from Sears Tower. Take Brown and Purple "L" Line to Loop Washington and Wells stop. Walk west 2 blocks.

Nearby Attractions: Chicago Board of Trade Visitors Gallery, Eli's Cheesecake World, Chicago Tribune tour, and U.S. Post Office tour (see pages 149, 152, 151, and 160); Federal Reserve Bank Visitors Center and tour (call 312-322-5111); Sears Tower.

Freedom Center, 777 West Chicago Avenue, Chicago, IL 60610

(312) 222-2289

www.chicago
tribune.com

Chicago Tribune

The *Chicago Tribune* printed 400 copies of its first issue on June 10, 1847. It now prints that many papers in less than a second on 10 massive offset presses that produce up to 55,000 newspapers per hour and more than 1 billion copies per year. This tour gives you a firsthand look at how the *Tribune* is printed, inserted, bundled, and delivered by one of the world's largest and most technologically advanced newspaper-printing facilities.

In the mammoth newsprint warehouse area, about the size of two football fields, the amount of paper used to print this popular newspaper seems overwhelming. Newspaper rolls are the size of small cows. The *Tribune* uses an average of 3,600–3,900 one-ton paper rolls every week. Newsprint produced by the *Tribune's* major suppliers is made from 30–35 percent recycled paper. Train tracks run alongside the warehouse to accommodate 18 railroad cars full of newsprint rolls, receiving deliveries five days per week (72 railroad cars' worth!).

Tower printing presses move so fast that the newspaper looks like a gray checkerboard blanket rolling up and down along the plates and cylindrical drums. Each press is a series of 10 units. The *Tribune* is proud of its increased color-printing capacity, achieved by installing three additional color tower units. The color tower units contain four vertically stacked printing machines, one each for blue, red, yellow, and black ink. Each press also cuts and folds the paper into sections.

In the busy daily packaging area, advertising sections are inserted by machine into a jacket, which is bundled, palletized, and sent out to delivery carriers for insertion into the completed paper. In the Sunday collating plant, a large crane inducts and retrieves preprint pallets. This is where advertisements, known as preprints, are placed into a sealed clear plastic bag and sent to the distribution network to be inserted into the Sunday newspaper for delivery to readers of the *Chicago Tribune*.

Cost: Free

Reservations Needed: Yes (call 312-222-2289).

Days and Hours: Press area is under construction; tours are very limited and may not be available. Tuesdays 10:00 AM–2:00 PM.

Plan to Stay: 1 hour.

Minimum Age: 12

Disabled Access: Yes. One attendant needed for each individual using a wheelchair.

Group Requirements: Maximum 15 people; 1 adult for every 7 children. Reserve as far in advance as possible.

Special Information: This is a manufacturing company, so strict safety regulations are enforced. No open-toed shoes are allowed. Presses may not be running during your visit. [Note: Most local newspapers give tours; contact your local paper for tour information.]

Gift Shop: Not in Freedom Center. Store in *Tribune* Tower (435 N. Michigan Ave.) sells *Chicago Tribune* merchandise (books, clothing, etc.). Open Mon–Fri 8:00 AM–6:00 PM and Sat 10:00 AM–4:00 PM. Call (312) 222-3080.

Directions: From I-90/94, take the Ohio St. exit. Turn left on Orleans St. and left on Chicago Ave. The guard in the security booth will direct you to the visitors' parking.

Nearby Attractions: Chicago Board of Trade, Chicago Mercantile Exchange, and U.S. Post Office tour (see pages 149, 150, and 160). Chicago's attractions include Sears Tower, Shedd Aquarium, Adler Planetarium, Lincoln Park Zoo, and the Museum of Science and Industry.

6701 West Forest Preserve Drive,
Chicago, IL 60634

(773) 736-3417
(800) 999-8300

www.elicheesecake.com

After its public debut at the Taste of Chicago in 1980, Eli's Cheesecake has become a sweet symbol of success for the Windy City. Eli Schulman, a guy from the "West Side of Chicago," created a special dessert for his restaurant, Eli's The Place for Steak. His son Marc continues Eli's level of dedication and commitment to making the best quality cheesecake.

Before starting your tour, notice the mural highlighting Eli's Cheesecake's history. In the back of this bright, atrium café, look through the glass window into the research and development department. This 62,000-square-foot bakery, built in 1996, uses more than 4 million pounds of cream cheese, 500,000 pounds of eggs, 250,000 pounds of butter, and 13,000 pounds of Bourbon vanilla annually.

After donning your hair net, walk through the double doors. Racks filled with all-butter cookie crusts baked twice the previous night await today's production. In the mixing area, a crane system lifts up and tilts the mixing bowl, which contains 500 pounds of batter for each batch of cheesecake. A big spatula with a black plastic paddle fills each crust. Up to 18,000 cheesecakes march along the conveyor through the 70-foot tunnel oven. Stand on the royal blue nonskid path observing rows 10 cheesecakes wide emerge.

After baking, the cheesecakes take a leisurely two-hour journey spiraling up and back down a two-story cylindrical cooling tower. This densely coiled spiral cooler slowly cools more than 2,000 cheesecakes at one time. Cheesecakes travel single-file down the conveyor belt and are depanned individually by hand.

In the blast freezer, cakes freeze solid in eight to ten hours. More than 30 trained pastry chefs and cake decorators hand-decorate some two-thirds of Eli's cheesecakes. Decorating a cheesecake involves great teamwork, taking up to three different steps.

After decorating, cheesecakes are sliced, packaged, and shipped.

Cost: Adults, $3; children under 12, $2 (costs go to Eli's Charitable Fund to support the community).

Freebies: Cheesecake slice.

Video/DVD Shown: Slide show on Eli's history and the baking process.

Reservations Needed: No, for the 1:00 PM "Sneak Peek" tour. Yes, for groups over 10 people and for "quiet tours" (no production) on weekends.

Days and Hours: Mon–Fri 8:00 AM–6:00 PM Tour packages available for groups of 10 or more. Call ahead to confirm the bakery is in production, otherwise Eli's offers a modified tour.

Plan to Stay: 25 minutes for tour, plus additional time in the retail store.

Minimum Age: 3

Disabled Access: Modified tour available.

Group Requirements: Groups over 10 people should schedule at least 2 weeks in advance, with contract and payment. Enjoy tour packages such as "Lunch & Munch," "The Ultimate Eli's Experience" (participate in "Quality Star" taste test and decorate your own cheesecake), and "Sail and Dine" (includes sightseeing cruise plus lunch). Group discount in café. Maximum group size is 45.

Special Information: No photography or strollers. Must wear rubber-soled, low-heeled shoes, otherwise receive modified tour. The Cheesecake Festival is in September.

Retail Store: Café sells many of Eli's 100 cheesecake varieties and logoed merchandise including hats, T-shirts, and polo shirts. Selection ranges from Original Plain (for the "cheesecake purist") to indulgent Belgian Chocolate Hazelnut, plus holiday specials like Egg Nog. Open Mon–Fri 8:00 AM–6:00 PM, Sat 9:00 AM–5:00 PM, Sun 11:00 AM–5:00 PM. Order Eli's C-Cake from website, picking from some 600 combinations of decorations and toppings.

Directions: From I-90/94 West, take Montrose St. Turn left. At light, turn left just before factory onto Forest Preserve Dr. Turn right into parking lot.

Nearby Attractions: Chicago Board of Trade and Chicago Mercantile Exchange tours (see page 149 and 150); Chicago's attractions include Sears Tower, Shedd Aquarium, and Lincoln Park Zoo.

See color photos, page 10.

205 / 207 South Main Street, Galena, IL 61036

(877) 777-KORN
(800) 235-8160

www.greatpopcorn.com
www.rmcf.com

Although separate stores, the Great American Popcorn Company and the Galena Rocky Mountain Chocolate Factory franchise share a common family and a delicious motto: Try anything to see if it tastes good. Charles and Ann Henle bought the Rocky Mountain franchise in 1990. About 70 percent of their handmade candy comes from the Durango, Colorado, factory. David Lewis and Catherine Henle-Lewis had been involved in her parents' business, Rocky Mountain Chocolate, for nearly 12 years before opening the Great American Popcorn Company next door in 1994.

Dave and Catherine hear the words, "I didn't know you could do this with popcorn!" all the time. They create new popcorn flavors by imagination or customer request, swirling in experiments at whim alongside their steady production of sweet Vanilla Caramel and Amaretto & Almonds, cheesy Bacon & Cheddar and Sour Cream & Chives, and spicy Blazing Saddles and Hellfire & Damnation.

At the start of the tour, hear the science behind corn popping before corn kernels stream into the middle vat of a five-foot-tall popper. Special mushroom corn makes a ball shape when popped and does not break into pieces like butterfly corn. Two heads shoot out the corn, which goes into giant bulk bags. To make caramel corn, brown sugar, corn syrup, and butter heat together in a "coater cooker," a 10-gallon automatic round drum. Then the popcorn tumbles in the mixture, giving each piece a rich coating. Popcorn rarely makes it from the cooling trays to storage bags; the warmth and aroma entices customers to buy on the spot.

Next door at Rocky Mountain, Truffles, the signature Rocky Mountain bear, sits four feet tall in a rocking chair out front to greet visitors. His sign says: "I will work for chocolate." Store workers break 10-pound blocks of milk and dark chocolate into pieces and melt them down in the large tempering kettles. Looking like witches with a brew cauldron, they mix in and cook the sugar, corn syrup, evaporated milk, and butter with a wooden paddle until

the fudge reaches 231°F. The fudge ripples over a 700-pound granite slab and mixes with chocolate liqueur before workers form it into fudge loaves. Taster spoons, loaded with warm, gooey fudge and given out several times during production, are the highlight of the tour.

Cost: Free

Freebies: Popcorn, fudge, chocolate bark.

Video Shown: No

Reservations Needed: No, except for groups larger than 15.

Days and Hours: Daily 9:30 AM–5:30 PM. June 1–November 1; extended hours Fri and Sat 9:30 AM–9:00 PM.

Plan to Stay: 20–25 minutes for each tour.

Minimum Age: None

Disabled Access: Yes

Group Requirements: Groups of 15 or more will be split between the 2 stores. Call at least 1 day in advance.

Special Information: No video or photography of specific items, but can take pictures with store owners. No smoking. Customers can call ahead to request production of specific items.

Retail Stores: Sell all Rocky Mountain candies and gift items, hundreds of popcorn flavors by bag or tin, gift baskets, ice cream, figurines, and stuffed animals.

Directions: From Chicago, take Rt. 20 West to Joe Davis County. Rt. 20 turns into Main St. Go through floodgates. Great American Popcorn and Rocky Mountain are on the same block.

Nearby Attractions: Ulysses S. Grant's home; Galena Water Park; Stillman Bed and Breakfast tea room; historic mansions of Galena.

7 Maiden Lane, East Dundee, IL 60118   (847) 783-5420
(847) 426-3441   www.haeger
potteries.com

Founded by David Haeger in 1871, Haeger Potteries today is directed by Alexandra Haeger Estes—the fourth generation of the Haeger family to be involved with the company. Started as a brickyard that helped rebuild Chicago after its Great Fire, Haeger Potteries is now one of the world's largest art pottery factories. While you can no longer tour the factory, you can watch the pottery production video and visit the historic Haeger Museum.

After an introductory talk about the production process, your video tour begins. Watch the automatic casting machines fill plaster molds with slip—liquid clay. Notice the hanging trolley system that slowly travels its four-mile course with dried pottery (greenware) perched on wooden shelves that look like birdcage swings.

Workers carefully pry the molds open, then give each artwork a hand sponge bath before drying. The block-long kiln and the round kiln are located in the Great Kiln room, where you'll almost feel the heat. The brown brick kilns are 220°F at the entrance and 2,000°F in the center. Workers neatly stack the greenware pieces—close to each other but not touching—onto railcars headed for a 12-hour trip through the kiln.

After its first kiln baking, the bisque is hand-dipped into a water-based glaze. The glaze, absorbed into the dry, porous bisque, dries almost immediately. A worker then takes the piece from a lazy-Susan table and showers it with glaze in a spray booth. These alternative glazing methods give the pottery its vibrant colors when it's fired again in the kiln.

The Haeger museum includes a vase determined by the *Guinness Book of World Records* to be one of the world's largest. Made in 1976 by Haeger's master potter, it took three months and 650 pounds of clay to complete. Among other Haeger items, the display cases show discontinued ceramic animal designs, a Harley-Davidson hog bank, a sculptured bust of Carl Sandburg, and a large Hummel figure (Hummel and Haeger exchanged artworks on Haeger's 100th anniversary). Explore the 25,000-square-foot, seven-showroom outlet store that sells most of Haeger's 800 different items.

Cost: Free

Freebies: No

Videos/DVDs Shown: 15-minute video on manufacturing process; 10-minute video on company history.

Reservations Needed: No

Days and Hours: Mon, Thur, Fri 10:00 AM–6:00 PM, Sat, Sun, 11:00 AM–5:00 PM. Closed Tue and Wed, and July 4th.

Plan to Stay: 35 minutes for video tour, plus time for museum and outlet store.

Minimum Age: 4, when accompanied by responsible adult; 5, for school groups.

Disabled Access: Outlet store and museum are accessible.

Group Requirements: None

Outlet Store: Sells pottery lamps, vases, bowls, sculptures, the best-selling *Stalking Panthers,* dried and silk floral arrangements, slightly imperfect items, overruns, and one-of-a-kind and discontinued pieces. Open Mon, Thur, and Fri 10:00 AM–6:00 PM; Sat and Sun 11:00 AM–5:00 PM.

Directions: From Chicago, take I-90 West to Rt. 25 North. Turn left onto Rt. 72. Turn left onto Van Buren St. Haeger Potteries is on your right.

Nearby Attractions: Spring Hill Mall; Santa's Village Amusement Park and Racing Rapids Water Park; Fox River State Recreational Trail; the Milk Pail Village; Chicago's attractions include Chicago Mercantile Exchange, Chicago Board of Trade, McDonald's Museum, and U.S. Post Office tours (see pages 150, 149, 158, and 160) 45 minutes away.

Harvester Works, 1100 13th Avenue,
East Moline, IL 61244

(800) 765-9588
(877) 201-3924

www.johndeere.com

JOHN DEERE

The harvester, or "combine" as it's called in the trade, is one of the machines that revolutionized farming and made possible America's tremendous production of grain and corn. For example, a combine with a corn "header" attachment can harvest as many as 12 corn rows at a time, picking and shelling the ears along the way. At John Deere Harvester, the world's most advanced combine factory, you'll see many steps involved in making its STS combines.

The techniques definitely differ from those used by pioneer blacksmith John Deere when he started the company in 1837. Along with the hissing and thumping machines heard at most factories, you'll also see robots welding, lasers cutting steel, and electrical charges applying paint in this world-class manufacturing plant. Considering this factory's size, don't be surprised to see workers getting around on Gator™ Utility Vehicles. Your John Deere tour guide will hand you a piece of metal. Feel the smooth cut on it, made by the combination laser-and-punch machine. Sparks fly as hooded welders apply their skills on smaller pieces, while robotic arms on the automated welding systems seal frames and grain tanks.

Watch a combine body slowly emerge and then hover on its hoist after being dipped into an electrically charged bath of green paint. The electric charge bonds the paint to all exposed surfaces on the submerged combine, even in joints and hidden crevices. After seeing several subassembly stations, you'll watch combines come to life on the main production line. Assemblers carefully position completed parts, such as the cab, feeder house, and engine. You will sense the pride of the worker who smoothly applies the finishing touch: the John Deere decal.

Cost: Free

Freebies: Brochure with description and pictures of the manufacturing process.

Video/DVD Shown: No

Reservations Needed: Yes

Days and Hours: Mon–Fri 8:00 AM, 10:00 AM, and 12:30 PM. Closed major holidays, week between Christmas and New Year's, and 2 weeks in the summer (usually end of July and beginning of August). Tours subject to change. Please call above numbers for tour availability.

Plan to Stay: 1.5 hours.

Minimum Age: 12

Disabled Access: Yes. You ride through the factory in a tram pulled by a small John Deere tractor.

Group Requirements: Make reservations at least 1 month in advance. Maximum size is 80 people.

Special Information: No video cameras or sandals allowed. Closed-toe shoes required. Visit John Deere tractor plant in Waterloo, IA (see page 279) and John Deere Pavilion in Moline, IL (see page 156).

Gift Shop: Adjacent to the new John Deere Pavilion at the John Deere Commons. Sells a variety of John Deere memorabilia, replica toys, and logoed clothing.

Directions: When you make reservations, ask the Guest Services Department for a map, since many area highways have multiple designations—almost guaranteeing confusion. From Chicago, take I-88 to the exit for Hwy. 5. Turn right at 70th St., which becomes 7th St. Turn right on 13th Ave. Look for the big green John Deere STS combine parked on the factory's front lawn. From Iowa, take I-80 to I-74 East. Get off at the John Deere Rd. East exit. Turn left at 70th St. and follow the above directions.

Nearby Attractions: John Deere Pavilion features interactive displays about agriculture, plus modern and vintage farm equipment (see page 156); Deere & Co. World Headquarters displays current and historical John Deere products, Girard Mural (includes more than 2,000 farming-related historical items dated 1837–1918), and video tour of this architecturally famous world headquarters; Collectors Center displays antique tractors; John Deere Historic Site in Grand Detour.

1400 River Drive, Moline, IL 61265

(309) 765-1000
(800) 765-9588

www.johndeere
pavilion.com

John Deere
PAVILION

The John Deere Pavilion, the world's largest agriculture museum, celebrates the past, present, and future of agriculture, as well as the history of the company. The 14,000-square-foot Pavilion is like one you'd see at a fairground, except the walls are made almost entirely of glass. Inside, stop at reception to request your own personal tour guide, likely a Deere retiree, who will happily customize your visit any way you like.

If you've never been on a farm, this is your chance to climb aboard a brand-new, shiny green tractor or combine that sits on the Pavilion floor. How has equipment like the tractor changed over the years, since Deere made the 1918 Waterloo Boy model? To find out, compare the new machines to their antique counterparts, also on display at the Pavilion (but don't climb on the antiques—they're too fragile). To see a tractor or combine in action, take a virtual tour at one of the touch-screen displays. "Tour" the combine factory and watch employees assemble this boxy piece of machinery, then see the machine harvest wheat, soy, and corn. At another station the "tour" shows workers assembling tractors. Notice all the different attachments—each attachment performs a different task on the field.

"Cornucopia" is a touch-screen exhibit that takes you from the beginning of a product's life until it gets to market. Learn the life story of apples, pork, or cotton. Another interactive exhibit called "The Past" walks you through the history of agriculture, while "The Future" educates guests about how the world will feed its booming population, which may double in the next 40 years. Like many guests, you may find yourself returning to the Pavilion again and again simply to reminisce and share experiences of life on the farm.

Cost: Free

Freebies: No

Video/DVD Shown: 14-minute film shown on a new high-definition screen system, "Anthem," about global farming practices.

Reservations Needed: No

Days and Hours: Mon–Fri 9:00 AM–5:00 PM, Sat 10:00 AM–5:00 PM, Sun 12:00 PM–4:00 PM. Closed Easter, Thanksgiving, Christmas, and New Year's.

Plan to Stay: 1 hour for tour and "Anthem," plus time to visit the John Deere Store and John Deere Collectors Center, just a few steps away.

Minimum Age: None

Disabled Access: Yes

Group Requirements: Groups of 30 or more should call in advance if possible.

Special Information: No videotaping of "Anthem." Visit John Deere factory tours in East Moline, IL (see page 155) and Waterloo, IA (see page 279).

Gift Shop: John Deere Store sells a variety of items emblazoned with the company logo, from baseball caps and towels to fishing lures and mailboxes. January–February: Mon–Sat 10:00 AM–5:00 PM, Sun 12:00 PM–4:00 PM. March–December: Mon–Fri 10:00 AM–6:00 PM, Sat 10:00 AM–5:00 PM, Sun 12:00 PM–4:00 PM. Closed same days as the Pavilion.

Directions: From the east, take I-74 West into Moline. Take the 7th Ave. exit (last Illinois exit). Turn left on 7th Ave. Go 4 blocks and turn right on 15th St. Go 4 blocks. From the west, take I-80 to I-74 East. Follow I-74 East across the Mississippi River to Illinois. Take the River Dr. exit (the first exit). Turn left on River Dr. and go 4.5 blocks. John Deere Pavilion is on the corner of River Dr. and 15th St.

Nearby Attractions: John Deere Harvester Works tour (see page 155); John Deere Collectors Center half block away on John Deere Commons (call 800-240-5265); Mississippi River; Historic Deere family homes; Deere & Company World Headquarters; Tournament Players Club at Deere Run.

See color photos, page 32.

333 Lexington Drive, Buffalo Grove, IL 60089 | (888) 459-3100 | www.longgrove.com

Tours of Long Grove Confectionery Company start in the shadow of a nine-foot-high Statue of Liberty, sculpted in solid chocolate with elaborate detail, that weighs over a ton. A 500-pound chocolate Santa Claus greets visitors throughout the year, and chocolate reproductions of paintings by Monet and Seurat adorn the walls elsewhere. These works are a fitting introduction to Long Grove, which has been combining art and chocolate in a big way since 1975.

However, as a tour of the chocolate factory reveals, much of the company's work occurs on a miniature rather than a colossal scale. After seeing a brief video on how chocolate is made from the seed of the tropical cacao tree, visitors embark on a tour of the factory and view production areas through windows. The strong, sweet smell of chocolate pervades every corner of this immense facility, which sprawls over 85,000 square feet.

The first stop is the kitchen area. Depending on the schedule, visitors may see homemade caramel as it cooks in copper kettles, English toffee on hot and cold tables, or caramel apples, which workers roll in pecans and drizzle with milk chocolate. You may also see how Long Grove makes its own cream and peanut-butter fillings in a huge mixer—a giant version of a kitchen blender.

The two vital zones for handmade chocolate are the molding and unmolding areas. The decorative use of colored chocolate is a signature of Long Grove. Staff paint colored elements by hand in the molds before chocolate is poured. The results, after over an hour in the cooling chamber, are intricately colored sculptures. The workers in the unmolding area then trim excess chocolate by hand with a small knife. Why doesn't the chocolate melt in their fingers? Depending on its chemistry, chocolate melts between 86°F and 90°F; the unmolding area is maintained at 60°F, and the bundled-up workers wear cotton gloves. After trimming, each piece is ready for wrapping.

Other chocolates are made for boxed collections in the enrobing area, where a machine coats each filling center with chocolate and sends it on a belt to the cooling tunnel. (Although visitors cannot see this area, a video shows the process.) After cooling, the chocolates ride into the packaging area, a large space where staff box them. Molded chocolates also end up here. Elegant decorations are another signature of Long Grove: workers dress each handmade piece in a careful raiment of cellophane, bows, and sometimes seasonal ornaments. A tasting of fresh chocolate ends the tour.

Cost: $2 per person.

Freebies: Free tasting of chocolate.

Video/DVD Shown: Various videos (total: 20 minutes) on manufacturing and on company background.

Reservations Needed: Yes

Days and Hours: Daily by appointment. Closed holidays.

Plan to Stay: 1.5 hours.

Minimum Age: None

Disabled Access: Yes

Group Requirements: No

Gift Shop: The shop sells the full range of chocolates. Open Mon–Sat 9:30 AM–5:30 PM, Sun 11:00 AM–4:00 PM. Closed holidays.

Directions: From I-94 East, take exit for Lake Cook Rd., turn right at end of ramp, drive 4 miles, and turn right on Lexington Dr. From I-94 West, take Lake Cook Rd. exit, turn left at end of ramp, drive 3 miles, and turn right on Lexington Dr.

Nearby Attractions: Haeger Potteries (see page 154); in Chicago (45 minutes away), Chicago Mercantile Exchange, Chicago Board of Trade, McDonald's Museum, and USPS mail-distribution center (see pages 150, 149, 158, 160).

See color photos, page 34.

If you're a hungry traveler, the sign advertising 15-cent hamburgers may beckon you like a desert mirage. But after parking next to a vintage Chevrolet Bel Air coupe and walking up to this retro-restaurant's counter, you'll realize that what you've discovered is not the cheapest burger this side of 1960, but the McDonald's Museum.

The museum is a restoration of the first McDonald's corporation franchise that opened on this site in 1955. Clean-cut mannequins tend the restaurant, serving up a simple menu: burgers, cheeseburgers, fries, shakes, milk, coffee, and soda. Most of the compact, clean operation is open to the customers' view. Outside on the original sign, Speedee, a winking little logo-man with a hamburger head, advertises "speedee" service and 15-cent burgers.

Red-and-white restaurants like this launched the McDonald's empire, which now includes more than 30,000 restaurants in more than 119 countries. In 1954, milkshake multimixer salesman Ray Kroc, intrigued by an order for eight machines, flew out to California to observe the restaurant operation of brothers Dick and Maurice McDonald. While his original intent was to sell them more multimixers, Ray Kroc saw his future in franchising McDonald's restaurants. Kroc left California as the brothers' franchise agent and opened his first franchise in Des Plaines, Illinois, on April 15, 1955.

Right away, you'll notice the quintessential seating and drive-thru are missing, just as they were from the original operating restaurant. During winter months, a removable Plexiglas "winter front" was added to the front of the building so customers would not have to stand in the cold at the service window.

While visitors are not allowed to enter the kitchen area, most of it is visible from the outside. In the customer service and food preparation areas, you'll see the authentic equipment used in those days. Hamburgers and cheeseburgers were grilled; fresh potatoes were washed, sliced, blanched, and fried; milkshakes were whipped up, of course, on multimixers. Although these techniques may not strike you as antiquated, the prices will. The most expensive item on the menu was a 20-cent milkshake. Downstairs, in the small exhibit area, you will see historic photos, the daily sales log from April 1955, and a short video.

Cost: Free

Freebies: Postcard of museum.

Video/DVD Shown: 3-minute video on company history.

Reservations Needed: No

Days and Hours: Memorial Day–Labor Day: Thur–Fri 10:30 AM–2:30 PM, Sat 10:00 AM– 4:00 PM, but call to confirm since entire schedule changes every year. Closed balance of the year.

Plan to Stay: 20 minutes.

Minimum Age: None

Disabled Access: Restricted to upper floor.

Group Requirements: None

Special Information: The oldest operating red-and-white McDonald's restaurant is in Downey, CA. The restaurant has a small gift shop and historic exhibit area. Call (562) 622-9248.

Gift Shop: No, but if you're hungry, a real McDonald's is across the street.

Directions: Located in vicinity of O'Hare Airport. From the south, take I-294 (Tri-State Tollway) North to Dempster West exit. Go west on Dempster (U.S. 14) to Lee St. Turn right onto Lee and go about 2 blocks. Just before Lee converges with Rand Rd., you'll see the museum on your left. From the north, take I-294 to Golf Rd. West exit. Go west on Golf Rd. (Rt. 58) to Mannheim Rd./River Rd. (U.S. 45). Turn left on U.S. 45 and proceed south. Just after you cross Rand Rd., you'll see the museum on your right.

Nearby Attractions: Botanic Gardens; Des Plaines Historical Museum; Woodfield Mall, about 20 minutes away; Chicago's attractions, including the Sears Tower, are about 30 minutes away.

100 North Mitsubishi Motorway,
Normal, IL 61761

(309) 665-0033
(800) 433-8226

www.mitsubishicars.com

Mitsubishi Motors began producing cars at its only North American automobile manufacturing facility in 1988, originally in a joint venture with Chrysler Corporation under the name Diamond-Star Motors. The company name was changed in 1995 to Mitsubishi Motor Manufacturing of America, and in 2001, all North American operations of Mitsubishi Motors were consolidated into Mitsubishi Motors North America (MMNA). Situated on 636 acres in central Illinois, the plant occupies more than 2.5 million square feet—the equivalent of approximately 52 football fields. With more than 1,900 employees, the factory produces such popular models as the Mitsubishi Eclipse coupe, Eclipse Spyder convertible, Galant sedan, and Endeavor SUV.

The catwalk tour shows you how the production line is designed to accommodate several different models intermixed on one assembly line and the just-in-time inventory management that have made the facility one of the most technologically advanced auto assembly plants in the world.

The plant is made up of five shops: Stamping, Body, Plastics, Paint, and Trim & Final. Representing a truly integrated manufacturing facility, MMNA Manufacturing stamps more major body panels and injection-molds most bumper fascias in-house, ensuring excellence in build. However, you can't miss the automated guided vehicles (AGVs) that transport parts and equipment between the Stamping and Body Shops. Without any apparent human intervention, the AGVs follow locator plates and wires in the floor to deliver racks to waiting workers.

The plant has more than 1,000 robots to perform monotonous, cumbersome, and more dangerous tasks. The Body Shop is 90 percent automated, with robots installing doors and hoods according to a highly synchronized order. With colorful sparks flying, the robots, which look and move like metallic and wire-filled praying mantises, precisely fit and weld the vehicle bodies together. More robots assist workers on the Trim & Final assembly line, installing seats, tires, batteries, windshields, instrument panels, and all fluids except gasoline.

Cost: Free

Freebies: Brochure

Video/DVD Shown: A video provides background on the plant and shows all stages of production, including those not seen on the catwalk tour.

Reservations Needed: Yes. Contact the Bloomington-Normal Area Convention and Visitors Bureau at (309) 665-0033 or (800) 433-8226.

Days and Hours: Tours are offered on Thurs only. Subject to change due to production schedule changes. Closed holidays and weekends. No tours during model changeover period. Some extended shut-down periods.

Plan to Stay: 1.25 hours for video, discussion, and tour.

Minimum Age: 10

Disabled Access: Yes

Group Requirements: Maximum group size is 50.

Special Information: No photography. More than a half mile of walking.

Gift Shop: No

Directions: From Rockford or Chicago, once on I-55/74, follow I-74 West toward Peoria (Exit 163). Off I-74, exit at Mitsubishi Motorway (Exit 125). The facility will be on your left. Follow the signs to the visitor parking north of flagpoles. From Decatur, St. Louis, or Champaign, once on I-55/74, take Rt. 9 (Exit 160B). Turn right on Mitsubishi Motorway. Factory will be on your right. Follow signs for visitor parking north of flagpoles.

Nearby Attractions: Beer Nuts Factory Outlet, with video of Beer Nuts being made (call 309-827-8580); Bloomington's other attractions, including Prairie Aviation Museum and Illinois State University Planetarium about 20 minutes away.

Cardiss Collins Processing & Distribution Center,
433 West Harrison Street, Chicago, IL 60607

(312) 983-7550

www.usps.com

UNITED STATES POSTAL SERVICE

Video/DVD Shown: No

Reservations Needed: Yes

Days and Hours: Mon–Fri 10:30 AM and 12:30 PM. Closed national holidays.

Plan to Stay: 1–2 hours depending on what areas you visit.

Minimum Age: 10

Disabled Access: Yes

Group requirements: Can handle groups of up to 100 people with at least 1 week's advance notice. Lunch available in cafeteria with advance notice.

Special Information: Substantial walking involved. Guides can individualize tour to special interests, which is why tour length varies. Many post offices like to give tours, so contact your local P.O. for information.

Gift Shop: Postal Store in retail lobby sells a large collection of commemorative stamps and books. Open Mon–Sun 24 hours a day.

Directions: From I-90/94, take the exit for Congress Pkwy. East. Take the Canal St. exit and turn left. Post office is located on corner of Harrison and Canal. From I-290, take the Canal St. exit. Free customer parking on Harrison side of building entrance ramp next to river.

Nearby Attractions: Chicago's attractions include CME (Chicago Mercantile Exchange), Chicago Board of Trade, and Eli's Cheesecake World (see pages 150, 149, and 152), Sears Tower, Shedd Aquarium, Adler Planetarium & Astronomy Museum, Lincoln Park Zoo, Art Institute of Chicago, and the Museum of Science and Industry.

There are few things we take more for granted than the delivery of our mail. After the tour, you'll no longer wonder what happens to your letter between the time you drop it in the mailbox and the time it's delivered. You'll discover the steps involved in processing the mail, from initial cancellation of postage stamps to final sorting by carrier route.

Automation plays a big role. Mail sorting relies on high-tech equipment that moves at lightning speed, using bar code technology and optical character readers (OCRs) to sort the mail. The OCR scans the address and sprays a bar code on the bottom of each letter at a rate of 11 pieces of mail per second. The OCR does a rough sort by region, with other machines reading the bar codes to sort by delivery route. The mail moves so quickly through these machines that it looks like one continuous stream of paper. The mail races through the bar code readers and parks itself in the proper zip code slot.

Machines in other areas cancel the stamps, weed out oversized pieces, or handle bundles and large flat pieces. Computers then automatically direct the sorted mail to the proper transportation route. The next time you open your mail, you'll appreciate what that envelope has been through.

Cost: Free

Freebies: No

52886-A State Road 13, Middlebury, IN 46540   (574) 825-1185   www.ahfurniture.com
(800) 870-2524

Company founder R. Gene Beachy's great-grandfather was an Amish farmer in northern Indiana who built furniture in his spare time. Out of respect for this elder, the tour begins in front of an elegant, popular piece of furniture the company calls "Grandpa's Secretary," a desk-and-cabinet reproduction that dates back to 1892. While the company's construction methods make use of electric saws, planers, drills, and sanders, reminding you of a modern woodshop, you'll also see carpentry techniques that would make great-grandfather proud.

The company's workforce is almost entirely Amish. The scarcity of farming jobs has led the Amish to work in factories such as this one. If your only experience with the Amish is watching them in horse-drawn buggies, you may be surprised to see men and women skillfully handling power tools. Except for the sneakers, the men wear the typical Amish plain pants and hats, and the women wear solid-colored dresses and bonnets—very different than the T-shirt and jeans worn by many American factory workers.

The furniture's solid-lumber construction begins with piles of pine, oak, or cherry boards cut to the required length in the mill area. To make the wood panels used to build the furniture, the boards interlock by tongue-and-groove cutouts and are placed on what looks like a steamboat's paddle wheel. Glue is placed between each pair of boards, and the pressure applied produces an almost seamless wood panel.

Each piece is then individually bench-built, so you can watch a craftsperson use panels or wood spindles to construct a desk, table, chair, or dresser. Workers sand the wood, spray stains, and hand-rub oil finishes. Hovered over a dresser, for example, you may see a worker hammering nails, fitting a mortise-and-tenon joint, or showing pride in the furniture's quality by signing and dating the piece.

Cost: Free

Freebies: No

Video/DVD Shown: 10-minute video on furniture making runs in showroom area.

Reservations Needed: Yes, for guided tour. No, to watch production from observation window in back of showroom.

Days and Hours: Mon–Fri 1:30 PM and 3:00 PM for guided tour. Can watch production through window Mon–Fri 9:15 AM–12:00 PM and 12:30 PM–4:00 PM. Closed holidays.

Plan to Stay: 20 minutes for tour, plus time for showroom.

Minimum Age: 6, for guided factory floor tour; none, to observe from window.

Disabled Access: Yes

Group Requirements: No maximum size. Larger groups will be split into 12 people per tour. Prefers 2 days' advance notice.

Special Information: No photography, since the Amish do not want photographs taken of themselves. Audio-cassette driving tour for area furniture-makers (for information contact Elkhart Convention and Visitors Bureau, 800-262-8161).

Showroom: Sells all furniture made at factory, including dining-room tables, chairs, desks, dressers, and bed frames. Occasional discounts available. Open Mon–Fri 9:00 AM–5:00 PM, Sat 10:00 AM–5:00 PM. Closed holidays.

Directions: From I-80/90 (Indiana Toll Rd.), take Exit 107. Turn right onto SR 13 South. Company is ahead on left.

Nearby Attractions: RV tours, including Coachmen, Jayco, and Monaco (see pages 164, 165, and 167); Walter Piano's tour (see page 169); Deutsch Kase Haus cheese factory, with observation windows in back of gift shop (call 219-825-9511 about production schedule); Shipshewana Flea Market and Auction, the Midwest's most popular outdoor flea market; Swartzendruber Hardwood Creations, located in the restored Old Bag Factory in Goshen, has an observation deck (call 219-534-2502).

350 Pearl Street, Fort Wayne, IN 46802 (219) 422-5631 ext. 276
(800) 995-8245 ext. 276
www.auntmillies.com

Food manufacturing is highly automated in big bakeries with lopsided ratios of workers-to-units produced. Aunt Millie's Bakeries has about 30 production people who make 180,000 loaves per day of such well-known breads as Sunbeam and Aunt Millie's. This tour shows you high-speed bread making at its most mechanized, with techniques very different from those used in 1901, when the company started baking wafers.

As you would do at home, Aunt Millie's combines ingredients in the mixer, bakes dough in the oven, and slices the bread before eating. But there the comparison ends, since the process at Aunt Millie's is much bigger, faster, and more intensely aromatic. About every 10 minutes, a trough filled with 2,000 pounds of dough rises above a "J" divider and drops a fresh blob of dough into a machine, which separates it into softball-size portions. A "rounder" machine then rounds and flours the dough before it heads for the "proofer."

Once the dough comes out of the overhead proofer, it moves through a "sheeter," which rolls it flat to remove gases and air bubbles. Then it falls into pans on five-across trays. Even the ovens seem to be in constant motion, welcoming and expelling loaves after an 18-minute baking. The depanners magically lift the hot bread from the pans using small suction cups. The baked loaves cool on a one-mile overhead conveyor-belt cooling system. While cooling, the bread is inspected for foreign objects; occasionally you'll see a loaf almost mysteriously flying off the line.

Slicing and packaging must be done quickly, while the bread is still warm; otherwise, the slices

lose moisture that keeps the loaf fresh. The tour guide explains some nuances of slicing bread, such as why pumpernickel is sliced thinnest. The bagging process is like inflating a balloon, except that the loaf follows the air into a bag that is then automatically tied. After watching state-of-the-art mass bread production, you'll never again take for granted that bread in your local supermarket.

Cost: Free

Freebies: Samples of warm bread with jam and margarine; coupons.

Video/DVD Shown: 12-minute video on bread production.

Reservations Needed: Yes

Days and Hours: Tue and Thur at 1:30 PM by appointment only.

Plan to Stay: 1.5 hours for talk on nutrition and company history, video, tour, and sampling.

Minimum Age: 5th grade and up.

Disabled Access: Yes

Group Requirements: Book 2 weeks in advance.

Special Information: No photography. No jewelry allowed. Warm during summer tours.

Thrift Store: Located on the west side of building. Breads near sell-by date are sold at discount. Open Mon–Fri 10:00 AM–6:00 PM and Sat 9:00 AM–4:00 PM. Closed holidays.

Directions: Atop the bakery is a unique billboard of bread slices continuously spilling from a bag of Sunbeam bread. More than 750 million slices have "fallen" from the yellow wrapper. Find this billboard and bakery from I-69 by taking Exit 102 to the east (Hwy. 24 W). This becomes Jefferson Blvd. Follow Jefferson Blvd. into the city. Turn left (north) onto Ewing St., right onto Main St., and immediate left into the Aunt Millie's parking lot.

Nearby Attractions: Sechler's pickles tour (see page 168); Fort Wayne Newspapers; Botanical Gardens; Science Central.

Step into an Old World oasis in the middle of Indiana. Settled by Mennonite immigrants from Canton Bern in Switzerland, Berne, Indiana, is known for its Amish village, quaint Swiss chalets, flower boxes, and congenial atmosphere. In the midst of it all, you'll find Berne Furniture, established in 1925 by Swiss settlers. Today Berne Furniture is still highly dedicated to the quality and excellence of Swiss custom upholstery.

Wood from nearby lumber mills is brought directly to Berne Furniture. Inhale the fresh smell of cut wood and brace yourself against the whir of the saw blades. Watch a craftsman guide a wood block against the jigsaw to achieve the perfect curve for a chair back. After the pieces are cut, holes are bored into the wood so the pieces can be connected, without nails, by inserting dowels.

After the frame is complete, steel springs are attached by hand. The worker tacks down the rows of springs along the seat of the frame, a mass of coils bobbing and swaying slightly like an exhibit of modern art. Each spring is then hand-tied with twine in eight directions for stability, so the base looks like a spider's web. Each end of the twine has to be nailed to the base. Hold your breath as the craftsman holds the nails in his mouth! With a magnetic hammer, he grabs a nail from his mouth and swiftly pounds it into the frame.

In the cutting room, 1,000 different fabrics of every color and texture line the wall. Cutting tables 13 yards long fill the room, making it look like a giant banquet hall. Cutters use heavy cardboard patterns to determine the piece shapes. Each cutter pays special attention so that the design on the fabric will match from one piece to another. They cut meticulously straight edges with heavy, 13-inch-long shears.

You will be surrounded by the whirring and click-ing of 30 sewing machines as you walk right through the middle of the sewing room. On your right, seamstresses nimbly maneuver fabric for cushions and throw pillows. On your left, they work on the pieces that will upholster the arms, backs, and bases. Not quite like your grandmother's sewing machine, these computerized electronic machines help the seamstresses be efficient and precise.

The upholsterers wrestle the fabric into exactly the right position before tacking it to the frame with an air-powered staple gun. When the master upholsterer is finished, another person will apply a hand-tailored skirt or artfully carved legs. Finally, all the loose threads are cut, stray padding is brushed away, and the Berne label is applied to every cushion.

Cost: Free

Freebies: Brochure detailing the company's history, products, and process.

Video/DVD Shown: No

Reservations Needed: Yes, 1 day in advance.

Days and Hours: Mon–Thur 9:30 AM, 10:30 AM, and 12:30 PM. Closed holidays and July 4th week and between Christmas and New Year's.

Plan to Stay: 1 hour.

Minimum Age: 12, although younger children may attend if well supervised.

Disabled Access: Yes

Group Requirements: Maximum group size 25–30 people. Larger groups can be split.

Special Information: Visitors are required to wear safety glasses.

Gift Shop: No. Will provide directions to local dealers.

Directions: From Fort Wayne, take Hwy. 27 South to Rt. 218 East (Main St.). Turn left on Behring St. Berne Furniture is on the corner of Berne and Behring Sts.

Nearby Attractions: Hitzer Stove Factory tour (call 260-589-8536); Swiss Heritage Village; Amishville USA; July Swiss Days Festival.

The RV industry has many start-up stories as colorful as Bill Gates' at Microsoft and Steven Jobs' at Apple Computer. The Corson brothers (Tom, Keith, and Claude) founded the company back in 1964, naming it after an inn Tom spotted along the Ohio Turnpike. From a meager start in capital, Coachmen now has record sales growth and revenues exceeding $500 million.

At this sprawling industrial complex, you'll get picked up for your tour at the Coachmen Caravan Visitors Center in a modern bus or a new motor home like those coming off the line. On the way to the tour site, the guide (who is also a sales representative) points out the buildings where the cabinets are made and where the floors, walls, and ceilings are formed and laminated in the vacubond process. Across from the chassis prep/frame shop/body shop building sits what looks like a football field's worth of Ford and Chevy chassis.

Walking through the travel trailer building, you can see these RVs come to life. At each station along the line, a different feature is added, whether it is the flooring, walls, or the familiar Coachmen Dalmatian logo. Saws buzz, overhead cranes lift front and rear fiberglass RV cabs and walls, and workers nimbly insert wiring and plumbing.

The motorized home tours usually occur after production ends at that plant for the day. Therefore, it offers a quieter industrial experience that gives you time to explore the RV innards. At one point on the tour, the RV just has its floors, then the next RV also has its side walls, and the next has its appliances, and so on. Near the end of the line is a big "rain booth" that exposes the finished RV to storm conditions for up to one hour, revealing any leaks.

Cost: Free

Freebies: No

Video/DVD Shown: Yes

Reservations Needed: Yes, call one week in advance.

Days and Hours: *Tours can be arranged only through dealers.*

Plan to Stay: 1 hour for tour, plus time for gift area in Visitors Center.

Minimum Age: 5

Disabled Access: No

Group Requirements: None

Special Information: Travel trailer and fifth-wheel tours available at the Fitzgerald, GA, plant (call 229-423-5471).

Gift Area: Coachmen Caravan Visitors Center sells Dalmatian-logoed items including T-shirts, jackets, key chains, and Dalmatian beanies. Open Mon–Fri 8:00 AM–5:00 PM. Closed holidays. Price list available at 888-422-2582.

Directions: From I-80/90 (Indiana Toll Rd.), take Exit 107. Turn right onto SR 13 South, which becomes Middlebury's Main St. At the north end of Middlebury, you'll see a friendly billboard at entrance to company complex. Tour begins at Caravan Visitors Center.

Nearby Attractions: RV tours, including Jayco and Monaco (see pages 165 and 167); Elkhart County is the RV manufacturing capital of the world. Local Convention & Visitors Bureau lists companies that give tours (call 800-262-8161). RV/MH Heritage Foundation Museum (call 574-293-2344); Amish Heritage Furniture tour (see page 161); Deutsch Kase Haus cheese factory, with observation windows in back of retail store.

AMERICA'S MOST **LIVEABLE** RVS

Since the mid-1960s, when Jayco founder Lloyd Bontrager first built his pop-up camper prototypes in a converted chicken coop, family members and friends have been an integral part of Jayco's success. Watching the construction of Travel Trailers and Fifth Wheels, both towable RVs, you still sense that family feeling, even though Jayco is the largest privately held RV manufacturer in the country. About 70 percent of Jayco's 1,500 workers are Amish or Mennonite, and their dedication to quality is evident as you travel through the factory.

Every Jayco trailer begins with a tubular steel frame built by a firm that specializes in RV frames. Workers lay tongue-and-groove plywood floor, insulate with fiberglass, and use Polyflex fabric on the bottom. Following these steps, you'll see the entire trailer flipped upside-down, like an immense turtle on its back. Workers attach axles and wheels to the underbelly and install a fresh-water tank. The unit is turned back over and placed on dollies that run down a track to various workstations in the plant.

Next, they lay the carpeting and linoleum. Workers then attach white-pine sidewalls, which have the interior paneling fastened with glue and brand nails. Look up, and you'll see the cabinet shops above the plant floor. Wood from the mill room is assembled into cabinets. Each production line, for the Jay Flight, Jay Feather, Eagle, and top-of-the-line Designer Fifth Wheels, has its own cabinet shop. Carpenters slide the finished cabinets down a ramp to the production area.

Toward the end of the RV's construction, workers attach the roof. They screw on tapered trusses or two-by-fours for the rafters, then stretch a rubber or aluminum roof over them. The area resounds with noises of drills, routers, and sanders. The RV's "skin" of .024-gauge aluminum or fiberglass is then secured onto the units. Once the RV's body is complete, appliances, drawer and cabinet fronts, windows, and custom-made upholstery are added. Afterward, at your leisure, you can view completed trailers displayed in a campground setting.

Cost: Free

Freebies: Product brochures.

Video/DVD Shown: 15-minute video on the company's history and production methods.

Reservations Needed: No, except for groups larger than 15 people.

Days and Hours: Tours Mon–Fri 12:00 PM; June–August a second tour is added at 9:30 AM. Display area and Visitors Center open Mon–Fri 8:00 AM–5:00 PM. Closed holidays. No production July 4th week and week between Christmas and New Year's.

Plan to Stay: 1.5 hours for video and tour, plus time for gift area, display area, and Visitors Center.

Minimum Age: None

Disabled Access: Limited, although must be careful of tools and wires on factory tour. No wheelchairs; call for more information.

Group Requirements: Groups larger than 15 people need to make reservations 10 days in advance. Maximum group size is 50.

Special Information: No photography or video equipment of any kind allowed on tours. Upon request, tours are available of the mini–motor home production buildings. Visitors Center displays Jayco memorabilia, including brochures from 1968.

Gift Area: Sells logoed items, including mugs, apparel, and miscellaneous gifts. Open same hours as Visitors Center. Closed holidays.

Directions: From I-80/90 (Indiana Toll Rd.), take Exit 107 for SR 13 South to Middlebury. Located on right, just south of the intersection with U.S. Rt. 20.

Nearby Attractions: Monaco and Coachmen tours (see pages 167 and 164). Elkhart County is the RV manufacturing capital of the world. For a list of tours, call (800) 262-8161. The RV/MH Heritage Foundation (call 574-293-2344) features museum, library, exhibition hall, and Hall of Fame dedicated to recreational vehicle and manufactured housing industries.

See color photos, page 30.

GREAT LAKES

Spiritual stained-glass church windows and drooping floral-patterned Tiffany lampshades are some of the most common uses of Kokomo opalescent glass. Founded in 1888, the company prides itself on having created its sheet glass the same way for more than 118 years. The company, now run by the great-grandsons of the founders, is the oldest maker of opalescent glass in the world. It originated the cat's-paw texture for Tiffany & Co.

Nestled into the back of the factory is the company's newest division, the Hot Glass Studio. Artists, or gaffers, and their talented assistants create functional and decorative blown-glass items, such as whimsical suncatchers, vases, bowls, and paperweights, using the remelted remnants from the sheet glass production.

As soon as you walk into the factory, you feel the heat wafting from the 2,600°F circular furnace. Each of the 12 fiery-orange glowing portholes of the furnace contains a cherry clay pot that holds 1,000 pounds of molten glass.

Once the table man rings a bell, each ladler scoops up to 70 pounds of molten glass out of the furnace and skips along the concrete floor, bouncing the ladle to keep the glass from hardening, looking almost like a ceremonial dance. Since up to five colors can be cast per sheet of glass, five men follow each other in rapid succession, repeating this dance. Using a long-handled, two-pronged pitchfork, the table man blends the glass, swirls it around, stretches it, tosses it like pizza dough, and almost effortlessly eases this 50-pound glob of molten glass onto the rollers. The rollers swallow up the glass and flatten it, with the bottom roller controlling the texture.

The one-eighth-inch-thick glass sheet travels through the 140-foot-long annealer for its one-hour cooling. As the glass hardens, its colors and patterns reveal themselves. Using T-squares and glass cutters, workers trim off the excess glass to create 32-by-80-inch sheets. Room 4, the stockroom, houses sheets of glass in narrow, wooden, two-

tiered racks. Since Kokomo makes approximately 540 colors and color combinations of sheet glass, this room contains a paint box of color and texture. Next time you go to your church or synagogue, you'll admire the stained-glass windows, wondering whether they were newly created or restored with Kokomo Opalescent Glass.

Cost: Free

Freebies: No

Video/DVD Shown: No

Reservations Needed: No, except for groups over 6 people.

Days and Hours: Wed and Fri 10:00 AM. Closed holidays. No tours in December. Call first, since company shuts down occasionally for repairs.

Plan to Stay: 1 hour, plus time in Op Shop.

Minimum Age: None, but must be extremely careful since you are near people carrying hot molten glass, and broken glass is on floor.

Disabled Access: Yes, but please call in advance.

Group Requirements: Groups larger than 6 people should call 2 weeks in advance.

Special Information: The extreme heat, especially in summer, can cause heat exhaustion for older visitors. No open-toed or open-heeled shoes. No photography.

Gift Shop: Op Shop sells paperweights, perfume bottles, vases, and suncatchers utilizing Kokomo opalescent glass. Hobbyists can buy sheets of rolled art glass by the pound. Custom design work is also available upon request. Open Mon–Fri 9:00 AM–5:00 PM. May–September: Sat 9:00 AM–1:00 PM. October–April: Sat 9:00 AM–5:00 PM.

Directions: From Indianapolis, take Hwy. 31 North. Turn left onto Markland Ave. in Kokomo. Turn left onto Home Ave. Turn right onto State St. Cross railroad tracks. Kokomo Opalescent Glass is at the corner of State and Market Sts.

Nearby Attractions: Other glass-related attractions, including nearby Seiberling Mansion, utilize Kokomo glass; Greentown Glass Museum; several companies 30 miles away in Elwood give tours, including the House of Glass (call 765-552-6841); Elwood Haynes Museum (invented first successful gasoline-powered car).

606 Nelson's Parkway, Wakarusa, IN 46573   (800) 650-7337   www.monaco-online.com

The roots of Monaco Coach Corporation run back to 1968 and the formation of Caribou Coach Corporation. They soon evolved into Monaco Motorhomes, Inc., and out of that organization, Monaco Coach Corporation was born in 1987. There are many milestones in the history of the evolution of the number-one highline diesel motor home manufacturer in the world. One of the most significant was the acquisition of Holiday Rambler in 1996. Holiday Rambler, which began in 1953, adds its names to the other brands now produced under Monaco Coach Corporation: Beaver, Safari, and McKenzie.

Today, Monaco is headquartered in Coburg, Oregon, with additional manufacturing facilities in Elkhart and Wakarusa, Indiana. At the Wakarusa, Indiana, location the following RVs are built: Holiday Rambler Scepter, Endeavor, Ambassador, Vacationer, and Atlantis. The Elkhart, Indiana, location produces all towable trailers and fifth wheels under the Holiday Rambler and McKenzie brand names.

Your guide will tell you about the company's history and the production of premium recreational vehicles. You will visit the factory floor to watch the construction of the RVs as they move down the assembly line. Monaco is especially proud of its Alumaframe construction. This durable, lightweight frame interlocks by C-channel studs at the joints, then each joint is double-welded together. Your tour guide will also take you through the finished RVs, brimming with top-of-the-line amenities and sophisticated interior decors.

All wood cabinets are made in-house of oak, cherry, and other select wood. Peek inside at the wooden cabinets and lush interiors—you'll be reminded more of a luxury hotel than wilderness. Enjoying the great outdoors does not have to include "roughing it"!

Cost: Free

Freebies: Product literature.

Video/DVD Shown: No

Reservations Needed: No, but arrive 15 minutes before tour time to sign in.

Days and Hours: Mon–Fri 10:00 AM and 2:00 PM; arrive 15 minutes in advance. Closed holidays.

Plan to Stay: 2 hours.

Minimum Age: 2; no baby strollers.

Disabled Access: Yes, please make arrangements in advance.

Group Requirements: No

Special Information: No photography or open-toed shoes. Tours are given at all locations Mon–Fri 10:00 AM and 2:00 PM. Contact numbers: Wakarusa, IN (800) 650-7337; Elkhart, IN (800) 866-6226; Coburg, OR (800) 634-0855.

Gift Shop: No

Directions: From the west, take Tollroad 80/90 East to the first South Bend exit. Take Hwy. 20 Bypass East to SR 19 South, then go south 7 miles to Wakarusa. Turn right at second traffic light onto Nelson's Pkwy. Monaco will be on the left. From the east, take Tollroad 80/90 West to Elkhart exit. Take SR 19 South. Proceed as above. Monaco will be on the right.

Nearby Attractions: RV tours, including Coachmen and Jayco (see pages 164 and 165). Elkhart County is the RV manufacturing capital of the world. Local Convention & Visitors Bureau lists companies that give tours (call 800-262-8161). The RV/MH Heritage Foundation (call 574-293-2344) features museum, library, exhibition hall, and Hall of Fame dedicated to recreational vehicle and manufactured housing industries.

5686 State Route 1, St. Joe, IN 46785

(219) 337-5461
(800) 332-5461

www.sechlers
pickles.com

GREAT LAKES

Like all pickles, Sechler's start out as cucumbers, salt, and water. Now in its third generation, Sechler's started making pickles in 1921. The first packing was done in the basement of Ralph Sechler's home, now the plant's office.

Trucks full of fresh cucumbers are unloaded into zigzagging grading machines. From a 20-foot elevation, the cucumbers fall into slats; smaller cukes roll through the first slats, and larger ones fall through slats at the end. Once sorted into seven sizes, the cukes are weighed in 20-bushel (1,000-pound) boxes. Farmers are paid by the number of pounds of each size cucumber; midgets (or "gherkins") are the most expensive.

In the tank yard, 120 10-foot-high wooden pickle vats stand in neat rows. Each holds up to 750 bushels (or 37,000 pounds) of pickles. The cucumbers are placed in these tanks by size, salt brine is added, and the tanks are closed with wooden lids. The pickles are usually in these tanks for at least 10 weeks but may stay as long as one -and -a half years, depending on demand and the cycle relative to next year's crop.

In the processing room, pickles cook in 110–140°F water for 24 hours to remove some of the salt. Cutting machines slice, dice, chip, grind, and chop the inspected pickles into numerous shapes and sizes. The pickles marinate for one to two days in dill brine, or seven to ten days in vinegar and spices for sweet flavoring. Smells of hot peppers, raisins, or oranges fill the air, depending on the variety in production.

Workers stand at a stainless-steel table hand-packing spears and peppers. Machines pack whole pickles, relishes, and hamburger chips. Jars move along the conveyor belt single-file, filling with pickles. The excess pickles roll into a cylinder below and recirculate back to the top of the machine. Down the line, the "juicer" overflows the jars with juice or brine. As the cap is put on, a burst of steam shoots

across it, cooling, condensing, and pulling down the center of the lid to form a pressure seal. The "dud" detector measures the jar's resulting vacuum level by measuring the recess in the lid. If the center isn't pulled down enough, the machine rejects the jar and sends it back through the line.

Cost: Free

Freebies: Paper hat and samples of all varieties in the showroom.

Video/DVD Shown: Sechler's 75th-anniversary video, with historic and product footage. Request to see video in showroom.

Reservations Needed: No, except for groups over 6 people.

Days and Hours: Tours only April 1–October 31: Mon–Fri 9:00 AM–11:00 AM and 12:30 PM–2:00 PM, every half hour. Closed holidays.

Plan to Stay: 30 minutes for tour and tasting, plus time in showroom.

Minimum Age: None

Disabled Access: Yes

Group Requirements: Groups larger than 6 people should call 2 days in advance. No maximum group size.

Special Information: Wear comfortable shoes. Be alert for wet floors and forklift.

Showroom: Sells over 30 varieties of pickles, such as orange-flavored spears and candied raisin crispies. Display cases show company history. Open year-round Mon–Fri 8:30 AM–4:30 PM, Sat 8:30 AM–12:00 PM. Closed major holidays. Mail-order form available from (800) 332-5461.

Directions: From Fort Wayne, take I-69 North to Dupont exit. Turn right on Dupont. Go straight through traffic light onto SR 1 North. Sechler's is 20 miles ahead (through farm country) on your left. From Auburn, take SR 8 East. Turn right onto SR 1 South. Sechler's is on your right.

Nearby Attractions: Auburn Cord Duesenberg Museum; National Automotive and Truck Museum; Fort Wayne's attractions, including Aunt Millie's Bakery (see page 162), are 20 miles away.

Walter Piano

25416 County Road 6, Elkhart, IN 46514

(574) 266-0615
(574) 674-0467

www.walterpiano.com

Elkhart, Indiana, is probably the musical instrument manufacturing capital of the U.S.A., with major saxophone, clarinet, flute, and other companies located in this area. The most accessible general-public tours are at Walter Piano, one of the only six piano manufacturers left in the U.S. Walter Piano, a family-owned company which started making high-end consoles and upright pianos in 1970, is as much cabinetmaker as piano-maker.

It takes four to five weeks to make one complete piano. You'll first feel like you've walked into a large cabinet shop. Workers hand-sand, saw, and drill cherry, oak, or mahogany cabinet parts. The cabinet parts for four pianos travel together on each cart. In spray booths, workers spray various stains, sealers, and lacquers.

In another area, a worker attaches the cast-iron piano plate to a wooden soundboard/frame assembly. More than 400 bridge pins are hammered by hand at an angle into the treble and bass bridge. With an air hammer, the worker punches in about 250 shiny nickel-plated tuning pins, then slides the frame assembly over to the next station. Pulling wire from coils overhead, the stringer hand-threads the wire through the hole in each tuning pin, snips it, and wraps the wire around the pin three times with a special tool. The stringer weaves the wire around the bridge pins and back through and around the next tuning pin for all 250 pins. It takes an experienced stringer one hour to do it all, while a new stringer takes eight hours.

After the cabinet and strung back are mated, soundboards travel through the factory to receive actions, hammers, and keys. (Since actions and keys are no longer made in the U.S., they are the only non–U.S.-made parts.) Pianos are tuned, weighted, and adjusted at each stage before final tuning and regulation.

The company also makes grand pianos, so you may be lucky enough to catch them bending the rim for one. This may be the only time you'll see a grand piano standing vertically, six feet tall. Strips of veneer, 16 feet long, are first glued together. A small crane raises the center of the glued strips, allowing the veneer to droop around the inside rim bending form, called an "inner cull." The outer cull is then lowered, and workers clamp the two culls together to compress and mold the layers of veneer.

Cost: Free

Freebies: Felt-covered piano hammers.

Video/DVD Shown: No

Reservations Needed: Yes

Days and Hours: Mon 1:00 PM, unless special arrangements made. Closed holidays, first 2 full weeks of July, and week between Christmas and New Year's.

Plan to Stay: 45 minutes for tour, plus time in the showroom.

Minimum Age: None

Disabled Access: Yes

Group Requirements: Minimum group size is 12 people; maximum group size is 30. Groups of 20 or more can be accommodated with additional tour times. Call at least 2 days in advance.

Special Information: While there are strong lacquer fumes in the finishing room, it is possible to bypass this room. No photography.

Showroom: Wide variety of console and grand pianos made by Walter Piano as well as other manufacturers. Also sells grandfather clocks. Open Mon–Fri 10:00 AM–5:00 PM (Mon and Thur until 7:00 PM), Sat 9:00 AM–1:00 PM.

Directions: From I-80/90, take Elkhart Exit 92. Turn left onto Cassopolis St. At second traffic light, turn left onto CR 6. Walter Piano is about 1 mile ahead on your right.

Nearby Attractions: Other musical instrument manufacturers give tours on a limited basis. Contact the Elkhart Convention & Visitors Bureau for a list (call 800-250-4827); Amish Heritage Furniture, Jayco RV, and Coachmen RV tours in Middlebury (see pages 161, 165, and 164); Amish Acres.

Alticor (formerly Amway)

HOUSEHOLD AND
PERSONAL CARE PRODUCTS

7575 Fulton Street East, Ada, MI 49355

(616) 787-6701

www.alticor.com

ALTICOR

Alticor, parent company of Amway, Quixtar, and Access Business Group, is a global enterprise committed to helping people live better lives.

The entrance to the Visitor Center features a global map of key markets, a list of core values, and a tribute to company cofounders. Watch a welcome video about the entrepreneurial spirit of Alticor. The video screen then rises to the ceiling, revealing doorways into the heart of the exhibit. A 24-foot wall of backlit photographs introduces you to some of Amway's independent business owners (IBOs), representing varied markets around the world. Amway and Quixtar IBOs distribute more than 450 products manufactured by Access Business Group—including personal care and cleaning products, water treatment systems, Artistry skin care and cosmetics, and Nutrilite vitamins and food supplements.

In contrast to a photo display highlighting Nutrilite's farming and production practices, step onto a simulated metal factory floor as you enter the Access Business Group exhibit. Take a virtual tour of three production lines to see how Access makes powder, toothpaste, and printed products. Access delivers 30 million orders each year to global destinations, and you'll see a busy conveyor moving overhead, carrying some of these products. Watch a lively video on distribution logistics, accompanied by a distribution center diagram that lights up during each process step. The research and development section features interactive displays on thermal imaging and magnification.

In the Artistry section, you can evaluate how much your skin has been exposed to the sun. From different computers, log onto the Quixtar visitor site and browse through products available from this popular online shopping service and business ownership opportunity.

At the end of your visit, you will have a new appreciation for the spirit of free enterprise that has inspired people to build this American-made venture into a global business.

Cost: Free

Freebies: Travel-size product samples.

Videos/DVDs Shown: 10-minute video introduces the global nature of the enterprise.

Reservations Needed: No, except for groups of 10 or more people.

Days and Hours: Mon–Fri 8:30 AM–12:00 PM, 1:00–5:00 PM. Call ahead for holiday schedules.

Plan to Stay: 45 minutes, depending on your use of the interactive exhibits.

Minimum Age: None, although children under 16 must be accompanied by an adult.

Disabled Access: Yes

Group Requirements: Groups of 10 people or more please make reservations as far in advance as possible. Maximum group size is 70 people.

Gift Shop: No. Catalog available (call 800-544-7167).

Directions: From Grand Rapids, take I-196 East, which becomes I-96, to Exit 39 for M-21. The exit road becomes Fulton St. In about 5 miles, turn left into the Amway World Headquarters Building. Look for the row of international flags in front.

Nearby Attractions: Van Andel Museum Center; Grand Rapids Art Museum; Gerald R. Ford Museum; Grand Rapids Symphony Orchestra; Frederik Meijer Gardens and Sculpture Park; John Ball Zoo.

8066 U.S. 31, Acme, MI 49610

(231) 938-1644
(800) 298-3409

www.amonorchards.com

Northern Michigan calls itself the cherry capital of the world. The roads in and around Traverse City are lined with bright red cherry trees during the summer. Stands selling the juiciest, freshest cherries you've ever tasted appear along most roads.

David Amon accurately predicted a sharp drop in the price of cherries and added tourism and specialty products to Amon Orchard's agriculture business. The company also branched out to other types of fruit production and now enjoys taking visitors through the fields to see and learn about it all.

Relax as you ride in a shaded, canvas-topped, open-sided trolley that meanders through rows of eight- to ten-foot-tall trees on this 200-acre, family-run orchard. Your driver (perhaps David himself) spouts interesting facts you probably never knew about cherries. You learn that the "fresh" cherries with stems in your supermarket were probably handpicked in Oregon or Washington long before they were ripened.

The driver stops the trolley to let you pull a ripe fruit from a tree, perhaps one of the three different apricot or nectarine varieties or seven different types of peaches they grow. From the trolley, you can also reach some red tart, light, or dark sweet cherries. The juice from these fresh, ripe fruits will squirt into your mouth and, if you're not careful, onto your shoes!

One of Amon's missions through the tour is to teach people about the changes in agriculture, such as integrated pest management systems that use "good" bugs to eat "bad" bugs, thus requiring less pesticide. Another proudly pushed theme is that cherries aren't just for dessert anymore. Creative uses of cherries include many of the specialty products you'll want to sample in the retail store before or after the tour.

Cost: $1 donation for trolley ride.

Freebies: Ripe fruit from trees, cherry juice, gourmet product samples, recipe brochure.

Video/DVD Shown: No

Reservations Needed: Only during National Cherry Festival (first or second week in July). Advance notice required for motor coaches.

Days and Hours: *Call for hours and availability (800-298-3409).* Open mid-July and during Cherry Festival week and weekends in October, based on planting schedule and staffing. Arrangements can be made for motor-coach groups year-round.

Plan to Stay: 1 hour for trolley tour, petting farm, u-pick (call for the Ripe and Ready Report and map, telling you what months are best for picking different fruits), and retail store. In October, wander around the maze carved through 8-foot-tall cornstalks.

Minimum Age: None

Disabled Access: Yes

Group Requirements: Call at least a few days in advance for motor-coach group tours year-round. Call for group tour rates.

Special Information: Orchard is particularly scenic during spring blossom season, with special tours available. Family Fall Festival on October weekends features u-pick pumpkins.

Retail Store: Grandma Amon's Country Market and gift shop sells fresh-picked fruit from orchard, jams, and gourmet cherry products, including "Fudgie" sauce, cherry hot-pepper jelly, cherry Mexican salsa, dried cherries, and baked goods. Daily in-store specials. Mid-June–October: Mon–Sun 10:00 AM–6:00 PM. November–December: Tue–Sat 10:00 AM–5:00 PM. Catalog available from above number.

Directions: From Traverse City, take U.S. 31 North. Orchard is about 8 miles ahead on your right. From Mackinaw City, take I-75 South to U.S. 31 South. Orchard is on your left 10 miles south of Elk Rapids.

Nearby Attractions: National Cherry Festival week (first or second week in July) events include cherry pie–eating contests, Cherry Royale Parade, and Taste of Cherries. Kilwin's Chocolates tour (see page 178); Good Harbor Vineyards tour (call 231-256-7165); the Music House; Grand Traverse Bay.

"JIFFY" mixes

You recognize "JIFFY" mixes by their little blue-and-white boxes and low prices, not by any supermarket coupons or fancy advertising campaigns. Chelsea Milling Company, founded in 1887, prides itself on this and has been producing its all-purpose JIFFY Baking Mix in a low-key fashion since 1930. Grandma Mabel Holmes named the famous biscuit mix (arch rival of General Mills' Bisquick) after hearing her father's housekeeper say, "The muffins will be ready in a jiffy." Howdy Holmes, former race car driver, is now at the helm of this family-run business.

The family feeling extends to the tour program. The head tour guide has been conducting tours for more than 25 years—following in the footsteps of her mother, who also led tours for nearly 20 years. After watching the slide show, you walk upstairs into the factory to watch the packaging process.

The dark blue, heavy, well-oiled, vintage 1950s and '60s machinery hisses as it works hard 24 hours a day. As you walk next to the circular box-making machine, a stack of flat boxes (or "shells") feeds into the machine. Simultaneously, a roll of waxed paper threads through and is cut and shaped around a metal block. The cardboard boxes form around the waxed paper.

As you walk to the filling area, notice the floor vibrating under your feet. For corn muffin mix, the number-one prepared food mix in the U.S.A., maize-colored powder funnels down from the second floor to fill each box, one at a time. Along each of the 16 small box lines, funnels fill the boxes in a two-step process. The boxes march single file along a conveyor belt over a scale and to the box top-sealer. At this circular machine, each station around the wheel performs one step toward sealing the waxed paper and then the box.

Workers hand-pack 24 small boxes into each case, and two cases of like product are glued together to form a piggyback carton. These piggyback cartons travel along a roller-coaster conveyor belt to the warehouse. And, if the boxes are not dizzy enough already, a driver will release two double-stacked pallets onto the Lanwrapper, which spins the cartons around as they are covered with heavy-duty shrink-wrap.

Cost: Free

Freebies: Recipe booklet; small box of "JIFFY" mix (2 boxes for people 13 years old or older).

Video/DVD Shown: 15-minute slide show covers company history, flour-milling process, and packaging.

Reservations Needed: Yes

Days and Hours: Mon–Fri 9:00 AM–1:30 PM. Closed holidays. Closed between Christmas and New Year's.

Plan to Stay: 1.5–2 hours.

Minimum Age: 6

Disabled Access: Some accessibility. Call for more information.

Group Requirements: Groups should call at least 1 week in advance for reservations. Regular group maximum is 45 people; however, special arrangements can be made for larger groups.

Special Information: No photography inside factory.

Gift Area: Guests can purchase 24-pack variety tour case containing an assortment of mixes and a recipe booklet. Also, individual products can be purchased by the case.

Directions: From I-94, take M-52 North (Exit 159). As you roll into Chelsea's Main Street, go through 4 traffic lights. As you cross the railroad tracks, notice white, 120-foot-high silos with blue "JIFFY Mixes" lettering to your left. Take 1st left onto North St. and park on right.

Nearby Attractions: The Walter P. Chrysler Museum tour (see page 181); Jeff Daniels' Purple Rose Theater; Stagecoach Stop U.S.A.; Ann Arbor's attractions, including University of Michigan, are 20 minutes away.

DeKlomp/Veldheer

12755 Quincy Street, off U.S. 31,
Holland, MI 49424

(616) 399-1803
(616) 399-1900

www.veldheer.com

Holland, Michigan, is full of Dutch re-creations, at least one of which you'll feel enticed to visit. The Tulip Time Festival (a 10-day event beginning the first weekend of May) will pleasantly overwhelm you with the dazzling colors of millions of tulips in full bloom. At DeKlomp, the only delftware factory in the U.S.A., watch delftware and wooden shoes being made through windows in the back of the large retail store. Also enjoy Veldheer's tulip farm and show garden.

Delftware originated with pottery brought to the Netherlands from the Orient in the 13th century. In 1310, Dutch artists in the village of Delft adapted the Oriental patterns, giving birth to the familiar blue-and-white hand-painted floral designs and Dutch scenery. Much of what passes for delftware in this country is actually mass-produced and stencil-decorated. However, DeKlomp's small staff of artisans paint each individual piece with the blue-and-white designs.

Dressed in traditional Dutch costume during Tulip Time, the artisans happily discuss each step of the production process, from molding the clay to decorating the final product. All materials—clay, molds, and machinery—are imported from the Netherlands. Walk by the paint room, where pottery is hand-painted and signed on the bottom.

At the next window, notice the unique machines used to create wooden shoes; ask to see them in action. Using a dual-action shaper machine and a pattern, a worker makes the left and right shoes simultaneously. By rotating a block counterclockwise, the machine traces a mirror image, thus producing a matched pair. The narrow shelves along the wall contain wooden shoe patterns. A worker places one of these patterns on the center rod of the dual-action carving machine, which carves out the interior of each pair of shoes. The right rod carves the left shoe, and the left rod, the right shoe. You will also see the only automated wooden shoe carving machine in the U.S. and a shaper machine that makes souvenir 3.5- to 12.5-centimeter shoes—sometimes as many as five in a row, resembling a totem pole.

Cost: Production viewing: free. Tulip farm: adults, $6.

Freebies: No

Video/DVD Shown: No

Reservations Needed: No

Days and Hours: April–December: Mon–Fri 8:00 AM–6:00 PM, Sat and Sun 9:00 AM–5:00 PM. January–March: Mon–Sat 9:00 AM–5:00 PM. Tulip Time Festival (10 days in May, starting the first weekend): Mon–Sun 8:00 AM–8:00 PM. Closed Thanksgiving, Christmas, and New Year's. Wooden shoes not carved January–March. Painting and shoes sometimes not in production at other times during the year.

Plan to Stay: 45 minutes for self-guided tour of production through windows in the back of the retail store, plus time for gift shop and Veldheer's Tulip Gardens.

Minimum Age: None

Disabled Access: Yes

Group Requirements: Groups over 20 should call in advance to arrange a guided tour. No maximum group size.

Retail Store: Large gift shop carries all of the shoes and delftware made in the factory, including delft canister sets and Christmas ornaments, miniature wooden-shoe souvenirs, and a wide variety of Dutch gifts and foods. A separate store sells tulip bulbs. Open same hours as tour. Price list available from above number.

Directions: From Grand Rapids, take I-196 West to Exit 55 (Business Rt. 196 West). Then exit at U.S. 31 North and follow it 2.5 miles to Quincy St. The factory is at the corner of Quincy St. and U.S. 31.

Nearby Attractions: Downtown Holland's art galleries; Dutch Village; Holland State Park Beach; Windmill Island; Saugatuck, an artists' colony; Saugatuck Dune Rides; Saugatuck Boat Cruises.

The Henry Ford, 20900 Oakwood Boulevard, Dearborn, MI 48124

(800) 835-5237   www.hfmgv.org/rouge

From 1928 through the 1940s, the Rouge complex was the capital of Henry Ford's industrial empire. It once employed more than 100,000 workers and produced a new car every 49 seconds. The Rouge had its own power plant, police and fire departments, hospital, and railroad.

Though not as large as it was, the Rouge (now known as the Dearborn Truck Plant) still makes vehicles, including Ford's F-150 pickup truck. You can visit parts of it on tours run by The Henry Ford, a nonprofit educational institution (not affiliated with Ford Motor Company or the Ford Foundation).

Departing in buses from the Henry Ford Museum (see page 175), tours begin with a look at famous landmarks. After you arrive at the Rouge, a short video introduces you to its history. From the past, you move to the present in the virtual-reality theater, where a 360-degree presentation shows the process of making automobiles in the 21st century. The show includes not only the sights and sounds of production but also, through modern technology, the smell of the plant. To top off the experience, the sequence on how vehicles are painted includes the distribution of a light water mist over the audience, approximating the feel of paint sprays.

Next you ascend an 80-foot observation deck to see Ford's 10-acre "living roof," a sprawling garden that flourishes atop the truck plant. Planted in thick mats of vegetation, the expanse of greenery absorbs rainwater to help prevent local flooding.

The tour's last stop brings you into the thumping heart of the modern Rouge factory. From an elevated walkway, you can take 20–30 minutes to view the final assembly area of the truck plant. If the factory is operating during your visit, you experi-ence the bustle and noise of production as workers put together F-150 trucks and other vehicles with remarkable speed and precision.

Cost: Adults, $14 (members $12); children, $10 (members $8.50); children 2 and under, free.

Freebies: No

Video/DVD Shown: A 12-minute video on the Rouge's history plus a 14-minute presentation on manufacturing automobiles.

Reservations Needed: No, but strongly recom-mended; tours often sell out months in advance.

Days and Hours: Tours leave from the Henry Ford Museum every 30 minutes Mon–Sat 9:30 AM–2:30 PM; during summer, also Sun 9:30 AM–2:30 PM (call 800-835-5237 for current hours). Closed Thanksgiving and Christmas.

Plan to Stay: Up to 3 hours for tour (also, visitors must arrive at bus stop at least 30 minutes before scheduled departure).

Minimum Age: No

Disabled Access: Yes

Group Requirements: Maximum 75. Large groups should reserve several months ahead of the desired tour date.

Special Information: No photography or videotap-ing in the theaters and factory. Tours are not guar-anteed to see the Dearborn Truck Plant in full op-eration (workers are usually in action Mon–Fri).

Gift Shop: Henry Ford Museum Store sells souve-nirs, toys, and miscellaneous items related to the his-torical themes of the museum. Open daily 9:30 AM–5:00 PM. Closed Thanksgiving and Christmas.

Directions: From I-94 or I-75, get on Southfield Fwy. North (M-39), exit at Oakwood Blvd., turn left on Oakwood, and drive 1.8 miles. From I-96, get on Southfield Fwy. South (M-39) and exit at Michigan Ave. Stay left on service drive and turn right at en-trance to Henry Ford on Village Rd.

Nearby Attractions: The Henry Ford complex also includes the Henry Ford Museum and Greenfield Village (see page 175). Also in the Detroit area, Wal-ter P. Chrysler Museum, Chelsea Milling, and Lionel trains (see pages 181, 172, and 179).

Henry Ford Museum and Greenfield Village

U.S. MANUFACTURING AND CARS

The Henry Ford, 20900 Oakwood Boulevard, Dearborn, MI 48124

(313) 982-6001
(800) 835-5237

www.TheHenryFord.org

GREAT LAKES

America's Greatest History Attraction

The history of American technology and manufacturing is the focus of the constantly improving Henry Ford Museum (not affiliated with Ford Motor Company or The Ford Foundation). Among many other exhibits, spanning such subjects as transportation, agriculture, and clockwork, the "Made in America" installation will appeal especially to people who love factory tours.

The size of a football field, the exhibit area greets visitors with a clanking machine that assembles electrical switches and a swinging robotic arm that sprays paint on a farm-tractor chassis. Encircling the exhibit area is a constantly moving overhead conveyor belt with chairs, propellers, wheels, bike frames, sinks, and more hanging from it. Full-size displays, videos (many showing historic footage), photographs, talks, and hands-on activities offer a creative look at U.S. manufacturing history and processes.

While you'll be fascinated by the machines, such as one for making light bulbs from ribbons of molten glass, take time to read the text descriptions and watch the videos scattered throughout. Displays explain workers' roles and the good and bad effects machines had on them. For example, the display of the "clean room" used in fabricating computer chips explains the stress-related injuries that workers in this controlled environment can suffer.

"Made in America" has a few historical displays on car manufacturing, such as the area devoted to Ford's Highland Park plant of the 1920s, whose moving assembly line revolutionized mass production. Car buffs will want to visit another area of the museum for the exhibit called "The Automobile in American Life." It's filled with a number of big and intriguing artifacts. These include the actual 1961 Lincoln car in which President Kennedy was assassinated and the experimental automobile (quadricycle) that Henry Ford invented in 1896.

Nearby Greenfield Village features the original buildings and homes of famous American inventors and industrialists, such as Thomas Edison, the Wright brothers, and Henry Heinz. The Henry Ford

Museum is also the starting point for the tour of the Ford Rouge vehicle-making plant (see page 174).

Cost: Museum: adults, $14; senior citizens 62 and over, $13; children 5–12, $10; children under 5, free. Greenfield Village: adults, $20; seniors, $19; children 5–12, $14; children under 5, free.

Freebies: Drawings made by rubbing crayons over brass etchings in Henry Ford Museum.

Videos/DVDs Shown: Video clips and features are everywhere.

Reservations Needed: No

Days and Hours: Museum and Village open Mon–Sat 9:00 AM–5:00 PM., Sun 12:00 PM–5:00 PM. Closed Thanksgiving and Christmas. Village building interiors closed January–March.

Plan to Stay: A few days to see all attractions. Combination tickets (FunPack) available.

Minimum Age: None

Disabled Access: Yes

Group Requirements: Groups of 15 or more should call 2 weeks in advance for reservations and group discounts. Educational programs for school groups: call 2 weeks in advance.

Special Information: Special events throughout the year at the Henry Ford; see the website for schedule.

Gift Shops: Sells souvenirs, toys, and miscellaneous items related to the historical themes of the museum. Open daily 9:30 AM–5:00 PM. Closed Thanksgiving and Christmas.

Directions: From I-94, exit on northbound Southfield Fwy. (M-39), drive 1.8 miles to Oakwood Blvd. (Exit 4), take a left onto Oakwood, and drive 1.8 miles. From I-75, exit on northbound Southfield Fwy. (M-39), drive 4.1 miles to Oakwood Blvd. (Exit 4), take a left onto Oakwood Blvd., and drive 1.8 miles. From I-96, exit on southbound Southfield Fwy. (M-39), drive 4.5 miles to Michigan Ave. (Exit 6), stay to left on service drive, then take right at entrance on Village Rd.

Nearby Attractions: The Ford Rouge Factory Tour leaves from the museum (see page 174). Also in the area: Walter P. Chrysler Museum (see page 181); Henry Ford Estate—Fair Lane tour (call 313-593-5590); Automotive Hall of Fame.

Hoegh Industries

317 Delta Avenue, Gladstone, MI 49837

(906) 428-2151

www.hoegh
petcaskets.com

Hoegh Industries is the world's largest manufacturer of pet caskets, cremation urns, and memorial plaques. Dennis Hoegh began the business in 1966, after meeting a dog owner who could not find a casket worthy of his beloved sled dog. The company now produces more than 30,000 caskets annually in eight sizes and 22 styles, ranging from a hamster-sized 10-inch case to a 52-inch box fit for the grandest Great Dane. Molded of high-impact styrene plastic and equipped with a padded cloth interior, the caskets are made by a crew of eight workers.

Your tour starts near the computerized ovens; each one heats and softens four pieces of plastic simultaneously. Plastic sheets in different sizes—some pink, some blue, most buff—line the corridor waiting their turn in the ovens. Entering the oven as a rigid sheet clamped into a metal frame, the plastic undergoes a startling transformation. The rigid sheets become flexible, clothlike membranes, vibrating and jiggling as they're pulled out of the oven. As a plastic sheet hovers in the air, a mold rises up to meet it. Vacuum pumps suck all the air from the space between plastic and mold, and a pet casket is formed.

Once cool, molded bottoms are lifted out of the frame so a worker can cut off the flashing and scrape the edges. One worker collects this excess plastic and feeds it into a waist-high grinder, creating tiny plastic pebbles. Beyond the grinder machine you can see where the polyurethane foam is added. The casket bottom sits in a wooden support, while a worker sprays a thin stream of superheated chemicals along the bottom inside edge. The worker must quickly insert, brace, and clamp down the interior wall, since the chemicals immediately begin to expand like exploding meringue. Confined by the interior and exterior casket walls, the foam expands within the cavity into a sturdy insulation, creating a double-walled eternal vessel. Home workers sew the cloth interiors for the caskets.

Step outside to admire the model pet cemetery. Most intriguing is a wall of remembrance plaques. A pet's photograph can be engraved onto a durable metal plaque, along with a name, dates, and a brief comment. Look for the plaques for Chuck the lizard, Fruit Loops the toucan, and the pet turkey who would walk on a leash, who died at age 13.

Cost: Free

Freebies: Postcards, brochures, rulers, pencils, pens, occasionally calendars.

Video/DVD Shown: Optional 17-minute video highlights the production process and shows a model pet cemetery. Video usually shown in winter or bad weather; also can be sent to groups, upon request.

Reservations Needed: No, however preferred for groups larger than 10 people. Individuals and families may want to call ahead (same day) to give the factory notice.

Days and Hours: Open Mon–Fri 8:00 AM–4:00 PM. Lunch break from 12:00 PM–12:30 PM. Closed holidays.

Plan to Stay: 30–45 minutes.

Minimum Age: No minimum if accompanied by a parent. Children in groups should be 10 years old.

Disabled Access: Yes

Group Requirements: Groups larger than 10 people should call at least 1 day in advance.

Gift Shop: No

Directions: Take I-75 North. At the Mackinac Bridge, follow U.S. 2 West. When you reach Gladstone, turn left on Delta Ave. The factory is on the right.

Nearby Attractions: DeLoughary's Sugar Bush maple syrup and cream tour (call 906-466-2305); Fayette Historic State Park; Seney National Wildlife Refuge; Hiawatha National Forest.

Kellogg's Cereal City USA

171 West Michigan Avenue,
Battle Creek, MI 49017

(269) 962-6230
(800) 970-7020

www.kelloggs
cerealcity.org

Twelve years after Kellogg Company discontinued its popular plant tours in 1986, the Heritage Center Foundation opened Kellogg's Cereal City USA. Tony the Tiger welcomes you inside the 45,000-square-foot extravaganza, named by the Discovery Channel as the second best factory tour for kids on the planet, and into the history of breakfast cereal, which all started in Battle Creek, Michigan.

At the simulated Cereal Production Line, Jill and Mr. Grit describe how a grit—the heart of the corn—becomes a golden corn flake. The video tour replicates every facet of the production process.

In the simulated production line, the aroma of the grain at each processing step is reproduced. Every few minutes an overhead car full of kernels of corn and flavoring travels the rail and stops to release its contents into the cooking tank. See the corn pass through on metal screens as it dries. Learn that tempering equalizes the moisture in the grain and is therefore the single most important step in the process. A large, loud re-creation of a separator divides the tempered corn into single kernels before the pressing units roll them into flakes. You can even try some warm corn flakes right off the line.

Step into the Historical Timeline's old-time nickelodeon theater and listen as Duff, a local historian, brings to life the early history of Battle Creek, the Battle Creek Sanitarium, and the cereal boom. At the '50s and '60s exhibit, learn how the Kellogg Company developed Saturday morning television programming and reminisce about shows like *Arthur Godfrey*, *The Beverly Hillbillies*, *Rin Tin Tin*, and *The Monkees*.

In the Cereal City cinema, "A Bowl Full of Dreams," watch Bob Keeshan, better known as Captain Kangaroo, narrate a film on Kellogg Company marketing campaigns and reminisce during the vintage commercials that follow. Finish the day with a Froot Loops sundae at Sullivan's ice-cream counter.

Cost: Adults, $7.95; seniors 65+, $6.50; children 3–12, $4.95; children under 2, free. Annual individual and family passes available.

Freebies: Single-serving box of cereal.

Videos/DVDs Shown: The Bijou Theater shows a 20-minute video, "Best to You Revue," on the cereal industry, Kellogg brothers, and Kellogg characters. You feel as though you've been shrunk to the size of a salt shaker while viewing oversized spoons, bowls, and cereal boxes. Videos in each exhibit area.

Reservations Needed: No, except groups over 20 people.

Days and Hours: Open year-round. Times vary by season. Call ahead or check website.

Plan to Stay: 2.5 hours plus time for shopping and eating.

Minimum Age: None

Disabled Access: Yes

Group Requirements: Discounts for groups of 20 or more. Call 2 weeks in advance. Educational group tours available.

Special Information: Battle Creek festivals include: The World's Largest Breakfast Table, the second Saturday in June; Team USA Hot Air Balloon Championship in July; and the International Festival of Lights, late November–December. Visit website for new exhibits and shows, or call the visitor center at (800) 397-2240 for information.

Gift Shop: Factory Store sells more than 500 items, including Ron Lee collectible Kellogg character figurines, clothing, kitchen items, and souvenirs. Become a "Famous Flake!" by getting your photo on a commemorative 20-oz. box of Kellogg's Corn Flakes. Also shop online at above website.

Directions: From I-94, take exit 98B to Downtown Battle Creek. Continue about 5 miles to the second light and turn left onto Michigan Ave. Kellogg's Cereal City USA is located about 4 blocks on the left.

Nearby Attractions: Binder Park Zoo; Full Blast Family Entertainment Center; Kalamazoo Air Zoo; Kalamazoo Valley Museum; Gilmore Car Museum.

Kilwin's Chocolates

FUDGE, CHOCOLATES, AND ICE CREAM

355 North Division Road, Petoskey, MI 49770 | (231) 347-3800 | www.kilwins.com

Kilwin's

Among its popular tourist attractions, Northern Michigan and Mackinac Island have an abundance of candy and fudge shops, with few more respected than Kilwin's. At most of its 54 retail stories, you can watch them make creamy fudge. All of the stores' chocolate candies and brittle are made and shipped from this small factory on the outskirts of Petoskey, the resort town where Don and Katy Kilwin opened their first shop in 1947 as a sideline to their bakery business.

What we like about tours of small to midsize candy companies is how close you get to the action. In the production area, you may see candies boxed, cream centers mixed, peanut brittle poured, chocolate blocks warmed in melters, liquid chocolate funneled into molds, or pecans marching through the enrobing machine. Making peanut brittle is at least a two-person operation that requires more muscle than you might expect. Two workers pick up a copper kettle and pour its dense, hot mixture of mostly peanuts, sugar, and butter onto a cold steel or marble table. Once the brittle is partially cool, the rubber-gloved workers slice the nine-foot slabs into three pieces. They then hover over the pieces, flipping and stretching out each part so it's not too thick with peanuts.

To make the solid milk chocolate tool kits and ice-cream-cone suckers, liquid milk chocolate is poured into molds, which cool on metal trays in a nearby room. A worker then adds the decorations to create the ice-cream effect. Watch a worker gently dip the top part of the sucker into white chocolate. It's a real skill to get just the right amount of white chocolate onto the candy so that the cone-looking part stays dry. Sprinkling jimmies (sprinkles) on top completes this production feat.

Cost: Free

Freebies: Sample of one of their popular chocolates, such as the tuttle (caramel, pecans, and chocolate).

Video/DVD Shown: No

Reservations Needed: No, during summer season, except for groups over 10 people. Yes, for remainder of year.

Days and Hours: June, July, August (sometimes September): Mon–Thur 10:30 AM, 11:00 AM, 2:00 PM, and 2:30 PM. Tours only by special request other months of year. Closed holidays and during unscheduled plant shutdowns.

Plan to Stay: 20 minutes for tour, plus time in retail store.

Minimum Age: None

Disabled Access: Yes

Group Requirements: Motor-coach tours can visit all year with 1 week's advance notice. Call (231) 347-4831.

Special Information: Production changes daily, so call ahead if you have favorites. Limited ice-cream production on tour.

Retail Store: Sells full line of 300 confectionery products, including fudge, tuttles, truffles, and sugar-free chocolate. Open year-round Mon–Fri 9:00 AM–5:00 PM. Closed holidays. Catalog and franchise information available at above number.

Directions: From the south, take I-75 North to Gaylord Exit 282. Turn left on Rt. 32 West to Rt. 131 North. Turn right to Petoskey. Turn left onto Division Rd. Kilwin's is immediately on left. From the Upper Peninsula, take I-75 South and exit at Indian River Exit 310. Turn right onto Rt. 68 West. Take Rt. 31 South to Petoskey. Turn left onto Division Rd. Kilwin's is on the right at top of hill.

Nearby Attractions: Boyer Glassworks (call 231-526-6359); Petoskey's Gas Light District; Lake Michigan's beaches; Mackinac Island (self-proclaimed fudge capital of world), 35 miles away.

26750 Twenty-Three Mile Road,
Chesterfield, MI 48051-2493

(586) 949-4100,
ext. 1211

www.lionel.com

Just about every American over 35 recognizes the Lionel brand name. Back in 1949, people of all ages used to stop by the company's showroom on East 26th Street in New York City to see the famous miniature railroad display. Store buyers and collectors would come to watch as small locomotives pulled freight cars through pretend towns and over imitation mountains. In 1964, the showroom closed its doors. But today, thanks to the hard work, dedication, and volunteer efforts of the employees at Lionel's Michigan headquarters, you can once again enjoy seeing Lionel trains in action and learning the story behind the company that started in 1900.

Your visit begins with a video about Lionel, its heritage, and its manufacturing. Then you enter the showroom. Lights rise slowly over the 14-by-40-foot railroad display, illuminating a fascinating arrangement of trains, tracks, and scenery that will remind kids (and kids at heart) why they love collecting model trains.

This classic display features multiple levels of tracks with many different rail lines. Buttons around the display allow visitors to operate accessories themselves, including trains on a smaller layout just for young kids.

The design of the main display's bottom level includes elements from the original 1949 layout, such as the underground passenger platform and the yard and roundhouse area. The next level reveals more modern-era trains, including more freight cars and diesel- or steam-powered engines. The top, overhead level uses the American Flyer line, which, although different in size from the other model trains, fits in perfectly with the rest of the display.

While watching the chugging, rumbling trains, don't forget to enjoy the impressive scenery of a small, semireal city. The workers who created this extraordinary display thought of every detail, right down to the park statues, rail yard workers, and store signs. Also notice the company timeline on the wall, illustrating more than 100 years of model train history. It includes rare and unique prototype train models, artifacts, historic ads, and photos.

Cost: Free

Freebies: Souvenir pin and product catalog.

Video/DVD Shown: 10-minute video on company history and manufacturing process.

Reservations Needed: Yes

Days and Hours: Wed and Thur 10:00 AM, 3:00 PM, and 4:00 PM; Fri 10:00 AM, 1:30 PM, and 2:30 PM; Sat 9:00 AM, 10:00 AM, 11:00 AM, and 12:00 PM. Times change seasonally, so call for recording. Closed holidays.

Plan to Stay: 1 hour for video and tour of visitors center, plus time for gift shop.

Minimum Age: None

Disabled Access: Yes

Group Requirements: For groups of 20 or more, additional visitors center tour times may be available. Maximum group size is 60 people.

Special Information: Information available about Railroader Club membership.

Gift Shop: Sells the Visitors Center Boxcar (available only at this store), other trains, starter sets, train accessories, and logoed items including T-shirts, signs, and clocks. Discount for Railroader Club members. Open Tue–Fri 1:30–4:30 PM, Sat 10:00 AM–12:30 PM. (Call ext. 1443 for seasonal hours.)

Directions: From I-94, take Exit 243 (Twenty-Three Mile Rd./New Baltimore exit). Veer left at exit if coming from Detroit and stay on Twenty-Three Mile Rd. Turn left at 3rd light onto Russell Schmidt Rd. (You'll see "Lionel" sign.) Turn right into visitor parking.

Nearby Attractions: The Walter P. Chrysler Museum tour (see page 181); Morley Candy Factory tour (groups only, call 586-468-4300); Yates Cider Mill; Anchor Bay Aquarium; Selfridge Military Air Museum; Detroit's attractions about 30 minutes away.

Simplicity Pattern Company has been synonymous with sewing since 1927. The Niles facility, built in 1931 and expanded in the 1970s, covers 750,000 square feet. Retiree-led tours are available for groups of 12 or more.

Over the noise of the paper mill, a supervisor describes the production of the tissue paper upon which one of Simplicity's 800-plus current patterns will be printed. Simplicity recycles paper from various sources by mixing it with water and then running the pulp through a paper-making machine that steams the water out. The paper is wound around a cardboard core. The resulting tissue-paper roll, weighing in excess of 4,000 pounds, is then cut into various widths for use on the pattern presses.

In the prepress department, electronic files are received from the corporate office in New York. Then the files for envelopes, instruction sheets, and patterns go to a large format platesetter, and a laser burns the images onto an aluminum printing plate.

Your guide takes you to the envelope manufacturing area to watch a four-color press print envelopes on a sheet of 48-by-55-inch flat stock paper using black, blue, red, and yellow inks. A guillotine blade cuts the envelopes, stacked in quantities of 2,450 sheets, into 21 rectangular sections. A die-cutter trims them to the exact envelope shape.

A Stevens press prints, cuts, and folds instruction sheets from a continuous roll of newsprint that is over 48,000 feet long. A single web press prints the pattern (2–30 pieces, depending on the level of detail) on tissue paper received from the mill area, then cuts and folds the tissue into individual patterns.

In the pattern finishing area, machines fold the envelopes and glue the sides together. The inserting machine utilizes a separate hopper for the finished envelopes, instruction sheets, and pattern tissue. Vacuum pulls a pattern tissue and an instruction sheet in between belts where they are electronically timed to come together. Vacuum also pulls the envelope into a Ferris wheel pocket where air is used to open the envelope. The pattern and instruction sheet drop into the envelope and the flap is tucked in. A small hydraulic press compresses and bundles pattern packets for shipping worldwide.

Cost: Free

Freebies: Pattern and booklet.

Video/DVD Shown: No

Reservations Needed: Yes. Tours are only for groups of 12 or more.

Days and Hours: Tue–Thur 10:00 AM. Closed holidays. No tours in December or January.

Plan to Stay: 1.5–2 hours.

Minimum Age: 12

Disabled Access: Yes, although a lot of territory is covered.

Group Requirements: Groups over 12 people should call 1 month in advance. No maximum group size. No open shoes allowed in factory.

Special Information: Sometimes strong smells in the mill.

Gift Shop: No

Directions: From I-80/90 in Indiana, take IN-933 North (becomes M-51 in Michigan). In Niles, turn right onto Main St. Go one block and turn left onto 13th St. Continue one block past the second four-way stop and turn left onto Merrifield St. From U.S. 31, take U.S. 12 East to M-51 North. Follow above directions.

Nearby Attractions: Four Flags Antique Mall; Fernwood Botanical Garden and Nature Preserve. Attractions in Elkhart, IN, including Walter Piano tour (see page 169), are 45 minutes away.

Walter P. Chrysler Museum

One Chrysler Drive, Auburn Hills, MI 48326   (888) 456-1924   www.chrysler heritage.com

WALTER P. CHRYSLER MUSEUM

This 55,000-square-foot polished granite and glass building was modeled after the adjacent DaimlerChrysler Headquarters and Technology Center. The futuristic 35-foot tower in the two-story atrium catches your eye. Three spectacular Chrysler production and concept vehicles rest on platforms that jut out from the tower. As you stare at these rare vehicles, notice that the tower slowly rotates, allowing you to view each of the cars without moving an inch.

The museum's ground floor traces the auto industry's first 50 years from the perspective of Chrysler—both the man and the company. Rare vehicles date back to the early 1900s, and a timeline wall details the key executives and predecessor companies that shaped today's DaimlerChrysler. Life-size dioramas depict key moments in Chrysler's life as well as corporate milestones—one features a realistic-looking Walter P. Chrysler circa 1908, examining his handiwork in his workshop. Classic advertising and photos and newsreel-style videos highlight important historic and social world events since the 1920s.

More than 65 vehicles are on display. You'll see the 1924 Chrysler, a sleek black touring-car prototype; big-engine muscle cars of the 1960s and 1970s; and current production vehicles and concepts. Accompanying labels allow you to compare salaries to the costs of vehicles and goods, both in the past and today.

Did you know that Chrysler was the first to develop an aerodynamically efficient design? If you compare the Airflow design to its squarish predecessors, you'll notice that most cars were quite boxlike and vertical before the futuristic 1934 Airflow introduced the sloping windshield and front, along with a tapered tail. Several interactive displays throughout the museum highlight the Chrysler Corporation's innovations in design and engineering. Visitors can even try their hand at vehicle design, selecting the shape, color, equipment, and other features of a new model that earns either a thumbs-up or -down from the rest of the team.

Cost: Adults, $6; seniors, $3; children 6–12, $3; DaimlerChrysler employees, retirees, and children under 6, free.

Freebies: No

Video/DVD Shown: Three 10-minute films: "Inside DCTC" shows how DaimlerChrysler develops cars; "The Early Years" is on Walter P. Chrysler and the young company; and "Speed and Power" is on Mopar muscle cars. Interactive video stations on specialized topics.

Reservations Needed: No

Days and Hours: Tue–Sat 10:00 AM–6:00 PM, Sun 12:00 PM–6:00 PM. Closed Easter, July 4th, day before Thanksgiving, Thanksgiving, Christmas Eve, Christmas, New Year's Eve, and New Year's Day.

Plan to Stay: 1.5 hours for tour and films, plus time for store.

Minimum Age: None

Disabled Access: Yes. Most videos are closed-captioned.

Group Requirements: Groups of 15 or more should call 24 hours in advance. Group rate is $3 per person.

Museum Store: Sells a variety of exclusive Chrysler Heritage Brand items, such as apparel, books, magazines, and a wide selection of die-cast Chrysler-related model automobiles.

Directions: Located in the DaimlerChrysler complex in Auburn Hills, MI, approximately 30 miles north of downtown Detroit. From I-75, take the Chrysler Dr. exit and follow the museum signs to the southeast corner of the complex (intersection of Featherstone and Squirrel Rds.).

Nearby Attractions: Chelsea Milling, The Henry Ford, and Lionel tours (see pages 172, 175, and 179); Marvin's Marvelous Mechanical Museum (248-626-5020); Meadow Brook Hall Museum, a house built in 1929 by the widow of one of the Dodge brothers; Great Lakes Crossing mall; Olde World Canterbury Village; Morley Candy; Henry Ford Estate; Cranbrook Art Museum and Science Institute; Detroit Zoo.

203 Waterfront Drive, Two Harbors, MN 55616   (218) 834-4898   www.lakecounty historicalsociety.org

Every great company has humble beginnings. The famous 3M company began in this small, green, square building in 1902, with the original goal of mining corundum. The five businessmen who founded Minnesota Mining and Manufacturing signed the articles of incorporation here, and it served as the original office and headquarters. In 1991, the Lake Country Historical Society purchased the building (phone number above is for the LCHS) and renovated it, and it now showcases both the past and present of 3M. If you like corporate history, as well as the nearby lighthouses, original big old trains just down the street, and other Lake Superior attractions, then this museum is worth a visit.

The building, which pays tribute to the birthplace of 3M, its early struggles, and its current successes, has different exhibit areas packed neatly into the small space. The displays include a recreation of the company's first office, with original artifacts and documents, a history of the company in photos, a "lab" area showcasing 3M's commitment to research and development and product diversification—featuring a hologram wall that displays old and new products—and a few hands-on technology applications.

Sandpaper is a product that fueled 3M's original growth. The museum pays tribute to this product with a jumbo roll of sandpaper, before it is cut into smaller pieces, and a colorful sandpaper mosaic. Another well-known company product, Scotch Tape (invented in 1925), is featured in a timeline that shows how this product has evolved. The story behind Post-its, a big winner for 3M, is also revealed.

Innovation is at the heart of 3M. You may be surprised by all the products you see that you didn't realize the company had developed. These diverse products on display range from the synthetic rubber used in astronauts' space boots to labels used to tag monarch butterflies. When the company says that one out of four people in the world use a 3M product every day, this museum brings to life the reality of this statement.

Cost: Adults, $2.00; age 9–17, $1; children under 8, free.

Freebies: No

Video/DVD Shown: Some of the displays have accompanying interactive kiosk with videos.

Reservations Needed: No, except for groups over 10.

Days and Hours: Open late May–October only. Mon–Fri 12:30 PM–5:00 PM, Sat 9:00 AM–5:00 PM, and Sun 10:00 AM–3:00 PM. Closed November–April. Guided tours given by request, otherwise self-guided.

Plan to Stay: 30 minutes.

Minimum Age: None

Disabled Access: Entire museum display area on first floor.

Group Requirements: Groups over 10 must call a few days in advance. Groups can request guided tour. Bus groups can combine tour with visits to other area historical attractions.

Special Information: The local Two Harbors lighthouse offers bed-and-breakfast accommodations with reservations through the number above.

Gift Shop: Located down the street at the Lake County Historical Society Depot Museum, 520 South Ave. Sells variety of Lake Superior, lighthouse, and other local gifts and souvenirs. Mon–Sat 9:00 AM–5:00 PM and Sun 10:00 AM–3:00 PM.

Directions: From Duluth area, take Rt. 35 North to Hwy. 61 North into Two Harbors. Turn right onto Waterfront Dr. Building at corner of 2nd Ave.

Nearby Attractions: Lake County Historical Society Depot Museum, which features in front of the building the wood-burning Three Spot, the first engine train used in the area, and a Mallet, one of the world's most powerful steam locomotives; Two Harbors Lighthouse; and Gooseberry Falls State Park. Duluth attractions include Stora Enso paper tour (see page 189), S.S. *William A. Irvin* cargo boat tour, and Great Lakes Aquarium about 30 minutes south. The Split Rock Lighthouse is 30 minutes north.

GREAT LAKES

Andersen WINDOWS·DOORS AW TM

Windows have long symbolized clear observation and understanding, so it is fitting that Andersen Windows gives visitors an unusually close look at its manufacturing operation. After an introduction to company history and culture, the tour brings you right to the start of the manufacturing process. From the lumberyard, pine wood arrives from various timber sources and enters the cutting and milling area. As you stand nearby, inhaling the wholesome smell of fresh pine, computer-controlled machinery cuts the lumber into planks in a continuous flow process that handles 100 million board feet (or square feet) of wood a year.

Next you see (and hear) the noisy area of the ripsaw. This huge cutting machine sections planks of lumber into usable pieces that are then sorted by size and quality (or "grade"). Your up-close view of the action makes this the loudest part of the tour, as the ripsaw handles 300 feet of lumber every minute in front of you. From the ripsaw and automatic sorters, the wood travels at 400 feet a minute to the staging areas. Stacked and tallied, the pieces await processing.

Your tour then visits the finger-jointing area. Highly concerned with environmental matters, Andersen ensures that little (less than one percent) goes to waste in its operation. Small bits of wood that would be otherwise unusable are "finger-jointed" into usable pieces for manufacturing. This process involves a strong adhesive that can hold up to 180 pounds per square inch.

In the milling area, you meet the Mattison and Weinig molders. These machines shape the wood into stiles, the vertical parts of a window sash, and rails, the horizontal parts. You also see how Andersen colors these parts in the electrostatic-coating area. Whether they are coated entirely in one color, only on the exterior, or with a split finish of two colors, one million stiles and rails every week un-

dergo this cycle of coating and drying, which lasts 90 minutes.

The last major stop on the tour is the final assembly line where Andersen's workers put together tilt-wash windows (the type that slide up and down and tilt inward for cleaning) or casement windows (which open and shut like a door); workers also assemble patio doors of various kinds. The two tilt-wash lines are capable of producing over 100 different sizes of frames. Each shift in the 24-hour working day produces between 800 and 1,000 units. As you stand among the workers on their shift, you can sense the amiable solidarity that defines the company culture of Andersen windows.

Cost: Free

Freebies: No

Video/DVD Shown: Yes

Reservations Needed: Reservations preferred for all tours and required for groups of 10 or more. Smaller groups can walk in and tour without prior arrangements.

Days and Hours: Tours run on demand Mon–Fri, 9:00 AM–3:00 PM. Closed major holidays.

Plan to Stay: 2 hours

Minimum Age: 16

Disabled Access: Yes, with prior arrangements.

Group Requirements: Groups of 10 or more people must reserve. Each tour accommodates a maximum of 15 people, so larger groups will be split into more than one tour.

Gift Shop: At the time of writing, a planned gift shop was due to open by 2007.

Directions: From St. Paul, take I-94 East about 20 miles and exit on Hwy. 95 North. Turn left at end of ramp and drive 3 miles into downtown Bayport. Turn right on Fourth Ave. North and drive 2 blocks (cross railroad tracks). Visitor parking is on right. Front entrance is behind flags and fountain.

Nearby Attractions: Faribault Woolen Mills, SPAM Museum (see pages 186 and 188); Minnesota Transportation Museum.

601 Brooks Avenue South,
Thief River Falls, MN 56701

(218) 681-8558
(800) 279-0179

www.arcticcat.com

ARCTIC CAT®
World Class Snowmobiles™

The Arctic Cat snowmobile has often set the standards for the North American snowmobile industry. In 1962, the Arctic Cat was the first front-engine snowmobile ever produced in this country; in the early 1970s, it was the top-selling snowmobile. Tough times for the industry and the U.S. economy in the late 1970s halted production. During the early 1980s, the "Boys from Thief River" restructured the company; now, once again, it manufactures award-winning racing and touring snowmobiles. The company also produces Arctic Cat ATVs, which now account for at least a third of their business.

Depending on the month, your tour shows what's involved in making the Arctic Cat snowmobiles or ATVs (although not in sequential assembly order) and numerous subassembly steps. The first thing you see is a line hanging with parts that have been through the powder paint shed, on their way to an oven that bakes the paint into the metal parts. Throughout the tour, you often see parts on conveyors moving in and out of cleaning, priming, and painting booths.

Robots and workers weld together the chassis. Workers put the parts in the jig, a frame that holds them together during assembly. With sparks flying, a robotic arm moves from spot to spot welding the chassis. Down the line, workers bolt some parts and robotic arms weld others to the chassis, including the skis.

The foam cushion seats start as liquid chemicals, with the mix determining the desired plushness. This mixture is squirted into preheated molds and, within a few minutes, out pops a cushion. After the vinyl is stretched around it, the seat is ready for the silk-screened logo. In the main assembly area, each chassis moves down the line with a parts cage that contains all its pieces; workers pull out parts as needed. When they test the engine, you think about the fun of riding the machine.

Cost: Free

Freebies: May give out balloons, bumper stickers, decals, product literature.

Video/DVD Shown: No

Reservations Needed: No, except for groups larger than 10.

Days and Hours: Mon–Fri 1:00 PM. Closed holidays and usually the week of July 4th. Special arrangements possible for other tour times. Occasional shutdowns when waiting for parts, so call ahead about the day you want to visit.

Plan to Stay: 45 minutes for tour, plus time for gift counter.

Minimum Age: None

Disabled Access: Yes

Group Requirements: 1 week's advance notice for groups larger than 25 so that additional tour guides will be available.

Special Information: No photography.

Gift Shop: Sells logoed items, including T-shirts, caps, mugs, and scale-model Arctic Cats and trucks. Open Mon–Fri 1:00–4:00 PM or after tour, if earlier. Catalog with full line of clothes and accessories available at above number. Information about Cat's Pride, the world's largest organized snowmobile owners' club, available from (800) 279-8558 (800-461-1987 in Canada).

Directions: From Hwy. 2, take Hwy. 59 North through center of Thief River Falls. Turn left onto Brooks Ave. (Bowling Center on the corner). Arctic Cat is on your right. From Hwy. 32, turn left at Brooks Ave.

Nearby Attractions: Christian Brothers hockey stick factory tour in Warroad (see page 185); Polaris snowmobile tour (see page 187) in Roseau; Red Lake River; Pioneer Park; Agassiz Wildlife Reserve.

Christian Brothers

HOCKEY STICKS

Highway 11, Warroad, MN 56763

(800) 346-5055
(218) 386-1111

www.hockeystick.com

GREAT LAKES

Who is better equipped to make hockey sticks than a former hockey star and Olympic Gold medalist, or two? Brothers Roger and Billy Christian combined their hockey acumen—honed during the 1960 (U.S.A.'s first Olympic gold in hockey) and 1964 Winter Olympics—and their carpentry skills to found Christian Brothers in 1964 with Hal Bakke. Today the company is one of the world's best-known hockey-stick manufacturers, only two of which are in the U.S.A. Your tour guide explains some of the company history.

Particularly during winter, you can follow along as workers create sticks for National Hockey League (NHL) professional hockey players and silk-screen the famous players' names onto the shafts. Whether the sticks are for a schoolyard team or the NHL, they start as ash and elm blanks, cut to the general length and width of a handle. A grader, using a specially designed bending machine, tests the wood for strength and integrity. (In fact, all of the factory's machines were custom-designed for the Christians; several are one-of-a-kind inventions.) Workers then add a block of wood to the handles, slice the block, and glue the blade form together. A carousel-like machine heats the sticks two by two, setting the glue and bonding blade and handle together. Each time the machine turns, workers add two more sticks.

After going through a sander machine so powerful that its operation shakes the ground around it, the sticks enter the steamer for softening. Workers hand-press the curve into the blades. Each NHL pro who uses a Christian stick has sent the factory a sample stick with a blade curve that lies on the ice just the way he likes. New sticks are made with the exact dimensions of this template.

Christian Brothers' best playmaker is a machine

that forces a fiberglass-like tube over the blade and cuts it off, edge-free, with air scissors. After another hand-smoothing and an epoxy bath, 1,200 sticks per hour pass through the silk-screener, which affixes the company's name (and, for custom orders, the player's name) to three sides of each handle.

Cost: Free

Freebies: Posters, brochures, sometimes miniature hockey sticks (drink stirrers).

Video/DVD Shown: No

Reservations Needed: Yes

Days and Hours: *Call ahead, because tours are irregularly scheduled.* Closed holidays and the week between Christmas and New Year's.

Plan to Stay: 20 minutes.

Minimum Age: None

Disabled Access: Yes. A few aisles may be too narrow for wheelchairs.

Group Requirements: Groups larger than 40 people should call 1 week ahead. Large groups will be split into groups of 15.

Special Information: No photography. Factory filled with sawdust. Winter visits are the best time for seeing NHL pros' custom orders. Plant busiest with retail stock orders April–December. Company also manufactures protective equipment for hockey and in-line skating but at other plants.

Gift Shop: Christian Brother's hockey sticks and athletic wear are available at retail stores in Warroad.

Directions: From the east, take Hwy. 11 West to Warroad, which lies 6 miles south of the U.S./Canada border. Christian Brothers sits prominently on your left. From I-29, take Hwy. 11 East to Warroad.

Nearby Attractions: Polaris snowmobile tour (see page 187) in Roseau; Arctic Cat snowmobile tour in Thief River Falls (see page 184); Marvin Windows tour (call 218-386-1430); Warroad Library & Heritage Center; Lake of the Woods Recreational Area.

GREAT LAKES

⊂FARIBAULT MILLS

We blanket the world. Since 1865!

Long ago, 800 central-U.S. mills made woolen blankets. Today only three carry on, the largest being Faribault Woolen Mills. Faribault produces more than half the wool blankets made in the United States. It is one of the few "fully vertical" mills left (a soup-to-nuts mill, starting with raw wool and ending with a finished blanket). Although automated machines help with the weaving, the process is still labor intensive. Workers handle fibers, comb batting, spin yarn, and finish and bind woven pieces— human touches that machines cannot replicate.

In the wool stock area, huge bales of raw wool await inspection. You may catch the scent of wet wool. Touch Faribault blankets' three component fibers: domestic wool, merino wool, and acrylic. Each fiber feels softer than the next. Scouring and blending operations clean the wool stock before the dyeing vats color it. In carding, the fibers are combed into huge fluffy sheets of batting. Workers card the wool into ends of roving. Your tour guide may let you feel how soft and weak the roving is, easily torn by the gentlest tug. Then try tearing the spun yarn apart—you'll hurt your hand before you succeed!

In the weaving room, elephantine computerized looms transform the yarns into blankets. Shuttles fly from side to side on the looms so rapidly that the human eye cannot follow. Horizontal "packing bars" move back and forth to pack in the just-woven yarns. Faribault's 26 automated looms can create over 2,000 items a day. Watch the careful inspectors at the burling station, where each woven piece is backlit and inspected, inch by inch, for snags, flaws, and finished quality, then measured and sized.

The final stop is the finishing area. Massive presses pull the blankets and throws, squaring them, truing the edges, and preparing them for the sewers. Using yarn as thread, the sewers add silken tapes to bind blankets' edges or overstitch the edges with

sergers. These laborious personal touches continue as the final products are carefully prepared for shipment worldwide.

Cost: Free

Freebies: Logoed souvenir.

Video/DVD Shown: 15-minute video runs continuously in the retail store, featuring a mother sheep describing the blanket-making process to her lamb.

Reservations Needed: Yes, for groups of 10 or more.

Days and Hours: Mon–Fri 10:00 AM and 2:00 PM. Closed New Year's, Easter, last week in June, the first 2 weeks in July, Thanksgiving weekend, and 2 weeks around Christmas. Plan to arrive 15 minutes before tour.

Plan to Stay: 40 minutes for tour, plus time for retail store.

Minimum Age: None, for families; 12, for groups.

Disabled Access: Only to the first floor of the factory (can see everything except the first and last production steps).

Group Requirements: Groups larger than 10 people should make reservations at least 1–2 weeks in advance. Large groups will be split into groups of 12–14.

Special Information: Automated looms in the weaving area are loud, and portions of the tour can be hot during summer.

Retail Store: Sells Faribault first-quality blankets and throws as well as discontinued lines and irregulars, various manufacturers' all-season clothing for men, women, and children, and one-of-a-kind antique bobbins. Open Mon–Sat 9:00 AM–5:00 PM, Sun 12:00 PM–5:00 PM. Closed holidays. Catalog available from (800) 448-WOOL.

Directions: From Minneapolis, take I-35 South to Faribault. Then follow billboards directing you to factory and store.

Nearby Attractions: Rice County Historical Museum; Alexander Faribault Park; Cannon River Dam.

Polaris is the world's largest manufacturer of snow-mobiles and also a major producer of all-terrain vehicles (ATVs), as well as the new Victory motor-cycle. Its resurgence is somewhat similar to that of Harley-Davidson, which regained competitiveness after its management buyout from AMF. Polaris was a division of Textron, a multinational conglomerate, before its own management buyout in 1981. At that low point in Polaris's history, the company had about 100 employees and the Roseau plant was shut down. Now it has more than 2,500 workers and over $1 billion in annual sales.

Even with the company's big investment in la-bor-saving technology and robotics, this huge plant in rural northwestern Minnesota, 10 miles from the Canadian border, has become one of the big-gest employers in the region. The tour lets you see firsthand how Polaris assembles snowmobiles and ATVs (all the parts are made in other Polaris plants in Osceola, Wisconsin; Spirit Lake, Iowa; and a Hudson, Wisconsin, engine plant jointly owned with Fuji Heavy Industries). You can walk between the two snowmobile and two ATV lines, observing the subassembly, preassembly, final assembly, and testing areas of the line.

In the snowmobile subassembly area, workers and robots put the parts together and prepare the skis and frame. Most of the metal parts are E-coated, submerged in black liquid paint primer for corrosion resistance, then sprayed with a powder-coat finish. Preassembly adds the chain case, suspension, and tracks. Heading over to the final assembly area, no-tice the finished hoods hanging from the monorail on their way from the plastics area. A visitor favorite is watching the motor being hoisted, lowered, and quickly fastened into place.

After all the final parts, tubes, and wires are con-nected, finishing touches such as the reflector tape and Polaris nameplate are added. Finally, the snow-mobile or ATV travels to the test shacks that sit near the ends of each line. The workers give them a little gas, start the engines, and test all the parts and critical features.

After watching production in action, walk through the Experience Center and see Polaris's product lines from the very beginning to present day.

Cost: Free

Freebies: Small packet with decals, stickers, and pin.

Video/DVD Shown: Yes, theater shows DVD movies featuring athletes using various Polaris products.

Reservations Needed: No, except for groups over 15 people.

Days and Hours: Mon–Fri 4:00 PM. Closed holidays.

Plan to Stay: 2 hours.

Minimum Age: None, but quite noisy for young children.

Disabled Access: Yes

Group Requirements: Headphones available only to groups smaller than 10 people. Large groups should call at least 2 days in advance. No maxi-mum group size, but ratio is 10 people per guide.

Special Information: Noisy; groups receive head-phones or earplugs depending on number of people on tour. No photography. Tours also available of the Polaris Spirit Lake, IA, plant that manufactures ATVs and Victory motorcycles (call 712-336-6702).

Gift Shop: Sells snowmobiles, logoed clothing, and other accessories. Located in Experience Center.

Directions: From the west, take Hwy. 11 East. At the first traffic light in Roseau, turn right at Hwy. 89 (also 5th Ave., SW). Polaris will be on your right. From the east, take Hwy. 11 West and turn left at Hwy. 89 in Roseau. Polaris will be on your right. From the north, take Hwy. 310, which becomes Hwy. 89 in Roseau; plant is a few blocks ahead on right.

Nearby Attractions: Christian Brothers hockey stick and Arctic Cat snowmobile tours (see pages 185 and 184); Marvin Windows tour and Infor-mation and Training Center (call 218-386-4222); Roseau River Wildlife Area; Lake of the Woods; Ro-seau City Park and Museum.

Processed meat never had it so good—the SPAM Museum features SPAM and Hormel Foods milestones from the late 1800s to the present day. The museum is 16,500 square feet, with 16 exhibit areas where you discover the invention of SPAM luncheon meat, how SPAM is canned, and other Hormel Foods history.

In the lobby, notice the large photomosaic on the wall—it appears to be photographs of the 1937 and 2001 SPAM cans, but actually consists of more than 1,200 photographs. On the wall opposite the photomosaic, more than 3,390 SPAM cans are assembled around a globe, depicting SPAM's global presence.

Walk up to a huge, unlabeled SPAM can. Before the entrance, pause at the 1920s telephone switchboard, slip on a headset, and listen to "party line" conversations concerning Hormel Foods–related stories, such as employee Cy Thompson's embezzlement of over $1 million in 1921. When you've had your fill of corporate gossip, enter the can and watch a puppet play called "SPAM Is BORN," all about the invention of SPAM and how it got its name. As you exit the can, notice that it now features the SPAM label, a testament that you truly witnessed the product's birth.

Move on to the Marketing exhibit, which features the KSPaM radio station, the Hormel Girls Theater, Hormel Foods print advertising, and Hormel Foods television commercials. Listen as the KSPaM booth broadcasts remote, live radio from around the world and 1940s radio commercials. Next door at the Hormel Girls Theater, you hear what it was like to be a Hormel Girl from three former Girls.

Next, get ready to see how SPAM is canned. You won't be able to enter an actual production plant, but you can watch a video of the entire process. Afterwards, you can practice canning SPAM yourself at an interactive area where you stuff the "meat," a

pliable pink beanbag, into a can. After you attach the lid and cook the can in a mock oven, you slap on a label and pack the can into a cardboard carton. At the push of a button, a screen displays your production time as well as the number of cans produced at the Austin plant, so you can have an idea of the rate of speed necessary during production.

Like SPAM luncheon meat, the new museum features a little bit of everything and teaches the public why SPAM's appeal both as a food item and a souvenir generator just might last as long as the product's shelf life!

Cost: Free

Freebies: No

Videos/DVDs Shown: 18-minute film dedicated to people who love SPAM and various video presentations that include interviews, commercials, chef demonstrations, and production.

Reservations Needed: No, except for guided tours.

Days and Hours: After Labor Day–April 30: Thur–Sat 10:00 AM–5:00 PM, Sun 12:00 PM–4:00 PM. May 1–Labor Day: Tue–Sat 10:00 AM–5:00 PM, Sun 12:00 PM–4:00 PM. Closed New Year's, Easter, Thanksgiving, Christmas Eve, and Christmas.

Plan to Stay: 1.5 hours, plus time for SPAM store.

Minimum Age: None

Disabled Access: Yes

Group Requirements: Guided group tours for museum and SPAM café can be arranged through the Austin Convention and Visitors Bureau (800-444-5713, ext. 300).

SPAM Shop: Sells logoed T-shirts, hats, and other merchandise. Mon–Sat 10:00 AM–5:00 PM, Sun 12:00 PM–4:00 PM. Hormel Foods gift catalog available (call 800-588-7726).

Directions: From I-90, take Exit 178B. Bear to the right and follow signs.

Nearby SPAM/Hormel Foods Attractions: Jay C. Hormel Nature Center (hiking, canoe rentals, skiing); George A. Hormel Historic Home; annual SPAM Jam.

Duluth Paper Mill, 100 North Central Avenue,
Duluth, MN 55807

(218) 628-5312
(218) 722-6024

www.storaenso.com

After waiting in the entrance area of the mill tower, you walk upstairs past individual offices. In this massive brown complex, the only ribbon of windows is along the walkway to the offices. From a video and your tour guide's introduction, you learn that Stora Enso, domiciled in Helsinki, Finland, is one of the leading forest products manufacturers in the world. Each year, the Duluth mill can manufacture 240,000 tons of supercalendered paper used for four-color printing in magazines, newspaper advertising inserts, and catalogs. Users include *Better Homes and Gardens* magazine, and JC Penney and Target catalogs and newspaper inserts. Approximately 45 truckloads of logs arrive each day, allowing this mill to be the largest producer of this high-quality, glossy paper in the United States.

Your guide explains the blue paper machine model, just a portion of the $1.5 million scale model paper mill. Wearing headphones and safety glasses, follow your tour guide downstairs to the "wet end" where pulp slurry, 99 percent water and 1 percent pulp, jets between two wire screens. In the press section, water is squeezed out of the paper sheet. Acting as a sponge, felt absorbs 40 percent of the water.

Walk alongside the long steel Northern Star trainlike paper machine. The paper travels at about 53 miles per hour from the wet end to the dry end of the machine. It takes approximately 45 minutes to make a 24-foot-wide, 9-foot-diameter reel of paper weighing about 30 tons. In the dryer section, the paper weaves between 53 steam-heated drying canisters.

The remote-controlled, yellow overhead crane system transports the paper rolls to the massive supercalender machines. Here, the paper weaves in and out of 12 calender rolls. Steam, heat, and pressure smooth the surface of the paper. The supercalender polishes the paper to give its shine.

Cranes transport the huge supercalendered paper reels to the winders. The paper runs under the floor in a single sheet. Slitters, resembling saw blades, cut the reels into smaller rolls based on customer orders. After the paper is rewound onto a cardboard core, each roll slowly glides by on the in-ground, orange conveyor system to an elevator that delivers it downstairs to the rollwrap and shipping area.

Cost: Free

Freebies: Brochures about forestry.

Video/DVD Shown: 6.5-minute video provides company information and shows papermaking process.

Reservations Needed: Yes, pick up free tour tickets at Duluth Visitor Information Office on Harbor Drive by the Vista Boats. Groups of 10 or more, see below.

Days and Hours: Public tours Memorial Day–Labor Day only. Mon, Tue, Fri 9:00 AM, 10:30 AM, 1:00 PM, and 3:00 PM. Closed July 4th and occasional maintenance shutdowns.

Plan to Stay: 1 hour.

Minimum Age: 10

Disabled Access: Yes

Group Requirements: Maximum group size is 25. Call (218) 628-5312. Group tours also offered during the summer months by appointment. Call (218) 722-6024 for summer reservations.

Special Information: No cameras, high heels, or open-toed shoes permitted. Expect warm temperatures and to walk approximately 0.5 mile. Call (218) 628-5312 at least 48 hours in advance if you need special accommodations. Paper mill tour in Wisconsin Rapids, WI (see page 217). Stora Enso also gives recycling tour in Wisconsin Rapids (call 715-422-3789).

Gift Shop: No

Directions: From Duluth, take I-35 South to Central Ave. exit. Turn left at bottom of ramp. Parking lot will be on your left. Tour begins at the mill's entrance tower. From Minneapolis/St. Paul, take I-35 North. Take Central Ave. exit in West Duluth. Turn right at bottom of ramp. Follow above directions.

Nearby Attractions: 3M Museum tour (see page 182); Lake Superior Gardens Center; S.S. *William A. Irvin* Ore Boat floating museum; Great Lakes Aquarium; North Shore Scenic Drive; Willard Munger State Trail.

AIRSTREAM

Wally Byam invented the Airstream back in 1932 because his wife refused to go camping unless she could take her kitchen. He decided to build a trailer with built-in comforts that copied the sleek, bullet-shaped design of an airliner, which could travel the roads like a "stream of air." Little could he have imagined that it would become the Rolls-Royce of RVs, one of the finest examples of American industrial design, and be used as television and movie stars' offices and dressing rooms on studio back lots.

The tour at this Thor Industries subsidiary (Thor is the second-largest RV manufacturer in the U.S.A.) shows you what makes these trailers and motor homes so unique: aircraft-style manufacturing. To build the shiny aluminum shell, the individual sheets of aluminum are laid up and measured for the curved roof and side walls, drilled, and then riveted together and connected to the end cap and interior metal ribs. Approximately 4,000 rivets are installed by hand. Spaces for the doors and windows are cut out of this aluminum shell.

In another area, the chassis rails are laid down. A high-grade aluminum skin seals the underbelly from beneath. Fiberglass insulation is inserted before workers put down the tongue-and-groove plywood floor that seals the chassis from above. Hoists lift the aluminum shell and place it gently on the chassis, which sits on special leveling jacks. Workers then bolt the chassis and shell together.

Once the exterior shell is sealed and married to the chassis, it's thoroughly checked for water leaks. In the water check, huge pumps spray hundreds of gallons of water on the top and sides of the RV body. Meanwhile, workers inside the RV use flashlights to help search for any leaks at the seams and rivet holes. Any needed additional caulking and weather sealing is done from the inside.

With the outside and chassis completed, the workers turn to the trailers inside. The toilets are always the first interior objects installed. Although the interiors can be highly adjustable, the toilet has to go over the septic-tank hole, and everything else goes in around it. Workers then rivet on the interior skin. Electrical wiring, carpeting, plumbing, and furniture are installed. All cabinets and furniture, built at the plant, are anchored to the interior metal frame. When complete, the units go to the mechanics building, where they are inspected.

Cost: Free

Freebies: No

Video/DVD Shown: No

Reservations Needed: No, except for groups over 20 people.

Days and Hours: Mon–Fri 2:00 PM. Closed holidays, weeks around Christmas and New Year's, and usually at beginning of July.

Plan to Stay: 1.5 hours for tour and gift shop.

Minimum Age: 16

Disabled Access: Yes

Group Requirements: Groups over 20 people should call 2 days in advance. No maximum group size. Special tour times can be arranged.

Special Information: No photography. Wally Byam Caravan Club International headquarters in town (call 937-596-5211 about Airstream company and WBCCI rallies).

Gift Shop: The Wally Byam Store at the Factory Service Center sells full collection of logoed items and accessories, including T-shirts, caps, and scale-model RVs. Open Mon–Fri 8:15 AM–4:45 PM. Closed holidays, but not during factory shutdown periods.

Directions: From I-75, take the Indian Lake/Jackson Center Exit 102. Take SR 274 East and head into Jackson Center. Plant is on left.

Nearby Attractions: Wally Byam Memorial Park; Neil Armstrong Air & Space Museum; Dayton's attractions, including Wright-Patterson Air Force Base, 50 miles away.

American Whistle

6540 Huntley Road, Columbus, OH 43229

(614) 846-2918
(877) 876-2380

www.american
whistle.com

"How does that little ball get into the whistle?" is the question asked by most curious children (and adults) who tour the American Whistle Corporation. The answer is, "The corking machine does it." You'll have to go on the tour to find out what that means.

The corking machine is just one of the many whistle-making steps you'll see at the only metal-whistle manufacturer in the U.S.A. As you journey through the factory's work stations, with the din of the press in the background, you'll be amazed to learn from your tour guide that more than 1 million whistles are manufactured each year in this neat, compact facility. Watch whistles being cut, stamped, soldered, baked, bathed, polished, and packaged.

The press is your first stop, after an initial briefing by your tour guide. Here, in rapid succession, a 37-ton press fitted with a die (a piece similar to a cookie cutter) stamps whistle pieces out of a brass ribbon. One after another, brass cutouts resembling miniature sets of Mickey Mouse ears are punched out. In a later process, the ears fold upward to become the sides of the whistle.

During another part of the tour, you are privileged to view the whistles in their own private bathing area—a tiny room off the main factory floor. Here, in a large, open, circular trough called a vibratory, the whistles take a stone bath. The stones resemble rough jade pieces and are placed in with the whistles and a tiny bit of liquid. Then the trough vibrates for seven hours to smooth any rough edges off them. The finished, bright, shiny whistles, lined side -by side for inspection and packaging, are the same whistles you see being tooted by policemen at busy traffic intersections or by referees at the Super Bowl.

Also learn how to use a whistle as a safety tool. American Whistles are four decibels louder than their nearest competitors, and the company sponsors a Whistle Defense Program to encourage safety awareness. While a piercing whistle can scare away attackers and bring help, it cannot be used against the victim.

Cost: $4 per person.

Freebies: New "American Classic" chrome whistle.

Video/DVD Shown: No

Reservations Needed: Yes. Individuals and families must join scheduled group tour.

Days and Hours: Mon–Fri 10:00 AM–4:00 PM. Closed holidays.

Plan to Stay: 1 hour for tour.

Minimum Age: None

Disabled Access: Yes

Group Requirements: Minimum group size of 15 people, or $45. Call at least 1 week in advance. Maximum 65 people per group.

Special Information: Photography restricted in parts of the factory.

Gift Shop: Display case is located in the factory at the end of the tour. Metal whistles (even 24-karat gold), lanyards, and mouthpiece covers available in many colors. Catalog available from above number.

Directions: From I-71, exit for Rt. 161 (Dublin-Granville Rd.). Go west on Rt. 161 to Huntley Rd. Turn right onto Huntley Rd. Factory is on the right in about 1 mile—roughly halfway between Rt. 161 and Schrock Rd.

Nearby Attractions: Anthony-Thomas Candy tour (see page 192); Krema Peanut Butter tour (call 614-299-4131); other Columbus attractions include State House, Columbus Zoo and Aquarium, and Center of Science and Industry.

GREAT LAKES

Anthony-Thomas®
Chocolates

Few companies design their factories with tours in mind. The Anthony-Thomas Candy Company, however, built its chocolate factory in 1994 specifically to accommodate visitors, who safely view (and smell) the candy-making operations from the unusual perspective of a suspended catwalk with a glass enclosure. This provision has paid off well: the company estimates that 50,000 people visit the factory and the retail shop every year.

From the starting point in the retail shop, tours go straight to the walkway above the immense factory, which covers 152,000 square feet. It is a busy panorama: eight lines of workers produce 25,000 pounds of chocolate candies here during every shift—a total of 25 tons a day. Their labors are supplied by a unique network of pipes wrapped in silver foil that carry liquid chocolate throughout the facility.

In the kitchen area, you gaze down on copper kettles that cook the various filling centers, which include butter cream, mint cream, chocolate mousse, cappuccino, rum, amaretto, and raspberry kirsch. The kitchen also produces an almond-butter blend of English toffee, which the staff prepare on tables, cut into squares, and coat in milk chocolate. Nuts are a basic element in the Anthony-Thomas universe of candy, and the kitchen roasts its own cashews, pecans, almonds, and Brazil nuts for a later coating of chocolate. Caramel falls on beds of pecans to create turtles (or "dainties").

Filling centers move to the enrobing lines, where machines coat them with silky liquid curtains of milk or dark chocolate supplied by the network of silver-wrapped pipes. After the coating, the chocolates ride on belts to the cooling tunnels and thence into the packaging area, where staff wrap and box them for the regional retail stores of the company.

Being an Ohio company, Anthony-Thomas naturally makes its own buckeye candy (milk chocolate around a filling of especially rich peanut butter) in the factory's four-stage molding plant. Tours may also see the molding machine that shapes whimsical novelties, including golf balls of white chocolate and lettered plaques in high and low relief.

Cost: Free

Freebies: A big sample of chocolate at the end of the tour.

Video/DVD Shown: No

Reservations Needed: No

Days and Hours: Tue and Thu 9:30 AM–2:30 PM. Closed holidays.

Plan to Stay: 45 minutes for the tour plus time for the retail shop.

Minimum Age: No

Disabled Access: Yes

Group Requirements: No. Reservations are appreciated for school groups of over 10 people. Groups of more than 20 may make a reservation for times outside the normal hours.

Special Information: On the Saturday two weekends before Easter, Anthony-Thomas holds an open house for families with children that includes a tour of the factory. Visitors at this time of the year see the special seasonal work of making cream-filled eggs and molded chocolate bunnies.

Gift Shop: The retail shop sells the full range of chocolates. Open Mon–Fri 9:00 AM–5:00 PM and Sat 9:00 AM–5:30 PM.

Directions: From I-70 East or West, take the exit for N. Wilson Rd. At the end of the ramp, turn right on N. Wilson Rd. and drive about 1 mile. Turn left on Trabue Rd. Take the first right on Arlingate Rd. Anthony-Thomas is on the left.

Nearby Attractions: American Whistle and International Trucks (see pages 191 and 197); Motorcycle Hall of Fame Museum (call 614-856-2222); Early Television Museum (call 614-771-0510).

CAROUSEL Magic!

Ah, the beauty and wonder of a carousel. Who among us does not stand back and gaze at the colorful animals as they bring smiles and happiness to children and adults alike? Enter a world where these animals come to life. Your tour guide leads you onto the carving floor through large, glass-paneled, wooden double doors in the back of the gift shop. Carousel Magic!, one of only two carousel-carving factories in the U.S.A., and the only major U.S. producer of full-size carousel horse carving kits, dedicates itself to preserving and fostering the tradition of carousel making, through building, restoring, and repairing carousels.

Begin by seeing a kiln-dried, 12-inch-high block of basswood, made of several layered boards. Not yet completely glued together, your tour guide "opens" the block into its two halves and, to your surprise, it is hollow! This construction method makes the body stronger than a solid block would, permits expansion and contraction of the wood, prevents considerable cracking or warping, and reduces the animal's weight by 25 to 30 percent.

Nearby, small and large chunks of wood soar through the air as mallet meets gouge (chisel) to remove excess bulk from a larger block of wood. On another workbench, the apron-clad master carver firmly places the bottom of the gouge's wooden handle in the palm of his right hand, wraps the four fingers of his left hand around the middle of the tool, supports its underside with his left thumb, and delicately applies pressure as the curved, U-shaped blade carves detail into a horse's mane. The thin sliver of wood curls up and gently falls to the shaving-covered, hardwood floor. Touch the smoothness of the resultant groove.

Proceed up a flight of steps to the art department, where the tip of a painter's thin brush, covered in bright red, colors an intricate rose carved on the horse's saddle. Run your fingers along the shiny body of a finished animal, examine its trappings, and be dazzled by the glass eyes and jewels. Inspired by this process, you can order a carving kit, start creating, and become a part of this magical tradition.

Cost: Adults, $4; children 5–12, $1; children 5 and under, free when accompanied by an adult.

Freebies: No

Video/DVD Shown: No

Reservations Needed: No, except for groups of 10 or more.

Days and Hours: Tue–Sat 10:00 AM–4:00 PM. Closed holidays and December 22nd–April 2nd.

Plan to Stay: 30–45 minutes, plus time for gift shop.

Minimum Age: None

Disabled Access: Yes

Group Requirements: Groups of 10 or more should call a few days in advance. Maximum group size is 47 people. Special rates for school groups and home school groups.

Gift Shop: Sells carousel-related music boxes, stickers, jewelry, and books. Open Mon–Sat 10:00 AM–5:00 PM. Call to check for special holiday hours.

Directions: From the north, take I-71 South to Rt. 30 West (Exit 176). Take SR 13 South. Turn right onto Fourth St. Carousel Magic! is on the right. From the south, take I-71 North to SR 13 North (Exit 169). In Mansfield, SR 13 becomes Diamond St. Turn left onto Fourth St. Carousel Magic! is on the right.

Nearby Attractions: Carousel District in downtown Mansfield, which includes the Richland Carousel Park (contains a working carousel of 52 animals and 2 chariots, the first hand-carved wooden carousel built in the U.S. since 1930), boutiques, art galleries, and bookstores; Richland Discovery Center and Academy (technological discovery zone).

Creegan

510 Washington Street, Steubenville, OH 43952   (740) 283-3708   www.creegans.com

The coal- and steel-industry problems in this tri-state area of West Virginia, Pennsylvania, and Ohio may have left a void in Steubenville. However, few places have more vigor than the family-owned and -operated Creegan Company, the nation's largest manufacturer of animated and costume characters. You may recognize Beary Bear, Plentiful Penguin, or Strawberry Bunny from your local retail store windows and seasonal mall displays. Creegan also designs characters for Sea World, Hershey's Chocolate World, and Walt Disney World. Inside the former Montgomery Ward department store, Creegan employees bring an array of characters to life.

Your guide leads you into a virtual craft heaven containing what must be thousands of spools of ribbon of every color, pattern, and texture. Puppet heads, scenery, and props lurk behind silk flowers and craft paraphernalia. A large, lifelike white gorilla stands beside three rosy-cheeked elves. During some tours, an employee dressed as Beary Bear wanders around. Up a wide staircase is the art shop, where workers make costumes and paint faces on molded plastic heads. On the main floor, a huge vacuum-form machine presses out the puppets' faces. Here you may see sheets of stark white plastic being pressed over molds into various facial configurations.

Downstairs in the sculpting area, one woman sculpts all of the character-head molds. Shelves contain hundreds of plaster molds shaped like heads, feet, hands, and animals. Farther along is the mechanics/electronics department, full of workbenches laden with toolboxes, handsaws, lathes, vises, and drill presses. Peek inside some headless mechanized bodies to discover some figures' detailed electronic insides and to see how the parts unite to produce a character's body movements. After a tour of the Creegan Company, you will agree with its motto: "We make things move."

Cost: $1

Freebies: Cake, candy, or cookie samples from Fancy Food section of the store.

Video/DVD Shown: Yes, "Made in America" with John Ratzenberger.

Reservations Needed: Preferred

Days and Hours: Mon–Fri 10:00 AM–4:00 PM, Sat 10:00 AM–2:00 PM (tours by request on Saturdays from November 1st–Christmas). Call for extended tour hours November 1–December 31. Closed Easter, Christmas, and New Year's.

Plan to Stay: 30 minutes, plus time for shops.

Minimum Age: None

Disabled Access: Yes

Group Requirements: 1 day's advance notice is requested for groups larger than 10 people. Inquire about group discounts on store merchandise.

Special Information: Individuals not part of a group may walk through the factory on their own or may join a group led by one of the entertaining tour guides.

Retail Stores: Showroom displays and sells Creegan's most recent animated figures and scenery. Year-round Christmas shop offers ornaments, gifts, and novelties. Retail store carries a variety of items, including cake-decorating and candy-making supplies and seasonal decor items. Open Mon–Fri 10:00 AM–5:00 PM, Sat 10:00 AM–2:00 PM, Sun by appointment; November 1–December 31, Mon–Thur 10:00 AM–5:00 PM; Fri–Sun 10:00 AM–2:00 PM. Creegan's record collection, as well as some collectable coins and stamps, by appointment. Catalog available.

Directions: From I-70, take SR 7 North to Steubenville. Turn left on Washington St., then left on 5th St. Creegan's is on the corner of Washington and 5th Sts.

Nearby Attractions: Homer Laughlin China and Senator Heinz History tours (see pages 145 and 130); Weirton Steel Mill tour (call 304-797-8597); Welsh Jaguar Classic Car Museum. Steubenville is the "City of Murals," with 25 beautifully painted historic murals throughout the city.

5353 Lauby Road, North Canton, OH 44720   (330) 494-0833   www.harrylondon.com
(800) 321-0444

A triangular glass portico entrance, a classy maroon awning, and the meticulously landscaped grounds welcome you to Harry London Candies. Before the tour, a friendly white-smocked tour guide offers you a sample of delicious chocolate, and your taste buds come alive!

Stroll past the Chocolate Wall of Fame. Old photographs and memorabilia show how Harry London first started manufacturing his quality chocolates out of his Ohio home in 1922. Gleaming white tanks and large vats swirl, mix, and heat up to 80,000 pounds of the rich, smooth brown confection a day. Foot upon foot of tubing starts here and transports the warm, liquid "food of the gods" (from the Latin meaning of "cacao") to the state-of-the-art candy-making processes you witness along the rest of your tour.

Floor-to-ceiling glass walls separate you from the fast-paced and efficient world of mass-producing quality chocolate. Look down on four 80-foot-long enrobing lines.

The candies proceed through the cooling tunnel and then on to packaging. Videos and signs explain as you watch employees operate the wrapping machine (it wraps 72–100 pieces per minute) and the centrifugal-force table, where chocolate is spun into every conceivable shape. After this spellbinding trip through the world of Harry London candy making, you'll agree that "any sane person loves chocolate."

Cost: Adults, $3; children 3–18, $2; children 2 and under, free.

Freebies: Chocolate samples on arrival and at end of tour. Samples also available in store while you shop.

Videos/DVDs Shown: 7-minute video covers history of Harry London Candies and of chocolate manufacturing, plus 1-minute videos along tour path describing various candy-making procedures.

Reservations Needed: Yes

Days and Hours: Mon–Fri 9:00 AM–3:30 PM. Tours run every hour. Closed major holidays.

Plan to Stay: 1 hour for tour, plus time for retail store.

Minimum Age: None

Disabled Access: Yes, first floor only.

Group Requirements: Groups should call at least 1 month in advance for reservations. No maximum group size. Call for special tours to be given to groups with a specific interest (such as marketing students or small children).

Special Information: No photography, cell phones, or recording devices.

Chocolate Store: The 2,400-square-foot retail store features over 500 varieties of chocolate and gourmet candy, including Pretzel Joys, chocolate peanut butter Buckeyes, and Hawaiian Gold. The store is designed with a lot of natural light and a large brick fireplace. Open Mon–Sat 9:00 AM–6:00 PM.

Directions: Take I-77 to Exit 113 for Akron-Canton Airport. Turn right onto Lauby Rd. Turn right at the second entrance and "Harry London Candies" sign.

Nearby Attractions: Hoover Historical Center tour (see page 196); I-77 is known as the "Hall of Fame Highway," including Rock and Roll Hall of Fame and Museum, National Inventors Hall of Fame, and NFL Pro Football Hall of Fame.

Hoover Historical Center/ Walsh University

VACUUM CLEANERS

1875 East Maple Street,
North Canton, OH 44720-3331

(330) 499-0287

www.walsh.edu

Surrounded by elegant decor and antique furnishings, you tour two buildings and see as many as 75 vacuum cleaners exhibited in the Tannery, plus a Victorian Italianate-style farmhouse, once the boyhood home of William Henry "Boss" Hoover, founder of the Hoover Company. The Center is now home to the "Sweeping Changes" display, which chronicles the history of the Hoover family and company and the evolution of the vacuum cleaner.

The Tannery is an 1840s building that served as the Hoover family home until they built their farmhouse in 1853. The house contains family history and tools used in the original Hoover business of tanning and making leather goods. There is also a display of cleaning devices used from the late 1800s to the early 1900s, ranging from primitive brooms to manual cleaners.

The Hoover vacuum history unfolds in the Victorian farmhouse. Inspect the 1908 Hoover Model "O," the world's first commercially successful, portable, electric vacuum cleaner. "Take a ride" on a replica of the 1910 manual Kotten suction cleaner. Step up onto the oval platform and rock side to side. Watch as the bellows on each side of the platform activate, and cause the attached nozzle to sweep up the sand on the floor. Push a button to hear a recording of Hoover salesmen singing "All the Dirt, All the Grit," the company theme song of the 1920s and 1930s. Touch products that were made by Hoover for WWII to aid the war effort.

Read the history of the Hoover family and company while you look at family photographs housed in elaborate frames. View four generations of Hoovers in one photograph. Learn about the business relationship that began between William and janitor James Murray Spangler, upon Spangler's creation of the "electric suction sweeper," a device made from

a tin soap box, a fan, a motor, a sateen pillowcase, and a broom handle.

If you visit during the summer, enjoy a pleasant walk through the Center's fragrant and colorful herb and flower gardens. Don't forget to stop in Bitzer Park, in the center of town, which holds a life-sized bronze statue of William walking and talking with a young boy. It represents his reputation as a gifted mentor and is a tribute to his entrepreneurship and philanthropy.

Cost: $3.00; 12 & under, free.

Freebies: No

Video/DVD Shown: No

Reservations Needed: No, except for groups of 18 or more.

Days and Hours: Tours are conducted hourly 1:00–4:00 PM, Wed–Fri in February, Wed–Sat March–December. Closed major holidays and through January. For groups of 8 or more, morning reservations are available Mon–Fri.

Plan to Stay: 1 hour for tour and gift shop.

Minimum Age: None

Disabled Access: Tannery is one floor. Ramp for access to Victorian house, first floor only.

Group Requirements: Groups of 8 or more should call at least 2 weeks in advance. Maximum group size is 40.

Special Information: No video cameras.

Gift Shop: Sells vacuum-shaped chocolates, toy Hoover vacuums, key rings, pens, postcards (one of a vintage Hoover ad), and baseball hats and T-shirts with the Hoover logo. Open same hours as museum.

Directions: From I-77, take exit 111 and turn east on Portage St. Drive past Whipple Ave. and turn right at the next light onto Wise Ave. At the 4-way stop, turn left onto Maple St. The Center is located about 2 miles past the Hoover Company on the left side of the street, opposite Walsh University.

Nearby Attractions: Harry London Candies tour (see page 195); Bitzer Park; Canton Museum of Art; William McKinley Presidential Library & Museum; National First Ladies' Library; Canton Classic Car Museum; Maize Valley Farms; Maps Air Museum.

Springfield, Ohio, is home to numerous International-manufacturing facilities; the company's roots in the community date back to 1806. However, the company's vehicles, which become utility trucks, rental trucks, pickup and delivery trucks, and tow trucks, are seen everywhere—delivering farm produce to market, transporting school children to classes, and moving freight. In Springfield, you'll learn how these massive vehicles are made in the Assembly Plant, which features the main tour, the Cab Assembly and Stamping Facility, Paint Facility, and Body Plant.

One of the largest plants in the country, the Assembly Plant comprises 33 acres under roof. In the Assembly Plant, you'll see the complete assembly process of International trucks, beginning with a steel frame rail and ending as a completed truck rolls off the line. Highlights of the tour include the frame inverter, cab mount, and new cab trim line. The process of inverting frames is fairly new in the large truck industry. Key processes like u-bolt tightening, prop-shaft installation, and axle squaring and pinning can be completed while the frame is inverted, thus making them more ergonomic and ensuring quality. On the plant's new cab trim line, a glass bonding cell installs the front and rear windows of the cab using a robotic glue-dispensing station, air cylinders, and suction cups to aid in lifting and installing the glass. Also on the cab trim line, the driver control module and the instrument panel are combined and inserted through the cab door.

Upon request, you can also tour the adjacent Cab Assembly and Stamping Facility (CAS), opened in 2001, and the Paint Facility. Watch cabs for the new trucks being stamped and assembled using state-of-the-art robotic equipment, tooling, and processes. Completed cabs move on to the Paint Facility, where colors of all varieties are applied using electric paint robots. Then, they are ready to be sent to the Assembly Plant, where they are added to chassis traveling down assembly lines. After seeing the full assembly, stamping, and paint process, you'll understand what goes into these high-performance trucks.

Cost: Free

Freebies: Educational brochures about the company and Springfield operations.

Video/DVD Shown: No

Reservations Needed: Yes

Days and Hours: *Regular tour program has been discontinued. Call for information about when and whether it has resumed.*

Plan to Stay: 1.5 hours for Assembly Plant, plus 1 hour for additional facilities.

Minimum Age: 14

Disabled Access: Yes

Group Requirements: Must call in advance.

Special Information: No photography, open-toed shoes, shorts, or personal radios. Safety goggles provided. Can be hot in summer and noisy any time. Cab Assembly and Stamping tours as well as Paint Facility tours available by special request.

Gift Shop: Eagle's Nest sells logoed T-shirts, hats, pens, and model trucks. Open Mon–Fri 12:00 PM– 12:30 PM, 3:30–4:30 PM. Hours subject to change (call 937-390-4118).

Directions: Take I-70 to Rt. 68 North. Follow Rt. 68 to County Line Rd. exit. Turn right. At 1st traffic light, turn right onto Urbana Rd. At traffic light by the large company sign, turn right. Park in visitor's section and proceed to main lobby.

Nearby Attractions: Dayton's attractions, including Wright Memorial Air Force Museum, are 15 miles away.

KitchenAid®
e x p e r i e n c e

If you have a KitchenAid stand mixer on your countertop, you can be sure it was made in Greenville, Ohio. In its factory on the city's outskirts, KitchenAid produces all of its famous stand mixers and ships them throughout the world.

The facility is easy to find. Visible as you approach from Route 127, and bearing the name of Whirlpool (the parent company), the giant factory stands prominently on its own in a large field. Tours start in the vestibule. While you wait, you can brush up on the history of KitchenAid's mixers by studying the displays that adorn the walls.

But the academics end there—now for the action. Literally pulled from the assembly line for this tour, your guide is an experienced member of the manufacturing staff. In addition, workers may pause in the middle of their duties to explain the tricks of their trade. With this wealth of expertise to look forward to, you don your protective eyewear (provided and necessary), step onto the factory floor, and enter their world.

Sparks fly in the machine shop, where the die-cast parts of the mixers are individually worked. Although KitchenAid has moved from two-person workstations to an assembly line, the manufacturing process is still highly manual. The sparks that catch your eye come from the smoothing of rough spots and bumps that inevitably appear on the metal cases when they are cast. Next you see the paint procedure, which wields a remarkably diverse palette of 23 colors. Every hue—from a stately brown to a couple of pretty hot pinks—glows on the countless exterior cases that hang from racks in the painting zone.

In the subassembly area, as some workers wrestle with wire whips for blending, others bring parts of the motor together. In the zone of final assembly,

all parts of the mixers unite in the finished product, which is immediately inspected and boxed for the last stage: shipping. Immense even by factory standards, the shipping area is lined with a breathtaking multitude of boxes—enough mixers for the whole world. There can be no more dramatic reminder of the fact that every KitchenAid stand mixer on the planet is made here.

Cost: $5 per person.

Freebies: Visitors receive a gift product after the tour (product varies).

Video/DVD Shown: No

Reservations Needed: No, except groups of over 8.

Days and Hours: Mon–Fri 10:00 AM and 1:00 PM. Tours are subject to manufacturing schedules, so call ahead. Closed Thanksgiving, Christmas, New Year's, Easter, week of July 4th, and week after Christmas.

Plan to Stay: 1 hour.

Minimum Age: 12

Disabled Access: Yes

Group Requirements: Groups larger than 8 need an appointment.

Special Information: Protective eyewear is issued before the tour.

Gift Shop: KitchenAid Experience (2 miles away at 436 South Broadway in downtown Greenville) sells the full range of KitchenAid portable products. It offers free cooking classes (call ahead for schedule). Open Mon–Sat 10:00 AM–6:00 PM, Sun 12:00 PM–5:00 PM. Closed Thanksgiving, Christmas, New Year's, and Easter.

Directions: From I-70, take Rt. 127 North into Greenville. Turn left on Township Hwy. T-33, left on KitchenAid Way. From 1-75, take Rt. 36 West into Greenville. Turn right on Rt. 127 North, left on Township Hwy. T-33, left on KitchenAid Way.

Nearby Attractions: Bear's Mill Pottery (call 937-548-5112); Ghyslain Chocolates (call 765-964-7905); Winery at Versailles Tour & Tasting (call 937-526-3232).

Lee Middleton Original Dolls

1301 Washington Boulevard, Belpre, OH 45714

(740) 423-1481
(800) 233-7479

www.leemiddleton.com

THE *Middleton*
DOLL COMPANY

Lee Middleton began creating dolls at her kitchen table in 1978, using her children as the first models. While the kitchen table may have given way to a 50,000-square-foot "dollhouse" factory (hidden behind a pastel-colored Victorian gingerbread facade), the same detailed, labor-intensive production process continues. Today, Middleton Doll Company is the area's No. 1 tourist destination. The tour shows the intricacy involved in making her vinyl collectible baby dolls.

All dolls start with molds for heads, forearms, and lower legs. A measured amount of liquid vinyl fills metal mold trays. The vinyl cures to a solid state in rotational molding ovens. After the molds cool, workers pull a small plug from each one. Then they use pliers to magically yank warm, hollow vinyl parts from each mold's tiny opening.

Stencils are used in painting vinyl doll faces. One head may require different stencils for eyebrows and lips, while blush on the cheeks is done freehand. Air is pumped into the head, temporarily expanding it like a balloon and enlarging the eye sockets. Workers then insert eyes into the openings and focus them, before delicately applying eyelash strips. When the heads, arms, and legs are attached to polyfill-stuffed bodies to complete the dolls, you appreciate the "labor" involved in their birth. The doll makers include a Bible with each of their "babies" because Lee Middleton wanted to thank God for giving her the talents that make her collectible dolls so special.

Cost: Free

Freebies: No

Video/DVD Shown: No

Reservations Needed: No, except for groups over 10 people. Scheduled tours take precedence over walk-ins.

Days and Hours: February 1–December 31: Mon–Fri 9:00 AM, 10:15 AM, 11:00 AM, 12:30 PM, 1:15 PM, and 2:15 PM. January tours by appointment only.

Plan to Stay: 20 minutes for Legacy Doll House Museum and 15–20 minutes for factory tour, plus time for gift shop.

Minimum Age: None

Disabled Access: Yes

Group Requirements: Groups of 10 or more must call in advance. Maximum group size is 60 people.

Special Information: No photography during tour.

Gift Shop: Sells limited-edition, first-quality Middleton Dolls, store edition dolls, Small Wonder Play Babies, designer doll accessories (including clothing and nursery furnishings), and other gift and souvenir items. Store has an Adoptable Nursery. Baby receives a birth certificate for the trip home. Open January: Mon–Fri 12:00 AM–5:00 PM, Sat 9:00 AM–5:00 PM; February–April: Mon–Sat 9:00 AM–5:00 PM; May–December: Mon–Fri 9:00 AM–6:00 PM, Sat 9:00 AM–5:00 PM, Sun 12:00 PM–4:00 PM.

Directions: Take I-77 to Rt. 50 West (Athens). Take Division St. exit and turn right. Cross Little Kanawha Bridge, then Belpre Bridge. Turn left at bottom of the bridge and go about 1 mile. Factory is on the left.

Nearby Attractions: Fenton Art Glass tour (see page 144); Stahl's Christmas Shop; Children's Toy and Doll museum; Doll Showcase store; Historic Marietta, OH; Blennerhassett Island Historical State Park and Museum.

Longaberger®

Tree-lined streets and beautifully restored Victorian houses create historic charm in Dresden, Ohio, the home of The Longaberger Company and its famous baskets. The tour of the manufacturing campus is self-guided, but guides are available to answer questions. Along the way, you learn the history of Longaberger and how it makes its baskets, and see all of the company's current products.

After entering the basket-making facility, you proceed along a quarter-mile mezzanine above the manufacturing floor. Look down to a view of hundreds of basket weavers working.

Maple wood provides the raw material for baskets. Logs are "cooked" for eight hours and then cut and measured into wood strips of the proper length for each style of basket. Weavers' fingers nimbly maneuver the moist, flexible maple strips to create the mosaic of the weave. The basket gradually takes shape as the craftsperson weaves and then taps the weave with a hammer to ensure a secure, tight, durable result.

Near the end of the process, the basket receives a "haircut" to trim away excess upsplints (the basket's vertical strips of wood). The weaver wraps the last band of wood around the circumference of the basket, hand-tacks it into place, and then dates and signs the completed artwork.

After the weaver finishes, the basket is sent to be stained. In this process, baskets are hooked onto circular overhead racks called "spinners." As the spinners rotate them, the baskets move down a conveyor belt through the chamber, where they are doused with stain.

Cost: Free

Freebies: No

Video/DVD Shown: No

Reservations Needed: No, except for groups of more than 15 people.

Days and Hours: Mon–Sat 9:00 AM–5:00 PM, Sun 12:00 PM–5:00 PM. To see weaving, tour the basket-making facility Mon–Fri before 2:00 PM. No weaving on Sat or Sun. Weaving demonstration on the mezzanine 7 days a week. Closed holidays. Hours may vary, so call ahead.

Plan to Stay: 1.5–2 hours.

Minimum Age: None

Disabled Access: Yes

Group Requirements: Groups of more than 15 people should call 3 days in advance to arrange a tour. No maximum group size.

Special Information: An on-site shuttle bus provides transportation to and from parking and between buildings.

Gift Shop: The Just for Fun Shop, at the middle point of the tour, sells selected Longaberger baskets, the only baskets available without contacting a Longaberger independent home consultant. Logoed T-shirts, gifts, and basket accessories are also available. Guests may also weave their own baskets in the Make A Basket Shop, located at the end of the tour (reservations are recommended). Both shops are open during the same hours as the tours. A "Wish List" catalog with the entire Longaberger basket and pottery line is available from an independent home consultant at (800) 966-0374.

Directions: Take I-70 to Zanesville and then travel 3 miles on Maple Ave./SR 60 North. Turn right onto North Pointe Dr. and go 8 miles. As North Pointe becomes SR 60 North, continue for 3 miles. Turn left onto Raiders Rd. Plant is ahead 2.8 miles on your right. Enter through the Longaberger Homestead entrance.

Nearby Attractions: Longaberger Homestead; Longaberger Golf Club; The World's Largest Basket.

13400 Brookpark Road, Cleveland, OH 44135   (216) 362-8700   www.malleys.com

You cannot miss the enormous ice-cream sundae that adorns the top of Malley's Chocolates' 60,000-square-foot building. This landmark commemorates Malley's first ice-cream and chocolate shop, opened in 1935. Like all the best candy-factory tours, this one begins with a sample, great chocolate smells, and a brief introduction to chocolate making. To put you in the right mood, they pipe in sounds of the tropical rainforest. The immediate landscape is festooned with banana and cacao trees hand-painted in lively pastels. Temporarily you return to the very origins of chocolate—to the tropics where cocoa beans grow.

As you gaze out over the expansive, modern candy kitchen, your tour guide describes chocolate's journey from its birth in the cacao plantations to the creamy liquid that you see swirling and churning in the 500-pound chocolate melting pot. This is Malley's secret chocolate recipe, which is kept under lock and key. Meanwhile, in the center's kitchen, anything from flavored to rich, creamy caramel centers may be bubbling away in copper kettles on gas stoves. Amid all this modern equipment, look for the antique gas stove dating back to the company's inception.

Your attention is drawn to the center of the room, where the automated kettle-lift pours 60 pounds of chewy, gooey hot caramel onto one of several cooling tables. Like a construction worker hurrying to smooth out a layer of concrete before it hardens, a chocolatier uses a huge spatula to quickly spread and smooth the thick caramel. A large rolling-and-cutting instrument is used to cut the still-soft caramel into pieces.

In another area, you see the enrober automatically coating the candy centers with chocolate. Before your tour concludes, you pass by the design center to glimpse some of Malley's specialty items.

Cost: $3; children under 2, free.

Freebies: Samples during your tour, and a take-home chocolate bar treat.

Video/DVD Shown: 3-minute video describes hand-packing process.

Reservations Needed: Individuals and families must join a scheduled group tour.

Days and Hours: Mon–Fri 10:00 AM–3:00 PM. Call for seasonal hours. Closed holidays.

Plan to Stay: 1 hour for tour, plus time in retail store.

Minimum Age: Not recommended for children under 3.

Disabled Access: Yes

Group Requirements: Minimum group size is 10 people; maximum is 50. Reservations needed 2 weeks in advance (4 weeks during holiday seasons).

Special Information: Best days to see production are before major holidays. No photography, please.

Retail Store: Sells full selection of Malley's chocolates including assorted chocolate creams, molded chocolate-covered peanut butter dinosaurs, and, of course, Grandpa Malley's favorite "Bordeaux." Hand-painted walls and floral prints add to the flavor of a real sweet shop. Open Mon–Sat 9:00 AM–6:00 PM. Catalog available from (800) ASK-MALL (275-6255).

Directions: From the east, take I-480 west to West 130th St. exit. Turn left onto West 130th. Turn right on Brookpark Rd. Malley's is on the right. From the west, take I-480 east to West 130th St. exit. Turn left at end of exit ramp. Malley's is on the left.

Nearby Attractions: *Cleveland Plain Dealer* newspaper tour (call 216-999-5665); Great Lakes Brewing Company tour (call 216-771-4404); NASA Glen Research Center (call 216-433-2000); Cleveland's attractions include Cleveland Zoo, Tower City, The Flats, Rock and Roll Hall of Fame and Museum, Great Lakes Science Center, and Cleveland Museum of Art.

9279 Cadiz Road, Cambridge, OH 43725   (740) 439-1827   www.mosserglass.com

MOSSER GLASS
M
CAMBRIDGE, OHIO

A beautiful country landscape is the backdrop for the little red farm cottage located conveniently just off the road. The front porch framed in white columns beckons you in. As you enter Mosser's "Little Red House" showroom, the sparkle of glass from every corner catches your eye. In this glass menagerie, you see glass of all colors and shapes. Walls are decorated with everything from miniature punch bowls to figurines of clowns and frogs—samples of what you will see made in the factory downstairs.

The first part of the tour takes you through the shipping area. After viewing hand-packing, your guide points out a display case of colored particles. These are the various chemicals used in Mosser's recipes for coloring glass. What really catches your eye, however, is stacks of over 200 intricately designed cast-iron molds, used in creating all of the hand-pressed glass shapes.

As you move past the batch room, you see machines that resemble inverted cement mixers forming an initial mixture of silica sand and soda ash. Large furnaces that heat the mixture to about 2,500°F then come into view as you enter the open, high-ceilinged, cement block factory. From this point on, the pressing of each piece of glass is done by a four-person human assembly line. While you watch glass being made, you are facing a furnace and its four-person team; beyond is an enormous factory window fitted with huge exhaust fans. The window is wide open to a panoramic view of the Ohio countryside.

Watch the glassmaking team in action as the glowing molten mixture is removed from the furnace by the "gatherer." Another person cuts and then presses the hot material into the mold. A third worker removes the hot piece of glass from the mold and puts it onto the fire polisher, which smoothes any rough edges or mold marks left from pressing.

Finally, the last worker places the glass piece onto a slow conveyor belt for the "lehr," or cooling oven, where it undergoes a gradual, three-and-a-half-hour cooling process.

As your tour ends at the lehr, you see the warm finished shapes being removed from the conveyor belt. Along one wall you observe glass figures receiving an acid rinse in a large tub to produce the soft, brushed effect of frosted glassware.

Cost: Free

Freebies: Yes

Video/DVD Shown: No

Reservations Needed: No, except for groups larger than 15 people.

Days and Hours: Mon–Fri 8:00 AM–3:00 PM. Lunch break from 10:30 AM–11:00 AM. No tours at that time. Closed holidays, 2 weeks in July, and last week of December.

Plan to Stay: 15 minutes for tour, plus time to browse Little Red House showroom.

Minimum Age: None

Disabled Access: Yes, for factory; 4 steps into showroom.

Group Requirements: Groups larger than 15 should call a few days in advance for reservations. No maximum group size, since large groups will be split into groups of 8.

Special Information: No sandals or open-toed shoes. Factory can get quite warm in the summer.

Gift Shop: Little Red House showroom offers everything from glass candlesticks, paperweights, and miniatures to antique reproductions. Open Mon–Fri 8:00 AM–4:00 PM. Closed holidays.

Directions: From I-77, take Exit 47. Take SR 22 West. Mosser Glass is 0.5 mile ahead on the right.

Nearby Attractions: Boyd's Crystal Art Glass tour (call 740-439-2077); Degenhart Paperweight & Glass Museum (call 740-432-2626); Salt Fork State Park and Lodge; Cambridge's antique shops and glass museums.

965 East Midlothian Boulevard,
Youngstown, OH 44501

(800) 860-2867   www.schwebels.com

If you like the idea of watching a ton of dough fall into a giant baking pan, this tour is for you. Schwebel Baking Company produces breads and related products with century-old baking techniques. Now over a century old, it runs an empire of bakeries and bakery outlets in Ohio, Pennsylvania, and New York that produces and delivers nearly a million loaves and packages of buns every day for retail stores, restaurants, and supermarkets of the region.

You can tour the bakery at the headquarters of Schwebel in Youngstown, Ohio. After visitors assemble in the conference room, your guide starts by giving a five-minute history of the company. In 1906, Dora and Joseph Schwebel started their enterprise in their kitchen in Youngstown, where they baked 40 loaves of bread a day for local residents. The business grew from there. At Schwebel's 100th anniversary in 2006, the company had more than 30 outlets and over 1,400 employees.

After the introduction, the tour begins. Because the noise in the bakery requires the guide to speak through a microphone, visitors receive portable radios with headphones, along with the obligatory hairnets, before they enter. (The bakery is also quite warm. In fact, Schwebel does not give tours during the summer, when the temperature can rise to 125°F.)

The tour consists mainly of viewing Schwebel's bakery equipment. You first see the huge bread mixer, about 12 feet tall and six feet wide, which prepares the dough. After the mixing process, the falling ton of dough comes into play: all 2,000 pounds emerge at once from the mixer into a huge metal trough. The following machine cuts the dough to size, and the next one rolls up the cut dough and drops it into pans for baking.

A conveyor belt shuttles the goods to the proof box, where the nascent bread rises for an hour. The next stop is the oven. A typical loaf of bread bakes here for 20 minutes and then spends an hour in circulation on the conveyor belt to cool it. The loaf then proceeds to the slicer and the wrapper and thence to the trays and racks that are the first step of distribution.

Throughout the tour, the tantalizing smell of baking bread hangs richly in the air. By the time you return to the conference room after the tour, nothing could be more welcome than the free loaf of fresh bread that you receive on your way out.

Cost: Free

Freebies: A loaf of bread, plus other items for both adults and children.

Video/DVD Shown: No

Reservations Needed: Yes. Individuals may be booked with an already scheduled group.

Days and Hours: Tues 6:00 PM and Wed 10:00 AM–3:00 PM, September–May (no tours during summer). Closed major holidays and the weeks of Thanksgiving and Christmas.

Plan to Stay: 1 hour.

Minimum Age: 5

Disabled Access: Yes

Group Requirements: Maximum of 25 people.

Special Information: Visitors may not wear jewelry during the tour. Schwebel also offers tours at its bakery outlets in Cuyahoga Falls (call 330-920-9610) and Solon (call 440-248-1500), both in suburban Cleveland.

Directions: From I-76 or I-80, take I-680 toward Youngstown. From I-680 North, take exit for Midlothian Blvd. (Rt. 625). Turn left at end of ramp and left on E. Midlothian Blvd. Schwebel is a half mile down on left. From I-680 South, exit to Midlothian Blvd. (Rt. 625). Turn right at end of ramp on E. Midlothian Blvd. Schwebel is a half mile down on left.

Nearby Attractions: Youngstown Historical Center of Industry & Labor (call 330-743-5934).

Velvet Ice Cream

State Route 13, Utica, OH 43080

(740) 892-3921
(800) 589-5000

www.velvet
icecream.com

GREAT LAKES

Since 1914 **Velvet** Ice Creams

A picturesque farm-country landscape welcomes you to Velvet Ice Cream's 20-acre site. The scene is complete with a mill stream, pond, ducks, and an 18-foot antique water-powered grist mill, taking you back in time to another century. Ye Olde Mill, whose original hand-cut stone foundation dates back to 1817, is featured on the company's ice-cream cartons. It's hard to imagine that adjacent to it is Velvet Ice Cream's modern, state-of-the-art ice-cream factory, capable of producing over 2,000 gallons of ice-cream products each hour!

The company has been owned and run by the Dager family since 1914. A stroll through their ice-cream museum reveals some of the antique ice cream–making equipment used throughout history—and lots of fun facts about America's favorite dessert. You can just picture the workers slowly and laboriously turning cranks by hand in what must have been a tedious, painstaking process. The museum also tells the history of milling, the world's oldest industry.

Your guided tour starts in the barnlike visitor center. Walk to the factory. A sign near the viewing windows proudly boasts: "Welcome to Ohio's Ice Cream Capital." Your attention is drawn to hundreds of feet of stainless-steel tubing, which seems to outline every corner and angle of the factory. The cold mixture of cream, milk, and sugar is pumped through this labyrinth of tubing to the processing machinery.

You might see juicy red strawberries being dumped into the mix at the flavor vats. The filling operation follows, as the ice cream is pumped into carton after carton. A maze of conveyor belts transports the filled containers as they are lidded and wrapped in polyethylene for shipping. They finally disappear into freezer storage where, within a few hours, they are frozen. Look for the novelty machines making ice-cream sandwiches, pushups, or the 1817 gourmet ice-cream bar—vanilla and peanut-butter ice cream coated in chocolate—yum!

Cost: Free

Freebies: No

Video/DVD Shown: 12-minute video shows the history of Velvet Ice Cream and the ice cream–making process.

Reservations Needed: No, except for groups larger than 15 people that want a guided tour of the factory or a group larger than 15 for the restaurant.

Days and Hours: May 1–October 31: Mon–Fri 11:00 AM–3:00 PM on the hour for guided tour. No weekend production. Restaurant, ice-cream parlor, interactive ice-cream and milling museums, picnic area, and park are open seven days a week; See Gift Shop section below for restaurant and museum days and hours. Closed November–April.

Plan to Stay: 1 hour for guided tour plus time for self-guided visit to museum, a stop in Ye Olde Ice Cream Parlor, and a stroll through the scenic grounds.

Minimum Age: None

Disabled Access: Yes

Group Requirements: Groups larger than 15 people for a guided tour or lunch reservation should call 1 week in advance. All groups welcome. School groups receive ice-cream sample.

Special Information: Arrive before 3:00 PM Mon–Fri to see production. Annual Memorial Day Weekend Ice Cream Festival; Fall Harvest Days every Sunday in October, with pumpkins, live music, petting zoo, and hayrides.

Gift Shop: Ye Olde Mill contains a replica of an old-fashioned early-1800s ice-cream parlor, as well as a restaurant and gift shop. Restaurant offers homemade food and, of course, ice cream. Gift shop sells nostalgic gifts, Ohio-made handcrafted items and food products, and velvet logoed items, T-shirts, hats. Hours for museum, restaurant, ice-cream parlor, and gift shop are seven days a week: May 11:00 AM–8:00 PM, June–August 11:00 AM–9:00 PM, September–October, 11:00 AM–8:00 PM.

Directions: Take SR 62 to Utica. Turn onto Rt. 13 South and go 1 mile. You're there when you see Ye Olde Mill.

Nearby Attractions: The Longaberger Company (see page 200); Dawes Arboretum; The Works: Ohio Center for History, Art & Technology; Midland Theater.

201 East Seven Hills Road,
Port Washington, WI 53074

(262) 235-6000

www.allen
edmonds.com

Allen Edmonds

Allen-Edmonds shoes some of the most famous feet in the world. Visitors to Allen-Edmonds Shoe Corporation may see the inaugural shoes worn by three U.S. presidents and the size 24 EEEEEEs handcrafted for a teenager in Seattle. Shoes from the collection are rotated regularly. For added fun, step into the red, white, and blue clown shoes worn by Oscar- and Emmy-winning actor Ernest Borgnine.

Walk into the atrium gallery of Allen-Edmonds Corporate Centre in Port Washington, Wisconsin, and you'll see the Allen-Edmonds Shoe Revue, a distinctive changing collection of men's footwear worn by presidents, kings, sports celebrities, and film stars. There is even a pair of brown cordovan loafers presented to the Pope by Allen-Edmonds' president and owner, John Stollenwerk. Along the atrium-viewing gallery are movie posters with displays of the Allen-Edmonds shoes featured in major films and highly rated television shows.

From glass windows along the atrium walkway, notice the use of "cellular manufacturing." A group of procedures is performed on the shoe within a "workcell," then the shoe is passed to a different "cell" where further work is done. You may see a worker guiding a shoe through a machine that stitches around the insole. This 360-degree welting process has been a tradition since the company was founded in 1922. Visitors may also see worn Allen-Edmonds being recrafted into almost-new condition (they recraft more than 1,500 pairs each week).

Between the video and what you can see from the atrium windows, you will learn the entire hand-crafting process. Each pair of Allen-Edmonds shoes requires 212 production steps—from the inspection of the leather to the final shine.

In the finishing department in the back, each new pair is blanketed in soft burgundy flannel and tucked into an elegant black and gold box. They await shipment to a major department store, high-end specialty store, shoe salon, or the Shoe Bank, an 11,000-pair on-site shoe store that will undoubtedly be your final destination.

Cost: Free

Freebies: Catalog

Video/DVD Shown: 12-minute video demonstrates the complex steps in shoe production.

Reservations Needed: No, the tour is self-guided.

Days and Hours: Mon–Fri 7:00 AM–9:00 PM, Sat 9:00 AM–9:00 PM, Sun 9:00 AM–6:00 PM. No production on Fridays or weekends.

Plan to Stay: 25–30 minutes for atrium gallery and video, plus time in Shoe Bank.

Minimum Age: None

Disabled Access: Yes

Group Requirements: None

Outlet Store: The Shoe Bank offers full line of Allen-Edmonds first-quality men's shoes (some brand-name women's shoes also) at 25 percent off standard price. Open Mon–Fri 7:00 AM–9:00 PM, Sat 9:00 AM–9:00 PM, Sun 9:00 AM–6:00 PM. Recrafting services available. Annual Summer Tent Sale is a big event. For catalog and dates of Tent Sale, call (262) 284-7158.

Directions: From Milwaukee, take I-43 North to Exit 100. Look for big American flag at Allen-Edmonds entrance.

Nearby Attractions: Kohler design center and tour (see page 212); Lake Michigan; Cedarburg.

Carr Valley Cheese

S3797 County G, La Valle, WI 53941

(608) 986-2781
(800) 462-7258

www.carrvalley
cheese.com

Named after its location, Carr Valley Cheese is one of the few companies that produces cheddar cheese the old-fashioned way. Many Wisconsinites remember the 1930s and 1940s, when, as kids, they snacked on fresh curd from cheese factories that dotted Wisconsin's countryside every few miles. Here, you can taste fresh, warm curd that squeaks against your teeth and observe how it is turned into cheese.

In the retail store, a glass wall runs the length of the production area, where you may see owner Sid Cook, a fourth-generation cheese maker, clad in bib overalls. Since each of the four 19-foot-long stainless-steel vats is at a different production stage, it helps to review the picture board and audiotape before taking your self-guided tour. Each day, 52,000 pounds of pasteurized milk are filtered from holding tanks into cheese vats, which resemble single-lane lap-swimming pools. A large agitator twists and turns as it travels the length of a vat and back. A culture (which begins the ripening process and tastes like sour milk) and rennet (which causes milk to solidify) are added, and a wire harp cuts the mixture into small curds. As the whey (liquid) is removed, a separator extracts the cream. The cheese remains in the vat.

Once solid, the cheese is cut into 20-by-2-inch slabs. While they're stacked like slices in a loaf of bread, excess moisture drains from the slabs. The curd mill chops them into small chunks, and workers fill small black metal buckets with 25 pounds of curd. You can see curds weighed, poured into forms, and pressed into wheels.

Walk around to the back of the plant to see wheels waxed and packaged. In the wax room, a rack of cheese wheels is lowered into a two-foot-deep vat of 200°F clear, red, or black wax (color depends on the cheese's age). The wax seals out air and protects the cheese from mold as it cures in the warehouse for up to two years (longer aging means sharper cheddar).

Cost: Free

Freebies: Samples of curds and cheeses.

Video/DVD Shown: Yes, 10-minute video about cheese making.

Reservations Needed: No, except for groups larger than 30 people.

Days and Hours: Mon–Sat 8:00 AM–4:00 PM. Best time is 10:00 AM. Closed Thanksgiving, Christmas, and Easter.

Plan to Stay: 30 minutes for self-guided tour and retail store.

Minimum Age: None

Disabled Access: Yes, but difficult to get into wax room.

Group Requirements: Groups larger than 30 should call 1 day in advance to schedule tour guide; will be split into smaller groups.

Special Information: Can watch video and some production of European cheeses at their other facility, Wisconsin Pride, in Mauston WI (call 608-847-6632).

Retail Store: Sells full line of Carr Valley cheese. Wheel sizes: 3-pound "gem," 5.5-pound "favorite," up to 23-pound "daisy," and 72-pound "cheddar" (once the industry standard). Also sells cut cheese, curds, sausages, and Wisconsin-made jams, jellies, and honey. Sells cheese production video. Open Mon–Sat 8:00 AM–4:00 PM. Catalog available from (800) 462-7258.

Directions: From I-90/94, take Hwy. 12 South. Take Hwy. 33 West through Reedsburg (look for Carr Valley Cheese signs) to La Valle. Go straight onto Hwy. 58 South through Ironton. After 1 mile, turn left onto County G. Brick plant is 2 miles ahead on right.

Nearby Attractions: Wisconsin Dells casinos and boat cruises, about 25 miles away. For complete list of Wisconsin cheese plants, write: Cheese Plants, Wisconsin Milk Marketing Board, 8418 Excelsior Drive, Madison, WI 53717.

General Motors

SPORT-UTILITY VEHICLES AND PICKUPS

Truck Group, 1000 Industrial Avenue,
Janesville, WI 53546

(608) 756-7681   www.gm.com

GREAT LAKES

North American Truck Platforms

General Motors has been building vehicles in Janesville since the Samson Tractor in 1919. Through the years, this plant has produced a range of vehicles including Chevys, Buick Skyhawks, and now the popular Suburban, Yukon, Tahoe, and medium-duty trucks. During World War II, the factory made artillery shells. With the factory's long history, it's no surprise that this plant and the retiree who leads your walking floor tour exude a sense of pride. It's also one of the few automotive tours that individuals and families can take without advance reservations.

You'll see plenty of robots assisting the workers. In the Suburban body shop, over 160 robots perform about 70 percent of the welds. These robots, which look more like bird beaks, bend over from their bases to apply spot-welds. The colorful shooting sparks make you realize how much safer it is for robots to perform this task than workers, who mostly program, monitor, and repair this equipment.

Once the steel body-frame is assembled, it moves through a dimensional vision system that uses laser beams to check the frame parts' sizes against their ideal measurements. In other parts of the factory, robots also apply the base-coat paint in enclosed booths and put the prime and urethane on the window glass before workers pop it into place. While the body frame is being constructed, other lines build the chassis. Workers assemble the underneath part first, and a turnover hoist flips the chassis over like a pancake.

In the final assembly lines, an overhead hoist lowers the vehicle body onto the chassis, and workers bolt them together. To the music of air tools, parts such as fenders and grills seem to arrive from every direction for attachment. You will see the dynamic vehicle-test area, where the vehicles sit on rollers and accelerate to 60 mph so major features can be tested. At this point, the assembly process is complete, and you're tempted to hop in and hit the road.

Cost: Free

Freebies: None

Videos Shown: 9-minute pre-tour video, which overviews the plant history and vehicle production, and 13-minute video on plant history and components of building an SUV.

Reservations Needed: Yes

Days and Hours: Tour times change with production schedule. Call tour hotline for times at (608) 756-7681. Closed holidays, week between Christmas and New Year's, and 2 weeks in July.

Plan to Stay: 1 hour for video and tour.

Minimum Age: None, although children under 5 may be frightened by noise and sparks. Children under 10 must be accompanied by an adult.

Disabled Access: Yes

Group Requirements: Groups of 10 or more should make reservations as early as possible—tours fill quickly, especially in spring and summer. Maximum group size is 60.

Special Information: No video equipment or cameras allowed. For security reasons, no bags, backpacks, or purses permitted. Vehicle painting by robots is not on tour, but you see plenty of robots perform other tasks.

Gift Shop: No

Directions: From I-90, take Hwy. 351 West. Turn right at stop sign and proceed north on Hwy. G (Beloit Ave.). Turn left at Delavan Dr. and left at plant. Enter through doors in center of building, directly under flagpole on roof. From Hwy. 14 West, go straight onto O, which becomes Delavan Dr., then turn left at plant. Call above number for maps to plant from other directions.

Nearby Attractions: Wisconsin Wagon group tours (call 608-754-0026); Rotary Gardens; Palmer Park; Tallman House; Milton House.

GREAT LAKES

11700 W. Capitol Drive, Wauwatosa, WI 53222

(414) 343-7850
(877) 883-1450

www.harley-davidson.com

Since the company started in 1903, Harley-Davidson® has come to represent a lifestyle of individuality, freedom, and passion for adventure. There is nothing quite like the feel of a Harley-Davidson motorcycle and the camaraderie at H.O.G.® (Harley Owners Group) events. You can enhance your connection with these motorcycles by watching how they are made at one of their factories. The Capitol Drive powertrain plant is the only Harley-Davidson plant offering public tours in Wisconsin.

The Capitol Drive Tour Center offers a trip through history: a timeline traces the development of Harley-Davidson engines, from the classic "Knucklehead" to the contemporary Twin Cam 88®. Watch employees turn out 883cc and 1200cc XL V-Twin engines for Sportster® and Buell® motorcycles. Follow an XL engine from forgings through finished product. Displays along the tour route highlight the machining and finishing processes that create key components used in Sportster and Buell powertrains. This demonstration of how powertrain parts are createdgives you a hands-on approach to learning about Harley-Davidson products.

Get up close and personal with Genuine Motor Parts and Screamin' Eagle® manufacturing processes. Whether the goal is to beef up the performance of a Fat Boy® motorcycle or to replace powertrain components on a '72 Sportster, the Genuine Parts Manufacturing Group puts it all together. See skilled powertrain machinists manufacture replacement parts for noncurrent Harley-Davidson engines and Screamin' Eagle performance parts.

In the Engine Remanufacturing Department, the last stop on the tour, Evolution® and Twin Cam 88 engines get a new lease on life. Watch skilled technicians completely disassemble engines, replace worn parts, and then reassemble and hot-test engines to meet strict Harley-Davidson quality standards.

In the Tour Center, you are encouraged to "try on" many current models of Harley-Davidson and Buell

motorcycles. You can sit on the Buell bike display, which is stabilized at a 45-degree angle to give you the feel of leaning into curves.

Cost: Free

Freebies: Collectible badge and *The Enthusiast* magazine.

Video/DVD Shown: Yes

Reservations Needed: No, except for groups of 10 or more. Call ahead; plant tour times and availability may change.

Days and Hours: Tours available Mon–Fri 9:30 AM–1:00 PM on a first-come, first-served basis. Tour Center open Mon–Fri 9:30 AM–2:30 PM. Closed on major holidays and for year-end maintenance. Tours may be modified at any time due to manufacturing requirements and during model year changeover. Please call ahead for complete details.

Plan to Stay: Allow 1.5–2 hours for the factory tour, exhibits, and gift shop.

Minimum Age: 12

Disabled Access: Yes (call ahead).

Group Requirements: Groups of 10 or more must reserve at least 14 days in advance.

Special Information: Fully enclosed, low-heeled (one inch or lower) shoes required. Photography is permitted in the Tour Center but not in the factory. Tour participants aged 18 and over must present a valid, government-issued photo ID or passport and complete a registration card. Visitors must pass through a metal detector before entering the plant. Tours are also available at the company's plants in York, PA (see page 123), and Kansas City, MO (see page 287).

Gift Shop: Offers a selection of Harley-Davidson souvenir merchandise and features a penny press machine. Open Mon–Fri 9:30 AM–2:30 PM. Closed on major holidays and for year-end maintenance.

Directions: From I-94, take Hwy. 45 North to W. Capitol Dr. (Hwy. 190). Take the industrial ramp over to the factory. Plant entrance signs identify location.

Nearby Attractions: Milwaukee attractions include Miller Brewing Company (see page 213); Milwaukee Art Museum and Milwaukee County Zoo are about 30 minutes away.

See color photos, page 18.

Imagining what a million of anything looks like is not an easy thing to do, but taking the tour at Hillestad Pharmaceuticals will certainly make it easier. They keep over 5,000 different materials in inventory including high-quality, natural sources, ready to make into millions of different tablets, protein powders, creams, lotions, and liquids. Their machines are capable of producing millions of tablets a day. Small-time production is not what you'll see here.

The first step in making a tablet is similar to combining ingredients for a cake. After the ingredients are weighed, they are granulated in a blender. Then they are combined with water and other ingredients and mixed together. They are put through a low-temperature dryer before moving to the next step.

A unique two-layer tablet is created at the tablet presses. The vitamins are not mixed with the minerals as in most tablets, but are brought together into layers by an upper and lower punch (the machine that presses the tablets). The punch exerts 10,000 pounds of pressure per square inch and can produce over one million tablets each day.

Next, the tablets are coated by machine or by hand. The coating is sprayed into a large, spinning kettle that can hold 400,000 tablets. The tumbling tablets coat each other when they come into contact. Many different kinds of coatings can be applied in this department, ranging in a spectrum of color, coating over 400,000 tablets each batch.

The freshly made tablets then go through packaging. Watch machines rapidly count tablets into bottle-sized portions. Other machines label and code the bottles. There is a machine that does the bottling, and another that seals them. It's a busy room, and it is the last step before shipping.

The final part of the tour features a mechanical "stomach" where tablets are tested for disintegration. The stomach's acids are duplicated in a pan, and the tablets are placed with the liquids. An apparatus moves the tablets around in the acids, simulating the digestion process. It's a simple test that will give you a visual demonstration what happens to vitamins and supplements inside your body.

Cost: Free

Freebies: Sample of a multivitamin and a catalogue.

Video/DVD Shown: No

Reservations Needed: No

Days and Hours: Mon–Fri 9:00 AM–3:00 PM.

Plan to Stay: 30 minutes, plus time to look around the outlet store.

Minimum Age: No

Disabled Access: Yes; call (800) 535-7742 with any questions.

Group Requirements: No

Outlet Store: Sells all the products made in the factory, along with a few healthy snacks. Open Mon–Fri 8:00 AM–4:30 PM, Sat 9:00 AM–12:00 PM.

Directions: Drive along Hwy. 51 North. At Woodruff, Wisconsin, pass the intersection with Hwy. 47. Continue north on Hwy. 51 for two blocks. Hillestad Pharmaceuticals is on the right, across from Perkins.

Nearby Attractions: Paul Bunyan's Restaurant; Peck's Wildwood Wildlife Park & Nature Center.

GREAT LAKES

Founded in rural Wisconsin by a German beekeeper in 1852, Honey Acres not only harvests honey from its bees but also makes several honey-based products. Although it has an obvious business interest in honey, a main theme of the company's tour program is the overall environmental importance of bees. Bees and other pollinating insects are a vital presence on our planet: without them, flowering plants would fail, along with most of our agriculture.

Every tour begins with a 20-minute slide show on the common honeybee *(Apis mellifera)*. One remarkable fact about bees is that they produce different types of honey according to the available flowers. During spring and summer, the bees of Honey Acres produce a light honey from clover, which thrives in those months. Later in the year, the bees make a dark and robust honey from the stronger nectar of the buckwheat and wildflowers that flourish during fall.

After the slide show, your tour visits the museum. The queen of the exhibits here is a window on a living bee colony—a natural factory. Though at first the humming mass of insects may seem chaotic, a close inspection reveals that it is anything but disorganized. You can see individual workers (all sterile females) in a number of specialized tasks. The most incredible is the communicative dance that an individual bee performs for her colleagues after discovering a new source of nectar-rich flowers. The movements of her abdomen tell her co-workers which directions to take to find the windfall.

Your tour then moves on for a glimpse of the human workers at Honey Acres. The factory operations that you briefly see involve the automated machines that fill jars with honey and then cap, label, and box the jars. The associated sweet smell hangs richly in the air. Fittingly, your tour concludes by visiting the shop for free tastings of honey and related products. Among the company's wares are honey-based energy bars that have helped to sustain rugged explorers in Antarctica and on Mount Everest. Thus energized, you may be in the mood for a nature ramble on a trail through the woods and meadows of the 40-acre property.

Cost: Free

Freebies: Free tastings of honey after the tour.

Video/DVD Shown: A 20-minute slide show introduces bees, beekeeping, and the annual cycle of harvesting honey.

Reservations Needed: Yes, for tour; reserve at least a week in advance. Reservations not needed for museum.

Days and Hours: Tours are available Mon–Fri 9:00 AM–3:30 PM. (See Group Requirements, below, for more information.) The museum is always open during these hours and requires no reservations (May 15–October 30 the museum is also open Sat–Sun 12:00 PM–4:00 PM, but no tours are available at these times). Closed holidays.

Plan to Stay: 1 hour for slide show, museum, and tour.

Minimum Age: None

Disabled Access: The tour involves stairs, but access for wheelchairs can be arranged with advance notice.

Group Requirements: Tours require a minimum of 10 visitors and must be reserved. Call (800) 558-7745. Individuals can be accommodated with a group tour that has already been scheduled.

Gift Shop: The shop sells the full line of honey and honey-related products. Open Mon–Fri 9:00 AM–3:30 PM (May 15–October 30 open also Sat–Sun 12:00 PM–4:00 PM).

Directions: From Milwaukee, take I-94 West to Hwy. 67 North. Drive 15 miles on Hwy. 67 North. Honey Acres is on left. From Madison, take I-94 East to Hwy. 67 North and follow directions above.

Nearby Attractions: Trek, Miller Brewing, and Allen-Edmonds tours (see pages 218, 213, and 205).

Since Jelly Belly's Fairfield, California, factory tours (see page 369) have become so popular, the company expanded in 2001, opening a warehouse and distribution center in Pleasant Prairie to supplement the tours in California. Now you can hop on the Jelly Belly Express Train and ride around the new warehouse, stopping to learn about the Jelly Belly Candy Company's production process and sample flavors.

When you arrive, a 30-foot-tall, inflatable Jelly Belly bean with a candy corn hat greets you. Walk into the store and line up next to Jelly Belly Junction—a train station entry to the tour. Inside the warehouse, you will board the Jelly Belly Express, a colorful, four-car electric train with no tracks. Your tour guide drives the train, making commentary between stops.

First, watch the Welcome Video on a large-screen display, which details the company history. After you're on your way, you may be tempted to hop off the train for a moment or two once you see the boxes of candy stacked to the rafters. Be patient—sampling comes later. At the raw materials station, try to count how many sacks of ingredients it takes to produce a day's worth of candies.

Unlike tours of modern factories, you stop at the Candy Kitchen, which displays a mini-museum of reproduced equipment from the company's early days, including old candy machinery and candy kettles. The Panning Process shows off what makes Jelly Belly beans so special—machines add candy shells to intensely flavored centers; non–Jelly Belly beans have no flavoring in the center.

As you pass through Candy Alley, three-dimensional beans fly overhead. While viewing the Jelly Belly bean mosaics, you might recognize some of your favorite presidents, artistically rendered in lemon, cotton candy, and green apple flavors, among others. The dancing chorus line of animated Jelly Belly characters sends you along to the Shipping Department. Reward yourself after the tour with a trip to the tasting bar, where you can create your own Jelly Belly recipes by combining multiple bean flavors.

Cost: Free

Freebies: 3-ounce bag of jelly beans. Sample over 100 candies at tasting bar.

Videos/DVDs Shown: Large screen videos of production and distribution processes shown during ride on Jelly Belly Express.

Reservations Needed: No, except for groups over 10 people.

Days and Hours: Mon–Sun 9:00 AM–4:00 PM. Closed New Year's, Easter, Thanksgiving, and Christmas.

Plan to Stay: 40 minutes for train tour and sampling, plus time for retail area and snack bar.

Minimum Age: None

Disabled Access: Yes

Group Requirements: Groups of 10 or more should call in advance.

Special Information: No photography. Fairfield, CA, factory tour (see page 369).

Retail Store: Sells all Jelly Belly beans and Goelitz Confections, Belly Flops (discounted, irregular beans), gift baskets, jelly bean trinkets, hot dogs, ice cream, and desserts. Open Mon–Sun 9:00 AM–5:00 PM.

Directions: From Milwaukee, take I-94 (U.S. 41) South to Exit 347. Turn left (east) onto SR 165 (Lakeview Pkwy.). Turn left (north) on SR 31 (Green Bay Rd.). In 0.25 mile, turn left (west) on Jelly Belly Ln. into the Jelly Belly Center. From Chicago, take I-94 (U.S. 41) North into Wisconsin, to Exit 347. Stay on left side of ramp. Turn right (east) onto SR 165 (Lakeview Pkwy.) and follow above directions.

Nearby Attractions: McDonald's #1 Store Museum tour (see page 158); Great America Theme Park; Chicago's attractions, including Chicago Mercantile Exchange, Chicago Board of Trade, Eli's Cheesecake World, and U.S. Post Office tours one hour away (see pages 150, 149, 152, and 160); Milwaukee's attractions, including Miller Brewery tour (see page 213), Milwaukee County Zoo, Boerner Botanical Gardens, and Milwaukee Art Museum, are about 45 minutes away.

KOHLER.

A visit to Kohler is more than just a tour of the world's largest plumbingware manufacturer. The factory tour begins and ends at the Kohler Design Center, a three-level showcase of products and bathroom layouts that are so attractive you'll want to move in. The Design Center also houses the company museum, which chronicles Kohler history since 1873, and Kohler's own colorful "great wall of china."

Guided by a company retiree, your tour begins in the pottery building's molding area, a humid place where bare-chested men smooth wet clay toilets with large sponges. Next come the kilns: long, brick ovens that bake glazed clay fixtures into vitreous chinaware. Stroll among glossy stacks of Thunder Grey sinks and Innocent Blush commodes. Watch inspectors "ping" the chinaware with hard rubber balls and listen for cracks.

Next, enter Wisconsin's largest iron foundry. Its electric melt system eliminates the smoke and fumes previously associated with foundries. It's still an imposing place, full of molten metal, warning lights, and hissing machinery—a highly memorable industrial experience. Here you'll discover how they make molds to form cast-iron tubs, sinks, and engine blocks. The concrete floor shudders with the heave and thud of massive presses that create sand molds. You'll feel the heat from the "ladles" of glowing molten iron traveling by on forklifts. Deeper inside the building, an automated production line turns out one bathtub casting every 30 seconds.

In the enamel building, workers gingerly remove red-hot bathtubs, lavatories, and kitchen sinks from ovens. Enamel powder that melts into porcelain is quickly sifted onto each fixture. Finally, pass into the whirlpool-bath section, where up to seven tubs bubble serenely. After three hours of touring this enormous plant, you may be more than a little tempted to flop into the water and relax.

Cost: Free

Freebies: Product-line books in Design Center.

Video/DVD Shown: 20-minute video in Design Center shows Kohler history and Kohler Village highlights.

Reservations Needed: Yes, for plant tour. No, for Design Center.

Days and Hours: Factory tour: Mon–Fri 8:30 AM. No tours on holidays, week between Christmas and New Year's, first week of July, or first week of August. Design Center: Mon–Fri 8:00 AM–5:00 PM and Sat, Sun, and holidays 10:00 AM–4:00 PM. Closed Thanksgiving and Christmas.

Plan to Stay: 2–3 hours for factory tour, plus time for video, museum, and Design Center.

Minimum Age: 14, for tour; under 18 must be accompanied by adult. None for Design Center.

Disabled Access: Discouraged for tour, because of stairs. Design Center is fully accessible.

Group Requirements: Kohler requests that you call for complete group information. Groups larger than 8–10 people will be split.

Special Information: No photography on tour. Up to 2.5 miles of walking, including some outdoors. Be careful where you walk. During tour, you'll see examples of works produced by artists in the Arts/Industry Residency program.

Gift Counter: Design Center sells postcards, polo shirts, and Kohler-logoed items.

Directions: From Chicago and Milwaukee, take I-43 North to Kohler exit. Follow signs into Kohler—the company is the town. Stop at Kohler Design Center for orientation information and start of plant tour. From Madison, take I-94 East to Milwaukee, then I-43 North. Follow above directions.

Nearby Attractions: Shops at Woodlake Kohler; The American Club "five diamond" resort hotel; Blackwolf Run championship golf courses; Waelderhaus, replica Austrian chalet in style of Kohler family's ancestral home tour (call 920-452-4079); Whistling Straits, home of 2004 PGA Championship.

Visitor Center, 4251 West State Street, Milwaukee, WI 53208

(414) 931-BEER (2337)

www.miller brewing.com

MILLER BREWING CO

SINCE 1855

MILWAUKEE, WIS. USA

In 1855, German immigrant Fredrick Miller purchased the Plank Road Brewery. Surrounded by woods, the small brewing operation was no bigger than a Victorian house. Today, a replica of the Plank Road Brewery is just one of the historic highlights in Milwaukee's Miller Valley—the home of the nation's second largest brewer, Miller Brewing Company.

Walk outdoors and upstairs to Miller's packaging-center balcony. A blur of cans roars along conveyor belts that wind through wet machinery, packing up to 200,000 cases of beer daily.

The next stop is Miller's mammoth distribution center that covers the equivalent of five football fields. Typically, you can see half a million cases of beer.

In the brew house, Miller makes its beer, up to 8.5 million barrels annually in Milwaukee alone. Climb 56 stairs to look down on a row of towering, shiny brew kettles where "wort," a grain extract, is boiled and combined with hops. Stroll through Miller's historic Caves, a restored portion of the original brewery where beer was stored before the invention of mechanical refrigeration.

Finish your tour at the Bavarian-style Miller Inn and sample a Miller beer or soft drink. Be sure also to take a few minutes to inspect the impressive collection of antique steins. In the summer, you can enjoy your beverage in an adjoining beer garden enlivened by music.

Cost: Free

Freebies: Beer (for those 21 years of age and older with proper ID), soda, peanuts, and postcards (Miller will cover postage to any world destination).

Video/DVD Shown: 15-minute video shows brewing process and overview of Miller's history, information about their present operation, and the future of the company.

Reservations Needed: No, but recommended for groups of 15 or more.

Days and Hours: Mon–Sat 10:30 AM–3:30 PM. Closed holidays and week between Christmas and New Year's.

Plan to Stay: 1 hour for video and tour, plus time for product sampling and gift shop.

Minimum Age: No

Disabled Access: Plant tour: no. Visitor Center (includes video), Miller Inn, and Caves: yes.

Group Requirements: Groups of 15 or more should call at least 1 day ahead for reservations. Maximum group size is 105. Limited reservations on Saturdays.

Special Information: Best time to see production is weekdays. Miller Brewing Company also gives tours and has a gift shop in Tumwater, WA (call 360-754-5217), and the Miller Marketplace and Brew Kettle Museum in Ft. Worth, TX (call 817-568-BEER).

Gift Shop: Girl in the Moon Brewery Shop sells clothing, caps, glassware, steins, mirrors, tap handles, and other Miller-logoed items. Open Mon–Sat: summer 10:00 AM– 5:30 PM; winter 10:00 AM–5:00 PM.

Directions: From Chicago, take I-94 West to 35th St. Turn right (north) on 35th St. Turn left (west) onto State St. Pass through "Miller Valley" (well marked) to last building on left, Miller Visitor Center and Gift Shop. From Madison, take I-94 East to Hwy. 41 North to the State St. exit. Follow signs to right, down hill to traffic light. Turn left onto State St. Visitor Center is 1 block ahead on right.

Nearby Attractions: Quality Candy/Buddy Squirrel factory tour (see page 215); Miller Park (home of Milwaukee Brewers); Milwaukee County Zoo; Mitchell Park Horticulture ("The Domes"); Milwaukee County Museum; Milwaukee Art Museum; Boerner Botanical Gardens; Cedar Creek Winery. Miller Visitor Center front desk has information on and directions to many local attractions.

See color photos, page 40.

4300 Highway CR, Manitowoc, WI 54220

(920) 758-2500
(800) 558-3535

www.naturalovens.com

Natural Ovens Bakery

Paul Stitt founded Natural Ovens in 1976, after discovering that many food companies were adding appetite stimulants to their products to increase sales. A biochemist, Paul believes food should be good for you, filling, and satisfying. Now he and his wife, Barbara, supply fresh breads to over 1,200 grocery stores in a handful of states. When you tour the facility, you'll notice that in their employee cafeteria, junk food has been replaced by delicious foods made with fresh vegetables, fruits, and grains, some even grown on company grounds.

Your tour begins in the huge lobby in front of an 11-by-17-foot stained-glass window depicting the museum, as well as the growing and harvesting of flax. In 1986, Paul rediscovered flax, which has been proven beneficial in reducing the risk of heart disease. Flax is used in almost all of the bakery's products.

View the bakery through a series of windows. The bakers arrive at midnight to begin mixing the dough for the bread. The bakery uses three semi-truckloads of flour a week—60 acres of wheat! After the sponge rises for three hours, it's put into the mixer, and the rest of the ingredients are added to make enough dough for 550 loaves. You may gasp as the enormous blob of dough is dumped out of the mixer. After the dough has risen twice and been mixed three times, the huge mass goes through the dough divider, making more manageable two-pound pieces. The smaller clumps look like little rabbits as they flop from the divider into the molder, where they're kneaded and shaped into loaves.

After rising, the dough moves to the 120-foot-long indirect brick oven. In just one hour, 4,000 loaves will travel from one end of the oven to the other.

Smell the heavenly aroma as you watch thousands of golden loaves emerge right under your nose. Within 16 hours, those same loaves will be sitting on a grocery shelf somewhere far away from Manitowoc.

Cost: Free

Freebies: Hot samples of baked goods.

Video/DVD Shown: 8-minute video provides close-up look at the mixing and baking process. Shown when no production.

Reservations Needed: No, except for groups larger than 10 people.

Days and Hours: Tours: Mon, Wed, Thur, Fri 9:00 AM, 10:00 AM, and 11:00 AM. The baking is completed by 2:00 PM. No baking on Tue. Self-guided viewing of bakery when lobby is open, Mon–Fri 8:00 AM–5:00 PM. Closed Thanksgiving, Christmas, and New Year's.

Plan to Stay: 1–1.5 hours for bakery tour.

Minimum Age: None

Disabled Access: Yes

Group Requirements: Groups over 10 people should call at least 4–6 weeks in advance. Maximum group size 55 people.

Gift Shop: The lobby of the factory sells a complete selection of Natural Ovens products, plus specialty items including books, vinegars brewed locally, almond butter, aprons, T-shirts, and maple syrup. Open Mon–Fri 8:00 AM–5:00 PM, Sat 8:00 AM–3:00 PM.

Directions: From the south, take I-43 North to Exit 144. Turn right on Hwy. C. Turn left on CR. Bakery is 2.5 miles ahead on left. From the north, take I-43 South to Exit 149. Turn left onto Hwy. 151 East. Turn right onto CR. Bakery is 1 mile ahead on right.

Nearby Attractions: Wisconsin Maritime Museum; Rahr-West Art Museum; West of the Lake Gardens (open May–October); Lake Michigan Car Ferry.

1801 East Bolivar Avenue, St. Francis, WI 53235 | (414) 483-4500 | www.qcbs.com
(800) 972-2658

GREAT LAKES

This factory tour is actually two tours in one. In 1916, Polish immigrants Joseph and Lottie Helminiak opened Quality Candy Shoppes in Milwaukee's popular Mitchell Street shopping district. In 1960, Buddy Squirrel, the premier nut shop, was purchased by Quality Candy. Today, the two product lines are housed in a 45,000-square-foot factory and warehouse, with a 14,000-square-foot distribution center. The family-owned company operates more than 12 stores in Wisconsin. This joint tour allows you to see how Quality Candy makes award-winning chocolate candies and how Buddy Squirrel processes popcorn, nuts, and snack mixes.

Your tour begins in the Quality Candy kitchens. Here, candy makers prepare and mix the ingredients for the chocolate candies' centers. Centers, made from scratch in these kitchens, include caramel, creams, toffee, cordials, marshmallow, and nougat. From a viewing corridor, you see the centers embark on a short journey to the enrobing room, where they are engulfed in a fountain of either milk or dark chocolate before going through the cooling tunnel. One of the highlights of the Easter tour is watching over 80 seasonal solid chocolate moldings being made, varying in sizes from one ounce to a 67-pound rabbit. All the candies then travel to the packing area to be boxed and sent off to a Quality Candy store or wholesaler.

The Buddy Squirrel segment adds some "pop" to the tour. Tons of corn kernels dive into giant poppers, in which they become popcorn. The popcorn is then seasoned with butter, cheese, caramel, and other flavorings. Once again, your taste buds are tempted by the scents in the air. The popcorn meets up with the nuts (also made by Buddy Squirrel but not seen on tour) in the packing room, and the goodies are prepared for their voyage to candy and nut stores all over the region.

Cost: Adults, $2; children 10–13, $1; children under 10, free.

Freebies: Samples of candy and caramel corn.

Video/DVD Shown: No

Reservations Needed: Yes. Individuals and families need to join scheduled group tour or form group of at least 10 people.

Days and Hours: Tue–Thur 10:30 AM and 1:00 PM. No tours on holidays, November and December, 2 weeks before Easter (except for Annual Open House), and 1 week at the beginning of July and August.

Plan to Stay: 45 minutes, plus time for Kitchen Store.

Minimum Age: 10

Disabled Access: Yes

Group Requirements: Groups of at least 10 people should call 4 weeks ahead. Maximum group size is 50 people.

Special Information: Annual Easter Open House (the second Sunday before Easter from 10:00 AM–4:00 PM—call for date) features Mr. & Mrs. Easter Bunny and special factory tours with free Easter treats.

Retail Store: Kitchen Store sells all Quality Candy/Buddy Squirrel products, including award-winning Butter Almond Toffee, Pecan Caramel Tads, popcorns, and nuts. Open Mon–Fri 9:30 AM–4:30 PM and Sat, 9:30 AM–3:00 PM. Closed holidays. Catalog available from above number.

Directions: Take I-94 to Layton Ave. exit. Turn left onto Brust, then right on Whitnall. Make a quick left on Kansas St. Quality Candy/Buddy Squirrel factory is on right. Enter under bright red awning on south side of building.

Nearby Attractions: Miller Brewery tour (see page 213); Milwaukee County Zoo; Mitchell Park Horticultural Conservatory ("The Domes"); Milwaukee County Museum; Milwaukee Art Museum; Boerner Botanical Gardens; Cedar Creek Winery.

GREAT LAKES

A FAMILY COMPANY

In 1886, Samuel Curtis Johnson (at age 53) created and marketed a paste wax formula to sell as a sideline to his parquet flooring business. It became so successful that he expanded his line to introduce wood dyes, dance wax, and paints. In 1939, SC Johnson moved into a building designed by Frank Lloyd Wright and eventually branched out to manufacture such familiar products as Edge, Glade, Off!, Pledge, Raid, Scrubbing Bubbles, Shout, Windex, and Ziploc.

In the company's corporate display room, pictures, products, and descriptions illustrate the company's unique development. The unfaltering dedication to business is depicted in the presented histories of the company's four generations of chairmen. See a display of various SC Johnson global consumer products. In the Golden Rondelle lobby, see some of the prestigious awards presented to the company for marketing environmentally friendly products.

Strolling through the company's global headquarters, you will be dazzled by the interior of the Administration Building. Wright built this massive, futuristic "Great Workroom" using 21-foot columns that shoot up and expand outward as they reach the ceiling. Illuminated Pyrex glass tubing wraps around the building, allowing natural sunlight, yet not one real window exists!

Although excluded from the tour, equally impressive in its shape is the Research Tower, rising over 150 feet into the air. Designed using the cantilever principle, which is similar to the root, trunk, and branch system of a tree, the tower appears to hang suspended in the air. Also not on the tour, the company's nearby production facility, "Waxdale," covers nearly 2.2 million square feet, equivalent to 36 football fields. Waxdale's aerosol lines can fill up to 500 units per minute. As the company's primary U.S. manufacturing plant, it is one of the most modern and efficient production, warehousing, and shipping centers in the world.

Cost: Free

Freebies: Brochures on Frank Lloyd Wright designs of SC Johnson.

Films Shown: "Carnauba, A Son's Memoir" and "To Be Alive," both shown in the Golden Rondelle Theater.

Reservations Needed: Yes

Days and Hours: Tours and movies are offered on Fri. Call for times. Closed holidays and week between Christmas and New Year's.

Plan to Stay: 45 minutes for architectural tour, plus up to 2 hours for films.

Minimum Age: None, but children must be accompanied by an adult.

Disabled Access: Yes

Group Requirements: Groups should call no less than 2 weeks in advance. Maximum group size is 40 people.

Gift Shop: No

Directions: Take I-94 to Hwy. 20 East (Washington Ave.). Continuing east for about 8 miles, Hwy. 20 East curves left. Do not take curve but go straight (east) onto 14th St. Golden Rondelle Theater is 3 blocks ahead.

Nearby Attractions: Racine Arts Museum (RAM); Wustum Art Museum; Racine Zoo.

STORAENSO

The forests of the Upper Midwest help make Wisconsin the nation's leading paper producer. In the middle of the state lies Wisconsin Rapids, home of Stora Enso, North America's largest manufacturer of coated printing papers used in magazines, catalogs, annual reports, and brochures. Set inside a concrete and brick building several stories high and stretching five city blocks, Stora Enso's largest machine produces enough paper to create a 19-foot-wide strip from Chicago to New York City every day.

At the head box, the start of the paper machine, a mixture of 99 percent water and 1 percent wood fiber is sprayed onto a rotating fabric mesh screen. A combination of gravity and suction drain most of the water as the sheet of paper forms on the wire. The remainder of the water is removed by squeezing the sheet between giant rollers and then drying it with steam-heated dryers. Five hundred feet away, the newly formed paper wraps onto giant spools at the end of the paper machine in only 20 seconds. If you time it right (about every 40 minutes), you can see a "turn-up," where a new reel of paper is started without ever slowing down or stopping the process.

The 20,000-pound reels of paper move onto a 475-foot machine that applies coating layers to each side of the sheet. The next stop is the supercalenders, which iron and polish the sheet to a high gloss. Finally the reels of paper, now weighing as much as 33,000 pounds, are taken to the rewinder, where they are cut into smaller rolls for shipment to customers or conversion to sheets.

Your guide will then escort you to Stora Enso's sheeting operations. Computer-controlled automated guided vehicles (AGVs) transport rolls of paper across 7,000 feet of predetermined routes in the floor. At the facility's sheeters, rolls of paper are cut

to size, packaged, and labeled. The AGVs take the finished paper to a cavernous warehouse that can store more than 20 million pounds of paper.

Cost: Free

Freebies: Small writing pad, brochure, poster, and postcard.

Video/DVD Shown: 10-minute overview of the mill's operation, including pulp-making and forestry program.

Reservations Needed: No, except for groups of 5 or more.

Days and Hours: Wed, Thur, and Sat at 10:00 AM. Other times by prior arrangement. Closed some holidays.

Plan to Stay: 1.5 hours for tour and video.

Minimum Age: 5 years and older. Children under 18 must be accompanied by an adult.

Disabled Access: Yes. Advance notice requested, so adequate number of guides can be available.

Group Requirements: Groups should call at least 1 week in advance. For specially arranged tours, minimum group size is 5 people. Maximum group size is 60 people.

Special Information: Closed-toed shoes are required. Summer paper mill tour at subsidiary in Duluth, MN (see page 189 or call 218-628-5100).

Gift Shop: Sells T-shirts, pens, mugs, hats, and puzzles. Open when there are tours.

Directions: From Madison, take I-90/94 West to I-39 North (Exit 108). Take Hwy. 73 West and turn right on Hwy. 13 North. Cross the Wisconsin River. Turn right onto West Grand Ave. Turn left on 4th Ave. Mill tour entrance is 1.5 blocks on right.

Nearby Attractions: Stora Enso's Stevens Point Mill tours (call 715-345-8060); Wisconsin Dairy State Cheese tour (see page 219) about 30 minutes away; Stevens Point Brewery tour (call 715-344-9310). Wisconsin Paper Council publishes a brochure of Wisconsin paper tours (call 920-722-1500).

801 West Madison Street, Waterloo, WI 53594   (920) 478-2197   www.trekbikes.com

When does a bike start to look like a bike? At the Trek plant, not until it reaches final assembly. Here the lean frame, little more than a wisp of painted geometry, meets pedals, cables, handlebars, and wheels, which are then boxed together for shipment to bike stores worldwide.

You'll see how Trek, which started in 1975 with four employees building frames for Midwestern bicycle dealers, has innovated bike production. Metal frames take their form in the welding area. Thousands of metal pipes and joints, looking like bins of plumbing fixtures, are arranged precisely on steel tables and soldered together. It's a crackly, clattery region made brilliant with spits and stripes of green flame from the welding torch. Trek's frames of carbon fiber, a lightweight, almost ethereal compound, are built in an adjoining area. Workers hustle around the mounted carbon frames, spreading the fast-drying glue before it stiffens and sets. These newly glued frames are baked in an oven, then sanded smooth.

All frames, metal or carbon—about 1,000 a day—go to the paint department. They hang like coats on conveyor hooks that trundle toward large sheet-metal closets: the painting booths. Meanwhile, robots in a nearby department join rims to hubs, creating the wheels that will eventually meet up with the frames. On the glossy floor, heaps of fresh black tires, with the incarnate odor of a bike shop, are stacked hundreds deep. See the spokes bending and weaving into position and the "hop and wobble" process of computer-monitored "rim truing." On your way out, notice the "Employee Park-

ing" area, an indoor rack some 50 yards long that's crowded with colorful bikes. If you drive your car to Trek, the largest manufacturer of quality bicycles in the U.S.A., you'll find a large paved lot with plenty of places to park!

Cost: Free

Freebies: No

Video/DVD Shown: No

Reservations Needed: Yes

Days and Hours: Wed 10:00 AM. Closed holidays. Closed for 2 weeks around the end of June and beginning of July. Tour schedule subject to change.

Plan to Stay: 45 minutes for tour.

Minimum Age: None

Disabled Access: Most of tour is wheelchair accessible.

Group Requirements: Groups larger than 12 must call 1 week in advance. Maximum group size is 15. Does not want traditional bus tours.

Special Information: No video cameras. Photography restricted in some areas. Trek factory in Whitewater, WI, also offers tours (call 262-473-8735).

Gift Shop: No

Directions: From I-94, take Marshall/ Deerfield exit. Travel north on Hwy. 73 toward Marshall. Turn right at Hwy. 19 (Main St. in Marshall). Trek plant is 4 miles ahead on right.

Nearby Attractions: In Waterloo, inquire locally about tour of local pickle factory Little A-Merrick-A Amusement Park in Marshall; John Deere lawn tractor plant tour in Horicon (call 920-485-4411); Madison's attractions, including Arboretum, Vilas Park Zoo, and State Capital tours, about 40 minutes away.

The Dairy State Cheese plant, owned for generations by the Moran family, is fronted by a busy little shop. Look through the bank of windows either upstairs or downstairs from the shop, and you'll see a vast room filled with stainless-steel pipes, vats, and tables. A few workers move about in hair nets and rubber boots, but much of the "Stirred Curd Cheddar" process you're watching is highly automated. Given the size of the production room, the near absence of people is conspicuous, a testimony to the efficiency of state-of-the-art cheese-making equipment.

Off to your left rise several immense silos filled with thousands of gallons of pasteurized and cultured milk. Ten pounds of milk are used in producing every pound of cheese. A network of pipes carries the milk from the silos to four vats, each one longer than a school bus. All day the upright enclosed vats are filled and emptied. The curds and whey are pumped over to long tables. A "forker" swirls as it drifts up and down the length of the long narrow vat, beginning the process of separating the liquid (whey) from the milk solids (curd).

When the whey is drained off, what remains is a warm mass of glossy curds. The final step is to salt the curds. The fresh curds are automatically fed into presses, where they are compacted into 700-pound blocks of brand-new cheese. The massive orange or white blocks are then sealed into wooden boxes for aging. After about one month, the cheese is shipped to Kraft for cutting. When your tour ends, be sure to return to the shop and browse among the coolers stocked with 85 varieties of cheese. Buy yourself a bag of curds so fresh they'll squeak on your teeth.

Cost: Free

Freebies: Cheese samples.

Video/DVD Shown: Optional 23-minute film promotes Wisconsin cheese and details manufacturing process.

Reservations Needed: No, except for groups larger than 25 people.

Days and Hours: Mon–Fri 8:30 AM–4:30 PM. Production ends around 4:00 PM. Sun 9:00 AM–12:00 PM, but no production. Call to confirm holiday hours.

Plan to Stay: 15 minutes for self-guided viewing, plus time for video and cheese shop.

Minimum Age: None

Disabled Access: Yes

Group Requirements: Groups larger than 25 should make reservations 2 days in advance. Ice-cream cones and cheese samples provided for school tours.

Special Information: Guide available by request with 2 days' notice.

Retail Store: Cheese shop sells wide selection of cheeses, sausage, and locally made ice cream. Open Mon–Fri 8:30 AM–5:15 PM, Sat 8:30 AM–5:00 PM. Sun 9:00 AM–12:00 PM. Call about holiday hours. Catalog available from above number.

Directions: Take U.S. 51 North to the Hwy. 73 exit at Plainfield. Turn left (west) on Hwy. 73 to Hwy. 13. Turn right (north) and go through Wisconsin Rapids, following signs for Hwy. 34 North. Enter town of Rudolph, and Dairy State Cheese is on right.

Nearby Attractions: Stora Enso tour (see page 217); Stevens Point Brewery tour (call 715-344-9310); Rudolph Grotto Gardens and Wonder Cave. For complete list of Wisconsin cheese plants, write: Cheese Plants, Wisconsin Milk Marketing Board, 8418 Excelsior Dr., Madison, WI 53717.

INDIANA

OHIO

see Mid-Atlantic
page 93

BUFFALO TRACE DISTILLERY
REBECCA-RUTH CANDIES

Charleston

WEST
VIRGINIA

VIRGINIA

TOYOTA

St Louis

Frankfort

COLONEL HARLAND SANDERS MUSEUM
LOUISVILLE SLUGGER MUSEUM
LOUISVILLE STONEWARE
AMERICAN PRINTING HOUSE FOR THE BLIND
FORD

OLD KENTUCKY CANDIES

Norfolk

Jefferson City

ILLINOIS

CHURCHILL WEAVERS

WILD TURKEY
THREE CHIMNEYS
MAKER'S MARK DISTILLERY

KENTUCKY

MISSOURI

REPLACEMENTS LTD

Raleigh

Springfield

CORVETTE
NATIONAL CORVETTE MUSEUM

BILL DAVIS RACING
FURNITURE DISCOVERY CENTER

SEAGROVE AREA
POTTERIES

NORTH
CAROLINA

PURITY DAIRIES

Nashville

BLUE RIDGE
MOTION PICTURES

BMW

NISSAN

see Heartland
page 277

TENNESSEE

Jonesboro

GM SPRING HILL

MASTERCRAFT

Wilmington

ARKANSAS

Memphis

JACK DANIELS
DISTILLERY

Columbia

GIBSON

SOUTH
CAROLINA

Little Rock

WORLD OF COCA-COLA
CNN

Atlanta

AMERICAN CLASSIC TEA

Charleston

VIKING RANGE

Birmingham

MISSISSIPPI

MERCEDES-BENZ

ROBINSON IRON

ALABAMA

LANE PACKING

GEORGIA

Savannah

PEAVEY
ELECTRONICS

HYUNDAI

Montgomery

Monroe

Jackson

Shreveport

LOUISIANA

SALLY CORPORATION

Jacksonville

Tallahassee

WHETSTONE CHOCOLATES

TONY CHACHERE'S

Baton Rouge

KLIEBERT'S TURTLE AND ALLIGATOR TOURS

E-ONE

KONRIKO

NEW ORLEANS ARTWORKS
BLAINE KERN'S MARDI GRAS WORLD

CORRECT CRAFT

MCILHENNY
COMPANY

New Orleans

DISNEY-MGM STUDIOS

Orlando

KENNEDY SPACE CENTER

MOTIVATIT SEAFOODS

Tampa

GONZALEZ Y MARTÍNEZ

NEW PIPER AIRCRAFT

FLORIDA

HOFFMAN'S

G u l f

Miami

o f

M e x i c o

0   80 mi

0   80 km

This tour is not just for car buffs but for anybody interested in modern manufacturing methods. Robots and people work together in futuristic harmony, and the atmosphere is friendly rather than forbidding. People wave a lot. During the tour, your guide may point out a (human) Team Member and encourage you to raise a cheer of support.

Guests gather in the visitor center and start the tour in the auditorium with an overview of Hyundai and a video about the manufacturing operation. Donning headsets for hearing your guide's commentary, you put on safety glasses and board the tour's electric tram, which your guide drives into the plant.

In the stamping shop, rolls of coiled steel are cut and then stamped under great pressure into 17 different vehicle body parts. Here you meet your first Hyundai robots, which collect the parts and store them. More robots (over 250) await you in the corridors of the weld shop. They weld together, with precision and a lot of flying sparks, the stamped metal parts into the recognizable body of a car. These skeletal cars proceed by overhead trestle to the paint shop, where they turn 11 somersaults in a preparatory bath before robots spray on their coats of color and glossy finish.

Your tour moves to the next area for general assembly. Through modern ventilation and conveyance, this zone is surprisingly clean, cool, and quiet. Humans join robots here: over a thousand Team Members install the parts and pieces of each vehicle, including wiring, brake controls, engine, drive train, tires, battery, doors, seats, and glass. However, robots play an important role even here. One of the most striking sights of the tour is the snakelike robot that places the windshields; when the glass is perfectly poised and ready, it lunges forward like a Hollywood dinosaur and sets the windshield in place.

After receiving oil, coolant, gasoline, and other fluids, the car undergoes rigorous quality tests. Your tour follows this process outside to a two-mile test track, where the examinations include a check of the brakes and a ride along a rough road to listen for rattles and loose parts.

The Montgomery facility has its own shop for making V6 engines, and this is the last stop on your tour. Having seen the installation of the engines back in general assembly, here you can learn about their construction. Feel free to browse through the visitor center and gift shop after the tour.

Cost: Free

Freebies: No

Video/DVD Shown: An 8-minute overview before the tour explains the process of making vehicles.

Reservations Needed: Yes. Visit www.hmmausa.com/tours.cfm and click on the "Book a Tour Today" link, or call the reservation line (334-387-8019), Mon–Fri 9:00 AM–4:00 PM.

Days and Hours: Tours: Mon, Wed, and Fri at 9:30 AM, 12:30 PM, and 2:00 PM. Visitor center: Mon–Fri 9:00 AM–4:00 PM. Closed holidays.

Plan to Stay: 1.5 hours.

Minimum Age: First-graders with parent or guardian; third-graders for school groups.

Disabled Access: Yes, please call ahead to make arrangements.

Group Requirements: The tour permits a maximum of 32 people. Larger groups must schedule more than one tour.

Gift Shop: The shop sells Hyundai promotional merchandise. Open Mon–Fri 9:30 AM–5:30 PM (closed 12:45–1:15 PM). Closed holidays.

Directions: From I-65, take Hope Hull/Hyundai Blvd. exit, travel west about 0.7 mile, merge on Hyundai Blvd., and drive east for 1.3 miles. Plant is on left. Look for Visitor Entrance and Visitor Parking. Tell security you are there for tour.

Nearby Attractions: Rosa Parks Library and Museum; Civil Rights Memorial; Hank Williams Museum.

See color photos, pages 26.

1856 Robinson Road, Alexander City, AL 35010   (256) 329-8486   www.robinsoniron.com

Robinson Iron

Have you ever taken the New York City subway from Astor Place and admired the cast-iron kiosk entrance? If so, you've already seen Robinson Iron's handiwork. Perhaps you've sat on its benches, which line Pennsylvania Avenue in Washington, D.C., or daydreamed while watching water flow through the 12,000-pound Court Square Fountain in Montgomery. Robinson restored the fountain, as well as the intricate ironwork at Singapore's renowned Raffles Hotel. Although you cannot tour the foundry, where 2,500°F molten iron flows like melted butter, you can watch skilled ironworkers turn the raw castings into ornate fountains, urns, lampposts, garden statuary, or perhaps customized railings for subway stations.

As you enter the shop, welding arcs hiss, grinding wheels squeal, and drills buzz, leaving no doubt that you're surrounded by heavy ironworking. Masked welders in the fabrication area wield plasma arc cutters, which produce a light as bright as a laser. A metallic, flinty odor fills your nose. When the sparks clear, you'll find the raw castings have become a 16-foot multitiered fountain for a municipal park, or a 400-pound deer, complete with antlers, for someone's backyard.

In the finishing area, workers spray-paint Charleston Green, Gloss White, or Black in a painting booth. An overhead crane lifts the mammoth ornaments into place, so workers can construct shipping crates around them. Before you end the tour, head outside down the path to the Pattern Shop, to see how the whole process starts. Pattern makers follow blueprints from Robinson's designers to custom-carve, detail, and create a wooden master, which is then used to fashion a plastic or metal working pattern. The foundry uses the pattern to produce a hollow sand mold into which molten iron is poured. The raw casting it creates will go to the workers in the fabrication area, where you began. In the Atrium Showroom, finished pieces stand ready for your close inspection, admiration, and purchase.

Cost: Free

Freebies: No

Video/DVD Shown: No

Reservations Needed: Yes. Call for reservation.

Days and Hours: Mon–Fri 8:00 AM–4:00 PM. Closed holidays. Production decreases during 4th of July week and Christmas week.

Plan to Stay: 45 minutes, plus time in showroom.

Minimum Age: None, although some areas are restricted for children under 5, who might stay in the Atrium Showroom to watch the fountain.

Disabled Access: No

Group Requirements: Groups of 8 or more should call 1 day in advance.

Special Information: Plant can be quite noisy at times.

Showroom: The Atrium Showroom features a representative collection of ironworks from the company's catalog (available in showroom or from above phone number or website), including small garden statuary, ornamental urns, and animal sculptures. Open same hours as tour.

Directions: From Birmingham, take Hwy. 280 East to Kelleton. Turn left on Business 280 (*not* Bypass 280). In 2 miles, where the road widens, watch on the right for Robinson Foundry. Take the first right after the foundry. Cross the railroad tracks. Robinson Iron is the brown metal building on your right. From Montgomery, take Hwy. 231 North to Wetumka. Turn right on Hwy. 9 North. Turn right on Hwy. 22 East. Turn left onto Hwy. 280 West. In a little over 1 mile, turn right on Robinson Rd. Bear right at the fork, and watch for Robinson Iron on your left.

Nearby Attractions: Russell Corp. clothing manufacturer tour (call 256-329-4000); Martin Lake; Kowaliga Marina; Horseshoe Bend National Military Park.

SOUTH

1 Mercedes Drive, Vance, AL 35490

(205) 507-2253
(888) 286-8762

www.mbusi.com

Mercedes-Benz

Most Americans credit Henry Ford with the invention of the automobile. However, as you'll learn from the History Exhibit at the 24,000-square-foot Mercedes-Benz Visitor Center, the first automobile came to be known as the Mercedes-Benz (invented in 1886).

The Racing Exhibit portrays Mercedes' long and illustrious racing career through photographs of all the cars' famous drivers, historical racing footage, and a historical Mercedes-Benz racing vehicle. Many safety features were first tested in race cars and then incorporated into passenger cars.

Sheet-metal panels for the M-Class, a sport-utility vehicle, come into the plant prestamped and subassembled on a just-in-time basis. The panels are welded together in the body shop. The vehicle leaves the body shop complete with four doors, tailgate, and hood, but it's only a colorless shell. Look through windows into the paint shop, where cars enter on the mezzanine level as raw steel precision-shaped bodies. In this clean room, workers wear astronaut-like suits and hair nets. The cars zigzag their way back and forth along the whole length of the paint shop, alternating between dip tanks and oven lines, and come out in front of you in glossy painted colors. The selectivity bank shuffles the cars around into assembly sequence as if it's playing checkers.

In assembly, one of the highlights is the "marriage" station on the final line, where the completed chassis is bolted to a completed body. You'll wish you had arranged for factory-direct delivery so you could drive your new M-Class vehicle right out of the Visitor Center.

Cost: Visitor Center: free; call for information and reservations for factory tour.

Freebies: No

Video/DVD Shown: Plans for video uncertain.

Reservations Needed: Yes, for factory tour. No, for Visitor Center, except for groups of 100 or more. Factory tours are limited in size, so call well in advance.

Days and Hours: Factory tour: Mon–Fri by appointment. Visitor Center: Mon–Fri 9:00 AM–5:00 PM and 1st Sat of month 10:00 AM–5:00 PM. Both closed holidays. Factory closed July 4th week and week between Christmas and New Year's. Mercedes-Benz reserves the right to cancel the factory tour for production or safety reasons.

Plan to Stay: 1 hour each for factory tour and Visitor Center, plus time for Mercedes Boutique.

Minimum Age: 12 for tour; none for Visitor Center.

Disabled Access: Yes

Group Requirements: Groups over 10 people should call at least 1 week in advance for the Visitor Center and 1 month for the factory tour. Maximum group size is 25 people for factory tour.

Special Information: No photography in factory.

Gift Shop: Mercedes Boutique sells logoed key chains, caps, T-shirts, coffee mugs showing the Visitor Center's silhouette, plus other Mercedes-Benz merchandise. Also carries lifestyle items such as hiking equipment and water bottles. Open same hours as Visitor Center. Closed holidays.

Directions: From Birmingham, take I-59/20 West to Exit 89. Turn left over the Interstate. Bear right onto Mercedes Dr. Visitor Center is first building on left.

Nearby Attractions: Tannehill State Park; Tuscaloosa's attractions, including Paul (Bear) Bryant Museum, Mound State Monument, and antebellum homes, about 17 miles away.

SOUTH

A MBUSI Team Member carefully welds the body of an M-Class.

The Mercedes-Benz U.S. International plant in Vance, Alabama, is home to the Mercedes-Benz M-Class. A $600-million expansion doubled the size of the facility and its workforce.

6100 South Orange Avenue,
Orlando, FL 32809

(800) 346-2092   www.correctcraft.com

Nautiques™
BY CORRECT CRAFT ❚ SINCE 1925

After seeing the water-ski extravaganza at nearby Sea World in Orlando, you may wonder how Ski Nautiques, its official ski towboats, are made. A tour of Ski Nautique manufacturer Correct Craft shows you in one hour the two-week process of building the premier inboard water-ski towboat. Correct Craft, started in 1925 by W. C. Meloon, is now a third-generation family business.

Starting with a mold, fiberglass boats are actually built from the outside in. To create the shiny, colorful stripes of the hull's exterior, the interior surface of the mold is sprayed in sections with gelcoat. Then workers wearing floor-length aprons and safety gear use spray guns resembling oversized dentist-drill arms to apply the initial "skin coat" of fiberglass. A mixture of fiberglass and epoxy resin shoots out of the gun, looking like cotton candy when it hits the mold. Next, the entire inside of the mold is coated with clothlike fiberglass sheets to form a solid unit. Workers use hand rollers to smooth the hull's surface and inhibit the development of air pockets.

In another area, you can touch a smooth hull or deck just hoisted out of its mold. To reduce vibration and noise, ISODAMP CN (used by the Navy) is put on the inside of the hull's walls and the floor. In the engine area, a carousel-like crane swings around to lower an engine onto its frame. After the engine is bolted into place, workers install the dashboard, carpeting, interior trim, and seating. Each boat is tested under actual running conditions for at least 30 minutes in a lake before decorative decals and graphics are applied. The water-skiers who go on this tour will immediately want to take one of the boats out for a pull.

Cost: Free

Freebies: Stickers

Video/DVD Shown: Upon request, a detailed 15-minute video on company history and production process is shown in the waiting area.

Reservations Needed: Yes

Days and Hours: *Company moving into new product facility and headquarters in Fall 2006. Tour availability and schedule TBD.*

Plan to Stay: 1 hour.

Minimum Age: 10

Disabled Access: Yes

Group Requirements: Groups should call ahead. Large groups will be split into groups of 10–15 people.

Special Information: Even though it's an open-air facility, you'll get a strong resin smell in the area where the fiberglass is applied. Watch out for forklifts moving through the maze of hulls and decks in various stages of production. Look for a 1934 wooden replica of a Correct Craft displayed in the waiting area. Future plans are to move to a new facility.

Gift Area: Fashion Nautique carries a wide array of Correct Craft clothing and accessories.

Directions: *Call or check website for directions.*

Nearby Attractions: Magic of Disney Animation Studios (see page 227); Regal Marine tour (call 800-US-REGAL); Sea World; Wet 'n' Wild. In Sarasota, on Florida's west coast, Wellcraft boat manufacturer gives tours (call 941-753-7811).

SOUTH

The Magic of Disney Animation

Disney-MGM Studios,
Walt Disney World Resort,
Lake Buena Vista, FL 32830-0040

(407) 824-4321   www.disneyworld.com

The Walt Disney Company, with its giant theme parks, real estate holdings, and Oscar-winning movies, started as an animation studio in 1923. Whether you wonder how cartoon characters (like the ubiquitous Mickey Mouse) are drawn or what the newest Disney animated film will be, the answer is found on the Magic of Disney Animation tour at Disney-MGM Studios. This creative heritage comes to life in entertaining videos throughout the tour, samples of art from current movies, and lobby displays of Oscars that Walt Disney Studios has won.

Animators have assigned roles, much like the characters they draw. Some animators sketch the character only at its furthest points of movement, while other artists add the in-between positions, redraw the series to refine the detail, or create special effects and the "sets" on which the animated characters perform. Guests can try their hand at sketching a famous Disney character and even take their sketch home with them.

Cost: Included in admission charge to the theme park at Walt Disney World Resort.

Freebies: A self-drawn sketch of a Disney character.

Videos Shown: Guests can view a video presentation called *Drawn to Animation,* featuring Mushu from the animated feature *Mulan.*

Reservations Needed: No

Days and Hours: Mon–Sun 10:00 AM–7:00 PM. Most activity Mon–Fri. Hours change depending on theme park hours and season. Open 365 days a year.

Plan to Stay: All day at Disney-MGM Studios. The Magic of Disney Animation tour runs in continuous 15-minute blocks (add time to wait before the tour).

Minimum Age: None

Disabled Access: Yes

Group Requirements: Groups larger than 10 people can call (407) 824-6750 in advance to order tickets to the theme park.

Special Information: Take this tour in the morning to avoid the longest lines, and try to go during the workweek. Tour is available on weekends and holidays, and you'll sometimes see an animator hard at work on a project. Other animation tours for student groups available through Youth Group Programs. Call (800) 833-9806 for more information.

Gift Shop: The Animation Gallery sells figurines and cels of your favorite animation characters, along with books, videos, and other Disney cartoon character items. Open same hours as theme park.

Directions: From Orlando, take Exit 67 off I-4 and follow the signs. From Tampa, stay on U.S. 192 and take Exit 62.

Nearby Attractions: All attractions and shows at Disney-MGM Studios. The Studios' Backlot tour teaches you about moviemaking and television production and provides glimpses of current Disney projects in production.

SOUTH

Whether you've wanted to be a firefighter since childhood or you've just watched the trucks careen around street corners, this will give you a new appreciation for fire trucks. E-ONE has become one of the world's leading manufacturers of emergency vehicles, building a complete line of fire and rescue vehicles, including airport crash fire firefighting (ARFF) trucks.

To enable the fire and emergency services to save lives and protect property, E-ONE manufactures fire apparatus to meet the varying needs of the customers. As you proceed through the factory-floor tour, notice the many different fire truck varieties (aerials, pumpers, and rescue vehicles), as well as the many cab, body, and chassis designs.

In the body plant, power shears resemble guillotines as they chop diamond-patterned aluminum sheets. See sparks fly as a face-shielded worker welds the body frame together. Once the body is structurally sound, sanders and grinders transform it into a bright, shiny fire engine. In the paint shop, you'll notice that there is no one official "fire-engine red."

In the assembly area, raw black chassis patiently await their bodies and other accessories, such as pumps and electrical wiring. At the end of the line, a crane lowers a freshly painted custom cab onto its chassis. Check the shipper ID label on the dashboard window or cab—some fire-fighting vehicles are headed for Small Town, U.S.A., others to some exotic South Pacific island. At the end of the tour, you'll want to climb up into a fire-engine cab, sit in the thickly padded seats, touch the sophisticated control panel, and turn the steering wheel, pretending you're a firefighter.

Cost: Adults, $6; seniors age 55 and above, $4; children 6–12, free. Firefighters with identification, free.

Freebies: No

Video/DVD Shown: Yes, in the reception area.

Reservations Needed: Yes

Days and Hours: Based on demand and weather conditions, tours are scheduled for Mon–Fri 9:00 AM, 11:00 AM, and 1:00 PM. Closed holidays and the week between Christmas and New Year's.

Plan to Stay: 1 hour, plus time for the gift shop.

Minimum Age: 6. Children under 6 receive a 20-minute abbreviated tour of the vehicle delivery center, provided at 8:30 AM, 10:30 AM and 12:30 PM.

Disabled Access: Yes

Group Requirements: Based on availability. Group size limited to 20 people. Call at least 2 weeks in advance.

Special Information: The use of cameras and cell phones is strictly prohibited within the facilities. Comfortable, closed-toe shoes are required. Safety glasses are provided and must be worn in the required areas. Occasionally, you may hear the sound of a fire-truck siren. Don't worry, it's just a test.

Gift Shop: The Fire Locker, exclusive shop for E-ONE merchandise, sells apparel, hats, mugs, and miscellaneous merchandise. Open Mon–Fri 8:30 AM–12:30 PM and 1:30–5:00 PM. For more store info, call (352) 861-3521 or check www.firelocker.com.

Directions: From the Florida Tnpk. (south of Ocala), take I-75 North to Exit 352 Hwy. 40 (the second Ocala exit). On I-75 North, you can see the plant on the right (east side). Go right at exit (going east). Turn right at S.W. 33rd Ave., then right at S.W. 7th. Follow service road that cuts back to left. The Welcome Center is on the left.

Nearby Attractions: Silver Springs attractions; Wild Waters; Don Garlits Museum of Drag Racing; Appleton Museum of Art.

SOUTH

Gonzalez y Martínez

2103 East 7th Avenue, Tampa, FL 33605

(813) 248-8210
(888) 805-5897

www.gonzalezy
martinez.com

Even though we don't write about tobacco tours in this book, we include this more as a history lesson than as a factory tour; cigar making is the industrial history of Tampa. In 1885, Don Vicente Martínez Ybor, a Cuban cigar factory owner, fled Cuba's political unrest to establish his cigar empire in a section of Tampa. Referred to first as "Mr. Ybor's City," later as Ybor City, this district, at its peak, had 200 cigar factories with 12,000 *tabaqueros* (cigar makers). Only a handful of master *tabaqueros* still hand-roll cigars in Tampa.

The Gonzalez y Martínez family tradition of cigar making was born shortly after the turn of the 20th century, after their recent arrival from Cuba and the marriage of Marcelíno Gonzalez to Francísco "Don Pancho" Martínez's daughter. Four generations later, Richard Gonzmart, Don Pancho's great-grandson, continues the family tradition.

You enter this cigar factory and store through a separate entrance of the famous Columbia Restaurant, recognizable by its colorful fruit-bouquet Spanish tile. Opened in 1905 and now in its fourth and fifth generations of family ownership and operation, the Columbia Restaurant is the oldest restaurant in Florida and the largest Spanish restaurant in the world.

Inside, the *tabaquero* sits at a dark brown wooden desk, surrounded on three sides by cases displaying cigars and a packing area behind him. The *tabaquero* classifies and separates the best leaves for filler, binder, and wrapper. From a pile on his desk, he selects several brown, almost-brittle, paper-thin, whole tobacco leaves. Next, he deveins these wrapper leaves. With a small water spray bottle, he moisturizes the leaves to obtain flexibility and restore silkiness. Stretching the wrapper leaves for rolling, he tightly rolls them around scraps of dried tobacco leaves, "filler," and twists the ends shut.

After he chops off the excess with a blade, he carefully stacks each cigar on top of the desk, getting them ready for storage in their walk-in humidor.

Today Ybor City is being revived. Restored red-arched brick buildings with second-floor latticework balconies line the cobblestoned streets of 7th Avenue, the main thoroughfare. And traces of its cigar-making history still survive.

Cost: Free

Freebies: No

Video/DVD Shown: No

Reservations Needed: No

Days and Hours: Mon–Sat 10:00 AM–4:00 PM.

Plan to Stay: 10 minutes, plus additional time in the store and Columbia Restaurant.

Minimum Age: None

Disabled Access: Yes

Group Requirements: None

Special Information: Personalized cigar labels can be made for special corporate or personal occasions such as births, anniversaries, and wedding announcements.

Retail Store: Sells cigars ranging from Don Casimiro Collection, handmade in Tampa, to Private Batch Bourbon Cigars and cigar-related paraphernalia. Open Mon–Thur 10:00 AM–9:00 PM., Fri–Sat 10:00 AM–11:00 PM.

Directions: From I-275, take I-4 East. Take Exit 1. Turn right off ramp. Turn left onto 21st St. Will be on left at corner of 7th Ave.

Nearby Attractions: Ybor City State Museum provides cigar-making demonstrations on weekends. Exhibits tell about immigrants' lives and Ybor's history. Down the street, visit tiny restored "casitas," cigar workers' shotgun-style houses (call 813-247-6323); Ybor City State Museum provides map for Heritage and Factory walking tour of Ybor City; Columbia Centennial Museum (call 813-241-6971); Tampa Rico Cigar Company tours (call 813-247-6738); Ybor City Brewing Company tours (call 813-242-9222); Busch Gardens; Adventure Island; Museum of Science and Industry.

SOUTH

5190 Lake Worth Road, Greenacres City, FL 33463 | (561) 967-2213 | (888) 281-8800 | www.hoffmans.com

Begun in 1975, when Paul Hoffman and Theresa Hoffman Daly paid $1,400 at an auction for an existing candy shop, this family-operated company now makes 200,000 pounds of candy per year. In this Tudor-style chocoholics' heaven, viewing windows at the right side of the store overlook the kitchen.

Directly in front of the observation window, the enrobing machine coats candy centers with an avalanche of chocolate. You may be lucky enough to watch peanut brittle or "jitterbugs" being made. Two workers pour a 300°F mixture of butter, sugar, and peanuts from a copper kettle onto a marble slab. They spread the mixture with metal spatulas, cut it in half with a pizza cutter, and flip it over. Then, with a comblike spatula, they spread out the edges to "stretch" the peanut brittle.

Farther back in the kitchen, buttercream centers proceed on a wire belt to another enrober. A worker waits for the chocolates to emerge, then hand-marks the type of center (for example, "R" for raspberry). After watching these candies being made, you'll be ready to sample some, especially the famous chocolate-covered pretzels.

You can walk off these extra calories in Hoffman's three-quarter-acre botanical gardens. Stroll among exotic and rare plants, a rainforest area, a miniature cacao plantation, and a fruit-salad section with pineapple, banana, and orange trees.

Every holiday season the garden is transformed into Hoffman's Holiday Wonderland, sparkling with more than 100,000 lights. It includes a giant gingerbread house, animated carolers, a custom-made menorah, a 15-foot Christmas tree, a life-size nativity scene, and Santa's North Pole Village.

Another garden highlight is the Candyland Railroad, a G-scale model community with more than 500 feet of track. Railcars make stops at Coconut Cream Cottage, Rocky Candy Mine, and Pecan

Truffle Pond. The formal garden features topiaries shaped like a golfer, unicorn, and reindeer.

Cost: Free

Freebies: Sample chocolates.

Video/DVD Shown: 13-minute video about chocolate making, the botanical gardens, and Candyland Railroad.

Reservations Needed: No, except for groups larger than 15 people.

Days and Hours: Mon–Fri 9:00 AM–3:30 PM. Closed Thanksgiving, Christmas, New Year's, and Easter.

Plan to Stay: 25 minutes for self-guided viewing through observation window and video, plus time for gardens, trains, and Chocolate Shoppe.

Minimum Age: None

Disabled Access: Yes

Group Requirements: Groups larger than 15 people should call 1 week in advance to arrange a video presentation. Groups over 40 people will be split into smaller groups. No maximum group size.

Special Information: Best time to see production is from August 15 to Easter. During summer, call ahead for production schedule.

Retail Store: Chocolate Shoppe sells Hoffman's 80 varieties of chocolates. Open Mon–Sat 9:00 AM–8:00 PM, Sun 9:00 AM–6:00 PM, and from Thanksgiving to December 31, daily 9:00 AM–10:00 PM. Closed Thanksgiving, Christmas, New Year's, and Easter. Catalog available; call (888) 281-8800.

Directions: From I-95, exit at 6th Ave. South in Lake Worth. Head west approximately 2 miles to Military Trail. Turn right onto Military Trail. Turn left onto Lake Worth Rd. Hoffman's is down the road on left. From Florida Tnpk., take Exit 93 (Lake Worth Rd.). Turn left and travel about 3 miles. Hoffman's is on right.

Nearby Attractions: International Museum of Cartoons; Kravis Center; Lion Country Safari; Palm Beach Community College Museum of Art; Morikami Museum and Japanese Gardens; Lake Worth Beach.

SOUTH

Kennedy Space Center

VISITOR COMPLEX

No manufacturing operation in the United States is more ambitious than the NASA space program. Kennedy Space Center, its central "spaceport" on Cape Canaveral, gives visitors a detailed view of our past, present, and future technology for propelling astronauts into orbit, to the moon, and perhaps even to Mars. In addition to spacecraft exhibits and two IMAX® cinemas, the Kennedy Space Center offers a basic tour that is included in general admission and special tours that require separate tickets.

Leaving by bus from the Visitor Complex, the basic tour is available every 15 minutes and makes three stops. The first, Launch Complex 39 (LC 39), is where the space shuttles take off. A nearby observation platform, rising 60 feet high, gives visitors a fine view of the two immense launch pads. You can also see the Launch Control Center and the vast Vehicle Assembly Building, perhaps the biggest hangar in the world.

Another stop is the facility in which NASA prepares parts of the International Space Station (ISS). You can walk through an actual-size mock-up of the interiors where astronauts will work and sleep. From the observation room, you see the processing bay in which elements of the space station are prepared. You also visit the Apollo/Saturn V Center. This cavernous facility preserves memories of the Apollo program, which culminated in the moon landings. The centerpiece is one of the original giant Saturn V rockets, the size of a building.

In special tours, which last up to three hours, guests travel to areas where NASA assembles spacecraft. You may enjoy an up-close visit to the Vehicle Assembly Building, the enormous Crawler Transporters, and the Shuttle Landing Facility.

The Astronaut Training Experience (ATX) is an all-day interactive program that gives you a taste of the rigors that NASA crews must endure to prepare for missions. The day also includes a general tour of Kennedy Space Center, simulators, and a simulated space-shuttle mission. Because the ATX is interactive, special requirements apply (call for details).

Cost: Standard admission: adults, $31; children (aged 3–11), $21. Special tours cost extra (call or check website for schedule and prices).

Freebies: No

Video/DVD Shown: The facility has two IMAX® theaters. Tours may also see videos.

Reservations Needed: Not for general admission. Required for special tours.

Days and Hours: Daily 9:00 AM–5:00 PM. Buses for the basic tour leave every 15 minutes. Closed Christmas and certain launch days.

Plan to Stay: Several hours, depending on interests.

Minimum Age: None

Disabled Access: Yes

Group Requirements: Reserve special tours at least a few weeks in advance.

Special Information: All visitors must pass through metal detectors. No guns, other weapons, or sharp items are permitted. Coolers and large bags are not allowed; small bags are inspected. Backpacks are not permitted on launch days. Operational requirements may close or alter tours.

Gift Shop: The shop sells NASA apparel, toys, memorabilia, books, DVDs, and souvenirs. Open daily 9:00 AM–5:00 PM. Closed Christmas and certain launch days.

Directions: From Orlando, take SR 528 East to SR 407 toward Kennedy Space Center. When SR 407 ends, turn right on SR 405 and follow signs. From 1-95 South, take SR 50 and turn left at end of ramp on SR 50. At next intersection, turn right onto SR 405 and follow signs. From I-95 North, take Hwy. 50 toward Kennedy Space Center. Turn right on SR 405 and follow signs.

Nearby Attractions: Magic of Disney Animation and Correct Craft (see pages 227 and 226).

SOUTH

Freedom of flight

The Piper name has been synonymous with small aircraft since the introduction of the Piper Cub in the late 1930s by a former Pennsylvania oilman, William T. Piper. After producing thousands of bright yellow Cubs for pilot training during World War II, Piper moved its base from central Pennsylvania to a sprawling facility in Florida where it has developed more than 100 single- and twin-engine models and built more than 150,000 planes. In the summer of 1995, New Piper Aircraft Inc. became a reality when President/CEO Charles Suma and a nucleus of employees took over the assets of the Piper Aircraft Corporation. Today retired company workers conduct informative, in-depth tours of New Piper's 1.2 million-square-foot plant, where you will learn all about the planes in which many pilots are first taught how to fly.

Your tour begins in Building 1, appropriately where the manufacturing process itself begins with the making of the custom tools and dies used to manufacture various parts of the finished aircraft. Next, watch as workers put 4,000-pound rolls of raw aluminum through giant shearing machines to cut the metal to a workable size. As you move along, you'll see this metal transform into the skin and bones of an airplane.

Parts like wing flaps, landing gear, and hydraulic lines fill in the skeletal airframe; discover how they are made in the subassembly areas, fastened in place, and calibrated. Watch computer-controlled milling and routing machines robotically cut, drill, bore, and shave these parts into shape while spewing tiny shards of metal. Get a glimpse at nearly completed aircraft ready for its first test flight before heading to the most exciting part of the tour: the mating of the wings and fuselage. An overhead crane sets the fuselage down over the single, continuous wing piece as it is held steady by a jig. With this step, the elaborate birth of an airplane seems complete, and your imagination can take flight.

Cost: Free

Freebies: Brochures on Piper aircraft.

Video/DVD Shown: 5–10-minute video on company history and safety.

Reservations Needed: Yes

Days and Hours: *Not giving tours during plant construction. Call to find out if tours have resumed.*

Minimum Age: 5

Plan to Stay: 1–2 hours.

Disabled Access: Yes

Group requirements: Groups should call 1 week in advance. No maximum group size.

Special Information: Piper Aviation Museum in Lock Haven, PA, covers some of the history of the original Piper Company. Call (570) 748-8283.

Gift Shop: Piper Pilot Shop sells a variety of logoed merchandise, including miniature airplane models, clothing, and luggage. Open Tue–Fri 9:00 AM–5:00 PM. Online ordering is available through the Pilot Shop website (www.newpiper.com).

Directions: From I-95 South, take Exit 68 (Vero Beach exit). Turn left onto Rt. 60. Turn left on 34th Ave. Turn right on Aviation Blvd. Turn right onto Piper Dr. and pass 2 parking lots on right. Make a right just before the white stone company sign.

Nearby Attractions: Kennedy Space Center in Cape Canaveral (see page 231) is 50 miles away.

SOUTH

A dark ride is an enclosed attraction, such as those at theme parks, in which a vehicle conveys you through passages that entertain with fantastic or grotesque scenery, moving figures, and coordinated sounds. They have come a long way since the days of the tacky haunted house. Dark rides are also no longer found only in theme parks: museums, corporate exhibitions, retailers, and even restaurants now employ these forms of entertainment (or at least their robots).

The Sally Corporation, one of the major creators of dark rides, uses robotic technology and sculptural artistry to make anything their clients imagine—whether dinosaurs in lush Jurassic landscapes, unquiet mummies in lavish Egyptian tombs, or faithful renditions of classic cartoon characters. Sally's work can be seen at Six Flags, Universal Studios, and FAO Schwartz.

You can tour Sally's factory, located at its colorful headquarters in the palm-lined downtown district of Jacksonville, Florida. Tours begin in a small theater, where a live presentation introduces the art of the dark ride. At the core of this craft is the science of animatronics: the construction of robots, in accurate likenesses of humans and animals, that are programmed to perform intricate lifelike movements, synchronized with a recorded soundtrack. A demonstration, including an interactive game for the audience, illustrates the complex technology that shapes these displays.

The heart of the tour is a detailed look at the areas where the creative staff build their dark rides. After ideas take shape in the design studio, they come to life in the various workspaces of the production floor. Populated with a weird and wonderful array of heads and creatures, the sculpting room is where the animatronic figures acquire their basic forms before the technicians integrate the robotics that make them move. The finish-art department gives them their personality: artists skillfully apply skin tone, hair, and the other attributes that endow their creations with vivid and sometimes startling

realism. In the programming area, the movements and sounds of each figure are coordinated with life-like precision. Meanwhile, the scenic-painting room is where artists color the outlandish dreamscapes of Sally productions.

However, the biggest wows occur in the main space of the production floor itself, where all the elements come together. Depending on where the production cycle is during your visit, you may see the spectacular culmination of the current big project or watch the industrious beginning of the next. Whatever the case, you will certainly see the huge resident Tyrannosaurus rex, rising with menace (and many teeth) from its metal enclosure. But this sample colossus is at only one end of the creative staff's dynamic range and virtuosity. Nearby, a tropical display features tiny singing birds, an exquisite achievement of animatronics on a small scale.

Cost: Free

Freebies: No

Video/DVD Shown: No

Reservations Needed: Yes

Days and Hours: Tue and Thu 9:00 AM, 10:00 AM, 11:00 AM, 12:00 PM, 1:00 PM. Closed July 4th, Thanksgiving, Christmas, New Year's, and the week after Christmas.

Plan to Stay: 1 hour for the tour.

Minimum Age: 5

Disabled Access: Yes

Group Requirements: Maximum of 30 people per tour.

Special Information: Make reservations well in advance. Tours are often solidly booked for several months ahead.

Gift Shop: No

Directions: From I-95, take Forsyth St. exit in downtown Jacksonville. On Forsyth St., drive 7 blocks. Sally is at intersection of Jefferson St.

Nearby Attractions: Whetstone Chocolates (see page 234); San Sebastian winery tours (call 904-826-1594); St. Augustine's Historic District (includes Nation's Oldest House); Castillo de San Marco Spanish fort; Spanish Quarter Museum; Lighthouse Museum and Lighthouse; coastal beaches.

SOUTH

Whetstone Chocolates

100 S. Ponce De Leon Boulevard,
St. Augustine, FL 32084

(904) 825-1700

www.whetstone
chocolates.com

The small ice-cream and candy shop founded by Henry and Esther Whetstone in 1967 is now a 94,500-square-foot facility that produces 500 to 1,800 chocolates per minute. This self-guided tour provides a view of the major steps in making Whetstone's specialty chocolates. Although much of the production is now automated, many areas of production still use a hands-on approach.

Start with a 15-minute video about the history of chocolate, its harvesting, and the journey from bean to finished product, including a complete tour of the plant when all chocolate is in production. Afterwards, meet and activate a robot used on the factory line and see a kettle full of 500 pounds of melting chocolate.

In the molding room, the chocolate begins its 35-minute journey from liquid to finished product. Approximately 400 molds, each containing as many as 24 cavities, wait patiently to be filled with chocolate from a 10,000-pound melter. The melter maintains the chocolate at a temperature of 115°F. The chocolate is pumped from the melter into a tempering machine, which cools it to 85°F by moving it through a series of cooling chambers, giving the chocolate a shiny appearance. The tempered chocolate is then sent through heated pipes to the depositors, which funnel it into the molds. If the product requires a filling (such as a nut, caramel, or fruit piece), the molds are sent to another filling station. After filling, more chocolate is added to finish the piece.

As you walk along the factory's elevated, glass-enclosed walkway, signs above the machines give a brief description of the processes below. The chocolates move into the packing room, where stacks of boxes await filling. Here, the pieces are inspected for flaws (unacceptable chocolates are recycled) and then hand-packed. Some varieties of Whetstone chocolates are individually adorned with brightly colored foil wrap by a wrapping machine before being packaged.

Watch Whetstone's famous chocolate seashells go from liquid chocolate to scalloped, molded shells. Also see how they make the chocolate

orange, which breaks into 18 slices when whacked. At the enrobing machine, nuts, toffee crunch, caramels, and caramel pecan monkeys ride along a conveyor belt and pass under a chocolate waterfall. Whetstone continually researches and tests new flavors and shapes of chocolate, so there is always something new to discover on the tour.

Cost: Free

Freebies: Chocolate seashell sample.

Video/DVD Shown: 15-minute video in theater shows the history and technology of chocolate making.

Reservations Needed: No, except for groups larger than 15 people.

Days and Hours: *A new factory is planned to open in early 2007. Please check the website to confirm days and hours prior to visit.* Mon–Sat 10:00 AM–5:00 PM. Best time to view production is Mon–Fri 10:00 AM–2:00 PM. Limited production on Saturdays. Closed Thanksgiving and Christmas. Since factory production schedules frequently change, call (904) 825-1700, ext. 25.

Plan to Stay: 30 minutes for self-guided tour and video, plus time for the Factory Outlet Store.

Minimum Age: None

Disabled Access: Yes

Group Requirements: Groups larger than 15 people can request a special guided tour by calling (904) 825-1700, ext. 24, in advance. Large groups will be split into groups of 25 people. Bus groups welcome.

Outlet Store: The Factory Outlet Store sells entire selection of Whetstone chocolates and candies (such as assorted chocolates, caramel pecan monkeys, seashells, chocolate oranges, and Scenes of St. Augustine candy bars) and gift items. Call (800) 849-7933 or visit above website to order.

Directions: *A new factory was planned to open in early 2007. Please check the website for exact directions prior to visit.*

Nearby Attractions: San Sebastian winery tours (call 904-826-1594); St. Augustine's Historic District includes the Nation's Oldest House; Castillo de San Marco Spanish fort; Spanish Quarter Museum; Lighthouse Museum and Lighthouse; coastal beaches.

One CNN Center, Atlanta, GA 30303

(404) 827-2300
(877) 4CNNTOUR

www.cnn.com/
studiotour

CNN Center's naturally lit atrium greets you at the global headquarters of Turner Broadcasting System. Your tour of the world's news leader begins as you ride one of the world's largest free-standing escalators (eight stories) to an area exhibiting CNN's growth paralleling world events from the past 25 years. Next, step inside a re-creation of CNN's main control room where you can see and hear behind-the-scenes elements of the network live.

Follow your tour guide into CNN Studio 7E. Examine the TelePromTer. It is like those used in newsrooms around the world. Watch your guide on a monitor point to various graphics just as your favorite newscaster points to a weather map.

Peer through glass walls high above the main newsroom floor and observe the researching, gathering, and reporting of news. The tour guide explains how producers, writers, and anchors work together on the complex news-gathering process, which continues 24 hours a day, seven days a week. Everywhere you look on the news floor, dozens of neatly dressed people seem to be staring intently, either up at the news monitors, ahead at their computer screens, or down at their keyboards and notes while talking on phones. Satellites feed the news from around the world into hundreds of computer terminals.

Cost: Adults, $12; seniors 65 and older, $11; youth 4–18, $9.

Freebies: Replica CNN press pass.

Video/DVD Shown: Short video in the tour finale.

Reservations Needed: No, but advance reservations recommended. Same-day reservations are not available by phone.

Days and Hours: Mon–Sun 9:00 AM–5:00 PM, except Thanksgiving, Christmas, and Easter. Each day's tour tickets go on sale at 8:30 AM.

Plan to Stay: 55 minutes including video and tour.

Minimum Age: none

Disabled Access: Yes, with 1 day's notice.

Group Requirements: Groups of 20 or more must call 24 hours in advance for reservations and group discounts.

Special Information: Photography allowed only in selected areas.

Gift Shop: The Turner Store, on the retail level of CNN Plaza, sells logoed merchandise including CNN, TBS, TNT, the Cartoon Network, and Turner South Network. Open Sun–Thurs 9:30 AM–6:00 PM, Fri–Sat 9:30 AM–7:00 PM. Closed Thanksgiving, Christmas, and Easter. Call (404) 827-2100.

Directions: By train, take MARTA to Stop W1, "Omni, World Congress Center, Georgia Dome." By car, take I-75/85 North to Exit 96 (International Blvd.). Follow signs to the Georgia World Congress Center. From I-75/85 South, take Exit 99 (Williams St./Downtown). Again, follow signs to the Georgia World Congress Center. CNN Center is on the corner of Centennial Olympic Park Dr. and Marietta St. in downtown Atlanta, across the street from the Georgia World Congress Center and next door to the Omni.

Nearby Attractions: Downtown Atlanta's attractions, including World of Coca-Cola Atlanta (see page 237), World Congress Center and Georgia Dome, Underground Atlanta, Centennial Olympic Park, Imagine It! The Children's Museum of Atlanta, and Georgia Aquarium.

SOUTH

Highway 96 East & 50 Lane Road,
Fort Valley, GA 31030

(478) 825-3362
(800) 277-3224

www.lanepacking.com

Did you know that there are over 40 varieties of peaches grown in the state of Georgia, and that more than 30 are grown at Lane Packing Company? June-gold, Southern Pearl, Rubyprince, Lane Luck—you'll find these varieties and many more, with equally pretty-sounding names, at this peach-packing operation. A fifth-generation family business that farms approximately 2,500 acres of peaches and 2,000 acres of pecans, it houses one of the most modern peach processing facilities on the East Coast.

From a 59-inch platform overlooking this operation, with the aid of informational signs describing each process, see firsthand how fresh-from-the field peaches make their journey through the processing facility. During your self-guided tour, hear the children around you giggle with happiness as the automatic dumping system releases approximately 1,000 pounds of peaches per minute into a large bath of flowing, 36°F water. Gently bobbing up and down, they take a relaxing ride to their next stop: the grading area. Here, standing on both sides of several conveyor belts, white-gloved workers inspect, by touch and sight, the slowly moving peaches. Deemed too soft or as having other physical defects, some of the peaches depart from the others on the number two line, where they are regraded, packed, and sold at a reduced price.

Meanwhile, proudly standing in single file on a conveyor belt, each of the peach elite is electronically weighed and labeled with a PLU sticker, after having been washed and waxed. They then proceed to one of 12 filling stations according to their size. At each station, 25 pounds at a time slide down a chute into a half-bushel box waiting below. After packaging, they are loaded into a refrigerated truck and await departure for their next destination.

In most cases, this next destination is a home where the customers enjoy the peaches in their simplest form. However, after your tour, explore the variety of peach products at the Peachtree Café, Roadside Market, and Just Peachy Gift Shop: peach ice cream, amaretto and peach syrup, peach butter, and peach tea. Discover there's no end to the delights of peaches, and see them all at Lane Packing Company.

Cost: Free

Freebies: Samples of peaches and peach products.

Video/DVD Shown: Video that describes the peach-packing process is shown in the retail area.

Reservations Needed: No, but recommended for groups of 20 or more people.

Days and Hours: Mid-May–mid-August: Mon–Sun, 8:00 AM–8:00 PM, depending upon the availability of peaches.

Plan to Stay: 20 minutes for the tour, plus additional time for eating at the café and browsing the gift shop and market.

Minimum Age: None

Disabled Access: Yes

Group Requirements: Groups of 20 or more should call in advance, but not necessary. You can request to have a tour guide.

Gift Shop, Roadside Market, and Café: The Just Peachy Gift Shop sells peach-themed jewelry, shirts, toys, dishes, and baskets. Roadside Market offers fresh farm produce, as well as peach and vidalia onion products. Peachtree Café serves a variety of food, including barbecue sandwiches, a daily fresh fruit bar, peach and blackberry cobbler, and peach ice cream. Open year-round, Mon–Sat 9:00 AM–5:30 PM, Sun 12:00 PM–5:30 PM.

Directions: From I-75, take Exit 142 GA Hwy. 96 West approximately 5 miles. Lane Packing Company is on the right.

Nearby Attractions: Andersonville National Cemetery and Historical Site; Georgia Music Hall of Fame; Georgia National Fairgrounds and Agricenter; Georgia Sports Hall of Fame; Hay House, The Palace of the South; Massee Lane Gardens; Museum of Aviation.

SOUTH

55 Martin Luther King Jr. Drive S.W.,
Atlanta, GA 30303-3505

(404) 676-5151
(800) 676-COKE

www.worldof
coca-cola.com

A mammoth neon logo and colorful flags from more than 200 Coca-Cola–enjoying nations welcome you to this Coca-Cola attraction. At this three-story, multimedia celebration of Coke, you will learn about the savvy marketing that catapulted what originally started as a headache remedy into the world's number-one soft drink. In fact, if all the Coca-Cola ever produced were placed in eight-ounce bottles and laid end to end, the line would stretch to the moon and back 1,323 times. (This and other impressive facts are continuously flashed on an electronic billboard.)

View the "Bottling Fantasy," a whimsical sculpture that turns the bottling process into art. Then take a nostalgic journey through 100-plus years of history, past display cases showing early bottling equipment and advertisements, billboards, and trinkets featuring 1920s vaudeville stars. For more interactive time travel, step into giant Coca-Cola cans called "Take 5 Units" and touch the video screens inside. Five-year sips of world events and lifestyles from 1886 to the present are combined with Coca-Cola history. Sit in a replica 1930s soda fountain, while a soda jerk flicks the fountain handle one way for fizz and the other way for flavored syrup.

The Coca-Cola Great Radio Hits kiosk blares with music stars singing Coke radio jingles from the 1960s to the present. (Even the Moody Blues sang "Things Go Better with Coke"!) View Coke's classic television commercials.

In Club Coca-Cola, aerial liquid jets deliver your free soft drink. Once you place your cup under the fountain, an infrared sensor triggers overhead spotlights that illuminate your cup. The glass tubing and neon around you begin to pulsate, and soda arches 20 feet from a hidden high-pressure nozzle, scoring a hole-in-one into your cup. After leaving this futuristic soda fountain, be sure to watch the international Coca-Cola commercials and sample exotic flavors (like Fanta Peach from Botswana).

Cost: Adults, $9; seniors 60+, $8; children 4–11, $5; 3 and under (with adult), free. Prices subject to change.

Freebies: Large variety of Coca-Cola products, plus 20 exotic flavors not available in the U.S.A.

Videos/DVDs Shown: Optional 10-minute presentation called "Every Day of Your Life," shown in large-screen, high-definition cinema. Other videos shown throughout the exhibits. Videos closed-captioned for the hearing impaired.

Reservations Needed: No, but recommended for groups over 20 people.

Days and Hours: Mon–Sat 9:00 AM–5:00 PM, Sun 11:00 AM–5:00 PM. Expect long waits during holidays and Atlanta-area events. Closed Easter, Thanksgiving, and Christmas and at 3:00 PM Christmas Eve and New Year's Eve.

Plan to Stay: 1.5 hours for displays, plus time for gift shop and waiting.

Minimum Age: None

Disabled Access: Yes

Group Requirements: Groups larger than 20 people can make reservations in advance to receive express entry and discounted admission. Call (404) 676-6074 Mon–Fri 9:00 AM–5:00 PM.

Special Information: Foreign language brochures available. Arrive earlier in day to avoid longest wait. *New World of Coca-Cola planned for 2007. The new address had not been determined at publication.*

Retail Store: Everything Coca-Cola features logoed clothing, gifts, and collectibles. Open same hours as attraction.

Directions: From I-75/85 North, take Exit 246 (Central Ave. exit). Follow Central Ave. as it goes over expressway to Martin Luther King Jr. Dr. Museum is at intersection. From I-75/85 South, take Exit 248A (State Capitol/MLK Dr.). Go straight on Martin Luther King Jr. Dr. 3 blocks to intersection with Central Ave.

Nearby Attractions: Downtown Atlanta's attractions, including CNN tour (see page 235); Underground Atlanta; State Capitol; Georgia World Congress Center; Atlanta Heritage Row (history museum).

1839 Frankfort Avenue, Louisville, KY 40206 | (502) 895-2405 | www.aph.org

American Printing House for the Blind (APH) is the world's oldest (founded in 1858) and largest non-profit company devoted to making products for visually impaired people. The company likes to say that the tour through this multimedia company teaches visitors about a "world they never saw before."

Your journey begins in the display room surrounded by the range of APH products, including a *Reader's Digest* in braille. Turning a print book into braille is not a simple process in which workers magically scan in a print page and out pops a perfect braille version. It begins with computers and software that help workers with the first step in translating the written text into braille.

Proofing this computer-generated output is the key to the braille publications' accuracy. A proofreader reads an entire book aloud from the brailled proof pages, while a second person follows along in the print copy, marking both errors and corrections. Once the corrections are made on the computer disk, the disk output may be sent to a braille embosser that prints directly on heavy braille paper, or in some cases, the output may be sent to a machine that punches the raised dots of the braille alphabet onto printing plates. You can see the modified rotary and clamshell presses as they spin out braille pages from these plates.

APH has 11 recording studios for turning print books into talking versions. Peek in at the professional narrator and technicians at work.

The last stop on your tour will be the award-winning APH Callahan Museum, which chronicles the international history of education for blind people. Visitors can write in braille, see the first book embossed for blind readers, play a computer game designed for blind students, and much more.

Cost: Free

Freebies: A braille copy of a special edition of *My Weekly Reader,* the grade school–age magazine in braille and print, and a braille alphabet card.

Videos/DVDs Shown: 3 brief videos on history of braille, the process of printing a braille book, and how a talking book is made.

Reservations Needed: No, except for groups of 10 or more.

Days and Hours: Plant tour: Mon–Thur 10:00 AM and 2:00 PM. Museum: Mon–Fri 8:30 AM–4:30 PM. Call for Saturday Museum Hours. Closed holidays.

Plan to Stay: 1.5 hours, plus time for museum and gift counter.

Minimum Age: No required minimum for museum or plant tour for small groups, but recommend 2nd grade and up.

Disabled Access: Yes

Group Requirements: Groups over 10 people can receive guided tour of the plant and/or museum by calling a minimum of 1 week in advance. Maximum size is usually about 50 people (one busload). Minimum age for school groups for plant tour is 4th grade. School groups of 1st- to 3rd-graders will have hands-on museum tour and plant tour that focuses on braille production. Pretour education materials are sent to school groups.

Special Information: No photography in plant. National Braille Press in Boston, MA, also offers public tours (see page 74).

Gift Counter: Sells T-shirts with braille alphabet, braille key chains, art calendar, and note and holiday cards featuring art by visually impaired artists. Open during tours, but you can purchase items online at above website. Catalog available for all APH products by calling (800) 223-1839.

Directions: From I-64 East, take Exit 7, Story Ave. Then immediately turn left at Spring St. Turn left again at Mellwood Ave. After you go under highway, turn right on Frankfort Ave. APH is at top of hill on left. From I-64 West, take Exit 7 for Mellwood Ave. Turn right onto Frankfort Ave. and follow directions above. For directions from different locations, see website or call company to fax them to you.

Nearby Attractions: Louisville area attractions, including Colonel Harland Sanders Museum, Ford, Louisville Stoneware, and Louisville Slugger Museum tours (see pages 239, 245, 247, and 246).

SOUTH

Colonel Harland Sanders Museum

KFC Headquarters, 1441 Gardiner Lane, Louisville, KY 40213

(502) 874-8300

www.kfc.com

WE DO CHICKEN RIGHT

In Japan, Colonel Sanders is Ohji-san, or "Grandfather," and his statue stands near every one of the restaurants he inspired. A life-size statue honors the man who above all else demonstrated that the little guy can succeed in America.

Harland Sanders, born in 1890, held many jobs to support his family—streetcar conductor, cook, justice of the peace, and automobile mechanic. At his museum, an animated Colonel Sanders "speaks" to you.

Some of the rare photos show Sanders' Court Restaurant. About 1930, Sanders began cooking chicken for customers at his auto service station (later a restaurant) along busy U.S. 25. At Sanders' Court, he perfected his famous secret blend of 11 herbs and spices, and developed the innovation of frying chicken in a pressure cooker. The original cooker made such a difference. In 1935, Governor Ruby Laffoon made Sanders an honorary Kentucky colonel for his contribution to the state's cuisine. At his museum, an animated Colonel Sanders "speaks" to you.

Unfortunately, a highway bypass closed the restaurant in the early 1950s. After paying his bills, Sanders had nothing to live on except his Social Security check. With his wife, Claudia, he hit the road, making samples of his chicken and offering franchise deals to restaurant owners. The idea was so successful that, in 1964, he sold his interest in Kentucky Fried Chicken and became the company's spokesman, wearing his now-famous white suit.

The Colonel traveled extensively around the world, met many dignitaries and celebrities, and gave millions of dollars to charities. The Colonel's favorite award was a wire chicken presented to him by the National Restaurant Association. KFC is the world's most popular chicken restaurant chain—10,800-plus restaurants in 91 countries and part of Yum Brands, Inc. However, after visiting this museum, you'll forever associate KFC with the 66-year-old man who began an empire with a $105 Social Security check.

Cost: Free

Freebies: No

Video/DVD Shown: No

Reservations Needed: No, except for groups larger than 15 people.

Days and Hours: Mon–Fri 8:00 AM–5:00 PM, Fri 8:30 AM–12:30 PM. Closed standard holidays. *Only can see small portion of Sanders' office. Visit Corbin, KY, to see more. See special information below.*

Plan to Stay: 10 minutes.

Minimum Age: 8

Disabled Access: Yes

Group Requirements: Groups of 15 people or more should call at least 2 weeks in advance. Maximum group size is 35.

Special Information: In the lobby of the KFC/Yum Brands corporate headquarters, so dress appropriately. The café and motel in Corbin, KY, where the Colonel concocted his secret recipe, has been restored to its mid-1940s glory (call 606-528-2163).

Gift Shop: No, but the closest KFC is on Bardstown Rd.

Directions: Take I-264 to Newburg Rd. exit. Go south and turn right onto Bishop Ln. Turn right onto Gardiner Rd. Museum is in KFC/Yum Brands corporate headquarters, which has an antebellum plantation facade.

Nearby Attractions: Ford, American Printing House for the Blind, and Louisville Stoneware tours, and Hillerich & Bradsby (Louisville Slugger) Museum (see pages 245, 238, 247, and 246); Hadley Pottery tour (call 502-584-2171); Louisville's attractions include J. B. Speed Art Museum, Churchill Downs/Kentucky Derby Museum, and Kentucky Art and Craft Center.

1001 Wilkinson Boulevard, Frankfort, KY 40601   (502) 696-5926   www.buffalotrace.com
(800) 654-8471

BUFFALO TRACE™

DISTILLERY

It's no wonder Buffalo Trace is so proud of its heritage: it is one of only four continuously running distilleries. Most distilleries did not make it through Prohibition; this distillery was allowed to make bourbon for medicinal purposes. While the distillery has had many names, its latest incarnation and renovation came in 1999 as Buffalo Trace Distillery, named after buffaloes' path, or trace, to the Kentucky River over two centuries ago.

While a regular tour covers parts of the operation, a more thorough hard-hat tour requires a reservation. On both, you enjoy the scenic grounds, dotted with buffalo-themed art. The red brick historic buildings create a sense of richness and heritage.

As you enter the aging warehouse, you will smell what is known as the "angels' share," evaporated bourbon. Your tour guide will explain that a full barrel holds 53 gallons (550 pounds). In the first year, 10 percent is lost (7 percent seeps into the fresh oak barrel and 3 percent evaporates into the air—hence "angels' share"). Every subsequent year 3 percent is lost. Particularly on a warm day, you will be pleasantly surprised by the cool temperature in the warehouse. The low seven-foot beamed ceilings further envelop you in the coolness and the rich bourbon aroma. Walk along the 12-inch-wide worn wooden plank floor between rows of barrels stacked three high on "ricks."

For the hard-hat tour, you walk inside the mash house and listen to the hissing of steam as ground corn, wheat, or rye, barley, and water cook for three hours to become sweet mash. Stand next to 90-gallon fermentation tanks as sour mash ferments the sweet mash (similar to the process of using sour-dough starter to make sour-dough bread) for three to five days. Notice the natural bubbling at the surface of the tanks. Walk across a narrow catwalk, like an airplane jetway, to the top floor of the still house. Here the useable portions of the bourbon

separate from those portions that are sent to perfumers and the petroleum industry.

Now that you feel a little intoxicated from the "angels' share" and interesting facts, you can sample some bourbon and vodka in the tasting room at the end of the tour.

Cost: Free

Freebies: Bourbon and vodka samples, bourbon chocolate. Root beer for minors.

Video/DVD Shown: No

Reservations Needed: No, except for hard-hat tours, groups, and special tour times.

Days and Hours: Open year-round Mon–Fri 9:00 AM–3:00 PM. Sat 10:00 AM–2:00 PM; tours on the hour. However, bourbon-making occurs only from mid-September–mid-April. Closed holidays.

Plan to Stay: 1 hour for regular tour, 2 hours for hard-hat tour, plus additional time in the gift shop.

Minimum Age: None

Disabled Access: Yes for regular tour, no for hard-hat tour.

Group Requirements: Groups over 20 people need to make a reservation at least one week in advance.

Special Information: Many stairs involved in this hard-hat tour.

Gift Shop: Sells the full line of bourbon and vodka products, as well as a wide assortment of shirts, sweatshirts, and jackets in rich signature earth-tones with buffalo embroidered logo. Offers novelties such as mouse pads, leather belts, glasses, etc. Open Mon–Fri 9:00 AM–4:00 PM, Sat 10 00 AM–3:00 PM. Closed holidays. Merchandise available online.

Directions: From I-64 East, take U.S. 127 North to U.S. 421 South (Wilkenson Blvd.) Turn left onto U.S. 421 South. Distillery is on left. From I-64 West, take U.S. 60 West to U.S. 421 North and follow to distillery.

Nearby Attractions: Rebecca Ruth, Wild Turkey, Three Chimney horse farm, and Toyota tours (see pages 251, 254, 252, and 253) Kentucky Bourbon Trail (www.kybourbon.com); Kentucky Bourbon Festival (call 800-638-4877).

bottles of Buffalo Trace bourbon being filled by hand

barrels of aged bourbon being dumped in preparation for bottling

100 Churchill Drive, Lorraine Court,
Berea, KY 40403

(859) 986-3127

www.churchill
weavers.com

CHURCHILL WEAVERS

It takes hard work and heritage to hand-weave a beautiful Churchill Weavers blanket or throw. Churchill Weavers, nestled in a small college town where Kentucky's Bluegrass meets its Cumberland Mountains, encompasses history, pride, and craftsmanship. MIT graduate and industrial engineer Carroll Churchill and his wife, Eleanor, an English schoolteacher, returned from missionary work in India to found Churchill Weavers in 1922. Eleanor chose Lila and Richard Bellando to continue the Churchill legacy. In 1996, Crown Crafts, a leader in home fashion textiles, acquired Churchill Weavers. Today Lila and Richard still carry on the leadership of this unique company.

Your self-guided tour includes the historic loomhouse, residence of almost 50 looms. Notice that the weathered brown of the looms matches the building's ceilings, walls, and wooden plank floors. In the loomhouse is the waterwheel-like "warper." Threads are wrapped around it according to a written pattern, then wound onto a warp drum that fits into the back of a loom.

The highlight of the tour is watching wooden looms in action, as weavers create baby blankets, throws, table linens, scarves, and fabrics for other products. Watch an agile weaver alternate between pulling the beater forward with her left hand and "throwing" the shuttle with her right. At the same time, as if playing an organ, she steps on foot pedals to create a pattern. The rhythm of the weavers at their looms sounds like the hoofbeats of galloping horses. The rhythm breaks only when a weaver stops to replace a yarn-filled bobbin in the shuttle, then it begins again.

Menders check newly woven cloth on light boards and repair flaws. From warping to weaving to tying the fringes, you will observe this timeless, hands-on process of "constructing" fabrics. These beautiful "high-touch" items, made by loving hands, help balance the high-tech, fast-paced world in which we live.

Cost: Free

Freebies: No

Video/DVD Shown: 4-minute optical video in gift shop shows the company's history and its weaving process.

Reservations Needed: No, for self-guided tour. Yes, if groups want tour guide.

Days and Hours: Mon–Thur 9:00 AM–12:00 PM, 12:30 PM–4:00 PM. Call about Fri hours. Loomhouse hours vary seasonally. Closed Christmas and New Year's.

Plan to Stay: 20 minutes for tour, plus time for video and gift shop.

Minimum Age: None

Disabled Access: Yes

Group Requirements: Maximum group is 40 people. Tour guide can be arranged if booked 3–4 days in advance.

Special Information: Due to the intense concentration required by the weaving process, please do not disturb the weavers at work.

Retail Store: Sells baby blankets, scarves, stoles, throws, and decorative pillows made by Churchill Weavers, and pottery, candles, baskets, and woodcrafts from all over the U.S.A. The outlet room sells woven seconds and overruns by Churchill craftspeople. Open Mon–Sat 9:00 AM–6:00 PM, Sun 12:00 PM–6:00 PM. Catalog available from the above number.

Directions: From Lexington, take I-75 South to Exit 77. Follow Walnut Meadow Rd. to second traffic light. Turn left onto Rt. 25 North and pass Berea Hospital. Bear right onto Hwy. 1016. Follow the signs to Churchill Weavers. From the south, take I-75 North to Exit 76. Stay on Rt. 25 North through town, past Berea Hospital. Continue with above directions.

Nearby Attractions: Berea is the folk arts and crafts capital of Kentucky. You can purchase the works of local craftspeople while observing them in their studios scattered throughout the town. At Berea College, you can watch students produce a variety of crafts.

Cones of yarn are carefully and methodically turned into warps on one of the two pre-World War II warpers.

Just as it has been for the past 85 years, a weaver works on a handmade fly shuttle loom built by the craftspeople at Churchill Weavers.

600 Corvette Drive, Bowling Green, KY 42101   (270) 745-8019   www.bowlinggreen assemb yplant.com

SOUTH

Since it was first built in 1953, General Motors' Corvette has become an American automotive icon, representing muscle, fantasy, and youth. The television series *Route 66*, about two bachelors who traveled American highways in their 'Vette, increased the car's popularity. In 1981, GM moved Corvette assembly to the Bowling Green complex, the size of 22 football fields. Bowling Green also assembles the Cadillac XLR, which is included in the tour.

Led by a guide who points out the car's special features, you'll walk on the plant floor to witness the major steps in the sports car's production. See the windshields attached, and the joining of the chassis and body.

Computerized robots weld the steel frame together before the Corvette receives its signature fiberglass body panels. Once the panels are painted, they return to the main assembly floor, where workers install them along with other parts such as seats, wheels, and removable roof. While the car's body is being assembled in the trim area, the engine and drivetrain are assembled in another area. When the two come together, it's called "body marriage," with workers scampering underneath the car to connect the chassis and body.

Almost everywhere you look, Corvettes in some stage of assembly move past on a multilevel network of conveyors that cover about seven miles. A worker sits in the car and starts the engine. Like a baby's first cry, the engine makes its initial roar. It may take a couple of seconds for the car to start but, once running, it idles for some time while workers make various checks throughout the car. Only when the car is fully built do all four wheels touch the ground for the first time. Even if you didn't arrive as a die-hard Corvette enthusiast, you'll leave as one.

Cost: $5 per person.

Freebies: Postcard

Video/DVD Shown: 6-minute video on plant safety regulations, plus steps not on the tour, such as body painting.

Reservations Needed: Reservations recommended but not required, except for groups of 10 people or more. Register online.

Days and Hours: Mon–Fri 9:00 AM and 1:00 PM CST. Closed holidays, week between Christmas and New Year's, 2 weeks in summer (usually starting early July), and for model changes and production shutdowns. Always call ahead.

Plan to Stay: 1.5 hours for tour and video, plus time in gift corner.

Minimum Age: Must be at least 7 years old. School groups minimum 4th grade.

Disabled Access: Yes

Group Requirements: For groups larger than 10 people, log onto www.bowlinggreenassemblyplant.com.

Special Information: No photography on tour. No electronic devices, purses, bags, backpacks. 1 mile of walking. No open-toed shoes.

Gift Corner: Sells Corvette memorabilia including T-shirts, hats, and key chains. Open during tour hours.

Directions: From I-65, take Exit 28. For plant, turn right at Corvette Dr., then right after entering the gate. Follow signs to tour parking. Allow extra time for long walk from parking lot to tour entrance. For museum, turn left at Corvette Dr.

Nearby Attractions: National Corvette Museum (see page 249); Beech Bend Raceway Park, Lost River Cave, and Mammoth Cave National Park.

Fern Valley Road at Grade Lane,
Louisville, KY 40213

(502) 364-3551   www.fordvehicles.com

Since 1913, Ford has had operations in Louisville, which now includes both the Louisville Assembly Plant and its massive heavy-truck plant. Ford made 12 Model Ts a day back in 1913. Now the home of the popular Explorer, Ranger, and Mercury Mountaineer, this plant has substantially quickened its pace to 87 vehicles per hour (the auto industry norm is 60, making this plant possibly the fastest in the world). You get to see almost all the production steps, although not in the order of assembly, as all the vehicles are built on one long line.

The body area is always one of the most exciting places to visit at an automobile plant. It's the scene most often shown of car factories on TV: skeleton car bodies and robots marching together in perfect unison, with colorful sparks flying. Here you can watch the real thing. With the help of more than 140 robots, the stamped sheet metal that comes from other Ford plants is precision-fitted and welded to exact specifications. The robots help transfer parts, spot-weld, and apply sealer. The body then heads to the paint area, which is usually not on the tour.

In the trim area, most of the vehicles' insides are added, filling up the painted shell. It's truly an industrial symphony of sounds from the machines and tools that buzz, crunch, and hiss. With robots' assistance, workers bend, twist, and reach to install various interior and exterior parts, such as wiring, door glass, windshields, door handles, instrument panels, and horns.

The chassis is built in another area. Notice how the frame is actually upside down when workers install the fuel and brake lines, body mounts, and wiring. The frame is then flipped over before the bumpers are added, along with the engine, transmission, and driveshaft. Another favorite site is the "body drop." The body, hanging from a part of the 20-plus miles of conveyors in the factory, is lowered and secured to the frame. After more parts are added, including the all-important tires and seats, the vehicle is started and heads off for final inspection. The inspectors act like the pickiest buyers, checking even the tiniest mechanical and visual details.

Cost: Free

Freebies: Brochures about the history of Ford in Louisville and the assembly process.

Video/DVD Shown: 10-minute video of material similar to that covered in the brochure.

Reservations Needed: Yes

Days and Hours: Please call to see if tours are being scheduled. Special tours occasionally arranged.

Plan to Stay: 2 hours for talk, video, and tour.

Minimum Age: None, but young children could be intimidated by the noises.

Disabled Access: Yes

Group Requirements: The total number of visitors is limited to 150 each session. Groups need to schedule months in advance to ensure space availability.

Special Information: Will walk approximately 1.5 miles during tour.

Gift Shop: Yes

Directions: From I-65, exit at Fern Valley Rd. Plant is visible from exit regardless of which direction you travel. Drive to plant entrance and park in administrative lot.

Nearby Attractions: Louisville's attractions, including Louisville Stoneware and American Printing House for the Blind tours and Louisville Slugger and Colonel Harland Sanders (KFC) Museums (see pages 247, 238, 246, and 239); Muhammad Ali Center. Churchill Downs/Kentucky Derby Museum, are about 30 minutes away.

Hillerich & Bradsby Co., 800 West Main Street,
Louisville, KY 40202

(502) 588-7228
(877) 7-SLUGGER

www.slugger
museum.org

The Louisville Slugger bat, created by Bud Hillerich in 1884, has been called "one of the greatest original American products ever made." In 1996, Hillerich & Bradsby Co. opened the Louisville Slugger Museum, a tribute to baseball's greatest hits and hitters. You'll see actual bats swung by such legendary sluggers as Ty Cobb, Lou Gehrig, and Joe DiMaggio, plus the bat Babe Ruth used during his 1927 record-setting 60-home-run season. Listen to Hall of Fame broadcasters call baseball's greatest moments. Take the field in a replica of Camden Yards. Choose a famous pitcher to throw the ball in your direction at 90 miles per hour, crawl through a giant ball and glove sculpture, or step into a batting cage and take a few swings of your own.

After walking through the museum and a replica of a Northern white ash forest, take a guided tour of the plant. With the ever-present smell of wood in the air, H&B turns the Northern white ash and maple billets into bats. Most of the bats are made on automatic lathes.

It takes about 40 seconds to make a bat on the tracer lathes. Workers use a metal pattern of the exact bat shape and guide the machine to trace this pattern, a process similar to copying a key at the hardware store. All of the Major League bats are made on a special CNC lathe, the only one of its kind in the world.

With sizzle and smoke, the famous oval trademark, bat model number, and the player's autograph are still seared into the "flat of the grain" on some bats. Bats can also be foil-branded with either gold or silver. Behind the branders are large cabinets holding more than 8,500 professional baseball players' autograph brands. You'll leave the museum and tour having witnessed a part of true Americana.

Cost: Adults, $9; seniors 60+, $8; children 6–12, $4; children 5 and under, free.

Freebies: 18-inch miniature wood bat.

Video/DVD Shown: 13-minute film, "Heart of the Game," relives some of the greatest hits in baseball. Overhead flat screen monitors show close-up production at various stops.

Reservations Needed: No, except for groups larger than 20 people.

Days and Hours: Mon–Sat 9:00 AM–5:00 PM, year-round; open until 6:00 PM in July; also open Sun 12:00 PM–5:00 PM, April 1–November 30, but no bat production. Production at other times varies based on factory needs. Closed holidays.

Plan to Stay: 1.5 hours for tour and museum, plus time for gift shop.

Minimum Age: Discourages children under age 5.

Disabled Access: Yes

Group Requirements: Reservations needed for groups over 20 people. At least 1-month advance notice suggested for summer tours. Call (502) 588-7227.

Special Information: No photography in plant.

Gift Shop: Sells Louisville Slugger logoed items, including T-shirts, hats, towels, gym bags, and pen bats. Personalized bats are also available. Open same hours as tour.

Directions: From Indianapolis, take I-65 South to I-64 West. Exit on 3rd St. Turn right onto River Rd. Turn left onto 8th St. You can't miss the Louisville Slugger Museum—just look for the world's tallest bat. From Cincinnati, take I-71 South to I-64 West and follow above directions.

Nearby Attractions: Colonel Harland Sanders (KFC) Museum, Ford, Louisville Stoneware, and American Printing House for the Blind tours (see pages 239, 245, 247, and 238); Louisville Science Center (across the street from the Louisville Slugger Museum); Frazier Historical Arms Museum; Muhammad Ali Center, Kentucky Derby Museum; Churchill Downs.

See color photos, page 36.

Louisville Stoneware

731 Brent Street, Louisville, KY 40204

(502) 582-1900
(800) 626-1800

www.louisville
stoneware.com

Raw clay, mined from western Indiana, forms a small hill against the back wall of the clay-making room. Since 1815, this has been the main ingredient for the artistic, durable, authentic American pottery made by Louisville Stoneware. The guided tour includes the clay-making room, where clay is vigorously mixed with water to make a clay "soup." Under high pressure, a press pushes liquid clay through filters with water dripping out the bottom. In the pug mill, the resulting firm cakes of fine clay are chopped into soft mud or turned into liquid slip clay. In a process called "slip casting," this fluid is poured into angular plaster molds to form items such as bird feeders and birdhouses.

The guided tour shows you "jiggering," glazing, hand-painting, and kiln-loading. Jiggering, another process of romancing the clay, is used for more concentric shapes. Leaning over a spinning pottery wheel, a potter places clay onto a concave plaster mold (shaped like the inside of a bowl) and then lowers the "shoe" to form the plate or bowl. The potter uses a water-drenched sponge to smooth the clay's surface. Each plate dries on its individual plaster mold. Throughout the factory, you will see stoneware drying on 6- to 20-foot-high storage conveyors, whose shelves can be rotated or advanced when full.

You can stand next to the artists as they hand-paint traditional patterns directly onto the dried clay pieces. At first appearing pastel, the final underglaze colors reveal themselves only after a white translucent glaze is applied and the piece is fired at a high temperature. You'll feel the heat emerging from the three kilns, which hold 500 pieces each. The whole firing process takes almost a full day—10 hours to reach 2,350°F, and then 12 hours to cool.

Cost: Adults $5, seniors 55+ $3, children 12 and under, free.

Freebies: No

Video/DVD Shown: No

Reservations Needed: No, except for groups larger than 8 people.

Days and Hours: Mon–Fri 10:30 AM and 1:30 PM. Closed holidays.

Plan to Stay: 40 minutes for the tour and video, depending on whether you see the clay-making process, plus time for outlet store.

Minimum Age: None

Disabled Access: Yes

Group Requirements: Groups larger than 20 people should call 1 day in advance for desired time. Large groups will be split. Group cost is $3 per person.

Special Information: Since there are 3 firing kilns, the factory can be hot in summer.

Gift Shop: Visitors center sells colorful dinnerware, giftware, bakeware, birdhouses, flowerpots, and spiritual items. Ask about personalized services and bridal registry. Bring the kids to Paint Your Own in the pottery studio. Sells factory seconds up to 40 percent off regular prices. Annual tent sale in July sells seconds at additional savings. Open Mon–Sat 9:00 AM–6:00 PM. April–December, also open Sun 1:00–5:00 PM. Catalog available from (800) 626-1800.

Directions: From Lexington, take Rt. 64 West to 3rd St. South (one way). Turn left onto Broadway, then right onto Brent St. before the railroad overpass. Located 2.5 blocks ahead on left. From the Louisville area, take Rt. 65 North to Broadway exit. Turn right onto Broadway, then right onto Brent St.

Nearby Attractions: Louisville Slugger Museum, Colonel Harland Sanders (KFC) Museum, Ford, and American Printing House for the Blind, tours (see pages 246, 239, 245, and 238); Hadley Pottery tour (call 502-584-2171); Speed Art Museum; Churchill Downs/Kentucky Derby Museum; Kentucky Museum of Art & Craft.

SOUTH

3350 Burks Spring Road, Loretto, KY 40037   (270) 865-2099   www.makersmark.com

Maker's ☆S IV Mark ®

An illustration of the Maker's Mark distillery appears on its bottles; the label invites you to visit "any time you're in the neighborhood," so you know the place must be special. Just as Bill Samuels Sr. wanted to create his own distinctive bourbon by using gentle winter wheat instead of rye, he wanted to restore a historic distillery complex into the home of Maker's Mark.

Your tour of this National Historic Landmark distillery begins near the stonewalled creek that runs through the peaceful, landscaped grounds, where you'll hear a brief history of the distillery. Its black buildings feature bright red shutters with a Maker's Mark bottle cutout. Unlike larger distilleries' 600-barrel-per-day production, Maker's Mark crafts its bourbon in 19 barrel batches.

In the still house you'll smell corn, wheat, and malted barley cooking. The bubbling yellow mash ferments in century-old cypress vats. Vaporization of the mash in the shiny copper still separates out the whiskey, which is placed in charred oak casks for aging. When you enter the aging warehouse's ground floor, the aromas alone tell you what's in the barrels. Barrels reach maturity only after completing a rotation system in which the newest barrels are placed on the warehouse's hot upper floors and are rotated to the cooler lower levels after about three years.

Only in the bottling house does the production pace quicken. Near the end of the line, each bottle's glass neck is hand-dipped into red sealing wax and then twisted to allow the excess to drip off and run down the neck. Notice each worker's distinctive dipping and twisting technique.

Cost: Free

Freebies: Water and lemonade; bourbon ball sample; great smells.

Video/DVD Shown: No

Reservations Needed: No, except for groups larger than 25 people.

Days and Hours: Mon–Sat 10:30 AM, 11:30 AM, 12:30 PM, 1:30 PM, 2:30 PM, and 3:30 PM, Sun 1:30 PM, 2:30 PM, and 3:30 PM. Closed on Sundays in January and February. No production from mid-August–mid-September, but tour still runs. Limited weekend production. Closed Thanksgiving, Christmas Eve, Christmas Day, New Year's Day, and Easter Sunday.

Plan to Stay: 45 minutes to an hour for the tour, plus time for visitors center and Quart House. Once a pre–Civil War distiller's home, the visitor's center has pieces from the Samuels' collection of early-1800s furniture and other historical and craft items. The Quart House, oldest standing package liquor store in America, is a restored pre-Prohibition retail store.

Minimum Age: Recommends that children under 10 be accompanied by an adult. You must be 21 to purchase and dip your own bottle of Maker's Mark.

Disabled Access: Yes. Paved walking paths between buildings.

Group Requirements: Requests prior notice for groups of 25 people or more.

Special Information: The Bottling line does not run every day, but visitors can purchase souvenir bottles to dip in the signature red wax every day except Sunday.

Gift Shop: The Gift Gallery in the visitor center sells logoed and craft items, including shirts, sweaters, jackets, key chains, and shot glasses. Also, gourmet sauces and candies made with Maker's Mark. Open Mon–Sat 10:00 AM–4:30 PM, Sun 1:00–4:30 PM.

Directions: From Bardstown, take KY 49 South and follow signs to distillery. You're there when you see the sign that says, "You've Just Found the Home of Maker's Mark."

Nearby Bourbon-Related Attractions: Heaven Hill Distillery tour (call 502-348-3921); Oscar Getz Museum of Whiskey History (call 502-348-2999); Jim Beam's American Outpost (call 502-543-9877); Annual September Kentucky Bourbon Festival in Bardstown.

See color photos, page 38.

350 Corvette Drive, Bowing Green, KY 42101

(270) 781-7973
(800) 53-Vette

www.corvette
museum.com

Touring the Corvette assembly plant and visiting the National Corvette Museum are two experiences about which many Corvette enthusiasts dream. In addition, it is possible to take delivery of your brand-new Corvette right from the National Corvette Museum. Even current owners can get a day in the spotlight through the NCM Xperience. All this happens on two sides of I-65 in Bowling Green, Kentucky, rendering it mecca to the Corvette owner.

As you enter this 68,000-square-foot museum, you will notice a white 1953 (the year it all began) Corvette to your left. Your self-guided tour will take you into the large Chevrolet theater. Next you walk through the Nostalgia area. Stroll down Main Street of "small town" U.S.A. A recreated Mobil Gas station depicts America's romance with performance cars in the late 1950s. Notice the quarter-scale 1957 Corvette.

In the Corvette Performance area, you will walk along a slanted curved "racetrack" inside an 80-foot diameter room surrounded by a giant panoramic mural of famous Corvette racing scenes. The Design and Development area pays homage to the great people behind this great car. Life-size clay mannequins of chief designers and chief engineers such as David Hill are represented in recreated work scenes. A crashed up model car with shattered glass and exposed crushed body demonstrates crash performance testing.

At the far end of the museum, you walk into one of the most recognizable areas of the museum—the 11-story Corvette Skydome—140 feet in diameter with a nearly 100-foot-high glass ceiling. The 30 cars displayed in this area, as in every part of the Museum, are constantly being changed and rotated. Walk inside the center red cone whose spire juts out the top of the glass ceiling of this yellow Sky-

dome. This tribute to Dale Earnhardt includes Dale Earnhardt cereal boxes, miniature race cars, action figures, Winston Cup Championship mugs, even a copy of the Daytona Beach Newspaper from Monday, February 15, 2001, denoting Dale Earnhardt's death with "Black Sunday" as the headline.

Lastly, walk along the 240-foot showcase atrium. Here cars wait for their owners to arrive. You can also sit inside a Corvette. You will leave even more revved up about the Corvette than when you entered the museum.

Cost: Adults, $8; youth (6–16), $4.50; children (5 and under), free; family rate, $20. AAA, group, senior, and military discounts available.

Freebies: No

Video/DVD Shown: Film shows every 15 minutes on the 16-by-28-foot screen in the 200-seat Chevrolet theater. Covers the history and mystique of the Corvette.

Reservations Needed: No

Days and Hours: Mon–Sun 8:00 AM–5:00 PM. Closed Thanksgiving, Christmas Eve, Christmas Day, and New Year's Day.

Plan to Stay: 1–2 hours plus additional time in the Corvette store.

Minimum Age: No

Disabled Access: Yes

Group Requirements: Groups of 15 or more should call 14 days in advance for guided tour of museum.

Special Information: For more information about National Corvette Museum Delivery (Option R8C), NCM Xperience, and events calendar, check www.corvettemuseum.com.

Gift Shop: The Corvette store sells logoed apparel, leather jackets, and license plates from each year since 1953. Open same hours as museum. Online store also available.

Directions: From I-65, take Exit 28. Turn left on Corvette Dr. Wind your way towards the yellow Skydome. If you own a Corvette, you can park in the special Corvette row closest to the museum entrance.

Nearby Attractions: Corvette assembly plant (see page 244); Beech Bend Raceway Park; Lost River Cave; Mammoth Cave National Park.

SOUTH

SOUTH

Bourbon Chocolates, Bourbon Cherries, Chocolate Thoroughbreds, and Kentucky Derby Mints—the names alone are enough to attract you to this candy-factory tour. Combine the tour with plentiful free samples before, after, and even right off the assembly line, and you have the makings of a tasty experience.

The chocolate in these famous Kentucky candies starts as 10-pound bars of Guittard chocolate. In the molding area, melted chocolate sits in a mixer while a rotating blade slowly turns it into a creamy paste. While the tour guide is pointing to overhead photographs and explaining how cocoa beans are harvested and the chocolate is made, you'll be tempted to sneak your finger into the mixer for a taste. Nearby are stacks of Old Kentucky's popular molds, including a 75-pound Easter bunny, dentures, and a horse's behind.

As you stroll through the candy "kitchen," you often see 8-by-3-foot slabs of fudge and candy centers cooling before they are cut with a ridged rolling pin. In the production room, glass jars of maraschino cherries may be marinating in 101-proof Jim Beam bourbon. Stand next to the conveyor belt while the candies receive a bottom chocolate base then go through a "chocolate car wash" that coats them in chocolate. Looped chains drop down to caress the tops of the candies, creating a swirl design. After the candies exit the cooling tunnel, workers carefully hand-pack the chocolates—a job that must require great willpower to prevent nibbling.

Cost: Free

Freebies: Plentiful candy samples, including a candy directly off the assembly line.

Video/DVD Shown: No

Reservations Needed: Yes. Individuals and families may have to join a group tour.

Days and Hours: Mon–Thur 10:00 AM–3:00 PM. Closed holidays.

Plan to Stay: 20 minutes for tour, plus time for gift shop.

Minimum Age: None

Disabled Access: Yes

Group Requirements: 1 day's advance notice for groups. No maximum size. Large groups split into groups of 25 people.

Special Information: If interested in seeing specific candies made, ask when you book the tour.

Retail Store: Sells all of the company's different kinds and shapes of candies. Look for gift baskets shaped like horse heads, horseshoes, and Kentucky maps. Glass showcases filled with truffles sit next to canisters of various free samples. On the store's front table, notice the upside-down mushroom-shaped jar filled with cherries aging in bourbon. (Unfortunately, once the cherries are aged, Kentucky liquor laws do not allow the sale of this cherry-flavored bourbon.) Open Mon–Fri 9:00 AM–6:00 PM, Sat 9:30 AM–5:30 PM, Sun 1–5:00 PM. Catalog available from above number.

Directions: From Cincinnati, take I-75 South to Exit 115 for Newtown Pike. Go west on Circle 4 (New Circle Rd.). Take exit for Harrodsburg Rd. toward Lexington. Turn right onto Lane Allen Rd., which becomes Rosemont Garden. Turn right onto Southland Dr. Old Kentucky is on the right. Factory is in the back of its retail store, in a shopping center. From Louisville, take Rt. 60 East to New Circle Rd. exit. Make immediate left onto Nicholasville Rd. Turn left onto Southland Dr. and go past railroad overpass. Old Kentucky is on the left.

Nearby Attractions: Rebecca-Ruth Candies, Toyota, and Three Chimneys horse farm tours (see pages 251, 253, and 252); Kentucky Horse Park; Boonesborough State Park; Fort Harrod State Park.

Rebecca-Ruth Candies

CHOCOLATES AND BOURBON BALLS

112 East 2nd Street, Frankfort, KY 40601

(502) 223-7475
(800) 444-3766

www.rebeccaruth.com

Kentucky's famous 100-proof bourbon whiskeys—and a lot of local pride—are key ingredients in this family-owned company's world-renowned chocolates. These chocolates are as rich as the history surrounding the Rebecca-Ruth name itself. Founded in 1919 by two uncommonly courageous schoolteachers, Rebecca Gooch and Ruth Booe, the company's popularity grew as a result of the women's highly acclaimed chocolates and was aided by their creative sales techniques—which included loudly plugging their products on street corners. Ruth Booe originated the "Bourbon Ball." Made with real Kentucky bourbon and crowned with a Southern pecan, this confection has become the treat of the South.

The bright red awning shading this small, house-like store and factory creates an unpretentious atmosphere. The 10 to 15 employees (some of whom have been here for over 30 years) make about 100,000 pounds of confections a year.

In the cream-candy room are articles about Rebecca-Ruth from national magazines such as *Southern Living* and *Gourmet*. Workers pull candy cream on a hook by hand and then use a taffy-pull machine. When it's "just right," the rope of candy is cut into pieces and left to sit. It becomes very creamy, rich, and flaky. Peanut brittle and toffee are also made in this room.

In the kitchen, the cast-iron candy furnace and copper kettles emit the sweet scent of hand-stirred, melting sugars. In the production area, large mixers prepare rich fillings for their assembly-line journey down the enrobing line. First the candy dough is extruded onto a belt, and then it goes through a "chocolate waterfall." Two workers personally apply the finishing touches: a luscious southern pecan, sprinkles, or a swirled flourish on top.

A tour highlight is seeing "Edna's table." For close to 70 years, Edna Robbins handmade delicacies on the same marble table used by Rebecca and Ruth. (Ruth bought "Edna's table" for $10 in 1917.)

Cost: 75 cents per person.

Freebies: Samples of the original Bourbon Balls and other chocolates (children receive liquor-free samples only).

Video/DVD Shown: 8-minute video on candy production.

Reservations Needed: No, except for bus groups.

Days and Hours: January–November Mon–Sat 9:00 AM–12:00 PM and 1:00–4:30 PM. No tours 4 days before Valentine's Day, Mother's Day, and Easter.

Plan to Stay: 45 minutes, plus time in retail store.

Minimum Age: Young children should be accompanied by an adult.

Disabled Access: No

Group Requirements: Bus operators should call (800) 444-3766, or visit the website, to make reservations or obtain additional information, or send email to tours@rebeccaruth.com.

Special Information: Video cameras not allowed. Production more likely in mornings.

Retail Store: Sells a wide variety of liquor-cream chocolates (including Bourbon Balls, Kentucky Irish Coffees, and Kentucky Mint Juleps), and liquor-free chocolates, including nut clusters, butter creams, and Kentucky Creamed Pull Candy. Open year-round Mon–Sat 9:00 AM–5:30 PM. Closed Thanksgiving, Christmas, and New Year's Day. Catalog available from 800 number above.

Directions: From Lexington, take I-64 West to Frankfort Exit 58, then take U.S. 60 West. Turn left onto Second St. Rebecca Ruth is on left. From Louisville, take I-64 East to Frankfort Exit 53. Take Rt. 127 North to U.S. 60 East, which becomes Second St. Stay on Second St. Cross over Capital Ave. Rebecca-Ruth is on left.

Nearby Attractions: Three Chimneys horse farm, Toyota, and Buffalo Trace Distillery tours (see pages 252, 253, and 240).

SOUTH

See color photos, page 46.

1981 Old Frankfort Pike, Versailles, KY 40383

(859) 873-7053

www.three
chimneys.com

THREE CHIMNEYS

The Idea is Excellence.

Although a tour of a horse-breeding farm is a slight diversion from the other companies in this book, we decided to include Three Chimneys because the thoroughbred industry is the third-largest industry and the number-one tourist attraction in the state of Kentucky. In fact, Kentucky-bred horses are a majority among winners of the world-famous Kentucky Derby.

As you leave the city of Lexington and drive along the Old Frankfort Pike, you will be calmed by the gently rolling hills and the black or white ribbons of fencing that zigzag across green pastures dotted with sleek brown horses. Enjoy this scenic drive past other horse farms while watching for the low, forest-green sign that identifies Three Chimneys.

Make your way to the charming visitor center, adjacent to the farm's state-of-the-art veterinary laboratory. Down the red brick path, past the great oaks, is the limestone stallion barn. This five-star equine hotel, lined with oak panels, trimmed with Palladian windows, and topped with a skylight in a cupola, is home to champion racehorses, now studs worth millions of dollars. Each 16-foot-square stall has black bars with black-and-gold engraved nameplates. Grooms attend to the stallions' every need.

These knowledgeable grooms are available to answer all your questions and list each of their charges' accomplishments; for example, fan favorite Smarty Jones retired to Three Chimneys in 2004 and is the fifth-richest American thoroughbred of all time, earning $7,613,155 and winning eight of his nine career starts by an average margin of six lengths. Point Given, the only horse in history to win four consecutive million-dollar races and Horse of the Year for 2001, occupies a nearby stall.

Every day, the stallions graze and stretch their legs in their individual one- to two-acre paddocks.

They are also ridden or walked daily for exercise. Breeding sessions are twice daily, February through July. To ensure the safety of mares and stallions, the round walls of the breeding shed are lined with foam-rubber-padded vinyl, and the floor is covered with wood chips and a raised cocoa mat. Five grooms assist with the breeding—a brief act, but one that can be worth $100,000 to Smarty Jones' owners.

Cost: Free. Tips to grooms are appreciated.

Freebies: No

Video/DVD Shown: No

Reservations Needed: Yes. For tours in April, July, and September–November call 2–3 months in advance; other times of the year, call at least 2 weeks ahead of time.

Days and Hours: Tue–Sat 1:00 PM by appointment only. Closed holidays.

Plan to Stay: 1 hour.

Minimum Age: None

Disabled Access: Yes

Group Requirements: Standard bus tours are discouraged.

Special Information: Please respect the grounds and horses. This is neither a zoo nor a public riding stable.

Gift Shop: No

Directions: From Lexington, take Rt. 4 (New Circle Rd.) to Old Frankfort Pike. Drive west for 8 miles, passing a red brick church on your right. The farm is 0.5 mile ahead on your left. From Cincinnati, take I-75 South to I-64 West to Midway exit. Follow signs on Rt. 62 West through Midway 2 miles to a 4-way stop. Turn left onto Old Frankfort Pike. Farm is a half-mile ahead on your right.

Nearby Attractions: Toyota tour (see page 253); Kentucky Horse Park; Keeneland Racecourse and Calumet Farm tours (organized through Horse Farm Tours Inc. at 859-268-2906).

SOUTH

1001 Cherry Blossom Way,
Georgetown, KY 40324

(502) 868-3027
(800) 866-4485

www.toyota
georgetown.com

SOUTH

Toyota's largest vehicle manufacturing plant outside of Japan is located in this growing community in Kentucky's Bluegrass Region. Toyota Motor Manufacturing, Kentucky (TMMK), covers 7.5 million square feet of floor space, the equivalent of 156 football fields. But don't worry about your legs getting tired on the plant tour, because you'll be riding comfortably in one of their trams.

TMMK employs about 7,000 team members who build nearly 2,000 quality vehicles each day. A "takt time" of 55 seconds on both of the vehicle assembly lines means that two new Toyota vehicles are built in Georgetown every 55 seconds!

TMMK began production in 1988 with the popular Toyota Camry sedan. The Avalon sedan was added in 1994, while the Sienna minivan was produced from 1997 to 2002. Production of the Camry Solara coupe began in 2003.

Toyota vehicles get their start in Stamping, taking shape from huge coils of cold-rolled steel. The steel is cleaned, straightened, and stamped into sheet-metal components that make up the vehicle bodies. With hundreds of tons of force, the automatic presses shape the steel into doors, hoods, roofs, and many other parts.

The sheet-metal components then move to Body Weld, where team members and computer-controlled robots perform the welding that results in a completed body shell. The new vehicle bodies then travel by overhead conveyors to Paint before moving on to the Trim, Chassis, and Final lines in Assembly.

As you tour TMMK, your guide points out the foundations of the world-renowned Toyota Production System. These will include examples of *kaizen,* or continuous improvement; just-in-time parts delivery; and the *andon* system, where team members can stop the line at any time to address quality concerns or any problems.

In the TMMK Visitor Center, you will see current models of the vehicles and engines built in Georgetown, plus the very first Camry produced by team members in May 1988. The Visitor Center also includes interactive video displays and exhibits on Quality, Teamwork, the Toyota Production System, and hybrid technology.

Cost: Free

Freebies: Toyota vehicle (in the form of a refrigerator magnet!).

Video Shown: 10-minute video provides a brief plant overview, including sections not included on the tour.

Reservations Needed: Yes, but walk-ins will be accommodated as space permits.

Days and Hours: Plant tour: Mon–Fri 10:00 AM, 12:00 PM, and 2:00 PM, Thur also 6:00 PM. Closed holidays. Visitor Center: Mon–Fri 9:00 AM–4:00 PM, Thur until 7:00 PM. *Toyota reserves the right to cancel or reschedule tours at any time.*

Plan to Stay: 1.5–2 hours for plant tour, video, and exhibits.

Minimum Age: Plant tour: 1st grade for public tours and 4th grade for school tours. Visitor Center: no minimum age.

Disabled Access: Yes

Group Requirements: Maximum group size is 64 adults. Large groups must call several months in advance.

Special Information: Photographs and video and mechanical recordings are allowed in the Visitor Center but not during the plant tour.

Gift Shop: Sells logoed golf shirts, T-shirts, caps, etc. Open same hours as Visitor Center.

Directions: From Lexington, take I-75 North to Exit 126 (Georgetown/Cynthiana). Turn right onto U.S. 62 (Cherry Blossom Way). Drive exactly 2.5 miles and turn left at Visitor Entrance sign.

Nearby Attractions: Three Chimneys horse farm, Rebecca-Ruth Candies, Buffalo Trace Distillery, and Old Kentucky Candies tours (see pages 252, 251, 240, and 250); Kentucky Horse Park; Keeneland Racecourse; Calumet horse farm; Georgetown College.

See color photos, page 50.

1525 Tyrone Road, Lawrenceburg, KY 40342   (502) 839-4544   www.wildturkey
bourbon.com

The Wild Turkey Bourbon Distillery sits on a hill next to the Kentucky River. Water from this naturally filtered limestone riverbed and corn from nearby farmers are the main ingredients in Wild Turkey bourbon, a uniquely American whiskey. This tour shows almost all steps in crafting the bourbon named after distillery executive Thomas McCarthy's private stock, which he often took on wild turkey hunts.

The first surprise is the metal-barred windows on the big, gray, square warehouses throughout the grounds. They provide vital air circulation to the rack houses where the bourbon ages. The government once required installation of the bars to prevent any barrels from leaving without proper fees being paid.

The initial step in producing bourbon is mixing corn, rye, and water. The mix is cooked and cooled, and then malted barley is added. With special yeast added, this sour mash ferments in stainless-steel tanks. Watch the slow, gentle swirl of the thick yellow mash in the vats; carbon-dioxide bubbles rise to the surface as the yeast changes sugar to alcohol, called "distiller's beer." Stand next to the 40-foot-high copper still, where the alcohol is separated in a vaporization process.

New charred white oak barrels then become the colorless whiskey's home. The tour guide explains that the burnt layers of wood inside the barrel give bourbon its distinctive flavor and color (whiskey must be aged in new, charred-oak barrels for two years to be legally called "bourbon"). Inside a cool warehouse amid racks of barrels on wood planks, you'll enjoy the sweet bourbon smell. The entire process is not much different from what it must have been 100 years ago.

Cost: Free

Freebies: Food made with Wild Turkey, such as a bourbon brownie, lemonade, and coffee.

Video/DVD Shown: In 15-minute video, "A True Kentucky Legend," master distiller Jimmy Russell covers the history of bourbon, Wild Turkey distilling, and its products.

Reservations Needed: No, except for groups of 20 or more people.

Days and Hours: Mon–Fri 9:00 AM, 10:30 AM, 12:30 PM, and 2:30 PM. Saturday tours also available. Always call ahead.

Plan to Stay: 45 minutes for tour, plus time for snacks and visitors center. The visitors center is in a restored building with historical mementos, a scale model of the bourbon production process, and a gift shop.

Minimum Age: None

Disabled Access: Visitors center is fully accessible. Remainder of the facility has gravel paths and flights of stairs to some areas.

Group Requirements: Advance notice requested for groups of 20 or more. No maximum size.

Special Information: Wear comfortable walking shoes. Tour runs all year but not all areas are in production during certain weeks in July and August.

Gift Shop: Sells wide range of merchandise from T-shirts to barbecue sauce, so you can take a piece of Kentucky tradition home with you. Open Mon–Fri 8:30 AM–4:30 PM. Call for Saturday hours.

Directions: From Louisville, take I-64 East to Rt. 151 South to Rt. 127 South. Turn left on Rt. 44, which turns into U.S. 62 East. Bear right onto Tyrone Rd. (Rt. 1510) to distillery. From Lexington, take U.S. 60 West (take Business Route at split) to Versailles to U.S. 62 West to distillery. You're almost there when you see billboards announcing "Bourbon Lovers—Welcome to Paradise."

Nearby Attractions: Beaver Lake and Taylorville Lake; Ripplewood Estate.

233 Newton Street, New Orleans, LA 70114

(504) 361-7821
(800) 362-8213

www.mardi
grasworld.com

You know this tour is going to be fun as soon as you arrive. Colorful Mardi Gras props—such as a gigantic jester, alligators, and Marilyn Monroe—perch in front of this fantasy factory. Blaine Kern, known locally as "Mr. Mardi Gras," is the world's largest float builder. His family-run company, begun in 1947, creates 75 percent of Mardi Gras–parade floats. The Kern Companies also build props for casinos and amusement parks, plus floats for up to 60 parades worldwide annually.

After a guide and a video explain the history of Mardi Gras and the company, you can dress up in authentic Carnival costumes. Don sequined headdresses, gowns, and regal coats of armor and imagine yourself as a noble king or queen of the ball! You'll enter a maze of amazing props with a 15-foot torso of Cleopatra standing nearby.

Follow the yellow arrows to the next "den" (float artists' warehouse). It's a big carpentry and paint shop, where workers build sensational floats for each Mardi Gras "krewe" (club). Artists, painters, and sculptors decorate each float with brightly colored themed scenes. Gold and silver foil on the sides of the floats glistens and flutters in the breeze. The floats are as colorful and animated as Saturday morning cartoons, and strings of lights trace their outlines at night.

In den 7, also used as a function room for parties, gigantic King and Queen Kong figures flank the performance stage. Completed tractor-trailer-sized floats constructed of wood, papier mâché, fiberglass, and Styrofoam rest here waiting to be set free along their parade routes. Notice the famed "Bacchasaurus" float, with stairs under its belly to assist the krewe members in climbing onto the float. It's the Trojan Horse meets *Jurassic Park!*

The Mardi Gras floats come alive when krewe members dance, sing, throw kisses, wave their arms, and toss beads, doubloons, stuffed animals, and cups from their floats.

Cost: Adults, $15; seniors, $11; children under 12, $7.25; under 3, free.

Freebies: Mardi Gras Jester Bead King Cake sample and coffee.

Video/DVD Shown: 11-minute video covering Mardi Gras and company history.

Reservations Needed: No, except for groups over 25 people.

Days and Hours: Mon–Sun 9:30 AM–4:30 PM. Closed Mardi Gras, Easter, Thanksgiving, and Christmas. Depending on the season, time, and day, you will see differing amounts of float-building activity.

Plan to Stay: 1 hour for introductory talk, video, costume try-on, and tour, plus time for the gift shop.

Minimum Age: None

Disabled Access: Yes

Group Requirements: During Carnival Season (January 6 to the day before Ash Wednesday), groups of 10 or more people should call 2 weeks in advance. Otherwise, 1 day is sufficient. Group discounts available.

Special Information: King Cake and coffee included (the King Cake tradition is that whoever eats the piece containing a baby figure must host the next party). Cooking demonstrations with lunch (tour included) are offered daily for $25 per person. Excellent site for parties, complete with miniature parades and lit floats. Call (800) 362-8213.

Gift Shop: Sells Carnival paraphernalia including beads, cups, and doubloons, plus T-shirts, books, and posters. Ships King Cakes. Open same hours as tour.

Directions: From New Orleans, cross Crescent City Connection to Westbank. Take General De Gaulle Dr. East exit. Turn left onto Shirley Dr. Follow signs to Mardi Gras World. From downtown/French Quarter, take free Canal St. ferry and then free shuttle bus. Future plans for paddle-wheel steamboat directly to Mardi Gras World dock.

Nearby Mardi Gras–Related Attractions: Arnaud's Restaurant.

SOUTH

Kliebert's Turtle and Alligator Tours

41083 West Yellow Water Road,
Hammond, LA 70403

(985) 345-3617
(800) 854-9164

www.klieberttours.com

Harvey Kliebert knows a good business opportunity. After raising turtles for 35 years and alligators for 25 years, in 1984 he decided to turn the farm into a tourist attraction. This example of agritourism has not only added to his income but also turned the colorful Harvey and his farm into celebrities. While you're there, you can check out the airboat used in the Burt Reynolds' movie *Gator.* Harvey himself appears occasionally in MTV interviews.

It's still an authentic turtle and alligator farm, dotted with duckweed- and clover-covered ponds that the breeding turtles and alligators call home. Over 17,000 laying turtles produce more than 1 million eggs per year. Once the turtles lay their eggs, which they do up to three times between April and August, Harvey and his crew dig up the eggs from the dirt nests on the pond banks. They then dip the eggs in a pressure machine that removes salmonella. All of the hatchlings are sold outside the U.S.A. for aquariums, children's pets, or food.

The gator breeding pond provides the most excitement for visitors, with gators lounging at the water's edge. Egrets and herons nest in trees overhead. Harvey has about 250 breeder alligators, all born in 1957. The big ones grow to 14 feet long and 1,200 pounds. If you watch the workers throw the gators dead chicken, fish parts, or ground nutria, you can happily assume that they're not too hungry during your visit.

Around June 1 of every year, the female gators start building their nests, piling dirt and grass in mounds two feet high. They then lay eggs just once per year, sometime between June 15 and July 1. As the tour guides/alligator farm workers glibly explain, the female will attack any animal or person that comes around the nest. Fortunately, Harvey and his crew have developed methods of chasing the female away so they can grab her eggs. After incubation, the gators live in pens until they are sold for their meat and hides, or sold to breeders in Florida.

Cost: Adults, $6; children, $3; children under 2, free.

Freebies: Recipe sheets.

Video/DVD Shown: No

Reservations Needed: No, but recommended for groups over 20 people.

Days and Hours: Open March 1–October 31 Mon–Sun 12:00 PM until dark. Call ahead. The farm is open only during the afternoon so visitors don't scare nesting turtles. No tours during extreme cold or storms. Closed holidays.

Plan to Stay: 45 minutes for tour, plus time for gift shop.

Minimum Age: None

Disabled Access: Yes

Group Requirements: Groups over 20 people should call 1 week in advance. No maximum group size. Group discount of 25 percent off for 10 or more people. School groups receive 50 percent discount.

Special Information: Turtles lay eggs April–July; alligators lay eggs June 15–July 1. Annual Alligator Day the third Saturday of August, although may be moved up 1 month.

Gift Shop: Sells alligator heads, fingers, teeth, jewelry, turtle-foot back-scratchers, and just about any gift or food you can imagine that can be made and sold out of alligator or turtle parts. Open March 1–October 31 Mon–Sun 12:00 PM until dark. Call for additional days and hours. Closed holidays. List of products available from above number.

Directions: From New Orleans, take I-10 West to I-55 North to the Springfield exit. Take LA 22 West, which crosses over I-55. Turn right onto the frontage road to the north that runs parallel to I-55. Turn left onto Hoffman Rd. Turn right on Yellow Water Rd. and follow signs. From Baton Rouge, take I-12 East to I-55 South. Take Springfield exit. Take LA 22 West and follow directions above.

Nearby Attractions: Abita Brewing Company tour in Abita Springs (call 504-893-3143); Global Wildlife Center in Folsom.

307 Ann Street, New Iberia, LA 70560

(800) 551-3245

www.conrad
ricemill.com

The best place to start a tour of the Konriko Rice Mill is in the Konriko Company Store, a replica of an old plantation company store next to the mill. While you wait for a tour to begin, the friendly Cajun staff offers you a cup of strong, flavorful South Louisiana–style coffee. Something is always cooking for visitors in the store, too—one day it might be Konriko red beans and rice; another day, Konriko's jambalaya mix with rice. Once you've sampled some good Cajun coffee and cooking, the tour officially begins.

After watching an informative slide presentation, you move next door to America's oldest rice mill. Konriko's mill was built by founder Philip Conrad in 1912 and has been in continuous operation ever since. Made of wood and corrugated tin, the mill is loud and rickety when in operation. But it has great character and is on the National Register of Historic Places.

Before entering the mill, you'll see the outdoor scale and dryer that weighs and dries the unmilled rough rice local farmers deliver. An average truckload of rice is about 30,000 pounds. Next to the dryer is a bin that stores the rice before it is processed. When full, the bin holds 1 million pounds of rice—about $100,000 worth.

Inside, your guide uses a scale model of a mill as a visual aid to explain how different varieties of rice are milled. Walk on the wooden floors between boxes of rice, piles of cardboard containers, burlap bags, and packaging machines. You'll enter several aromatic rooms where workers mix and package Konriko rice and seasonings. Peek into the rice-cracker production room. If you're lucky, your tour guide will give you a hot rice cake fresh from the oven to top off the tour.

Cost: Adults, $4.00; seniors 62 and over, $3.50; children (3–11), $2.25.

Freebies: Fresh, hot coffee; cooked Konriko products; and recipes.

Video/DVD Shown: 20-minute "historically correct" slide presentation on Cajun culture and Konriko's development.

Reservations Needed: No, except for groups over 15 people.

Days and Hours: Mon–Sat 10:00 AM, 11:00 AM, 1:00 PM, 2:00 PM, and 3:00 PM. No production on Saturdays, holidays, and during factory repairs, but tours usually run.

Plan to Stay: About 40 minutes for video and tour, plus time for gift shop.

Minimum Age: None

Disabled Access: Full access to Konriko Company Store. 4 steps lead to mill.

Group Requirements: Groups over 15 people should call 2 weeks in advance. Maximum group size is 50. Group rates available for 30 or more. Special tour times can be arranged.

Special Information: Mill can be loud. Hot in the summer.

Gift Shop: Konriko Company Store sells local foods and crafts, complete assortment of Konriko rice cakes, brown rice crackers, famous Wild Pecan Rice, mixes, T-shirts, novelty items, even Cajun dance video and music tapes. Open Mon–Sat 9:00 AM–5:00 PM. Closed Thanksgiving, Christmas, New Year's, and July 4th. Catalog available at above number.

Directions: From I-10, take Lafayette/U.S. Hwy. 90 exit (Exit 103), and follow U.S. 90 through Lafayette toward New Iberia. At LA 14 (Center St.) in New Iberia, exit and turn left. Turn right on St. Peter St., then right on Ann St. Rice mill is on left.

Nearby Attractions: McIlhenny Tabasco sauce tour (see page 258); Shadows-on-the-Teche; Rice Museum in Crowley; Delcambre Shrimp Boat Landing; Vermilionville, Acadian Village, and Jean Lafitte National Historical Park/Acadiana Cultural Center in Lafayette.

SOUTH

Avery Island, LA 70513

(337) 365-8173
(800) 634-9599

www.tabasco.com

This concentrated hot pepper sauce, first created after the Civil War on an exotic 2,200-acre island in the South Louisiana bayou country, has such a lively flavor that it is now sold in more than 160 countries and territories around the world, and its labels are printed in 21 languages and dialects. McIlhenny Company grows the *Capsicum frutescens* peppers (tabasco peppers) in several countries to ensure a good harvest. But there is only one Tabasco sauce factory, and you'll recognize this modern redbrick building as soon as you open your car door and catch a whiff of the piquant pepper aroma.

A film explains that McIlhenny planted hot pepper seeds from Mexico or Central America. He created his sauce (brand-named Tabasco, a Mexican-Indian word) by mashing the peppers with Avery Island salt, aging the mash in wooden barrels, adding vinegar, and then straining the mixture.

Along a corridor in the modern factory, observe four lines of Tabasco sauce bottling from behind a long glass wall. The smell here isn't nearly as strong as it must be inside the packaging room. Some lines produce more than 300 bottles of Tabasco sauce a minute, helping the factory produce at least 600,000 bottles a day.

After the bottles are spun around in the carousel and injected with the hot red pepper sauce, they journey naked down the assembly line. Machines automatically clothe the bottles with the familiar bright red octagonal caps, green foil neckbands, and diamond-shaped labels. The dressed bottles are then mechanically packed in boxes, ready to travel. Their final destination will be dining tables from Pennsylvania to Peking, where their red caps will be removed and they will "drop in" to spice up a meal.

Cost: Free

Freebies: Miniature Tabasco sauce bottle and samplings of other McIlhenny products.

Video/DVD Shown: 11-minute overview of McIlhenny's history and operations, as well as Tabasco sauce origins and the full processing, including harvesting of peppers, mashing, aging, mixing with vinegar, and bottling.

Reservations Needed: No

Days and Hours: Mon–Sun 9:00 AM–4:00 PM. May not see production Fri–Sun. Closed major holidays.

Plan to Stay: 25 minutes for video and tour, plus time for gift shop and grounds.

Minimum Age: None

Disabled Access: Yes

Group Requirements: None

Special Information: Some production process details are in photos and captions above the viewing window.

Gift Shop: Country Store sells a wide variety of Tabasco specialty foods and novelty items, from pepper earrings to lithographs, toys, cookware, ties, cookbooks, and spices. Open same hours as tour. Gift shop at Jungle Gardens entrance open until 5:30 PM (sells similar items). Catalog available at (800) 634-9599.

Directions: From New Orleans, take I-10 West to Exit 103A. Follow U.S. 90 through Lafayette toward New Iberia. Exit at LA 14 and turn left. At LA 329 junction, turn right. Stay on LA 329 approximately 6 miles. The road dead-ends at Avery Island, where the toll road has a nominal charge per vehicle. Signs will direct you to factory.

Nearby Attractions: Konriko tour (see page 257); Jungle Gardens and Bird City on Avery Island.

SOUTH

Louisiana is known for its tasty seafood, and few factories process more of it than Motivatit. The Voisin family, owners of the company, has been involved in the seafood industry since their ancestors arrived in Louisiana from France in 1770. The oyster plant shucks 400 to 500 burlap sacks (40,000 to 50,000 pounds) of oysters daily. This company pioneered the use of High Hydrostatic Pressure (HHP) to process oysters and clams and was the first to apply the technique commercially. The use of HHP technology increases the yield on products, while reducing bacteria and extending shelf life.

Most food-processing plants you visit seem highly automated. Workers appear to spend their hours monitoring or assisting the computerized, fast-moving machines. But this is not so at seafood-processing plants. Sure, you'll see half-shelled oysters move down an assembly line, and modern refrigeration units, but human hands do the real work of getting the meat from the shell.

You enter what looks like the world's largest raw-oyster bar. If you close your eyes, you can easily imagine that you're next to the ocean listening to carpenters build a house. Rows of rubber-aproned workers stand in front of metal tables piled with fresh, salty-smelling oysters. These professional shuckers, working on one oyster at a time, pry open the oyster, scoop out the meat with a small knife, and toss the meat and shells into separate buckets. The best shuckers can repeat this rhythmic prying and tossing at a rate of almost 500 oysters per hour.

Cost: $5 per person.

Freebies: Occasionally, a dirty-colored Louisiana oyster.

Video/DVD Shown: No

Reservations Needed: Yes. Individuals need to either join a scheduled group tour or form a group.

Days and Hours: Mon–Fri 8:00 AM–5:00 PM. Before 11:00 AM is best time to see production. Closed holidays.

Plan to Stay: 30–45 minutes for tour.

Minimum Age: None, but children must be supervised.

Disabled Access: Yes

Group Requirements: 1 week's advance notice; longer during peak travel seasons.

Special Information: Floors are wet. Oyster production is busiest, as the locals say, in the "months with the Rs" (September–April).

Gift Shop: No

Directions: From New Orleans, take Hwy. 90 West to Houma. Take exit 210 and head west on Hwy. 182. Turn left at Gum St. Oyster plant and corporate headquarters are at the corner of Gum and Palm Sts.

Nearby Attractions: Southdown Plantation Home/ Terrebonne Museum; swamp tours; Louisiana Universities Marine Consortium (LUMCON) Marine Research Facility tour in Chauvin (call 504-851-2800). Annual Breaux Bridge Crawfish Festival (first full weekend in May) 2 hours away.

SOUTH

The New Orleans Arts District was unaffected by Hurricane Katrina, and it offers visitors plenty to do. Located in a restored 19th-century brick building, the New Orleans School of GlassWorks & PrintMaking Studio lets you watch artisans use their skills in glassblowing, printmaking, bookbinding, and related crafts in jewelry, metal sculpture, and papermaking.

The heart of this facility is the two continuous-melt furnaces, encircled by three fully equipped traditional European glassblowing benches. After you walk through the store and enter the studios, you'll immediately notice the teams of glassblowers as they jump, jive, and wail in the glassblowing arena to the sounds of New Orleans music. They like to say their maneuverings are similar to the choreography of swing dancers, as they "swing out" their vessels to lengthen them and skillfully balance the glowing, honeylike molten glass on the end of their blowpipes.

Faculty members occasionally narrate for the crowd as they instruct students making Venetian-inspired blown- and cast-glass creations. You may be invited to take part in the final step, known as the "fiber optic pull." Notice the special skills involved in "torch working" glass objects into such shapes as sea creatures or beads. These are made from rods and tubes of colored glass (called cane) that become soft and malleable when heated by the flame of a tabletop torch. The techniques used by flame-working artists often resemble those used in glassblowing, but are just much smaller in scale. Gravity, heat, and simple steel hand tools are the basic provisions they need to shape glass into sculptural designs.

You're encouraged to stroll through each studio to discuss the processes with the artists at work in the open studios. Papermaking equipment fills the back area of this studio, a 25,000-square-foot space with skylights. You see an etching press, automated letterpress, and other machines used to hand-make and marble paper and to bind books. Note how printmakers use acid to etch copper plates, set lead type for hand-bound books, and make custom wedding invitations and "shoot screens" for hand-printed fabric designs.

Cost: Free

Freebies: None

Video/DVD Shown: No

Reservations Needed: Reservations are required for groups of more than 10 people and for hands-on participatory events to accompany demonstrations.

Days and Hours: Mon–Sat 10 00 AM–5:00 PM (September–May); Mon–Fri 10 00 AM–5:00 PM (June–August). Closed major holidays. Production varies. Call for details.

Plan to Stay: 30 minutes for a self-guided tour, plus time for gift shop/crafts store in front area.

Disabled Access: Yes

Group Requirements: Groups of 10 or more should contact GlassWorks to reserve guided tours.

Special Information: During summer, local culinary artists create chocolate and sugar sculptures. If you call at least 2 days in advance, you can design a colorful ornament, have a glass impression of your hand cast in solid glass, create a glass bead, or make your own prints on the star wheels press. Regularly scheduled classes, workshops, and private lessons are available (call 504-529-7277).

Gift Shop: Gallery store sells glass, metal, marble, and print creations made in studios.

Directions: From I-10 (toward Mississippi Bridge), take St. Charles Ave. exit. Continue on Calliope (under interstate) for 3 lights, until Camp St. Turn left on Camp St. Continue on Camp St. and turn right on Girod. Take another right on Magazine. GlassWorks is on Magazine, between Girod and Julia.

Nearby Attractions: The Ogden Museum of Southern Art; Contemporary Arts Center; various art galleries; D-Day Museum; RiverWalk; Convention Center. French Quarter is a 30-minute walk away.

See color photos, page 44.

We love stories about people who start new businesses at the age most people focus on retirement. The late Tony Chachere started his third career at the age of 67. Having retired from successful stints in pharmacy and insurance, he decided to fulfill a lifelong desire to write and publish a cookbook. While a member of Cooks Unlimited, a men's cooking club, he had developed a "secret" spicy seasoning mix that he used in many of the book's recipes. The popularity of the seasoning recipe in his cookbook encouraged Tony to start manufacturing the blend for consumers. Today the seasoning is the number-one-selling spice mix in the Cajun/Creole category.

After a brief talk about Tony's and the company's histories, your tour guide leads you into the refrigerated ingredients room. It's piled high with boxes and burlap bags filled with spices. Smell the pungent aromas emanating from the boxes of ground red pepper and oregano. The company uses more than 8.5 million pounds of ingredients each year, and it all begins here.

Because of the overwhelming smell on the second floor, you can't observe the actual mixing together of the spices. Even on the first floor, you'll notice that workers wear portable air units that filter the pungent air around them. Next, your guided factory-floor tour takes you into the packaging area. The spices drop down through overhead pipes to several different fast-moving assembly lines. Each day, the auger processor fills 2,000 cases of eight-ounce "little green cans" with the seasoning mix. On another line, gumbo and jambalaya mixes are automatically sealed between two sheets of foil (creating bags) and inserted into boxes.

During the current tour, you walk through the warehouse. Here, finished products of all types and sizes wait in large brown boxes for shipment to stores and distribution points worldwide. As you pass by the food scientists' kitchen, you may smell the product being tested. In the UPS shipment area, used for smaller orders, you'll be surprised to see a popcorn popper. The company uses popcorn as a more environmentally conscious packing material than Styrofoam. A true indicator of where you live may not be the zip code on your UPS package, but rather the size of the can of Tony Chachere's Creole Seasoning you order—locals always keep 17-ounce cans on their kitchen tables.

Cost: Free

Freebies: Bag of souvenir items, including catalog, pamphlet cookbook, and product samples.

Video/DVD Shown: No, but one is planned.

Reservations Needed: *Call ahead, as tour program has been discontinued during plant construction.*

Days and Hours: *Not certain of schedule and tour restart date. Call for information.*

Plan to Stay: 30 minutes for tour.

Minimum Age: 7

Disabled Access: Yes

Group Requirements: Groups over 10 people should call 2 weeks in advance. Special times can be arranged. No maximum group size.

Special Information: No photography.

Gift Shop: Sells all of their seasoning and rice mixes, including Original Creole Seasoning, and both of Tony's cookbooks. *Cajun Country Cookbook* and *Tony Chachere's Second Helping* contain mouthwatering recipes accumulated through a lifetime steeped in Cajun culture and Southern hospitality. Free catalog available at number above. While the gift shop is closed for construction, items will be sold through the front desk of the office.

Directions: From I-10, take I-49 North to U.S. 190 West. Turn right onto Lombard St. Factory is 5 blocks ahead on left.

Nearby Attractions: Opelousas Museum and Interpretive Center; Opelousas Museum of Art; Opelousas Vieux Village; Chretien Point Plantation.

SOUTH

Peavey Visitors Center and Museum,
4886 Peavey Drive, Meridian, MS 39305

(601) 486-1460   www.peavey.com

LISTEN TO THIS™

Hartley Peavey, founder of the world's largest music and sound equipment manufacturer, grew up in this eastern Mississippi railroad town. As a teenager in 1965, he constructed his first guitar amp in his parents' basement. Today his company employs 2,000 workers in Mississippi, Alabama, and England, and markets amplifiers, guitars, keyboards, and sound systems in 103 countries. Every form of music—from punk to polka, from country to classical—has been touched by Hartley Peavey's products.

Though its factories are not open for tours, the company celebrates its history—research and development and manufacturing—at the Visitors Center. In its first life, the building was a U.S. Department of Agriculture research facility, specializing in sugar-producing crops. Peavey lovingly restored the exterior to its original Federalist style. But the interior is now strongly postmodern, with splashes of chrome, teal, yellow, and black—colors found on many of Peavey's products.

Called the Peavey World Tour, the center presents exhibits and video programs and has become a mecca for musicians of all types who trust their stylings only to equipment bearing the Peavey logo. The first-floor galleries provide a personal view of the company's founder. Look for a 1901 photograph of Hartley Peavey's grandfather and the original lightning-bolt logo drawn on notebook paper. One room re-creates the basement where Hartley made his first amplifier, complete with tools and old issues of *Popular Mechanics* and *Popular Science.* Upstairs galleries chronicle the company's growth from this basement workshop to 19 facilities.

Follow the yellow banister downstairs to today's "world of Peavey" and make your own music on some of the world's most sophisticated and coveted sound systems. Test the full Peavey line, including electric guitars, electronic keyboards, amplifiers, and complex studio mixing equipment. Peavey

Electronics designed this hands-on space for visitors of all ages. Several guitars are mounted on the floor, giving toddlers a chance to pluck away at the taut steel strings.

Cost: Free

Freebies: Copy of *Monitor,* the company magazine, and guitar picks.

Videos/DVDs Shown: 18-minute video on company history and goals; 7-minute video on media matrix computer sound system.

Reservations Needed: Yes

Days and Hours: *Closed temporarily for remodeling. Call ahead for information.*

Plan to Stay: 1 hour for museum and playing instruments, plus time in gift shop.

Minimum Age: None

Disabled Access: 5 steps to first-floor historical exhibits. Staircase down to video theater and hands-on equipment display.

Group Requirements: Groups of 50 or more need reservations. Call (601) 484-1460.

Special Information: Set up for self-guided tours, but guided visits can be arranged.

Gift Shop: Gear shop sells logoed items from key chains, T-shirts, and coffee mugs to $100-plus satin tour jackets. Open center hours. Catalog available from (800) 752-7896 or above website.

Directions: From Jackson, take I-20 East through Meridian as it changes to I-20/59. Take Exit 157B for Hwy. 45 North. Take the first exit (for Sonny Montgomery Industrial Park). At bottom of ramp, turn right onto Marion Russel Rd. After you cross railroad track (about 1 mile), turn right into the center's parking lot.

Nearby Attractions: The Jimmie Rodgers Museum (Meridian is the birthplace of Jimmie Rodgers, the father of country music); Annual Jimmie Rodgers Country Music Festival; Grand Opera House of Mississippi (tours of "The Lady" are available; call 601-693-LADY); Merrehope Mansion; Dunn's Falls Water Park; the Dentzel Carousel.

SOUTH

VIKING

VIKING RANGE CORPORATION

What might you find in the homes of many rich and famous people or on the set of *Iron Chef America?* A Viking Range, manufactured in the heart of the Mississippi Delta. On the tour, it's hard to determine which is more surprising—the vast array of products, colors, and sizes available or the fact that such a big company manufactures the majority of its parts right at this local, small-town plant. In 1983, founder Fred E. Carl Jr. developed the first commercial-type range for home use when he wanted a heavy-duty range for his new house. The cooktops, ovens, ventilation products, refrigerators, dishwashers, waste disposers, and outdoor grills that the company added to its line since then can be found in the homes of celebrities and professional cooks alike.

In the receiving area, forklifts heave large quantities of raw materials such as sheet steel and wiring into the factory. The Vipros turret punch press, one of the company's most powerful and most impressive machines, loads the sheet metal mechanically onto the press table. Silver shavings drop soundlessly to the floor as the machine's sharp prongs drill screw holes. Intricate software allows the Vipros to seem as if it runs on its own. Once the Vipros makes enough of one part, it automatically makes the required number of another part. Hydraulics keeps this giant press running more quietly than you would expect.

After the drilling stage, other machines fold the shiny metal with ease. You'll recognize the oven bases as the shaped pieces move down the assembly line. Because they're built from the bottom up, each oven part fits into the next: the sides into the base, the windows into the front door panel, the cut-outs for the burners, and knobs into the stove top.

The expertise required by the workers themselves, who wire the ovens for their features, is as impressive as the machines. Reaching into the cavity of a nearly completed oven, the workers intricately connect wires of different shapes and sizes. With the insides in place, workers add the exteriors. Since they are custom-made, the assembled appliances vary from one to the next. In vibrant shades such as stainless steel, cobalt, eggplant, and lemonade, the ovens resemble sculptured works of art, inspiring enough to make you want to fire up the burner and cook something!

Cost: Free

Freebies: No

Video/DVD Shown: No

Reservations Needed: Yes. Call 1 week in advance.

Days and Hours: Mon–Thur 1:00–4:00 PM. Closed holidays. No production during the weeks of Christmas and July 4th.

Plan to Stay: 45 minutes.

Minimum Age: 18

Disabled Access: Yes

Group Requirements: Groups over 10 people should call 2 weeks in advance. Maximum group size is 20 people.

Special Information: No photography.

Gift Shop: No

Directions: From Memphis, take I-55 South to Grenada. Take Hwy. 7 South to Greenwood and turn right on Hwy. 82. Take Main St. exit. Bear right onto Main St. and turn right on Market St. Turn left at traffic light onto Viking Rd. Factory is on left in about 1 mile. From Jackson, take I-55 North to Winona. Take Hwy. 82 West to Greenwood and take Main St. exit. Bear right onto Main St. Turn right on Market St. and turn left at traffic light onto Viking Rd. Factory is on your left in about 1 mile.

Nearby Attractions: Historic Cotton Row District of Greenwood; Mississippi Delta; Cottonlandia Museum.

SOUTH

300 Old Thomasville Road, High Point, NC 27260   (336) 887-2222   www.billdavis racing.com

Die-hard NASCAR fans are in for a treat when they visit Bill Davis Racing. Compared to other shops in the industry, this one allows the fans to walk through the assembly room, take pictures of the cars, ask the mechanics questions, and get an up-close look at the production side of racing. This is a self-guided tour that allows you to relish the race environment for as long as your heart desires.

In the large assembly room, you'll see a row of cars lined up, ready for racing. Although the cars look the same, they have been custom made for the racetrack they will eventually race on. There are also cars in various stages of production. You might see an engine being guided into place, or the mechanics working on the drive components of the car. If you have a question, feel free to speak up. This shop is devoted to its fans and encourages interaction with its mechanics. You can find out that a car takes five and a half weeks to construct from scratch, that it weighs 3,500 pounds, and can cost as much as $210,000 to make. Ask about its horsepower, how it handles, or what happens if it crashes.

If you want to see the tractor-trailers that transport the cars to races, be sure to plan your tour for the middle of the week. The trailers are loaded up on Wednesdays and are gone by Friday. The trailers are mobile shops that travel with the cars. You'll get a peek inside and see how the team prepares during the week for a weekend race.

You'll also get to look inside the fabrication shop.

From behind glass, you'll see new cars being put together and wrecked cars being repaired. Mechanics hand-piece the bare chassis, work 24-gauge sheet metal into body form, and tack weld it all together. Everything on the car is handmade in the metal shop and then painted in the paint shop.

The only thing missing from this tour is a look at how the engine is put together, which is not open to the general public. Some things have to remain secret.

Cost: Free

Freebies: Postcards of the drivers.

Video/DVD Shown: No

Reservations Needed: No

Days and Hours: Mon–Fri 8:30 AM–4:00 PM.

Plan to Stay: 30 minutes for tour, longer if you have lots of questions.

Minimum Age: No

Disabled Access: Yes

Group Requirements: For groups of 10 or more, call ahead to schedule a tour.

Gift Shop: Sells souvenirs and apparel online at www.billdavisracing.com.

Directions: From I-85 North, follow the signs for Thomasville. Exit at Old Thomasville Rd. and turn left. Just after the intersection at Market Center, Bill Davis Racing is located on both sides of the street. Begin the tour on the left side.

Nearby Attractions: Furniture Discovery Center (see page 266); Petty Museum; Richard Childress Racing and Winery; All-a-Flutter Butterfly Farm; Historic Castle McCulloch Gold Mill; Maize Adventure; Mendenahll Plantation; Museum of Old Domestic Life.

12 Old Charlotte Highway, Asheville, NC 28803   (828) 296-1499   www.blueridge
motionpictures.com

Don't go looking for the waterfall out of *The Last of The Mohicans,* filmed here in 1992—you won't find it. Instead, you'll learn how it was constructed on the wet stage and filmed to look real. You'll also see photographs of many other scenes you thought were real on screen, but were actually elaborate effects created at Blue Ridge Motion Pictures. Although it might be a letdown to find out that your favorite movie scenes were actually sets invented to deceive the viewer's eye, you'll be let in on the secrets that made those scenes happen.

Blue Ridge Motion Pictures films commercials, marketing, infomercials, parts for independent films, and feature films. Depending on the production schedule, you might see any part involved in creating these film moments. As part of the pre-production process, you might see the set of your next favorite movie under construction. The crew of model and prop makers can create any scene or prop that is needed in a movie, from the oval office to a chamber of horrors. If you're there during the production of a movie, you might see how a set works during filming, such as how the cameras and lighting equipment are used, or what a grip is. The studio also deals in aspects of postproduction. You'll get a look at the small fleet of computer screens and equipment that aid in the editing process. Postproduction also includes adding special effects, so maybe you'll finally learn how they make the ball of fire that erupts after an explosion.

There are several sound studios at Blue Ridge Motion Pictures, including a wet stage, sound stages, green screens, and "Stage X," a creepy set built in a labyrinth of rusting pipes. Outside the main building is a set of industrial buildings, all set for the climactic scene the protagonist always seems to find himself in at the end of an action movie. Also outdoors are 18 acres of wooded land, complete with a pond and winding trails and roads, perfect for a multitude of outdoor scenes.

Cost: Adults, $10; seniors 65+ and students under 18, $8; children under 5, free.

Freebies: No

Video/DVD Shown: A 6-minute video about movie production is shown.

Reservations Needed: No, except for groups of 15 or more.

Days and Hours: Tours are Sat at 10:30 AM.

Plan to Stay: 1.5 hours.

Minimum Age: No

Disabled Access: Yes

Group Requirements: Reservations needed for groups of 15 or more. Call (828) 296-1499.

Retail Center: Sells pencils, pens, mugs, and other items bearing the Blue Ridge Motion Pictures logo. Open Mon–Fri 9:00 AM–5:00 PM.

Directions: From I-240, take exit 8 and turn onto 74 A West. Drive 0.5 mile and turn right onto Old Charlotte Hwy. The Blue Ridge Motion Pictures entrance is the second left. From I-40, take exit 53 B to exit 8 off I-240 and follow the directions above.

Nearby Attractions: Grandfather Mountain; Linville Caverns; Oconaluftee Indian Village; Biltmore Estate; Great Smoky Mountains Railroad.

SOUTH

High Point Museum, 1859 East Lexington Avenue, High Point, NC 27262

(336) 885-1859

www.highpoint museum.org

While most of High Point's famous furniture factories no longer give public tours, you'll experience the furniture manufacturing process from A to Z at this unique interactive museum. The displays in the main exhibit area, set up to simulate the "flow of production" in an ideal furniture factory, offer a comprehensive look at the detailed production involved in crafting dressers, china cabinets, highboys, and upholstered chairs.

Approach a designer's studio desk, where manufacturing always starts, and pick up the drafting tools and wood samples. Mascots "Joe" and "Josephine"—life-size blueprints detailing the measurements of an average-size man and woman—stand upright as a reminder of the human dimensions of furniture design.

Visit Harvey Hardwood, a 500-pound solid red oak that gives a two-minute lesson about forestry and the use of hardwood. His animated face and motion-triggered presentation entertain children and adults alike.

A giant blueprint of a Queen Anne highboy greets you in the case goods section, where your "factory tour" officially begins. Displayed (although not running) are the machines used to shape, carve, sand, and assemble. You can grip the handles of band saws, lathes, and drills. The multispindle carver is fascinating; follow the contours of a model and see how spinning blades produce 16 identical matches.

Grab an air-powered nail gun in the upholstery section and begin simulating the assembly of a frame for a loveseat. A large blueprint outlines the furniture's design. Touch more than 15 samples of fabric and then select your favorite on the interactive computer, which allows you to design your own sofa by picking a style and watching it come together frame by frame on the screen. Sit on an upholstered chair, and you'll appreciate the sturdy craftsmanship and design.

In the special exhibit area, the Serta Miniature Bedroom Collection contains reproductions of famous bedrooms, such as King Tut's and Kublai Khan's (whose round, moon-shaped, carved bed is a favorite among visitors). Crafting large or small furniture requires precise measurements, a steady hand, and an eye for detail—all of which are comprehensively explained in the heart of High Point, the furniture-making capital of the world.

Cost: Free

Freebies: No

Video/DVD Shown: No

Reservations Needed: No, except for groups of 15 or more people.

Days and Hours: *FDC is closed. Aspects of the museum will be relocating to High Point Museum. Call (336) 885-1859 or check www.highpointmuseum. org for information.*

Plan to Stay: 1 hour, plus time for gift shop.

Minimum Age: None

Disabled Access: Yes

Group Requirements: Groups of 15 or more should make reservations 2 weeks in advance for a guided tour.

Gift Shop: Sells a wide selection of furniture books, furniture-shaped chocolate, jewelry, logoed T-shirts, and bookmarks. Open same hours as museum.

Directions: From I-85, take Hwy. 311 North to College Dr. Turn right onto College Dr. Go approximately 4 miles. Turn right or Lexington Ave. Museum will be on left. From I-40, take Hwy. 68 South to Centennial St. Turn left on Centennial St. for 1 mile. Turn left on Lexington Ave. for 0.25 mile. Museum is on the left.

Nearby Attractions: Krispy Kreme doughnut tour (call 336-885-8081), Angela Peterson Doll and Miniature Museum; High Point Museum and Historical Park.

SOUTH

REPLACEMENTS, LTD.

For a special dinner party, you carefully set the table with the fragile bone china Aunt Millie willed you. But a guest accidentally dropped a precious teacup while helping clear the table. Once you see Replacements, Ltd.'s rows of shelves (62,000, to be exact!) stacked 16 feet high with 160,000 different patterns of china and crystal, you will feel confident about matching Aunt Millie's teacup. Replacements, the world's largest supplier of discontinued and active china, crystal, and flatware, receives 15,000 pattern requests every month.

In the research department, "detectives" identify discontinued china, crystal, and flatware patterns for desperate customers, who send pictures, photocopies, or pencil rubbings of their treasures. The researchers use old catalogs (one prize possession is a 1936 Fostoria Catalog) and pictures to identify patterns. Antique dealers and a 700-buyer network receive Replacements' 1,000-page quarterly wish list of customer requests. Buyers scour auctions, estate sales, and flea markets worldwide in search of specific patterns.

Wearing goggles that protect their eyes, skilled restoration-area workers carefully smooth out small (less than one-eighth of an inch) chips in crystal. Besides restoring crystal to its original beauty, workers reglaze and fire certain china pieces to remove scratches. Paintbrushes in hand, these artists expertly dab special paint onto the gold and platinum trim on ornate, elegant porcelain.

One tour highlight comes when your guide leads you down an aisle of the 10 million–piece warehouse. Looking without touching is difficult—but required—as you peer at towering shelves and spot anything from the elegant stem of a Baccarat crystal to a Limoges dessert plate. Equally impressive is the flatware department. Here you see gleaming silver serving spoons and shiny butter knives being inspected, identified, and inventoried. Workers polish precious pieces on high-speed buffing machines, then seal them in their own plastic bags to retard tarnishing. You leave with a true appreciation of the effort and dedication involved in researching, restoring, and replacing the "irreplaceable."

Cost: Free

Freebies: Logoed magnet.

Video/DVD Shown: No

Reservations Needed: No, except for groups larger than 25 people.

Days and Hours: Mon–Sun 9:30 AM–6:30 PM, every 30 minutes. Closed major holidays.

Plan to Stay: 20–30 minutes, plus time in showroom and museum.

Minimum Age: None

Disabled Access: Yes

Group Requirements: Groups larger than 25 should call 2 days ahead; will be split into smaller groups.

Special Information: Wear comfortable shoes. Museum adjacent to showroom focuses on Ohio River Valley's early-20th-century glass industry.

Retail Store: 12,000-square-foot showroom displays porcelain, crystal, and metal collectibles in antique mahogany, oak, and walnut showcases (some dating back to the 1800s, and many with their original glass!). Also, Masons' lamps (Wedgwood), crystal perfume bottles, and jewelry. Open Mon–Sun 8:00 AM–9:00 PM.

Directions: Take I-85/40 and exit at Exit 132. Go north (left if coming from Greensboro, right from Burlington) on Mt. Hope Church Rd. and turn left on Knox Rd. Replacements is on left.

Nearby Attractions: Seagrove Area Potteries tours about 40 miles away (see page 268); Thomas Built Buses gives limited tours (call 336-889-4871); Greensboro's attractions include Colonial Heritage Center, Greensboro Arboretum, Greensboro Cultural Center at Festival Park; Burlington Factory Outlets. Winston-Salem's attractions are 25 miles away.

SOUTH

Museum of North Carolina Traditional Pottery,
122 Main Street, Seagrove, NC 27341

(336) 873-7887
(336) 873-7300

www.seagrove
potteryheritage.com

MUSEUM
OF NORTH CAROLINA
TRADITIONAL POTTERY

More than 100 pottery studios scattered across the countryside make up the Seagrove pottery community. Within a 20-mile radius of the tiny, rural town of Seagrove (population approximately 357), the potteries are located along Route 705, Potters' Row, and its snaking secondary roads. Hand-painted 12-foot wooden signs point up different roads toward clusters of studios. At the Museum of North Carolina Traditional Pottery, you can obtain a map marking all the locations, find help focusing your exploration, and view a sampling of the pottery styles made in the area.

Starting in the 1750s, English potters migrated to the Seagrove area for its good clay and its location on a major commercial road. Despite the influx of 20th-century mass production, several potteries have persevered; some are now in their eighth and ninth generations. Now the largest community of potters in the U.S.A., Seagrove maintains the feeling that its people have been making pots for a long time.

In this laid-back, Old World–style community, many of the potteries are small family operations. Some are in backyards; some have dirt or brick floors, covered with clay dirt. Many use North Carolina native clay, which fires up to a light orange/brown terracotta color.

In a low-ceilinged log building with an earthen floor, Vernon Owens, owner of Jugtown Pottery, and his wife make salt-glazed crocks, milk churns, molasses jugs, and other traditional pieces. They throw salt onto the pots during the firing inside the 2,300°F wood-burning kiln. The salt melts, bonds with the silica in the clay, and leaves a clear, bumpy, orange-peel texture. At Holly Hill Pottery, one of the area's larger potteries, you'll see up to four potters transforming mounds of clay into tea glasses or dinner plates. Another potter may be loading the 1,000-cubic-foot gas-fired kiln. As you visit many potter-

ies, you'll recognize their distinctive characteristics. In fact, by looking at the shapes and silhouettes of each potter's antiquelike pitchers, experienced eyes can classify them not only as North Carolina pots, but also specifically as Seagrove pots.

Cost: Free

Freebies: Map of Seagrove Area potteries available at the Museum of North Carolina Traditional Pottery and at all the potteries.

Video/DVD Shown: No

Reservations Needed: No, unless motorcoach groups want a guide (see below).

Days and Hours: Generally Mon–Sat 9:00 AM–5:00 PM. Call the above numbers regarding schedules.

Plan to Stay: 1–2 days, although it's impossible to visit every pottery shop.

Minimum Age: None

Disabled Access: Yes, for most studios.

Group Requirements: Call 1 week in advance (336-873-7300) to arrange for a motorcoach step-on guide.

Special Information: Kilns are especially hot in the summer. The Seagrove Pottery Festival, held the weekend before Thanksgiving, features pottery demonstrations and sales.

Gift Shop: No

Showrooms: Each studio sells wares, including face jugs, grape pitchers, Seagrove traditional and functional stoneware, and contemporary stoneware with pastel designs. Open generally Mon–Sat 9:00 AM–5:00 PM. Closed holidays

Directions: From Greensboro intersection of I-85 and I-40, take I-73/I-74 South (old Rt. 220). After sign for area potteries, take Seagrove Exit 45. Turn left onto Rt. 705. Museum of North Carolina Traditional Pottery is in an old brick building on right.

Nearby Attractions: North Carolina Zoological Park; Richard Petty Museum; North Carolina Aviation Museum; Southern Pines and Pinehurst golf communities.

SOUTH

Charleston Tea Plantation,
76617 Maybank Highway,
Wadmalaw Island, SC 2948

(843) 559-0383
(800) 443-5987

www.charleston
teaplantation.com

On a small island 25 miles south of Charleston, the last 11 rural miles along a dead-end road, lies the only commercial tea plantation in the U.S.A. Charleston Tea Plantation is a tea farm rather than an Old South plantation with white columns. But the farm, with its long rows of perfectly manicured five-foot-wide tea hedges set among grand oak, is just as enchanting.

Start outside by looking at the tea fields: rows of tea bushes stretching over acres of land. Make sure to look at the propagation demonstration, a display of tea plants in various stages of growth. Each plant comes from a clone, not a seed, so the traits of each plant are carefully controlled. Out in the tea field, you might see the Green Giant, a hybrid cotton picker and tobacco harvester used for gathering tea leaves. The Giant drives between the rows while its blade swings over the tops of the bushes, clipping just the top few leaves. A fan under the Giant blows the newly clipped leaves up into a basket, which are collected later and brought into the factory.

Inside the factory, you'll stand on a walkway above the factory floor and look down. Mirrors hang above each machine so you can see what is happening below. Initially, the freshly harvested leaves are placed on a withering bed for 12 to 18 hours. Natural air blows over the leaves, reducing their moisture from 80 percent to 68 percent. Afterward, the leaves are chopped up and sent to the oxidation bed. To make black tea, the only tea made in this factory, the leaves remain on the bed for 55 minutes until they turn coppery orange. Then they are put into an oven and baked for about 28 minutes. The moisture remaining in the leaves determines these baking times. If the leaves aren't baked just right, the quality of the final product will be compromised. Finally, the sticks and fibers are sorted out from the tea leaves, and the leaves are ready for packaging.

The best time to see the harvesting and tea-making process is between May and October. If you can't make it then, you'll miss out on the sounds of the machines and the smell of the tea in the factory, but you will see a video detailing every step. After the tour is over, head to the Gift Shoppe for a sample of fresh American Classic Tea.

Cost: Free

Freebies: American Classic Tea sampling.

Video/DVD Shown: 8-minute video overviews entire production process, from harvesting to factory.

Reservations Needed: No

Days and Hours: Wed–Sat 10:00 AM–4:00 PM, Sun 12:00 PM–4:00 PM.

Plan to Stay: 45 minutes–1 hour.

Minimum Age: None

Disabled Access: Yes

Group Requirements: None

Special Information: Wear comfortable shoes and clothing for the outdoor walk.

Gift Shoppe: Carries a wide selection of teas, tea-related items, local Lowcountry food items, art, and souvenirs.

Directions: From Charleston, take Ashley River Bridge (U.S. 17), stay left to Folly Rd. (SC 171), turn right onto Maybank Hwy. (SC 700) for 18 miles. Look for entrance signs on the left.

Nearby Attractions: Atlantic Littleneck Clam Farm tour (call 843-762-0022), 25 miles away; Angel Oak Park, 11 miles away; Kiawah Island Resort, 22 miles away.

SOUTH

BMW Zentrum

The BMW Zentrum Visitors Center seems to appear out of nowhere as you approach it. The Zentrum (German for "center") sits in front of BMW's first manufacturing facility outside of Germany. Ten white flags wave in front of the white horseshoe-shaped building nestled on BMW's 1,039 acres. Inside the 28,000-square-foot Zentrum, the past, present, and future of BMW come together in a one-of-a-kind building, the only BMW visitors center in North America, located next to the only BMW manufacturing plant in the U.S. Part meeting and events center, part café, part gallery, and part time machine, the Zentrum gives you views of famous BMW race and art cars and a sneak preview of the experimental BMW cars of the future.

Follow a covered walkway from the Zentrum into the quiet factory that produces the sporty Roadsters, Coupes, and X5s. In the Communications Plaza, the plant's "town center," the three main manufacturing areas—body, paint, and assembly—physically intersect.

In the body shop, workers in green fire-resistant jackets weld the steel parts together at a marriage station, while bursts of sparks fly into the air. The paint shop is seven stories high (only three stories above ground), protected by a glass wall, and pressurized to keep debris from contaminating the paint environment. Cars pause at each station to be cleaned and coated with a sealant to reduce noise and water leakage before being primed, color-coated, and clear-coated.

In assembly, the painted bodies are placed on a rotating conveyor and tilted 90 degrees so workers can install the parts in the car's underbody without bending or stooping. Both the X5 and Z4 travel along the serpentine one-line assembly process where associates install the interior parts, such as the engine, fuel lines, gas tank, dashboard, seats, and radio.

Finally the cars are rigorously tested and prepared to be shipped to over 130 different markets worldwide.

Cost: Zentrum, free; plant tour, $5.

Freebies: No

Video/DVD Shown: 15-minute movie "Birth of a BMW," a virtual factory tour. Shown every half hour in the surround-sound theater.

Reservations Needed: No, for Zentrum; yes, for the plant tour.

Days and Hours: Zentrum: Mon–Fri 9:30 AM–5:30 PM. Closed holidays. Plant tours: Available by reservation only. Plant tours may be abbreviated or canceled due to new model development and unreleased automobile designs.

Plan to Stay: 1 hour for Zentrum, 1.25 hour for tour, plus time in gift shop and café.

Minimum Age: None, for Zentrum; 12, for plant tour.

Disabled Access: Yes

Group Requirements: Groups should call 888-TOUR-BMW or write BMW Manufacturing Corp., P.O. Box 11000, Spartanburg, SC 29304. Maximum group size is 50 people. BMW confirms reservations up to 90 days ahead. BMW Car Club and student discounts available.

Special Information: No photography in plant.

Gift Shop: Sells BMW memorabilia and BMW model cars. European-style café serves German beer, pretzels, and cappuccino. Open same hours as Zentrum.

Directions: From I-85, take Exit 60 for Hwy. 101 South toward Greer. Entrance into BMW will be ahead on your left. Follow signs for "BMW Visitors Center."

Nearby Attractions: Biltmore House in Asheville, NC, and Blue Ridge Mountains are 1 hour away.

PURE *Gibson*

Whether you are a music lover, a woodworker, or are fascinated by an American business success story, the tour lets you experience the making of this world-famous electric guitar. The company started in 1894 when Orville Gibson created a whole new family of guitars and mandolins. Through the years, the company has had different owners, each facing successes and challenges. The Gibson Corporation of today, dedicated to both its history and innovation in wood technologies, has grown a long way from when it was purchased from bankruptcy for $5 million in 1986.

You walk on the factory floor, within nose length of 16 different workstations for making electric guitars. Although guitar making involves many steps that require hand workmanship, this facility, completed in late 2000, showcases state-of-the-art guitar manufacturing. You see millions of dollars of guitars in various stages of production, from bare woods to finished products. The tour begins with the initial body building from maple and mahogany woods and goes all the way to the last steps when they put on the strings to tone it for final inspection.

Each step has its unique process that combines handwork and machines. For example, the binding process puts a white plastic trim around the outside rim of the guitar to both protect it and make the instrument more attractive. A limber five-foot piece of plastic is put through the glue pot and then wrapped around by hand. A harness is then used to "mummify" it until dried. In a later stage, after the guitar is sprayed with a solvent-based paint, they scrape off the excess so you can still see the shiny white trim.

Notice the special care that goes into the neck fitting, as it is slid into a slot on the body. Hand scrapers are used to make it smooth and straight. At the very end, the electronic parts are put on, including the two pickups, the control pod assembly, the tuner knobs, and the machine heads for the strings. These are used for the sound to resonate through the amplifier. Next time you hear the B. B. King Lucille, the Les Paul Classic, or the Flying V, you will know all about its birth.

Cost: $10 per person.

Freebies: No

Video/DVD Shown: No

Reservations Needed: Recommended

Days and Hours: Mon–Sat 10:00 AM, 11:00 AM, 1:00 PM, 2:00 PM, 3:00 PM, and 4:00 PM; Sun 1:00 PM, 2:00 PM, 3:00 PM, and 4:00 PM. Closed Thanksgiving, Christmas Eve, Christmas, and New Year's.

Plan to Stay: 45 minutes.

Minimum Age: 12, unless can be ensured one-to-one ratio of adults to children. No minimum for museum.

Disabled Access: Yes

Group Requirements: Groups broken into 15 people per group. $2-per-person discount available.

Special Information: No video cameras allowed. Factory is part of a manufacturing and expanding entertainment complex.

Gift Shop: Gibson Store sells logoed merchandise, plus selected guitar models. Open Mon–Sat 10:00 AM–6:00 PM.

Directions: Located downtown, about 1 block south of Beale St.

Nearby Attractions: Sun Studios (birthplace of rock and roll, where Elvis recorded his first song); National Civil Rights Museum; Mississippi River; Graceland is about 8 miles away.

SOUTH

Welcome Center, 100 Saturn Parkway,
Spring Hill, TN 37174

(931) 486-7787 Welcome Center
(800) 326-3321 Plant Tour

www.saturn.com

To many Americans, the Saturn car represents the rebirth of U.S. automobile manufacturing. Since the first General Motors Saturn rolled off the line in 1990, these import-fighting cars have earned a reputation for their high quality, the no-haggle sales approach by retailers, and enthusiastic customers. The manufacturing plant began offering regular public tours in the summer of 1997. A horse barn has been renovated into the new Saturn Welcome Center. The Welcome Center's theme is the "Birthplace of Saturn" and consists of interactive displays and exhibits on the Saturn story.

This highly integrated manufacturing complex includes the power train, general assembly, and body systems buildings. General Motor's Spring Hill site sits on some 2,400 acres of what was previously farmland—in fact, the company currently farms approximately 1,200 acres of land, raising corn, wheat, and soybeans. The GM Spring Hill Manufacturing plant has been designed to blend into the countryside, so very little of the plant can be seen from the highway or the Welcome Center. To see the manufacturing plant, you will need to register for a plant tour and take a 10-minute bus ride from the Welcome Center to the plant.

Near the entrance to the Welcome Center is a kiosk that gives you a short introduction to the company. The displays are arranged in eight horse stalls that can be viewed by starting at either end of the barn. The history stall contains mementos from the site and the founding of Saturn. Other stalls contain videos and memorabilia on teamwork, owner's letters, and community activities. Three of the stalls are dedicated to the manufacturing story.

Cost: Free

Freebies: Product brochures.

Video/DVD Shown: 15-minute video entitled "One Car at a Time" covers Saturn production.

Reservations Needed: No, for Welcome Center; yes, for plant tour. Occasional last-minute cancellations allow walk-in visitors to take a plant tour. Call (800) 326-3321 for information and reservations.

Days and Hours: Welcome Center: Mon–Fri 8:00 AM–5:00 PM. Plant Tour: Mon, Tue, Thur, Fri 8:30 AM, 10:00 AM, 1:00 PM, 2:30 PM; Wed 10 00 AM, 1:00 PM, 2:30 PM. Plant closed holidays, including the day after Thanksgiving, the week between Christmas and New Year's, Good Friday, and 2 weeks in July. Call Welcome Center for hours during holiday weeks.

Plan to Stay: 2 hours for Welcome Center and plant tour.

Minimum Age: 6 with parents, 9 in school groups, for plant tour; none for Welcome Center.

Disabled Access: Yes, for Welcome Center. Call above number for accommodations on plant tour.

Group Requirements: No maximum for Welcome Center, although advance notice appreciated. Maximum 30 people per plant tour time period. Reservations accepted up to 3 months in advance.

Special Information: No cameras, bags, purses, cell phones, or carry-ons of any sort. Visitors must wear safety glasses on tram tour. No shorts. Please call for potential schedule changes.

Gift Shop: No

Directions: From Nashville, take I-65 South. Exit at Rt. 396, Saturn Pkwy. West. Take Hwy. 31 South. Watch for sign.

Nearby Attractions: Rippavilla Plantation; Natchez Trace State Park; Nashville's attractions, including Purity Dairies tour (see page 276) and Grand Ole Opry, about 40 minutes away. Local area around Spring Hill and Columbia includes many antebellum homes and Civil War sites.

SOUTH

Lynchburg, TN 37352   (931) 759-6180   www.jackdaniels.com

In the heavily vegetated, woodsy, hilly terrain of south-middle Tennessee, you feel like you're visiting a national park rather than the world's oldest registered distillery (1866) when you tour Jack Daniel's. A babbling brook follows you through the entire tour. You learn from the tour guide that the water is no coincidence, that Jasper Newton (Jack) Daniel chose this property because of Cave Spring's iron-free water. This pure limestone water flows at 56°F year-round and is one secret of Jack Daniel's fine whiskey.

Your tour begins with a short minivan ride up the hill to one of 45 aging houses. The large wooden structure's air is thick and musty with the smell of whiskey and wood. Your eyes take in only a small fraction of the 20,164 barrels of aging whiskey lined up seven stories high. Four years of warm days and cool nights inside these white-oak barrels give Jack Daniel's whiskey its flavor and color.

In the stackyard (called the "rick yard," for its ricks, or piles of wood), Moore County hard sugar-maple wood is burned to make charcoal. In charcoal mellowing vats the distilled, fermented whiskey seeps through 10 feet of charcoal and a wool blanket at a rate of less than six gallons an hour.

You'll see another interesting whiskey-making step in the hot, noisy mash room. Here, in large tanks called mash tubs, corn, rye, barley malt, water, and yeast ferment for four days. A panel measures the liquid's progress toward becoming 140-proof whiskey.

A wooden structure that resembles an old Southern country farmhouse is actually Jack Daniel's original office, which dates back to 1878. Still in its natural setting, it is filled with period furniture, old file cabinets, and ledgers that documented the company's financial transactions.

Cost: Free

Freebies: Ice-cold glass of lemonade in White Rabbit Saloon after tour.

Video/DVD Shown: Video at tour's beginning explains Jack Daniel's and whiskey making.

Reservations Needed: No, except for groups larger than 30 people.

Days and Hours: Mon–Sun 9:00 AM–4:30 PM. Closed Thanksgiving, Christmas Eve, Christmas Day, New Year's Eve, and New Year's. During 2-week July shutdown, you follow standard tour route, even though distillery isn't in production.

Plan to Stay: 1 hour for videos and tour.

Minimum Age: None

Disabled Access: Yes. Specially designed van tour for people in wheelchairs.

Group Requirements: Groups larger than 30 should call on Thursday of week before visit.

Special Information: Lots of walking, so wear comfortable shoes. Tour booklets available in major foreign languages. Distillery is designated a National Historical Landmark.

Gift Shop: Just about every store in Lynchburg sells Jack Daniel's souvenirs but no whiskey. Lynchburg Hardware and General Store has largest selection, including old-time saloon mirror, wooden whiskey chest, stoneware jugs, and playing cards. Catalog available at above number.

Directions: From Nashville, take I-24 East to Exit 111. Turn left onto Hwy. 55 and follow it through Mancester and Tullahoma to Lynchburg. The visitors center parking lot is on the left. From Chattanooga, take I-24 West to Exit 111. Follow above directions.

Nearby Attractions: Lynchburg is filled with Southern charm and hospitality. Visit courthouse and Miss Mary Bobo's Boarding House (Southern-style food served).

SOUTH

MasterCraft

Knoxville, Tennessee, is to boats what Detroit, Michigan, is to cars. More boats are made in Knoxville than anywhere in the world. MasterCraft, the largest inboard boat manufacturer in the world, builds about 3,500 boats per year. Their boats are in high demand, especially by water-skiers and wakeboarders—more world records have been shattered behind MasterCraft ski boats than any other boats.

Unlike cars, which are painted last, boats are spray-painted first. In the 72,000-square-foot lamination building, workers spray gel coat into each boat mold. Afterwards, they peel the masking tape off and then spray colored stripes. Fiberglass is hand-laid into the mold. After unfurling each cloth-like layer of fiberglass, the worker uses a hand roller to pop out the air bubbles. For each boat, a worker repeats this laying out and rolling process for up to 22 layers of fiberglass. During your tour, you see 40 to 50 boats in different stages of production. Each day, 18 boats start the cycle and 18 boats finish. Notice that most of the process is done by hand—there's hardly any automation, another difference between boat and car assembly.

After lamination, each boat is pushed outdoors on its dolly to the adjacent 72,000-square-foot rigging building. Pass by the sewing department. Rolls of upholstery are cut and sewn. On dollies, boats move along the rigging line for assembly. Decks are attached. While the boat is hoisted up, the engine slides in and a mechanic tightens the bolts. After the steering wheel is inserted, the upholstery is set over the seat bracing.

Once assembled, each boat is water tested for 45 minutes to ensure optimal performance, testing out the RPMs and turning radius. As you watch the water test on beautiful Lake Tellico, located in front of the factory, you'll wish you were skiing or wakeboarding behind the boat.

Cost: Free

Freebies: Commemorative tour T-shirt.

Video/DVD Shown: Plays in lobby.

Reservations Needed: Highly recommended.

Days and Hours: Mon–Thur 2:00 PM. No production Fridays. Closed between Christmas and New Year's and during model changes for 1–3 weeks in July.

Plan to Stay: 40 minutes, plus time in the gift area.

Minimum Age: None, however small children must be able to wear the supplied safety glasses.

Disabled Access: Yes

Group Requirements: Maximum 10–12 people. Call at least 1 week in advance.

Special Information: No photography. Noisy in lamination building.

Gift Shop: Sells license plates and logoed merchandise, including logoed life jackets. Located in sportswear coordinator's office. Open Mon–Thur 9:00 AM–5:00 PM.

Directions: From Knoxville, take Rt. 129 South, which runs into Hwy. 411 South. Travel through Vonore. Turn right onto Hwy. 72 West. Turn into Tellico West Industrial Park. Follow signs. From the south, take I-75 North. At Exit 72, turn right onto Hwy. 72. Travel 17 miles. Turn left into Tellico West Industrial Park. Follow signs. From the north, take I-75 South. At Exit 72, turn left onto Hwy. 72. Follow above directions.

Nearby Attractions: Sea Ray boat tour (call 423-884-6631); Great Smoky Mountain National Park; Knoxville attractions 50 minutes away include University of Tennessee.

SOUTH

NISSAN

Imagine 94 football fields side-by-side and back-to-back, all under one roof! That would be an unfathomable size for a sports complex, but it is the size of Nissan's first U.S. manufacturing plant. Since the plant began production in 1983, the unemployment rate in Rutherford County has been cut in half. On your tour, you are shuttled through an enormous facility, where 6,700 Nissan employees and 2,400 contractors and on-site suppliers build Frontier trucks, Xterra sport utility vehicles, Altima sedans, Maxima sedans, and Pathfinder sport utility vehicles.

Zigzagging through the massive welding operation, you feel as if you are on a movie set. Look up at the conveyor systems suspended from the ceiling as sparks fly from tentacle-like robot arms welding together the main body parts of the vehicle shell. The Intelligent (or "smart") Body Assembly System (IBAS) is a mixture of automation and computerization. IBAS robots replace the conventional jigs that hold steel panels together as the Altima body is welded. The computerized capabilities of the system allow for more than one model of vehicle to be assembled in the system before lasers check the accuracy of the welds.

As your tour guide maneuvers the shuttle along the maze of aisles, the unmistakable smell of fresh paint begins to fill your nostrils. While in the paint facility, gaze through glass that encloses the paint lines. Here, in a precise and lengthy process, robots and humans apply layers of protective coatings, primer, and paint. Employees carefully check each vehicle's finish as part of the quality control system. You can feel the heat as you pass the enclosed paint-bake ovens, where the paint finish is baked onto each vehicle.

In the final assembly areas, you see the human touch. With heads bowed in concentration and fingers flying, people install the hundreds of parts that transform the painted vehicle shells into dynamic

machines. It's fun to witness the finishing touches in the final production stages as workers put in seats or install tires on the moving production line, where up to 550,000 vehicles are produced each year.

Cost: Free

Freebies: Yes, collectible Nissan magnet featuring a Nissan vehicle.

Video/DVD Shown: 10-minute overview of Nissan North America operations, including manufacturing at the Smyrna and Canton, MS, vehicle assembly plants and the nearby Decherd, TN, engine assembly plant.

Reservations Needed: Yes. Maximum of 50 people per tour, whether individuals, families, or groups. Occasional last-minute reservations, so it's worth a call to see if you can fit into tour.

Days and Hours: Tue and Thur 10:00 AM and 1:00 PM. Closed holidays, week between Christmas and New Year's, and 1 week in early July.

Plan to Stay: 1.5 hours for video and tour.

Minimum Age: 10 (5th grade).

Disabled Access: Yes

Group Requirements: Maximum of 50 people per time period. Reservations accepted up to 3 months in advance.

Special Information: No photography or shorts. Tours are also offered at Nissan's Canton, MS, vehicle assembly plant by calling (601) 855-TOUR and at Nissan's Decherd, TN, engine assembly plant by calling (931) 962-5624.

Gift Shop: Yes

Directions: From Nashville, take I-24 East toward Chattanooga. Take Exit 70 (Almaville Rd.) and turn left toward Smyrna (Almaville Rd. becomes Nissan Dr.). Nissan is about 3 miles ahead on right. Enter Gate 1.

Nearby Attractions: Sam Davis Home; attractions in Murfreesboro (geographic center of Tennessee) include Stones River Battlefield, Oakland Mansion, and antique stores. Nashville's attractions, including Purity Dairies tour (see page 276) and Grand Old Opry, are 20 miles away.

SOUTH

A cheery ice-cream parlor welcomes you to Purity Dairies' ice-cream plant. In the tour room, the 81-year-old company shows a film about milk and the manufacturing of their dairy products. Then the big blue curtain opens, revealing a huge window with a panoramic view of the ice-cream factory.

Seeing the production of ice-cream sandwiches or Nutty Buddies is almost like watching a live theater performance, with each player taking a specific role. The show is a continuous interaction of machinery, humanity, and ice cream. In the foreground, two women handle the sandwich or Nutty Buddy machine. One feeds chocolate wafers or sugar cones into the machine, which squirts out the exact amount of vanilla ice cream filling for each novelty product. The other worker boxes the products after they have been automatically wrapped. A complicated labyrinth of overhead piping, frosty and dripping with condensation, runs throughout the plant. A milk-based mixture is pumped to various stainless-steel machines, where it is flavored, transformed into ice cream, and shot into individual cartons. The cartons are automatically shrink-wrapped and sent to the freezer for hardening.

Across the lot is the milk plant, where 15,000 gallons of milk are processed and packaged daily. The daily production of 10,500 pounds of cottage cheese causes a natural sour odor in the room where Purity makes Little Miss Muffet's curds and whey. An enormous stainless-steel tub filled with the white lumpy stuff comes into view, and your guide explains the intricacies of separating curds and whey to produce cottage cheese.

In another part of this facility, Purity manufactures its own plastic milk containers. It takes 7,754 plastic beans to make a gallon jug. At the end of the tour, visitors convene at the weigh station and the group is collectively weighed. Here the Purity trucks are also weighed before heading out to make deliveries. The loud moo you might hear is the horn on one of Purity's special home-delivery trucks, painted white with large black spots that resemble a . . . guess what? (The horn is a hint.)

Cost: Free

Freebies: Ice-cream samples and goody bags.

Video/DVD Shown: 15-minute movie about Purity's milk and other products.

Reservations Needed: Yes, please call (615) 760-2271, ext. 489.

Days and Hours: Mon–Fri 10:00 AM, 11:00 AM, and 1:00 PM.

Plan to Stay: 1 hour for video and tour.

Minimum Age: None

Disabled Access: 10 steps leading up into plant entrance.

Group Requirements: Adult tours need at least 4 months' advance reservations; children's tours, 8 weeks ahead. Group tours are booked far in advance. Maximum group size is 40.

Special Information: Because company has expanded marketing territory, tour is very popular. Book as far ahead as possible.

Gift Shop: No

Directions: From Alabama, take I-65 North to I-440 Knoxville. Take Murfreesboro Rd. exit. Go down to the light. Turn left onto Murfreesboro Rd. Purity Dairies is 1.5 miles on the right.

From Kentucky, take I-65 South to I-40 East. As soon and you pass Downtown Nashville and are on I-40, take exit for Fesslers Lane. At end of the ramp, turn right at the light. At next light, turn right onto Elm Hill Pike. Purity Dairies is 0.25 mile down on the right.

Nearby Attractions: Nissan tour (see page 275); Grand Old Opry; Opry Mills.

Heartland

CANADA

MONTANA

Billings

see Rocky Mountains
page 321

WYOMING

I-25

Laramie

Denver

COLORADO

Colorado Springs

80 mi

80 km

NORTH DAKOTA

Minot

Bismarck

I-94

PIPESTEM CREEK

Grand Fork

SOUTH DAKOTA

HOMESTAKE GOLD MINE

SIOUX POTTERY AND CRAFTS
MT RUSHMORE GOLD

Rapid City

Pierre

I-90

MINNESOTA

Duluth

St Paul
Minneapolis

WINNEBAGO INDUSTRIES

NEBRASKA

I-80

AFFINITY

KOOL-AID

Lincoln

HARLEY-DAVIDSON MOTOR COMPANY
HALLMARK VISITOR CENTER

Topeka

Kansas City

HALLMARK CARDS

REUTER ORGANS

I-70

KANSAS

Wichita

KEEPSAKE CANDLES

FRANKOMA POTTERY

Tulsa

Oklahoma City

OKLAHOMA

I-35

see Texas
page 297

Lubbock

TEXAS

I-20

see Southwest
page 311

Santa Fe

Albuquerque

I-40

Amarillo

NEW MEXICO

Lake Superior

MICHIGAN

WISCONSIN

Green Bay

I-94

Madison

I-43

Lake Michigan

Lansing

IOWA

JOHN DEERE

KRAUSS FURNITURE SHOP

Des Moines

see Great Lakes
page 147

I-80

ILLINOIS

INDIANA

Springfield

Indianapolis

I-70

St Louis

BOEING
ANHEUSER-BUSCH

PURINA FARMS

MISSOURI

I-44

I-55

KENTUCKY

I-65

WAL-MART VISITORS CENTER

ARKANSAS

I-40

Nashville

I-40

TENNESSEE

Memphis

Little Rock

see South
page 221

ALABAMA

MISSISSIPPI

Birmingham

105 North Main Street, Bentonville, AR 72712   (479) 273-1329   www.walmart
stores.com

The Wal-Mart retail empire, with more than a million employees (called "associates") and billions of dollars in yearly revenues, began in the building that now houses the Visitors Center. From the outside, it's an exact replica of the first Walton's 5 & 10, opened by Sam and Helen Walton in 1950. The folksy center brings together the history, growth, philosophy, and present-day scope of the company. As you walk on the original checkerboard red and green linoleum tile floor, examining the displays and watching the videos, you're surrounded by a true American business success.

Merchandise from the 1950s and '60s sits in the front window. In the lobby is a cut-out figure of Sam Walton (the store's first manager) next to a huge mural showing a typical 5 & 10 of the early '50s. Family portraits and other murals of the company's operations also hang throughout the center, along with early newspaper ads and memorabilia. The center has more than 40 separate displays. The most popular are the laser video programs on the history of the company and on the Walton family. One large exhibit is a timeline that traces the Wal-Mart story from its variety store roots to the present day. Mementos, photos, and products such as old Barbie dolls fill the display. At the push of a button is a narrated, illuminated photomap tracking the nationwide spread of Wal-Mart stores.

The Visitors Center holds many of Sam's prized possessions. The Presidential Medal of Freedom, the nation's highest civilian award, which Sam Walton received in 1992, is proudly displayed. So are his old red pickup truck and original office, complete with the apple crate used as a chair for guests. Other exhibits include Wal-Mart and Wall Street, Community Involvement, Satellite Communications, and Saving the Environment.

The Buy American exhibit features a changing display of the American-made products that Wal-Mart sells and the jobs created by this partnership of retailers and domestic manufacturers. The long-range goal of the Buy American program is to re-establish the competitive position of U.S.–made goods. You leave understanding more about the people and heritage behind what has been called "the retailing phenomenon of the century."

Cost: Free

Freebies: No

Videos/DVDs Shown: Several video programs on the company, the Walton family, the Medal of Freedom, and conversations between Sam and his brother.

Reservations Needed: No, however, recommended for groups of 10 or more.

Days and Hours: Tue–Sat 9:00 AM–5:00 PM. Closed Thanksgiving, Christmas, and New Year's.

Plan to Stay: 30 minutes, plus time for videos.

Minimum Age: None, but recommends children be at least 10 to appreciate and enjoy the exhibits.

Disabled Access: Yes

Group Requirements: Groups of 10 or more should call 2 days in advance.

Special Information: Exhibits change to reflect Wal-Mart developments. You may want to schedule your visit around Wal-Mart Stores, Inc.'s annual meeting (usually first week in June) in nearby Fayetteville. Tens of thousands attend the largest annual meeting in the U.S.A., which features live entertainment, enthused employees, and a real sense of the corporate culture.

Gift Counter: Sells Wal-Mart and Visitors Center logoed items, including mugs, key chains, and T-shirts. Open same hours as Visitors Center.

Directions: Take Hwy. 71 or Hwy 71B to Hwy. 72. The Visitors Center is on the west side of the square in downtown Bentonville. Look for the big American flag and the building that says "Walton's 5 & 10."

Nearby Attractions: Terra Pottery Studios tour, 20 miles away, in Fayetteville (call 479-643-3185); University of Arkansas; Beaver Lake; Eureka Springs.

HEARTLAND

Waterloo Works, 3500 East Donald Street,
Waterloo, IA 50701

(319) 292-7668
(800) 765-9558

www.deere.com

Deere began building tractors in downtown Waterloo in 1918 and moved to the current location in 1981. Many of the old two-cylinder John Deere tractors, manufactured from 1918 to 1960 and affectionately known as "Johnny Poppers," are still in active use. The tour shows you manufacturing techniques to make their highly rated tractors.

A company retiree leads your tour through the tractor assembly buildings (48 acres). The air is filled with the scent of machine oil and the sound of laser welders and robots. Tractor-building requires many subassembly steps, such as constructing the cab, before the main assembly lines put it all together. An automatic system-guided vehicle pulls the tractors through assembly, keeping computerized tabs on parts drawn from some 40,000 storage bins. Lasers cut out plates for the sides of fuel tanks. Robotic welders join parts with impressive consistency and rainbows of sparks.

Three chassis lines and three final assembly lines move at a synchronized pace. In about two hours, the tractor frames become complete machines. Notice how carefully the cab and other parts are lowered from an overhead conveyor hoist and mounted on the tractor frame. Near the end of the line, after fluids are added, workers test wheel-less tractors for such features as engine start-up, speed and power levels, and brake and park/lock security.

Tractors are assembled using a modular, team concept. The production area is arranged in process groups called "cells," with each cell's operators responsible for assembling a related family of parts. Once a cell's work is completed and checked, the tractor moves to the next cell.

Cost: Free

Freebies: Brochure on tractor production.

Video/DVD Shown: 16-minute video overviews the entire John Deere Waterloo Works.

Reservations Needed: Preferred for individuals. Required for groups and families.

Days and Hours: Mon–Fri 8:00 AM, 10:00 AM, and 1:00 PM. Closed major holidays and week between Christmas and New Year's. Summer shutdown first two weeks of August. (Call about more extended summer shutdown.)

Plan to Stay: 2 hours.

Minimum Age: 13

Disabled Access: Yes

Group Requirements: Groups larger than 6 people should make reservations 10 days in advance.

Special Information: No cameras, cell phones, or video cameras. For information on John Deere factory tours nationwide (including Davenport, Dubuque, Des Moines, and Ottumwa, IA), call Visitors' Services at Corporate Headquarters in Moline, IL (800-765-9588). East Moline, IL, plant produces harvesters (see page 155). John Deere Pavilion in Moline, IL, displays history of agriculture exhibits (see page 156).

Gift Shop: The Deere Crossing sells a wide variety of logoed items, including T-shirts, hats, and belt buckles. Open to tour visitors. Call (319) 292-7564 about other hours.

Directions: From Dubuque, take Hwy. 20 West to Exit 68 North in Waterloo. Follow exit road north. Turn left onto Gilbertville Rd. Turn right onto North Elk Run Rd. Turn left onto East Donald St. From Des Moines, take I-80 East to Hwy. 63 North. Exit at Hwy. 20 East to Waterloo Exit 68 North. Follow the directions above.

Nearby Attractions: Other John Deere tours in Waterloo available at the Foundry, Drive Train, and Engine Works (call 319-292-7668 for information); Grout Museum of History and Science; Waterloo Community Arts Centre; George Wyth Memorial State Park.

HEARTLAND

Krauss Furniture Shop

2783 Highway 6 Trail, South Amana, IA 52334   (319) 622-3223   (866) 272-6402   www.krauss furn ture.com

Krauss Furniture is located in Iowa's Amana Colonies, which were founded in 1855 by German immigrants escaping religious persecution. The Amana Colonies offer an abundance of family activities, including many craftwork tours. The moment you walk in the door at Krauss, the smell of walnut, cherry, and oak woods mixed with the odor of fresh varnish will tell you this is a furniture factory. As you saunter between the yellow lines on this self-guided tour, you watch as many as 15 craftsmen building custom-made tables, chairs, cupboards, bedroom sets, rockers, and clock cabinets. Krauss completes up to 1,000 pieces per year.

You'll see many different types of woodworking tools, some brand new and others over 80 years old. In the cutting area, workers dry, machine, glue, and rough-sand all the lumber used. A lathe worker, covered head-to-toe with sawdust and chips, turns spindles to make the furniture legs. Planers reduce the boards to equal thickness. They are then glued into panels, rough-sanded, and cut into rough lengths.

Krauss does not use an assembly line to make furniture. Each craftsman has his own workbench and builds the furniture, one piece at a time, from start to finish. The method is the old-time hand-fitted, dovetailed or mortise-and-tenon joinery. Woodworker hobbyists will covet these craftsmen's tools, time, and skill in building furniture. In the finishing area, the workers sand and finish the pieces. The finish, Krauss Furniture's pride, is painstakingly sprayed and brushed on (as many as seven coats) and sanded off until it is completely smooth. When the oil is finally applied for a hand-rubbed finish, workers show the same affection as parents brushing their children's hair.

Cost: Free

Freebies: Product brochure.

Video/DVD Shown: No

Reservations Needed: No, except for motor-coach tours.

Days and Hours: Mon–Fri 8:00 AM–4:00 PM. Sat 9:00 AM–4:00 PM. Not always in full production on Saturday, so call ahead. Closed major holidays.

Plan to Stay: 15 minutes for the self-guided tour, plus time for the showroom.

Minimum Age: None

Disabled Access: Yes

Group Requirements: Bus tour groups can get guided tour. Call 1 week in advance.

Special Information: Sawdusty setting.

Showroom: Sells all Krauss wood pieces, from large furniture to smaller gift items. Most smaller wooden items, such as magazine racks and picture frames, are made by local retired people. Picture albums show custom-designed furniture that can be built to order. Open Mon–Fri 8:00 AM–5:00 PM, Sat 9:00 AM–5:00 PM, and May–December also Sun 1:00–4:00 PM. Catalog available.

Directions: From I-80, take Exit 225 for Hwy. 151 North. At the T intersection with Hwy. 6 Trail, go left 2 miles. Krauss Furniture is on the north side of Hwy. 6 Trail (large clock outside building). From Hwy. 6 Trail West, Krauss is about 1 mile east of South Amana.

Nearby Attractions: The Amana Colonies have a number of attractions and a world-renowned tradition of craftsmanship. Some other local businesses that offer tours or work-area viewings include Amana Woolen Mill (call 319-622-3432), Schanz Furniture and Refinishing (call 319-622-3529), Amana Furniture and Clock Shop (call 319-622-3291), Ehrle Brothers Winery (call 319-622-3241), and Village Winery (call 319-622-3448).

Winnebago Industries was born in 1958, when a group of local businesses, worried about Iowa's depressed farm economy, persuaded Modernistic Industries of California to build a travel-trailer factory in Forest City. Local businessmen soon bought the factory and, in 1960, named it Winnebago Industries, after the county in which it was located. Since 1966, when the company started making motor homes, the name Winnebago has become synonymous with "motor home."

You will not doubt Winnebago's self-proclaimed position as an industry leader after touring the world's largest RV production plant. The company prides itself on its interlocking joint construction and on the fact that it produces the majority of parts in-house, including fabric covers for its seats and sofas. The 200-acre factory includes the main assembly areas (which you'll see on the tour), metal stamping division, plastics facility, sawmill and cabinet shop, and sewing and design departments.

In the chassis prep building (not on tour), parts of the all-steel frame are stamped out. Sparks fly as workers weld floor joints and storage compartments to the chassis. The completed RV (including windshield) will be set into this steel frame. The front end drops from a mezzanine onto the chassis and is aligned by laser beams.

The motor-home production lines are in a building employees affectionately call "Big Bertha." From your vantage point on the catwalk, you'll see the developing motor homes creep down three 1,032-foot-long assembly lines at 21 inches per minute. First, workers install a heat-resistant laminated floor. Next, they install the bathroom fixtures, then screw the Thermo-Panel sidewalls (made of block foam embedded with an aluminum frame and steel supports, interior paneling, and an exterior fiberglass skin) onto steel outriggers extending from the floor of the motor home. Farther down the line, cabinets are installed.

Finally, the entire unit receives a one-piece, fiberglass-covered, laminated roof. The motor home is then driven to the company's Stitchcraft building to receive its furniture and window coverings. The completed motor home is rigorously inspected in the test chambers, where it experiences severe "rainstorms." Select units also travel through a test track of road hazards.

Cost: Free

Freebies: Product brochures.

Video/DVD Shown: 22-minute "Winnebago Industries—A Closer Look" video takes you through a detailed view of the world's largest motor-home factory. When no factory tours, visitors can watch this video as well as informative videos on individual Winnebago and Itasca motor homes.

Reservations Needed: No, except for groups larger than 6 people.

Days and Hours: April–October: Mon–Fri 9:00 AM and 1:00 PM; November–mid-December: Mon–Fri 1:00 PM. No tours mid-December–March 31. Closed holidays and 1 week in July.

Plan to Stay: 1.5 hours for video and tour, plus time for Visitors Center motor-home exhibits and wall displays.

Minimum Age: No, but small children must be accompanied by an adult.

Disabled Access: Yes, for Visitors Center. Factory tour includes 3 staircases.

Group Requirements: Groups larger than 6 people should make reservations 2 weeks in advance.

Special Information: Photography allowed in Visitors Center but not in plant.

Gift Shop: Winnebago-Itasca Travelers Club gift shop sells logoed items, including jackets, shirts, and caps. Open 8:30 AM–4:00 PM year-round. Closed holidays.

Directions: From I-35, exit at Hwy. 9 West. At junction of Hwy. 9 and Hwy. 69, take Hwy. 69 South. Turn right on B14 and immediately turn right on 4th St. in Forest City. Visitors Center is on right.

Nearby Attractions: Pammel RV Park; Pilot Knob State Park; Mansion Museum; Waldorf College; Heritage Park.

HEARTLAND

See color photos, page 54.

Birthdays, graduations, weddings, and holidays all have one thing in common—they are perfect occasions to send a Hallmark card. Travel into the world of Hallmark and find out exactly what it takes to make a card at their 716,000-square-foot, two-story manufacturing plant in Topeka, Kansas. As you walk into the receptionist area, look to your right to see a wooden mural by former Hallmark artist Robert Sneeburg. After receiving safety instructions (stay between the marked lines), prepare to enter an enormous factory floor and experience why Hallmark can say, "When you care enough to send the very best."

Your tour guide, who works on the manufacturing floor, begins the tour at the foil department. Hallmark's reputation for intricate detail is evident as you watch gold, silver, and other color foils being applied to create captions, art design, and lettering on cards. In contrast, your next stop at the large die-cut area proves that Hallmark is an enormous operation. Massive machines standing taller and wider than a conversion van cut cards out of litho sheets and send them down a conveyer belt to be stacked.

Next, walk past the clang-clunk of the die-cut machines to the screen-print operation. Screen-printing applies ink to large sheets of stock. Each sheet that comes out travels along a 30-foot round conveyer to allow the ink to dry. See the end of the manufacturing process as you walk through folding, quality control, and packaging.

Your last stop on the first floor is envelope production. It's the nosiest and one of the busiest rooms in the factory, where envelope machines produce over 3 billion envelopes per year for all of Hallmark. Watch five-foot-high paper stock disappear into the machines and emerge as a completed envelope only a little larger than your hand.

The second floor is devoted to more detailing and packaging. Enter the Christmas card box-set area. From February to October, this area die-cuts, folds, and packages all the Christmas card sets you see in stores. Next, walk through the handwork area where employees perform miscellaneous packaging/repackaging and hand-finishing touches. Then walk into the "flitter" department, where they add that extra sparkle to many Hallmark cards. You can guess what their specialty is—glitter!

Cost: Free

Freebies: Hallmark pencil.

Video/DVD Shown: No

Reservations Needed: Yes, all groups must give notice at least 1 week in advance.

Days and Hours: Mon–Fri 8:30 AM–10:00 AM, 12:30 PM–2:00 PM.

Plan to Stay: 1 hour.

Minimum Age: 12

Disabled Access: Yes

Group Requirements: Groups of 10 or more should call at least 2 weeks in advance. Maximum group size is 45.

Special Information: No cameras allowed. No cell phones used in plant during tour. Hallmark Visitors Center in Kansas City, MO (see pages 286).

Gift Shop: No

Directions: From I-70 East, take Exit 183 for downtown and Salina. Get off at 4th St. exit onto Madison St. Turn left at stop light into Hallmark parking lot. From I-70 West, take 3rd St. exit. Continue through intersection to stoplight. Turn left at light onto 4th St. Hallmark parking lot will be on your left.

Nearby Attractions: State Capitol Building; Governor's Mansion; Kansas Museum of History; *Topeka Capital-Journal;* Air Museum (Forbes Field); Gage Park and Zoo.

Since 1917, Reuter Organ Company has produced custom-built organs for churches, universities, and homes. Housed in a 75,000-square-foot building, 50 craftsmen build 6 to 12 pipe organs per year. Construction of each organ takes two to four months, so you'll see several in progress during your tour.

No two organs are identical. Each organ's size depends on its site, so engineers draw individualized musical and architectural plans. Musical plans incorporate pipe scales and other aspects relating to acoustics. Architectural plans specify arrangement of the parts and perhaps a rendering of the finished and installed organ.

In the pipe department, workers cut sheets of zinc, copper, and spotted metal (a tin-lead alloy) to each pipe's size and shape. Metal is rolled on mandrels to form the pipes, then pipes are hand-soldered or tig-welded. Pipes range from 32 feet tall to the size of a pencil. The number of pipes in each organ varies from a few hundred to over 6,000. Pipes are arranged in ranks, a rank having 61 pipes. Each rank is analogous to an orchestral instrument. "Voicers" essentially "teach" these new organ pipes to "sing," then refine their sound so each rank's pipes sound like one voice.

As you tour this factory building, notice the skilled woodworkers and metalsmiths meticulously hand-fashioning organ parts. As you smell the raw wood and feel the sheepskin leather, appreciate the handwork that goes into each organ. The wood used for the console, organist's bench, and decorative case matches the purchaser's décor.

Everything comes together in the assembly room. Here, workers assemble the wind chest and build the framework that supports the organ. They test the organ musically, in the same arrangement as its final destination. Now you hear the full "color of sounds" that the different organ ranks create. Once you see the fully assembled creation, you'll understand why the pipe organ is known as the King of Instruments.

Cost: Free

Freebies: Brochures

Video/DVD Shown: No

Reservations Needed: Yes, please phone ahead to schedule tour.

Days and Hours: Mon–Fri 10:00 AM–2:00 PM, break from 12:00 PM–1:00 PM. Closed holidays and Christmas through New Year's.

Plan to Stay: 1 hour.

Minimum Age: No, for families; age 12, for groups.

Disabled Access: Yes

Group Requirements: Groups larger than 15 people will be divided into smaller groups, each with its own guide. Call 2 weeks in advance for reservations. Maximum group size is 25–30 people.

Special Information: Walking shoes recommended. Finished organs are not tested on every tour because an organ is completed every 1–2 months. Call ahead to arrange your tour accordingly.

Gift Shop: No

Directions: From Kansas City, take I-70 West to West Lawrence exit. Turn right at first light on Princeton. Turn right again at stop sign on North Iowa St. Proceed north on North Iowa St. about 1.5 miles. Round the corner at Lakeview Rd. and turn right onto Timberedge Rd. Enter the Reuter building on the west side. From Topeka, take I-70 East to West Lawrence exit and follow above directions.

Nearby Attractions: Historic Downtown Lawrence; Riverfront Mall; Kansas University; Haskell Indian Nations University; Hallmark Cards tour (see page 282) in Topeka, about 40 minutes away; attractions in Kansas City, MO, including the Hallmark Visitors Center (see page 286), are about 45 minutes away.

12th and Lynch Streets, St. Louis, MO 63118 | (314) 577-2626 | www.budweiser tours.com

The tour of the St. Louis brewery (founded 1852), located next to the Anheuser-Busch World Headquarters, puts a face on the world's largest brewer. As the tour guide leads you from the tour center to the Budweiser Clydesdale paddock and stable, lager cellar, Brew House, Lyon's Schoolhouse, and Bevo packaging plant, a sense of history and the smell of hops surround you.

The Budweiser Clydesdales tradition began in 1933 when August A. Busch Jr. presented his father with the first team of Clydesdales to celebrate the repeal of Prohibition. Today the gentle giants make more than 500 appearances annually with their bright red beer wagon. See where the beer is actually made in the historic six-story Brew House. Built in 1891, the Brew House is a tour favorite with its clock tower, ornate wrought-iron railings, and hop vine chandeliers from the 1904 World's Fair. The Lyon School House, built in 1868, is the oldest structure in the Anheuser-Busch complex. It served as the company's headquarters from 1907 until 1981.

Visit the beechwood aging and fermentation cellars and Bevo Packaging Plant. Anheuser-Busch is the only major brewer that still uses the famous beechwood aging process to age and naturally carbonate its beers. In the lager cellar, stainless-steel lager tanks are lined with a layer of beechwood chips, providing additional surface area to attract and retain yeast. Beechwood aging is part of the secondary fermentation. Each of the lager tanks holds enough beer to fill approximately 200,000 six-packs.

The Bevo Packaging Plant was constructed in 1917 and stands eight stories tall and houses 27 acres of floor space and over 25 miles of conveyor belts. You will see fast-paced action as bottles and cans are filled. Whimsical fox sculptures are perched on each corner of the building, all munching on chicken legs and holding a mug of Bevo, a nonalcohol cereal-based beverage that Anheuser-Busch produced during the Prohibition era.

Cost: Free

Freebies: For guests 21 or older, beer samples, soda, and snacks.

Videos/DVDs Shown: Brew House: multimedia presentation tells story of brewing process. Bevo Packaging Plant: 3-minute video tells how bottles and cans are filled with the world's favorite brews.

Reservations Needed: No, except for groups of 15 or more.

Days and Hours: March–May, Sept–Oct: Mon–Sat 9:00 AM–4:00 PM, Sun 11:30 AM–4:00 PM. June–Aug: Mon–Sat 9:00 AM–5:00 PM, Sun 11:30 AM–5:00 PM. Nov–Feb: Mon–Sat 10:00 AM–4:00 PM, Sun 11:30 AM–4:00 PM. Schedules change; visit website for up-to-date schedules. Call for holiday hours.

Plan to Stay: 1.25 hours for tour, plus additional time for gift shop.

Minimum Age: Under age 18 must be accompanied by adult.

Disabled Access: Yes

Group Requirements: Groups larger than 15 should call 1 week ahead.

Special Information: Anheuser-Busch also gives tours in Merrimack, NH; Jacksonville, FL; Fort Collins, CO; and Fairfield, CA. For general information on all tours, see above website. See page 77 for feature on Merrimack, NH, tour.

Gift Shop: The Anheuser-Busch Gift Shop sells clothing, hats, glassware, beach gear, framed pictures, and Anheuser-Busch logoed items. Gift shop closes 90 minutes after last tour.

Directions: Take I-55 to Arsenal St. exit. Follow signs to Tour Center (on 12th and Lynch Sts.).

Nearby Attractions: St. Louis area attractions include Boeing Museum (see page 285), Grant's Farm, St. Louis Zoo, Gateway Arch, Union Station and Science City, Missouri Botanical Garden, St. Louis Science Center, and International Bowling Museum & Hall of Fame. Tour Center front desk has information sheet with directions and hours for nearby attractions.

See color photos, page 2.

HEARTLAND

Boeing

James S. McDonnell Prologue Room,
McDonnell Boulevard and Airport Road,
Building 100, St. Louis, MO 63134

(314) 232-6896   www.boeing.com

The Boeing Company in St. Louis calls its company museum the Prologue Room, after William Shakespeare's comment that "what is past is prologue." To Boeing, past achievements are not history but the beginning of each new technical advancement. As you stand on the steps overlooking the museum room, you'll realize Boeing's part in aviation's past, present, and future. Models of commercial planes, missiles, spacecraft, and fighter jets of all sizes and colors seem to be everywhere.

Boeing aircraft built in St. Louis downed every enemy fighter shot down during Operation Desert Storm. With this track record, the display of military planes will pique your curiosity. A wide, oval glass case shows the evolution of Boeing military planes from aviation's golden age in the 1930s to the most current technology. In the center of the oval are one-seventh-scale models of the F/A-18 Hornet, F-15 Eagle, and AV-8B Harrier combat fighters, and the AH-64 Apache helicopter. A glass oval in the back of the museum has a similar display for the generations of the company's commercial aircraft, from the DC-1 (the first successful commercial passenger plane) to the Boeing 777.

Although the museum does not show how Boeing builds its products, displays do provide a complete history of its aviation products. Aviation buffs can study aircraft and fighter plane lineage charts and display cases depicting Boeing's numerous firsts, such as building the first planes to land at the North and South Poles. The center of the museum contains full-size engineering mock-ups of the Mercury and Gemini spacecraft that carried America's early astronauts into space. In the era before computer-aided design, engineers had to build these full-scale models to test the practicality of their hand-drawn designs.

Notice the aviation-art gallery, which features oil paintings by several artists whose work is also displayed in the National Air and Space Museum in Washington, D.C. You leave understanding how since 1916 Boeing products have affected wars' outcomes, made worldwide travel possible, and helped explore the universe.

Cost: Free

Freebies: No

Video/DVD Shown: Optional video in gallery area runs for 2 hours. Consists of shorter videos presenting company history, building of jet fighters, and Boeing planes in flight accompanied by music. Can watch 5 minutes of it or the entire video.

Reservations Needed: No

Days and Hours: June–August only, except for school programs, Mon–Sat 9:00 AM–4:00 PM. Closed July 4th.

Plan to Stay: 45 minutes for museum, plus time for video.

Minimum Age: None, but 6 years old recommended to appreciate displays.

Disabled Access: Yes

Group Requirements: Groups larger than 20 should call ahead to arrange a guided tour. During school year, programs available for 4th, 5th, and 6th graders, with maximum group size of 30.

Special Information: The Boeing Company in Everett, Washington, also gives tours (see page 346).

Retail Store: Located 5 minutes away at 5900 N. Lindbergh Blvd. (314-895-7019), corner of Lindbergh and McDonnell Blvd. Sells aviation posters, photos, and models, plus Boeing-logoed items including T-shirts, caps, jackets, mugs, and key chains. Open Tue–Fri 10:00 AM–6:00 PM and Sat 10:00 AM–3:00 PM year-round.

Directions: From downtown St. Louis, take I-70 West to I-170 North. Turn left onto Airport Rd. Enter through Boeing Executive Offices gate 2 blocks ahead on the right. Look for large black glass building.

Nearby Attractions: St. Louis's downtown attractions, including Anheuser-Busch (Budweiser) brewery tour (see page 284), are 20 minutes away.

HEARTLAND

Crown Center Complex, 2501 McGee,
Kansas City, MO 64141

(816) 274-3613

www.hallmark
visitorscenter.com

Hallmark

VISITORS CENTER

Hallmark's slogan, "When You Care Enough to Send the Very Best," applies to its visitors center. You will walk through 14 exhibits that tell the story of the world's largest greeting-card company. See a 40-foot historical timeline and learn how Hallmark started when a man named Joyce C. Hall began selling picture postcards from his fourth-floor room at the Kansas City YMCA. The timeline has memorabilia from Hallmark's history intertwined with world events.

During the six-minute multimedia film presentation on the essence of creativity, listen and watch Hallmark artists explain how the creative process works. Did you know that Winston Churchill was an artist? One of his paintings hangs in the visitors center along with other originals by Norman Rockwell, Grandma Moses, and Saul Steinberg.

Another area is devoted to the craft and technology of card production. You can watch a technician make engraving dies—the metal plates that raise the three-dimensional designs on paper—or cutting dies, which work like steel cookie cutters to make unusually shaped cards. Two presses churn out the cards you might purchase 10 months from now. At the touch of a button, you can watch a machine turn ribbon into a miniature star bow and take one home with you.

View clips from Hallmark commercials and Hallmark Hall of Fame television dramas. Costumes, props, and a real Emmy award are on display. Hallmark employees' affection for company founder Hall shows in a display of Christmas trees that employees gave Hall from 1966 to 1982. Each tree's decorations reflect a theme of importance to the company during that year. To experience Hallmark's international appeal (cards sell in more than 100 countries), rub the sheep dog's nose on the handrail of one of the cards to hear birthday greetings in 12 languages. One of the newest exhibits features the Hallmark Keepsake Ornament collection. You can see some of the most popular Keepsake Ornaments, like the Starship Enterprise, the 1957 Corvette, Peanuts characters, and sports heroes.

Cost: Free

Freebies: Postcard and a bow.

Videos/DVDs Shown: Short videos on topics related to the exhibits are shown throughout the visitors center.

Reservations Needed: No, except for guided tours for groups of 10 or more.

Days and Hours: Tue–Fri 9:00 AM–5:00 PM and Sat 9:30 AM–4:30 PM. Closed holidays and most holiday weekends. Also usually closed the first 2–3 weeks in January for yearly renovations.

Plan to Stay: About 1 hour, but can spend any amount of time for self-guided tour.

Minimum Age: None

Disabled Access: Yes. Call (816) 274-3613 for information or visit website.

Group Requirements: Escorted tours available for groups of 10 or more. Groups should make reservations 2–4 weeks in advance. School/youth groups need 1 adult for every 7 children. Call (816) 274-3613 or visit website.

Special Information: Hallmark Cards tour in Topeka, KS (see page 282). Some Hallmark Production Centers in other cities conduct tours by advance reservation; check with visitors center for information.

Gift Shop: Not in visitors center. The closest of the 47,000 independent retail outlets is in Crown Center.

Directions: Located in Crown Center Complex, about 1 mile south of downtown Kansas City. Take Grand Ave. to 25th St. and park in the Crown Center Parking Garage. Proceed to third level of Crown Center shops. The visitors center is located outside Halls department store.

Nearby Attractions: Liberty Memorial World War I Museum (call 816-784-1918); Kaleidoscope children's interactive exhibit (call 816-274-8301); Science City at Union Station (call 816-460-2020).

HEARTLAND

See color photos, page 14.

Kansas City Vehicle & Powertrain Operations, the newest of Harley-Davidson's plants, is the manufacturing home of the VRSC™, Sportster®, and Dyna™ families of motorcycles.

During riding season, note the many employee-owned motorcycles parked out in front as you approach the plant. Inside the Tour Center, view exhibits of models made here, including the second V-Rod® ever produced at this plant, covered with employee signatures. On the tour, you'll see the fabrication area, where sheets of steel go into a hydraulic press. The press lowers, and a fender or a fuel tank appears. Next, a laser cuts off the excess steel from the fender and cuts holes in it for wiring. In the polish area, a robotic arm with a buffer wheel buffs the tank. Watch as machines on the frame line bend steel tubes into the shape of a frame and workers fuse the tubes together. The finished frames pass through quality check and are taken to the paint line.

In the assembly area, each station adds different components of the motorcycles, from the kickstand to the headlamp. At one station, a hook lifts the powertrain (engine and transmission) into the frame. Using industry-leading processes, employees build quality into the motorcycle throughout the assembly operations. After assembly, the completed vehicle is ready for a test run. It is taken into the "roll-test" booth, which has two steel rollers in the floor. A tester rides the bike to check all functions, from the engine to the horn. Finally, the motorcycle is wrapped up in plastic and crated by a robot, before being shipped to a Harley-Davidson dealer.

On the tour, you'll also view assembly of the liquid-cooled Revolution® powertrain, the force behind the VRSC family of motorcycles. The tour wouldn't be complete without a stop in the company's Custom Vehicle Operations, where limited-edition factory custom vehicles are born.

Cost: Free

Freebies: Collectible badge and *The Enthusiast* magazine; product catalogs may also be available.

Video/DVD Shown: Yes

Reservations Needed: No, except for groups of 10 or more. Calling ahead is recommended, since plant tour times and availability may change.

Days and Hours: Tours available at regular intervals Mon–Fri 8:00 AM–1:00 PM. Tour Center open Mon–Fri 8:00 AM–3:00 PM. Closed on major holidays and for year-end maintenance. Tours may be modified at any time due to manufacturing requirements. Please call ahead for complete details.

Plan to Stay: Allow 1.5–2 hours for the factory tour, exhibits, and gift shop.

Minimum Age: 12

Disabled Access: Yes (call ahead).

Group Requirements: Groups of 10 or more must reserve at least 14 days in advance.

Special Information: Fully enclosed shoes are required. Photography is permitted in the Tour Center but not inside the factory. Tour participants aged 18 and older must present a valid government-issued photo ID and complete a registration card. Visitors must pass through a metal detector before entering the plant. Annual Open House during the month of September. Tours are also available at the company's plants in York, PA (see page 123), and Wauwatosa, WI (see page 208).

Gift Shop: Offers a selection of Harley-Davidson souvenir merchandise and features a penny press machine. Open Mon–Fri 8:00 AM–3:00 PM. Closed on major holidays and for year-end maintenance.

Directions: Take I-29 to the 112th St. Exit. Go east on 112th St. to end of street. Turn left on Congress. The factory is the first drive on the right.

Nearby Attractions: Zona Rosa (shopping, dining, and entertainment); Argosy Casino; Parkville; historic Weston; Weston Bend State Park.

HEARTLAND

See color photos, page 18.

Nestlé Purina PetCare Company,
200 Checkerboard Drive, Gray Summit, MO 63039

(314) 982-3232

events.purina.com
/dogs/farms

From its 1894 beginnings as a horse- and mule-feed store to its position today as the world's largest producer of pet food, Nestlé Purina PetCare Company remains focused on animal care and nutrition. Located on the grounds of the oldest and largest animal nutrition center in the world, Purina Farms wants visitors to gain a greater appreciation and understanding of their pets. While the Visitor Center has a few displays about Nestlé Purina PetCare and its products, the complex resembles a family-oriented petting zoo more than a promotion-laden company museum.

A timeline traces the company's 100-year-plus history and product development. You can see classic Purina commercials for products such as Dog Chow, the nation's leading dry dog food. A hands-on exhibit lets you experience the sights and sounds of a pet food factory. Interactive displays teach the basics of pet nutrition and the remarkable sensory and physical abilities of domestic animals. Scent boxes help you experience how a dog smells things, while other displays show the differences between your vision and that of dogs and cats.

The Farm Animal Barn contains sheep, cows, horses, hogs, rabbits, and turkeys. Roll up your sleeves here to romp in the hayloft, pull a rope to determine your "horsepower," pet piglets, or milk a cow. Inside the Pet Center, home for different breeds of dogs, cats, puppies, and kittens, you'll see cats lounging and climbing on a five-story Victorian mansion, complete with special windowsills, stairways, and mantelpieces. Petting windows and outdoor areas for dogs let you cuddle and play with them. The Pet Center also features videos and newsletters with tips on pet care, and next door are two areas for canine competition. You leave having learned more about your favorite pets and about Nestlé Purina PetCare's efforts to keep them well fed.

Cost: Free, except for some special events.

Freebies: Brochures on pet care and the company's products are available by request from front desk.

Videos/DVDs Shown: Video shown in a converted 48-foot grain barn provides a brief history of Nestlé Purina PetCare Company. Short videos shown at selected exhibits.

Reservations Needed: Yes, although they can usually accommodate a large number of visitors.

Days and Hours: Open mid-March–mid-November only. Spring and fall: Wed–Fri 9:30 AM–1:00 PM, Sat–Sun 9:30 AM–3:00 PM. Summer: Tue–Sun 9:30 AM–3:30 PM. Closed holidays.

Plan to Stay: 2 hours for displays in main building, videos, Farm Animal Barn, animal demonstrations, and Pet Center, plus additional time for wagon rides, dog shows, children's play areas, and gift shop.

Minimum Age: None

Disabled Access: Yes

Group Requirements: No maximum group size. Requests 1 week's advance notice for large groups.

Special Information: Special events scheduled throughout the year include "Easter Village," "Country Time," and the very popular "Haunted Hayloft." Hosts more than 60 canine events yearly: All Breed Shows, National Specialties, Herding Trials, Agility Trials, and Lure Coursing, among others. Call for schedule or visit the website.

Gift Shop: Sells animal-decorated items including mugs, cards, pencils, and banks; also logoed clothes and hats. Open same hours as visitors center.

Directions: From St. Louis, take I-44 West. Pass Six Flags Over Mid-America. Take the Gray Summit exit and turn right onto Hwy. 100. Turn left on Country Road MM. Follow signs to Purina Farms.

Nearby Attractions: Shaws Arboretum; Six Flags Over Mid-America.

1600 Center Park Road, Lincoln, NE 68512   (402) 423-6625   www.affinitysnacks.com

Since 1932, Weaver's Potato Chips, now Affinity, has used homegrown potatoes to produce some of the most popular potato chips in its area of the Midwest. It started on Ed Weaver Sr.'s stove with a scrub brush, knife, and kettle. More than 90 percent of Weaver's potato-chip ingredients come straight from Nebraska. Every day, 100,000 pounds of these potatoes are trucked into the factory, where they are dumped into large bins and sent on a short trip through the plant, then a longer trip to stores in 14 states as potato chips.

Unlike most snack-food companies, Affinity currently allows you to view the process up close, sometimes only five feet away from the machines, instead of seeing it from an observation deck or overhead walkway. You can watch as the whole, uncooked potatoes jump into the washers for a hot bath and scrub-down (they always scrub, rather than peel, the potatoes to retain the vitamins). The clean potatoes are then sent to the slicers, where razor-sharp blades quickly slice the potatoes into pieces one one-hundredth of an inch thin. A spiked roller pierces little holes in the chips to prevent blistering while they cook. The slices move to the 35-foot fryer and cook until crispy. You and the cooked chips then move ahead to the packaging room.

The potato chips enter a very modern, high-tech piece of chip-making machinery: an optic sorter. Although you will not be able to see this particular process up close, your tour guide will explain it to you. The optic sorter takes photographs of the chips as they move past the camera's lens. Dark brown, green, and other imperfect potato chips are actually blown off the conveyor by air jets. The rest of the chips move on to the packaging room. Chips are gently conveyed to the sophisticated packaging equipment that automatically weighs, fills, and seals bags. Workers inspect the bags and then hand-pack them into cardboard boxes for storage in the warehouse. Delivery trucks pick them up and deliver them to stores all across the Midwest. Be sure to taste your free sample on the way out.

Cost: Free

Freebies: Half-ounce bag of potato chips.

Video/DVD Shown: No

Reservations Needed: Yes, call at least 1 week in advance.

Days and Hours: Mon–Wed 9:00 AM–11:00 AM and 11:30 AM–1:30 PM. Closed holidays.

Plan to Stay: 30–40 minutes.

Minimum Age: None

Disabled Access: No

Group Requirements: Groups larger than 20 people will be split into smaller groups.

Special Information: Wear comfortable shoes, since there is a lot of standing and walking on the factory floor.

Gift Shop: No

Directions: From I-80, exit at Hwy. 2 in Lincoln. Follow Hwy. 2 West to Rt. 77 South. Take second left into the industrial park. Plant is red, white, and blue building on the left.

Nearby Attractions: Sugar Plum Candies tour (call 402-420-1900); Christian Record Services Braille Printer tour (call 402-488-0981); State Capitol; University of Nebraska; Pioneers Park Nature Center; Star City Shores; Folsom Children's Zoo; Lincoln Children's Museum.

HEARTLAND

Kool-Aid

Hastings Museum of Natural and
Cultural History, 1330 North Burlington Avenue,
Hastings, NE 68902

(402) 461-4629
(800) 508-4629

www.hastings
museum.org

Many of today's business leaders may remember starting down the road to financial success setting up a front-yard stand selling Kool-Aid for a nickel. Since 1927, Kool-Aid has provided young children with fun, fruity relief from summer's thirst, creating some of childhood's fondest memories along the way. In the summer of 2002, the city of Hastings celebrated the 75-year-old birthday of both Kool-Aid and the Hastings Museum by opening "Kool-Aid Discover the Dream." Located downstairs in the Hastings Museum, this 3,300-square-foot exhibit pays homage to Edwin Perkins, the inventor of Kool-Aid, the official soft drink of Nebraska.

As you enter the museum, the Kool-Aid kid draws you downstairs to the exhibit. You first walk into DM Perkins General Store, Edwin's father's store. In this turn-of-the-20th-century storefront, you can play store clerk selling merchandise behind the counter. In the next room, a display shows the birth of an entrepreneur. Starting as a kitchen chemist, Edwin invented many products before he hit upon Kool-Aid.

Next door, the Hastings Room shows the introduction of Kool-Aid. Print up a Kool-Aid packet, measure out the powder, and hand-fill a packet like it was done 75 years ago. Underneath your feet, follow the flowing, undulating ropes of fiber optics creating a river of green, orange, purple, and red Kool-Aid.

In 1931, the Perkins family moved to Chicago. The Chicago Room shows other products Kool-Aid produces, such as bubble gum, ice-cream mixes, and soda. Notice the display of premiums including the plastic pitcher produced in the summer of 1963 when the packages were redesigned to show the smiling pitcher. Try selling Kool-Aid at a 1940s stand offering "Kool-Aid 5¢ a glass." In a small theater, watch five-year segments of commercials spanning 40 years. Generation Xers remember 1970s commercials when the ground would rumble as the jovial Kool-Aid man would break through the nearest wall shouting "Oh yeah!" and provide pitchers of thirst-quenching Kool-Aid.

The General Foods room (Perkins sold his company to General Foods in 1953, which ultimately merged with Kraft in 1988) features an original red, 50-pound fiberglass Kool-Aid man costume. In a diorama, learn how the ad agency art director's son's traced patterns on a frosty windowpane led to the designer's doodles, which became the Pitcher Guy, the friendly, smiling Kool-Aid pitcher inviting young children to quench their thirst.

You leave this exhibit with a true understanding of the history behind Kool-Aid and Perkins's business prowess. And, of course, you'll want to find the nearest ice-cube–filled glass of your favorite Kool-Aid flavor—especially if you visit in the summer.

Cost: Museum: Adults, $6; seniors, $5.50; children 3–12, $4.

Freebies: No

Videos/DVDs Shown: Various DVD interactives show Perkins's early business years and nostalgic TV commercials.

Reservations Needed: No

Days and Hours: Mon–Thur 9:00 AM–5:00 PM, Fri–Sat 9:00 AM–8:00 PM, Sun 10:00 AM–6:00 PM. Extended summer hours Tues–Sun until 8:00 PM. Closed Thanksgiving and Christmas.

Plan to Stay: 30 minutes in exhibit, 3 hours in entire museum, including Super Screen Theatre, Planetarium, and the Museum Store.

Minimum Age: None

Disabled Access: Yes

Group Requirements: Groups over 15 people should call 2 weeks in advance for discount.

Special Information: During second weekend in August, Kool-Aid Days in various locations in Hastings feature entertainment, children's activities, and Kool-Aid man.

Gift Shop: Sells Kool-Aid logoed memorabilia. Open similar hours to museum.

Directions: From I-80, take Rt. 281 South (becomes Burlington Ave.). Turn left on 14th St. Turn right into parking lot.

Nearby Attractions: Stuhr Museum of Prairie Pioneer in Grand Island; Pioneer Village in Minden; The Arch and MONA (Museum of Nebraska Art) 1 hour away in Kearney.

HEARTLAND

Named for the beautiful, pristine stream that flows through the nearby prairie, Pipestem Creek makes an unusual natural product. Ann Hoffert, a former nurse practitioner, established Pipestem Creek in 1991 at her dad's 7,500-acre farm. Her wreaths and bird feeders are made of homegrown sunflowers, millet, barley, ornamental corn, burgundy amaranths, and everlasting flowers. The plants are carefully dried, preserved, and hand-fashioned into large and small edible wreaths, suitable for bird feeders or home decorations. Wreaths and home decorations are sold through national mail-order catalogs as well as in specialty shops and through direct orders.

The drive to Pipestem Creek takes you past acres of planted fields, towering grain elevators, and rumbling tractor/combines, which service the seed business run by Ann Hoffert and her husband on the family farm. Several red, wooden, historic granary buildings and a train depot were removed and restored by Pipestem Creek and house their drying, shipping, and gift-shop facilities. In the white production building, bedecked with vines in the summer and surrounded by flowering beds, workers at large tables carefully assemble the sweet-smelling sunflower heads, corn husks, amaranths, and sheaths of millet or green barley. It can take a worker over an hour to create one of the largest wreaths.

The head gardener comes and goes with armfuls of dried materials, distributing fragrant supplies to the workers. One wall is covered with pictures and informational materials spelling out Pipestem Creek's history and illustrating its varied marketing methods.

If you visit during summer, your tour guide (maybe Ann herself) will walk you past a big farmhouse and through the private gardens designed by her daughter to admire the 1,500 feet of rainbow-colored beds planted in everlastings. One of the tall, restored granary buildings houses edible crops while they're drying. In another, cast your gaze upward at the ceiling—you'll see a cornucopia of colorful varieties of flowers drying, free from destructive mold and hungry critters. Edible grains, along with sparkling burgundy amaranths and colorful heads of Indian corn, fill every blank space. Another granary on the tour, known as the "Cabin in the Woods," provides lodging for birders.

Cost: Self-guided tours: free. Guided tours: adults, $3; children 10–18, $1.50; children 9 and under, free.

Freebies: No

Video/DVD Shown: No

Reservations Needed: No, except for groups over 10 people.

Days and Hours: Mon–Fri 8:00 AM–4:00 PM, weekends by appointment or chance.

Plan to Stay: 1 hour, plus time for gift shop.

Minimum Age: None

Disabled Access: Grounds and gift shop accessible. Stairs in production areas.

Group Requirements: Groups larger than 10 people should call 1 week in advance. No maximum group size.

Special Information: August is the best month for viewing sunflower fields. To also see the everlasting flower fields, specialty crops, and gardens, tour from May–October.

Gift Shop: Features sunflower-based products, Sun Feeders, Sun Florals, and dried flower arrangements. Housed in a 10-sided wooden granary. Open same hours as tour. Free catalog available at above address.

Directions: From I-94, take Hwy. 281 North for 33 miles, then turn right onto Hwy. 9 East. Pipestem Creek is about 1 mile ahead on the right.

Nearby Attractions: Arrowwood National Wildlife Refuge; McHenry Railroad Loop (call 701-785-2163), Putnam House, Foster County Museum; Hawksnest Ridge; National Buffalo Museum and Frontier Village in Jamestown.

HEARTLAND

9549 Frankoma Road, Sapulpa, OK 74066   (918) 224-5511   www.frankoma.com
(800) 331-3650

FRANKOMA POTTERY

The name "Frankoma" combines founder John Frank's name with that of Oklahoma, a source of rich clay deposits. In 1927, Frank left Chicago to teach art and pottery at the University of Oklahoma. Five years later, equipped with one small kiln, a butter churn for mixing clay, a fruit jar for grinding glazes, and a few other crude tools, he started his own pottery studio. Several fires, expansions, and a generation later, Frankoma Pottery has grown to 70,000 square feet.

As your guide leads you through this facility, you will observe Frankoma's two methods of forming pottery. In the casting department, "slip" (liquid clay) is poured into plaster molds. The molds absorb water from the slip, leaving harder clay against the mold's walls. Excess slip is poured out. After four hours of drying, the piece is removed from the mold and allowed to dry overnight. The second, more interesting method is pressing, which is used for plates and flat pieces. A 50-ton hydraulic press slams down on a solid slab of clay to form each object. It smashes the clay around a mold, pushing excess clay out the sides. Regardless of how it is formed, each piece is taken to the trim line, where rough edges are hand-trimmed with a paring knife and smoothed with a wet sponge.

After the pottery is fired, it is ready for glazing. A hand-held air gun sprays glaze on flat pieces. Deep pieces are dipped in glaze to coat the inside and then sprayed on the outside. The brushing department "dry-foots," or removes the glaze from the pieces' bottoms, so they do not stick to the kiln.

Look through the continuously firing tunnel kiln, which is open on both ends. Long, pottery-filled kiln cars enter one end. Each kiln car reaches a maxi-mum temperature of 2,000°F at the center, allowing the clay to solidify and the glaze to melt and change color. The car emerges from the other end at 350°F. You will leave with a new appreciation for the hands-on nature and collectibility of Frankoma pottery.

Cost: Free

Freebies: No

Video/DVD Shown: No

Reservations Needed: No, except for groups larger than 10 people.

Days and Hours: April–December, Mon–Sat 9:00 AM–5:00 PM. Call to confirm times.

Plan to Stay: 30 minutes, plus time in gift shop.

Minimum Age: None

Disabled Access: Yes

Group Requirements: Advance reservations preferred for groups of 8 or more. Groups larger than 25 will be split into smaller groups. School groups get free clay to take back to their schools.

Special Information: Since kilns fire constantly, it can get hot in the summer.

Gift Shop: Sells full line of microwavable, oven-proof, and dishwasher-safe Frankoma dinnerware and accessories. Look for baking pans, relish dishes, and bean pots shaped like Oklahoma, Texas, Louisiana, and Arkansas. Seconds sold at discount. Open Mon–Sat 9:00 AM–5:00 PM. Closed holidays. Catalog available from above numbers.

Directions: Take Turner Tnpk. to Exit 215 (Sapulpa exit). Turn left on Hwy. 97, then right onto Hwy. 166 East to Old Hwy. 66 (Frankoma Rd.). Turn left; Frankoma is on your right, 0.5 mile down the road.

Nearby Attractions: Keepsake Candles tour (see page 293); Mr. Indian store; Tulsa's attractions, including Philbrook Museum of Art and Gilcrease Museum of the Americas, are about 20 minutes away.

HEARTLAND

Route 3, Bartlesville, OK 74003

(918) 336-0351
(888) 636-0351

www.keepsake
candles.com

Keepsake Candles®

Traditional
Handcrafted Quality

It's known as the "church fund-raising project that got out of hand." In 1969, Ed Ririe agreed to make candles molded in the shape of his mother's antique glassware for the church Christmas Bazaar. The color for the candles came, despite protest, from his daughters' crayons. Now Ed's wife, Alice Ririe, manages the company, and the candles are sold in all 50 states and around the world. Built in the 1950s by the government as part of a radar station, the factory was once a half-court gymnasium. You'll find other equipment of unique origin on your tour, such as worktables made from hospital gurneys, a melting vat that was once a dairy tank, and a storage cabinet that was formerly an analog computer.

Enter this unique structure, and you're confronted with a huge stack of wax slabs. The slabs are melted in a vat that can hold 1,400 pounds of liquid wax. The wax for the candles' outside shell is mixed with other substances in order to raise the melting point so the shell holds its shape as the candle burns down.

A shell maker takes a bucketful of melted wax and adds a wax-based dye. The shell maker then carefully pours some colored wax into a pliable silicon rubber mold. The worker hand-twists the mold to make sure all sides have an even coating of wax. After about four layers, the shell will be thick enough to stand on its own. Similar to a process the Romans used to make lead pipes 2,000 years ago, this is called slush molding.

A worker splits apart the flexible mold to reveal a brightly colored shell that resembles a piece of antique pattern glass. The shell is polished using panty hose, the same way you would use sandpaper on wood.

The worker uses an old coffeepot to pour the clear, scented, liquid wax into the shells. Depending on the day, peppermint, strawberry, or cinnamon may permeate the air around you. After it cools,

each candle is tagged with its color, scent, date, pattern, and style.

Cost: Free; Candle Critter Dipping for the kids, $1.

Freebies: No

Video/DVD Shown: 4-minute video covers manufacturing.

Reservations Needed: No, except for groups over 10 people.

Days and Hours: Mon–Sat 10:00 AM–5:00 PM. Closed holidays. Special holiday hours: November 1–December 24: Mon–Sat 9:00 AM–6:00 PM, Sun 1:00–5:00 PM. Holiday open house first weekend in November.

Plan to Stay: 15 minutes for talk, plus time in the Country Store.

Minimum Age: 6

Disabled Access: Yes

Group Requirements: Groups should call 1–2 weeks in advance. Maximum group size 45 people. Large groups will be split into groups of 10–12 people.

Special Information: Factory is not air-conditioned; it can be very hot in summer. Grounds have antiques, including farm equipment and buggy. Railroad cars and caboose in front of store.

Country Store: Shop has 5 rooms, each with its own theme. Candles are displayed on antique stoves, cupboards, and sewing machines. Seconds sold at discount. Also sells baskets, gourmet foods, candleholders, and seasonal items. Open Mon–Sat 10:00 AM–5:00 PM. Closed most holidays. Special holiday hours in effect November 1–December 24. Catalog available from above number.

Directions: From U.S. Hwy. 75, take U.S. Hwy. 60 West through Bartlesville; 2 miles past Phillips Research Center, turn right onto CR 3235. Keepsake Candles is at the top of Radar Hill.

Nearby Attractions: Frankoma Pottery tour (see page 292); Phillips' Mansion; Wild Horse Refuge; Woolaroc Museum and Game Refuge; Tallgrass Prairie; Frank Lloyd Wright's Price Tower; June Oklahoma Mozart Festival; Red Dirt Soap Company.

HEARTLAND

160 West Main Street, Lead, SD 57754   (605) 584-3110   www.homestake
visitorcenter.com

Not long after Custer's military expedition discovered gold in the Black Hills of South Dakota, prospectors rushed into the area of Deadwood Creek, panning the streams for the yellow nuggets they hoped would make their fortune. Once the gold in the stream had been "panned out," a few persistent individuals searched for a site where they could mine gold from rock. Among these were the Manuel brothers, who, in 1876, discovered an outcrop of ore called a "lead" (pronounced LEED), and went on to extract $5,000 worth of gold from it by the end of that spring. That site became the Homestake Gold Mine, the oldest underground gold mine in the western hemisphere, which operated for 125 years.

View the awesome Open Cut surface mine from the observation deck of the Homestake Visitor Center. In 1982, modern miners reentered the Manuel brothers' 19th-century workings. Between then and 1998, ore was blasted from holes drilled into the rock surface and hauled by truck to be processed into gold. Interpretive photos and signs provide detailed information about 20th-century techniques used in the Open Cut.

Board the HVC trolley for a tour of the historic city of Lead and surface workings of the Homestake Gold Mine. Today's tour takes you to the Homestake property, where you enter the Safety Building to visit the "dry" (a locker room for 1,000 men). You then continue down a ramp and past the boss's windows, where miners picked up orders and supplies for their working day. You continue past the Yates Shaft and through a tunnel into the Yates Hoist Room to view the enormous cable and machinery which moved men and supplies as far as 8,000 feet underground every day.

Reboarding the trolley, you continue past the Homestake Wastewater Treatment Plant, which removed cyanide and heavy metals from water used in the ore processing and released the clean water back into the streams.

Your tour goes past the Sawmill, Yates Shaft, and the mechanical shop yards. The last stop is the Gold Run Park, at the site of the South Mill Processing Plant, where you can view historic mining equipment and read interpretive signs.

Before closing in 2001, the Homestake Gold Mine produced 40 million troy ounces from the largest vein of gold ever discovered in its 125-year history. Today, the state of South Dakota is assuming ownership of the property and working with the National Underground Science Authority to develop the Homestake Gold Mine into a world-class underground research and development facility.

Cost: Adults, $6; seniors, $5.25; students (6–18), $5; under 6, free. Family special: two parents and their children, $20. Net proceeds are donated to local charities.

Freebies: Ore samples.

Video/DVD Shown: A 15-minute video shows underground mining and the refining process; the gift shop sells it.

Reservations Needed: No

Days and Hours: Visitor Center and Observation Deck open year-round. Tours available May–September. Closed major holidays.

Plan to Stay: 1 hour for tour plus time for shop.

Mininum Age: None

Disabled Access: Yes

Group Requirements: Groups over 20 people should call at least 1 week in advance. Inquire about group rates.

Special Information: Hard hats must be worn on tour.

Gift Shop: Sells Black Hills Gold jewelry, local history books, South Dakota products, and logoed items, including T-shirts, sweatshirts, and mugs.

Directions: From Deadwood, take Hwy. 85 North for 3 miles. You'll see signs for "Lead City Park" and a large surface mine.

Nearby Attractions: Mt. Rushmore, Crazy Horse, Adams Museum & Adams House, Broken Boot Gold Mine, Days of '76 Museum, and Black Hills Mining Museum.

Black Hills Gold jewelry first appeared after the Black Hills Gold Rush of 1876. By law, in order to use the name "Black Hills Gold," companies must manufacture the jewelry in the Black Hills of South Dakota. To produce Black Hills Gold's characteristic green tint, 12-karat gold is alloyed with silver; alloying gold with copper creates a pink tint. This tour shows you the ancient lost wax method of casting used to manufacture all Black Hills jewelry.

Imagine a golden leaf, precise in form and detail and smaller than a contact lens. At Mt. Rushmore jewelry, such minuscule foliage is commonplace. See workers with soldering needles tack tiny leaves and grapes onto the shanks of rings. At the "wriggling" station, watch a craftsperson wiggle a tool back and forth to etch ridges and veins into a leaf one-third the size of a corn flake. Artisans sit at rows of workstations equipped with small drills, jeweler's loupes, and plenty of tweezers.

All jewelry originates in the Design Room. Artists fashion rubber molds into which hot wax is shot. After the wax sets, the mold is pried apart, and the wax ring joins others on a wax "tree" about the size of a centerpiece. The tree is then dipped in plaster, and this plaster cast slides into a kiln. The wax melts, and liquid gold is injected into the resulting hollow cavity. When the metal has set, the hot cast is dunked in cold water. The plaster shatters, revealing an exact duplicate of the original wax model. This gold tree of rings is pruned, and each ring is ground, buffed, frosted, and polished. During busy holiday seasons, the company's 125 employees produce over 1,000 pieces of jewelry per day.

Cost: Free

Freebies: No

Video/DVD Shown: 7-minute video on company history, legend and history of Black Hills Gold, and production shown in showroom.

Reservations Needed: No, except for groups larger than 30 people.

Days and Hours: May–September: Mon–Fri 8:00 AM–3:40 PM, tours generally on the half hour; mid-September–mid-May: tours by walk-in or reservation. Closed holidays and week between Christmas and New Year's.

Plan to Stay: 30 minutes, plus time in factory showroom.

Minimum Age: None

Disabled Access: Yes

Group Requirements: No maximum group size. Large groups will be split. Requests 1 day's advance notice for groups larger than 30 people.

Special Information: This family-run business is one of the few jewelry manufacturers' tours that allows visitors directly onto the production floor.

Factory Showroom: Sells entire 3,600-style line of Black Hills Gold jewelry and 2,000 non–Black Hills Gold diamonds, rubies, emeralds, and sapphires. Rings are arranged in velvet cases among elegant watches, dishes, and crystal bowls. Open May–September: Mon–Sat 8:00 AM–8:00 PM, Sun 9:00 AM–6:00 PM; October–April: Mon–Sat 8:30 AM–5:30 PM. Closed Sundays, Christmas, Thanksgiving, and Easter.

Directions: From I-90, take Exit 57. Turn left onto Omaha St. Turn right onto Mt. Rushmore Rd. Mt. Rushmore Jewelry is at intersection of Fairmont Blvd. and Mt. Rushmore Rd. From Hwy. 79, travel west on Fairmont Blvd. to Mt. Rushmore Rd.

Nearby Attractions: Sioux Pottery and Crafts tour (see page 296); video and observation booth at Landstrom's Black Hills Gold Creations (call 605-343-0157 or 800-843-0009); Mt. Rushmore; Reptile Gardens; the Ranch Amusement Park; Museum of Geology at South Dakota School of Mines; the Journey Museum; Crazy Horse Mountain Carving.

HEARTLAND

Sioux Pottery and Crafts

1441 East Saint Joseph Street,
Rapid City, SD 57701

(605) 341-3657
(800) 657-4366

www.siouxpottery.com

The red clay used at Sioux Pottery comes from Paha Sapa, the Black Hills area, and is considered sacred. This clay is carefully fashioned into vases and pots whose exteriors are then graced with Sioux Indian designs symbolizing the Sioux culture, environment, activities, and dealings. For example, crossed arrows represent Friendship, a zigzag of lightning stands for Swiftness, and a diamond wedged between two backward Es connotes Horses Killed in Battle.

Along with the red clay, the craftspeople at Sioux Pottery also utilize a more secular variety from Kentucky. This white, elastic clay is used for certain pieces, such as those with handles, which are too delicate to withstand the pronounced shrinkage inherent in firing red clay. About 10 artists can be seen working at any one time, each one seated at an old kitchen table. The floors of their workspace are powdered with dust; boot prints lead to a dank back room where the red clay exists as "slip" (earthy red liquid). From outside, the slip is piped into concrete vats, where it is mixed and strained, then turned into clay.

The artists employ three different methods for turning clay into pots: casting, wheel throwing, and jiggering. In casting, slip is poured into plaster molds. The plaster absorbs the excess liquid, and the clay takes the shape of the mold. In wheel throwing, potters bend over spinning pottery wheels, hand-forming original pieces from balls of clay. The third method, jiggering, is used for flat plates and bowls. As the wheel spins, a potter lowers a blade that cuts out the shape. White or red, all unfired pottery is called "greenware." You'll see shelves of greenware, all dull and smooth. The Indian artists paint freehand designs and proudly sign their names on each piece.

Cost: Free

Freebies: No

Video/DVD Shown: No

Reservations Needed: No, except for groups larger than 12 people or to arrange tours outside regularly scheduled times.

Days and Hours: Self-guided tours: Mon–Fri 8:00 AM–5:00 PM. Best viewing days Tue–Fri. Guided group tours available upon request. Closed holidays and week after Christmas.

Plan to Stay: 20 minutes, plus time in gift shop.

Cost: Free

Minimum Age: None

Disabled Access: Yes

Group Requirements: Call 2–3 days in advance for groups larger than 12 people. Groups larger than 20 will be split into smaller groups.

Special Information: A lot of clay dust in the back rooms' air.

Gift Shop: Sells handmade pots, bowls, and dishware, as well as mandalas, dance shields, painted cattle skulls, and sacred medicine wheels, all created locally by members of Sioux nation. Factory seconds available at 50 percent off. Open May–August: Mon–Fri 8:00 AM–5:00 PM, Sat 10:00 AM–4:00 PM, Sun 12:00 PM–4:00 PM; September–April: Mon–Fri 8:00 AM–5:00 PM, Sat 10:00 AM–2:00 PM (in September, Sat 10:00 AM–4:00 PM). Catalog available by mail for $5.

Directions: From I-90 bypass, take Exit 59 and go south on LaCrosse St. Turn left (east) on East North St. to Cambell St. Turn right (south) on Cambell to St. Patrick St. Turn right again (west) on St. Patrick to East St. Joseph St. Sioux Pottery is 2 blocks ahead on your right.

Nearby Attractions: Mt. Rushmore Jewelry tour (see page 295); Black Hills National Forest; Mt. Rushmore; Geology Museum at South Dakota School of Mines; Reptile Gardens; the Ranch Amusement Park.

Texas

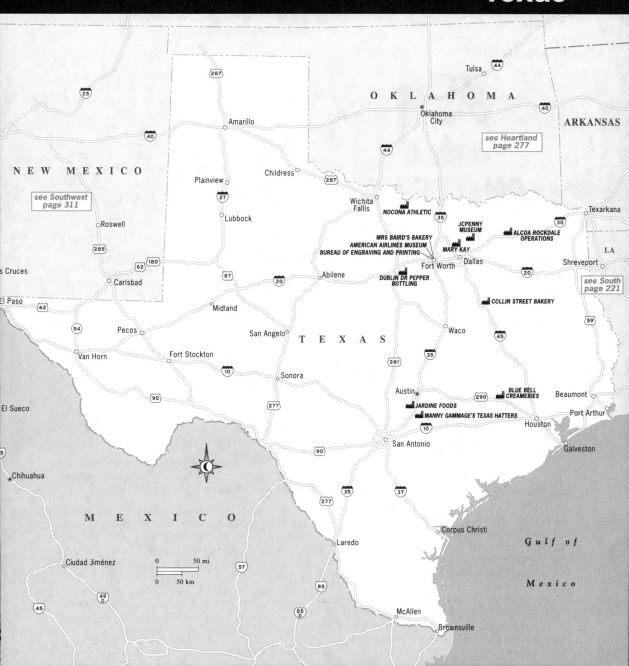

see Heartland
page 277

see Southwest
page 311

see South
page 221

OKLAHOMA

ARKANSAS

NEW MEXICO

TEXAS

MEXICO

LA

Tulsa

Oklahoma City

Amarillo

Childress

Plainview

Roswell

Lubbock

Wichita Falls

Texarkana

NOCONA ATHLETIC

JCPENNEY MUSEUM

ALCOA ROCKDALE OPERATIONS

MRS BAIRD'S BAKERY
AMERICAN AIRLINES MUSEUM
BUREAU OF ENGRAVING AND PRINTING

MARY KAY

Fort Worth

Dallas

Shreveport

DUBLIN DR PEPPER BOTTLING

Abilene

Carlsbad

s Cruces

El Paso

Midland

COLLIN STREET BAKERY

Pecos

San Angelo

Waco

Van Horn

Fort Stockton

Sonora

Austin

BLUE BELL CREAMERIES

Beaumont

JARDINE FOODS
MANNY GAMMAGE'S TEXAS HATTERS

Houston

Port Arthur

El Sueco

San Antonio

Galveston

Chihuahua

Gulf of

Corpus Christi

Mexico

Ciudad Jiménez

Laredo

0   50 mi

0   50 km

McAllen

Brownsville

Rockdale Chamber of Commerce,
1203 West Cameron Avenue (Route 79),
Rockdale, TX 76567

(512) 446-2030

Alcoa Rockdale is a vast operation that covers 35,000 acres in eastern central Texas. Its main purpose is producing aluminum for industrial use. But that is only part of the story. Alcoa Rockdale runs on energy from its own power plant, which uses lignite (a form of brown coal) that the company extracts from surface mines on its land. In short, it is a mining operation, power station, and industrial smelter in one site.

Alcoa Rockdale offers a tour on a suitably grand scale. Visitors gather 11 miles away at the Rockdale Chamber of Commerce and travel by bus to the facility. From the comfort and safety of the bus, they see the mining area, the power plant, and the smelter.

Yielding six million tons of lignite a year, Alcoa Rockdale's mining territory covers over 13,000 acres. At any given time, only some of the landscape is consumed by open surface mines, wide pits that give access to coal beds underneath deep layers of soil. Other areas are in a natural condition, either untouched or reclaimed from past mining. (Since 1980, Alcoa has restored over 5,000 acres of surface-mined land to a natural state.) Near the mining zone, you see the Sandow Power Plant, where lignite fuels the generation of electricity. The adjacent 1,000-acre reservoir supplies cooling water for industrial processes and bears its own water-treatment system.

Next to these, the massive smelter—the largest in the United States—is what all this fuel, water, and power are for. Smelting is the last step in making raw aluminum. Bauxite ore, mined from various sites around the world, is refined elsewhere into aluminum oxide, also called alumina. The alumina goes to smelting sites such as Rockdale. In the smelter, hundreds of pots, linked in configurations

called potlines, extract aluminum by passing electrical currents through molten alumina at extremely high temperatures (over nine times the boiling point). The Rockdale smelter can produce two million pounds of aluminum in a day.

Of the four aluminum products that Alcoa Rockdale makes, perhaps the most glamorous is powdered aluminum for solid rocket propellants. Alcoa Rockdale is the sole supplier of aluminum powder for fueling NASA's space shuttles.

Cost: Free

Freebies: No

Video/DVD Shown: At the Alcoa Training Center, visitors watch a short video that summarizes the operations of the plant.

Reservations Needed: Yes. Visitors often can book tours as late as a day in advance, but a week before the desired tour date is safer.

Days and Hours: Tours run on Wed and Sat at 9:00 AM. Closed holidays.

Plan to Stay: 2.5 hours.

Minimum Age: No

Disabled Access: Yes (visitors do not leave the bus except to watch the video).

Group Requirements: The bus carries a maximum of 24 passengers, but larger groups can arrange more than one tour on a given date

Directions: From Austin, take I-35 (Rt. 81) North to exit for Rt. 79 (E. Palm Valley Elvd.). Turn right at end of ramp and take Rt. 79 East for 45 miles into Rockdale. Rockdale Chamber of Commerce is on right. From Houston, take Rt. 290 West toward Austin for 67 miles. Rt. 36 North joins Rt. 290 at Brenham. When Rt. 290 splits away, continue straight on Rt. 36 North for 50 miles. Turn left on Rt. 79 West at Milano and follow t into Rockdale. Chamber is on left.

Nearby Attractions: In Brenham, Blue Bell Creameries (see page 300). In Austin, Austin City Limits television-studio tour (call 512-471-4811); Austin Steam Train (call 512-477-8468).

4601 Highway 360 at FAA Road,
Fort Worth, TX 76155

(817) 967-1560

www.crsmith
museum.org

You'll recognize the American Airlines C. R. Smith Museum, named after the man who served as company president for most of the years between 1934 and 1973, by the fully restored DC-3 (the *Flagship Knoxville*, which flew for American from 1940 to 1948) housed in a glass hangar. The Grey Eagles, a group of mostly retired American pilots, bought the *Knoxville*, which flew for American from 1940 to 1948) housed in a glass hangar. The Grey Eagles, a group of mostly retired American pilots, bought the *Knoxville*, and a team of American mechanics restored it to its current glistening condition. This 35,000-square-foot corporate museum contains informative interactive displays and video presentations.

The circular glass History Wall in the center of the open floor plan highlights company developments and memorabilia from the first airmail service (1918) to today, including a 767 maintenance manual on CD-ROM. Some of the oldest items, including a letter Charles Lindbergh carried on his first airmail flight from Chicago to St. Louis, bring America's heritage to life. Beyond this section is an "American Family" display, with lifelike mannequins representing American employees and videos describing their jobs and teamwork.

"Working in the Air," "Working on the Ground," and "Maintaining the Fleet" exhibits detail the equipment and procedures used in airline operations. You'll also get an up-close look at a jet engine, aircraft landing gear, and an air traffic control system. The "Flightlab" has a wind tunnel, test equipment, and simulators that teach the basic principles of flight. Near these more technical displays are brass-plate etchings of four different American Airlines planes. Put a piece of paper on your chosen plate and rub it with a crayon to make a souvenir. If only flying a real plane and running an airline were this easy!

Cost: Adults, $4; seniors 55+, $2; students (with ID), $2; children 2–12, $2; children under 2, free; organized groups of 10 or more, $1 per person.

Freebies: Brass rubbings (see above).

Videos/DVDs Shown: 14-minute film, *Spirit of American,* runs every hour on the half hour. Theater's all-around sound system and panoramic screen give you the feeling of flying on an American Airlines jet. Also, touch-screen videos throughout museum.

Reservations Needed: No, but recommended for groups larger than 10 people. Inquire about scavenger hunt.

Days and Hours: Tue–Sat 10:00 AM–6:00 PM. Call for holiday hours.

Plan to Stay: 1.5–2 hours for displays, videos, and film, plus time in gift shop.

Minimum Age: None

Disabled Access: Yes

Group Requirements: Reservations requested for groups of 10 or more people for self-guided tour and film.

Special Information: Special-event rental of museum available (call 817-967-5910). With the museum's open floor plan, the Map and Guide provide a helpful overview of the numerous displays.

Gift Shop: The Museum Store sells aviation-related items, such as models, crystal and porcelain eagles, clocks, mobiles, toys, and books; also, museum and American Airlines–logoed items. Closes half hour before museum.

Directions: From Dallas/Fort Worth Airport (3 miles away), take south exit and follow signs for Hwy. 360 South. Exit at FAA Rd. Turn right at stop sign. Museum is on right. From Hwy. 183 East, take FAA Rd./Hwy. 360 South exit. Turn right at stop sign. Museum is on right.

Nearby Attractions: Mrs. Baird's Bakery and Mary Kay museum (see pages 308 and 307); Dr Pepper Bottling Plant tour (call 888-398-1024); Six Flags over Texas; Fort Worth's attractions including Bureau of Printing and Engraving (see page 301), Fort Worth Zoo, and Fort Worth Museum of Science and History about 20 miles away; Downtown Dallas attractions, including JFK Museum, about 15 miles away.

TEXAS

This "Little Creamery in Brenham" maintains its small-town image through its advertising and girl-and-cow logo. At its headquarters, the 19th-century red brick schoolhouse offices, 1930s-replica refrigerated delivery truck, country store, and ice-cream parlor further that country feel. In the visitors center, see photos of Blue Bell and Brenham, and the company's original wooden time clock.

In the plant, look down through glass windows at the production floor's maze of stainless-steel pipes and various shaped tanks. Almost everything happens inside the tanks, so your tour guide explains the process. Base-mix ingredients are blended, homogenized, and pasteurized, then cooled and piped into refrigerated holding tanks. The tanks' huge round doors resemble ship portholes. Liquid flavorings are added in the rectangular flavoring tanks.

The mailbox-shaped freezer barrels whip and freeze the mixture to milkshake consistency. The ice cream and "dry" ingredients (fruit, cookie chunks, cookie dough, etc.) meet in the white pipes before traveling into containers. If the flavor of the day is banana split, workers peel and slice bananas in the behind-the-scenes kitchen. In the filler machine, empty, open, half-gallon round cartons spin to mix ice cream and ingredients as they flow into the cartons. Colorful lids slide down to cover the filled cartons.

Another room offers more movement as three-ounce Dixie cups are filled. Cups resting in a circular disk are filled two at a time; the disk rotates after every two are filled. You will be mesmerized by the repetitive spin-fill, spin-fill process. Nearby, ice-cream sandwiches start as chocolate wafers sliding down a V-shaped holder. Two wafers converge, and an ice-cream slice drops between them. Paper quickly wraps around the sandwich and helps maintain its shape. The sandwiches travel single file until they're mechanically pushed into cardboard boxes. All this whets your appetite for the samples you'll enjoy in the ice-cream parlor.

Cost: Adults, $3; children 6–14 and seniors 55 and older, $2; 5 and under, free.

Freebies: Ice-cream serving in the parlor; logoed paper hat with the tour.

Video/DVD Shown: Short video at beginning of tour covers company history.

Reservations Needed: No, except for groups of 15 or more. Everyone must make reservations during spring break.

Days and Hours: Summer: Mon–Fri 10:00 AM, 11:00 AM, 1:00 PM, 1:30 PM, 2:00 PM, and 2:30 PM. Fall and winter tour schedule varies; call for tour times and days. Closed holidays.

Plan to Stay: 40–45 minutes, plus time in visitors center, ice-cream parlor, and Country Store.

Minimum Age: None

Disabled Access: Yes

Group Requirements: Groups of 15 or more should call at least 2 weeks in advance. Call ahead for spring and summer tours. Maximum group is 45 people.

Special Information: March and April are busiest tour months because bluebonnets, the Texas State Wildflower, are in bloom. No photography in plant. Allow some waiting time during summer.

Gift Shop: Country Store sells custom Blue Bell items and a variety of unique gifts. Open year-round Mon–Fri 8:00 AM–5:00 PM. March–December, also open Sat 10:00 AM–4:00 PM. Closed holidays.

Directions: Take U.S. 290 to FM 577 North. Blue Bell is 2 miles ahead on right.

Nearby Attractions: Monastery of St. Claire; Antique Rose Emporium; Historic Downtown Brenham; annual Maifest; Washington County Fair.

TEXAS

Western Currency Facility Tour and Visitor Center,
9000 Blue Mound Road, Fort Worth, TX 76131

(817) 231-4000
(866) 865-1194

www.moneyfactory.gov

Did you know that the life span for a one dollar bill is 22 months, while the life span for a 100 dollar bill is nine years? Or that no one knows exactly why our money is green?

The Bureau of Engraving and Printing (BEP) strives to provide its visitors with many such facts, as well as the detailed history of paper currency in the United States. The earliest currency printing operations can be traced back to 1862, when six people worked in the basement of the Treasury building, separating and sealing each note by hand. Today, more than 2,500 people work in the Bureau both in Washington, D.C., and Fort Worth, TX.

The tour in the Fort Worth branch of the BEP begins on the first floor, where the visitor center is located. The exhibits and displays here depict the history of U.S. paper currency and the history of the BEP. There is also a restored spider press and engraver's bench from the turn of the century that give insight to the engraving process and the Intaglio printing method.

Upstairs, a 15-minute movie details the production process. Then the guided portion of the tour takes you across the quarter-mile-long elevated walkway above the currency production floor. You'll see the high-speed, sheet-fed rotary presses, capable of printing over 8,000 sheets per hour. Ink is put on the plates, and the surface is wiped clean while ink remains in the grooves of the plate. Each sheet is then forced with 20 tons of pressure into the grooves of the plate to pick up the ink. This process is called Intaglio printing and is the result of combined work by artists, steel engravers, and plate printers.

After the guided tour, take a close look at the exhibits highlighting the steps of currency production. At the west end, visit the mutilated currency redemption desk. You'll find out about the ways currency can be mutilated, and what the BEP does to redeem the destroyed currency.

Cost: Free

Freebies: Brochures, and educational material to children.

Video/DVD Shown: 15-minute film of the production process.

Reservations Needed: No, except for groups of 10 or more.

Days and Hours: Aug–May: visitors center Mon–Fri 8:30 AM–3:30 PM; tours every 30 minutes 9:00 AM–2:00 PM. June–July: visitors center Mon–Fri 10:30 AM–6:30 PM, with tours every 30 minutes 11:00 AM–5:00 PM. Closed on weekends, federal holidays, and the week between Christmas and New Year's.

Plan to Stay: Allow 45 minutes for guided tour, plus 30 minutes beforehand to clear security and 2–4 hours to explore the interactive exhibits.

Minimum Age: None. Exhibits are geared toward 5th grade and up, but younger children may also enjoy them.

Disabled Access: Yes. Wheelchairs may be requested for guided tours.

Group Requirements: Reservations required for groups of 10 or more. No more than 75 visitors per tour.

Special Information: Cell phones or any electronic equipment, backpacks, cameras, weapons, food, and drinks are prohibited. American Sign Language, Spanish, and assisted listening devices available on request for use in the theater.

Gift Shop: Sells uncut currency sheets, collectable coins, hats, T-shirts, pens, and other souvenirs.

Directions: From Dallas/Fort Worth, take I-35W North toward Denton, exit to Hwy. 287/81 North, proceed to 156/Blue Mound Rd., and turn left. Visitors' parking lot is 1 mile down on the left.

Nearby Attractions: Mrs. Baird's Bakery (see page 308), Cabellas outdoor store, Fort Worth Zoo, Fort Worth Museum of Science and History.

TEXAS

COLLIN STREET BAKERY

Collin Street Bakery (1896) is the oldest fruitcake bakery in the U.S.A. The family-owned company's history is as colorful as the cherries, pineapples, papaya, and pecans on its cakes. The Deluxe Fruitcake has circled the earth aboard an Apollo spacecraft and adorned the tables of royalty, famous entertainers, sports legends, and politicians.

A glass-windowed, metal door opens from the lobby onto a small elevated platform. (Tell someone in the Bake Shop that you want a tour; they'll admit you to the baking area and explain the action. Otherwise, you can watch through the window—minus the aroma and sounds.) From October to mid-December, what you see is one of the most memorable sights of any in this book. A sea of workers, standing in small stalls on both sides of at least three production lines, hand-decorate fruitcakes' tops with pecans and candied fruit. The cakes, at this point only dough in round baking pans, flow in from the left. Each worker grabs a cake, decorates it with pecans, and then places it back on the line headed for the ovens.

Another worker races about with a big scoop, keeping each decorator's holding bin filled with pecans. During this busy period, the staff increases from around 80 employees to over 650, and workers decorate over 30,000 Original Deluxe Fruitcakes each day, making more than 1.5 million each year. Workers have been known to burst into their own classic holiday song—"I've Been Working on the Fruitcake."

From the platform, look toward the back of the production area at a highly automated bakery operation. To the left, pecan-filled batter is mixed in vats, and dough is automatically deposited into baking tins and leveled by hissing machines. To the right, an oven consumes long trays of up to 2,800 cake pans in one swallow. The batter-filled tins travel a precisely timed journey through the long oven and cooling tunnel. As a testament to the fruitcake's quality, flags from some of the 200 countries to which Collin Street ships hang from the back of the production area (England is the top fruitcake importer).

Cost: Free

Freebies: Small samples and 10-cent coffee; postcards.

Video/DVD Shown: Optional 10-minute video on production process, shown in lobby area.

Reservations Needed: No, except for groups of 8 or more.

Days and Hours: Mon–Thur 9:00 AM–11:00 AM and 1:00–3:00 PM. Closed holidays. October 1–mid-December, you watch fruitcake production from small landing just inside production area. Other times, take guided tour through baking machinery. Any time of year, need to ask for tour in adjoining Bake Shop.

Plan to Stay: 10 minutes for viewing, plus time for video and Bake Shop.

Minimum Age: None

Disabled Access: Yes

Group Requirements: Requests 1 week's advance notice for groups of 10 or more. No maximum group size, although only 10 people can watch from landing at one time.

Special Information: No photography in plant.

Bakery Shop: Sells over 136 different baked items, including Deluxe Fruitcake, rum cake, pecan pie, and pecan bread. Ask about unboxed factory-second fruitcakes. Also sells logoed T-shirts, caps, and baskets. Open Mon–Thur 7:00 AM–5:30 PM, Fri–Sat 7:00 AM–6:00 PM, and Sun 12:00 PM–6:00 PM. Fruitcake catalogs available from (800) 248-3366, and Cryer Creek Kitchens food items available from (800) 468-0088.

Directions: From I-45, take exit for Hwy. 31 West; becomes 7th Ave. in Corsicana. Bakery is on your left.

Nearby Attractions: Navarro Pecan Co. group tours available through Chamber of Commerce (call 903-874-1503); Pioneer Village; Richland-Chambers Lake.

Old Doc's Soda Shop and Museum,
105 East Elm, Dublin, TX 76446

(254) 445-3939
(888) 398-1024

www.dublin
drpepper.com

In 1885, Wade Morrison named his newly developed soft drink after his former sweetheart's father, Dr. Pepper. But the drink was only served from the soda fountain at drugstores until a man named Sam Houston Prim started the Dublin Bottling Works. Opened in 1891 in Dublin, Texas, this is the World's Oldest Dr Pepper Bottling Plant, and it still cranks out returnable bottles of Dr Pepper with 1930s machinery. The late Bill Kloster, employee of the plant since 1933 and owner from 1991 to 1999, spent the better portion of 60 years amassing one of the largest collections of Dr Pepper memorabilia. The plant remains in the Kloster family, with grandson Mark overseeing the business.

On Tuesdays, when the plant bottles, a fruity fragrance fills the air as reusable bottles slowly and noisily shake, rattle, and roll past on the old machinery. Gears shift and bottles rise, drop, and turn like amusement park carousel horses, then do-si-do and waddle single file down the conveyor belts. Since parts are no longer available, many of these vintage machines are held together with ingenuity and baling wire. The bottles file past at what may seem like slow motion (32 per minute) compared to today's speedier bottling lines (1,500 per minute).

The filling process begins as bottles clatter through the 37-foot-long 1965 Miller Hydro Bottle Washer. Once washed, the bottles receive a squirt of syrup and then are filled with pure carbonated water. Once filled, the bottles rotate to the capper and then are mixed. Bottles turn over in three somersaults, then a worker grabs two bottles in each hand and sets them into bottle-shaped cutouts on a light board for inspection. After twirling each bottle to ensure consistent color (indicative of proper mixing) and crack-free bottles, the worker places 24 bottles into the pockets of each red or yellow wooden crate. People travel great distances to see this process and load their cars with these wooden crates of Dr Pepper, made with Imperial pure cane sugar (other bottlers use corn syrup).

In the museum rooms, Bill's artifacts trace Dr Pepper's heritage from its beginnings in an 1885 Waco, Texas, drugstore to the present. His exten-

sive collection, the largest in existence, includes Dr Pepper signs, billboards, advertisements, calendars dating back to 1905, clocks, and various treasures. His prized possessions were a life-size cardboard cutout of the red, white, and blue saluting Patriotic Girl, and attention-grabbing motion displays like the carousel with three airplanes bearing the numbers 10, 2, and 4 (representing the times you should drink Dr Pepper for some extra "pep").

Cost: Adults, $2; senior citizens, $1.50, children 6–12, $1; children under 6, free.

Freebies: Ice-cold Dr Pepper.

Video/DVD Shown: No

Reservations Needed: No, except for groups larger than 10 people.

Days and Hours: Mon–Fri 9:00 AM–5:00 PM. Sat 10:00 AM–5:00 PM. Sun 1:00–5:00 PM. No tours 12:00 PM–1:00 PM. Closed Thanksgiving, Christmas, and New Year's. Bottling is on a monthly or as-needed basis. When not bottling, a simulation is shown.

Plan to Stay: 30–45 minutes for tour and museum area, plus time in gift shop.

Minimum Age: None

Disabled Access: Yes

Group Requirements: Groups larger than 10 should call 2 weeks in advance. Groups over 20 will be split.

Special Information: Dr Pepper Museum located in a 1906 bottling plant in Waco, TX (call 254-757-1024). Dr Pepper Bottling in Irving, TX, offers tours of high-speed bottling plant (call 972-721-8112).

Gift Shop: Old Doc's Soda Shop sells logoed items including T-shirts, kitchen accessories, clocks, and memorabilia with vintage Dr Pepper logos and designs. Vintage soda fountain serves up Dr Pepper and ice cream and sandwiches. Purchase Dr Pepper by the case. Open same hours as above. Items can also be purchased online.

Directions: Dublin lies at the intersection of Hwys 377 and 6. From Fort Worth/Dallas, take Hwy. 377 South to Dublin. From Waco, take Hwy. 6 west to Dublin. Plant 1 block past center of town.

Nearby Attractions: Dublin Historical Museum; Dublin Rodeo Museum; Hoka Hey Foundry; Proctor Dam and Parks.

TEXAS

1 Chisholm Trail, Buda, TX 78610

(512) 295-4600
(800) 544-1880

www.jardinefoods.com

After touring Austin and Texas Hill Country sites, Jardine's authentic Texas-style foods round out a Texas gastronomic experience. The graceful live oak trees, restored chuck wagon, wisteria-covered gazebo, and oak rocking chairs on the wide front porch of the company's headquarters all welcome you to the Jardine ranch and invite you to "set a spell."

The "Jardine Outfit," the company's nickname for itself, immediately makes you feel at home. A visit to Jardine's combines ranch relaxation, a warm homey feeling, and an opportunity to view the bottling and packaging of hot sauce, barbecue sauce, chili, and jalapeño peppers through windows in the limestone ranch-house "factory."

Legend has it that after many years of cooking for cowboys on trail drives, D. L. Jardine settled in Texas Hill Country. As a chuck wagon "cookie," he added various combinations of salsa, chilis, peppers, and spices to beans, meat, and cornbread. Since 1979, the Jardine Outfit has produced foods based on these early recipes. To develop new recipes, the Jardine R&D Outfit (Rowdy & Dangerous) researches the history and culture of foods that characterize Texas heritage.

As you stroll outdoors under the sloped, ridged-tin roof and awning, look through several windows into a small section of the factory. If they're making Jardine's popular Chisholm Trail Texas Chili Bag O' Fixin's, watch hair-netted workers hand-fill reusable cloth bags with cellophane-wrapped spice packets. Seated at a long table, they grab packets from red plastic bins, insert them into the cloth bags, and pull a string to tighten each bag shut.

Through the last set of windows, you'll see the horseshoe-shaped automatic filling line. Sauces, such as barbecue and salsa, simmer in the three kettles to the left. The sauce passes through a pipe

and is funneled into the bottles, which are capped, suction-sealed, labeled, and sent along a conveyor belt to the shipping warehouse. You leave craving the nearest Texas-style restaurant or your own kitchen so you can whip up some of these specialties.

Cost: Free

Freebies: Bottle of Texas Champagne brand hot pepper sauce only if you mention this book; mail order catalog.

Video/DVD Shown: No

Reservations Needed: Preferred for groups larger than 15 people.

Days and Hours: Mon–Fri 9:00 AM–4:00 PM. Closed holidays.

Plan to Stay: 15 minutes for self-guided tour, plus time for grounds, historic graveyard, and general store.

Minimum Age: None

Disabled Access: Yes

Group Requirements: Groups larger than 15 should call 2 weeks or more in advance. Food tastings are arranged for groups of 15 or more.

Special Information: Picnic tables available on request.

General Store: Sells Jardine's authentic Texas-style foods, including salsas, condiments, spices, and other ranch-style recipes. Open Mon–Fri 9:00 AM–4:00 PM. Closed holidays. Catalog available from (800) 544-1880.

Directions: From I-35 South, take Exit 221 for Main St. toward Buda. Travel 1.1 miles and turn right just past the Jardine Foods sign. Turn right onto Chisholm Trail, which leads to the offices. Park on left. From I-35 North, take Exit 220. Follow access road to 2nd light (Main St.). Turn left onto Main Street and travel 1.1 miles (same as above).

Nearby Attractions: Manny Gammage's Texas Hatters tour (see page 306); Austin's attractions, including the State Capitol, Lyndon B. Johnson Library & Museum, and 6th Street, are 11 miles away.

TEXAS

JCPenney

In 1902, James Cash Penney opened "The Golden Rule" cash-only dry-goods store in the small mining town of Kemmerer, Wyoming. With 36 stores in 1913, the company was renamed JCPenney Company, and the "Penney Idea," seven mission-statement principles that guide the company today, was formulated. Now the company has over 1,050 stores nationwide and a thriving catalog, ecommerce, and drugstore business. You can visit its state-of-the-art home office and also the company's historical museum.

In the central rotunda at the heart of this 125-acre complex is a larger-than-life bronze sculpture of Mr. Penney. A replica of the first Golden Rule store is carved into his desk. A small, open museum area displays well-worn, yellowed early advertisements through recent catalog covers. A replica of the first Kemmerer store—including shopkeeper, dry goods, and original wooden counter—lines one wall. Other displays illustrate company development, including credit cards (1957) and the first electronic point-of-sale system (1960s).

You will be most impressed with the expansiveness of this three-story glass-atrium megastructure. With a portion of the profits from selling its 45-story New York City skyscraper (company headquarters from 1964 to 1987), Penney purchased 429 acres in rural Plano, Texas. This 1.9-million-square-foot office unites over 3,300 corporate "associates," Mr. Penney's name for his first employees, who worked "with" rather than "for" him.

The open floor plan and walkway seating areas facilitate communication between associates. Company day-care services and fitness facilities promote employee morale. A robotic mail-delivery system and on-site direct video broadcast system connecting all the over 1,050 stores enhance productivity. After seeing many of its features, you'll agree that this futuristic home office—located on Legacy Drive—is a legacy to the founder and to the company's associates.

Cost: Free

Freebies: Museum brochures.

Videos/DVDs Shown: Small theater shows short nostalgic films, including 1950s interviews with Mr. and Mrs. Penney.

Reservations Needed: No

Days and Hours: Mon–Fri 8:00 AM–5:00 PM.

Plan to Stay: 20 minutes for museum plus time for lunch in company cafeteria, where curved glass walls frame a water pool with fountain.

Minimum Age: None

Disabled Access: Yes

Group Requirements: None

Gift Shop: JC's, down the escalator from museum, sells logoed clothing and other items. Open Mon–Fri 8:00 AM–3:00 PM.

Directions: From Dallas, take Dallas Tollway North to Legacy Dr. exit. Turn left onto Legacy Dr., then right onto Communications Pkwy. Turn left onto Headquarters Dr. Park in North or South garage.

Nearby Attractions: American Airlines C. R. Smith Museum and Mary Kay factory and museum (see pages 299 and 307); Dr Pepper Bottling Plant tour (call 972-721-8112); Dallas's downtown attractions, including Dealey Plaza and JFK Sixth Floor Museum, are 20–30 miles away.

TEXAS

Manny Gammage's
Texas Hatters

CUSTOM-MADE HATS

911 S. Commerce Street, Lockhart, TX 78644

(512) 327-4287
(800) 421-4287

www.texashatters.com

By such titles as "Dr. of Mad Hattery," "Wizard of Lids," and "A 'Manny' of Many Hats," you know that the late Manny Gammage was no ordinary hat maker. Although his daughter, Joella, now leads the store's crew, composed mostly of family members, Manny's legacy as one of America's finest custom hat makers continues. In his time, he hatted such personalities as Ronald Reagan, Howard Cosell, Jerry Jeff Walker, Burt Reynolds, and Willie Nelson. Photographs, many autographed by the famous people wearing Manny's hats, form a collage on the shop walls and fill several large photo albums.

Once inside the small store, make your way over to the antique counter and take a stool. Ask Joella, a third-generation master hatter, to guide you through the swinging door marked "Employees Only," into the small production area. Be careful not to touch anything as you work your way through the cramped quarters to the back.

Hats start as unshaped blanks made of beaver and/or hare's hair. From cubbyholes lining the walls, a worker selects the correct solid wooden block for the desired hat style and the wearer's head shape. After steam-heating the hat, he/she uses his/her muscles to stretch it over the heavy block. The hatter irons out the crown as it slowly rotates on an antique crown ironing machine. Then, with an iron that weighs 12 pounds in the morning but feels like 45 pounds by evening, the hatter irons the brim. Finally, the hatter hand-sands the crown and brim to smooth the texture.

As you squeeze your way into the next area, Joella explains that there are many steps involved in making a hat. Study the well-worn poplar-wood disks, or "flanges," stored in slotted shelves. Look for the LBJ flange—you'll recognize it by the letters LBJ on the side. Sandbags are lowered onto a wooden flange to flatten the hat's brim. In the next area, an old Singer sewing machine puts bindings on the brim; leather sweatbands and satin linings are sewn in by hand. More personality comes from the hatband—elephant hide, snakeskin, lizard, leather, and feathers. Even if you don't buy a hat, you'll leave with some great stories.

Cost: Free

Freebies: A token souvenir, when available.

Video/DVD Shown: Occasionally

Reservations Needed: Yes, must call 1 month in advance, then 1 week before to confirm. Tours can be difficult to schedule since it's a small family business. No tours on Fri or Sat.

Days and Hours: Tue–Sat 9:30 AM–5:30 PM. Call ahead for Christmas and summer vacation dates.

Plan to Stay: 10–20 minutes.

Minimum Age: None, though not recommended for children under 2 due to the noises and steam. Children require adult supervision.

Disabled Access: Yes

Group Requirements: Groups larger than 5 will be split into smaller groups.

Special Information: Best time to watch workers is early in the week after lunch. Can be hot in summer. Very strict safety rules must be obeyed.

Retail Store: Sells custom-made hats for 2-week delivery. Most popular styles are Hi-Roller and Rancher. Open same hours as above. Catalog available from 800 number.

Directions: Take Hwy. 183 South from Austin, 25 miles from Austin-Bergstrom Airport. Take right onto Commerce and an immediate left into driveway.

Nearby Attractions: Jardine's Foods tour (see page 304); Kreuz Market; O'Brien's Antiques; Lockhart State Park; Gladder's Gourmet Cookies; Chisolm Trail Roundup (an annual event); Austin's attractions, including Sixth Street Lyndon B. Johnson Library and Museum, and Capitol Building, are approximately 30 miles away.

MARY KAY

Inscribed at the entrance to the company museum is the late Mary Kay Ash's motto: "You can do anything in the world that you want to do if you want it badly enough and you are willing to pay the price." This determination and Mary Kay's ability to motivate and reward her (mostly female) sales force made Mary Kay, Inc.—founded in 1963 by Mary Kay and her son Richard—into one of America's most admired companies.

Drive from corporate headquarters to the aromatic manufacturing facility, where 40 lines fill and package over 200 Mary Kay products. On the eyeshadow line, gray plastic bottoms, clear tops, and eye-shadow refills merge on a freeway system that, together with human hands, packages approximately 38,000 per 10-hour shift. Once mascara and lip-gloss tubes are filled, workers manually insert applicators with a gentle twist. In another line, watch as a highly automated process adds the applicators to these products. It's fun to follow a bottle through the fragrance line—filling, manually inserting pumps, stamping down lids, and hand-packing perfume bottles.

The tour highlight, however, is the waxy-smelling lipstick line. Liquid lipstick is pumped into oblong metal molds, which are stacked onto an iced cooling table to solidify. Workers manually insert each lipstick bullet into its tube. Upright tubes march into a glass-enclosed oven, where flames caress the outer layer to give the lipstick a brilliant shine. The next time you apply (or watch someone apply) lipstick, you'll appreciate this labor that enhances women's beauty.

The corporate tour's highlight is the late Mary Kay's personal office at the corporate headquarters, with its crescent-shaped pastel sofa and her desk, followed by a tour of the museum. While reservations are required for the tour that includes Mary Kay's office, reservations are not required to visit the museum only. Its art deco white, pink, and black granite floors and brass-trimmed dark wood cases display mannequins wearing the director's suits

since 1963, Mary Kay product lines, and many photographs and awards.

Cost: Free

Freebies: No

Video Shown: Several videos in museum cover company history, manufacturing process, company career opportunities, and annual seminars.

Reservations Needed: No, for museum only. Yes, for guided tours of corporate facility (including Mary Kay's office and museum) and manufacturing plant. Please call (972) 687-5720 at least 2 business days in advance to make reservations. Groups, see below.

Days and Hours: Museum: Mon–Fri 9:00 AM–5:00 PM. Guided manufacturing headquarters tours: Mon 2:00 PM only, Tue–Thur 10:30 AM and 2:00 PM, Fri 10:30 AM. Guided tours of corporate location: Mon–Fri 10:00 AM or 2:00 PM. Closed holidays.

Plan to Stay: 1 hour for Corporate and Manufacturing tours.

Minimum Age: 10, unless accompanied by an adult.

Disabled Access: Yes, for corporate building and most of factory tour (call ahead for arrangements for 1 flight of stairs). Wheelchairs are available.

Group Requirements: Groups larger than 25 must call at least 1 week in advance for reservations. Groups larger than 20 will be split into smaller groups.

Special Information: Photography allowed in museum and office, but not in plant.

Gift Shop: No

Directions: To corporate headquarters: From Lyndon B. Johnson Frwy. (I-635), take Dallas Tollway North and exit at Westgrove/Keller Springs. Follow service road through Keller Springs and turn left at Westgrove. Turn left back onto service road going south. Mary Kay is first big building on right. To manufacturing facility: from Stemmons Frwy. (I-35), take Regal Row exit. Head south on Regal Row. Plant is 2 blocks ahead on left.

Nearby Attractions: American Airlines C. R. Smith Museum (see page 299); Dr Pepper Bottling plant tour in Irving (call 972-721-8112); Cavanaugh Flight Museum; Downtown Dallas attractions include Sixth Floor Museum (JFK Museum), Dallas Museum of Art (including the Museum of the Americas wing), and West End MarketPlace.

TEXAS

Discover the bakery that introduced sliced bread to Texas. Now one of the most modern bread bakeries in America, Mrs Baird's started as a home-kitchen operation in 1908. Although the Baird children once delivered bread to the neighbors in baskets, a fleet of delivery trucks now journey the vast highways of Texas and the surrounding region. One thing has not changed since Mrs. Baird began baking in her home five generations ago: "Family pride" is still the final ingredient.

After donning a hair net, embark on a voyage into the bakery. Notice the smell of yeast permeating the air around you. Compare your own pantry to this fantastic food warehouse. Bags stacked high on metal shelves around you contain up to 2,000 pounds of ingredients, such as salt and powdered milk. Each of these "super sacks" of ingredients will eventually end up sifted together in the 25-foot-tall sifter and then moved to the mixers to become part of the bread dough. The company uses 100,000 to 200,000 pounds of flour each day to make up to 144,000 loaves of bread.

As you move out of the ingredient area and closer to the ovens, the aroma changes to that of fresh-baked bread. Machines drop fistfuls of dough for hamburger buns into baking pans. Turn around to see larger portions of dough for making loaves of bread fall into place. At times, you might witness Mrs Baird's specialty, hand-twisted white bread, the only exception to full automation in the plant. Watch the baker twist two long ropes of dough together like a braid to form one loaf. The dough is then placed in the pans and taken by conveyor to rise.

Gaze upward at a bumper-to-bumper highway of bread and hamburger buns traveling by on cooling tracks above your head. The depanner machine removes the fresh-baked bread from the pans with rows of suction cups. Blades, sharpened every five minutes, slice the 107°F bread. Then the fresh bread is popped into the bags you see in the store.

Cost: Free

Freebies: Hot slice of buttered bread, pencil, activity pamphlet, and a goodie bag of powdered doughnuts, freshly baked at the cake plant next door (cake plant is not open for tours).

Video/DVD Shown: 5-minute video on the nutritional importance of bread, the company history, and the baking process.

Reservations Needed: Yes, reservations should be made at least 2 weeks in advance. Call (817) 293-6230 and ask for the tour coordinator or call (817) 615-3050 to leave a voice-mail message.

Days and Hours: Tues–Thur 10:00 AM–4:00 PM. Closed holidays.

Plan to Stay: 45 minutes.

Minimum Age: 6

Disabled Access: Yes

Group Requirements: Maximum group size is 50 people. Larger groups will be divided. One adult is required for every 10 children.

Special Information: No photography. It's warm in the bakery, so dress comfortably. No shorts, sandals, or jewelry. Hand twisting can be seen only on occasion. Tours are available at 6 Mrs. Baird's bakeries. Tour schedules available on website. Reservations can be booked through website for all sites.

Gift Shop: No

Directions: From downtown, take I-35W South to Sycamore School Rd. Turn left under the highway overpass. Take an immediate left onto the service road. Turn right into the bakery and follow "Tour Visitors" signs.

Nearby Attractions: American Airlines museum and Mary Kay tour (see pages 299 and 307); Dr Pepper Bottling plant in Irving (cal 972-721-8112).

TEXAS

Nokona

Nocona, Texas, is the leather goods capital of the Southwest. Nocona Athletic Goods Company started making Nokona baseball gloves and other sporting goods during the Depression. While U.S. sporting-goods companies began shifting labor-intensive baseball-glove production overseas in the early 1960s, Nocona proudly stayed at home. (Currently, imports represent 98 percent of glove sales nationwide.) The Nokona ball glove is one of two glove lines still made in the U.S.A., and the plant tour gives you the chance to see all of the production steps. While workers have some help from machines, you'll notice that the process is far from automated.

Making baseball and softball gloves begins with selecting the correct leather, which Nocona does on-site, not overseas. The tour guide passes around pieces of cowhide and kangaroo leathers so you can feel the contrasting textures, and explains the differences between leather used in today's gloves compared to that of previous decades. Each glove's 14 to 18 leather pieces are die-cut from big leather sheets. Workers lay a metal frame in the shape of a hand on the correct spot and use a press to cut out a piece. They use experience gained from guiding patterns here for the past 50 years.

After stamping the name and logo on the leather, workers meticulously sew the pieces together. Up to this point the glove has been built inside out, so it's turned right side out one finger at a time on a hot iron. Workers then weave a long needle in and out of the glove to lace the leather together before stretching it on hot irons and applying leather-conditioning oils. You'll be tempted to pick up a glove and play catch in the middle of the factory.

From the aroma of leather, move to the smell of glue in the department that assembles football equipment, such as shoulder pads and helmets. Workers construct this equipment mostly from pre-molded plastic parts and shock-absorbing pads. Don't forget to visit the company's small collection of old leather baseball mitts and football helmets, conjuring images of Ty Cobb and Knute Rockne in the years of day games, grass gridirons, and U.S.A.–made sporting goods.

Cost: Free

Freebies: Product catalogs used for wholesale trade.

Video/DVD Shown: No

Reservations Needed: Preferred

Days and Hours: Mon–Fri 8:00 AM–12:00 PM and 1:00–4:00 PM. Closed holidays, 2 weeks at Christmas, and 2 weeks around July 4th.

Plan to Stay: 1 hour.

Minimum Age: None

Disabled Access: Yes

Group Requirements: No minimum. Maximum group size is 30 people with 1 day's advance notice.

Special Information: Glue smell may initially bother some people.

Gift Shop: Nokona Retail Outlet, within the factory, sells all Nokona gloves and equipment.

Directions: From Dallas, take I-35 to Hwy. 82 West exit in Gainesville. Stay on Hwy. 82 West into Nocona, turn right at Clay St., and left on Walnut. Company is in big red brick building on right.

Nearby Attractions: Justin Park; Lake Nocona.

TEXAS

Southwest

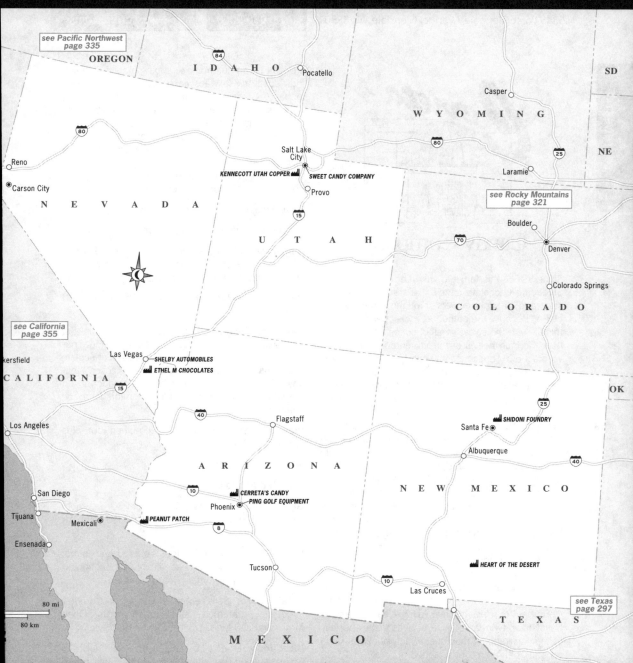

see Pacific Northwest
page 335

OREGON

IDAHO

84

Pocatello

SD

WYOMING

Casper

80

NE

80

Reno

Salt Lake City

25

Laramie

Carson City

KENNECOTT UTAH COPPER

SWEET CANDY COMPANY

NEVADA

Provo

see Rocky Mountains
page 321

15

UTAH

Boulder

70

Denver

COLORADO

Colorado Springs

see California
page 355

Las Vegas

SHELBY AUTOMOBILES

ETHEL M CHOCOLATES

kersfield

CALIFORNIA

15

OK

40

Flagstaff

25

SHIDONI FOUNDRY

Santa Fe

Los Angeles

ARIZONA

Albuquerque

40

San Diego

10

NEW MEXICO

Tijuana

CERRETA'S CANDY

PING GOLF EQUIPMENT

Mexicali

Phoenix

PEANUT PATCH

8

Ensenada

HEART OF THE DESERT

Tucson

10

80 mi

Las Cruces

see Texas
page 297

80 km

TEXAS

MEXICO

Cerreta's Candy

CHOCOLATES, CANDY,
AND CARAMEL POPCORN

5345 West Glendale Avenue, Glendale, AZ 85301   (623) 930-9000   www.cerreta.com

Candy Company

Since 1968, this family-owned company has been producing chocolate candy that's sold at its retail store and in supermarkets throughout the western U.S.A. Because the entire factory is open, your nostrils fill with the sweet smell of cocoa and your ears hear the loud noises of mixers, enrobers, and conveyors turning chocolate into candy. Cerreta's makes four types of chocolate candy in this factory: mints, creams, caramels, and clusters. Throughout the factory, you will notice workers hand-pouring and hand-mixing ingredients into oversized copper kettles.

Since this is a self-guided tour, overhead monitors along the walkway help explain the candy-making process. Lean against the waist-high railing to see the action. The long, yellow, automatic molding machine makes French mints. A pale green, minty liquid fills one plastic tray, containing 32 molds, every six seconds. The trays are flipped over to allow the excess to flow out. Once the mint cools, chocolate centers are injected and cooled again before dollops of mint are added, sealing the chocolate inside. Notice the mile-long spiral conveyor in the glass-enclosed chilling room. After the mints travel around and around up the spiral, workers release the candies from their molds, much like removing ice cubes from plastic trays. The released candies travel down twin-lane conveyor belts to the specially designed wrapping machine, which swallows them up and spits them out wrapped at a rate of 1,000 candies per minute.

In the background, watch as a worker pours liquid caramel from a copper cauldron onto a long, refrigerated stainless-steel table. Once solidified, the caramel is cut into long ribbons. Some of the ribbons

are fed into an automatic wrapping machine, which individually twist-wraps each caramel in clear cellophane. Unwrapped caramels and other centers, such as buttercreams and peanut brittle, travel to the enrobing machine. There, centers move along a wire conveyor belt and are drenched in chocolate. If they're making caramel popcorn, workers dig into the bowl to scoop and mix the coated popcorn to prevent sticking. It looks like so much fun, you'll want to put on a pair of rubber gloves and help them.

Cost: Free; chocolate pizza making, $7.

Freebies: Sample of Cerreta's candy.

Videos/DVDs Shown: Videos on overhead monitors along walkway provide up-close view of the entire chocolate-making process.

Reservations Needed: No, except for groups of 30 or more.

Days and Hours: Self-guided viewing: Mon–Sat 8:00 AM–6:00 PM. Guided tours: Mon–Thur 10:00 AM and 1:00 PM. Open-House chocolate pizza making year-round after tour. Closed holidays. Even though there is limited production on Saturdays, you can view video monitors and see equipment.

Plan to Stay: 20 minutes for self-guided tour, plus time for retail store.

Minimum Age: None

Disabled Access: Yes

Group Requirements: Groups of 30 or more should call in advance to arrange guided tours for special tour times.

Special Information: The tour is offered year-round; do call ahead, however, since limited production on Saturday and in summer. Hot in summer.

Retail Store: Sells entire selection of Cerreta's chocolates, caramels, and French mints. Open Mon–Sat 8:00 AM–6:00 PM. Closed holidays.

Directions: From I-10, take 59th Ave. North to Glendale Ave. Turn right, and Cerreta's will be on the right. You'll recognize the building by its upside-down copper cauldronlike awning.

Nearby Attractions: Ping Golf Equipment tour (see page 314); Saguaro Ranch Park.

4322 East County 13th Street, Yuma, AZ 85365

(928) 726-6292
(800) USA-PNUT

www.thepeanut
patch.com

The Peanut Patch has become a rich tradition in Southwest Arizona. A trip to or through Yuma would not be complete without stopping by for a visit to the George family, owners of the Peanut Patch. The Peanut Patch has come a long way from its humble beginnings as a local grower of peanuts. They no longer grow peanuts in Yuma, but they cook and sell peanuts of every description. You will get to see how a peanut plant grows and watch the preparation of some peanut treats, such as peanut brittle and peanut butter.

Start off the tour with a peanut-growing lesson. You may be amazed to learn that peanuts, as legumes, grow underground; they are planted in April and are harvested in October. A single peanut plant remains from the hundreds that once grew on the farm. Pictures of successive growth stages of the peanut plant are also on display.

Walk through the kitchens of the store and watch peanut treats being made. One kitchen is devoted to making peanut brittle. Smell the butter, peanuts, and sugar as they simmer together in copper kettles. The hand-stirred mixture is poured onto old-fashioned marble slabs for cooling, and later it's broken into pieces of peanut brittle. In the second kitchen, watch employees hand-dip candies into rich chocolate. Out in the store, look through a Plexiglas-

enclosed area at the fudge bubbling in a stainless steel double boiler. By the end of your tour, you will have worked up quite an appetite from the sights and smells of all these peanut treats. Luckily, you get to taste the treats you just watched being made!

Cost: Free

Freebies: Fudge and peanut samples.

Video/DVD Shown: No

Reservations Needed: No, except for groups larger than 10 people.

Days and Hours: October–November and January–April only: Tue and Fri, 10:00 AM. Closed Thanksgiving, Christmas, New Year's, and Easter.

Plan to Stay: 30 minutes, plus time for gift shop.

Minimum Age: None

Disabled Access: Yes

Group Requirements: Call at least 2 weeks in advance for reservations. Minimum group is 10 people. No maximum group size.

Gift Shop: Sells peanuts, other nuts, trail mixes, dried fruits, and candies. Offers unique Arizona specialties, such as cactus jellies and local farmers' products. Catalog available (call 800-USA-PNUT). Mon–Sat 9:00 AM–5:00 PM. Closed June 1–September 30, Thanksgiving, Christmas, New Year's, and Easter.

Directions: Take I-8 to Yuma. Take Ave. 3E exit. Go south to County 13th St. Turn left and travel 1.25 miles. The Peanut Patch will be on your left.

Nearby Attractions: Century House Museum; Yuma Crossing State Historic Park; Territorial Prison; Yuma River Tours.

2201 West Desert Cove, Building 120,
Phoenix, AZ 85029

(602) 687-5385

www.pinggolf.com

SOUTHWEST

Long before Karsten Solheim began playing golf at the age of 43, he had an interest in golf clubs. Solheim, one of the golf industry's most recognizable figures, started perfecting golf clubs with the goal of making a fiendishly fickle game easier to play. The first putter he developed made a loud, shrill "ping" sound; hence, the eventual name for his clubs. When Julius Boros won the Phoenix Open in 1967 with a Ping putter, the popularity of Ping golf clubs increased. That same year Solheim left General Electric as a project engineer to start Karsten Manufacturing Corporation, the parent company of Ping Golf Equipment, in a small 20-by-40-foot building. Today the company employs about 1,000 workers, and the site covers most of a city block.

Your tour begins after you view the displays of the company's golf clubs, woods, irons, putters, and bags in the visitors center. The guide, usually a former golf professional, leads you past the original 1967 building. Currently the repair department, it initially served as Karsten's production area, machine shop, reception area, order desk, and shipping department.

Because of the size of the "campus," you walk in and out of buildings based on proximity rather than order of production. Since the iron and putter grinding area is so noisy, the guide explains the process only outside the building. The irons, cast by the off-site foundry, require grinding and tumbling for further shaping.

In the iron, putter, and wood assembly areas, shafts are cut to the correct length and installed into club heads, while clubs wait on shelves for grips. To attach a grip, two-way adhesive tape is wrapped around the shaft. A solvent poured onto the tape turns it into glue, and the grip is slid onto the shaft. The club's lie angle is adjusted for the height and swing habits of its future owner. In the stamping area, the clubs are stamped with individual serial numbers. The last part of your tour takes you to Karsten Engineering, a subsidiary that assists in designing clubs and other products. See milling machines and examine their handiwork at nearby display tables. After the tour, you'll want to play golf at one of the many golf courses in the Phoenix area.

Cost: Free

Freebies: Information sheets, brochures, personalized fitting recommendations.

Videos/DVDs Shown: Yes

Reservations Needed: Yes

Days and Hours: Tue and Thur 9:30 AM. Call for availability and reservations 3–4 months in advance.

Plan to Stay: 2 hours for tour, videos, and questions.

Minimum Age: 9

Disabled Access: Yes

Group Requirements: Cannot handle group tours larger than 18 people.

Special Information: No photography. Wear comfortable shoes for the half mile of walking. Ping golf club owners and people interested in golf will enjoy the tour the most.

Gift Shop: No. Products sold through dealers and area golf courses.

Directions: From I-17, go east on Peoria Ave. Turn left onto 23rd Ave. Turn right on Desert Cove. Turn right on Karsten's Way and park in the lot on the left.

Nearby Attractions: Cerreta's Candy tour (see page 312); Metro Center Shopping Mall; Phoenix attractions include more than 100 golf courses.

Only in Las Vegas would a candy factory identify its product lines with flashing red neon signs. Thousands of people come here daily as a diversion from Las Vegas's casinos. Ethel M began in 1981 with one shop and now has around 16 in three states. A tour of the facility not only shows you how premium chocolates are made, but also offers you relaxation in its cactus garden.

Stroll along pathways that meander through the Ethel M cactus garden's 350 varieties of shrubs, succulents, and cacti. Species collected from South Africa, the Red Sea, South America, and Japan are up to 60 years old. The garden blossoms with red, orange, and purple flowers from late March to May, but the stone benches soothe visitors year-round.

The Living Machine, located adjacent to the cactus gardens, purifies the chocolate factory's wastewater. Visitors view over an acre of waste-consuming ecologies in tanks, marshes, and reed beds transforming wastewater into water clean enough to be used for landscape irrigation.

Start your self-guided factory tour at the kitchen. From a corridor, observe the chocolate making through glass windows. Depending on when you visit, you'll see different production steps. Batches of toffee bubble in copper kettles, then workers pour this Almond Butter Krisp onto cooling tables. Buttercreams (maybe raspberry or chocolate) or liqueur creams (perhaps Amaretto) swirl slowly in shallow, round mixers. Metal blades stir these candy centers until they're smooth.

Farther along the corridor, notice the two massive pale-yellow machines. Empty plastic coin-shaped molds, patterned after U.S. 1904 Series coins, methodically move along the conveyor belt through the long machine. Liquid milk or dark chocolate pours through spigots to fill the molds. Some even get mint cream centers. The molds are vibrated to shake out air bubbles, conveyed through a cooling tunnel, and then flipped over to release the chocolate coins. You exit into the retail store, where you are greeted with a sample chocolate of the day.

Cost: Free

Freebies: Sample chocolate of the day.

Videos/DVDs Shown: No

Reservations Needed: No

Days and Hours: Mon–Sun 8:30 AM–7:00 PM. Closed Christmas. No production for 1 week in July, but can visit cactus garden and view videos.

Plan to Stay: 15 minutes for self-guided tour and videos, plus cactus garden and shops.

Minimum Age: None

Disabled Access: Yes

Group Requirements: Can accommodate very large groups.

Special Information: Best times to see production are Mon–Fri 9:00 AM–2:00 PM. Special holiday season cactus garden display.

Gift Shop: Chocolate Shop sells entire Ethel M line—more than 50 varieties of chocolates. Offers 1-pound assortment gift boxes, the popular 29-ounce "Taste of Las Vegas" assortment, with a photograph of Las Vegas's neon lights on the cover, and silver "Las Vegas slot machines" filled with chocolate coins. Open same hours as tour. Closed Christmas and shorter hours on Thanksgiving. Catalog available from (800) 4-ETHELM.

Directions: From Las Vegas strip, drive east on Tropicana. Turn right onto Mountain Vista. Turn left onto Sunset Way (Green Valley Business Park) and follow signs. From Hoover Dam, take Boulder Hwy. to Sunset Rd. Turn left onto Sunset Rd. Turn right onto Sunset Way. Follow above directions.

Nearby Attractions: Clark County Heritage Museum; Sunset Station Casino.

SHELBY AUTOMOBILES

Carroll Shelby is a famous figure in the history of motor sports. During the 1950s, he set a new land speed record, won the famous 24-hour race at Le Mans in France, and achieved many other successes. However, he is equally esteemed for his later influence on automotive design. Developed in the early 1960s, his signature Cobra cars—light, fast, nimble, but well balanced—were the first to combine the handling of European race cars with the power of American engines. Shelby still designs and builds Cobra cars.

Appropriately, Shelby Automobiles sits at the entrance of the Las Vegas Motor Speedway, which sprawls at the edge of the vast Nevada desert. Tours start on the checkered floor of the Shelby Museum, which houses over a dozen Shelby cars of the past (including the first Shelby Cobra from 1962) and the future (prototypes of forthcoming models). Between 1965 and 1970, Shelby Automobiles produced its own line of Mustangs for Ford, and some of these historic vehicles are also present. This is an ideal setting to learn more about the Shelby tradition of automotive design, and your tour guide gives a brief talk on the history of the man and his machines.

You then move to the cavernous factory to see the stations where the workers build new cars. For safety reasons, visitors tour the plant while the workers are on break, but the excursion does cover well over half the 100,000 square feet of the manufacturing facility, including the area of research and development. With cars under construction both down on the floor and raised for underbody work, the tour keeps your gaze moving in many directions at vehicles in various stages of completion. Among the parts that you see are the chassis of the vehicles: the supporting frame and working parts, which include rack and pinion steering and specialized gears that can take the finished car from zero to 60 mph in 3.7 seconds. You also view the unfinished interiors. Among the stylish elements that go into each car is a classic 16-inch wood-rim steering wheel, a trademark of Cobras from their beginnings in the 1960s.

If you did not have enough time before the tour, you can return to the museum to view 45 minutes of videos about Carroll Shelby and his legacy. For sports-car enthusiasts who care to buy a Shelby vehicle of their own, the facility also includes a dealership.

Cost: Free

Freebies: No

Video/DVD Shown: Two videos (30 minutes and 15 minutes) run continuously in the Shelby Museum.

Reservations Needed: No

Days and Hours: Mon–Fri 10:30 AM. Closed holidays.

Plan to Stay: About 40 minutes for the tour, plus time for the Shelby Museum.

Minimum Age: No

Disabled Access: Yes

Group Requirements: Groups of over 30 people must reserve a tour in advance. Groups may arrange a tour for any time during the general hours of operation.

Special Information: The Shelby Museum contains over a dozen historic Shelby cars. Open Mon–Fri 8:00 AM–4:00 PM. Closed holidays.

Gift Shop: The shop sells Shelby apparel, souvenirs, and memorabilia. Open Mon–Fri 8:00 AM–4:00 PM. Closed holidays.

Directions: From I-15, take the Speedway Blvd. exit and get on Speedway Blvd. Shelby American is on the right, at the entrance to the Las Vegas Motor Speedway.

Nearby Attractions: Ethel M Chocolates (see page 215); Desert National Wildlife Refuge.

Heart of the Desert

Eagle Ranch, 7288 Highway 54/70, Alamogordo, NM 88310

(505) 434-0035

www.eagleranch pistachios.com

According to ancient Turkish legend, young lovers walked through moonlit pistachio groves to test their love. If they heard pistachios splitting open on the trees, they knew their love was indeed true. Centuries later, in another desert thousands of miles away, the Schweers family may have had this romantic legend in mind when they chose Heart of the Desert Pistachios as their trademark. As owners and operators of Eagle Ranch Pistachio Groves, New Mexico's first and largest pistachio farm, the Schweers have put years of love and hard work into producing these delicious nuts.

Tours are offered year-round, but if you visit Eagle Ranch in September, you can watch the mechanical shaking machines harvest the pistachios. The shakers clasp and vibrate the trees, releasing showers of nuts that are then transported into bins by conveyor belt. The pistachios move past a group of eagle-eyed workers who remove blemished or deformed nuts. The good pistachios enter a needle sorter, a six-foot-diameter barrel open at both ends. The needles that line the inside of the barrel hook into the split nuts' green meat, leaving the unsplit pistachios to roll out the bottom. The unsplit nuts are shelled, and these nutmeats are flavored, roasted, and packaged.

The split nuts, meanwhile, flow across a sloped, vibrating sizing machine composed of flat plates with various size holes. As the pistachios jump along the vibrating plates, the smaller nuts fall through the tiniest holes into bins underneath. The remaining nuts continue along the machine, dropping into openings of increasing size until each bin along the way holds larger-sized pistachios.

In another process, pistachios move downhill on a hopper that feeds into a seemingly benign color-sorting machine. Suddenly you may hear a machine gun–like blast as nuts shoot out of the color sorter. A jet of air kicks out those nuts whose hue does not match the machine's prescribed color standards. The remaining pistachios are either sprayed with chili flavors or salted, then roasted in a huge oven. Workers insert and remove 40-pound trays of nuts from the 10-foot-tall roaster in a nonstop workout. Meanwhile you can take a relaxed stroll into the gift shop, where you can sample and "go nuts" over Heart of the Desert pistachios.

Cost: Free

Freebies: Pistachio nut and candy samples.

Video/DVD Shown: Yes

Reservations Needed: No, unless groups larger than 10 people want different tour times.

Days and Hours: Memorial Day–Labor Day: Mon–Fri 10:00 AM and 1:30 PM. Labor Day–Memorial Day: Mon–Fri 1:30 PM. Closed Thanksgiving and Christmas.

Plan to Stay: 45 minutes for tour, plus time for gift shop, visitors center, and art gallery.

Minimum Age: None

Disabled Access: Yes

Group Requirements: Groups larger than 10 people should call 1 week in advance for alternative tour times. No maximum group size.

Special Information: Adjacent to gift shop is a visitors center with background information on the farm and pistachios, and an art gallery.

Retail Store: Sells pistachios, a wide selection of New Mexico wines, including their own Heart of the Desert Wine, and other gourmet gifts. Other items include Southwestern Indian jewelry, gift baskets, pottery, and T-shirts with Southwestern themes. Open Mon–Sat 8:00 AM–6:00 PM; Sun 9:00 AM–6:00 PM. Mail-order brochure available from (800) 432-0999.

Directions: From I-25 or I-10, take Hwy. 70 North. Eagle Ranch is 4 miles north of Alamogordo on Hwys. 54/70.

Nearby Attractions: Apache Trail attractions include White Sands National Monument, Space Hall of Fame, Ruidoso Downs Race Track, Lincoln National Forest, Hubbard Museum of the American West, Valley of Fire State Recreation Park, and Lincoln Historical District (Billy the Kid Museum and Lincoln County Heritage Center).

SHIDONI
Foundry • Gallery • Gardens

The bronze age lives on in the desert village of Tesuque, about five miles north of Santa Fe. Shidoni Foundry, which takes its name from a Navajo greeting, is a vital resource for artists who work in bronze—a lot of bronze. The foundry specializes in monumental casting: its projects include 13 life-sized horses for the racetrack in Lexington, Kentucky, and a 24-foot-long representation of a cattle drive that is now located in front of the Astro Hall in Houston, Texas. Shidoni pours five tons of bronze a month, and sometimes 700 pounds into a single mold. Without doubt, the best day to visit the foundry is Saturday, when metalworkers steer molten bronze into the ceramic shells to create the metal pieces that artists will assemble into their works.

Tours of the foundry are self-guided. Following red arrows on the floor, you see every step in the artists' process of making metal sculptures. First are the studios where artists create wax molds in the shapes of the various parts that will compose their works. The artists set each mold in a thick ceramic shell, a swollen impression of the shape the corresponding metal part will ultimately take. These ceramic shells receive the molten metal.

The climax of a visit to Shidoni is the spectacular pouring of hot liquid bronze, which occurs in the dip room (officially known as the "investment" room). Dressed like astronauts in silver suits with helmets, bronze-working experts prepare to deliver up to several hundred pounds of molten metal, heated to 2,100°F, into the molds. The preheat furnace rumbles loudly as it warms the ceramic shells; then it falls quiet, leaving a dramatic hush. The metalworkers bring out the molten bronze, which glows a brilliant golden orange in the relative gloom of the interior. As they pour the bright liquid metal, drops splash and spill, bouncing off the floor—a dramatic sight.

The last area of your tour is the metal shop, where artists assemble sculptures. All around, you see the sundry parts of perhaps half a dozen projects: a giant hand here, a horse's rear end there. Some finished works stand in the sculpture garden outside. You can also visit the Bronze Gallery, where you may survey the many unique small to mid-sized bronze sculptures that are for sale.

Cost: Free

Freebies: No

Video/DVD Shown: No

Reservations Needed: No (except for groups of 10 or more people).

Days and Hours: Sat 9:00 AM–5:00 PM (best day to visit; call for a schedule of bronze pourings). Also open Mon–Fri 12:00 PM–1:00 PM. Closed holidays.

Plan to Stay: 1 hour

Minimum Age: No

Disabled Access: Yes

Group Requirements: Groups of 10 or more should call to make arrangements at least a week in advance.

Gift Shop: Shidoni has 2 galleries: the Bronze Gallery, full of unique contemporary metal sculptures for sale, and an adjoining sculpture garden; and Shidoni Arts, an indoor and outdoor collection of fine American crafts. Open Mon–Sat 9:00 AM–5:00 PM.

Directions: From Hwy. 285 (St. Francis Dr.), take the Tesuque exit and follow the road straight into the village. After about 1.25 miles, take the hairpin right turn on Bishop's Lodge Rd. and drive about half a mile. Shidoni is on the right. From Santa Fe Plaza in Santa Fe, drive 5 miles north on Bishop's Lodge Rd. Shidoni is on the left.

Nearby Attractions: Santa Fe's attractions include Museum of Fine Arts, Museum of Spanish Colonial Art, Museum of Indian Arts, Wheelwright Museum of the American Indian, and a historic stretch of Route 66.

Kennecott's Bingham Canyon Mine
Visitors Center, 128 South Highway 111,
Bingham Canyon, UT 84006

(801) 569-6287   www.kennecott.com

If you moved Chicago's Sears Tower to the bottom of the Bingham Canyon Copper Mine, it wouldn't even reach halfway to the top of the mine. In fact, at over two-and-one-half miles across and one-half mile deep, this mine is the deepest human-made excavation on earth. In 1906, steam shovels began eating away at a mountain that divided Bingham Canyon. Today huge rotary drills and electric shovels have replaced steam shovels, and an open pit has replaced the mountain. Kennecott is still mining copper from Bingham Canyon, which has yielded over 17 million tons of copper—more than any other mine in history.

Your visit begins with an unbelievable view of the mine from an overlook. The view encompasses hundreds of millions of years of the earth's history and lots of brown dirt in a circular pattern. Look down at the workers and machines who remove about 400,000 tons of material daily, knowing that soon you will learn exactly how miners remove the copper ore from this canyon.

Inside the Visitors Center, eight exhibits teach you everything from the mine's history to the daily uses of copper and how Kennecott protects the environment through reclamation and revegetation projects. For those especially interested in history, one exhibit tells how the surrounding area of Utah developed and prospered along with the copper industry. You will also learn about the people of Kennecott and the company's community efforts.

In the center's 80-seat theater, watch a video, which provides a condensed explanation of the entire copper-mining process, as well as some of the history behind the mine and its neighboring communities. As you drive away from the Bingham Canyon Mine, be sure to glance back at the mountainside you saw as you drove in; you now have a new appreciation of the mining industry, copper, and Bingham Canyon.

Cost: $5 per vehicle, with all funds going to local charities.

Freebies: Company brochures.

Video/DVD Shown: 15-minute video explaining mine history and operation.

Reservations Needed: No, but call at beginning and end of season to verify Visitors Center is open.

Days and Hours: Open April–end of October, weather permitting: Mon–Sun 8:00 AM–8:00 PM. Closed holidays.

Plan to Stay: 1 hour.

Minimum Age: None

Disabled Access: Yes

Group Requirements: None. $50 entrance fee for tour buses. Free for school buses. Booklet available for educators and tour guides.

Special Information: Tour does not permit you to go down into the mine. However, observation deck and exhibits offer views of it. No motorcycles allowed.

Gift Shop: Sells souvenirs, T-shirts, and postcards, as well as educational books, small rocks, and minerals. Shop is operated by local Lions Club and is not part of Kennecott. Open same hours as Visitors Center.

Directions: From Salt Lake City, take I-15 South to 7200 South exit and turn right. Turn right onto 7800 South, which turns into Bingham Hwy. Take Bingham Hwy. toward Copperton. Mine is visible on mountainside ahead. Follow signs to Kennecott's Bingham Canyon Mine.

Nearby Attractions: Salt Lake City's attractions, including Sweet Candies tour (see page 320); Salt Lake Temple, Great Salt Lake, and ski resorts, are about 25 miles away; Mormon Church headquarters.

3780 West Directors Row (1100 South), Salt Lake City, UT 84104

(801) 886-1444
(800) 669-8669

www.sweetcandy.com

If your dream is to be surrounded by over 500 varieties of candy, then you should visit this factory. Sweet Candy Company has been in business since 1892 and is best known for Salt Water Taffy, Chocolate Covered Orange Sticks, and Cinnamon Bears. The company is still owned and operated by the Sweet family (yes, that is really their name) after five generations.

On the first stop of the tour, you will see the giant warehouse (50,000 square feet, three stories high) filled with hundreds of candy items, weighing almost three million pounds. Raw materials are stored at the far end of this warehouse. Sugar, the company's number-one ingredient, is stored in one-ton bags. It uses 40 bags of sugar, or 80,000 pounds, every week.

Next, your tour guide opens the big sliding doors to let you look into the taffy kitchen. Huge mixers whip the taffy, which is at 180°F. A crane pours the bucket of taffy over giant cooling wheels. Overhead pipes running through the factory provide sugar, corn syrup, and melted chocolate, both milk and dark, "on tap." Kids will wish they had this type of plumbing system at home: just turn the spigot to get sugar, corn syrup, or chocolate—what could be better! Watch how jelly beans are made and look at the mogul machines, which press shapes into cornstarch to create molds for candies.

Walk inside the chocolate-enrobing room. Flavored sticks are so popular that a whole "chocolate waterfall" is devoted to them. The other enrober covers other candy as it moves down the belt. Each enrober feeds into its own cooling tunnel. Using a vacuum, a specially designed machine picks up the flavored sticks, boxes them, and shrink-wraps the package. In fact, the entire process of making the candy sticks is so automated that no human hands are needed.

You will experience how Cinnamon Bears are formed and learn how many days it takes to make a jelly bean. You will marvel at machines that fill up to 90 candy bags a minute.

Cost: Free

Freebies: Several fresh candy samples along the factory tour route.

Videos/DVDs Shown: Short video about the history of the company. If you desire, you can watch a selection of other videos showing close-up views of candies being made.

Reservations Needed: Yes, call (801) 886-1444 for reservations.

Days and Hours: Reserved tour times are available Mon–Thu. Closed Fri (though the store is open till noon), weekends, and holidays.

Plan to Stay: 45 minutes, plus time for the candy store.

Minimum Age: Everyone who can keep a hairnet on is welcome.

Disabled Access: Yes

Group Requirements: Call for reservations. One adult required for every 8 children.

Special Information: No cameras, cell phones, purses, or bags are allowed in the factory. You will be required to remove jewelry. You may check items at the front desk.

Retail Store: Sells a wide selection of candies fresh from the factory including "Sweet Deal" seconds and closeouts. Open Mon–Thur 8:00 AM–5:00 PM, Fri 8:00 AM–12:00 PM.

Directions: From Salt Lake City airport or I-80, take Bangerter Hwy. South. Turn left on California Ave. Turn left on 3800 West. Sweet Candy will be on your right in 2 blocks. From I-215, take California Ave. West. Turn right on 3800 West. Sweet Candy will be on your right in 2 blocks.

Nearby Attractions: Six miles southwest of Utah's biggest tourist attraction is the Mormon (Church of Jesus Christ of Latter-day Saints) Temple Square.

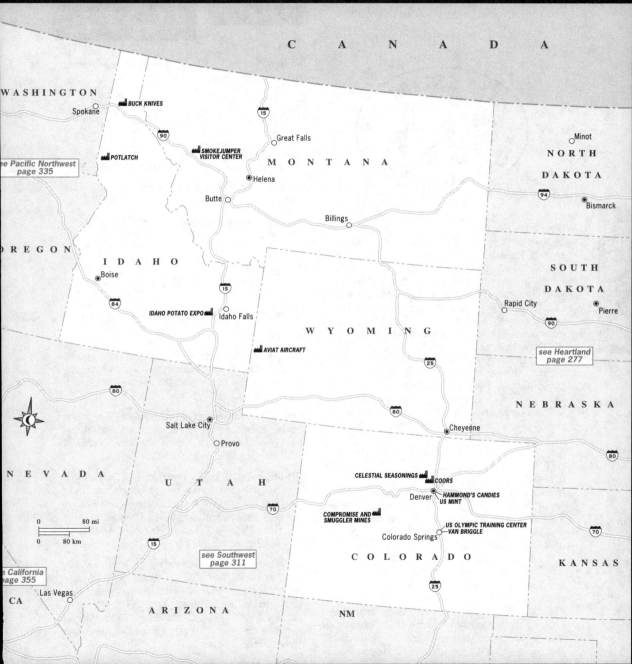

CANADA

WASHINGTON

BUCK KNIVES

Spokane

90

POTLATCH

15

**SMOKEJUMPER
VISITOR CENTER**

Great Falls

M O N T A N A

See Pacific Northwest
page 335

Helena

Butte

Billings

O R E G O N

I D A H O

Boise

15

84

IDAHO POTATO EXPO

Idaho Falls

AVIAT AIRCRAFT

W Y O M I N G

80

Salt Lake City

Provo

80

25

Cheyenne

N E V A D A

U T A H

70

CELESTIAL SEASONINGS

COORS

Denver

**HAMMOND'S CANDIES
US MINT**

**COMPROMISE AND
SMUGGLER MINES**

**US OLYMPIC TRAINING CENTER
VAN BRIGGLE**

Colorado Springs

see Southwest
page 311

15

C O L O R A D O

0   80 mi
0   80 km

see California
page 355

CA

Las Vegas

A R I Z O N A

NM

Minot

N O R T H

D A K O T A

94

Bismarck

S O U T H

D A K O T A

Rapid City

90

Pierre

see Heartland
page 277

N E B R A S K A

80

70

K A N S A S

25

4600 Sleepytime Drive, Boulder, CO 80301   (303) 581-1202   www.celestial seasonings.com

At the corner of Sleepytime Drive and Zinger Street, named after its two best-selling teas, lies the home of Celestial Seasonings. Since it began in 1969 with Mo's 36, founder Mo Siegel's own herbal tea blend, Celestial Seasonings has become the largest U.S. herbal tea manufacturer—1.6 billion tea bags per year. This tour offers much more than a standard factory-floor tour. You also learn about the company's marketing approach and get your sinuses cleared while visiting the Peppermint Room.

After an enthusiastic introduction by your guide in the welcoming area (be sure to hug the cuddly, six-foot Sleepytime Bear), you may participate in a consumer test. Next to the lobby is a gallery showing the original paintings for the tea box designs.

The storage and production areas are a maze of pallets stacked with burlap bags of herbs. In a mini botany lesson, learn that black, green, and white teas come from the *Camellia sinensis* tea plant, and herbal "tea" from a variety of plants and herbs. To prevent its absorbing other flavors, the teas are isolated in their own rooms, in wooden crates stenciled with their country of origin. As the tour guide raises the metal door allowing you to enter the world of mint, you will be bombarded with intense peppermint and spearmint aromas.

On the main production floor, rock and roll music plays over the roar of the machines. Here you'll see how tea gets into those little bags and brightly printed boxes. Package-forming machines simultaneously fold recycled cardboard and insert liners. Look for the big machines in the center of the production floor with wheels of porous, coffee filter–like paper and a hopper on top. As the continuous stream of tea drops between the merging top and bottom paper layers, the paper is heat-sealed to form the bags. Groups of 20 bags are then inserted into boxes. When the open boxes roll past you on

the conveyor belt, take a peek in at your freshly formed favorite flavors.

Cost: Free

Freebies: Samples of any or all iced or hot flavors at the tea bar.

Video/DVD Shown: In art gallery, 10-minute video on company history and manufacturing process.

Reservations Needed: No, except for groups of 8 or more.

Days and Hours: Hourly tours Mon–Sat 10:00 AM–3:00 PM and Sun 11:00 AM–3:00 PM. Closed holidays.

Plan to Stay: 45 minutes for tour, plus time in Tea Shop & Emporium, Celestial Café, herb garden, and tea sampling.

Minimum Age: 5, for factory floor.

Disabled Access: Yes

Group Requirements: Groups of 8 or more should call (303-581-1317) 1 month in advance for reservations. Groups larger than 20 will be divided into smaller groups.

Special Information: No photography. Flat shoes recommended. For busy summer tour season, arrive well in advance of desired tour time. Breakfast and lunch available at the Celestia Café.

Gift Shop: Tea Shop & Emporium sells all Celestial Seasonings teas and many logoed items, including mugs and magnets with tea-box designs, and Sleepytime Bear T-shirts, hats, and aprons. Bargain boxes of teas. Open Mon–Fri 9:00 AM–6:00 PM, Sat 9:00 AM–5:00 PM, Sun 11:00 AM–4:00 PM. Closed holidays.

Directions: From Denver, take I-25 North to U.S. 36 West. Take Hwy. 157 (Foothills Pkwy.) North, which becomes Hwy. 119 heading northeast. Turn right onto Jay Rd. Turn left onto Spine Rd., then turn left onto Sleepytime Dr. From Boulder, travel northeast on Hwy. 119 (Longmont Diagonal) and follow directions above.

Nearby Attractions: Leanin' Tree Museum of Western Art; Boulder's attractions, including Pearl Street outdoor mall and hiking in the Rockies, are about 15 minutes away.

You know you're in for an adventure as you ride up Aspen Mountain's Little Nell ski run in a white Suburban. Before you enter the cabin just outside the entrance to Compromise Mine, take in the panoramic view of Aspen. In the cabin, you don a hard hat and adjust its size to fit your head using a knob in the back. The tour guide, one of the owners of the mine, points out your location on the wall map.

Outside, board an 18-gauge tour car and ride 2,000 feet underground behind an electric mine locomotive. Chug along skinny tracks into the dark, narrow, cold tunnel. The pitch-blackness is sporadically punctuated by candles burning. The four-foot-wide, seven-foot-tall tunnel gives way to larger cavelike openings. These open stopes, or underground chambers, were created by the removal of ore. One of the stopes is more than 1,200 feet deep. Disembark at station No. 8. Look down a ladder that goes down 100 feet. A series of ladders go down 800 feet. With a constant underground temperature of 55°F, your breath makes white, puffy clouds.

On the tour, you learn that the Compromise Mine is one of the largest and richest silver mines in the Aspen Mining District. In the early 1880s, immense bodies of high-grade ore were discovered in the area mines. Often veins that contain silver continued between mines. Legal battles ensued over ownership. David M. Hyman tried to prove he owned a continuous vein, while Jerome B. Wheeler argued it was not continuous. In the end, a compromise was reached, thus the name Compromise Mine. The mine remained productive until 1893, when the demonetization of silver caused Aspen's mining industry to collapse. Subsequent intermittent mining ceased in the 1930s. Since 1986, Aspen Mountain Mining Corporation rehabilitates tunnels and drives new workings in search of silver ore deposits in Compromise Mine.

Since the grandfather of one of the current owners actually mined Smuggler Mine, the main focus is the preservation of Aspen history. A walking tour of Smuggler Mine covers two levels of the mine. Climb up stairs to the second level, which overlooks the first. Walk 1,200 feet into the mine. Smuggler Mine, on the National Historic Register, is steeped in history. It is one of Aspen's most famous silver mines and one of the few still open today. The world's largest nugget of silver, removed from the seventh level, weighed 1,840 pounds. As you take your next chairlift up Aspen Mountain, you now have a new appreciation of life underground.

Cost: Compromise: Adults, $30; children under 12, $20. Smuggler: Adults, $20; children under 12, $15.

Freebies: Ore samples.

Video/DVD Shown: No

Reservations Needed: Yes, 1 week in advance.

Days and Hours: Compromise: July and August Sat 9:00 AM, 11:00 AM, 1:00 PM, and 3:00 PM. Smuggler: Year-round, by reservation.

Plan to Stay: Compromise: 2 hours. Smuggler: 1.5 hours.

Minimum Age: 5

Disabled Access: Compromise: Need to be able to ride in Suburban and rail car.

Group Requirements: Smuggler: 4-person minimum.

Special Information: Wear warm clothing, as mine temperature is 55°F year-round. Dark, wet, slippery ground.

Gift Area: Sells T-shirts and hats.

Directions: Compromise: Downtown Aspen pickup. Smuggler: From Aspen, take Hwy. 82 toward Independence Pass. After small bridge, take 3rd left. Park Ave. runs into Park Circle, which runs into Smuggler Mountain Rd. Mine gate after one hairpin turn.

Nearby Attractions: Aspen and Snowmass Mountains; summer Aspen Music Festival; Snowmass Ranch; Maroon Lake Scenic Trail; Ashcroft ghost town.

Coors

13th and Ford Streets, Golden, CO 80401   (303) 277-BEER   www.coors.com

Coors®

The world's largest single-site brewery sits at the base of the Colorado Rockies between two "table-top" mountains. In addition to the distinctly non-industrial setting, the brewery tour has other memorable sights. The "Coors Copper Kitchen" brewhouse observation area is bordered on two sides by 50 handmade copper kettles, each the size of an above-ground swimming pool. Each kettle's sides are white ceramic tile, while its top is a dome of shiny copper with a long, narrow, copper neck. The kettles have assigned roles in the brewing process, which your guide will gladly explain.

Founded in 1873, Coors claims it is the only brewer in the U.S.A. to do most of its malting on-site. Before barley can be used in the brewing process, its starch must be converted into malt. The barley steeps in two-story-deep stainless-steel tanks, which prepares it for growth. Next, the barley is spread out on long screens called "germination beds." After the seeds sprout, the barley is roasted for 14 hours in immense kilns, then aged and milled.

The stillness of the malting process contrasts with the speedy aluminum-can packaging machine area. Thousands of cans converge here every minute and then roll by in 6-, 12-, and 24-pack cartons.

Cost: Free

Freebies: 3 beer samples in Coors' hospitality lounge for visitors age 21 or older, with picture ID. Serves most Coors brands and assorted soft drinks.

Videos/DVDs Shown: Peter Coors' welcome message, shown at tour entrance area. Another video shows can and bottle manufacturing, filling, packaging, shipping, and distributing.

Reservations Needed: No, except for groups of 20 or more.

Days and Hours: Mon–Sat 10:00 AM–4:00 PM. Closed holidays. Call for schedule around holidays.

Plan to Stay: 40 minutes for brewery tour, plus time for beer sampling, gift shop, and shuttle-bus tour from Coors parking lot through Historic Golden. Coors grounds also have interesting features, including a 16-foot-high, 13-foot-wide original copper brew kettle used in the 1880s. (It stands at the main entrance.) Veterans' memorial salutes the "Defenders of Freedom."

Minimum Age: Under 18 must be accompanied by adult.

Disabled Access: Yes, an alternative route is available.

Group Requirements: Groups of more than 20 people should make reservations 1 week in advance (call 303-277-2552).

Special Information: For special-needs tours, call 303-277-2552.

Gift Shop: Coors & Co. sells a wide range of logoed clothes and beer souvenirs, including mugs, glasses, bar stools, and tap handles. Look for the popular blinking bottle-cap buttons. Open Mon–Sat 10:00 AM–5:00 PM. Closed holidays.

Directions: From Denver, take I-70 West to Hwy. 58 West to Golden. Exit at Washington Ave. and turn left on Washington, then left onto 13th St. to Ford St. for visitors' parking. You're in Golden when you see the archway over the main street ("Howdy, Folks! WELCOME TO GOLDEN—Where the West Lives!") and smell the malted barley. Parking-lot shuttle takes you on a brief tour around Golden and then to brewery.

Nearby Attractions: Colorado Railroad Museum; Foothills Art Center; Buffalo Bill Memorial Museum and Grave; Rocky Mountain Quilt Museum; Golden Pioneer Museum; Heritage Square Village.

5735 North Washington Street, Denver, CO 80216   (888) CANDY-99   www.hammonds candies.com

Ever wonder how candy canes or other hard candies get their stripes? At Hammond's, you'll see how hard candy has been made by hand since the 1920s.

First, step into the packing room, where workers pack lollipops or candy canes. Next, through a wall of windows in the kitchen, you'll see large copper kettles. Inside, 50 pounds of sugar, water, and corn syrup heats to over 300°F. Two men lift and carry a huge kettle and pour the bubbling, amber-colored liquid onto a metal table. Next you may see the candy maker adding different colors to areas of this sheet of candy: for a candy cane, he scoops out some red paste with a spatula and mixes it into one section, then adds green in another corner. Another section remains clear. Finally, the "scrap"—the crushed beginnings and ends of other candy—is melted into another section: this will become the candy canes' center.

Once the sheet has cooled, the candy maker cuts the color sections with giant scissors—these will become the candy canes' stripes. A clear section is placed on a taffy-puller-like machine. As the machine pulls, it adds air, turning the candy white. Next the red, white, and green sections are laid out on a heated table in a long, flat "blanket."

The cooks then place the center piece on the puller, to add air (so it will melt faster in your mouth) and flavoring, like cherry. Next this centerpiece, which is shaped like a big duffel bag, is placed on the blanket of stripes, and the blanket is wrapped around it. The candy makers put this roll on a heated canvas mat. The mat is on a machine that rotates the bundle. When the bundle is hot enough, a cook takes one end in his hands and pulls it to the width of a candy cane. As the cook pulls, the machine rolls the bundle. This motion creates the twist

in the candy cane stripes. As the cook cuts the strip into pieces, a worker takes each piece and puts a crook in it. Other workers place the canes on trays to cool, and then they roll the finished candy canes into the packaging room.

Cost: Free

Freebies: Candy samples.

Video/DVD Shown: 10-minute segment about the tour, from a Food Network program.

Reservations Needed: No, except for groups over 10 people or special needs groups.

Days and Hours: Mon–Fri 9:00 AM–3:00 PM, Sat 10:00 AM–3:00 PM, every 20 minutes. Closed Easter, Memorial Day, July 4th, Labor Day, Thanksgiving, Christmas, and New Year's.

Plan to Stay: 30 minutes for tour and video, plus time for gift shop.

Minimum Age: None

Disabled Access: Yes, call a day ahead for reservations.

Group Requirements: Groups of 10 or more should call in advance.

Special Information: Must wear hairnets. Very small children may wear a hat. Strollers do not fit in factory. Tour can be hot in the summer in the cooking area. Candy Cane Festival held in December; call for dates.

Gift Shop: Sells factory seconds, a range of handmade candies, Christmas decorations, books on candy making, and T-shirts. Mon–Fri 9:00 AM–4:30 PM.

Directions: From I-25, take 58th Ave. east. Turn right onto Washington St. Take the first right into Mapelton Distribution Center and look for the Hammonds sign.

Nearby Attractions: U.S. Mint tour (see page 326); Denver Zoo; Denver Museum of Natural History; Denver Museum of Miniature Dolls & Toys; City Park and Botanical Garden.

See color photos, page 16.

ROCKY MOUNTAINS

The Denver U.S. Mint produces more than 10 billion coins per year. From a glass-enclosed observation area, you'll see many of the production steps. The Mint starts with preshaped blanks for pennies and 8,000-pound metal coils for other coins. These coils first pass through presses that punch out blanks, which are slightly larger than the finished coins. Blanks are very hard, so they are softened in a 1,400°F annealing furnace.

In the coin press room, shiny blanks are converted into their familiar identities. Watch workers dump crates of blanks into the top of the machine. The coin presses are sheltered in blue huts for noise abatement. The large blue Bliss press can produce about 800 coins per minute. Its smaller, longer counterpart, the Schuler press, can produce more than 800 coins per minute, with each die stamp lasting about 1 million strikes.

In the counting and bagging area, the enormousness of the production process becomes clear. Overhead hoists dump gondolas filled with shimmering coins into vibrating hoppers on top of the counting machines. Workers standing in front of the machines use hand-held sewing machines to seal each bag once it is filled with the proper number of coins. As the tour ends, you walk through richly decorated, marble-floored hallways of the original mint building, complete with nine grand turn-of-the-20th-century chandeliers. You will also see a sentry box by the stairs, the foremost means of dissuading robbers in the 1930s.

Cost: Free

Freebies: No

Video/DVD Shown: No

Reservations Needed: Yes, make reservations online.

Days and Hours: Mon–Fri 8:00 AM–3:00 PM, excluding Federal holidays.

Plan to Stay: 30 minutes for exhibits and tour, plus time for numismatic sales room.

Minimum Age: Children under 14 must be accompanied by an adult.

Disabled Access: Yes

Group Requirements: None

Special Information: No photography in building. Many personal items, including strollers, handbags, and shopping bags, will not be allowed inside. Expect lines to enter the building during summer, so arrive early in the day, since walk-up tour reservations are given out on first-come, first-served basis. Visitors must pass through a metal detector. Due to heightened security, tour hours and policies may change without notice. Tours available at U.S. Mint in Philadelphia, PA (see page 134).

Sales Room: Sells proof and commemorative sets, medals produced by U.S. Mint, and other numismatic items. Store is on Delaware St., just south of Colfax. Open same hours as tour. Closed government holidays. Catalog information at (202) 283-2646 or (800) USA-MINT.

Directions: Located in downtown Denver, between Delaware and Cherokee Sts. From I-25, take exit for downtown Denver and follow signs to Denver Mint. Look for the building with Italian Renaissance architecture. Park on the street or in a downtown lot.

Nearby Attractions: Hammond's Candies tours (see page 325); downtown Denver attractions, including the Denver Art Museum, Colorado History Museum, and State Capitol.

U.S. Olympic athletes are made here (or at least fine-tuned to compete against the world's best). Located within the U.S. Olympic Training Center, the Visitors Center provides information about the U.S. Olympic Committee, U.S. Olympic Training Centers, and the Olympic Movement. You learn what it takes to send an athlete to the Olympic games, including the three to five years of resident training and extensive support efforts. The center features numerous frequently changing art exhibits and displays of Olympic memorabilia.

Just outside the Visitors Center, walk through the Carol Grotnes Belk Sculpture Garden, featuring four bronze sculptures and a 12-foot-high Olympic Ring Wall amid a landscape of flowers and foliage. The rooftop terrace of the Visitors Center has an Olympic-flame display and offers panoramic views of the entire complex and the Irwin Belk Olympic Path, with its life-size figures and narrative panels about Olympic and Pan-American sports.

During the tour, view athletes and their world-class training facilities, including Sport Center Gymnasiums, weightlifting and wrestling facilities, the U.S.A. Shooting Center, Coaching & Sport Science, the Aquatics Center, Sport Medicine, and the flume. Notice the special features in each facility. For example, at the Aquatics Center, look for the overhead catwalk and underwater cameras used for filming athletes both above and below water for testing purposes. The Olympic Sports Centers contain six big gyms, which can accommodate the training requirements of 14 Olympic and Pan-American sports. The Shooting Center is the largest indoor center in the western hemisphere. Beyond all the equipment and scientific methods of training, however, it's watching athletes at work in their day-to-day routines that shows the sweat, dedication, and commitment it takes to be an Olympic star.

Cost: Free

Freebies: Various items at front desk, including pens and calendars.

Video/DVD Shown: 12-minute film with Olympic highlights.

Reservations Needed: No, except groups of 10 or more (call 719-866-4656).

Days and Hours: August 15–May 31 (winter hours): Tours run hourly Mon–Sat 9:00 AM–4:00 PM. Closed between Christmas and January 1. June 1–August 14 (summer hours): Tours run every 30 minutes Mon–Sat 9:00 AM–4:00 PM (no tour at noon). Self-guided maps of the Olympic Pathway are available. A USOC ambassador at the front desk shows the film and answers questions.

Plan to Stay: 1.5 hours plus time for grounds and store.

Minimum Age: None

Disabled Access: Yes, but wheelchairs are not provided.

Group Requirements: Groups of 10 or more must reserve (call 719-866-4656).

Special Information: Tours are available at the U.S. Olympic Training Center in Chula Vista, CA, near San Diego (619-482-6222), and the U.S. Olympic Training Center in Lake Placid, NY (518-523-2600).

Gift Shop: Olympic Spirit Store offers a wide assortment of unique Olympic and sport-specific merchandise, with lots of apparel and special items during Olympic years. Open Mon–Sat 9:00 AM–6:00 PM, Sunday 11:00 AM–6:00 PM (719-866-4792 and www.usolympicshop.com).

Directions: From I-25, take the Unitah exit; from Unitah, turn right on Union and then right on Boulder. Entrance to Olympic complex is off Boulder.

Nearby Attractions: Van Briggle Art Pottery (see page 328); Air Force Academy (call 719-333-2025), Patsy's Candies (call 719-633-6777); Seven Falls, Cheyenne Mountain Zoo, Royal Gorge Bridge, Pioneer Museum, Ghost Town, Cave of the Winds, Pike's Peak, Garden of the Gods, Old Colorado City.

ROCKY MOUNTAINS

600 South 21st Street,
Colorado Springs, CO 80904

(719) 633-7729   www.vanbriggle.com

The original designs for Van Briggle Art Pottery date back to 1899. Van Briggle's *Despondency,* a vase with a figure of a despondent man molded around the rim, was first exhibited in Paris in 1900, where it won first place. A reproduction can be viewed in the Van Briggle masterpiece reproduction area. In addition to winning many awards, Artus Van Briggle reproduced a creamy, dull glaze known as "dead" matte glaze, which had been used by 14th-century Chinese. A tour of the company gives you a sense of the man and of his wife's continuation of his legacy, and an understanding of the process of making art pottery.

At the beginning of the guided portion of your tour, a potter demonstrates throwing pottery on an original early-1900s Van Briggle kick wheel. Next you move into the casting department, where rows of white chalky plaster molds are used to duplicate sculptured and wheel-thrown pieces. Liquid clay, or "slip," is poured into these molds. As the slip conforms to the exact design of the mold, the mold absorbs moisture from the slip. The longer the slip stays in the mold, the thicker the piece becomes. Excess slip is poured from the mold, leaving a hollow clay piece that is removed by hand.

The balance of your tour is self-guided, allowing you to spend as much time as you want viewing different processes and reviewing the explanatory displays, tape, and historical photographs. In the etching department, watch workers use damp sponges, carving instruments, and small turntables to smooth and refine the patterns of the unfired clay pieces called "greenware." Pottery stacked on shelves awaits one of the two kiln firings required to finish a piece. Between the first (or "bisque") firing and the second, glaze is applied to add color. In front of the kilns, displays show the piece's progression from a mold to the finished work.

Follow the curved shape of the building, past one of the largest wheel-thrown vases, to the historical photographs of Artus Van Briggle and early studios. Additional photographs show the transformation of the 1899 Colorado Midland Railroad roundhouse, where trains once chugged under the building's archways, to the current home of Van Briggle Art Pottery.

Cost: Free

Freebies: No

Video/DVD Shown: Yes

Reservations Needed: No, except for groups larger than 20 people.

Days and Hours: Mon–Sat 8:30 AM–4:30 PM. Limited production on Saturday. Closed Thanksgiving, Christmas, and New Year's.

Plan to Stay: 20 minutes for partially self-guided tour, plus time in showroom.

Minimum Age: None

Disabled Access: Yes, but not to restrooms.

Group Requirements: Groups larger than 20 people should call 1 day in advance.

Showroom: Sells art nouveau decorative pottery and lamps. Also sells Van Briggle pottery collectors' books. Open Mon–Sat 8:30 AM–5:00 PM. Catalog available from (800) 847-6341.

Directions: From Denver, take I-25 South to Exit 141. Follow U.S. 24 West to 21st St. You're there when you see the curved shape and large tan bricks of this former railroad roundhouse, now on the National Registry of Historic Places. From Pueblo, take I-25 North to Exit 141. Follow the directions above.

Nearby Attractions: Olympic Training Center (see page 327); Air Force Academy (call 719-333-2025/7742), Patsy's Candies (call 719-633-6777); Seven Falls, Cheyenne Mountain Zoo, Royal Gorge Bridge, Pioneer Museum, Ghost Town, Cave of the Winds, Pike's Peak, Garden of the Gods, Old Colorado City.

ROCKY MOUNTAINS

660 South Lochsa Street, Post Falls, ID 83854

(208) 262-0500
(800) 326-2825

www.buckknives.com

First started in 1902 by Hoyt Buck, Buck Knives is a far cry from the five knives a day that Hoyt and his son Al hand-wrought in a 100-square-foot plant in 1947. Now run by the third and fourth generations, with a fifth-generation tour guide, the company flourishes in a 200,000-square-foot plant, producing well over 50,000 knives per week.

At the first of the 15 stations you visit on your tour, you see the fine blanking machines. Used for thinner blades such as Folding Hunter and pocketknives, the fine blanking machines, operating like large hydraulic cookie cutters, punch out parts from flat, uncoiled stainless steel. Farther down the line, notice the fiery red sparks underneath the thick steel at the laser machine. The laser cuts hairline patterns outlining the circumference of blades as well as decorative elk and deer profiles inside the blades. Double disk grinders put the first edge on the blades, and the hollow grinders create a concave finish, if needed. To harden, the blades travel through a 50-foot continuous furnace, which heats the steel to 1,976°F, then a deep freezer at 121°F below zero, and then another oven to raise the temperature.

On the oval assembly line, affectionately called "The Dog Track," blades and handles are riveted together. Watch a worker hold a knife against a laminated leather stropping wheel to achieve maximum blade sharpness, known as Edge2X technology. The C.A.T.R.A. machine tests the sharpness of the blades by lowering paper down so the knife can slice through it. A worker loads knives onto a conveyer belt, which feeds into the Harper Buffer, which, much like a car wash, rotates and polishes the brass and handles. After this tour, you'll want to peel an apple or cut some nautical rope with a new, sharp Buck knife.

Cost: Free

Freebies: No

Video/DVD Shown: No

Reservations Needed: No, but recommended. Required for groups over 12 people.

Days and Hours: Mon–Thur 10:00 AM, 12:00 PM, and 2:00 PM. Closed holidays and weeks around July 4th, Christmas, and New Year's.

Plan to Stay: 45 minutes, plus additional time in the company store.

Minimum Age: Children under 7 must be well supervised by an adult; call ahead if you have children under 7.

Disabled Access: Yes

Group Requirements: Groups over 12 people should call at least 2 weeks in advance. Groups larger than 12 will be split into 2 groups.

Special Information: Photography permitted only in designated locations. Very noisy, but headset blocks out noise so you can hear tour guide only. No open-toed shoes allowed.

Gift Shop: H. H. Buck and Son's Company Store sells Buck knives at a 20 percent discount, plus logoed T-shirts, mugs, etc. Open Mon–Fri 9:30 AM–4:00 PM., Sat 10:00 AM–3:00 PM. Closed holidays and weeks around July 4th and New Year's.

Directions: From the east, take I-90 West. Take the Pleasant View Rd. exit and turn left onto N. Pleasant View Rd. Turn right onto S. Locksa St. From the west, take I-90 East. Take the Pleasant View Rd. exit and turn right onto N. Pleasant View Rd. Turn right onto S. Locksa St.

Nearby Attractions: Serano Alpacas (call 208-773-9121); the attractions and museums of Coeur d'Alene, ID, and Spokane, WA, are less than 30 miles in either direction.

Idaho Potato Expo

130 N.W. Main Street, Blackfoot, ID 83221   (208) 785-2517   www.potatoexpo.com

You may hear the whistle of an enormous train passing by as you enter the 1912 railroad depot that houses the Idaho Potato Expo. Your first questions when visiting the potato state may be "What does a potato field look like? Did we pass one on the way here?" The answer is found on a huge photograph of a potato field displayed by the entrance. The museum displays tell the history of the potato. Proceed to the next room to watch a video on how the potato gets from the field to the grocery store.

The museum displays tell the history of the potato, from early Native American use, to photos and placards detailing potato farming through the centuries.

A commentator once said Marilyn Monroe's figure would look good even in a potato sack. You'll probably agree when you gaze at the photograph of Marilyn donning a burlap sack from a local market. Her agent set up the photo shoot as a publicity stunt, and you can take it home as a poster from the gift shop. Finally, check out the world's largest potato chip, over two feet in diameter on one side.

Cost: Adults, $3; seniors, 55+ and AAA members, $2.50; children 6–12, $1.

Freebies: One box dehydrated hash browns (serves 4 adults) per couple touring the museum.

Videos/DVDs Shown: 6-minute video showing how potatoes get from the ground to the grocery.

Reservations Needed: No, except for groups of 15 or more.

Days and Hours: April–October: Mon–Sat 9:30 AM–5:00 PM. From November–March: Mon–Fri 9:30 AM–3:00 PM. Closed December 25–January 1.

Plan to Stay: 30 minutes for museum and video, plus time for gift shop.

Minimum Age: None

Disabled Access: Yes

Group Requirements: Groups of 15 or more should call in advance. Group admission is $2 per person for 15 or more people.

Special Information: There is a park and picnic area immediately behind the Expo building.

Spud Seller Gift Shop: Sells potato cookbooks, potato fudge, potato lotion, potato soup, T-shirts, hats, shot glasses, mugs, huckleberry chocolate, bells, spoons, magnets, and much, much more.

Directions: From I-15, take Blackfoot exit 93. Go east to West Main St. and turn left. The Expo is 1.5 blocks down, on the right. Look for the old railroad depot. The Blackfoot Chamber of Commerce and visitors center are also located in the building.

Nearby Attractions: Bingham County Historical Museum (history of the Blackfoot area); Shoshone-Bannock Tribal Museum; Craters of the Moon National Monument and Preserve; Sun Valley; Yellowstone and Grand Teton National Parks are all less than 3 hours away.

Potlatch

LUMBER, PAPERBOARD, AND TISSUE

805 Mill Road, Lewiston, ID 83501

(208) 799-1429
(208) 799-0123

www.potlatchcorp.com

Potlatch

Potlatch's Lewiston complex is an integrated sawmill, pulp and paper mill, and tissue mill. The tour lets you see the transformation of wood into lumber, paperboard, and tissue products, all at one site. Wood waste from the lumber mill is used by the pulp mill and is also converted into energy for the entire complex.

The sawmill produces approximately 160 million board feet of lumber annually, enough to build about 10,000 average-size homes. The mill's saws are computer assisted and use laser scanners to determine the best combination of cuts. The buzz of saws and the clatter of chains and conveyors moving the logs through the process of debarking, squaring, edging, and trimming make the mill a very noisy place.

Large piles of wood chips and sawdust wait near the digesters that cook them into pulp. The digesters (not on the tour) break down the natural glue, called lignin, that holds the wood fibers together. The pulp goes to the fiber line, which removes additional lignin and purifies and whitens the pulp. The seemingly endless paper machines produce the paperboard used in milk and juice cartons, paper cups, and other food packages. The extruders laminate polyethylene to the paperboard to make liquid-tight containers.

The tissue machines produce paper towels, toilet paper, napkins, and facial tissue (at a rate of one mile per minute), which is sold under store labels by major supermarket chains. The mixture of pulp and water is formed on a screen that drains water from the sheet. Additional water is squeezed from the sheet before it circulates around a large, steam-heated "Yankee" dryer. A thin blade then peels the dried tissue sheet from the Yankee, and the tissue sheet is wound onto what looks like the world's largest paper-towel roll. For some products, such as bathroom and facial tissue, parent rolls are combined to make multiple-ply tissues. It's no surprise that Potlatch manufactures enough single rolls of toilet paper each year to supply the equivalent of at least one roll to every American.

Your tour ends in the calm of the greenhouse. Row upon row of young pine, fir, and cedar seedlings, each under one foot tall, illustrate how much wood is used in the production of lumber and paper products. The greenhouse produces more than 3.5 million seedlings per year for reforesting the company's lands.

Cost: Free

Freebies: Pencils and brochure about the company and its product manufacturing.

Video/DVD Shown: 5-minute video overviews tour safety precautions.

Reservations Needed: *Always call, as tours have been discontinued some years based on budget and personnel.*

Days and Hours: Production times vary. Call in advance. Closed holidays and during weeklong maintenance shutdowns.

Plan to Stay: 3 hours.

Minimum Age: Under 10 must be accompanied by adult.

Disabled Access: Stairs throughout tour route. Can do drive-through tour if prior arrangements are made.

Group Requirements: Groups larger than 15 people should make reservations at least 1 week in advance.

Special Information: Tours do not run every year. No flash photography. Some areas are very noisy and can be hot during the summer. Wear comfortable shoes for at least 1 mile of walking. Certain areas may not be open due to construction.

Gift Shop: No

Directions: In Lewiston, follow Main St. East to Mill Rd. You will see signs for Potlatch. Enter complex at the main gate. Guard will direct you to parking.

Nearby Attractions: Luna House Museum; Nez Perce National Historical Park; Hell's Canyon Recreational Area; Lewis and Clark Trail sites.

ROCKY MOUNTAINS

Aerial Fire Depot, 5765 West Broadway,
Missoula, MT 59808

(406) 329-4934

Smokejumpers are firefighters who parachute into remote roadless areas of forest to extinguish small wildfires before they become big. When forest lookouts or other observers spot a blaze, perhaps sparked by lightning, they call the smokejumpers. An aircraft rushes the firefighters to the burning location, where they parachute to a spot near the flames. If no safer landing zone exists, they will even drop into dense timber. Their cargo follows them: tools, food, and drinking water. The smokejumpers dig a line around the fire, cutting off its ability to spread. Then they begin the methodical hard work of putting out the flames with soil (called "mop-up"). When the job is done, usually a day or two later, the smokejumpers shoulder their heavy packs and become hikers, marching by map and compass through the wilderness until they reach the nearest trail or road—which can be anywhere between two and 50 miles away.

The dramatic occupation of smokejumping began in 1939 under the auspices of the U.S. Forest Service. Of the 10 smokejumping bases in the nation, one of the most active is the Northern Region headquarters in Missoula, Montana. Like all smokejumping stations, it fields an elite group; every year hundreds of firefighters apply for, at most, between only 10 and 20 positions. Tours of the facility, a concrete structure built in 1954, begin at the visitor center, where exhibits present the colorful history of smokejumping.

The firefighters themselves often lead the tours. You first visit the loft, where smokejumpers work when they are not fighting fires. This is called the manufacturing room—skilled with sewing machines, the firefighters make their own jumpsuits, packs, and harnesses, along with fireline equipment. They inspect, repair, and pack parachutes at the tower, a prominent 50-foot-high structure on which they hang parachutes to check them for damage. The ready room is where they suit up before missions.

As a constant reminder of the urgent summons that may come at any time, less than 50 yards from the building stand two aircraft that ferry the smokejumpers to remote wildfires: a DC-3 turboprop that carries 16 firefighters, two spotters, and two pilots; and a C-23 Sherpa, a robust, boxlike military aircraft that carries 10 firefighters, two spotters, and two pilots. If you are lucky, the smokejumpers will be called to duty during your tour, giving you a chance to watch them suit up and fly out.

Back in the visitor center, the National Smokejumper Memorial salutes firefighters who have died on duty. Tragic episodes include disasters that claimed the lives of smokejumpers in August 1949 and July 1994.

Cost: Free (donations appreciated).

Freebies: No

Video/DVD Shown: 2 videos (totaling 6 minutes) introduce smokejumping.

Reservations Needed: During summer, no (except groups of over 20). Appointments necessary rest of year.

Days and Hours: Daily 10:00 AM, 11:00 AM, 2:00 PM, 3:00 PM, and 4:00 PM, Memorial Day–Labor Day; Mon–Fri 7:30 AM–4:00 PM (by appointment only), Labor Day–Memorial Day.

Plan to Stay: Up to 1 hour for tour.

Minimum Age: None

Disabled Access: Yes

Group Requirements: Groups of over 20 may be split into different tours.

Gift Shop: Sells shirts, caps, books, and miscellaneous souvenirs (including the smokejumper action figure). Open daily 8:30 AM–5:00 PM, Memorial Day–Labor Day.

Directions: The base is located on the outskirts of Missoula International Airport. From I-90, take the Airway Blvd. exit and follow signs to the smokejumper base.

Nearby Attractions: Museum of Mountain Flying; Fort Missoula.

ROCKY MOUNTAINS

For 85-year-old aviation pioneer Curtis Pitts, an airplane is not only a means of transportation, it's also a piece of sporting equipment. Pitts designs acrobatic airplanes, the kind that dip, flip, and roll through the sky like a roller coaster at 4,000 feet. Aviat Aircraft custom-builds about a dozen Pitts Special planes each year; the aircraft often feature pert model names like Hot Stuff and Super Stinker and regularly rack up awards in aerobatic flying competitions. Aviat also manufactures the versatile Husky airplane, a two-seater renowned for its maneuverability and its STOL (Short Take Off and Landing) ability, especially in difficult terrain. Long a favorite among bush pilots, the Husky can be equipped with skis, floats, or even 31-inch tundra tires, enabling it to land virtually anywhere.

At the Aviat factory, adjacent to Afton Municipal Airport, you will see the entire production process of both Husky and Pitts Special planes. These rough-and-tumble flying machines begin as seemingly fragile steel airframes and gradually take shape as paneling, instruments, wiring, and wings are put in place. After a brief visit to the factory's shipping and receiving area, you'll arrive at "Husky Final" and "Pitts Final." Here, largely by hand, workers nestle a plane's engine into the fuselage and then secure the wings with nuts and bolts. See a plane that's ready to roll out of the factory and tackle its first test flight.

While observing other areas of the plant, like avionics, painting, and the "Fab shop," you'll notice that detailed inspections occur at every stage of production. The rigorous inspection process dates from when Pitts Specials were shipped as home-build kits for amateurs to construct themselves. You sense precision, not massiveness, at this factory. Absent is the din typically associated with airplane construction, since hands, not machines, do most of the work here.

Notice the careful craftsmanship in the factory's covering department, where workers use an eight-inch needle to stitch Dacron fabric securely over the open spars and ribs of a wing. The wing spars in the Pitts Special are made of spruce and mahogany wood rather than metal to give the plane flexibility and lightness for its aerobatic stunts. Finally, watch as painters use handheld sprayers to coat the plane with a gray, weatherproof epoxy primer, followed by as many as 18 layers of colorful paint. If you're suddenly in the mood to abandon your car and fly home, know that a Pitts Special, wings and all, easily fits into a two-car garage.

Cost: Free

Freebies: Brochures on Aviat's various aircraft.

Video Shown: No

Reservations Needed: Only November–May.

Days and Hours: June–October: Mon–Fri 11:00 AM and 2:30 PM. November–May: by appointment only. Closed holidays.

Plan to Stay: 30 minutes for tour, plus time for gift shop.

Minimum Age: None, but noise and fumes in factory may bother small children.

Disabled Access: Yes

Groups: Groups of 25 or more should call 1 day in advance.

Special Information: Photographs permitted from safety area. Noise and fumes in factory may bother some people.

Gift Shop: Sells jackets, hats, posters, and other Pitts and Husky aircraft memorabilia. Open Mon–Fri 7:00 AM–3:30 PM.

Directions: From Jackson Hole: Begin at Hoback Junction. Drive to Alpine Junction. Make a left onto Hwy. 89 South. Drive for 30 miles, through Afton, WY. Facility located on Hwy. 89.

Nearby Attractions: Star Valley Cheese restaurant, about 15 miles north (call 307-883-2510); Jackson Hole, 70 miles away.

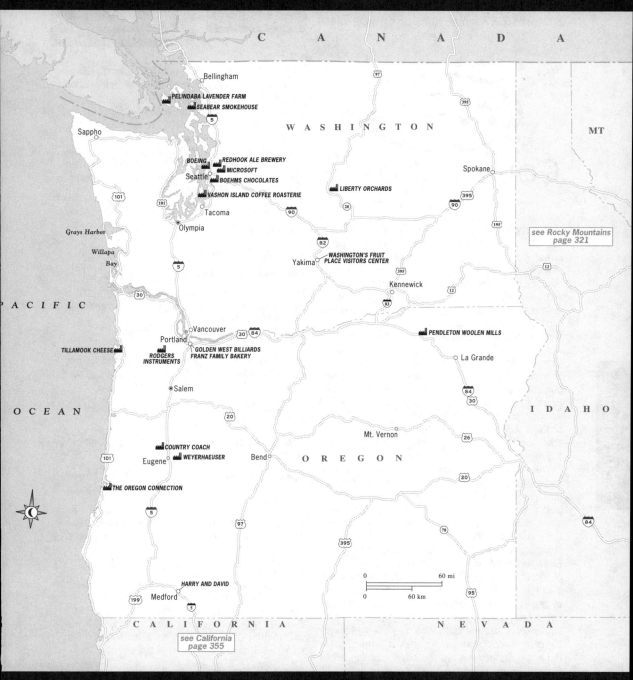

CANADA

Bellingham

PELINDABA LAVENDER FARM
SEABEAR SMOKEHOUSE

5

WASHINGTON

MT

Sappho

97

395

Spokane

BOEING   REDHOOK ALE BREWERY
MICROSOFT
Seattle   BOEHMS CHOCOLATES
VASHON ISLAND COFFEE ROASTERIE

LIBERTY ORCHARDS

395

90

101

101

Tacoma

90

28

195

Olympia

see Rocky Mountains
page 321

Grays Harbor

Willapa
Bay

82

WASHINGTON'S FRUIT
PLACE VISITORS CENTER

395

12

Yakima

5

Kennewick

12

82

PACIFIC

30

Vancouver

30 84

PENDLETON WOOLEN MILLS

Portland

TILLAMOOK CHEESE

RODGERS
INSTRUMENTS

GOLDEN WEST BILLIARDS
FRANZ FAMILY BAKERY

La Grande

84
30

OCEAN

Salem

IDAHO

20

COUNTRY COACH
WEYERHAEUSER

101

Mt. Vernon

26

Eugene

Bend

OREGON

20

THE OREGON CONNECTION

5

97

78

395

84

0   60 mi

0   60 km

HARRY AND DAVID

95

199 Medford

5

CALIFORNIA

NEVADA

see California
page 355

COUNTRY COACH

The motorcoach is the king of the recreational vehicle: a bus-sized movable living space with complete residential design, from kitchens to bathrooms. For over 33 years, Country Coach has been building diesel motorcoaches, and its operation now employs 1,600 workers in 450,000 square feet of manufacturing facilities (eight city blocks).

This makes a big tour. During about two hours, visitors to Country Coach not only walk but ride in a van from one manufacturing area to another. After leaving the Customer Care Center, the tour stops first in the factory where workers build motorcoach chassis: the steel frames, engines, transmissions, and other elements that form the mechanical foundations of the vehicles. This is a noisy, active place. Bright flashes of welding catch your eye while the wholesome smell of mechanical grease fills the nostrils. Anybody who is interested in automotive engineering and design will enjoy seeing the guts of the motorcoach drivetrain up close.

The second stage of the tour brings you into the immense space where testing and weighing occur. In a practice that is unusually thorough for its industry, Country Coach tests every chassis it makes with computerized diagnostic equipment. Hooked to the drivetrain, the stationary apparatus tests each chassis to a speed of 60 mph while reporting data. Elsewhere, instruments check not only the weight of each finished coach (up to 50,000 pounds) but also the balance of weight around the low center of gravity that such large and heavy vehicles must have. Another unit performs a full check of wheel alignment. If you are lucky, you may see brake testing of a motorcoach: at a signal, the driver guns the engine and slams on the brakes while special equipment measures the braking performance.

The third stage takes you into the factory where employees build the complex houses and interiors of each motorcoach, from the floor to the ceiling. Walls go up. Wiring and plumbing are installed, along with cabinets, carpeting, and tiles. Appliances are hooked up, including full-sized refrigerators worthy of any household.

The tour then visits the areas for painting and final finish. Although for safety reasons you do not enter a paint booth, you clearly see it through windows. Much sanding and buffing polish the exteriors. To complete your picture of the whole production process, the tour ends with a close inspection of a completed motorcoach.

Cost: Free

Freebies: No

Video/DVD Shown: No

Reservations Needed: No

Days and Hours: Mon–Thu 9:00 AM and 1:30 PM. Closed holidays, including the week between Christmas Eve and New Year's.

Plan to Stay: 2 hours.

Minimum Age: 7 (but not recommended for children under 14). There must be 1 supervising adult for every child.

Disabled Access: Limited. Call ahead to make special arrangements.

Group Requirements: Groups of over 10 should reserve a tour in advance.

Special Information: This tour is not recommended for people who are abnormally sensitive to industrial chemicals.

Gift Shop: The shop in the Customer Care Center sells clothing and RV–related items. Open Mon–Fri 8:00 AM–5:00 PM.

Directions: From I-5 South, take the Halsey/Brownsville exit. Drive 2 miles to Hwy. 99 and turn left (south). In Junction City, turn left on Sixth Ave. Country Coach is 4 blocks down on the left. From I-5 North, take Beltline Hwy. West to Hwy. 99 North. In Junction City, turn right on Sixth Ave. Country Coach is 4 blocks down on the left.

Nearby Attractions: Weyerhaeuser (see page 344); Willamette Valley Vineyards (call 503-588-9463); in Eugene, Conger Street Clock Shop & Museum, Oregon Air & Space Museum, and Science Factory Children's Museum.

PACIFIC NORTHWEST

Since its 1906 beginnings in a simple two-story frame home, Franz Bakery has fed millions of people in the Pacific Northwest. Franz's plant now covers six city blocks and turns out over 85 million pounds of baked goods each year. Your tour guide provides many impressive statistics, such as the company's daily production of 75,000 loaves, 684,300 buns, and 45,000 doughnuts from 250,000 pounds of flour. Yet, until you see the dough marching in and out of the ovens, it sounds impossible.

To create baked goods in these huge quantities, the process is highly automated with constant movement of dough and bread everywhere you look. Even with machines 100 times bigger than those you use at home, it takes 17 steps to make Franz bread, from the sifting of the flour to the loading of it on delivery trucks. You'll stare at dough being kneaded in mixers that work it into 1,200-pound pieces. The divider and rounder machines turn this hunk of dough into softball-size pieces that relax in the overhead proofer before being molded into loaf shapes and dropped into pans.

After the proof box, which allows the dough to rise to its proper size, the pans enter 100-foot-long ovens. Bread stays inside for 19 to 21 minutes, while buns only need a seven- to nine-minute experience. You'll enjoy the heat from these ovens on chilly, rainy Portland days. Once the pans move out of the oven, vacuum-suction cups gently lift the bread from the pans and place the hot bread onto a 4,000-foot-long cooling rack. After one hour and 18 minutes of cooling, the bread moves through machines that slice it, slip it into plastic bags, tie the ends, and code the packages. In the time it takes you to eat one slice of bread, 75 to 100 loaves are packaged.

Cost: Free

Freebies: Apple juice and bread; take-home Franz sack with bread miniloaf and goodies.

Video/DVD Shown: No

Reservations Needed: Yes. Tours for school and scout groups in the Pacific Northwest *only*. Not set up for regular public tours. Will not add individuals to existing group tours.

Days and Hours: *No regular tour hours. Limited availability. Call for hours, reservations, and availability.*

Plan to Stay: 1 hour for tour and tasting, plus time in thrift store.

Minimum Age: 7

Disabled Access: Yes, for most of tour.

Group Requirements: Minimum group size is 10; maximum is 60. Tours scheduled 4–6 weeks in advance.

Special Information: *Company is a local business and is very serious about limiting tours to groups in its geographic area.* No photography. Sneakers or walking shoes required. The intense smells may bother some people.

Outlet Store: Thrift store sells excess breads, buns, pastry, and muffins at discount. Open Mon–Fri 9:00 AM–5:30 PM, Sat 9:00 AM–5:00 PM. Closed holidays.

Directions: Company requests that you call above number for directions.

Nearby Attractions: Oregon Convention Center; Lloyd Center; Holladay Park; Portland's downtown attractions, including Rose Test Gardens and Japanese Gardens, are about 15 minutes away.

PACIFIC NORTHWEST

5505 Southeast Johnson Creek Boulevard, Portland, OR 97206

(800) 423-5702

www.billiardmfg.com

Playing pool (billiards to some) is a great American pastime. Golden West Billiards is the only maker of pool tables in the country that both manufactures and designs them entirely, all in one facility. This comprehensive process makes the company's factory tour an informative lesson in how pool tables are created.

Tours start in the showroom, which displays many samples of the billiard tables that have emerged from the factory since the company began in the 1960s. The range of styles is remarkable: from classic dark-wood frames of ornate Victorian elegance, some with hand-inlaid patterns, to streamlined modern designs that indulge the minimalism of the space age.

From this arena of finished products, your tour moves to the very beginning of the manufacturing process: the lumber area. Obviously, the wood frame is the foundation of a pool table, and Golden West deals in a lot of lumber. The company directly imports all the wood for its products: maple, cherry, oak, alder, mahogany, and exotic woods. It uses only hardwoods that have been thoroughly kiln-dried. The company's special care in these matters extends not just to its products but also to the environment the wood comes from. Golden West works with the National American Lumber Association to ensure that the trees were sustainably and responsibly harvested.

Most of your tour consists of walking through the factory, which covers 85,000 square feet. All of the manufacturing departments work in this immense open space. The masses of lumber you see become embellished frames through woodworking by machine and hand. You see some of the wood-carving process during your tour. After the wood is cut to length, the big carving machine shapes 16 legs at once—four tables' worth. For a woodworking aficionado, this is a powerful moment, full of noise and sawdust.

Once the wood has been carved, the assembly department puts together the frames. The turning department carves special details into the wood—those little touches that look so good under soft light in a cozy room on a winter evening. Yet another department paints the tables and applies finishing stain. Hundreds await this final step in giant stacks of 10. Amid the vast space of the manufacturing floor, this forest of billiard tables is impressive testimony to the high rate of productivity that runs through the various manufacturing departments you have just seen. It's a large output for what is still a small family-run enterprise.

Cost: Free

Freebies: No

Video/DVD Shown: No

Reservations Needed: No

Days and Hours: Tours may start at any time Mon–Fri 8:00 AM–4:00 PM. Closed holidays.

Plan to Stay: 1 hour.

Minimum Age: No

Disabled Access: Yes

Group Requirements: No

Gift Shop: The showroom sells billiard tables. Open Mon–Fri 8:00 AM–6:00 PM. Closed holidays.

Directions: From I-205 North, take exit for Johnson Creek Blvd. and turn left at end of ramp (from I-205 South, turn right at end of ramp) Drive 2 miles on S.E. Johnson Creek Blvd. Golden West is on right. From I-5 North, take exit for Terwilliger Blvd. and turn right at end of ramp on S.W. Terwilliger Blvd. (from I-5 South, turn left at end of ramp). Turn left on S.W. Taylors Ferry Rd., right on S.W. Macadam Ave., left on Sellwood Bridge to S.E. Tacoma St. After 1.5 miles, bear left on S.E. Johnson Creek Blvd., which turns sharply right after 0.75 mile. Golden West is halfway down on the left.

Nearby Attractions: In Portland, American Advertising Museum, Oaks Amusement Park, Oregon Maritime Center & Museum, Oregon Museum of Science & Industry. In the surrounding area, Rodgers Instruments, Tillamook Cheese (pages 342 and 343).

Harry and David®

Since brothers Harry and David Holmes began mailing succulent Royal Riviera pears around the country in the 1930s, their company has grown into a mail-order business whose gift baskets are an institution at holiday time. From an overhead balcony, watch workers hand-pack these beautiful baskets. Each packer receives a wooden box containing all of the components that go into the basket (which may include fruit, preserves, nuts, and candies), the basket itself, and a Styrofoam form that resembles a cowboy hat. After the packer fills the basket, it is transported by conveyor belt to workers who cover it with cellophane and send it to the shrink-wrap machine.

Around Christmas, you see the packing and wrapping of the Tower of Treats—five boxes, each containing a different product such as fruit, cookies, or cheese, stacked in a tower and wrapped with a ribbon. Each worker fills a box and passes it to the next person, who covers the box with a lid and adds another box on top. Once all five boxes are stacked, one member of a two-person team holds the ribbon, while the other wraps the ribbon around the tower and adds a pre-made bow and baubles on top. You see the ribbons flying as each team assembles up to 1,500 towers a day.

In the bakery, watch as fruit galettes, cookies, and cheesecakes are prepared by hand and placed into and removed from the ovens. Enter the candy kitchen, where the smell of chocolate wafts from vats that stir the brown liquid with rotating blades. Here you'll see the chocolate poured into molds and put through the enrober, the cooling chamber, and the cool room before being packed and frozen for later use in gift boxes.

Cost: $5

Freebies: Fruit galettes and chocolate samples; coupon for $5 off any $35 purchase in Harry and David store.

Videos/DVDs Shown: On bus ride: 5-minute company history video. In bakery and kitchen area: 3-minute operations video. In packing house: 3-minute videos on gift production.

Reservations Needed: Recommended for individuals, required for more than 10 people.

Days and Hours: Mon–Fri 9:15 AM, 10:30 AM, 12:30 PM, and 1:45 PM. Closed holidays, July 4th week, and Christmas week.

Plan to Stay: 1 hour for tour, plus time for Harry and David's Country Village and Jackson & Perkins Rose Garden.

Minimum Age: 7

Disabled Access: Yes

Group Requirements: Groups over 10 should call 1–2 months in advance. Maximum group size is 60.

Special Information: October–mid-December is the best time to see production. While the candy kitchen and bakery operate year-round, during the spring and summer, you'll see less packing of gift boxes.

Gift Shop: Harry and David's Country Village comprises a gift shop, pantry, and produce department. It carries many of the same gourmet gifts found in the Harry and David catalog. Open Mon–Sat 9:00 AM–8:00 PM, Sun 10:00 AM–6:00 PM. Closed holidays. Catalog and Fruit-of-the-Month Club information available (call 800-547-3033).

Directions: From Portland, take I-5 South. Take Medford Exit 27 onto Barnett Rd. Turn left at second light onto Center Dr. Store is on right. From San Francisco or Sacramento, take I-5 North to Medford Exit 27. Turn left after exiting and go over freeway. Turn left onto Stewart Ave., then left onto Center Dr. Store is on right. You will be transported to the plant, 1 mile away, by van.

Nearby Attractions: Britt Summer Music Festival in Jacksonville; the Oregon Shakespeare Festival in Ashland.

PACIFIC NORTHWEST

1125 South 1st Street, Coos Bay, OR 97420   (800) 255-5318   www.oregon connection.com

(The House of Myrtlewood)

The myrtle tree is a broadleaf evergreen found in a small area of the Pacific Coast. The wood looks yellow and brown when finished, and its fine grain makes it more durable than well-known redwood. At House of Myrtlewood, videos and guided tours reveal all the mysteries of this beautiful hardwood and how it's turned into everything from salad bowls to patented golf putters.

If you like the smell of freshly cut wood, you'll enjoy walking through the small sawmill area where logs are sliced into six- to eight-foot sections of varying thickness. Watch the workers use disks of various sizes as patterns to draw circles on the wood slabs, trying to avoid knotholes or other flaws. They cut out these circles, called "blanks," and drill holes in the center to prepare them for the initial "rough out" on the lathe. Large, wet wood chips fly off the lathe during the rough-out turning. Next the pieces go to the drying room, where it takes about nine weeks to dry the wood down from about 50 percent moisture to a 6.5 percent moisture content.

On the main factory floor, watch the "finish turning" of the dried rough-out. Turners do not use a pattern to shape bowls and trays. Instead, each piece is individually turned; no two pieces are exactly alike. Look up at the humming overhead driveline (whose design dates back to the 1850s and the Industrial Revolution), which powers the lathes. The pieces are then sanded and receive an oil finish. When workers burn in the company name, you appreciate the effort that went into that finished piece.

Cost: Free

Freebies: Homemade fudge samples in gift shop; coffee or tea.

Video/DVD Shown: 12-minute video describes myrtle tree, sawmill, and processing of myrtlewood products.

Reservations Needed: No, except for groups larger than 50 people.

Days and Hours: Mon–Sat 9:30 AM–5:00 PM, Sun 11:00 AM–4:00 PM. Factory operates Mon–Thur, but tours run every day. Closed Christmas, New Year's, Thanksgiving, and Easter. Call ahead to verify tour times.

Plan to Stay: 20 minutes, plus time for gift shop.

Minimum Age: None

Disabled Access: Yes

Group Requirements: Groups larger than 50 should call a day ahead.

Special Information: Limits on flash photography, for safety reasons. You may not see all 15 steps involved in making products.

Gift Shop: Carries full range of myrtlewood wares, from bowls, trays, cutting boards, and candleholders to Wooden Touch golf putters. (Putting green available for testing patented, handcrafted putter.) Also sells other gift items, homemade fudge, and Oregon gourmet foods. In the hobby room, craftspeople will find myrtlewood for turning and carving. Open same hours as tour. Catalog available from (800) 255-5318.

Directions: From Portland, take I-5 South to Hwy. 38 West. Then go south on Hwy. 101. Company is just off Hwy. 101 in South Coos Bay, in a wood building with large myrtle tree–shaped sign and American flag on top. From California, take I-5 North to Dillard-Winston exit and go west. Follow directions to Hwy. 42 West. Then go north on Hwy. 101. In approximately 5 miles, billboard will direct where to turn.

Nearby Attractions: The Real Oregon Gift ATV super center, gift shop, and mini-mart (call 541-756-2582); Tillamook Cheese factory tour, about 4 hours up the Oregon coast (see page 343); Oregon coast beaches; Shoreacres State Park.

Blanket Mill, 1307 S.E. Court Place, Pendleton, OR 97801

(541) 276-6911

www.pendleton-usa.com

Beginning by weaving Indian blankets in 1909, Pendleton Woolen Mills has expanded their product offering to include womenswear, menswear, blankets, and fabrics. The company operates on the "vertical" system of manufacturing, which means that it performs all the steps in processing raw wool all the way into finished products. In Pendleton, Oregon, you can tour the original Pendleton plant, which began as an Indian trading post. Pendleton does 95 percent of its manufacturing in the U.S., in contrast to 30 percent for others in the apparel industry.

Wool is received, graded, and washed before being dyed in the Washougal, Washington, mill. It is then shipped to this facility as big bales. Upstairs, the carding machines transform the loose wool into thin, straight, round strands called "roving." The spinning machines convert the roving to yarn by drawing out and twisting the fiber strands. The twisting gives the yarn its strength.

The first floor vibrates under your feet as you walk into the weaving room. The 8- to 10-foot-wide electronic looms pound as their harnesses move up and down. The 19 Jacquard looms produce complex patterns, such as Indian designs. A tape that carries a pattern of punched holes (similar to that of a player-piano roll) controls the sequence in which the yarns are raised and lowered. Depending upon the warp that was wound onto a loom (which could weigh over 1,000 pounds), it may require more than a month of weaving time.

Once completed, blankets and fabric are inspected before shipment to the Washougal Mill for finishing. Finished blankets are ready for distribution.

Cost: Free

Freebies: No

Video/DVD Shown: No

Reservations Needed: No, except for groups larger than 8 people.

Days and Hours: Mon–Fri 9:00 AM, 11:00 AM, 1:30 PM, and 3:00 PM. Closed holidays, 2 weeks in summer (usually August), and week between Christmas and New Year's.

Plan to Stay: 20–25 minutes, plus time for retail store.

Minimum Age: None, except difficult to keep ear protection on young children.

Disabled Access: Yes, for first floor. No, for second floor carding and spinning.

Group Requirements: Groups larger than 8 should call 1 week in advance.

Special Information: Company most interested in giving tours for local community. No photography. Pendleton's Washougal (WA) Weaving Mill (in Portland area) gives tours of the dyeing and fabric- and blanket-finishing process (call 360-835-1118).

Retail Store: Next to the Washougal mill is a retail store, which carries a full line of Pendleton womenswear, menswear, and blankets, and an outlet store, which carries discontinued items and seconds, sportswear, and blankets. Open Mon–Sat 8:00 AM–6:00 PM and Sun 9:00 AM–5:00 PM. Closed holidays.

Directions: From Portland, take I-84 East to Exit 210. Turn left under fwy. Turn left at stop sign at bottom of hill. Turn right under bridge (viaduct). Turn right at "Yield" sign onto S.E. Court Place. Pendleton will be on your left.

Nearby Attractions: Pendleton Underground Tours; Umatilla County Historical Society Museum; Wildhorse Gaming Resort; Tamastslikt Cultural Institute.

PACIFIC NORTHWEST

RODGERS®

Rodgers Instruments LLC

If you are ever in New York's Carnegie Hall or Philadelphia's Academy of Music, listen for beautiful sounds from an organ made by this leading builder of classic electronic and digital organs. Rodgers prides itself on technical innovation in organ building, whether by making the first transistorized organ amplifier (1958) or by introducing Parallel Digital Imaging technology to create warmer, more authentic pipe-organ sounds or it's new lead-free surface mount technology.

The guided tour shows all the steps involved in making organs, from the minute the raw wood comes through the back door until the finished product is loaded and shipped from the docks. Most products are available for customers in 4 to 6 weeks or less. Skilled workers painstakingly labor over each piece and sign their initials on whatever they do daily.

The wood used includes triple-A commercial-grade white and red oak from the northwest, Sitka spruce and sugar-rock maple from the Appalachian region, and mahogany. In the wood shop, Shoda Routers cut, grind, bevel, bore, miter, and do mirror-imaging cuts. An organ begins taking shape in the case-up area. The wood is counter-sunk screwed, glued, and clamped to form the organ's unique shape and design.

Organ parts are hand-sanded before staining. In the finishing department, instrument cases, benches, pedalboards, and music racks are stained with computer-precision machinery and given several lacquer-top coats for durability and appearance. Despite all the sanding and lacquering, reverse-air-flow generators mounted above the main staining areas keep this place dust free.

Along the tour are photos and posters of recent prestigious pipe combinations and individual church installations for guests to view and ask about. It's often the multiple ranks of 61 pipes each that give organs their powerful presence. Look for pictures of one of the largest organs Rodgers ever designed and built: the 194-rank organ (11,000 pipes) at Houston's Second Baptist Church, which took one

and a half years to build. Throughout the tour, you'll see and hear the roles that traditional external pipes and internal electronics (now mostly computer surface-mount circuit boards) play in organ music. This contrast of technology and traditional craftsmanship makes the tour diverse: in one room an artisan hand-sands wood cases, while a computer technician next door tests circuit boards.

Cost: Free

Freebies: Demonstration CDs, literature, and pens.

Video/DVD Shown: An episode of the Travel Channel's *Made in America,* in which Rodgers's history and organ construction are featured. Available for purchase upon request.

Reservations Needed: Yes. No drop-in tours.

Days and Hours: Tue and Thu 9:00 AM–12:00 PM. Closed for 1 week in the middle of August for annual maintenance.

Plan to Stay: Approximately 1 hour.

Minimum Age: No, but children must be able to wear safety glasses.

Disabled Access: Yes

Group Requirements: Groups must call 1 week in advance to make reservations. The maximum group size is 25 people. Exceptions are occasionally made for specified groups.

Special Information: Photography in the showroom only.

Directions: From Portland, take I-5 South to Rt. 26 West. Take Exit 61 at Shute Rd./Helvetia Rd. Turn left at the light, and head to Cornell Rd. Turn right onto Cornell. Immediately past Hillsboro Airport, turn right onto N.E. 25th Ave. Rodgers is on the right. You can also take the MAX rapid transit line from downtown Portland to the Hillsboro Fairgrounds exit. Take the Intel Shuttle and debark at Rodgers or walk half a mile from the Max Station.

Nearby Attractions: In Portland, Golden West Billiards (see page 338). Portland's attractions also include the Oregon Zoo, Washington Park, Oregon Math & Science Institute, and Willamette River attractions and boat cruises. In Hillsboro, Hillsboro Performance Center; Saturday Market; Hillsboro Blimp Factory.

PACIFIC NORTHWEST

4175 Highway 101 North, Tillamook, OR 97141   (503) 815-1300   www.tillamook
cheese.com

Tillamook County is known for green pastures, dairy cows, and cheese. In 1909, the Tillamook County Creamery Association (TCCA) began as a quality-control organization for the many small cheese plants that dotted the county. Today, TCCA is owned by nearly 150 family dairy farmers.

Guests at the Tillamook Cheese Visitors Center can take a self-guided tour. You are encouraged to set your own pace. Start with the video presentation downstairs, which describes the history of the cooperative, and then move upstairs to the observation area for a bird's-eye view of the cheese-making and packaging areas.

On the cheese-making side, you can watch the workers move among enclosed vats as they direct the process of turning milk into cheese. Each vat is filled with more than 6,000 gallons of milk. Though most of the action takes place in the enclosed vats and Cheddarmaster, videos show the different stages of cheese making. You can also watch the last step: 40-pound blocks of cheese are put into clear plastic bags in the pressing towers. The blocks of cheese continue down the belt to where they are vacuum-sealed and placed in cardboard boxes. Next they are sent to the aging room to be cooled. It takes 60 days at 40°F for Tillamook's medium cheddar to develop its flavor; the vintage white extra-sharp cheese takes over two years to mature.

On the packaging side, you can watch the aged 40-pound blocks of cheese change into smaller five-, two-, or one-pound blocks, packaged at a mesmerizing pace. Employees cut and weigh by hand, while fast-moving conveyors transport the cheese around the room to be packaged, sealed, and boxed.

If visitors are hungry for more information, they can spend time at the interactive kiosks, browsing among the nutritional information on all TCCA prod-

ucts. Visitors can then continue back downstairs for free samples of cheese.

Cost: Free

Freebies: Samples of Tillamook cheese and curd.

Videos/DVDs Shown: Throughout the self-guided tour, continuously running videos cover the creamery's history, its dairy operations, and the internal workings of cheese-making machines.

Reservations Needed: Not for the self-guided tour. Groups of 10 or more must reserve (call ahead if you plan to purchase breakfast or lunch in the café).

Days and Hours: Summer: Mon–Sun 8:00 AM–8:00 PM. Labor Day–mid-June: 8:00 AM–6:00 PM. Closed Thanksgiving and Christmas. Not always in full production on weekends and holidays.

Plan to Stay: 1 hour for self-guided tour, including videos, interactive exhibits, and historical dairy displays, plus time for cheese, gifts, and gourmet shops.

Minimum Age: None

Disabled Access: Yes

Group Requirements: Bus tours may call 1 week in advance to schedule an on-bus presentation.

Special Information: Interactive touch-screen kiosks provide separate modules for an in-depth look at the cheese-making process, complete products and nutritional listings, entertaining Kidz Zone, and the TCCA Time Machine, which explores the creamery's history.

Gift Shops: The cheese shop features all varieties and sizes of Tillamook cheese, ice cream, and other dairy products. The gourmet shop provides meats, seafood, jams, and other gourmet treats of the Pacific Northwest. The gift shop offers logoed items and unique farm- and beach-themed gifts. All open same hours as tour. The Farmhouse Café presents breakfasts, sandwiches, burgers, soups, salads, daily specials, and 35 flavors of Tillamook ice cream.

Directions: From Portland, take Rt. 6 West and go north on Hwy. 101. Factory is on right about 2 miles north of downtown Tillamook.

Nearby Attractions: Oregon Connection/House of Myrtlewood, down the coast about 4 hours (see page 340); Pioneer Museum; Latimer Quilt and Textile Museum; Oregon Air Museum; Three Capes Scenic Driving Loop; Oregon coast.

Weyerhaeuser

We make paper in many forms in the U.S.A., with much of it coming from the abundant forests of the Pacific Northwest. This Weyerhaeuser mill makes the ubiquitous brown paper that forms the smooth inside and outside layers of corrugated boxes. As in most paper mills, this one surrounds you with new sights, sounds, and smells.

To produce "linerboard," as it's called in the paper industry, Weyerhaeuser starts with a combination of wood chips from local sawmills and recycled paper. Before the plant opened in 1949, sawmills incinerated the chips as waste. Today these chips are a precious resource. In addition, recycled paper has become an important source of fiber. Weyerhaeuser uses more than 450 tons of recycled paper per day while producing linerboard with up to 40 percent recycled content. You'll notice hills of wood chips surrounding the mill buildings, with whole trucks being lifted skyward to unload more chips. The wood chips' density makes them look like a desert of light brown sand.

On your tour, you'll see stacks of huge bales of recyclable paper—corrugated boxes, office paper, and more. The bales are dropped into a massive blender that whirls the fiber into slurry. Nonpaper materials, such as adhesives, plastic liners, and dirt, are removed through a sophisticated screening process.

In the pulp mill, the chips are cooked to separate out the pulp (for safety reasons you do not see that process). Once cooked, the fibers are washed, refined, and blended with the recycled paper slurry. The mixture then enters a 500-foot-long machine that turns the pulp into paper at speeds of up to 2,250 feet per minute. Make sure you feel the pulp that the tour guide takes from the front of the machine. To some, it feels like thick applesauce.

Follow the pulp's path through the noisy machine, as it is transformed from slurry (99.5 percent water) into a finished sheet (8 percent water). It travels over and under rows of rollers, which press and dry out the water to make the paper that is then wound onto 30-ton reels. A new reel is produced about every 30 minutes. The reels, each holding 15 miles of linerboard, are cut into one- to two-ton rolls, banded, and shipped to Weyerhaeuser box-manufacturing plants via waiting trucks and boxcars.

Cost: Free

Freebies: Brochures and pamphlets.

Video/DVD Shown: No

Reservations Needed: Yes

Days and Hours: Mon and Fri by request and pending availability of tour guide. Closed holidays.

Plan to Stay: 1.5 hours.

Minimum Age: Children must be able to walk and wear earplugs and hardhats. No strollers.

Disabled Access: No, stair-climbing and extensive walking inside and outside the mill.

Group Requirements: Groups should call 3 weeks ahead. No maximum group size.

Special Information: As with all paper mills in the Northwest, this one can be hot, humid, and noisy, while outdoor weather may be cold and damp. Dress appropriately and wear sturdy shoes. No open-toed footwear.

Gift Shop: No

Directions: From I-5, take Hwy. 126 East to 42nd St. exit. Go south on 42nd St. Mill complex is about 1 mile ahead. Turn left at 3rd traffic light. Visitors must check in at main gate.

Nearby Attractions: Willamette Pass ski area; Lively Park Wave Pool; Lane County's Covered Bridges; Mt. Pisgah Arboretum and hiking trails; University of Oregon.

PACIFIC NORTHWEST

255 N.E. Gilman Boulevard, Issaquah, WA 98027   (425) 392-6652   www.boehms candies.com

A visit to Boehms tells a story, taking you through Julius Boehm's artifact-filled Austrian Alpine home, the candy factory he founded, and the chapel dedicated to mountain climbers. A climber himself, Boehm was lured to Washington's Cascade Mountains, "America's Alps." He was considered the oldest man, at age 80, to climb 14,000-plus-foot Mount Rainier. A lover of art and music, he filled his home with such items as a marble replica of Michelangelo's *David,* a wind-up music box, and a potpourri of Bavarian Old World artifacts.

Downstairs from Boehm's home is the candy factory. The pungent chocolate smell fills the air. Depending on the day, different sweets simmer in the kitchen. Mixers' metal blades stir Victorian creams. A worker with a wooden paddle stirs a truffle or peanut-brittle mixture in a copper cauldron before pouring it onto a steel cooling table and spreading it to the thickness of the steel bars at the long table's edges.

Women, trained in the art of hand-dipping chocolate, roll out the day's soft filling into round strips. With one hand they pinch off a portion, gently tossing it to the other hand, which continuously swirls the chocolate around on a marble slab to maintain the desired temperature. This process coats the filling and decorates the top. Other varieties of centers pass through the enrober's chocolate waterfall to get their chocolate coating. After traveling through a cooling tunnel, all chocolates are hand-packed into gift boxes for distribution to Boehms' retail stores.

Next visit the Luis Trenker Kirch'l, a replica of a 12th-century Swiss chapel near St. Moritz. Boehm built this masculine church with a boulder inside as a dedication to mountain climbers who died attempting to reach their mountains' summits. Current Boehms owner Bernard Garbusjuk, trained as a pastry chef in his German homeland, proudly boasts that your tour isn't too commercialized since it ends in the chapel and not at the gift shop.

Cost: Free

Freebies: Chocolate samples.

Video/DVD Shown: No

Reservations Needed: Yes, for guided tour; no, for self-guided tour.

Days and Hours: Factory floor guided tours available for individuals and families mid-June–end of August only; Mon–Fri (except Wed) 10:30 AM, 1:00 PM, and 2:15 PM, Sat–Sun 1:00 PM. Self-guided viewing through windows available year-round including weekends. Closed holidays.

Plan to Stay: 45 minutes for factory, home, and chapel tour, plus time for gift shop and grounds.

Minimum Age: None, for families. Children in groups must be 6 years or older with one adult for every 5 children.

Disabled Access: Yes, for factory and chapel. Difficult for home tour.

Group Requirements: Minimum group size is 15; maximum is 50. Groups should call 1 month in advance.

Special Information: Limited production on weekends. Foreign-language tours arranged with advance notice. Chapel available for rental.

Gift Shop: Sells all 160 luscious Boehms candies including Boehms' specialties, Mozart Kugeln (marzipan and filbert paste center double-dipped in chocolate) and Mount Rainier (caramel, fudge, and cherry center dipped in chocolate). Open year-round Mon–Sat 9:00 AM–6:00 PM, Sun 11:00 AM–6:00 PM. Closed some holidays. Call ahead to check. Mail-order brochure available.

Directions: From I-90, take Exit 17. Follow Front St. to Issaquah. Turn left onto Gilman Blvd. Two candy canes mark entrance.

Nearby Attractions: Boeing, Microsoft Museum, and Redhook Ale Brewery tours (see pages 346, 348, and 350); Lake Sammamish State Park; Snoqualmie Falls; Gilman Village; Issaquah Salmon Days Festival in October. Seattle's downtown attractions, including Pike Place Market and the Space Needle, 13 miles away.

Future of Flight Aviation Center,
8415 Paine Field Boulevard, Mukilteo, WA 98275

(800) 464-1476   www.futureofflight.org

Future of Flight™

AVIATION CENTER
& BOEING TOUR

Touring Boeing's 747, 767, and 777 aircraft plant is like visiting the Grand Canyon. You oversee the assembly areas from a third-story walkway, marveling at the size of the facility (it's the world's largest-volume building—11 stories high, 98 acres) while attempting to grasp the details of the process. As with the Grand Canyon, it's best to just take in the vastness, listen to your tour guide, and be awed by it all. After the tour, visit the Future of Flight's aviation gallery where you will experience interactive displays focused on the future of commercial aviation.

A short bus ride from this 1,000-acre complex's Future of Flight Aviation Center, a short walk though an underground tunnel, and an elevator ride take you to the open-air mezzanine observation deck. Gaze out over the subassembly floor as different airplane parts slowly come to life. The loud rivet-guns' spattering fills the air, as ear-muffed workers assemble plane wings, passenger bays, and nose cones. Overhead, cranes zigzag back and forth with plane parts.

You may see 747s, 777s, and soon the 787 Dreamliner on the final assembly floor at any one time. Don't expect to watch an entire plane created before your eyes. Notice the true colors of the jumbo jet's shiny metals and materials, the miles of wiring, the electronic components, and the other plane innards you take for granted at 30,000 feet. As the bus travels back to the Future of Flight Aviation Center & Boeing Tour, you'll pass the paint hangar. Sitting nearby on the runway waiting for flight tests are freshly painted jets headed for airlines around the world.

Cost: Adults, $15; seniors 52 and older, $14; and children under 15, $8.

Freebies: Brochure

Video/DVD Shown: All tours begin with one of several short videos.

Reservations Needed: Recommended Memorial Day–Labor Day, weekends, and holidays. Groups larger than 10 people should always call or book online in advance.

Days and Hours: Mon–Sun 9:00 AM–11:00 AM, and 1:00–3:00 PM, on the hour. Call (800) 464-1476 for additional tour times during peak season (May–October). Closed Thanksgiving, Christmas Day, and New Year's Day. Same-day tickets available from 8:30 AM and may sell out by 12:00 PM. Reservations available online.

Plan to Stay: 2 hours for video, tour, and aviation gallery. Allow time for the Boeing Store, to browse the Future of Flight Store, or to dine in the café. Hilton Garden Inn adjacent.

Minimum Age: Children must be 48 inches (122 cm) tall to take the Boeing Tour. No height restriction for aviation gallery.

Disabled Access: Yes

Group Requirements: Groups should make advance reservations by calling (800) 464-1476.

Special Information: No photography allowed on Boeing property. GrayLine of Seattle also offers tour with guaranteed entrance. The Boeing company museum in St. Louis, MO, also gives tours (see page 285).

Gift Stores: The Boeing Store sells souvenir and gift items with Boeing logo, including clothing, miniature airplanes, postcards, and aviation books and posters. The Future of Flight Store sells branded clothing, local Washington products, and premium Washington wines. Open Mon–Sun 8:30 AM–5:00 PM.

Directions: Located 25 miles north of Seattle. Take I-5 to Exit 189. Go west on State Hwy. 526 and follow signs to The Future of Flight Aviation Center & Boeing Tour Center.

Nearby Attractions: Boehms Chocolates, Microsoft Museum, and Redhook Ale Brewery tours (see pages 345, 348, and 350); *Seattle Times* North Creek tour (call 425-489-7015); Everett Center for the Arts; Animal Farm; Firefighters Museum; Kasch Park; Walter E. Hall Park and Golf Course; Silver Lake Park. Museum of Flight at Boeing Field in Seattle (call 206-764-5700). Tour Center desk has Everett Visitor's Guide, which includes all local attractions, accommodations, restaurants, and map.

117 Mission Street, Cashmere, WA 98815

(509) 782-4088
(800) 231-3242

www.liberty
orchards.com

LIBERTY ORCHARDS CO. INC.
CASHMERE, WASHINGTON 98815, U.S.A.

The story of Liberty Orchards is the story of two Armenian immigrants striving to succeed in the U.S.A. After failed attempts at running a yogurt factory and an Armenian restaurant, in 1918 they purchased an apple orchard, which they called Liberty Orchards to honor their new homeland. Aplets and Cotlets fruit candies, originally known as "Confections of the Fairies," grew out of a use for surplus fruit.

A guided tour of Liberty Orchards, now in its third generation, shows you how they create these natural fruit-flavored candies. Start your tour in the nut-sorting room, where California walnuts and Hawaiian macadamia nuts are sorted. Visit the Old-World kitchen where concoctions of fruit juices, fruit purees, pectin, sugar, and cornstarch cook at 230°F in stainless-steel kettles large enough to produce 256 pounds of candy. As the candy boils, steam emerges from the kettles, and a fruity, perfumed aroma fills the air. With long metal paddles, the cook stirs the bubbling concoction and then tastes it for correct consistency—a tough job, but someone has to do it. The cook's helpers pour the hot candy into smaller kettles and add nuts and natural flavoring. Then they pour the candy into long, plastic-lined wooden trays, roll it flat, and cover it for a day's rest in the cooler.

In the factory, workers flip the slabs of cooled candy out of their trays and coat the candy with cornstarch, which acts as a natural preservative to keep moisture inside. Candy-cutters cut the candy into bite-size cubes. Tumblers coat the sides of the cubes with cornstarch and then cover them with powdered sugar. Nimble-fingered packers hand-pack the candies into plastic trays at a rate of 4,000 to 5,000 per hour per packer. Fortunately the tour guides pass out free samples of these chewy treats, or you would be tempted to reach into the packing bins.

Cost: Free

Freebies: 3 different flavors of candies.

Video/DVD Shown: Yes, and you can purchase colorfully illustrated 20-page booklet called "The Story of Aplets & Cotlets," which covers family history, product and packaging development, and production process.

Reservations Needed: No, but preferred for groups larger than 12 people.

Days and Hours: April–December: Mon–Fri 8:00 AM–5:30 PM, Sat–Sun 10:00 AM–4:00 PM. January–March: Mon–Fri 8:30 AM–4:30 PM. Occasional weekend production. No production 11:00 AM–11:30 PM (lunch break) and after 4:00 PM. Tours run every 20 minutes, stopping half hour before closing. Closed New Year's, Christmas, Thanksgiving, Presidents' Day, and Easter.

Plan to Stay: 15 minutes, plus time for Country Store.

Minimum Age: None. Children under 16 must be accompanied by adults.

Disabled Access: Yes

Group Requirements: Groups larger than 12 people will be split into smaller groups. Call 2 days in advance.

Special Information: Floor can be slippery. Production generally Mon–Fri, plus occasional weekends. Liberty Orchards is in heart of Washington's apple industry, which produces 5 billion apples per year—half of all the apples eaten in America.

Gift Shop: Country Store sells all Liberty Orchards fruit and nut candies (such as Aplets and Cotlets), apple gifts, and Northwest products. Open same hours as tour. Catalog available from (800) 888-5696.

Directions: From Seattle, take U.S. 2 East. Take Cashmere exit, which puts you on Aplets Way. Follow Aplets & Cotlets signs. Turn left onto Mission St. Liberty Orchards is on left.

Nearby Attractions: Boeing Everett plant tour (see page 346); October Apple Days festival; Nearby Cascade loop attractions include Leavenworth Bavarian Village, Ohme Gardens, and Rocky Reach Dam.

PACIFIC NORTHWEST

This highly interactive visitor center offers a journey through the vision, technology, history, and culture of the Microsoft Corporation. Microsoft's original mission to have a personal computer in every home once seemed far-fetched. However, today it is close to reality. Take a self-guided exploration into the past, present, and future of Microsoft at the Microsoft campus in Redmond, Washington.

As you walk through the entrance, see an overview and display of Microsoft's vision, products, and services beginning with Microsoft's first software. Although they were only designed in the mid-1970s, some of the items are already considered archaic. Once you appreciate the origin of technology, prepare to experience present-day technology and look to the future.

Enter the first of four interactive exhibit areas: "Inside Microsoft." Explore the early history of Microsoft by looking at a 30-foot timeline highlighting company milestones, a Bill Gates exhibit, the world's first personal computer (the Altair 8800—Microsoft wrote its first piece of software for this machine), and other important company artifacts. Get a feel for Microsoft's corporate culture by looking at daily life. Next, move into the "Living Zone." Discover how technology is changing and shaping our everyday lives as you focus more on the desires of individual consumers. Here you can try out the latest PC games, the Xbox, MSN, WindowsXP, OfficeXP, and other products for home.

Once you feel like you've played enough, walk into the "Learning Zone." The "Learning Zone" focuses on how methods of teaching and learning are being transformed by technology. Learn about Microsoft's vision for a Connected Learning Community, a vast computer network for the purpose of sharing ideas and education. Also, test Microsoft's educational programs like Encarta and the Magic School Bus Series. Your last stop is the "Working Zone." Experience how continuous technological innovations at Microsoft have transformed the business world. Workplace products, such as mobile computing, the Tablet PC, and small business products are featured.

With so many interactive exhibits, the visitor center really engages its visitors and provides hands-on entertainment that is as informative as it is fun. With facts, history, and humor, the visitor center thoroughly captures Microsoft's distinctive culture, revealing the personalities behind the scenes.

Cost: Free

Freebies: Microsoft Visitor Center pencils and activity brochures for school groups.

Videos/DVDs Shown: Corporate videos highlight new Microsoft products and historical milestones.

Reservations Needed: No, except for groups of 10 or more.

Days and Hours: Mon–Fri 9:00 AM–7:00 PM. Call ahead if you want to visit after 5:00 PM; visitor center sometimes closes for special occasions.

Plan to Stay: 45 minutes–2 hours.

Minimum Age: None

Disabled Access: Yes

Group Requirements: Groups of 10 or more must call ahead or email mvc@microsoft.com The visitor center welcomes school field trips and community groups.

Gift Shop: For employees only.

Directions: Take SR 520 East toward Redmond to the N.E. 40th St. exit and turn left onto 40th St. Turn right onto 150th Ave. N.E. Continue about 1.5 blocks. Visitor center is in green building on the left side of street.

Nearby Attractions: Boehms Chocolates, Boeing, and Redhook Ale Brewery tours (see pages 345, 346, and 350); Lake Washington; Seattle's attractions, including Pacific Science Center, Pike Place Market, Boeing's Air and Space museum, and Space Needle, 13 miles away.

PELINDABA LAVENDER

SAN JUAN ISLAND

San Juan Island, the popular vacation destination in the Northwest, is also home to one of the premier lavender growers in the country. Your visit lets you see, smell, touch, and even taste what's involved in growing, distilling, and selling lavender-based products. Depending on the time of year and what's happening when you visit, you can walk through fields filled with the spiky, beautiful plants, help harvest lavender, watch the oil distillation, or taste lavender food products.

The husband-and-wife team of Stephen and Susan Robins began the company in 1999, originally just to preserve a beautiful valley as open space. Like many of the small businesses in this book, the founders did not expect their original enterprise, selling bulk crops to off-island flower brokers, to sprout into a tourism and manufacturing venture. Now about a third of its 20 acres is planted with purple lavender plants of 10 different varieties. Visit during July: your eyes and nose will be treated to the sights and smells of 14,000 fragrant organic lavender plants. Look for the signs in the fields and in the demonstration garden to guide your tour. Later, after harvesting, about half of these flowers are bundled and hung in the drying barn.

The other part of the harvest is used for oil distillation in an ancient steam-based process. You can peek at the machinery when it is not in use; if you're lucky, you can enjoy the treat of seeing it at work. Later in the year, the oil and dried lavender flowers and buds are processed into over 120 products, including bath soaps, fireplace sticks, candles, and vinegars.

Cost: Free

Freebies: The store has samples of various foods and personal-care products that use lavender. These vary according to when you visit. Samplings of teas, baked foods, lavender lemonade, and lavender ice cream are always available.

Video/DVD Shown: No

Reservations Needed: No, except for group tours of 10 or more.

Days and Hours: Open daily (including holidays) 10:00 AM–5:00 PM, May 1–October.

Plan to Stay: One hour or more for the self-guided tour of the fields, demonstration garden, distillery, and Gatehouse Store.

Minimum Age: None

Disabled Access: Yes, to the Gatehouse Store. Wheelchairs cannot easily go through the fields.

Group Requirements: Guided tours are available for groups of 10 or more at a cost of $5 per person (children under 12 free). Reserve 7 days in advance. Distillation process is available for viewing during group farm tours.

Special Information: The best time to see colorful lavender flowers is July–September. The Lavender Harvest Festival is held the third weekend of July. Call to check dates, or visit www.pelindaba.com for information.

Gift Shop: The Gatehouse Store sells over 100 lavender products for homes, kitchens, personal care, therapy, and even pets. Food and drink include lavender lemonade, lavender iced tea, scones, cookies, and ice cream (selection varies), plus fresh lavender bouquets (July–August) and dried wreaths and other arrangements. Open daily 10:00 AM–5:00 PM, May–October. Another store location in downtown Friday Harbor (150 First St.) has a similar selection along with a café and community events (open 7:00 AM–7:00 PM).

Directions: Take ferry to San Juan Island. In Friday Harbor, take Spring St. to Douglas Rd. and turn left. Douglas turns into Bailer Hill Rd. Follow this 5 miles to Wold Rd. and turn right. Farm is 1 mile on right. San Juan Transit bus also available.

Nearby Attractions: Westcott Bay Sea Farms (call 360-378-2489), San Juan Historical Park, Lime Kiln Whale Watch Park.

PACIFIC NORTHWEST

Founded in 1981, Redhook Ale Brewery has become one of the most respected regional breweries in the Northwest. Redhook blends perfectly the use of modern technology and old-world tradition, to brew its classic pub-style I.P.A. (India Pale Ale) and full, rich Redhook E.S.B. (Extra Special Bitter) ale, both of which have a loyal following in the region.

The 24-acre site was modeled after a Bavarian brewery in Andechs, Germany, and includes a Public House, outdoor beer garden, and pub. Enter the steel and concrete main building under the portico. Make your way to the Forecaster's Pub, where the tour guide begins with a brief history of Redhook.

Follow the tour guide to the Tour Gallery, where you are immediately aware of the sweet smell of hops and malt. Press your nose against the windows to look into the brewhouse. You'll notice computer control panels monitoring the amounts of malted barley, hops, yeast, and water. Proceed to the fermentation cellar, which houses numerous stainless-steel tanks—not a copper tank in sight! The rows of polished tanks, with their maze of pipes and valves, have automatic mechanisms to regulate temperature and pressure. The equipment even allows brewers to transfer batches from vessel to vessel without manual labor.

Then prepare your senses for the bottling hall. It's so loud, the guide stops speaking and lets the visual process explain itself. From your position on the open-air catwalk, watch the empty bottles get rinsed, filled, crowned, and labeled. You may experience déjà vu—the automated bottling line is reminiscent of the opening sequence in *Laverne and Shirley.* If you can sing the show's theme song, the guide will give you a free pint! Even if you can't, everyone of drinking age samples Redhook beers throughout the tour.

A century-old German company designed Redhook's brewing equipment, making it one of the most technically advanced breweries. However, although high-tech equipment may play a big role in Redhook's beer making, as a "craft" brewery, Redhook follows the German purity law, using only water, malt, hops, and yeast to create beer in the European tradition.

Cost: $1

Freebies: Samples of Redhook ales and souvenir tasting glass.

Video/DVD Shown: No

Reservations Needed: No

Days and Hours: Fall/Winter (Labor Day to Memorial Day weekend): Mon–Fri 2:00 PM and 4:00 PM; Sat and Sun 1:00 PM, 3:00 PM and 5:00 PM. Spring/Summer (Memorial Day through Labor Day): Mon–Fri 1:00 PM, 3:00 PM, and 5:00 PM; Sat and Sun 12:00 PM–5:00 PM on the hour. Closed Thanksgiving, Christmas, and New Year's. Bottling line runs Mon and Tue.

Plan to Stay: 1 hour for tour and beer sampling, plus time to drink and eat at Forecaster's Pub.

Minimum Age: None, however minors may need supervision.

Disabled Access: Yes

Group Requirements: None

Special Information: The company has an architecturally similar brewery in Portsmouth, NH. Call (603) 430-8600 for tour times.

Gift Shop: Forecaster's Pub sells shirts, beer mugs, and other accessories with Redhook logo or picture of brewery, along with catered menu and full selection of Redhook beers. Open Mon–Thur 11:00 AM–10:00 PM, Fri and Sat 11:00 AM–midnight, Sun 11:00 AM–7:00 PM.

Directions: From I-5, take I-90 East to I-405 North. Take Hwy. 522 East, Exit 23. Take Woodinville Exit and stay to the right. At the second light, turn right onto N.E 175th St. At the 4-way intersection, turn left onto Hwy. 202. Continue approximately 2 miles. Redhook Ale Brewery is just past Columbia Winery on the left.

Nearby Attractions: Boehms Chocolates, Boeing tours, and Microsoft Museum (see pages 345, 346, and 348); Columbia Winery (call 425-488-2776); Chateau St. Michelle tours and tasting (call 425-488-3300); Molbaks Nursery (call 425-483-5000).

SeaBear Smokehouse

WILD SALMON

605 30th Street, Anacortes, WA 98221

(360) 293-4661
(ext. 3001)

www.seabear.com

The Pacific Northwest is known for producing delicious smoked wild salmon. SeaBear has been smoking salmon using traditional Northwest methods since 1957. The company started as a backyard smokehouse, selling its product to local taverns. It has grown into one of the largest producers and shippers of packaged wild salmon products in the USA, using its patented "Gold Seal" pouch to preserve the salmon naturally without refrigeration. Located only about five miles from the Washington State Ferry Terminal to the popular San Juan Islands, the SeaBear tour captures the "flavor" of this regional industry.

Every day the tour can be different, depending on the type of salmon being prepared and the methods to flavor it. You'll learn about different salmon varieties, their oil content, and the range of smoking methods. After you walk through the warehouse, you may be greeted by big plastic totes (containers) filled with Alaskan salmon slacked (thawing) out in these tubs of water. Workers then hand-fillet the fish with specially designed filleting knives. They speedily cut off the fins and heads, split them, and lay the fish out onto the six-foot-high racks that ring the room. A skilled filleter can prepare a few hundred salmon per hour.

In the next area, you'll smell the fish smoker, though you cannot get too close. Inside, alder-wood chips slowly burn, filling the air with the distinct smoked-fish smell. After smoking, the filleted fish emerges as moist, flaky, cold-smoked Northwest salmon. It is unloaded from the racks, cut again into the appropriate portions, slid into the special foil packages for vacuum sealing, and then cooked

again with a steaming method that gives it a long shelf life. Stop in the storage freezer on the way out to meet "Fred" the King of King Salmon.

Cost: Free

Freebies: Samples of different salmon products available at retail counter.

Video/DVD Shown: No

Reservations Needed: No, except for groups of over 10 people. Reserve a few days in advance.

Days and Hours: Best time to tour is Mon–Fri 9:15–10:45 AM. This is when the salmon is filleted. The company also provides tours at other times. Production crew works until 3:30 PM. No weekend production or tours.

Plan to Stay: 20 minutes for tour, plus time in the retail store.

Minimum Age: None, although strong smells could bother some young children.

Disabled Access: Yes. Factory is on one level.

Group Requirements: Larger groups are split into tours of 10–15 people at a time.

Special Information: Be prepared to walk on the factory floor, which can be wet and slippery, right in the middle of production.

Outlet Store: Retail store has a wide selection of products, including various sizes of gift packs, along with individual and bulk packs of king, coho, sockeye, and keta smoked and pouched salmon. Frequent specials and outlet pricing on selected products, along with other fish, seafood, and Northwest gifts. You can even have your picture taken with a huge king salmon. Open Mon–Fri 8:30 AM–5:00 PM, Sat and Sun 10:00 AM–5:00 PM. Catalog: 800-645-FISH.

Directions: From I-5, take exit for Anacortes/San Juan Islands Ferry. Follow Hwy. 20 West into Anacortes to R Avenue exit. Turn right on 30th St., toward the water. SeaBear is one block ahead on the corner.

Nearby Attractions: Mt. Erie, Washington State Ferry Terminal, whale-watching, fishing, and various water sports.

PACIFIC NORTHWEST

The Vashon Island Coffee Roasterie

The Minglement, 19529 Vashon Island Highway, Vashon, WA 98070

(206) 463-9800

www.tvicr.com

The birth of America's love of gourmet coffee started in the Pacific Northwest, and this famous historic roasterie and storefront location has been a key player. The people of The Vashon Island Coffee Roasterie continue in the tradition of selecting the highest quality coffee beans and then hand roasting them on the original vintage roasterie coffee roaster. The historic building was constructed in 1914 and is home to specialty coffee pioneer Jim Stewart's original coffee company, The Wet Whisker, which eventually became known as Seattle's Best Coffee.

Before you enter this two-story converted country store (originally a dance hall over a dry-goods store), relax on the front porch chairs and enjoy the local flavor and friendly island residents. Inside, among art and antiques, your tour guide explains that roasting, the hands-on art that unlocks the coffee's flavor, is the most important process in coffee making.

You may be lucky enough to observe a professional cupping (tasting) in action. The heavy granite cupping table, which spins like a lazy Susan, is where they taste, evaluate, and create new coffee blends. Observe the experts as they sample a small spoonful of coffee, rapidly inhaling the coffee, forcing it to spray over their tongue while drawing in air. They swirl the coffee in their mouths and discard it into the two-foot high aluminum spittoons positioned at their feet. The cuppers evaluate each coffee for its aroma, acidity, body, and flavor.

Walk along the weathered wooden floor to the museum area, filled with art and coffee antiques. You will see coffee packages from Japan, Germany, and Saudi Arabia. Notice the collage of unusual items found over the years in the burlap bags of coffee beans it receives—soccer and lottery tickets, cigarette packages from Indonesia, belt buckles, and other common objects (coins, nails, etc.)—all screened out during the production process.

Look down over the balcony railing at the vintage red German Probat Roaster. Several times a week, it roasts 132-pound batches of organic coffee at a time. Afterwards, they cool in a stainless-steel pan at the lower side of the roaster. You'll leave with a new appreciation for the cup of coffee you drink every morning.

Cost: Free

Freebies: 4-oz. sample of the day. On front porch, coffee available for 75 cents per cup.

Video/DVD Shown: No

Reservations Needed: Yes. Call the day you plan to visit to see if they will be roasting.

Days and Hours: Mon–Fri 7:00 AM–5:00 PM. Closed Sun and major holidays. Since tours are informal here, just let the person behind the counter know you are here.

Plan to Stay: 15 minutes, plus time in store.

Minimum Age: None

Disabled Access: Yes, for retail store and museum area.

Group Requirements: None

Retail Store: Sells bulk and hand-packed fresh roasted coffees, specialty teas, herbs, and whole exotic spices, ceramics, gifts, and books. Open Mon–Fri 7:00 AM–5:00 PM, Sat 9:00 AM–4:00 PM. Closed Sun.

Directions: Take ferry from Seattle or Tacoma to Vashon Island. Vashon Hwy. is the main street off ferry. The Roasterie is located in the center of Vashon Island on the corner of Cemetery Rd. and Vashon Hwy.

Nearby Attractions: Vashon Island beaches, peaceful biking roads, kayaking, and bird-watching.

Washington's Fruit Place Visitor Center

FRUIT

1289 Pecks Canyon Road, Yakima, WA 98908 | (509) 966-1275 | www.treeripened.com

Never had the opportunity to walk through an apple or cherry orchard? Well, the Washington's Fruit Place Visitor Center sits in the middle of a real working cherry orchard. The visitor center also features a life-sized orchard photomural. Experience not only harvest time, but also the winter and spring orchard months—all at once! See an apple tree, its branches devoid of fruit, but covered in pretty, glistening snow. Gaze at a cherry tree, in bloom, dressed in blossoms of pink and white. Regard both kinds of trees heavy with fruit, so real that you are tempted to reach up, pluck a piece, and take a bite. On the photo wall, view ripe pears, apricots, and peaches. A spotlight shines on them, highlighting their beautiful green and orange colors.

From here, with photographs and step-by-step descriptions, learn the process that apples pass through, from orchard to shipping. Note that Washington's hot days and cool nights are the ideal conditions for the apples to thrive. As part of this exhibit, look through the window of a miniature controlled-atmosphere storage room. Observe the little bins of apples stacked one upon the other. Open the front door and listen to the revving of a forklift's engine. In this airtight room, the oxygen level is greatly reduced, the carbon dioxide is removed, and the temperature stays just above freezing. Essentially, the apples "take a nap" and remain as fresh as the day they left the orchard.

Next, join a crowd of many ages gathered around a large wall map. Watch as a curious child presses a button corresponding to a picture of a red apple. As she does so, the country of Spain lights up, instantly revealing where in the world Washington-grown red apples are shipped. Press the button corresponding to Italy, and discover what fruits are exported there. Keep pressing buttons, and be amazed at the areas of the world where Washington's apples, cherries, pears, plums, nectarines, peaches, and apricots travel.

For extra fun, tour the Visitor Center while the Cherry Harvest Festival or Apple Harvest Festival is taking place. Listen to live music. Shake hands or have your picture taken with Crispy Apple or Mr. Cherry Man, complete with his cherry head, top hat, and tuxedo. Watch as a red-haired clown paints a plum on a child's face. Sample many varieties of cherries and apples. Best of all, feast on wonderful sweets, such as chocolate-covered cherries and caramel-dipped apples.

Cost: Free

Freebies: Fruit samples, can of Tree Top Apple Juice, and recipes.

Video/DVD Shown: No

Reservations Needed: No, for self-guided tours. Yes, for guided tours and groups of 20 or more.

Days and Hours: Mon–Fri 9:00 AM–6:00 PM. May–December: also Sat 10:00 AM–5:00 PM and Sun 11:00 AM–4:00 PM. Closed holidays.

Plan to Stay: 45 minutes, plus time for the gift shop.

Minimum Age: None

Disabled Access: Yes

Group Requirements: Groups of 20 or more must make reservations.

Special Information: Cherry Harvest Festival occurs on July 4th weekend. Apple Harvest Festival occurs during October. Call for exact dates and times.

Gift Shop: Sells fruit-themed items, including preserves, apple butter, cider, clothing, toys, jewelry, and books. Open same hours as tour.

Directions: From I-82, take exit 31. From Hwy. 12, take the 40th Ave. exit. Turn right on Powerhouse Rd., pass Fred Meyer, turn left on Pecks Canyon Rd. and drive 0.25 mile to the Red Barn on the left.

Nearby Attractions: Sarg Hubbard Park; Yakima Greenway trail system; Yakima Area Arboretum; McGuire Playground; Washington Apple Commission Visitor Center in Wenatchee (approx. 2–3 hours from Yakima; call 509-663-9600 for more information).

PACIFIC NORTHWEST

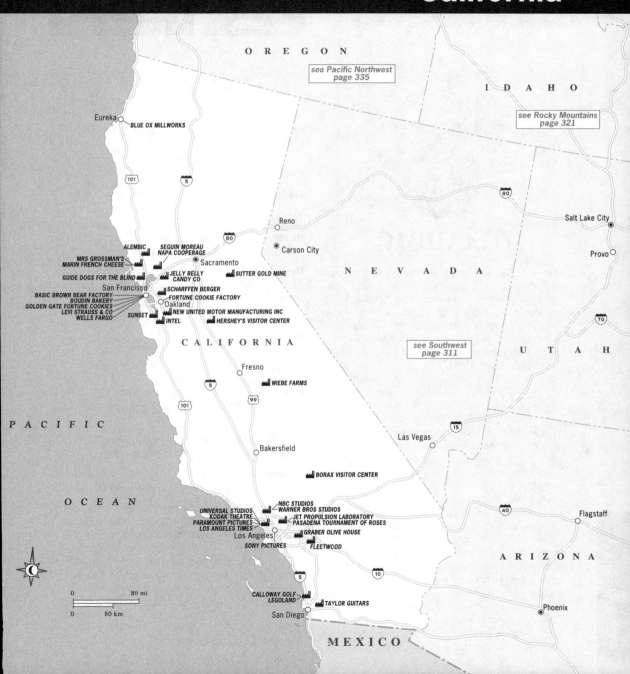

California

O R E G O N

see Pacific Northwest page 335

I D A H O

see Rocky Mountains page 321

Eureka

BLUE OX MILLWORKS

N E V A D A

Reno

Carson City

Salt Lake City

Provo

ALEMBIC
SEGUIN MOREAU
NAPA COOPERAGE
MRS GROSSMAN'S
MARIN FRENCH CHEESE
Sacramento
SUTTER GOLD MINE
GUIDE DOGS FOR THE BLIND
JELLY BELLY
CANDY CO
SCHARFFEN BERGER
San Francisco
FORTUNE COOKIE FACTORY
BASIC BROWN BEAR FACTORY
BOUDIN BAKERY
GOLDEN GATE FORTUNE COOKIES
LEVI STRAUSS & CO
WELLS FARGO
Oakland
NEW UNITED MOTOR MANUFACTURING INC
SUNSET
INTEL
HERSHEY'S VISITOR CENTER

C A L I F O R N I A

see Southwest page 311

U T A H

Fresno
WIEBE FARMS

P A C I F I C

Bakersfield

Las Vegas

BORAX VISITOR CENTER

O C E A N

Flagstaff

NBC STUDIOS
WARNER BROS STUDIOS
UNIVERSAL STUDIOS
KODAK THEATRE
JET PROPULSION LABORATORY
PARAMOUNT PICTURES
PASADENA TOURNAMENT OF ROSES
LOS ANGELES TIMES
GRABER OLIVE HOUSE
Los Angeles
SONY PICTURES
FLEETWOOD

A R I Z O N A

CALLOWAY GOLF
LEGOLAND
TAYLOR GUITARS
San Diego

Phoenix

M E X I C O

0   80 mi
0   80 km

101
5
80
70
15
99
40
10
5

3005 Wiljan Court, Santa Rosa, CA 95407 (707) 523-2611 www.alembic.com

ALEMBIC

Ron and Susan Wickersham started Alembic as a consulting firm that worked with the Grateful Dead, Jefferson Airplane, and Crosby Stills Nash & Young to improve the quality of live sound and recordings of live concerts. When Ron tried to craft a guitar with a higher bandwidth (and better sound quality), he ended up with low-output guitars. To make the sound louder, he designed the first active electric guitar amps to boost the signal—the birth of the modern-day electric guitar. While other companies focused on lead guitars, Alembic made instruments for bass guitarists and set the standard for bass design.

Inside the shop, see the complicated merging of electronics that create the electric guitar sound. Not many guitar companies make their own hardware, electronics, and pickups, and even fewer manufacture their own printed circuit boards like Alembic does. In the parts and subassemblies areas, watch as a worker assembles, winds, wires, tests, and casts the pickups for various instruments.

The CNC (Computer Numeric Controlled) machines drill the printed circuit boards and slot fingerboards for the frets while a worker buffs the brass parts so that they can be assembled to make a complete bridge. One of two giant glue presses clamps down on the necks to laminate them.

In the carving area, sawdust flies as workers sand contours into the wood before the necks are attached. After the guitar is assembled, it heads to finishing, where a worker wearing a space suit applies coats of spray to the instruments. The guitar sits for 24 hours between coats for the spray to cure before it is sanded and sprayed again—a high-gloss finish can require as many as 25 coats.

Finally, the guitar reaches set-up and inspection,

where workers level the fingerboard, press in the frets, and add the strings and meta tuners. After the finishing touches are applied comes the most popular job: plugging in and playing the guitars to check for buzzing and sound quality. One last person checks to make sure all the screws are in place, and the instrument gets approval to leave the factory.

Cost: Free

Freebies: No

Video/DVD Shown: No

Reservations Needed: Yes, call at least 1 day in advance, but they prefer one week's notice.

Days and Hours: First Wednesday of the month 11:00 AM–4:00 PM. Additional tour times can be scheduled by appointment.

Plan to Stay: 1 hour.

Minimum Age: None, but 1 adult required for every 2 children under 10.

Disabled Access: Yes

Group Requirements: Maximum group size is 20, but groups larger than 20 can be split into smaller groups.

Special Information: Tour is dusty and noisy. Dust masks and ear protection can be provided.

Showroom: Sells guitars and basses, strings, and guitar polish. Open Mon–Fri 10:00 AM–4:00 PM.

Directions: From San Francisco: Take U.S. 101 North over the Golden Gate Bridge. After about 45 minutes, take the Hearn Ave. exit. Turn left onto Santa Rosa Ave., left onto Hearn Ave., and go over the overpass. Take the first left onto Corby Ave. Corby makes a sharp right and becomes Bellevue. Take the first right onto Wiljan Ct. Alembic will be on your left. If you reach a stop sign, you've gone too far. From northern California: Take U.S. 101 South to the Hearn Ave. exit. Take the first left onto Corby Ave. and follow above directions.

Nearby Attractions: Luther Burbank Home and Gardens (call 707-524-5445); Martini & Prati Winery (call 707-823-2404). Calistoga attractions, including Old Faithful Geyser and the Petrified Forest, are about 30 minutes away. San Francisco attractions are about 1 hour away.

2801 Leavenworth St., San Francisco, CA 94133   (866) 5BB-BEAR   www.basicbrown bear.com

You'll enjoy playing teddy bear obstetrician on this tour. At this factory, discover how teddy bears are born and participate in their delivery. One of the few U.S. manufacturers of stuffed bears, Basic Brown Bear (BBB) lets you watch them handmake the cuddly creatures from start to finish.

In the cutting and sewing area, often the owner proudly explains her process. First, she draws each pattern on paper and makes a sample animal from the pattern. Workers use bandsaws to slice 24 layers of plush fabric into pattern pieces. Seamstresses sew together individual bear parts and outfits, stitching the sections inside out, then reaching inside to push out the bear legs, ears, and noses. Each seamstress can make about 35 baby bears or 10 grandparent bears a day, plus their clothes.

You learn that the first stuffed bears had shoe buttons for eyes. Now, grommets snap mushroom-shaped plastic eyes into place. A tour highlight is stuffing bears with polyester from a bright yellow machine used to fill life jackets during World War II. Now you can bring a bear to life by inflating it like a balloon. Wait on a line of yellow paw prints to push the filler's foot pedal. Out shoots a mixture of air and polyester. Another machine injects beans into bears. Once a bear is cuddly enough, its back is hand sewn shut.

At the beauty parlor, workers smooth out bear seams with an electric wire brush. A pressurized-air "bear bath" or "bear shower" (depending on the critter's size) removes fur "fuzzies." Children (and adults) giggle when they too receive a "bear shower" or give a bear a "bath." Bears are dressed in their outfits, including company-made wire-rim glasses. Visitors leave with a special affection for the bears they brought to life.

Cost: Free tour. Prices for stuffing your own animal run from $14 to $300.

Freebies: No

Video/DVD Shown: 20-minute Emmy award–winning video, "The Teddy Bear Factory," with its catchy tune, tells how teddy bears are made.

Reservations Needed: No, except for groups of 8 or more people.

Days and Hours: Mon–Sat 10:00 AM–6:00 PM, Sun 11:00 AM–6:00 PM, on the hour. Last tour at 4:00 PM. Closed holidays.

Plan to Stay: 30 minutes, plus time for stuffing and showering your own bear, and the gift shop.

Minimum Age: 3

Disabled Access: Yes

Group Requirements: Groups of 8 or more people should call 2 weeks in advance. Maximum group size is 40.

Special Information: Can also stuff your own animals at BBB's other stores in Old Town San Diego (call 877-234-2327) and in the Mall of America in Bloomington, MN (call 800-396-2327).

Gift Shop: More than 30 styles of stuffed bears (and other animals) and bear clothes, all handmade by BBB, are sold exclusively at this location.

Directions: Westbound from the Bay Bridge, take the Fremont St. exit. Turn left onto Fremont St. Fremont become Front St. Turn left onto Pine St. Turn Right onto Sansome St. Turn left onto Washington St. Make a slight right onto Columbus Ave. and another slight right onto Leavenworth St. From the South Bay, take U.S. 101 North, then merge onto I-280 North toward the Port of SF. Take the exit on the left, then merge onto King St. (becomes The Embarcadero). Turn left onto Bay St. Make a slight right onto Columbus Ave. Make another slight right onto Leavenworth St. Parking is available at the Anchorage Parking Garage located between Jones and Leavenworth Sts.

Nearby Attractions: Scharffen Berger chocolate tour, Boudin's Bakery tour, Golden Gate Fortune Cookies, and Wells Fargo Bank Museum (see pages 381, 360, 364, and 389). Fisherman's Wharf; Ghiradelli Square.

CALIFORNIA

See color photos, pages 6.

1 X Street, Eureka, CA 95501

(707) 444-3437
(800) 248-4259

www.blueoxmill.com

BLUE OX
MILLWORKS ◦ HISTORIC PARK
SCHOOL OF TRADITIONAL ARTS

A visit to Blue Ox Millworks means a first-hand look at craftsmanship techniques from the 1800s. Master craftsman Eric Hollenbeck produces authentic custom-quality architectural products such as balusters, wooden doors, and gable decorations. Visitors witness master craftsmen creating beautiful and unique products for the surrounding Victorian homes and for other Victorians around the world.

Once you have absorbed the magnificent redwoods and Victorian architecture in California's north coast city of Eureka, take the tour that begins as an enthralling history lesson. You'll listen to an introduction that includes a demonstration of the world's largest functioning collection of Barnes Manufacturing Human Powered tools, but the tour quickly switches from a history lesson to time travel when you stroll through a fully functioning Victorian era mill.

After the short introduction, the self-guided tour allows you to spend more time in the rooms you find most intriguing. You might enjoy watching a craftsman use an antique woodworking machine from the 1870s. If you have a passion for reading or writing, you'll likely find yourself captivated by the antique printing presses, and you might even see the 1890s press in use. If your second home is the water, you'll certainly be fascinated by the *Corrina Bella*, a 40-foot traditional sailing vessel being built by students at the mill school. When completed, the *Corrina Bella* will even provide a smooth ride along the Humboldt Bay. Visitors may also check out an apothecary where the stains and varnishes are produced.

For a more in-depth experience, consider one of the tour packages in which you can take part in ceramics and blacksmithing workshops. Learn how to make a ceramic tile, or hand forge your own nail.

Be sure to say hello to Babe and Blue, the Belgian Blue Oxen, before you leave.

Cost: Adults, $7.50; seniors 65+ $6.50; children 6–12, $3.50; children 5 and under, free.

Freebies: Children often walk away with a piece that was made while they are there.

Video/DVD Shown: No

Reservations Needed: No for self-guided tour; yes for package tours.

Days and Hours: Mon–Fri 9:00 AM–5:00 PM, Sat 10:00 AM–4:00 PM.

Plan to Stay: Introduction lasts 30 minutes–1 hour. After introduction, guests may stay as little or as long as they like.

Minimum Age: No

Disabled Access: Yes, in the outside areas, but some workshops have stairs.

Group Requirements: Special packages are available for groups. Basic Workshop Package includes a fully guided tour, ceramic workshop, and blacksmith workshop. 10–20 people, $25 each; 21–40 people, $22 each; 41–60 people, $20 each; 60 or more people, $18 each. Full Day of Activity Package includes a fully guided tour, a narrated tour of local Victorians, lunch served in the cook shack, a blacksmith workshop, ceramics workshop, slide show in an old-fashioned theater, and a demonstration by Babe and Blue (the oxen). $50 per person.

Special Information: Dress casually and wear low-heeled shoes.

Gift Shop: Sells blacksmithing, ceramics, woodworking, and printing projects created by students at the Blue Ox School of Traditional Arts.

Directions: From U.S. 101 North, turn left at T St., turn right at 1st St., turn right at X St. From Redwood Hwy. 199 South, merge onto U.S. 101 South, turn right onto X St.

Nearby Attractions: Arkley Center for Performing Arts, Clarke Museum, Samoa Cookhouse, The Carson Mansion, Ferndale, The Kinetic Sculpture Museum, Morris Graves Museum of Art, The Eagle House Victorian Inn.

CALIFORNIA

If you look up from this book, wherever you are, you will probably see several products that use borates. Comprising the basic element boron and other elements such as oxygen, calcium, and sodium, borates are inorganic salts that serve essential purposes in a huge variety of products for industry, agriculture, and households: soap, detergents, plastics, rubber, glass, fiberglass, ceramics, fertilizers, and more.

Between 18 and 12 million years ago, a giant mass of borate minerals formed under what is now the Mojave Desert in southern California. In 1925, the mining company Borax (now called Rio Tinto Borax) discovered the deposit, which is among the richest on the planet. The company now supplies nearly half of the world's demand for refined borates. Mining occurs outside the aptly named town of Boron in the largest open-pit mine in California: one mile wide, one and a half miles long, and 700 feet deep.

The Borax Visitor Center provides an insightful view of the mining operation. Located amid the austere beauty and arid heat of the Mojave Desert, Borax is a long drive from just about anywhere, and the visitor center feels like a cool oasis. Guests begin by seeing a video on the science of borates and the history of Borax. Then six exhibit areas await discovery. The first explains the geological history of the deposit and how mining works. Other exhibits explore the processes of refining and distributing borates for commercial use, and the safety programs and environmental efforts of the mining operation. A fun presentation illustrates the immense range of products that use borates. The last exhibit area shows the arduous early history of Borax in Death Valley during the late 19th century, when teams of men and mules toiled in extremely harsh desert conditions.

Save plenty of time for looking at the mine itself. A main viewing area outside the visitor center lets you gaze straight down into the vast depths of the open pit. For the adventurous, a rooftop viewing area on top of the visitor center provides an even better perspective on the abyss.

A colossal 240-ton mining truck stands on display outside. Not far away is an area where visitors may collect and keep their own minerals.

Cost: Gate admission: automobiles $2; buses $10; motorcycles $1. (Proceeds go to local nonprofit organizations.)

Freebies: A sample of "TV rock" (ulexite), whose crystals act like optical fibers: when you lay the bookmark over a printed page, the printing underneath appears on its upper surface.

Video/DVD Shown: A 17-minute video on borates and the history of Borax.

Reservations Needed: No

Days and Hours: Daily 9:00 AM–5:00 PM. Closed holidays. (If extensive rain has fallen, call ahead. On rare occasions, flash flooding can wash out the road to the visitor center.)

Plan to Stay: 1–2 hours

Minimum Age: No

Disabled Access: Yes (except rooftop viewing area).

Group Requirements: No

Special Information: As on any long drive through remote desert, bring water, food, blankets, extra fuel, and a mobile phone.

Gift Shop: The shop sells educational material and souvenirs, including books on minerals and mining, sample minerals, jewelry, and postcards. Open daily 9:00 AM–5:00 PM. Closed holidays.

Directions: From I-5 near Los Angeles, take Rt. 14 North 68 miles to Rt. 58 East (Mojave-Barstow Hwy.) and drive 25 miles. Take Borax Rd. exit and turn left at end of ramp on Borax Rd. Follow signs to visitor center.

Nearby Attractions: In Boron, Twenty Mule Team Museum records the history of borate mining in Boron and Death Valley.

CALIFORNIA

160 Jefferson Street, San Francisco, CA 94133 | (415) 928-1849 | www.boudinbakery.com

How can one batch of bread beget millions of loaves for over 150 years?

The story begins during the California Gold Rush, when a family of French bakers, the Boudins, combined the "sour" dough favored by miners with traditional old-world baking techniques, creating the original San Francisco sourdough French bread. Ever since, San Franciscans have kept up a steady demand, insisting that its characteristics remain the same: a crunchy dark-golden crust, a soft chewy center, and a distinctively tangy flavor. To make sure each loaf of bread is consistent, Boudin bakers have employed an ancient baking secret: the "mother dough"—a combination of wild yeast and lactobacillus, cultivated with a mixture of water and flour, which has been divided and replenished every day since the bakery began. Taking the place of commercial yeast, a portion of the mother dough is used to leaven the bread each day. This gives each batch the same flavor profile as the prior one, a lineage that dates back to the first loaves baked in 1849.

Boudin's self-guided Museum and Bakery Tour tells the story of the bakery against the backdrop of the City's events and personalities, from the gold rush to the present. There is a display of miners' and bakers' tools dating from the mid-1800s, historic images and artifacts, and a 100-foot timeline chronicling major events in the city and in the bakery.

Through exhibits in the interactive science section, you'll learn why sourdough is sour and how the mother dough has survived for more than 150 years. There is a video game that tests your skills as a baker and a quiz to determine your bread-type personality. Find out whether you are more like a walnut bread or a sweet baguette.

The bakery portion of the tour takes place on a catwalk above the demonstration bakery. You'll see flour pumped from the outside silo into the mixer, where it is blended into dough and then tossed from the mezzanine level to the ground floor before being hand finished and baked. Outside, a window gives a great view of the bakers sculpting the bread into such "critters" as crabs and turtles. The tour ends in the tasting room, where you can sample different kinds of breads and dipping oils.

Cost: Adults, $3; children under 12 free with parents.

Freebies: Free samples of bread in the tasting room.

Video/DVD Shown: A 3-minute montage of breads around the world includes old bread commercials and Charlie Chaplin slapstick. Another video discusses the last brick oven in San Francisco.

Reservations Needed: No, except for groups of 30 or more.

Days and Hours: Mon–Sun. Hours vary by season. Closed major holidays.

Plan to Stay: 45 minutes.

Minimum Age: No

Disabled Access: Yes

Group Requirements: Groups of 30 or more should call ahead.

Gift Shop: Sells dipping oils, jams, chocolate, wine, picnic supplies, and novelty items.

Directions: Located at corner of Jefferson and Taylor Sts. in Fisherman's Wharf. From the north, take U.S. 101 South across Golden Gate Bridge. Turn left on Van Ness Ave., right on Bay St., left on Mason St., left on Jefferson St. From the east, take I-80 West across Bay Bridge. Take Fremont St. exit, turn left on Fremont St., right on Howard St., left on Embarcadero/Herb Caen Way, slight right to stay on Embarcadero; stay straight for Jefferson St.

Nearby Attractions: Basic Brown Bear Factory, Fortune Cookie Factory, Scharffen Berger, and Guide Dogs for the Blind (see pages 357, 363, 381, and 366); Fisherman's Wharf and Pier 39.

Callaway GOLF

Callaway Golf Company designs and builds technologically advanced products to help golfers of all skill levels find more enjoyment from the game. The Carlsbad, California–based company revolutionized the industry with its Big Bertha line of drivers. The friendly, oversize clubs were named after a powerful World War I German cannon and helped position the company as the world's largest manufacturer of premium golf clubs. In recent years, the company has expanded its product line to include state-of-the-art golf ball manufacturing, as well as assembly of its best-selling Odyssey putter brand.

With some 25 golf club manufacturers in the area, Carlsbad is often called the Golf Club Capital of the United States. As the largest factory, Callaway Golf sprawls across more than 700,000 square feet of workspace in eight buildings, plus three greens at its private, 8.1-acre research facility, where pros often stop by to test and tweak the latest products.

You can tour its 80,000-square-foot club assembly plant, which utilizes cellular or "lean" manufacturing to efficiently speed the latest steel, titanium, or carbon composite clubs through teams of cross-trained employees. You can see how each clubhead and shaft are assembled by hand, then weighed and adjusted using computer technology to ensure swingweight accuracy within tenths of a gram. Clubs are then detailed, inspected, packaged, and sent to the distribution center for worldwide shipping.

Down the street, the 225,000-square-foot golf ball manufacturing facility has state-of-the-art equipment that makes golf balls from core to cover. You can see automated machinery mix, mill, and compress rubber and tungsten for the core, then send the spheres down the line for subsequent layers of ionomer and urethane that will be crafted by machines and robots into the company's premium two- and three-piece golf balls. The company's most advanced ball technology, the HX, features a revolutionary new cover pattern that replaces traditional dimples with a network of pentagons and hexagons for improved aerodynamic efficiency.

Cost: Free

Freebies: Catalog, logo golf ball, and coupon for free soft drink and cookie.

Video/DVD Shown: No

Reservations Needed: Yes; *always call ahead because tours have been discontinued, and it's uncertain when they will resume.* Groups, see below.

Days and Hours: Club assembly tour: Mon–Fri 9:15 AM and 3:30 PM. Ball manufacturing tour: Mon–Fri 11:00 AM and 2:00 PM. Arrive 10 minutes early to sign nondisclosure waiver. Closed holidays and occasionally for plant maintenance.

Plan to Stay: 45–60 minutes for each tour.

Minimum Age: 6. Children must be able to wear safety goggles.

Disabled Access: Wheelchairs permitted. No crutches, canes, or walkers.

Group Requirements: Groups larger than 120 people should call 2 weeks in advance. Large groups are divided into groups of no more than 50 people.

Special Information: Comfortable, flat-heeled, closed-toe shoes are required for 1 mile of walking. No photography in plant.

Gift Shop: Employee store is part of tour, not open to the public. Sells shirts, golf balls, and other logoed items. Maps available showing nearby dealers who sell Callaway golf clubs.

Directions: From San Diego, take I-5 North. Take Palomar Airport Rd. exit. Turn right at end of exit. Turn left onto College Blvd. into industrial park. Take first right onto Aston St. At dead end, turn right onto Rutherford Rd. Follow to second to last building on right.

Nearby Attractions: LEGOLAND and Taylor Guitars tours (see pages 372 and 386); Nearby golf-club manufacturers occasionally give tours: Taylor Made (call 760-931-1991) and Acushnet (call 760-929-0377); Aviara golf course; Old Carlsbad; Carlsbad State Beach.

CALIFORNIA

5300 Via Ricardo, Riverside, CA 92509

(800) 326-8633
(951) 788-2920
ext. 113

www.fleetwoodrv.com

FLEETWOOD.

With its many different brands of RVs, Fleetwood is the largest manufacturer of recreational vehicles in the U.S.A. You can tour the plant that produces the industry-renowned Bounder, as well as other widely respected products. When introduced in 1985, with its jumping kangaroo logo, the Bounder revolutionized the motor-home industry with its patented basement design and affordable price. Wearing a headset, you will get to watch just about everything it takes to build an RV, except for the 12-mile road test.

The chassis yard is where production begins. Sitting in the sunny Southern California weather are five acres of Ford and Workhorse chassis neatly arranged in long rows. Fleetwood's patented "Power Platform" is the foundation for building the motor home, which exceeds industry standards. Once you're inside the plant, with its giant horseshoe-shaped assembly line, the Bounder seems to come together like a big puzzle. In fact, when the dash assembly is put over the engine, this marks what's referred to as the "zero point" for the modular construction of the RV.

Observing the Vacubond process, which is used to build the walls, ceilings, and floors, is most visitors' favorite part. All the pieces that make up the wall, including the fiberglass outside, the steel frame, and the vinyl interior wallpaper, are placed on a big table. As each layer goes down, glue is automatically sprayed along its surface to unify all pieces. These walls-to-be are covered with what looks like plastic bags and are locked down to the table. Vacuum hoses suck out all the air for one hour. This intense suction creates a perfect seal between the wall's layers. Fleetwood pioneered the Vacubond construction for durability, plus thermal and sound insulation.

Once on the production line, a crane hoists the entire floor-and-basement assembly and sets it on the chassis as production staff scamper around to bolt the carriage together. Toward the back end of the horseshoe line, the motor home will be sent across the street to Fleetwood's brand new, state-of-the-art paint facility. Once the coach is painted, the unit will then be sent to the Final Finishing area as its production comes to a close. Although the production takes about four days, RVs move at a pace that allows you to see the Bounder in all production stages.

Cost: Free

Freebies: Product brochures.

Video/DVD Shown: 30-minute video on company history.

Reservations Needed: Required

Days and Hours: Mon and Wed at 10:00 AM. Closed holidays and between Christmas and New Year's. Tour times are subject to change; please call in advance.

Plan to Stay: 1–2 hours.

Minimum Age: 16

Disabled Access: Limited access.

Group Requirements: Maximum group size is 18, but call 2 weeks ahead for space availability. Special times can be arranged for larger groups, but must be arranged in advance.

Special Information: May also see Pace Arrow, Southwind, Bounder, Flair, Storm, Terra, and Fiesta. Class C tours are also available (Jamboree and Tioga). No photography. Must wear closed-toe shoes.

Gift Counter: Sells T-shirts, hats, and other logoed items. Open Mon–Fri 8:00 AM–3:30 PM. Closed holidays.

Directions: From Los Angeles, take -60 East. Exit at Market St. in Riverside. Turn left at exit onto Market St., right at Viacerro, which becomes Via Ricardo. Plant is on the left. Park in visitors' spaces at the appropriate plant.

Nearby Attractions: Graber Olive House tour (see page 365); Universal Studios, Paramount Pictures, and NBC Studios tours, approximately 60 miles west (see pages 387, 379, and 377); Lake Perris; Mission Inn; Disneyland, 45 miles west; Knott's Berry Farm, 40 miles west; Palm Springs.

CALIFORNIA

Fortune Cookie Factory

261 12th Street, Oakland, CA 94607

(510) 832-5552

Did you ever wonder how the fortune got inside a fortune cookie? Ever want to write your own fortune? What you may think of as Chinese culinary secrets are revealed at the Fortune Cookie Factory, a 30-plus-year-old family business. Don't be disappointed, however, when the owner tells you that fortune cookies were not created in Asia. No one knows who invented the fortune cookie, but it was first seen in the 1920s, served as a unique dessert, in San Francisco.

Fortune cookies start as a mixture similar to pancake batter, made of whole-wheat flour, cane sugar, water, and Egg Shade food coloring. Margarine, flavoring, and artificial coloring give the fortune cookies their golden color. A worker concocts 100 pounds of batter in a vertical electric mixer, then races across the floor to pour it into one of the seven custom-made fortune-cookie machines. You will be mesmerized by the circular, methodical motion of these groaning machines. Batter flows through a spigot into individual three-inch-diameter waffle irons. The individual plates clamp shut for their four-minute circular journey through the 225 piano-shaped ovens. Small, wafer-thin pancakes emerge, cooked on both sides and pressed to squeeze out all air pockets.

With great dexterity, the workers seated in front of each oven remove each pancake, randomly grab a fortune, place it on the pancake, fold the pancake in half like a taco, and bend it around a metal rod. For cooling, the cookies are placed points down in a holding tray. Each worker hand folds 15 to 16 fortune cookies per minute, or 50,000 per day.

Cost: $1 per person.

Freebies: A sample bag of fortune cookies.

Video/DVD Shown: No

Reservations Needed: Not for a self-guided walk-through tour, viewing the production process from the entrance to the production area. Yes, for a guided explanation group tour.

Days and Hours: Mon–Fri 10:00 AM–3:00 PM. Closed on major Chinese and U.S. holidays.

Plan to Stay: 15 minutes for viewing, plus time for gift counter.

Minimum Age: 4, unless with adult supervision.

Disabled Access: Yes

Group Requirements: Minimum group requirement is 10 people, with reservations 1 week in advance for a guided tour. Individuals are welcome for a self-guided walk-through tour.

Special Information: When the owner is there, he will gladly answer questions and tell you about his appearance on TV. Otherwise, look for a 1-page handout on the business, history, and fortune cookie–production process.

Gift Counter: Small retail shop at front of factory sells regular and flavored (e.g., strawberry, lime) fortune cookies, along with bible and X-rated versions. You can also order customized fortune cookies (various sizes and messages, even with an engagement ring, if desired) and purchase bags of "misfortunes," which are broken fortune cookies. Price information available at above number. Open Mon–Fri 10:00 AM–5:00 PM.

Directions: From north of Oakland, take I-980 South and get off at the 11th/12th St. exit. Make a left onto 11th St. Turn left onto Alice and left onto 12th. Look for the factory storefront on the left side of 12th St. From south of Oakland, take I-880 North to Oak St. Exit. Turn right at first intersection. Turn left on 12th. Storefront on left side.

Nearby Attractions: Golden Gate Fortune Cookies, in San Francisco's Chinatown, is a smaller business that has a viewing area near the retail counter *(see page 364)*; Lotus Fortune Cookies, near San Francisco's city hall, uses an automated system to insert fortunes (call 415-552-0759); Oakland's Chinatown; Madison Square Park; Lake Merritt; Oakland Museum of California; San Francisco's attractions are across the Bay Bridge.

CALIFORNIA

56 Ross Alley, San Francisco, CA 94108   (415) 781-3956

Tucked in a pedestrian alley in the heart of San Francisco's Chinatown is Golden Gate Fortune Cookies. Opened in 1962, Golden Gate is the only bakery in Chinatown that makes the cookies the old-fashioned way: by hand. Behind a black wrought-iron gate and a bright yellow sign, in a narrow, dimly lit room, two women seated on desk chairs toil at hand-folding fortune cookies.

Fortune cookies start as a creamy pale-yellow mixture, similar to pancake batter. Water, sugar, flour, eggs, vanilla, sesame, and butter combine to form this batter. Next, a machine, like an arm, pours the batter onto the bottom of pancake irons three inches in diameter. The top of each iron clamps shut. The pancakes travel through the circular oven for baking and come out of the oven standing on their sides. The pancake irons continuously revolve around the oven, requiring every worker to quickly remove each pancake and quickly shape it into a fortune cookie before the next pancake comes around. If the worker misses a few, she spears them off and these unfolded cookies are given away. Now she can catch up to the current pancake emerging from the oven.

With her left hand, the worker grabs a fortune from the tray and pulls a pancake off. She folds it in half and then bends it around a metal rod. With her right hand, she gingerly places the fortune cookie with its points down into a hole in the holding tray. When the cookies are hard, the worker gently places them in a big barrel ready to be packaged and shelved. With great dexterity, these two women can fold 10,000 fortune cookies each day.

Cost: Free, but a sign requests 50 cents for photos.

Freebies: Round, flat, fortune-less cookies.

Video/DVD Shown: No

Reservations Needed: No

Days and Hours: Mon–Sun 8:00 AM–8:30 PM.

Plan to Stay: 10 minutes.

Minimum Age: None

Disabled Access: Yes, but narrow and dimly lit.

Group Requirements: Since only a few people can enter at one time, large groups must be staggered into small parties.

Special Information: Dim lighting affects quality of photos taken.

Gift Counter: Small retail area at front of factory sells bags of unfolded fortune cookies, almond cookies, and mixed chocolate and regular fortune cookies. After you watch production for a few minutes, the staff strongly encourages you to buy their cookies. Open same hours as above. Order more than 50 cookies with custom fortunes from (415) 806-8243.

Directions: From Golden Gate Bridge, take U.S. 101 South. Turn left on Washington St. Ross Alley is a pedestrian street between Stockton St. and Grant Ave. From Bay Bridge, take I-80 South to Freemont St. exit. Cross Market St. on Front St. Turn left on California St. Park in garage on Kearney St. and walk to factory.

Nearby Attractions: Basic Brown Bear, Fortune Cookie Factory, Wells Fargo History Museum, and Levi Strauss Visitors Center (see pages 357, 363, 389, and 373). Mee Mee Bakery, also located in Chinatown, uses a more automated process in which a machine pushes down the fortune onto a flat pancake and then folds it (call 415-362-3204).

CALIFORNIA

315 East 4th Street, Ontario, CA 91764

(909) 983-1761
(800) 996-5483

www.graberolives.com

Graber Olive House

Companies that mass-produce California olives tell you that the black, pitted variety found on pizzas and supermarket shelves are natural and tree ripened. After visiting the Graber Olive House, you will know what these terms really mean. The C. C. Graber Co. is the oldest olive packer (1894) in the only U.S. state that produces olives.

A picker, who holds only a few olives in his hand at one time and drops them gently into a felt-bottomed bucket, carefully removes the cherry-red fruits from the tree. Mass-produced California "ripe" black olives are green when harvested and then oxidized a uniform black to hide bruises. Graber olives turn a natural nutlike color in processing.

After viewing pictures of the olives and groves, you're led through the company's production area. In the grading room, smock-clad women face a conveyor belt and carefully pick "culls" (overripe, underripe, or imperfect) out of the olive procession before them. More than 1 million olives roll by the graders during an eight-hour shift. The perfect olives then move to the vat room where, using the Graber family recipe, they are stirred, soaked, and tended for about three weeks in round concrete vats. After the careful curing process removes the olives' natural bitterness, they are ready to be canned.

The pampered olives undergo a thorough canning and sterilization process. Workers, using the "hand-pack filling machine," scoop olives into cans as they pass under a wheel. Paddles on the "Panama-paddle packer" rotate and push a small amount of water out of each can, forming a headspace for steam. The machine then hermetically seals each can. In the boiler room, carts filled with sealed cans of olives are rolled into a retort. The door is closed, and the olives are sterilized with 242°F steam from the boiler (like that on an old train) for more than an hour. Finally, the cans are labeled with the Graber name familiar to gourmets around the world.

Cost: Free

Freebies: The "hospitality bowl" is filled with free olive samples.

Video/DVD Shown: A 12-minute video on canning process.

Reservations Needed: No, except for groups of 10 or more people.

Days and Hours: Mon–Sat 9:30 AM–4:30 PM, Sun 10:00 AM–4:30 PM. Lunch break from 12:00 PM–1:30 PM. Tours are conducted all year, but grading, curing, and canning only take place in October and early November. Closed Christmas, Thanksgiving, New Year's, Easter, and July 4th.

Plan to Stay: 30 minutes for tour, plus time for museum and gift shop. Museum contains an original grading machine made by C. C. Graber and other items related to the olive business. Lawn area available for picnics.

Minimum Age: None

Disabled Access: Yes

Group Requirements: Groups larger than 10 people should call 1 week in advance. Large groups will be split into groups of 20.

Special Information: When the factory is not in production, tour goes through canning plant with a colorful explanation and photographs of the process.

Gift Shop: The Casa del Olivo Fancy Food and Gift Shop sells Graber olives, nuts, dates, fancy foods, gift baskets, candies, toys, cookbooks, and unusual pottery. La Casita sells kitchen supplies and works by local artists. Open Mon–Sat 9:00 AM–5:30 PM and Sun 9:30 AM–6:00 PM. Catalog is available at (800) 996-5483.

Directions: From Los Angeles and Palm Springs, take I-10 (San Bernardino Fwy.) to Ontario. Take the Euclid Ave. exit, then south to 4th St. Turn left onto 4th St. Graber Olive House will be on your left.

Nearby Attractions: Fleetwood Motor Homes factory tour (see page 362); San Antonio Winery tasting room (call 909-947-3995); Claremont Colleges; Griswald Center; Mission Inn.

CALIFORNIA

350 Los Ranchitos Road, San Rafael, CA 94903   (800) 295-4050   www.guidedogs.com

Guide·Dogs
FOR THE BLIND

After it was founded in the 1940s, Guide Dogs for the Blind taught wounded servicemen who had lost their sight in combat how to use and handle guide dogs. The school now instructs blind students from throughout the U.S. and Canada at no cost in a 28-day course. In addition, the school prepares dogs for service as guides. Each student leaves with a faithful companion: a fully trained guide dog between two and three years old. About 350 such teams graduate every year.

Tours begin at the visitor center with a five-minute video about the role of guide dogs in the lives of the visually impaired. You then proceed to the campus. At its center, sound from a fountain helps students orient themselves. Plants with strong scents, such as rosemary shrubs near the dormitory, help students recognize particular places.

If school is not in session, you may visit the dormitory. Braille signs and tactile maps guide students around the building, and the library offers books on tape to relax with in the evenings. The dormitory also has airline seats: flying home is often among the first things students do after they graduate, and here they can practice being on an airliner with a dog.

All tours visit the kennel complex, where 300 dogs live and train. You can watch the puppies, all born and weaned at the school. In the hallways, you witness training. An important function of a guide dog is keeping its owner safe in traffic, and dogs must know how to back away from a busy street in a straight line instead of turning in a loop that might expose the person to danger. Dogs learn this in a metal chute with food at one end: unable to turn around, they quickly acquire the skill of stepping backward for their reward.

You also see the kitchen where staff prepare food for the dogs and the "beauty parlor" where groomers bathe them. The last stop is the veterinary clinic that cares for the dogs' health.

Cost: $5 donation per person is requested.

Freebies: Giveaways may be available for children.

Video/DVD Shown: A 5-minute video introduces the role of guide dogs in the lives of the visually impaired.

Reservations Needed: Only for groups of 8 or more (call 800-295-4050). Smaller groups may drop in for a tour at the scheduled times.

Days and Hours: Drop-in tours run Mon–Sat at 10:30 am and 2:00 PM. Closed major holidays.

Plan to Stay: 75 minutes.

Minimum Age: 5

Disabled Access: Yes

Group Requirements: Groups of 8 or more (maximum 1 busload) must reserve. Call (800) 295-4050.

Special Information: Tours of the Oregon campus (in Boring, near Portland) are available by appointment only. Call (503) 668-2100.

Gift Shop: Sells clothing, products for dogs, souvenirs, and other items. Open Mon–Fri 9:00 AM–5:00 PM. Closed major holidays.

Directions: From U.S. 101 South, take Freitas Pkwy. exit, which becomes Del Presidio Blvd. Turn left on Las Gallinas Rd. and proceed around Northgate Mall. At corner of Northgate Dr., Las Gallinas becomes Los Ranchitos Rd. School's first driveway on left after cemetery. From U.S. 101 North, take Freitas Pkwy. exit. Stay to extreme right; exit merges into Civic Center Dr. Turn right at intersection of Civic Center Dr. and Merrydale overpass (first stoplight after exit). Turn left at Las Gallinas Rd. and follow directions above.

Nearby Attractions: Jelly Belly, Mrs. Grossman's, Marin French Cheese, New United Motor Manufacturing tours (see pages 211, 376, 375 and 378). San Francisco's attractions, including Basic Brown Bear Factory (see page 357), are 20 miles to the south.

Hershey Foods Corporation

"Wow, smell the chocolate!" will be your first words as you enter the Gift Shoppe. Hershey Foods Corporation, founded in 1894 by Milton S. Hershey in the small Pennsylvania town later named after him, is the country's largest candy maker; it makes approximately 33 million Kisses per day. Hershey's Oakdale plant makes fresh treats for the West Coast.

The video that is shown at the Gift Shoppe makes you feel as if you're in the factory. Listen to the history of Milton S. Hershey and how he started his successful chocolate factory. The video takes you through the process of where the raw ingredients come from right down to the finished chocolate bars. You will see the 10,000-pound vats called conch machines. The conch machines' granite rollers move back and forth on corrugated granite beds to create smooth chocolate paste from a mixture of cocoa butter, sugar, milk, and chocolate liquid.

You will see views of the high-speed computerized production lines that build well-known Hershey products such as the top-selling Reese's Peanut Butter Cups. After the brown paper cups land on a moving belt, they are lined with milk chocolate and then a layer of peanut butter. The top layer of chocolate is air-blown on and vibrated to ensure a smooth surface. In the wrapping and packaging area, the peanut-butter cups move so quickly on a sophisticated "freeway" system that they deserve a speeding ticket. Even watch on the video each Hershey's Kiss, one of the most recognizable shapes in the world, receive its own silver evening gown and paper necklace.

Cost: Free

Freebies: Free candy bar for scheduled school groups only.

Videos/DVDs Shown: 15-minute video, "The Cocoa Bean Story," about the production process; 22-minute video about Milton Hershey by Arts & Entertainment TV.

Reservations Needed: No, for Visitors Center. *Since 9/11 tours are no longer offered to the general public.* Prearranged school groups may go on factory tours.

Days and Hours: Mon–Sat 9:00 AM–5:00 PM, Thur until 7:00 PM. Closed holidays.

Plan to Stay: 30 minutes to watch tour video, plus time for Gift Shoppe.

Minimum Age: None

Disabled Access: Yes

Group Requirements: School groups only call (209) 848-5100, ext. 5625, at least 1 month in advance for a tour. No maximum group size. Prearranged scheduled school groups Tue, Thur, and Fri 8:30 AM–3:00 PM.

Special Information: See page 125 about the simulated factory tour at Hershey's Chocolate World in Hershey, PA.

Gift Shoppe: Sells Hershey's candy, T-shirts, and gifts, including teddy bears holding stuffed Kisses. Exhibits include a model 1915 wrapping machine. Open Mon–Sat 9:00 AM–5:00 PM, Thur until 7:00 PM. Closed holidays.

Directions: From San Francisco, take I-580 East to I-205 East. Take Hwy. 120 East to intersection of Hwys. 108 and 120. Go through intersection, travel 1 block, and turn left onto G St. Parking is on right. From Yosemite, take Hwy. 120 West. Continue on Hwy. 108/120 to Oakdale. Turn left onto Yosemite St. Turn left onto G St. Parking is on right. Phone recording has directions.

Nearby Attractions: Oakdale Cowboy Museum (call 209-847-7049); Oakdale Museum; Oakdale Brewing Company (call 209-845-BREW); Oakdale Cheese tour (call 209-848-3139); Delicato Vineyard tour (call 209-825-6212); Hershey's Visitors Center has list of additional nearby attractions and events.

CALIFORNIA

Corporate Museum, Robert N. Noyce Building,
2200 Mission College Boulevard,
Santa Clara, CA 95052

(408) 765-0503

www.intel.com/
go/museum

Few U.S. companies embody the computer revolution as well as Intel Corporation. Its 10,000-square-foot museum contains interactive displays that demonstrate how silicon chips are made, how they work, their effects on our lives, and their evolution. You'll also learn about Intel, the world's largest maker of silicon chips that power computers, cell phones, and thousands of other digital products.

Located at Intel's Santa Clara, California, campus in the heart of Silicon Valley, the museum offers a rare, inside look at a high-tech world where distance is measured in billionths of meters, and time in billionths of seconds. The Intel Museum is a self-guided experience that mixes Intel history, technology explanations, demonstrations, and popular culture in more than 30 exhibits.

The most recent additions chronicle the fascinating life of high-tech inventor and Intel cofounder Robert Noyce and show how digital technology has transformed how we record sounds, take pictures, and communicate. In the Intel Timeline, the history of Intel and the evolution of its products are depicted through artifacts and stories that entertain, whether or not you have technical insight.

Silicon chip manufacturing processes are shown in the "Intel Fab" exhibit area, where museum visitors, over closed-circuit flat-screen TV, watch Intel employees inside ultraclean "Fabs" (silicon chip factories) as they work wearing "bunny suits." No, these workers aren't dressed in costumes with floppy ears. The process used to manufacture silicon chips requires air many times cleaner than is found inside hospital operating rooms, so workers wear special white coveralls and head gear designed to prevent impurities from destroying sensitive silicon chips. You can even try on a bunny suit yourself and walk around on perforated flooring just like that through which purified air circulates in a real fab. A dazzling, 12-inch-diameter silver ingot of silicon on display may be the purest thing you'll ever touch.

The Intel Museum's exhibits appeal to all levels of technical knowledge and interest. Many exhibits are hands-on, like one that allows you to "spell" your name in the two-digit "binary" language of computers. Another exhibit allows you to place templates over a touch screen to replicate the steps taken to etch intricate circuitry onto silicon wafers. All the exhibits are informative and fascinating.

Cost: Free

Freebies: Occasionally for prescheduled tour groups.

Video/DVD Shown: Various video interviews with Intel engineers, scientists, and other employees, live video from an Intel factory, and more.

Reservations Needed: No, except for scheduled guided group tours.

Days and Hours: Mon–Fri 9:00 AM–6:00 PM, Sat 10:00 AM–5:00 PM. Closed holidays.

Plan to Stay: About 1–2 hours.

Minimum Age: None, but 8 is the recommended minimum. Displays have interactive components that are enjoyed most by children interested in computers or science.

Disabled Access: Yes

Group Requirements: Maximum group size is 20 people or 35 students. Minimum 8 people to be considered a group. Call (408) 765-0503 at least 6 weeks in advance to schedule a group tour.

Special Information: Bags and backpacks not permitted. No coat check. Cameras and handheld video cameras are allowed. Drop-in guided tours are available at preset times. Tours last approximately 1 hour. Please call for current tour times.

Intel Museum Store: Sells Intel branded merchandise, including apparel, pens, gifts, computer devices, toys, and other items. Open same hours as museum.

Directions: Take U.S. 101 to the Montague Expwy. East. Turn left onto Mission College Blvd. The Robert N. Noyce Building is on left. Museum is to the left of the lobby and can be entered through a plaza directly in front of the building.

Nearby Attractions: Stanford Linear Accelerator Center tour (call 650-926-2204); Tech Museum of Innovation (call 408-294-8324); San Jose Children's Discovery Museum (call 408-298-5437); Great America Theme Park (call 408-988-1776).

See color photos, page 28.

Jelly Belly Candy Co.

One Jelly Belly Lane, Fairfield, CA 94533   (707) 428-2838   www.jellybelly.com

If you question whether former president Ronald Reagan's policies were good for the U.S. economy or for kids, then you should visit this factory that produces millions of jelly beans per day, or 14 billion beans annually. The publicity surrounding President Reagan's fondness for gourmet Jelly Belly jelly beans led to increased demand, round-the-clock shifts, a new factory, and amusing tours for children and adults. The company has been making candy since 1898, but it was the introduction of the Jelly Belly in 1976 that spurred its modern growth.

While you'll see how the company makes a variety of creative candies, such as its line of Pet Gummi candies, the highlight is watching how it makes the Jelly Belly beans in more than 40 flavors. At the tour's beginning, you'll stare at large mosaic portraits of famous faces and figures such as Ronald Reagan and the Statue of Liberty, each made of 14,000 jelly beans. Follow your tour guide along Jelly Belly Candy Trail, an elevated walkway inside the 215,000-square-foot factory. View the beans at different stages of their creation. Be prepared for intense aromas. Unlike standard jelly beans, Jelly Belly beans are flavored both in the center and in the shell. Machines pour the special bean-center mixture into cornstarch molds that hold 1,260 centers per tray. Guess the exotic flavors, like strawberry daiquiri or peanut butter, as the bean centers travel by in the distance.

After the centers harden overnight, mechanical arms flip the trays over, and the centers are placed into spinning, open stainless steel drums. Here, workers add four layers of flavored syrup and sugars to create the outer shells. Each bean is automatically checked for correct size and color before traveling through the bagging and boxing machines. You'll look down at a hopper filled with a colorful and flavorful sea of jelly beans. The correctly weighed amount of jelly beans drops into plastic packets below. However, workers hand-pack the Gummi candies, which are too sticky for machines.

Cost: Free

Freebies: 2-ounce bag of Jelly Belly beans with an official menu matching colors to flavors. Logoed paper hat to wear during the tour.

Videos/DVDs Shown: Short videos show close-up view of candy making on weekends.

Reservations Needed: No

Days and Hours: Mon–Sun 9:00 AM–4:00 PM. No production on weekends, but see production video. No production on holidays and the last week in June through the first week of July.

Plan to Stay: 40 minutes, plus time for candy kitchen, café, and gift shop.

Minimum Age: None

Disabled Access: Yes

Group Requirements: None

Special Information: No photography on tour. Jelly Belly Center in Wisconsin also gives tours (see page 211). In exhibition candy kitchen, view candy makers hand-dipping chocolates and making toffee and caramel apples.

Retail Store: Sells more flavors of jelly beans than you can imagine (not only exotic fruit tastes, but also unusual flavors like toasted marshmallow, buttered popcorn, jalapeño) and sports beans, specially fortified to provide quick energy during exercise. Look for 2-pound bags of Belly Flops, factory seconds. Open Mon–Sun 9:00 AM–5:00 PM. Jelly Belly Café (open daily 11 AM–3 PM) serves Jelly Belly–shaped pizzas, hamburgers, and buns. Ice-cream counter.

Directions: From the San Francisco/Oakland area, take I-80 East to Hwy. 12 East. Turn right onto Beck Ave., right onto Courage Dr., right onto North Watney Way, and right onto Jelly Belly Ln. From Sacramento, take Abernathy exit left to Hwy. 12 East, then follow the above directions.

Nearby Attractions: In the same industrial park, Anheuser-Busch (Budweiser) Brewery tour (call 707-429-7595), Thompson Candy self-guided tour (call 707-435-1140), and VG Buck Olive Oil tasting (call 800-865-4836); Marine World Africa U.S.A.; Seguin Moreau barrel making tour (see page 382), Napa Valley wineries, and Culinary Institute of America located 20 minutes away.

CALIFORNIA

Jet Propulsion Laboratory

4800 Oak Grove Drive, Pasadena, CA 91109   (818) 354-9314   www.jpl.nasa.gov

NASA's Jet Propulsion Laboratory (JPL) is the Cape Canaveral of unmanned space exploration. Its teams of scientists and engineers, who have included the venerable Carl Sagan, work in numerous departments to plan, design, and build the spacecraft and satellites that probe our solar system. Among JPL's famous projects are the Viking Mars landers, the first spacecraft to touch down on another planet, in the 1970s; the Voyager deep-space probes that flew by the outer planets during the 1980s; the Galileo orbiter that explored Jupiter and its moons in the 1990s and early 2000s; and, more recently, the Mars rovers and the Cassini trip to Saturn. JPL also creates and commands satellites for monitoring Earth and its atmosphere and for studying the cosmos beyond our solar system.

The research and operational areas of JPL sprawl over a large campus. Depending on the interests of visitors and the focus of current missions, tours may visit any of several sites. Tours begin with a multimedia presentation on the history of JPL and its notable achievements. Visitors then go to the Von Karman Visitor Center, where they see models, on both small and actual scales, of past NASA spacecraft, including Galileo and the Pathfinder rover that explored Mars. Interactive exhibits illustrate the science and engineering of several missions.

Other areas you may visit include the mission-control center, which receives signals from spacecraft and satellites and controls their progress. The revealing images of Jupiter, Mars, and Saturn's moons that have stunned the scientific world were received here. You may see the Spacecraft Assembly Facility, where engineers clad in dust-proof suits build the spacecraft, probes, and satellites of JPL missions. Sealed to exclude foreign airborne particles that might interfere with electronic components, the assembly area enjoys fresh breaths of filtered air every 10 minutes from grates in the floor. Given NASA's recent activities on Mars, you may see the area where JPL tests new vehicles for exploring the Martian surface.

Cost: Free

Freebies: No

Video/DVD Shown: Tour starts with 20-minute multimedia presentation.

Reservations Needed: Yes. Call the Tour Reservation Line of the Public Services Office (818-354-9314).

Days and Hours: For individuals and for groups of up to 9 people, tours run once a week, generally on Mon or Wed, starting at 1:00 PM; reservations must be made about 2–3 months in advance. Larger groups may reserve tours about 6–9 months in advance; large group tours run Mon–Fri 9:30 AM or 1:00 PM.

Plan to Stay: 2.5 hours.

Minimum Age: None (tour may not be suitable for young children).

Disabled Access: The tour involves walking and stair-climbing, but wheelchair access can be arranged with advance notice (wheelchairs not provided).

Group Requirements: Groups of 10 or more (maximum 40) must reserve by telephone and submit a letter of confirmation within 10 days of initial contact. A roster of visitors is required about a month before tour. Changes to the roster are not permitted within 7 days of tour.

Special Information: Visitors must present government-issued photo ID. U.S. citizens may show a driver's license; foreign nationals must provide a passport or Green Card.

Directions: From Los Angeles, take the I-110 North until it becomes the Pasadena Fwy. North. Exit to Orange Grove Blvd. Turn right or California Blvd. and left on Pasadena Ave. Take I-210 (Foothill Fwy.) West. Exit at Berkshire Ave./Oak Grove Dr. Turn right at end of ramp and left at intersection (Oak Grove Dr.).

Nearby Attractions: In Pasadena, Mount Wilson Observatory (call 626-793-3100). In the nearby area, Los Angeles Times, Paramount Pictures, Universal Studios, Warner Brothers, NBC Studios (see pages 374, 379, 387, 388, and 377).

CALIFORNIA

6801 Hollywood Boulevard,
Hollywood, CA 90028

(323) 308-6300   www.kodaktheatre.com

Kodak THEATRE
at hollywood&highland center

Feel like a movie star when you tour the Kodak Theater in the heart of Hollywood. You are invited to stroll down an imaginary red carpet into a world of stardom as you step inside an elegant state-of-the-art facility designed by the renowned Rockwell Group. This tour is as close as many of us will ever get to participating in the Academy Awards.

Your experience begins on the street when you absorb the grand entrance to the theater. Stroll inside and relive past award shows as you view glass plaques for each Best Picture Oscar winner. The lobby exudes glamour, from the grand spiral staircase to the images of famous actors and actresses. Now that you have escaped from the busy sounds of Hollywood Boulevard, prepare yourself for a real golden man—the tour's first notable moment includes a display of an actual Oscar statuette. The celebrity treatment continues in your visit to the exclusive George Eastman VIP room.

Inside the 3,400-seat theater, your guide reveals where your favorite nominees sat during the last awards ceremony. From there, you'll gain a glimpse of the other side of the award shows, live concerts, and musicals with a behind-the-scenes view of producing a memorable show.

The tour focuses on providing historical and architectural highlights. An accompanying video explains the background of the marketing partnership with Eastman Kodak Company and offers details about the Academy Awards. At the tour's completion, you'll be given an exclusive postcard of the Kodak Theater and chance to browse a merchandising cart for tour members only.

Cost: Adults, $15; Seniors 65+ and children 17 and under, $10; children under 3, free.

Freebies: Postcard of Kodak Theater, not available anywhere else.

Video/DVD Shown: Short video describing Eastman Kodak Company and the Academy Awards.

Reservations Needed: No, tickets may be purchased up to 7 days in advance; tour included in the Hollywood CityPass.

Days and Hours: Daily 10:30 AM–4:00 PM June 1–Aug. 31; 10:30 AM–2:30 PM Sept. 1–May 31. Tours depart every half hour from Level 2 entrance.

Plan to Stay: 30 minutes for the tour.

Minimum Age: Children under 12 must be accompanied by an adult.

Disabled Access: Yes, with notice at time of ticket purchase.

Group Requirements: Groups of 15 or more are eligible for discounts and customized service. Reserve in advance.

Special Information: No photography or other recording devices. No food, beverages, chewing gum, or smoking during the tour. Stroller check is required.

Gift Shop: A cart sells merchandise, including Academy Awards posters, for tour customers only.

Directions: From the north, take U.S. 101 South and exit at Highland Ave. The street winds down and becomes three lanes as you approach the Hollywood & Highland Center. The parking entrance is on Highland Ave. next to the Renaissance Hollywood Hotel, north of Hollywood Blvd. From the south, take I-110 North to U.S. 101 North. Exit at Highland Ave. (stay on right-hand side of freeway as exit splits) and follow directions above.

Nearby Attractions: NBC Studios, Paramount Pictures, Universal Studios Hollywood, Warner Bros. Studios (see pages 377, 379, 387, and 388); Kodak Theater is a part of the Hollywood & Highland Center that includes multiple restaurants and shops.

CALIFORNIA

Thirty million LEGO bricks were used to create the 5,000 LEGOLAND models decorating the park. And they're not the simple constructions you may have built as a child. Miniland includes an incredibly accurate four-foot-tall replica of the White House, complete with tiny LEGO visitors. Near-life-size LEGO lions, giraffes, and elephants abound. Head over to the factory tour to see brick making, then to the model shop to watch model assembly.

At the Factory Tour, see animated miniaturized versions of the machines that mold, paint, and package LEGO bricks. In the first room, watch as the injection mold machine molds a brick. In another, see "partially assembled" pieces created, like little wheels being attached to little axles for LEGO cars.

In the Model Shop, watch the video in the breezeway and peer through the glass to see the model makers at work. You may see one of them sketching a building—like New York's Chrysler Building—or creating an architectural drawing on LEGO graph paper of a 1:20 scale model.

The next step in creating a LEGO model is the prototype. The prototype may be a smaller version or even just one section of the model; if the model is symmetrical, the model makers may build just half of it. For a LEGO Donny Osmond, half the head was created as a prototype and then a mirror was held up to see the complete Donny. A prototype's bricks are not glued together, making changes easier. Look for model prototypes displayed behind the glass at the Model Shop, and the finished models throughout the park.

Afterward, see the gluing of the model. Tubes with brushes on the ends hang from what look like IV bags suspended from the ceiling. The glue runs from the bag into the brush as the model makers brush the glue onto every LEGO brick, assembling the final model. Pipes suck glue fumes out of the air, protecting the model makers. Once the bricks are glued together, the model is coated with UV protectant so it can withstand the California sun.

Cost: Included in admission charge to the LEGOLAND Park.

Freebies: No

Video/DVD Shown: 10-minute video on model-making process at Model Shop and 5-minute video on packaging and shipping at Factory Tour.

Reservations Needed: No

Days and Hours: Hours change frequently. Please check the website.

Plan to Stay: All day at LEGOLAND. 15 minutes for Model Shop tour and video, 15 minutes for Factory Tour video and tour, plus time for gift shop.

Minimum Age: None, but it is designed for families with children ages 3–12.

Disabled Access: Yes

Group Requirements: School groups must make reservations 3 weeks in advance (call 760-918-KIDS). Groups may get discount if they call in advance, depending on size.

Special Information: Youth Group programs include day camps. LEGO is a contraction of the Danish words *leg godt,* meaning "play well." In Latin it means "I put together" or "I assemble."

Gift Shop: Seasonally sells make 'n' take models made at the model shop. Make your own LEGO creations and purchase what you make. Open same hours as LEGOLAND.

Directions: From I-5, take Cannon Rd. exit in Carlsbad. Go east, following signs to LEGOLAND Dr.

Nearby Attractions: LEGOLAND's 50 LEGO-themed attractions, rides, and shows; Callaway Golf and Taylor Guitars tours (see pages 361 and 386).

Levi Strauss & Co.

Levi's Plaza, 1155 Battery Street,
San Francisco, CA 94111

(415) 501-6000   www.levistrauss.com

Did you know that Levi Strauss & Co. created the world's first blue jeans in 1873? Levi's jeans were first called "waist overalls" until the turn of the 19th century and then "overalls" until 1960, when company catalogs and advertisements started reflecting what teenagers were calling them: jeans. A typical pair of Levi's 501 jeans requires approximately 1.75 yards of denim, 213 yards of thread, five buttons, and six rivets. These are some of the interesting facts you will learn at the Levi Strauss Visitor Center, located in the lobby of Levi's corporate headquarters in San Francisco.

The company used to manufacture its jeans in the United States and gave tours of two of its factories, which we covered in earlier editions of this book. It tried to continue manufacturing in the U.S.A. but was forced to move its production entirely overseas to remain competitive with other denim manufacturers.

Opened on May 1, 2003 (5-01, a reference to the original style of blue jeans), the Visitors Center commemorates 150 years of Levi history. You enter through the two-story glass wall into the 3,500-square-foot atrium lobby. This well-lit open space graduates in a step fashion to become seven stories tall at the rear. Every day employees walk through the "Latest and Greatest" tower in the center of the lobby. Look up at the oversized images spotlighting new products and media.

Sit inside the "Brand Builders" kiosk to watch television advertisements from four decades. The "Dear Levi" pavilion showcases enlarged consumer fan letters. You can even write your own letter. The "Product Innovations" pavilion chronologically displays individual garments such as a tattered pair of 501 jeans from 1890 and an Olympic track suit from 1984 (Levi's was the official outfitter for the U.S. Olympic team). Snake your way into the center to see a personal work of art using embroidery, buttons, paint, etc. created by one of the denim art contest winners in 1974.

Walk around the perimeter of the "Back to the Future" pavilion. Follow the timeline that ties Levi's history to popular cultural and world events. Starting with the birth of Levi Strauss in 1829 in Bavaria and his emigration to the U.S. in 1847, the exhibit chronicles many important dates, including 1971, the year the company went public, and 1985, when it became private again through one of the largest leveraged buyouts in history. While the only item that you see related to production here is a 1906 sewing machine, you will learn a lot about company history and innovations.

Cost: Free

Freebies: No

Video/DVD Shown: 20-minute video loop of television commercials over 4 decades.

Reservations Needed: No

Days and Hours: Mon–Fri 9:00 AM–6:00 PM, Sat–Sun 10:00 AM–5:00 PM. Closed holidays.

Plan to Stay: 20–30 minutes.

Minimum Age: None, but children will appreciate it more if they can read.

Disabled Access: Yes

Group Requirements: None

Special Information: None

Gift Shop: Flagship Levi's store at 300 Post St. in Union Square sells men's, women's, and some children's clothes. Open Mon–Sat 10:00 AM–8:00 PM, Sun 11:00 AM–6:00 PM (call 415-501-0100).

Directions: From Bay Bridge, take I-80 South to Freemont St. exit. Cross Market St. onto Front St. Turn left onto California St. Turn right onto Sansome St. Levi's Plaza will be right at intersection with Filbert St.

Nearby Attractions: Basic Brown Bear, Golden Gate Fortune Co., and Wells Fargo History Museum (see pages 357, 364, and 389). San Francisco's attractions include Coit Tower, Chinatown, Fisherman's Wharf, Lombard Street, North Beach, and Telegraph Hill.

CALIFORNIA

Los Angeles Times

If you ever wondered how that story in your newspaper got there, you'll enjoy touring the *Los Angeles Times*. The sound of clattering typewriters has given way to the relative quiet of computers in the newsroom. This tour of one of the world's great newspapers begins with the history of the *Times* and how it has grown along with the Southern California region. Then, you'll visit the newsroom, where a vast expanse of reporters work busily on late-breaking stories and rush to meet deadlines.

Discover that the Food Department has an ultramodern, full working kitchen, where staff members carefully taste-test dishes before the recipes appear in the paper. See how the Editorial Department works, learn about the paper's different editions, and walk by the library (known as the "morgue"). Photography buffs will enjoy the magnificent display of old cameras used by *Times* photographers. Huge black cameras with giant flashbulbs recall a time before television, when newspapers were almost our only eyes on the world.

The *Times* printing plant, two miles away, is open by reservation. You'll see the state-of-the-art pressroom, which extends nearly the length of two football fields, and the newsprint storage area, where robotlike automated vehicles carry 2,500-pound rolls of newsprint. While you'll see very few people, you will hear and see the beeping and flashing robots as they glide around. Visit plate making, where newspaper pages are converted from photographic negatives to aluminum printing plates, and observe the distribution system that takes newspapers from the press to the delivery truck. It's exciting to watch the newspaper-printing process in this massive, superautomated plant.

Cost: Free

Freebies: *Times* pencil, plus reporter's notepad for those 18 or under.

Video/DVD Shown: No

Reservations Needed: Yes, call at least 1 week in advance.

Days and Hours: Editorial tour and printing plant tour: Mon–Fri, 9:30–11:00 AM. Closed holidays.

Plan to Stay: 45 minutes to 1 hour for either tour.

Minimum Age: 10, or 5th grade.

Disabled Access: Yes

Group Requirements: Groups larger than 10 people need to call 1 month in advance. Group tours are by reservation Mon–Fri 9:30 AM, 11:00 AM, and 1:30 PM for either plant. Call (213) 237-5757 to schedule. Maximum group size is 20 people.

Special Information: The *Times'* Globe Lobby contains circa-1935 murals, a rotating globe of the world, and a historical display.

Gift Counter: (145 S. Spring St.) sells logoed pens, jackets, mugs, and shoulder bags. Open Mon–Fri 8:00 AM–4:00 PM.

Directions: Editorial Plant: From U.S. 101 South heading toward downtown L.A. (past I-110), take Broadway exit. Turn right onto Spring St. Pass the *Times* entrance at the corner of 1st and Spring Sts. and park in the *Times* garage at 213 S. Spring St. From I-10 East, exit onto one-way Spring St. Follow directions above. Olympic Printing Plant: directions provided with reservations.

Nearby Attractions: Paramount Pictures, Universal Studios, and Warner Bros. Studios tours (see pages 379, 387, and 388) are 7–15 miles away; NBC Studios tour (see page 377), about 30 minutes away; Museum of Contemporary Art (MOCA); The Music Center and Disney Concert Hall (213) 972-4399; Little Tokyo; Olvera Street.

CALIFORNIA

7500 Red Hill Road, Petaluma, CA 94952

(707) 762-6001
(800) 292-6001

www.marinfrench
cheese.com

Rouge et Noir

Thousands of miles away from France, this privately owned company has been making Camembert, Brie, and other soft-ripened French cheeses under the Rouge et Noir label for 140 years. The Marin French Cheese Company started in 1865, when they hand-dug the original cellar, which is still in use today. Until the 1950s, they made their own wooden boxes for the individual cheeses. At the London Cheese Awards competition, they won the "World's Best Brie" award against all world contestants.

Wait in the cool cellar for your tour to begin, then follow your tour guide down the hall to look through windows into each of the small cheese-making rooms.

In the Make Room, the white, chunky, cottage cheese–like curds are poured from buckets into rows of metal molds that resemble empty baked-bean cans. As the molds are filled with four inches of curd, white liquid whey pours out. The whey continues to drain out until the curd is only one inch thick. The cheese stays in the molds for approximately 18 hours.

Across the hall in the Salt Room, the cheese, now removed from the molds, soaks in salt brine. The Brie wheels soak the longest. Although you cannot go down to the aging cellars, the tour guide explains that the Camembert and Brie sit in the cellar for about 11 days so the edible mold can develop on the outside of the cheese.

Next, walk upstairs to watch men and women seated at a table hand-packing the 30 different cheese products. In the adjacent tasting area are historical photographs of the company's earlier cheese-making methods, awards its cheeses have won, and a display of all its products. On a red-and-white-checked tablecloth, cheeses for tasting sit invitingly on red-and-black logoed porcelain plates covered by glass cheese domes. After you sample the cheeses, you'll be ready for your own wine-and-cheese picnic.

Cost: Free

Freebies: Crackers and cheese samples in the tasting area and sales room; recipe brochure.

Video/DVD Shown: No (possible in future).

Reservations Needed: Yes

Days and Hours: Production times vary, but the factory is operating daily and tours are offered 7 days a week; call ahead. Tours generally on the hour Mon–Sun 10:00 AM–4:00 PM. Best time to see production is 11:00 AM, when the curds are poured. No production on weekends.

Plan to Stay: 20 minutes for tour, plus time in sales room and on 5-acre grounds, which include duck pond and picnic tables.

Minimum Age: None

Disabled Access: Yes

Group Requirements: Groups over 5 people should call in advance. No maximum group size.

Special Information: Two large barbecue areas may be rented for weddings and parties.

Sales Room: Sells all the Rouge et Noir cheeses (including goat and cow milk blue cheese), wine, bread, sandwiches, and other picnic supplies. Offers gift assortment packs and logoed aprons, wineglasses, T-shirts, and caps. Open Mon–Sun 9:00 AM–5:00 PM.

Directions: From San Francisco, take U.S. 101 North to Novato. Turn left onto San Marin Dr., right onto Novato Blvd., and left onto Petaluma–Pt. Reyes Rd. You can't miss the giant cheese-wheel sign 0.25 mile ahead on right. From Santa Rosa, take U.S. 101 South to Petaluma. Turn right onto E. Washington St., left onto Payran St., and right onto D St. Continue about 9 miles past the town. Marin French Cheese will be on your right.

Nearby Attractions: Sonoma and Napa Valleys; Pt. Reyes National Seashore; Bodega Bay; Petaluma Adobe State Historic Park; Petaluma Historical Museum/Library; The Great Petaluma Mill shops.

CALIFORNIA

MRS. GROSSMAN'S

Mrs. Grossman is Andrea Grossman—a name legendary among sticker collectors and scrapbookers. She is president and founder of Mrs. Grossman's Paper Company, the oldest and largest decorative sticker manufacturer in the U.S. Started in 1975 as a stationery line, Mrs. Grossman introduced Stickers by the Yard in 1979 after satisfying a customer's request for a simple red heart sticker for Valentine's Day. Now the company has a heart as a logo and a motto—its mission statement focuses on treating employees, vendors, and customers respectfully, caringly, and honestly.

When you walk into the 110,000-square-foot striking glass plant overlooking a bird sanctuary, you will feel like you have walked into someone's life. In the lobby, the soft-red furniture will welcome you. Walk up the glass stairs under the magical neon Mrs. Grossman's sign. Along the walls all around you is a sticker museum showing the sticker designs from the company's beginning—you may find yourself remembering some of the retired stickers such as the camel and the kangaroo.

After watching a video and perhaps winning some prizes during a question-and-answer session, venture into the factory. This is such a friendly place—wave to the employees and they will wave back. In the printing department, your tour guide may quiz you on how many hours it takes to print 400,000 stickers (10 hours—four to set up, four for printing, and two for cleaning and maintenance). Amazingly, eight massive 10-color presses pour out 400,000 stickers an hour. You may notice an ammonia smell—ammonia helps the ink dry faster.

A tour highlight is the high-tech, 20-foot-tall, computer-driven LaserWeb that resembles a space ship with flashing lights, countless control panels, and four monitors. A camera inside the machine allows you to watch as the laser passes over a copper template, shooting a design onto sticker paper. Watch on an overhead video screen as a 10,000°F laser causes paper molecules to explode, creating intricate, fanciful details such as lace for scrap-

books and heritage albums. Follow your guide into the warehouse where rolls of stickers are stacked 40 feet high, storing 3,000 miles of stickers. At the end of the tour, you can make a hands-on sticker art postcard. You leave with a feeling that loving kindness prevails—you may even want to work here.

Cost: Adults, $3; children 2 and under, free. Call for group rates.

Freebies: Stickers

Video/DVD Shown: 20-minute award-winning video narrated by the company's favorite dog, Angus, an Australian shepherd. Covers the life of a 20-cent sticker from concept to design, prepress to printing, and sales to shipping.

Reservations Needed: Yes; call for information.

Days and Hours: Mon–Fri. Times vary, so please call. Closed holidays.

Plan to Stay: 1.5 hours, plus additional time in the 2,000-square-foot retail store and to enjoy the walking path around bird sanctuary with geese, pelicans, ducks, and swans.

Minimum Age: None

Disabled Access: Yes

Group Requirements: Large groups will be split. Maximum 40 people.

Special Information: We hope you love dogs: Mrs. Grossman is often on the premises, along with the 5 dogs she and her son, Jason, own, plus employees' dogs are welcome too.

Company Store: Sells all 700 of the company's current designs, sticker kits and collections, and scrapbooking supplies. Open Mon–Fri 9:00 AM–5:30 PM. Closed some holidays.

Directions: From San Francisco, take U.S. 101 North. Turn left onto Lakeville Hwy. (Hwy. 116 East). Turn right onto South McDowell St. Turn right into parking lot.

Nearby Attractions: Marin French Cheese tour (see page 375); Petaluma Adobe State Historic Park; Shollenberger Park (great birding); Sonoma County wineries; San Francisco's attractions including Basic Brown Bear tour (see page 357), Golden Gate Bridge, and Fisherman's Wharf are about 1 hour away.

CALIFORNIA

NBC is the only major television network that provides tours to the public. Your tour guide will take you through the life of a television broadcast, from its conception to the building of the set, from the studio taping to your television at home. Visit the actual facilities as shows are taping in the studio next to you. Walk the halls of the stars and keep your eyes peeled for Jay Leno.

Begin your tour in the carpenter shop. Here, carpenters and artists work side by side to build and put the finishing touches on sets for NBC shows and events. Though sometimes huge, the sets are made with lightweight plywood and fiberglass brick so they don't become too heavy. The sets have to be fit together inside the studio due to the size limitations of studio doors.

Walk down the main hallway, cluttered with the sets for *Days of Our Lives*. Learn how this daily one-hour show is really a 24-hour-a-day operation. Sets are ever-changing. The show is taped year-round, unlike seasonal shows, which can run repeats in the summer. Peek into the studio if the door is open.

Follow your guide through the midway, where the stars park their cars. Check to see what Leno drove to work that day—he owns around 80 vintage cars and 50 motorcycles, including a Stanley Steamer, a classic Duesenberg, and a WWI–era motorcycle.

If the *Tonight Show* is not in session, go into Studio 3. Sit in the audience chairs and watch the bustle of setup onstage. The show is taped live with only about one and a half hours for editing before it is broadcast on the East Coast.

On the special-effects set, learn how the blue Chroma Key screen works, while a volunteer plays weatherman or flies like Superman. Your tour ends in the guest relations patio, which you may recognize as the Salem Place Mall from *Days of Our Lives*.

Cost: Adults $8.00; seniors (60 and over) $7.25; children (5–12) $4.50; under 5, free.

Freebies: No

Videos/DVDs Shown: A 6.5-minute video on the history of NBC and the tour, plus a behind-the-scenes look at production; 1-minute video on wardrobe and make-up techniques.

Reservations Needed: No, but tickets sold on first-come, first-served basis. Yes, for groups of 15 or more people.

Days and Hours: Mon–Fri 9:00 AM–3:00 PM. July and August also Sat 10:00 AM–2:00 PM. Tours every half hour. Closed some holidays.

Plan to Stay: 70 minutes, plus time for the gift shop.

Minimum Age: None

Disabled Access: Yes

Group Requirements: Groups of 15 or more people should call NBC Group Services at (818) 840-3551 at least 2 weeks in advance. Groups over 15 people will be split. Reservations may be difficult between Christmas and New Year's.

Special Information: No photography. Tours will not go into studios during production. Tours before 1:30 PM will likely include the *Tonight Show* studio. Free audience show tickets available daily at NBC's ticket counter on first-come, first-served basis. Send ticket requests to NBC Tickets at above address or call above number for more information. NBC Studios in New York City (see page 111) also gives tours.

Gift Shop: NBC Peacock Shop sells merchandise from NBC shows along with logoed souvenir items. Open same hours as tour.

Directions: From the south, take I-405 North to U.S. 101 East (to L.A.). From the left lane, merge onto Ventura Fwy. (Hwy. 134) East. Exit Buena Vista off-ramp. Turn left on Riverside Dr. Turn right on Bob Hope Dr. and follow signs to NBC Studios tour. From the east, take I-10 West to I-5 North. Exit Alameda Ave. West. Studio is 2 miles ahead, near St. Joseph's Hospital.

Nearby Attractions: Universal Studios, Paramount Pictures, and Warner Bros. tours (see pages 387, 379, and 388); Gene Autry Western Heritage Museum.

CALIFORNIA

Automobile factory tours always offer a special excitement. Because the General Motors/Toyota joint venture (nicknamed "NUMMI") uses this refurbished GM plant, it's a showcase of Japanese manufacturing techniques within the context of U.S. union-management relations. As your electric tram motors more than one mile over the factory floor, watch workers (called "team members"), giant machines, and robots build the Pontiac Vibe, Toyota Corolla, and Toyota Tacoma pickup truck.

Because of the plant's layout, your narrated trip does not follow the exact sequence of building cars and trucks. However, you will see most of the steps in the manufacturing process. Each of the plant's work areas—whether for stamping, body and welding, assembling, or inspecting—manufactures cars and trucks at a measured pace along the plant's 1.2 miles of assembly line. For example, as an engine is hydraulically lifted into the car engine compartment overhead, team members scramble to bolt the engine into place within 67 seconds, the scheduled time each unit spends at each workstation in the car-assembly area.

A cacophony fills the air: drilling, crunching, hissing, and buzzing. Since the plant has the largest metal parts–stamping facility on the West Coast, a constant thumping reverberates through part of the plant. Suddenly you may hear music playing. A team member on the assembly line has spotted a quality problem and pulled the Andon Cord. If the problem can't be resolved quickly, production stops on that section of the line, and the music keeps playing until the problem is fixed. (Each area has its own tune.) This cord empowers all team members to guarantee quality in the manufacturing process, what the Japanese call *Jidoka*. Even if you're not interested in the details of the Toyota production system, you'll marvel at the movements and flying sparks generated by more than 100 computerized welding robots.

Cost: Free

Freebies: Currently no souvenirs.

Video/DVD Shown: No, but captioned pictures in the tour waiting room explain the different manufacturing steps.

Reservations Needed: Yes; reservations made only online at www.nummi.com. Individuals and families must join a scheduled group tour.

Days and Hours: Tue–Fri 8:30 AM–2:30 PM. Tour content and schedule may change due to production requirements and model change activities. Closed holidays and week between Christmas and New Year's.

Plan to Stay: Approximately 2 hours, including introductory talk, tour, and wrap-up Q&A session.

Minimum Age: 10. Tours for children ages 10–18 require 1 adult for every 10 children.

Disabled Access: Yes, but not all parts of tour are wheelchair accessible. Call for special accommodations.

Group Requirements: Maximum group size is 50 people. Tours need to be scheduled 3–4 months in advance for larger groups.

Special Information: No photography. Because tour is by electric tram, there's not much walking.

Gift Shop: No

Directions: From I-880 North, use the Fremont Blvd. exit just past Mission Blvd. Turn right at first light and take immediate right. Visitor parking on left after three stop signs. If traveling south on I-880, use the second Fremont Blvd. exit, just past Auto Mall Pkwy. (Do not take the earlier Alvarado Niles/Fremont Blvd. Exit.) Plant is visible from freeway. Upon exiting, stay left to loop back over freeway. Turn right at first light. Follow above directions. Ask for map when making reservations.

Nearby Attractions: Intel Museum (see page 368); Great America Theme Park; Mission Peak Regional Park.

A Paramount Communications Company

Paramount Pictures, founded in 1912, shows the true TV and movie fan current moviemaking techniques while retaining its nostalgic charm. The only major studio still located in Hollywood, Paramount provides an exciting behind-the-scenes look at movie and television production. Tours of this original, classic studio are never exactly alike, since old sets are taken down and new projects begin every day.

Your tour guide will point out a number of famous Paramount landmarks along this two-hour tour. You will see various sets and soundstages of current Paramount productions. Stroll by the Camera Department, as well as a display of Oscars and Emmys on loan from stars who have awards to spare.

As you peer through the old Bronson Gate, the arched gateway entrance synonymous with Paramount Pictures, and gaze upon the famous Hollywood sign in the hills, you'll hear the story about this passage being the magic gateway to the Silver Screen for aspiring stars. Carefully study the roof architecture of some of the soundstages to identify the three film production companies located here before Paramount took over the site in 1928.

Notice the B tank, a body of water used for shooting miniatures and special effects, such as the parting of the Red Sea in the 1956 filming of *The Ten Commandments*. The 100,000-gallon-capacity water tower still marks the borderline dividing Paramount and RKO Studios, which was acquired by Paramount. Stroll through Production Park, not only the company's business hub, but also one of the most photographed areas in Hollywood. On screen, its buildings double as college campuses, foreign embassies, police precincts, hospitals, and more. At any point on the tour, you may suddenly see your favorite performer.

Cost: The studio tour is $35 per person.

Freebies: Tickets to the TV shows filmed at Paramount.

Video/DVD Shown: No

Reservations Needed: Yes, call up to 30 days in advance.

Days and Hours: *Studio tours depart four times a day every weekday. The tours will not operate on major holidays or weekends.*

Plan to Stay: 2 hours

Minimum Age: To go on the tour, 12. To be a member of the studio audience, 16.

Disabled Access: Yes

Group Requirements: Group tours are available; please call for information.

Special Information: The tour is by advance reservation only.

Gift Shop: Yes

Directions: From Los Angeles, take U.S. 101 North to Melrose Ave. exit. Turn left onto Melrose Ave. Parking information provided with reservation. From San Fernando Valley, take U.S. 101 South to Gower St. exit. Make a right onto Gower St., go down hill. Turn left onto Melrose.

Nearby Attractions: Universal Studios, NBC Studios, and Warner Bros. tours (see pages 387, 377, and 388); Mann's Chinese Theatre, with famous people's footprints in the forecourt; Downtown Hollywood's famous streets, including Hollywood Blvd., the Sunset Strip.

CALIFORNIA

391 South Orange Grove Boulevard,
Pasadena, CA 91184

(626) 449-4100

www.tournament
ofroses.com

Have you ever been awestruck by the amazing beauty and intricate detail of the floats as you watch the Rose Parade on New Year's Day? Have you ever dreamed of helping make those floats? While design and concept work begins a year in advance—it starts as soon as one Rose Parade is over, with construction throughout the year—the final fresh flowers cannot be applied until a few days before the Rose Parade. Not only can you view this process, you can actually help decorate the floats!

The process starts with a specially built chassis, upon which is built a framework of steel and chicken wire. In a process called "cocooning," the frame is sprayed with a polyvinyl material, which is then painted in the colors of the flowers to be applied later. Every inch of the float must be covered with flowers or other natural materials, such as leaves, seeds, or bark. Volunteer workers swarm over the floats in the days after Christmas, their hands and clothes covered with glue and petals. The most delicate flowers are placed in individual vials of water, which are set into the float one by one. An average float requires as many as 100,000 blossoms and costs upwards of $250,000.

Float decorating sites range from huge warehouse spaces to a gigantic circus-size tent in the parking lot of the Rose Bowl Arena. While some cities and individual companies self-build their floats, there are five major float design firms that build Rose Parade floats.

Phoenix Decorating is the only builder with permanent locations in Pasadena, California. All float construction and decoration takes place at its two facilities, close to the parade route and Tournament of Roses headquarters. These sites, the Rose Palace and Rosemont Pavilion, are the only facilities specifically designed to accommodate public viewing of float decoration.

As a volunteer decorator, you will work with adhesives, wet floral materials, and occasionally paint. You may also be climbing around on dirty scaffolding and ladders. All this hard work, buzz, and excitement to decorate beautiful floats in a few short (actually a few very long) days occurs so that they can majestically glide down Colorado Boulevard for the spectacular Rose Parade. This event precedes the Rose Bowl, the most famous/biggest of the Big 10 college football tournaments. Known as "The Granddaddy of Them All," the Rose Bowl began in 1902 and has run consecutively every year since 1916.

Cost: Watching: $5 for any two visits; under 3, free. Decorating: free. Advance tickets are available through Sharp Seating Company at (626) 795-4171.

Freebies: No

Video/DVD Shown: No

Reservations Needed: No, except there are long lines for viewing. Contact float builders directly up to 6 months in advance for tickets to help make floats. Some allow walk-ins, although work is not guaranteed.

Days and Hours: Watching: December 28 and December 29 9:00 AM–6:00 PM December 30 11:00 AM–6:00 PM, December 31st 11:00 AM–1:00 PM. Decorating: Same days, until 10:00 PM. If New Year's is on a Sunday, the decorating dates start one day later.

Plan to Stay: 4-hour minimum session for decorating.

Minimum Age: None, for watching; 14, for decorating.

Disabled Access: Yes, for Brookside Pavilion and Buena Vista Pavilion in Duarte.

Group Requirements: Groups of 25 or more must prearrange decorating assignments.

Special Information: Wear clothes which can get dirty and possibly damaged. Easier to volunteer at Festival Artists since it is located in Azusa, 45 minutes from Pasadena (call 626-388-1839).

Gift Shop: No

Directions: Check individual float builder's websites.

Nearby Attractions: Rose Bowl; Norton Simon Museum; Gamble House; Huntington Library.

CALIFORNIA

914 Heinz Avenue, Berkeley, CA 94710

(510) 981-4050
(510) 981-4066

www.scharffen
berger.com

★ ★ ★

SCHARFFEN BERGER

CHOCOLATE MAKER

If you're looking for supersweet American-style chocolate, this isn't the place—John Sharffenberger and Robert Steinberg founded Scharffen Berger Chocolate Maker in 1996 to celebrate a richer, older tradition of chocolate making. With vintage machinery and gentle hands, workers coax a blend of cocoa beans from small plantations near the equator into dense dark chocolate used for both baking and snacking.

Enter this refurbished 1906 vintage brick warehouse. Your tour guide tells the history of chocolate and the company (the only American chocolate-making company founded in the last 50 years), punctuated with samples of chocolate in every stage from cocoa bean to finished product. The pure, sugarless chocolate dissolves on your tongue with such an intense flavor that you might have a hard time finishing. Don't miss the cacao nibs: little, nutty nuggets of roasted and crushed cocoa bean.

The cleaned beans roast for one hour at 280°F before going into the winnower, where the nibs pour out from side holes into bins. Workers sift out the small nibs by hand: they will become Nibby Bars. Walk up the portable staircase to look down at the large nibs grinding inside the melanger. Two granite rollers spin in opposite directions on a rotating granite plate, crushing the nibs into chocolate liquor. Sugar, vanilla, soy lecithin, and cocoa butter complete the recipe. Scharffen Berger recipes vary; each country's beans have subtle, but distinct, flavors.

In the main tempering machine, the chocolate heats, cools, heats, and cools to become shiny with a good snap. Next, it shoots up a pipe, drops into molds, and travels through the cooling tunnel on its way to the assembly line. Workers hand-wrap the finished chocolates and send the slightly im-

perfect ones back to be remelted. This chocolate is intense—you will leave your tour still euphoric from the samples you ate an hour earlier.

Cost: Free

Freebies: Chocolate samples.

Video/DVD Shown: No

Reservations Needed: Yes. Individuals or small groups may reserve on website or call at least 2 weeks in advance. Groups larger than 15, see Group Requirements.

Days and Hours: Mon, Tue, Thur, Fri 10:30 AM, 2:30 PM, and 4:30 PM; Sun, Wed 10:30 AM, 2:30 PM, and 3:30 PM; Sat 10:30 AM, 11:30 AM, 2:30 PM, 3:30 PM, and 4:30 PM.

Plan to Stay: 1 hour for tour and sampling, plus time in gift shop.

Minimum Age: 10

Disabled Access: Yes

Group Requirements: Groups of 15 or more can email tours@scharffenberger.com or call (510) 981-4066 for 1:00 PM only. Groups cannot make reservations through the website. A $30 group tour fee, payable at time of reservation, is redeemable in gift shop. Maximum group size is 25.

Special Information: No open-toed shoes.

Gift Shop: Sells Nibby Bar, Mocha, Bittersweet, and Semisweet chocolate, cocoa powder, chocolate sauce, T-shirts, hats, books, fondue pots, and cooking utensils. Open Mon–Sat 10:00 AM–6:00 PM, Sun 10:00 AM–5:00 PM.

Directions: From San Francisco, take I-80 East. Take Ashby Ave. exit and keep left. Turn left onto Ashby Ave., left onto 7th St., and right onto Heinz Ave. Scharffen Berger will be on right.

Nearby Attractions: University of California at Berkeley Botanical Garden; Hooper's Chocolate factory tour (call 510-653-3703). San Francisco attractions, including Basic Brown Bear Factory (see page 357), Ghirardelli Square, Golden Gate Park, and Fisherman's Wharf are about 40 minutes away. Jelly Belly tours (see page 369) 30–40 minutes away; Intel Museum (see page 368) 1 hour away.

CALIFORNIA

While everyone knows that Napa Valley wineries offer tours, you may not know that in South Napa you can watch the ancient art of barrel making. Of 22 cooperages in the U.S. (most make whiskey barrels), only three are in Napa Valley. Seguin Moreau's Napa cooperage is a division of Seguin Moreau, France's oldest cooperage, established in the late 1800s.

As soon as your guide opens the doors to this cooperage built in 1994, you'll smell a pleasant vanilla aroma from the toasting barrels. You stroll along an open-air walkway just a few feet from the action. Brown overhead signs clearly mark all 12 of the production stations. Diagrams along the walkway show you which steps are performed in each of the two large, high-ceilinged rooms. With all the small fires in the first room, you wonder if some ancient witchcraft is brewing. Flames, water, and banging hammers are the key tools for shaping barrels. No glue is used. More modern woodworking machinery is used in the second room to finish the barrels.

American white oak, split from 90-year-old trees, is seasoned outdoors for two to three years to reduce moisture and tannins. Then the wood is ready to be cut into 37.5-inch-long staves and arranged in pairs—one wide, one narrow. With great skill, a master cooper "raises a barrel" by vertically arranging 27 to 30 of these alternating-width staves into a "rosette." He lines up the tops of the staves against the inside of a metal hoop, with the bottoms flaring out to form a tepee. If done correctly, the barrel could stand alone without the metal hoop; otherwise, the staves will fall into a tangled pile. To hold them tightly, metal hoops are pounded into place by the cooper circling the barrel in what's known as the "barrel-maker's dance." The staves are bent into the barrel shape with the help of moisture, heat, and an electric winch. The bending process takes approximately 20 minutes.

The barrels then move to the fires, where they are toasted for approximately one hour along a row of 12 small campfires. The coopers turn them over regularly so the insides toast evenly. The toasting releases natural flavors that enhance the taste of the wine that will eventually be put in the barrel. Barrelheads, assembled with wooden dowels and river reed, are toasted in a large oven. A cooper wedges the head into place with a shoehorn-like tool. At station 12 in the second room, the barrel rolls under the sanding belt. Each barrel takes 17 coopers about four hours to make.

Cost: Free

Freebies: Great toasting wood sme ls!

Video/DVD Shown: 10-minute video covers company history, where wood comes from, and barrel-making process at Seguin Moreau's French facility.

Reservations Needed: Recommended

Days and Hours: Mon–Fri 9:00 AM, 11:30 AM, and 1:30 PM. Closed week of July 4th and week between Christmas and New Year's.

Plan to Stay: 40 minutes for tour and video.

Minimum Age: None

Disabled Access: Yes

Group Requirements: Groups over 50 people will be split.

Special Information: No video cameras. Due to the flames, cooperage is very hot in the summer.

Gift Area: Sells logoed polos, mugs, and other items. Open Mon–Fri 8:00 AM–5:00 PM.

Directions: From Oakland/San Francisco, take I-80 East to Napa turnoff (Hwy. 37 West). Take Hwy. 29 North. After the Napa Airport on eft, you'll pass Seguin Moreau on your right. Turn right onto Hwy. 12 East. Turn left at traffic light onto N. Kelly Rd. and left onto Camino Dorado. Seguin Moreau will be on your right.

Nearby Attractions: Carneros area winery tours include Domaine Carneros Sparkling Wine (call 707-257-0101) and Artesa Vineyards & Winery (call 707-224-1668). For general information about Napa Valley winery tours, call (707) 226-7459.

10202 W. Washington Boulevard,
Culver City, CA 90232

(323) 520-TOUR

www.sonypictures
studios.com

Columbia Pictures, TriStar, and MGM are all well-known companies that are part of Sony Pictures Studios. The walking tour offers a look behind the scenes of this movie lot, once the home of MGM. Guides also work in the film industry and have a great historical repertoire, enlivening the tour with vivid anecdotes.

The tour varies according to what movies and TV shows are in production, and where access is permitted. You walk through warehouse-sized soundstages and through sets of current television shows, stopping to compare how the set looks in person with how it appears on the big screen or your television. Many famous movies were produced here. Visit the soundstages where Dorothy once skipped down the Yellow Brick Road in *The Wizard of Oz,* where agents in *Men in Black* battled aliens from outer space, and where the TV show *Charlie's Angels* was filmed. The tour guides recreate the feel of making these films and shows, coloring their accounts with little-known secrets about the stars and the productions.

If circumstances permit, your tour will also cover the arts of post-production. You may drop in on scenic artists painting colorful backdrops and the special rooms where sounds are created, recorded, edited, and mixed. You may learn some of the tricks the Foley artists use to supply the subtle noises that microphones miss but make a scene seem so real. Your tour may also include a segment on the musical scoring of movies.

Cost: $25 per person.

Freebies: Posters for new movies may be available.

Video/DVD Shown: A movie is presented at the start of the tour in a private screening room with plush seats. It presents the studio's history, includes clips of famous films it produced, and shows brief clips from upcoming productions.

Reservations Needed: No, but recommended.

Days and Hours: Mon–Fri 9:30 AM, 10:30 AM, 11:30 AM, 1:30 PM, and 2:30 PM. In summer there is a 12:30 PM tour. Closed weekends and all major holidays. Check in at least 30 minutes before tour time with a government-issued photo ID.

Plan to Stay: 2 hours for walking tour, plus additional time for shopping at Studio Emporium.

Minimum Age: 12

Disabled Access: Yes, but wheelchairs cannot be provided.

Group Requirements: Groups of 20 or more people get a discounted price of $20 per person. You must set the number of people a week before the visit.

Special Information: No cameras, large tote bags, or backpacks. Still photography is allowed in certain designated areas. The tour office is located in the Sony Pictures Plaza Building, which contains museum memorabilia and a café. If you want to watch a taping of *Jeopardy!* or *Wheel of Fortune,* call (800) 482-9840 to reserve. Eight-story atrium building lobby features historic movie posters and props from famous films, including Academy Award trophies.

Gift Shop: The Studio Emporium sells a selection of logoed hats, shirts, and other items that promote the studio and current movies.

Directions: From downtown L.A., take I-10 West and exit at Overland Blvd. Head south on Overland to Venice Blvd. Turn left on Venice to Clarington and turn right. Proceed 1 block across Washington Blvd. and turn left into the Sony Pictures Plaza Building. Tour department is in lobby.

Nearby Attractions: In the Los Angeles area, Getty Museum. Other studio tours include NBC (page 377), Warner Bros. (page 388), and Universal (page 387). In Beverly Hills, Academy of Motion Picture Arts and Sciences (call 310-247-3600).

CALIFORNIA

Sunset magazine was founded in 1898 by Southern Pacific Railroad Company as a promotional tool to encourage westward travel, and was named after the Southern Pacific's Sunset Limited train route. The magazine evolved into a gardening, travel, food, and home-improvement magazine for the West. The company now publishes seven monthly regional editions of *Sunset* magazine for 13 Western states. Each edition focuses on that region's needs and interests, particularly in travel and gardening. In 1931, Sunset published its first cookbook. You can take a self-guided walk through its display gardens.

Sunset's adobe-style home was designed by renowned architect Cliff May and opened in 1952. Enter the light, airy main lobby through the thick, hand-carved, 10-foot-tall front doors. Notice some of the interesting interior architectural features, such as the desert-tile lobby floor and the adobe brick walls— each brick is two feet deep and weighs 30 pounds!

Outside, stroll through the formal gardens created by landscape designer Thomas Church. This "Walk through the West" features native plants from Southern California to Washington, plus Hawaii. You'll first walk past the Old Man live oak, growing increasingly lopsided as it chases the sun.

Walk along the curved walkway to the Southwest Desert and Southern California section, which features cacti, succulents, and certain perennials that will grow under extreme drought conditions. Notice the large Southern yucca, which is probably 150 years old. Farther along the walkway is the Central California area. The lawn here is sometimes mowed into a putting green in the summer. Notice how the sun shines through the "Monterey Peninsula."

Huge coast redwoods reign over the garden's Northern California section. Look up at the magnolia blossom trees. Four Chardonnay and four Cabernet grapevines represent the Sonoma and Napa Valleys. Wet winters and cold temperatures characterize the climate for the Northwest. Here you'll see dogwood, firs, and many types of rhododendron, including azaleas.

After the peaceful, perfectly manicured formal gardens, you visit the organic test garden used for editorial projects. This 3,200-square-foot garden is divided into four test plots. Ever changing, the beds may contain 30 varieties of gourmet lettuce, or hyacinth and tulips in the spring. Next time you browse through *Sunset's* brightly colored garden photographs, you'll know where they were taken.

Cost: Free

Freebies: Walking tour map, which includes company history.

Video/DVD Shown: No

Reservations Needed: No, except for groups larger than 10 people.

Days and Hours: Mon–Fri 9:00 AM–4:30 PM. Closed holidays.

Plan to Stay: 20 minutes.

Minimum Age: None, however, children should be interested in horticulture.

Disabled Access: Yes

Group Requirements: None

Special Information: No professional photography allowed. Best times to tour are spring (when the gardens are in full bloom) and Christmas (when crafts projects are displayed in lobby).

Gift Shop: No; however, Sunset books are displayed and can be ordered by calling (800) 526-5111 or at www.sunset.com. Magazines are also sold in lobby. Subscribe to *Sunset* magazine by calling (800) 777-0117.

Directions: From San Francisco, take U.S. 101 South to Willow Rd./Menlo Park West exit. Follow Willow Rd. for approximately 1 mile. Sunset is on your left.

Nearby Attractions: Intel Museum (see page 368); Filoli Estate; Allied Arts Guild; Stanford Linear Accelerator Center tour (call 650-926-2204).

CALIFORNIA

13660 Highway 49, Sutter Creek, CA 95685

(209) 736-2708
(800) 225-3764

www.caverntours.com

If your only mining experience is watching the Seven Dwarves in *Snow White,* it might be time for you to witness the real thing. The Sutter Gold Mine tour focuses on educating people about life inside a mine, the safety issues involved, and what the earth looks like so far underground.

Safety is a priority right from the beginning. The guide counts everyone and "tags them in" by placing a metal tag over a number so everyone will be accounted for at the end of the tour. Then everyone is fitted with hard hats, an accessory you must wear throughout the tour.

A bus buggy shuttle, used in real mines, carries you to the entrance of the mine. The entrance is cut into the rocky hillside, framed by a metal gate and metal pipes. You'll hear a loud noise, which is the ventilation fan. Beyond the first 30 feet, the mine is pitch black.

As you tunnel down the mineshaft, you'll stop four times to view mining equipment exhibits. After traveling 1,850 feet down, you'll enter the safety chamber. The guide will tell you how the safety chamber works and will explain the map of the Motherlode. Next, you'll walk through the "comet zone," where gold-bearing quartz was extracted. Up some stairs and through a tunnel you'll see more mining displays depicting mining activity and see the drills that are used to extract ore. There are still places where gold can be seen in the walls of the mine, and you'll learn how to distinguish real gold from fool's gold.

You'll board the bus buggy shuttle to come back out of the mine, where you'll turn in your hard hat and be tagged out before going back above ground.

Be sure to save some time after the tour to pan for gold and do some gemstone mining.

Cost: Adults, $14.95; children, $9.95. Gold panning, $5 each; gemstone mining, $4.50 small bag, $6.95 large bag.

Freebies: No

Video/DVD Shown: Free movies about gold mining shown in the Gold Theater.

Reservations Needed: No, but groups of 10 or more should call ahead to make sure there will be space on a tour for them. School groups should also call ahead.

Days and Hours: Mid-May–mid-September: daily 9:00 AM–5:00 PM. Mid-September–mid-May: weekdays 10:00 AM–4:00 PM, weekends and holidays 10:00 AM–5:00 PM.

Plan to Stay: One hour for walking tour; up to all day for above-ground activities.

Minimum Age: 3 for underground tour, but recommended for 4 or older. No minimum age for above-ground activities.

Disabled Access: Yes, with advance notice.

Group Requirements: School groups and groups of 10 or more should call ahead. Group discounts available. Maximum of 23 persons on each tour, although larger groups can be accommodated; no minimum.

Special Information: Hard hats must be worn underground. Tour not recommended for people who are claustrophobic or have serious heart or lung problems.

Gold Store: Sells handmade gold nugget jewelry, books about the gold rush and gold mining, science activities, and lots of rocks. Open same hours as mine.

Directions: From Sacramento, take Hwy. 16 East to Hwy. 49 South. Look for entrance on the left approx. half a mile south of Amador City, just north of Sutter Creek. From the Bay Area, take U.S. 50 East to I-205 to Hwy. 120 East to Hwy. 99 North. Take Hwy. 88 East to Hwy. 49 North. Look for entrance on the right approximately 1 mile north of Sutter Creek.

Nearby Attractions: Black Chasm Cavern National Natural Landmark, California Cavern State Historic Landmark, Moaning Cavern, Kennedy Gold Mine, Indian Grinding Rock State Historic Park, The Miners Pick Antiques & Western Hardrock Mining Museum.

See color photos, page 48.

Kurt Listug and Bob Taylor started Taylor Guitars in 1974 in a dank, dusty warehouse where they turned out a couple of guitars each week and barely covered their costs. Gradually, Taylor's craftsmanship and Listug's sales skills attracted musicians like Neil Young and Bonnie Raitt. Sales to such well-known artists helped raise the public's awareness of the company. Today, Taylor Guitars creates 39,000 acoustic guitars per year and grosses over $40 million from production in its 143,000-square-foot facility. Listug and Taylor never gave up creative control, and the company continues to heighten industry standards with a combination of luck, intuition, and innovation.

On the tour, learn that Taylor accidentally revolutionized the neck attachment process because he did not know how to make a traditional dovetail to fasten the neck to the body. Instead of using glue, which impedes the transference of resonance and creates a deadening effect, he planed the surface of the body flat and bolted on the guitar neck, resulting in greater stability and a more articulate tone.

At the CNC (Computer Numeric Controlled) stations, peer through the bullet-proof plastic on both ends of the milling machines, where precision equipment produces necks and bracing materials to rigid specifications. To form curves and shapes, a vacuum holds blocks of tonewoods in place while the shaping tool glides vertically and the bed slides horizontally.

Computer-guided laser cutters work out the shapes of the top, back, and sides. The laser burnishes and heat-seals the edge of the wood—no saw blade lifts the grain and leaves a rough edge. Diamond-tipped cutting tools adjust the depth and width of the sound holes and decorative rosette for the tops. In the body department, a Multicam milling machine prepares the top, sides, and back for attachment to one another, perfectly fitting the pieces of wood together. Workers then check the glue joints with an ultraviolet light that illuminates any spilled glue.

The repair department provides some of the most unusual sights. Taylor veterans rescue forlorn guitars—run over by cars or dropped at airports—that bereaved owners send in, hoping to salvage at least part of a beloved instrument.

In the finish and final assembly area, preassigned necks and bodies meet according to the numerical tracking system, and each guitar bakes in ultraviolet light for three 23-second exposures to cure the finish, similar to the process used to finish airplanes. Try not to stare at the gleaming rows of finished Taylor Guitars like a child in a candy shop.

Cost: Free

Freebies: Logoed sound hole coasters cut from Taylor Guitar tops, catalogs, *Wood* & *Steel* publication, videos.

Video/DVD Shown: 40-minute video, "Taylor on Guitars: New Neck Designs," shown in lobby.

Reservations Needed: No, except groups larger than 10.

Days and Hours: Mon–Fri 1:00 P.M. Closed major and company holidays. Closed 2 weeks around Christmas and New Year's.

Plan to Stay: 1.5 hours.

Minimum Age: None, but children should have an interest in guitars.

Disabled Access: Yes

Group Requirements: Groups larger than 10 people should call 10 days in advance. Groups larger than 15 people will be split into smaller groups.

Special Information: Check website for Taylor performances and workshops held nationally.

Gift Counter: Sells Taylorware clothing and guitar straps. Open Mon–Fri 8:00 AM–4:30 PM. Taylor Guitars available from more than 800 dealers.

Directions: From San Diego, take I-8 East to El Cajon. Take Hwy. 67 North. Exit at Bradley St. Turn left (west) onto Bradley St. and right onto Cuyamaca St. Take left onto Gillespie Way. Taylor Guitars will be on the left.

Nearby Attractions: Callaway Golf and LEGOLAND tours (see pages 361 and 372); San Diego's attractions include San Diego Zoo, Wild Animal Park, and SeaWorld.

CALIFORNIA

100 Universal City Plaza, Universal City, CA 91608   (818) 622-3801   www.universalstudios
(800) 864-8377   hollywood.com

Film pioneer Carl Laemmle established Universal Studios in 1915 on a former chicken ranch. In the early days of silent pictures, visitors ate box lunches provided by the studio and sat in bleacher seats watching films being made. With the advent of "talking pictures," the tours stopped.

Largely as an effort to boost the lunchtime business at the Studio Commissary, Universal reopened its doors to the public in 1964. Millions of dollars and visitors later, Universal Studios Hollywood has developed its famed 420-acre studio lot into a first-rate theme park. Attractions provide a fun family experience through which to learn the secrets of motion picture and television production.

Universal Studios Hollywood really is a trip into what it feels like to be in a movie. It's not about what it's like to be an actor in a film, but rather what it's like to be a character in a Hollywood adventure story. While Charlton Heston or Ava Gardner did their *Earthquake!* scenes in hundreds of boring pieces, the tour puts the pieces together and plays them at full speed.

You can enjoy the behind-the-scenes Studio Tour, which visits famous production sets of the world's largest movie studio. You go past renowned sets from *War of the Worlds, Desperate Housewives, Jurassic Park, The Grinch Who Stole Christmas, Apollo 13, End of Days, Animal House,* and *Back to the Future,* among many others. Television sets you'll recognize include those from *Murder, She Wrote; Dr. Quinn, Medicine Woman; Leave It to Beaver; McHale's Navy;* and *Sliders.*

The Special Effects Stages provide insights into special effects used in *The Mummy* and *Shrek.* Several audience members can participate in the demonstrations. One show teaches how sounds and voices are dubbed into an already-shot film through Foley and ADR (automated dubbing replacement technique).

Cost: See website above for price and ticket-ordering information.

Freebies: No

Video/DVD Shown: Many attractions include videos.

Reservations Needed: No, except for groups of 20 or more people.

Days and Hours: Mon–Fri 10:00 AM–6:00 PM, Sat–Sun 9:00 AM–7:00 PM. Open 8:00 AM– 10:00 PM during peak days and in the summer. Box office opens 30 minutes before park. Closed Thanksgiving and Christmas.

Plan to Stay: All day at Universal Studios. The behind-the-scenes Studio Tour lasts 45 minutes.

Minimum Age: None

Disabled Access: Yes

Group Requirements: Groups of 20 or more people should call Group Sales (818-622-3771) 3–4 days in advance or write Universal Studios (at the above address) to reserve tickets. Groups receive a 10 percent discount off box-office prices.

Special Information: A booth at the studio offers free tickets to TV show productions; however, some of these shows are not filmed at Universal. In addition to the Studio Tour, other Universal Studios' movie-related attractions include Terminator 2: 3D, Nickelodeon Blast Zone, Animal Planet Live!, Jurassic Park—The Ride, Revenge of the Mummy—The Ride, Van Helsing: Fortress Dracula, Waterworld—A Live Sea War Spectacular, Back to the Future—The Ride, Backdraft, and Special Effects Stages; a new attraction is added each year.

Gift Shop: Many gift shops sell posters, videos, clothes, jewelry, mugs, and toys, with logos.

Directions: Located between Hollywood and the San Fernando Valley just off the Hollywood (101) Fwy., Universal Studios is accessible from either the Universal Center Dr. or Lankershim Blvd. exits. Follow "Universal Studios" signs and marquee to park.

Nearby Attractions: Paramount Pictures, NBC Studios, and Warner Bros. Studios tours (see pages 379, 377, and 388); Audiences Unlimited offers free tickets for taped TV shows (call 818-506-0067); Universal CityWalk.

CALIFORNIA

4000 Warner Boulevard, Burbank, CA 91522   (818) 977-1744   www.wbstudiotour.com

By some estimates, entertainment is the United States's second-largest export and pumps $50 billion into the U.S. economy. Begun in 1918, when films were silent, today Warner Bros. displays the latest technological advances in filmmaking.

The Warner Bros. tour is different from any other studio tour in California. Here, you will take an exclusive VIP tour designed for small groups seriously interested in the inner workings of a major studio. Because this is a VIP tour, production schedules are checked every morning to ensure that visitors see the most action possible. Some of the biggest stars, both human and animated, have worked at Warner Bros.—since this is a busy studio, don't be surprised if you see one of them walk by!

You will travel by electric cart to a variety of television and movie sets. Since these sets change with each new film, you may find yourself under a blazing sun in the Sahara, in romantic moonlight on Paris's Left Bank, or on an exotic, narrow avenue in crowded old Shanghai, all while actual movies or TV shows are being filmed.

Your guide may take you into the extensive Prop Shop and explain, "No, it's not a garage sale or fire sale, it's the Prop Shop." Or you may visit the impressive Wardrobe Department (with one of the world's largest costume collections) or the Mill (where sets are created). You may explore exterior sets like Laramie Street, used in a number of Warner Bros. westerns, and French Street, where many scenes from *Casablanca* were filmed. Discover that these exterior sets are basically shells with open backs. At the Sound Facilities, you may catch a symphony orchestra recording a movie's theme song, actors redoing dialogue that couldn't be properly recorded on the set, or technicians creating sound effects.

Opened in 1996, the Warner Bros. Museum features costumes, props, animation cels, and film clips. See the black-and-white hats from *My Fair Lady,* original correspondence about Humphrey Bogart, and candid shots of Errol Flynn. Stand between Bugs Bunny and Daffy Duck in a human-scale animation cel to see how you would look in cartoons.

Cost: $39 per person ($4 AAA discount).

Freebies: A VIP tour brochure.

Video/DVD Shown: 10-minute video shows highlights from Warner Bros. films since the first talking film, *The Jazz Singer,* in 1927.

Reservations Needed: No, but recommended.

Days and Hours: Mon–Fri 9:00 AM–3:30 PM, every half hour. Tour schedule can vary. During summer, some holiday tours can be specially arranged.

Plan to Stay: 2.25 hours for video, museum, and tour, plus time for gift shop.

Minimum Age: 8

Disabled Access: Yes

Group Requirements: Electric cart capacity is 12 people. Groups larger than 12 take walking tour of 110-acre lot. Call in advance for reservations. $7 discount per person for groups larger than 20 people.

Special Information: Wear comfortable walking shoes. Limited photography. Four-hour deluxe tours can be arranged.

Gift Shop: Sells T-shirts, pins, and hats with W.B. logo. Open Mon–Fri 9:30 AM–4:00 PM.

Directions: From San Fernando Valley, take U.S. 101/Hwy. 134 (Ventura Fwy.) East to Pass Ave. exit. Turn right onto Pass Ave. Turn left onto Riverside Dr. Turn right onto Hollywood Way; the Hollywood Way gate (Gate 4) is 1 block down the street. From Hollywood, take U.S. 101 (Hollywood Fwy.) North. Take the Barham Blvd. exit. Turn right onto Barham Blvd., and when you cross the Los Angeles River, Barham becomes Olive Ave. The studio is on your right. Stay on Olive Ave. as it curves around the studio, until you reach Hollywood Way. Turn right into the studio and park at VIP tour center.

Nearby Attractions: NBC Studios Paramount Pictures, and Universal Studios tours (see pages 377, 379, and 387).

CALIFORNIA

420 Montgomery Street,
San Francisco, CA 94163

(415) 396-2619

www.wellsfargo
history.com

Wells Fargo runs nine free history museums in many states, including California, Minnesota, and Alaska. Each museum presents Wells Fargo's role in the growth of America and the growth of the area of the country where the museum is located. You can see original stagecoaches, banking and express documents, working telegraphs, western art, gold coins, old money, and more.

Here we focus on the site in San Francisco where Wells Fargo first opened for business in 1852. From the street, look though the two-story glass windows to see the 1867 Wells Fargo Overland stagecoach, which was drawn by six horses and carried passengers and gold across the western plains. You can climb into one of these stagecoaches on the second floor of the museum. You'll find a recreated early Wells Fargo office—including telegraphs (you can send messages between two desks with Morse code), an agent's desk, documents, and package scales. Opposite the gift counter, in a glass-enclosed display case, note the impressive gold dust and ore from California's Gold Country.

Children can participate in a scavenger hunt around the museum. You can learn more about company history by watching a video. Learn about the Pony Express: from April 1860 to October 1861, mail was carried almost 2,000 miles from Missouri to Sacramento, California, in only 10 days.

On the second floor, you can climb into a cutaway stagecoach seat and even hold the leather reins. Next squeeze into a stagecoach without wheels. Note how cramped the interior space is; passengers facing each other knock their knees. (Grateful to be riding in the stagecoach, passengers overlooked these tight quarters.) Along the back wall you can pull out tall narrow wooden drawers to reveal a special collection of Gold Rush letters carried by hundreds of express companies.

After learning the history of Wells Fargo, you can walk through the back of the first floor of the museum into a very active branch lobby of the Wells Fargo bank. Another stagecoach resides here as well.

Cost: Free

Freebies: Facsimile reprint of Wells Fargo overland stagecoach ticket and brochures, some in many languages.

Video/DVD Shown: 2 videos, 15 minutes each, cover the company's history.

Reservations Needed: No, except for groups over 10 people.

Days and Hours: Mon–Fri 9:00 AM–5:00 PM. Closed banking holidays.

Plan to Stay: 45 minutes, or up to 1.5 hours, depending on level of engagement.

Minimum Age: None

Disabled Access: Yes

Group Requirements: Groups over 10 people should call in advance to guarantee admission.

Special Information: Other Wells Fargo History Museums exist in 2 parts of Sacramento, CA (call 916-440-4161 and 916-440-4263); in Los Angeles, CA (call 213-253-7166); in San Diego, CA (call 619-238-3929); in Minneapolis, MN (call 612-667-4210); in Portland, OR (call 503-886-1102); in Phoenix, AZ (call 602-378-1852); and in Anchorage, AK (call 907-265-2834). Information about these museums can be found on the website (www.wellsfargohistory.com). Educational programs available for school groups.

Gift Shop: General Store counter sells postcards and miniature stagecoaches, ranging from pennants to Limoges figurines. Open same hours as museum.

Directions: From Golden Gate Bridge, take U.S. 101 South. Turn left on California St. to Montgomery St. From Bay Bridge, take Freemont St. exit. Turn left on Fremont St. Crossing Market St., Fremont St. becomes Front St. Turn left on Pine St. Turn right on Sansome St. Turn left on Sacramento St. Turn left on Montgomery St.

Nearby Attractions: Basic Brown Bear, Golden Gate Fortune Cookies, and Levi Strauss (see pages 357, 364, and 373). Attractions in downtown San Francisco include Chinatown, North Beach, and Union Square.

CALIFORNIA

5351 Avenue 424, Reedley, CA 93654   (888) 441-5117   www.wiebefarms.com

The sun-drenched San Joaquin Valley of central California is among the most productive agricultural regions in the United States. Hot summers, moist winters, and rich soil make it ideal for the cultivation of many fruits and vegetables. As you drive through it on ruler-straight roads, you can see why this area is called "the nation's salad bowl": lush fields and orchards stretch in all directions.

Since founder Louis Wiebe planted his first orchard in 1956, Wiebe Farms has grown peaches, plums, and nectarines. Starting at the barn, tours show you the fields for a lesson in the cultivation of fruit trees. Next you visit Wiebe's own packing shed to learn how the fruit actually goes from farm to market.

Grafted from mature specimens, young trees are planted by hand in straight rows. As they grow, expert pruners shape them every winter into a form that yields the best amount, quality, and size of fruit. Each generation of trees lives about 15 years. The farm rotates the orchards continually, so you can see all stages of the trees' development.

Under the hot sun of spring, blossoms flourish, pollination occurs, and fruit swells. When the fruit is the size of a walnut, the farm's staff thin the branches (called "hangers") of extra fruit, leaving only enough to permit further growth. Harvest time at Wiebe runs from mid-May to mid-September. Balanced on their aluminum ladders, the farm's experienced pickers have a keen sense of what fruit is ready for eating and what must still develop. The difference can be too subtle for the untrained eye.

After nature has done its part, technology takes over. Ripe fruit moves in bins to the packing shed, which buzzes with machinery and busy staff. After unloading the fruit, employees wash it and treat it to retard decay; graders reject fruit that is not up to USDA standards. A conveyor belt passes the ap-proved fruit by a camera that sends images to a computer which sorts it by size and color. Another machine adorns the fruit with PLU (product lookup) stickers. Finally, a conveyor belt whisks the fruit to the packing department.

Packers perform the final inspection and place the fruit in shipping boxes that eventually reach markets all over the world. Packed, stamped, and stacked, the boxes travel in huge numbers to a nearby cold-storage facility. You can contemplate the whole process while you munch on free fresh peaches and nectarines.

Cost: $10 per person; $5 per student for school groups.

Freebies: Peaches, nectarines, and other peachy treats.

Video/DVD Shown: A 45-minute video about the farm.

Reservations Needed: Yes. School groups of any age are welcome.

Days and Hours: Mon–Sat 8:00 AM–4:00 PM (by appointment only), including holidays. Closed Sundays. Tours can be scheduled year-round, but packing shed is open June–August.

Plan to Stay: Average 1.5 hours, but tour can be extended according to the interest level of the group.

Minimum Age: No

Disabled Access: No

Group Requirements: Minimum 10 people (preferred); no maximum.

Special Information: Each tour is tailored to visitors' interests. The order of the tour depends on the time of day and farm scheduling.

Gift Shop: Open only for tour groups at start or end of visit.

Directions: From Hwy. 99, take Mountain View Ave. East (becomes West El Monte Way). Turn left on Rd. 52, right on Ave. 424. Barn is on right.

Nearby Attractions: King's Canyon National Park; Sequoia National Park.

Alaska, Hawaii, and Caribbean

ALASKA

RUSSIA

A L A S K A

CANADA

Nome

Fairbanks

ALASKA WILD BERRY PRODUCTS
ALASKA MINT

MUSK OX FARM

Anchorage

Valdez

ALASKAN
BREWING

P A C I F I C

O C E A N

0   200 mi

0   200 km

HAWAII

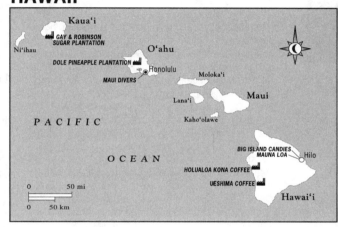

Kaua'i

GAY & ROBINSON
SUGAR PLANTATION

Ni'ihau

O'ahu

DOLE PINEAPPLE PLANTATION

Honolulu

MAUI DIVERS

Moloka'i

Lana'i

Maui

P A C I F I C

Kaho'olawe

O C E A N

BIG ISLAND CANDIES
MAUNA LOA

Hilo

HOLUALOA KONA COFFEE

UESHIMA COFFEE

Hawai'i

0   50 mi

0   50 km

CARIBBEAN

TORTUGA RUM

CUBA

DOMINICAN
REPUBLIC

US VIRGIN
ISLANDS

CAYMAN
ISLANDS

HAÏTI

BACARDI

APPLETON ESTATE

PUERTO
RICO

CRUZAN RUM
DISTILLERY

JAMAICA

A T L A N T I C

100 mi

100 km

O C E A N

Alaska Mint

429 West 4th Avenue, Anchorage, AK 99501

(907) 278-8414
(800) 770-6468

www.alaskamint.com

ALASKA, HAWAII, AND CARIBBEAN

You won't want to miss out on what could well be the highlight of your Anchorage visit. A tour of Alaska Mint is a golden experience. In business since 1991, Alaska Mint is the northernmost mint in the United States, and they are unique in that they make their own products, including the official medallions for the state of Alaska and the Iditarod Trail Committee.

On the self-guided tour, you can watch jewelers craft gold nugget and gold into quartz masterpieces, such as snowflake broaches, sparkling earrings, or teardrop pendants. Large glass windows allow visitors to peer into different show rooms, so a curious tourist really feels included in the professional process. An advantage of this self-guided tour is that you're welcome to linger at your favorite areas.

Alaska Mint provides reading materials, videos, and, best of all, finished goods. Take a look at the incomparable medallions, which are designed, molded, and etched on-site. You are sure to find a medallion that interests you, with choices that range from the Aviation medallion to the Gold Rush medallions.

You'll also surely be awed by the 10-foot gold scale, made in 1816 and used by the Philadelphia Mint, as well as the 1915 cash register that displays old U.S. currency from the 1840s and 1900s. You can share your golden moments at Alaska Mint by taking home one of their one-of-a-kind, dazzling gifts.

Cost: Free

Freebies: No

Video/DVD Shown: There are multiple videos throughout the tour and an up-close camera view that shows the coins being struck on the hydraulic press.

Reservations Needed: No

Days and Hours: January–May: Mon–Fri 9:00 AM–6:00 PM, Sat 10:00 AM–5:00 PM, closed Sun. June–August: 8:00 AM–7:00 PM. September–December: Mon–Fri 9:00 AM–6:00 PM, Sat 10 00 AM–5:00 PM, Sun 12:00 PM–5:00 PM.

Plan to Stay: Approximately 30 minutes.

Minimum Age: No

Disabled Access: Yes

Group Requirements: A group larger than 10 should call ahead.

Special Information: A coffee shop is on-site, offering juice, soda, and coffee drinks.

Gift Shop: Yes

Directions: Downtown Anchorage, corner of 4th and E Sts.

Nearby Attractions: Alaska Wild Berry Products (see page 393); downtown Anchorage features excellent shopping, eating, and sightseeing, including the Imaginarium.

5225 Juneau Street, Anchorage, AK 99518

(907) 562-8858
(800) 280-2927

www.alaskawildberry
products.com

Sauces and ketchups were hard to come by in Alaska in 1946. In Homer, Alaska, Kenneth and Hazel Heath decided to make their own, gathering low-bush berries outside their cozy cabin and mixing them with ingredients found in their home. The Sourdough Sauce was born, along with a handpicking tradition that is unique to the products made by Alaska Wild Berry. The company gets its berries from Alaskans throughout the state who go out into the wilderness to gather basket- and bucketfuls. The company has since moved its operations to Anchorage and added candies and chocolates to the production list, most notably the chocolate-covered wild-berry centers.

The world's largest chocolate fall, 25 feet tall and using 3,400 pounds of chocolate, is the opening feature of the tour. As you move on to the self-guided tour behind glass, be sure to read the posters explaining what the kitchen equipment is used for, how much candy is produced, and exactly how it is made. In the first kitchen, you'll see how jams and jellies are produced, cooking away in 80-gallon kettles. In the second kitchen, look for the large copper kettles and the creamer machine the candies are made in, and the cooling table they rest on. You may feel like you are in a scene right out of *I Love Lucy* in the third kitchen. There are three enrobing machines that coat candies, popcorn, and wild-berry centers in chocolate as they move along a conveyer belt. After being coated in chocolate, they are marked with designs by the kitchen crew and moved to a cooling chamber. You may get a glimpse of the crew packaging the candies in shrink-wrappers toward the back of the kitchen. The final kitchen is where chocolate shapes are made. Dark chocolate, milk chocolate, and white chocolate come out of the faucets of three machines and are set into the shapes that you might sample after you leave the fourth kitchen.

After you've seen the factory and tried the delicious samples in the store, go outside and walk around the Wild Berry Park and Village. You can take a nature walk and visit the live reindeer exhibit, giving you a thoroughly Alaskan experience.

Cost: Free

Freebies: After the tour, sample a variety of jams, jellies, sourdough sauce, candies, and chocolates in the Alaska Wild Berry Products store.

Video/DVD Shown: A demonstration video runs continuously in the store.

Reservations Needed: Only for groups of 20 or more (call 800-280-2927).

Days and Hours: June 1–September 1, daily 10:00 AM–11:00 PM. Tours are available whenever the store is open, but the kitchen is in operation Mon–Fri 10:00 AM–5:00 PM.

Plan to Stay: 30 minutes for the tour, plus time for the gift shop and nature walk (about 2 hours in total).

Minimum Age: No, but minors must be accompanied by an adult.

Disabled Access: Yes. Call (800) 280-2927 with questions.

Group Requirements: Call for group requirements (800-280-2927).

Special Information: Tours are available in the winter by arrangement. Also, the original factory in Homer, Alaska, still sells Alaska Wild Berry Products and features a display of Alaskan artifacts.

Gift Shop: Sells jams, jellies, syrups, candy, fudge, and boxed chocolate. The retail store also sells locally made souvenirs, gifts, and clothing.

Directions: From downtown Anchorage, take C St. South. Turn left on International Airport Rd. Just after Old Seward Hwy., turn right on Juneau St. Factory is on left.

Nearby Attractions: Wild Berry Park and Village; Alaska Mint (see page 392).

ALASKA, HAWAII, AND CARIBBEAN

Small, family-like Alaskan Brewing Company brews Alaskan Amber (based on a Gold Rush–era recipe from the local extinct Douglas City Brewing Co.), Alaskan Pale, Alaskan E.S.B., Alaskan Stout, and seasonal beers. Since its start in 1986, Alaskan Brewing Company's beers have won awards for quality at annual beer festivals. To expand its production space, the brewery took over a golf driving range in the other half of this wooden building (to this day, some golf balls linger in the roof's insulation) and built two new additions.

The tour starts off right—with a glass of Alaskan Pale (its lighter, fruitier beer). Now that you're in the spirit, walk into the tour hallway. You can look through glass walls into the brewhouse at three 310-gallon kettles known as the mash tun, lauter tun, and brew kettle. If you're lucky, you'll see activity here—a worker transferring mixtures from kettle to kettle or shoveling "spent" (already used) barley. The majority of Alaskan beer is brewed in a new 100-barrel brewhouse, also visible from this area. In show-and-tell, the tour guide hands out malted barley (tastes like Grape Nuts) and hops (a bittering herb). Notice what used to be "Alaska's biggest six-pack," six 10-foot-high stainless steel fermentation tanks stacked in a row. Now there are 46 fermentation tanks, each 20-plus times the size of the small ones in the tank area.

Walk outdoors and upstairs to a landing. Through windows, peer inside at the bottling operation. In the hospitality room and gift shop, admire the national/international bottle collections on display. Find your home state's beer. If your local brewery is not represented, be sure to send Alaskan one for its extensive collection when you get home.

Cost: Free

Freebies: 5-oz. glasses of beer.

Video/DVD Shown: No

Reservations Needed: No, but prefer a week's notice if the group is larger than 20.

Days and Hours: May–September: Mon–Sun 11:00 AM–5:00 PM, every 30 minutes, last tour at 4:30. October–April: Thur–Sat, same time schedule. Closed July 4th, Thanksgiving, Christmas, and New Year's.

Plan to Stay: 30 minutes, plus time in gift shop.

Minimum Age: No, but proof of age required. Anyone under 21 years old must be accompanied by a parent or guardian. You must be 21 years old to sample beer.

Disabled Access: Yes

Group Requirements: Prefers 1 day's advance notice for groups larger than 10 people. Groups larger than 35 people will be divided into smaller groups.

Special Information: Best days to see bottling are Monday through Friday. If your timing is right, you can sample seasonal beers (usually made in the spring and fall) or one of the R&D brews called "Rough Draft."

Gift Shop: Sells T-shirts, sweatshirts, and baseball caps with beer label designs. Offers bottle-cap fishing lures with the "Made in Alaska" bear design on a crown, and collectible pint glasses. Open same hours as tour. Merchandise is available on the website (www.alaskanbeer.com). Gift shop displays historical photographs and artifacts of Alaskan breweries from the 1800s to today.

Directions: From Juneau, take Egan Dr. to stoplight at the base of Vanderbilt Hill. Turn only way possible onto Vanderbilt Hill Rd. Turn right onto Anka Dr. Take second right onto Shaune Dr. The brewery is 1.5 blocks ahead on the left. You'll smell the strong scent of malt and hops as you approach on brewing days.

Nearby Attractions: Alaska Seafood Co. tour (call 800-451-1400); Mendenhall Glacier; DIPAC (salmon hatchery); Historic Downtown Juneau's attractions include the Capitol building and the Alaskan Bar & Hotel (features Alaskan's beer on tap); sport fishing.

Mile 50 Glenn Highway, Palmer, AK 99645   (907) 745-4151   www.muskoxfarm.org

The name "musk ox" (the Eskimo word is *oomingmak*) is a misnomer—the animals neither have musk glands nor belong to the ox family. Rather, they are short, stocky beasts. Underneath the shaggy carpet of the musk ox's brown guard hair is a coat of fine, soft, warm hair called "qiviut." In the winter, qiviut protects the musk ox against wind and bitter Arctic temperatures. In spring, musk oxen shed their qiviut naturally. This "down," or underwool, is combed out of their coats, spun into yarn that is eight times warmer than sheep's wool, and knitted by Eskimo women into beautiful lacy stoles, scarves, and hats. The Musk Ox Farm is a nonprofit organization formed to breed and study musk oxen and to provide a native-run and -owned cottage knitting industry. It is the only herd of domesticated oxen in the world.

At the farm, you see extensive displays describing the history and background of the animals and the special project of the Anchorage cooperative that sells the knitted qiviut items. Next you are shown where and how the furry beasts are combed. At a fenced-in walkway by the ox pens, the guide describes the animals' lives and habits, both in the wild and in captivity. In the wild, two bulls contest for dominance by banging their heads together. After circling around and challenging each other, they may back away as much as 50 feet and then run straight at one another, crashing their horns together in a sound that can be heard up to a mile away. You probably won't see any head-banging, but these curious creatures, who can weigh as much as 900 pounds, may approach and eat grass from your hand.

Stay as long as you like to observe these unique animals, or venture 50 miles away to the "Oomingmak" Co-operative in Anchorage. Here you'll see the lacy qiviut items that the Eskimo women made being washed, blocked (stretched on a pattern board to straighten the sides), and packaged at the front table of the small shop.

Cost: Adults, $9.00; seniors (65+), $7; children 5–12, $6.00; children under 5 accompanied by an adult, free.

Freebies: No

Video/DVD Shown: No

Reservations Needed: No, except for groups larger than 12 people and for winter tours.

Days and Hours: Mother's Day through end of September: Mon–Sun 10:00 AM–6:00 PM. Tours run every 30 minutes. Open summer holidays. Winter tours by appointment only. Call ahead.

Plan to Stay: 30–45 minutes, plus time in gift shop.

Minimum Age: None

Disabled Access: Yes

Group Requirements: Groups of 12 or more people should call at least 1 day in advance. Groups larger than 50 people will be split into 2 or more staggered-time tours. Group rate is $7 per person.

Special Information: The animals are more active in the morning. Early groups on Monday, Wednesday, and Friday mornings can see the oxen being fed.

Oomingmak Musk Ox Producers' Co-operative in Anchorage: Watch the final blocking process of caps, scarves, and other knit items with each Eskimo village's signature knitting pattern. Call (907) 272-9225.

Gift Shop: Sells qiviut items such as scarves, hats, and stoles. Also sells musk ox mementos such as stuffed animals, toys, mugs, and T-shirts. Open same hours as tour.

Directions: From Anchorage, take Glenn Hwy. North, through Palmer. About 2 miles past Palmer (at Mile 50), turn left onto Archie Rd. Follow signs to Musk Ox Farm, which is about o.25 mile down the road on left.

Nearby Attractions: Reindeer Farm; Palmer Visitors Center; Iditarod Trail Headquarters and Dorothy Page Museum in Wasilla (about 11 miles away); Hatcher Pass; Independence Mine State Historical Park.

585 Hinano Street, Hilo, HI 96720

(808) 935-8890
(800) 935-5510

www.bigisland
candies.com

You may be surprised at how far Big Island Candies will go in order to keep its customers entertained. Priding itself on its uniqueness, the company tries dipping almost anything in chocolate, and some of its successful (albeit unusual) experiments have produced chocolate-covered animal crackers, fortune cookies, and even *ika* (cuttlefish). Its more conventional products include original and chocolate-dipped shortbread and local favorites such as macadamia ("mac") nuts. Big Island Candies has been producing high-quality chocolates since 1977, when owner Allan Ikawa sold everything, including his boat and his house, to open the company.

On a self-guided tour, you may be tempted to dive through the factory's big glass windows into one of the cylindrical white melters that melt up to 1,000 pounds of chocolate into liquid form. The stainless-steel melters also temper the chocolate, thus ensuring that it will have a glossy finish. As you move to the next window, smell the shortbread cookies baking in the factory's six ovens. Big Island Candies is one of the few facilities of this size that still does hand-dipping, making chocolates the old-fashioned way. Dippers clad in black aprons walk over to the melters to fill their bowls with the sweet brown liquid.

Returning to their station, the dippers pour mac nuts into the chocolate-filled bowl. Skillfully grabbing a nut (or a cuttlefish, cookie, or animal cracker) with one hand, they smother it with more chocolate with the other hand and pop it into the cavity of a candy tray that stands on a scale in front of them. The scale ensures that each tray of candy has the proper weight. You may be amazed by the swiftness with which some of the dippers cover items with chocolate, deftly filling their trays at top speed and with incredible dexterity.

Knowing that many visitors come to Big Island

Candies in search of *omiyage* (gifts bought for friends and family, following an Asian tradition), the company creates distinctive packaging for its candies. You leave Big Island Candies knowing that the gourmet candies and chocolates inside those beautiful boxes are made with skill and care.

Cost: Free

Freebies: Chocolate, cookie, and Kona coffee samples.

Video/DVD Shown: No

Reservations Needed: No

Days and Hours: Daily 8:30 AM–5:00 PM, with the best time to see production Mon–Fri before 3:30 PM. Limited production on weekends and holidays.

Plan to Stay: 30 minutes for the self-guided tour, plus time in gift shop.

Minimum Age: None

Disabled Access: Yes

Group Requirements: None

Special Information: Japanese-speaking sales representatives are available.

Gift Shop: Sells all of the company's products, including chocolate-covered mac nuts, rocky road (mac nuts, marshmallows, and chocolate), crunchies (mac nuts, potato chips, and chocolate), crunch (mac nuts, crisp rice, and chocolate), and chocolate-dipped shortbread cookies, fortune cookies, animal crackers, and *ika*. Open Mon–Sun 8:30 AM–5:00 PM. Open every day of the year. Gift guide available from above number.

Directions: From Hilo airport, go through 1 traffic signal and take third right onto Hinano St. Big Island Candies will be on the corner. From Hamakua coast, stay on Kamehameha Ave. Turn right onto Kanoelehua Ave, right onto Kekuanaoa St., and right onto Hinano St. Big Island Candies will be on right.

Nearby Attractions: Mauna Loa Macadamia Nuts, Holualoa Kona Coffee, and Ueshima Coffee tours (see pages 401, 399, and 402); Hilo Bay; Hawaii Volcanoes National Park (with its live volcano).

64-1550 Kamehameha Highway,
Wahiawa, HI 96786

(808) 621-8408

www.dole-plantation.com

When you think of Hawaiian products, pineapple is likely at the top of your list, with Dole the most well-known brand name. Founded in Hawaii in 1851, Dole Food Company, Inc., is the largest producer and marketer of fresh fruits and vegetables in the world. Dole has offered different types of visitor experiences on Oahu, including tours of its canning operation that closed in 1993 (converted into a retail and office complex). The Dole Plantation, located on Oahu's North Shore on the same site the company first used to grow pineapples, offers a retail, historical, agricultural, and gastronomical experience.

When you first drive up, you see a splendid re-creation of a plantation mansion. The roof is tall and peaked, sheathed in materials that show the tin roofs of the old-time plantation building. Surrounding the center of the building is a traditional cooling verandah, ringed by tall trees and lush landscaping. Off to the right in front is the Pineapple Garden Maze, a fun challenge listed in the *Guinness Book of World Records* as the world's largest maze.

Inside the building, high ceilings with a rough-hewn finish attempt to give the appearance of a traditional pineapple warehouse. Special areas sell a variety of goods, foods, and snacks, designed to represent a traditional marketplace, a country store, and a series of building facades reminiscent of old Haleiwa Town. Look on the walls for displays chronicling the history of pineapple and for the dozens of oversized pineapple cans sporting authentic Hawaiian pineapple labels. Spend time learning from Dole's experts how to choose and slice pineapples.

There's also the Pineapple Express Train Tour, which takes you on an educational and informative two-mile loop behind the plantation, and The Plantation Garden Tour, which provides you with an up-close look at a wide variety of crops being grown on the North Shore of Oahu. After experiencing these

attractions, you'll enjoy the frosty Dole Whip back inside the plantation.

Cost: Plantation and display gardens: free. Maze: adults, $5; children 4–12, $3. Train Tour: adults, $7.50; children 4–12, $5.50. Garden Tour: adults, $3.75; children 4–12, $3.

Freebies: Pineapple chunks after cutting demonstration.

Video/DVD Shown: 20-minute continuous loop video on pineapple processing.

Reservations Needed: No, except for groups over 25.

Days and Hours: Daily 9:00 AM–5:30 PM (June–August 9:00 AM–6:00 PM).

Plan to Stay: 1 hour, plus time for the Maze, Train, and Garden Tours.

Minimum Age: None

Disabled Access: Yes

Group Requirements: Groups over 25 people, $4 for the Maze, $5.75 for the Train Tour, and $3.25 for the Garden Tour.

Special Information: A complete food and beverage facility was added in early 2006.

Gift Shop: The Dole Plantation is mostly a large themed retail store dedicated to everything pineapple, with hundreds of pineapple-related and Dole brand products, including pineapple candy, chocolates, cakes, cookies, and Waialua brand coffee. You can also purchase fresh pineapples to ship anywhere. Plus, it sells a variety of other goods, from local handicrafts to jewelry from Maui Divers. Outside along the lanai are tables for eating your pineapple snacks.

Directions: From Waikiki, take H1 West to H2 North. Continue to Kamehameha Hwy. 99. Located just North of Wahiawa.

Nearby Attractions: Wahiawa Recreation Area & Botanical Gardens; Honolulu attractions, including Maui Divers tour (see page 400) about 40 minutes away; Pearl Harbor 30 minutes away.

2 Kaumakani Avenue, Kaumakani, HI 96747 | (808) 335-2824 | www.gandrtours-kauai.com

The folks at Gay and Robinson Sugar Plantation know what kids' favorite food group is: Sugar! The sugar plantation tour is the perfect opportunity to explore the world of sugarcane. How is sugarcane grown and processed? How did the Hawaiian sugar industry become the world leader in sugar technology, research, and plant science? You'll learn the answers on the only tour of a working plantation in Hawaii—a fun and educational experience for the whole family.

Wilfred Ibara is the friendly and knowledgeable tour guide who will take you through the lush green fields. Have your camera ready, because you're in for an extraordinary view of the mill set against the ocean on one side, and acre after acre of sugarcane on the other. Wilfred will describe the two-year ripening process that sugar goes through, and then he'll wield his machete as if it were a paring knife to present you with a piece of cane to suck.

While the mill is most active from April to October, the tour is interesting no matter the season. The intelligence and creativity of the people who developed the factories will leave you in awe. Who would have thought that the sugarcane plant alone could produce material to fuel the factory, distill water, and produce sugar crystals and molasses? Almost everything is reused here at the last operating sugar plantation on Kauai, and one of two remaining in Hawaii. The plantation is one of the highest yielding sugar plantations in the world, averaging the highest tons of sugar per acre.

Visiting the Gay and Robinson Sugar Plantation will not only tantalize your taste buds, but it will also provide the chance to witness first-hand the industry that sustained the Hawaiian economy for 165 years. The folks at Gay and Robinson are working hard to preserve tradition as well as agricultural lifestyle. Sugar might be a kids' favorite food group, but grown-ups and kids alike are sure to come away with more than a satisfied sweet tooth.

Cost: Visitors center and museum, free. Adults, $30 for plantation tour, $60 for Olokele tour; children, $21 for plantation tour, $45 for Olokele tour.

Freebies: Fresh sugar cane and raw sugar are offered, and a recipe book.

Video/DVD Shown: No

Reservations Needed: Yes, for tours.

Days and Hours: Visitors center and museum Mon–Fri 7:00 AM–4:00 PM, Sat 9:00 AM–3:00 PM, Sun closed. Plantation tours Mon–Fri 9:00 AM and 1:00 PM. Olokele Overlook tour Mon–Fri 8:30 AM (includes lunch).

Plan to Stay: 2 hours for plantation tour, 3 hours for Olokele tour.

Minimum Age: 8 during harvesting, 5 during off-season.

Disabled Access: Limited access, can tour through plantation itself but not through factory.

Group Requirements: Maximum of 8 adults (or 11 passengers if some are children) for Olokele tour; parties of 12 or more may make special arrangements for plantation tour.

Special Information: All persons entering factory must wear shoes and safety equipment. Tours may be canceled due to bad weather. Tours can be hot, dirty, and noisy.

Gift Shop: Yes, open Mon–Fri 7:00 AM–4:00 PM, Sat 9:00 AM–3:00 PM.

Directions: From Lihue Airport, take Hwy. 50 just past mile marker 19. Turn left at Kaumakani Ave. Watch for yellow signs at entrance to avenue and parking.

Nearby Attractions: Kauai Coffee Company estate, a few miles from Poipu. Farther away on the west side of the island is Waimea Canyon.

Holualoa Kona Coffee

77-6261 Mamalahoa Highway,
Holualoa, HI 96725

(808) 322-9937
(800) 334-0348

www.konalea.com

When you sit down to drink your morning coffee, do you know whether you're drinking peaberry, extra fancy, or triple X? Did you know that it takes 100 pounds of picked coffee cherries to produce just 15 pounds of roasted coffee? Become an informed coffee consumer and watch coffee being processed and roasted at Holualoa Kona Coffee Company, located in the heart of Kona coffee country, a 50- to 60-mile region on the western side of the Big Island. Hawaii is the only state in the U.S.A. that produces coffee, and only coffee grown in this region may carry the Kona label.

At Holualoa, your guide describes the life of the coffee bean from the moment it's picked from the tree as a red "cherry," until it's dried to become the beige bean called "parchment." Then you see the hulling process, where parchment beans are dumped into a tall, thin elevator. The elevator pours the parchment into the huller, which removes the parchment skin from the beans to reveal green coffee beans, which are then dropped by another elevator into the grader. The grader comprises a series of screens with different-size holes stacked one atop another. The screens shake, causing the coffee beans to fall through the appropriately sized holes. The largest (and best) beans, including grades like peaberry, extra fancy, and fancy, are separated from the smaller, lower grades such as number one, prime, and triple X. Peaberry, the most valuable bean, has a distinct flavor and shape. A gravity table further separates the coffee, this time by density.

In the next building, you'll watch the coffee whirling around in the 40-pound roaster, which resembles a large air popcorn machine. During roasting, air from a blower tosses the coffee beans around to prevent burning. The person who does the roasting

explains how to take care of your coffee and how to distinguish good beans from low-quality ones. You'll learn that medium-roast coffee has more caffeine than dark roast because the longer coffee is roasted, the more caffeine is roasted out. By the end of this tour, you'll have a good understanding of what it takes to get the coffee from the tree to your cup.

Cost: Free

Freebies: Cup of fresh-brewed coffee.

Video/DVD Shown: No

Reservations Needed: No, except for groups larger than 10 people.

Days and Hours: Mon–Fri 8:00 AM–4:00 PM, with the best time to see production from 8:00 AM–3:00 PM. Closed holidays.

Plan to Stay: 30 minutes, plus time in gift area and working farm.

Minimum Age: None

Disabled Access: Yes

Group Requirements: Groups of over 10 people should call 1 day in advance. Groups of over 30 people will be divided into smaller groups.

Gift Area: Holualoa T-shirts and coffee are sold in the packaging room, where the tour ends. Open Mon–Fri 7:30 AM–4:00 PM. Brochure available from above number.

Directions: From Keahole Airport, take Hwy. 11 South. Turn left at the sign for Holualoa. Go all the way to the top of the mountain and turn right onto Mamalahoa Hwy. Turn left at the sign for Holualoa Kona Coffee. From the south, take Hwy. 11 North. Turn right at sign for Holualoa/Keauhou. Turn left onto Mamalahoa Hwy. Turn right at sign for Holualoa Kona Coffee, just past the mile 2 marker.

Nearby Attractions: Big Island Candies, Mauna Loa Macadamia Nuts, and Ueshima Coffee tours (see pages 396, 401, and 402); Kona Coffee Country driving tour map available from Kona-Kohala Chamber of Commerce (call 808-329-1758); November Kona Coffee Cultural Festival; Punalu'u (southernmost bakery in U.S.A.) viewing windows (call 808-929-7343); Kailua-Kona, a resort town.

The Maui Divers Jewelry Design Center,
1520 Liona Street, Honolulu, HI 96814

(808) 943-8383

www.mauidivers.com
www.mauidiverstour.com

MAUI DIVERS
OF HAWAII

Black coral is the official Hawaii State Gemstone, and this tour shows you why. Since its days of filling scuba tanks, back in 1958, Maui Divers has become the world's largest precious coral jewelry manufacturer. The company's founders initially experimented, making jewelry with rare black coral from the deep waters off Lahaina, branched out into pink and gold coral, then moved the company to Oahu. The video and tour show how they make their unique jewelry, which combines coral with gold, diamonds, pearls, rubies, or other precious gems.

You can watch most of the detailed process through glass windows that put you close to the deeply focused, blue-smocked workers. You see the design, waxing, casting, polishing, lapidary, and assembly areas. Designers make sketches for the goldsmiths, who then turn the drawings into three-dimensional jewelry carved from gold. The lost-wax casting process involves wax patterns of the jewelry being assembled into what looks like a small tree. Plaster molds are formed around this tree and heated in an oven to melt away the wax patterns, hence the name "lost wax." Gold is poured into the plaster molds. Once shattered, the molds reveal an exact gold replica of the wax tree. Gold rings and pendants are cut from the tree, then sanded and polished.

Notice the vacuum hoods under many of the machines in the finishing areas. These draw the gold mist into a central water bath, which is then refined. This process recovers over $500,000 in gold per year.

The tour guide escorts you through other areas, where skillful workers carefully cut, solder, polish, and inspect the gold pieces, or set precious gems into them. Notice the "Million Dollar Wall" in the coordinating area. Here, diamonds, pearls (some from the South Seas), emeralds, and sapphires are sorted and sized.

Cost: Free

Freebies: No

Video/DVD Shown: 9-minute video on deep-sea coral mining, company history, and jewelry production. Available in major foreign languages.

Reservations Needed: No, except for groups larger than 50 people.

Days and Hours: Mon–Sun 8:30 AM–5:00 PM. Usually no production Sat, Sun, and holidays, although visitors will still see video and manufacturing area and display cases on production steps.

Plan to Stay: 30 minutes for video and tour, plus time for showroom and gift store.

Minimum Age: None

Disabled Access: Yes

Group Requirements: 2 hours advance notice requested for groups larger than 50 people. No maximum group size. Translators and light refreshments for groups on request.

Special Information: No photography.

Showroom: Tour ends with store selling the world's largest selection of original fine coral jewelry designs, including black, red, and pink coral rings, earrings, cufflinks, and pendants in 14-karat gold settings; pearl and South Sea pearl earrings and necklaces; and gold dolphins, pineapples, and whales. Open same hours as tour. Second-floor stores have costume jewelry, local art, gift items, and a selection of designer items. With escort, can visit both stores without touring.

Directions: Free shuttle bus available from many hotels. Within walking distance of A a Moana Shopping Center. If driving, take Ala Wai Blvd. Turn right onto Kalakaua Ave. Turn left at Beretania St., left at Keeaumoku St., and left at Liona St. Maui Divers is on your left. Take elevator up to lobby entrance.

Nearby Attractions: Dole Pineapple Plantation (see page 397); Waikiki Beach; Ala Moana Shopping Center; Academy of Art Museum; Capitol Building; Iolani Palace.

Macadamia Road, Volcano Highway,
Hilo, HI 96720

(808) 966-8618
(888) MAUNA-LOA

www.maunaloa.com

Few factory tours offer the sweet smells of roasting nuts and melting chocolate along with a nature trail to walk off the free samples and goodies available at the gift store. Although almost all the macadamia nuts (or "mac nuts") sold worldwide are produced in Hawaii, the nut is actually native to Australia and wasn't grown in Hawaii until 1921. When Mauna Loa began marketing mac nuts under the Mauna Loa brand in 1976, their popularity mushroomed. This tour of the world's largest mac nut company provides a look through gallery windows at mac nut processing and packaging and at chocolate production.

Fresh from the 40-foot-high macadamia tree, the mac nut kernel sits inside a leathery brown, extremely hard shell. After shelling (burnt shells and husks fuel the entire plant), the nuts enter the main processing factory. Electric eyes automatically grade and sort the nuts, allowing only light, uniformly colored specimens to continue along to the roaster. Blue-hatted workers stand over the conveyor belt, also searching the stream of nuts for rejects.

The nuts are dry-roasted in large rectangular ovens, traveling slowly through the ovens on conveyor belts for 15 minutes. When roasting ends, the nuts are sorted again, and some are salted, candy-glazed, or made into mac nut brittle. Watch the packaging machine shoot them into fast-moving open metal tins, which then move down the line for vacuum-sealing.

Walk across the parking lot and up a staircase outside the building to look in the exterior windows into the factory. Inside, the smell of chocolate replaces the aroma of mac nuts in the candy factory, where chocolate waits in big steel melters. The nuts drop onto chocolate pads, then travel through the enrobing machine that covers them in a wave of chocolate. Rows of white-gloved, blue-smocked workers neatly hand-pack the chocolates in boxes after they leave the long cooling tunnels.

Cost: Free

Freebies: Samples of nuts and candy.

Video Shown: 7-minute video on mac nut farming, harvesting, and production. Shows continuously on the lanai near the gift store. Available in Japanese.

Reservations Needed: No, for self-guided tours. Yes, for guided tours.

Days and Hours: Self-guided tour and video: Mon–Sun 8:30 AM–5:30 PM (longer when cruise ships are in port). Guided tour: production times vary; call in advance.

Plan to Stay: 15 minutes for self-guided tour, plus time for video, nature walk, and gift store.

Minimum Age: None

Disabled Access: Yes, for candy factory; 20 stairs in the mac nut processing factory.

Group Requirements: Groups larger than 50 people should call 5 days ahead to schedule guided tour. No maximum group size.

Special Information: September–February is busiest production schedule.

Gift Shop: Sells all Mauna Loa mac nuts and candies, mac nut ice cream, mac nut popcorn, and logoed items including shirts and hats. Gift shop and Snack Bar open Mon–Sun 8:30 AM–5:30 PM (longer when cruise ships are in port). Catalog available from (888) MAUNA-LOA.

Directions: Located between Hilo and Keaau. Take Hwy. 11 to Macadamia Rd. Turn left if coming from Hilo and right if coming from Hawaii Volcanoes National Park. Drive through the Keaau Orchards to the yellow-and-blue Mauna Loa Macadamia Nut Visitor Center on left.

Nearby Attractions: Big Island Candies, Holualoa Kona Coffee, and Ueshima Coffee tours (see pages 396, 399, and 402); Kailua Candy Co. (call 800-622-2462); Hawaii Volcanoes National Park; Mauna Loa Village and open market about 2.5 hours away.

82-5810 Napoopoo Road,
Captain Cook, HI 96704

(808) 328-5662
(888) 822-5662

www.ucc-hawaii.com

UESHIMA COFFEE COMPANY

EST. 1933

While you likely know that you can spend a few days in Napa Valley in California touring wineries, very few people know that they can do the same with coffee-growing farms and roasting facilities in the Kona region of the Big Island of Hawaii. On the western side of the island, Kona's rich volcanic soil and moderate climate nurture the production of this world-famous coffee.

At the Ueshima Espresso Bar & Roastery store, peer through big glass windows to witness the roasting, grinding, and packaging of the coffee. A side room includes panels and displays about the farming and milling of coffee. The store is part of a coffee mill originally built to process pineapple, a crop that never became a commercial success in Kona.

The company claims that this is the only facility on the west side of the island where you can observe the entire process, from roasting to packaging. Coffee roasting begins with the raw green beans that the state of Hawaii has certified as "Kona" in both origin and quality. About 135 pounds of beans, already sorted by size and grade, are fed into the roaster that aromatically spins around and around.

To preserve the balance, flavor, and unique acidity of this exquisite coffee, the company cooks the certified Kona to a "city" roast that maximizes the body for which Kona is known. To ensure the coffee reaches this optimal roast each time, look for the color meter they use with each roasting.

If the coffee is ground here, they use the "crackulator," a specially designed grinding machine. It looks like a big steel tub connected to vacuum tubes. The crackulator reduces the amount of heat in the grinding process compared to a normal grinder, thus preserving the quality of the coffee. A vacuum process removes more of the chaff or "silver skin" found on the roasted coffee bean. Through other windows you see the conventional grinders, flavoring equipment,

and row of packaging machines filling bags of this coffee lovers' delight, for your brewing pleasure.

Cost: Free, unless combined with a tour to roast your own coffee.

Freebies: Fresh-brewed coffee, macadamia nuts, kona coffee choco-cookies, and chocolate-covered Kona beans.

Video/DVD Shown: Short videos in adjoining room that also has displays on coffee farming and history of the company and mill.

Reservations Needed: No, except for groups over 20 people and for personal roasting tour.

Days and Hours: Mon–Sun 9:00 AM–5:00 PM. Closed Thanksgiving and Christmas.

Plan to Stay: 15 minutes for tour, plus time in gift shop.

Minimum Age: None

Disabled Access: Yes

Group Requirements: Groups over 20 people should call ahead.

Special Information: Farm tours available Mon–Sun 9:00 AM–4:00 PM. Private roasting tours available that allow you to roast your own coffee and put it into bags with your picture on it for $30 per person. Japanese translators available most days.

Gift Shop: 100 percent pure Kona coffee (both ground and whole bean), including Kona Peaberry. This special type of coffee bean is usually found only at the tip or upper part of each coffee branch and makes up less than 5 percent of Kona's total coffee production. Also sells shirts, local island souvenirs, chocolate-covered coffee bean and mac nut candies, and cold drinks.

Directions: From Hwy. 11 South, turn right down Napoopoo Rd. Store is on the right.

Nearby Attractions: Holualoa Kona Coffee, Big Island Candies, Mauna Loa Macadamia Nuts tours (see pages 399, 396, and 401); Kona Coffee Country driving tour map available from Kona-Kohala Chamber of Commerce (call 808-329-1758); November Kona Coffee Cultural Festival; Kailua-Kona, a resort town.

Appleton Estate, now owned by Wray & Nephew, is the oldest and most famous of all of Jamaica's sugar estates. This industrial-looking facility sits in the picturesque, fertile Nassau Valley spanning both sides of the Black River in the Southwest of Jamaica. The origins of Appleton Estate date back to 1655, when the English captured Jamaica from the Spaniards. Appleton Estate was an established rum-producing sugar plantation by the year 1749, and it has been in continuous operation for two and a half centuries. From its pot and column stills, the distillery can produce up to 10 million liters of its unique estate rums per year.

As with other distillery tours, this experience provides plenty of smells, tastes, and sights, providing an enjoyable alternative to another day on the beach. You discover the intricate history of the estate and the details of the rum-making process. Plus, in the air-conditioned Appleton Lounge, which is the base for your visit, you will have plentiful opportunities to savor and appreciate the subtle differences in rum flavors and textures. Before this part of your visit, you sample during the tour juice freshly pressed from sugar cane, thick molasses, wet sugar, and "high wine," all by-products of the stages in the transformation of sugar cane to rum.

Look for the production steps that are special to Jamaican rum. For example, the tour starts with a trip to the original cane yard where a donkey walked around a circle path to power a simple press that squeezed the liquid from sugar cane. Pot still distillation is the traditional Jamaican method of separating the alcohol from water in the fermented molasses. It uses copper or copper-lined kettles to hold the "dead wash," and along with steam, concentrates and condenses the alcohol vapors.

On a hot day, the walk through the rack houses where Appleton Rums age provides a cool, energizing experience. The "rum conditioning" results from the rum vapors passing through the pores of the barrel. In another area, workers may be hand assembling the 40-gallon aging barrels in the cooperage. It is filled with the sounds of the coopers hammering the wooden hoops into place. The sound is similar to old-time Jamaican spiritual music, helping you stay in a vacation mode.

Cost: Adults, $12; children under 15, $6.

Freebies: Samples of different types of rums and 2 drinks per person. Small sample bottles.

Video/DVD Shown: 12-minute video on history of estate, barrel making, and Jamaican rum production.

Reservations Needed: Recommended. Required for groups over 50 people. Tours are arranged through local tour companies, Caribic Vacations (call 876-953-9878), Tourwise (call 876-974-2323), or Glamour Tours (call 876-979-8207), or from hotel tour desks.

Days and Hours: Mon–Sat 9:00 AM–3:30 PM. Closed Christmas, Easter Monday, and Boxing Day.

Plan to Stay: 45 minutes for tour, plus time for tasting and gift shops.

Minimum Age: None

Disabled Access: Steps with some ramps throughout facility.

Group Requirements: Can handle large groups. The bar area seats 200 and they cater events for 250 people.

Special Information: Foreign-language tours available.

Gift Shop: Selection of standard and unusual Jamaican souvenirs from T-shirts to crafts. Also snack bar, lounge, and liquor shop. Open same days and hours as tour.

Directions: From Negril or Montego Bay, there are directional signs to follow, although most people come by tour bus. Last few miles you drive through sugar cane fields and along curvy, bumpy Bamboo Ave., under tunnel created by bamboo trees.

Nearby Attractions: Y. S. Waterfalls; Cashew Ostrich Park; Black River Safaris; Pickapeppa Sauce Factory tour (call 876-603-3441); High Mountain Coffee tour (call 876-963-4411).

Casa Bacardi Visitor Center

RUM

Route 165, Intersection Route 888,
Cataño, Puerto Rico 00962

(787) 788-1500

www.bacardi.com

BACARDI CORPORATION

After soaking up the tropical sun and culture of Old San Juan in Puerto Rico, you may want to relax and cool off at the Casa Bacardi Visitor Center, located on the campus of the Bacardi Rum Distillery in nearby Cataño. This lush 127-acre estate glows with palm trees, other tropical flora, and well-manicured grounds.

Though the company was founded in Cuba by Don Facundo Bacardí in 1862, it relocated to Puerto Rico in 1936. This sprawling site boasts the largest rum distillery in the world. Despite modern technology, the company still produces rum with the secret strain of yeast that its founder isolated back in 1862. Adjacent to the distillery is the 17,000-square-foot visitor center, a lavish one-level building marked at its entrance with the company's striking symbol of a fruit bat, representing good health, fortune, and family unity.

With the aid of a handheld audio guide and headset, your tour through the seven opulent rooms of the visitor center is self-guided. In a replica Spanish colonial courtyard, you gain a sense of the historical context in which rum was first distilled in the Caribbean, and you learn how Don Facundo was able to experiment with the distillation of rum and eventually create his signature variety.

In other rooms of the visitor center, you discover details of the intricate process involved in making rum. Molasses from sugarcane is the key raw ingredient. In a controlled fermentation, yeast converts the sugars of the molasses into alcohol. Next comes the distillation, which separates water from the alcohol. This process heats the liquid and passes it through stainless-steel and copper stills. Once distilled, the raw rum undergoes purification by filtering through natural charcoal in a special process the company's founder pioneered. Like whiskey, the rum must age sufficiently (though the tropical heat makes a year of aging here equal to three years of

aging in chilly Scotland). Lastly, the rum is blended to create the smooth-drinking final products, which you can compare in "nosing booths" that let you smell eight kinds of Bacardi rum.

The lounge is what many guests most enjoy. Designed in the opulent Art Deco style of the 1930s, this room contains an "executive bar" at which professional bartenders explain the history of famous Bacardi rum cocktails and demonstrate their proper mixing. If you are at least 21 years old, you may taste the results.

Cost: Free

Freebies: Mixed rum drinks; soda and juice for minors.

Video/DVD Shown: A 10-minute movie tells the story of the Bacardi family and the company's rise to success.

Reservations Needed: No, except for groups larger than 20 people.

Days and Hours: Open Mon–Sat 8:30 AM–5:30 PM (last admission at 4:15 PM) and Sun 10:00 AM–5:00 PM (last admission at 3:45 PM). Closed major holidays.

Plan to Stay: 1.5 hours for self-guided tour and sampling.

Minimum Age: None, but children must be accompanied by an adult. Visitors must be 21 or older to consume alcoholic beverages.

Disabled Access: Yes

Group Requirements: Groups larger than 20 people should call 2 days in advance.

Gift Shop: Sells logoed T-shirts and a large assortment of gift packs of Bacardi rum. Open Mon–Sat 9:30 AM–5:30 PM and Sun 11:00 AM–5:30 PM. Closed major holidays.

Directions: From Old San Juan, take ferry at pier #2 to Cataño. Take public bus or taxi to Bacardi campus. Driving from Old San Juan, take Hwy. 22 West to the Cataño exit and take Rt. 165 North. Bacardi campus is on right at intersection with Rt. 883.

Nearby Attractions: Cabras Island; El Morro Castle in Old San Juan.

West Airport Road, Route 64,
St. Croix, U.S. Virgin Islands

(340) 692-2280   www.cruzanrums.com

CRUZAN RUM DISTILLERY

Rum tours can be sensory experiences, with the smells and tastes, the sounds and sights involved in both the manufacturing and craft of distilling. The Virgin Islands have been making some of the finest rums in the world since the early 1650s. At this historic location still stands the old windmill used for power before electricity and other remnants of an old plantation. International flags surround the stone fortresslike castle entrance. As you walk the grounds, you may see the centuries-old art of barrel making by coopers, as well as modern bottle machines.

The rum-making process begins with high-quality molasses received from Caribbean sugar plantations at the nearby dock. In what looks like a large, deep above-ground swimming pool, the molasses gets diluted with tropical rainwater pumped from a local aquifer. Cruzan adds its proprietary yeast cultures to begin fermentation of this mix into alcohol. Notice the bubbles rising to the top of the rich, brown, puddinglike mass in the holding tanks.

You might get a chance to talk with the Master Distiller at work with Cruzan's modern, five-column, stainless-steel and copper still. You might see the rum flowing through tubes in the top of each column of the still. The rum distillate goes into American oak barrels. Walk into the barrelhouse where the rum ages for a minimum of two years—or for up to 12 years. Surrounded by barrels from floor to ceiling, with the sweet smell of rum in the air, you'll be surprised to learn that over half of the rum evaporates during this stage. The properly aged rum is then charcoal filtered and diluted to 80 percent proof with more local rainwater. Finally, the bottling building (not always in operation) fills bottles with the self-proclaimed "The World's Finest Rum" and prepares it for shipping.

Cost: Adults, $4; children under 18 (drinking age), $1.

Freebies: Small samples in bar area of different types of mixed drinks, such as a Cruzan Rum Piña Colada.

Video/DVD Shown: An illustrated board lights up at each step along production process, accompanied by audio explanation.

Reservations Needed: Groups over 20 people should call at least 1 day ahead.

Days and Hours: Mon–Fri 9:00 AM–11:30 AM and 1:00–4:15 PM. Closed major holidays.

Plan to Stay: 20 minutes for walking tour, plus time for rum samples.

Minimum Age: None

Disabled Access: Stairs throughout complex.

Group Requirements: Reservations requested for large groups.

Special Information: For some visitors, the smells can be overpowering.

Gift Shop: Sells duty-free Cruzan rum and rum cakes; logoed items, including T-shirts, golf shirts, caps, pennants, flags, and shot glasses. Logoed items can be ordered from website above.

Directions: From Christiansted, take Rt. 70 West. Get on Hwy 66 (Melvin Evans Hwy.). Pass airport. Make right onto Rt. 64 West. Distillery is a quarter mile up the road on the right. There is a Cruzan Rum sign at entrance.

Nearby Attractions: St. George Village Botanical Gardens (340-692-2874); Whim Sugar Cane Plantation (340-772-0598); Fort Christianvaern; beaches; rainforest; national park.

Tortuga Rum Cake

Tortuga Rum Avenue, Industrial Park,
George Town, Grand Cayman,
Cayman Islands, B.W.I.

(345) 949-7701
(345) 949-CAKE

www.tortugarums.com

TORTUGA RUM CO. LTD.

After you spend your time scuba diving, lounging on the beaches, and perusing the shops in George Town, you can visit the factory that makes the Cayman Island's No. 1 export. While rum cakes have a long history in the Caribbean, Tortuga Rum Company is the first to commercially market these delicious treats. The founders, Carlene and Robert Hamaty, first baked them from home in 1987 using a 100-year-old family recipe. Now their growing enterprise features a 10,000-square-foot headquarters with a state-of-the-art bakery. It prides itself on plentiful free samples and big observation windows to see the baking, glazing, and packing process.

This facility is able to produce between 8,000 and 10,000 Tortuga Rum Cakes each day in seven flavors and three sizes: the 32-oz. large size, the 16-oz. medium size, and the 4-oz. mini. Listen to the live steel drum band playing in the background, while you admire the big revolving ovens that bake 52 sheet pans at a time. The pans look like they are going on a Ferris wheel ride up and around the oven. Their path in the oven takes one and a half hours at 350°F. The bakers gingerly remove the pans, hand glaze the tops with five-year-old premium rum, turn the cakes upside down, and place them on metal trolleys.

The cakes then spend at least two hours in the sterile cooling room. Notice the vacuum machine used to seal the cakes. Its two chambers force out the air from around the cake, wrap it, and preserve the cake's freshness without using chemicals. This vacuum-sealing process ensures a shelf life of six months (indefinitely if refrigerated or frozen). Quick hands put the cakes into individual boxes before another machine shrink-wraps them. The boxed cakes travel through the tunnel and into even bigger boxes for shipment around the world.

Cost: Free

Freebies: Cake samples and fruit punch.

Video/DVD Shown: 3-minute video about the company history, rum making, and cake production.

Reservations Needed: No, except for special groups requesting tour guide.

Days and Hours: Mon–Fri 7:00 AM–5:00 PM and Sat 7:00 AM–2:00 PM. Sunday when cruise ship in port. Closed Cayman Islands' public holidays, unless cruise ship in port.

Plan to Stay: 10 minutes, plus time for the grounds and gift shop.

Minimum Age: None

Disabled Access: Yes

Group Requirements: No maximum group size. Organized tours that want a guide should call 1 week ahead. Bus tours through cruise ships include guide.

Special Information: Eventually may be able to view the mixing area. Landscaped grounds for picnics, with local antique windmills, 300-year-old cannons (from the shipwreck of the *Ten Sails*), tropical birds, and other ancient artifacts.

Gift Shop: Sells over a dozen varieties of Tortuga Rum and other brands (this is largest duty-free liquor business in the Cayman Islands, including specially blended rums made in Jamaica, Barbados, and Guyana), Tortuga Rum specialty foods, including coffee and sauces. Also sells standard island souvenirs, "Caribbean Rhythms" music, and rum cakes in all 7 flavors: golden original, chocolate, Blue Mountain coffee, banana rum, coconut, pineapple, and key lime. Smaller Tortuga bakeries in West Bay near the Turtle Farm and in downtown George Town; franchise bakeries in Jamaica, Barbados, and the Bahamas. Except for the rum, can order from website above.

Directions: On North Sound Rd., follow signs for Airport from Seven Mile Beach. You will see from North Sound Rd. the complex on the right, with ornate wrought-iron gates and the big company sign.

Nearby Attractions: Well-known beach and water attractions; Island Glassblowing Studio (call 345-946-1483); Stingray Beer (call 345-947-6699); Cayman Turtle Farm (call 345-949-3893).

Day-Trip Itinerary Planner

We suggest that you use a detailed map of the region you are visiting and plan your trip carefully. AAA offers members a route-planning service, highlighting the best roads and highways that lead to your destination. Also, www.mapquest. com provides planning assistance, including directions, estimated travel time, and rest stops along your route. Google Maps (http://maps. google.com) offers a similar service and also pairs each map with a satellite image of the area the map covers. This allows you to actually see an aerial photograph of a particular street, intersection, or highway exit, providing a better sense of local conditions. We also suggest calling the destinations to verify times and directions between locations.

Atlanta's Pride

CNN (television news), page 235.

World of Coca-Cola Atlanta (soda), page 237.

Chicago Area for Fun

Eli's Cheesecake World (cheesecake) in Chicago, page 152.

Haeger Potteries (artwork pottery) in East Dundee, page 154.

Long Grove Confectionery Company (chocolate) in Buffalo Grove, page 157.

Chicago on Business

(Try to squeeze one in during your next trip.)

Chicago Board of Trade (grain and financial futures and options), page 149. (See the Nearby Attractions under Chicago Board of Trade for more sites related to finance.)

Chicago Mercantile Exchange (agricultural and financial futures), page 150.

U.S. Post Office (mail), page 160.

Traveling to or from O'Hare International Airport:

McDonald's #1 Store Museum (fast food) in Des Plaines, page 158.

Dallas/Fort Worth Area's Big Business and Government

Bureau of Printing and Engraving (U.S. paper money) in Fort Worth, page 301.

JCPenney Museum (retail stores and catalogs) in Plano, page 305.

Mary Kay (cosmetics and skin-care products) in Addison, page 307.

Traveling to or from Dallas/Fort Worth Airport:

American Airlines C. R. Smith Museum (air travel) in Fort Worth, page 299.

Detroit Transportation

Ford Rouge Factory Tour (cars and trucks) in Dearborn, page 174.

Henry Ford Museum and Greenfield Village (U.S. manufacturing and cars) in Dearborn, page 175.

Lionel (model trains and accessories) in Chesterfield, page 179.

Fort Wayne Food

(David Letterman's home state, Indiana)

Aunt Millie's (bread), page 162.

Sechler's (pickles) in St. Joe, page 168.

Kona Coffee Hawaii

Holualoa Kona Coffee in Holualoa, page 399.

Ueshima Coffee in Captain Cook, page 402.

Kona Coffee County driving tour map available from the Kona-Kohala Chamber of Commerce; see Nearby Attractions under both listings.

Las Vegas—Beyond the Casinos

Ethel M Chocolates (chocolates) in Henderson, page 315.

Shelby Automobiles (sports cars), page 316.

Louisville Charm

American Printing House for the Blind (Braille and large-type publications, audio books, and educational aids), page 238.

Colonel Harland Sanders Museum (fast food), page 239.

Louisville Slugger Museum (baseball bats), page 246; see color photos, pages 36–37.

Louisville Stoneware (pottery), page 247.

Minnesota—Winter Sports

Arctic Cat (snowmobiles and all-terrain vehicles) in Thief River Falls, page 184.

Christian Brothers (hockey sticks) in Warroad, page 185

Polaris (snowmobiles, all-terrain vehicles, and personal watercraft) in Roseau, page 187.

New York City on Business

(Try to squeeze in at least one during your next trip)

CNN New York (television news), page 105.

NBC Studios (television programs), page 111.

Sony Wonder Technology Lab (electronics), page 115.

Traveling to or from LaGuardia Airport:

Steinway & Sons (pianos) in Long Island City, page 116.

Northern Indiana— RV Capital of the World

Coachmen in Middlebury, page 164.

Monaco in Wakarusa, page 167.

Jayco in Middlebury, page 165.

RV/MH Heritage Foundation Museum and local Convention & Visitors Bureau lists other RV company tours (see Nearby Attractions under Monaco).

Northern Michigan— Chocolates and Cherries

Amon Orchards (cherries and cherry products) in Acme, page 171.

Kilwin's Chocolates (fudge, chocolates, and ice cream) in Petoskey, page 178.

Oregon Coast

Country Coach (luxury motorcoach) in Junction City, page 336.

Oregon Connection/House of Myrtlewood (wooden tableware and golf putters) in Coos Bay, page 340.

Tillamook Cheese (cheese) in Tillamook, page 343.

Traveling to or from Portland:

Golden West Billiards (pool tables) in Portland, page 338.

Rodgers Instruments (electronic and electronic-pipe combination organs) in Hillsboro, page 342.

The Guest Relations Association (GRA) is an organization for companies across all industries who host visitors through some type of unique experience in the form of a tour of their museum, factory or visitor center. The authors appreciate the GRA's support for *Watch It Made in the U.S.A.*

GRA Members included in *Watch It Made in the U.S.A.* with tours or museums open to the general public:

- Alticor – Ada, MI (see page 170)
- Andersen Windows – Bayport, MN (see page 183)
- Anheuser-Busch – St. Louis, MO and Merrimack, NH (see pages 284 and 77)
- Ben & Jerry's – Waterbury, VT (see page 82)
- Blue Ox – Eureka, CA (see page 358)
- Buffalo Trace Distillery – Frankfort, KY (see page 240)
- Caterpillar – Peoria, IL (see page 148)
- Celestial Seasonings – Boulder, CO (see page 322)
- Coors – Golden, CO (see page 324)
- Corvette – Bowling Green, KY (see page 244)
- The Crayola FACTORY – Easton, PA (see page 122)
- Guide Dogs for the Blind – San Rafael, CA (see page 366)
- Hallmark Visitors Center – Kansas City, MO (see page 286)
- Hammond's Candies Since 1920 – Denver, CO (see page 325)
- Harley-Davidson Motor Company – York, PA, Kansas City, MO, Wauwatosa, WI (see pages 123, 287 and 208)
- Herr's Snack Factory Tour – Nottingham, PA (see page 124)
- Hershey's Chocolate World – Hershey, PA (see page 125)
- Hope Acres – Brogue, PA (see page 126)
- Hyundai Motor Manufacturing Alabama – Montgomery, AL (see page 222)
- Jack Daniel's Distillery – Lynchburg, TN (see page 273)
- Jelly Belly Candy Co. – Fairfield, CA and Pleasant Prairie, WI (see pages 369 and 211)
- John Deere Pavilion – Moline, IL (see page 156)
- Kellogg's Cereal City USA – Battle Creek, MI (see page 177)
- Kohler – Kohler, WI (see page 212)
- Longaberger – Newark, OH (see page 200)
- Long Grove – Buffalo Grove, IL (see page 157)
- Louisville Slugger Museum – Louisville, KY (see page 246)
- Maker's Mark Distillery – Loretto, KY (see page 248)
- Martin Guitar – Nazareth, PA (see page 128)
- Miller Brewing – Milwaukee, WI (see page 213)
- Purina Farms – Gray Summit, MO (see page 288)
- QVC – West Chester, PA (see page 129)
- SC Johnson – Racine, WI (see page 216)
- SPAM Museum – Austin, MN (see page 188)
- Stora Enso – Wisconsin Rapids, WI (see page 217)
- Sweet Candy – Salt Lake City, UT (see page 320)
- Toyota – Georgetown, KY (see page 253)
- Velvet Ice Cream – Utica, OH (see page 204)
- Vermont Teddy Bear – Shelburne, VT (see page 92)
- Wells Fargo – San Francisco, CA (see page 389)
- Wolfgang Candy – York, PA (see page 137)
- World of Coca Cola – Atlanta, GA (see page 237)

For more information about the guest relations association visit www.guestrelationsassociation.org

Company Index

Walter P. Chrysler Museum:181
Walter Piano: 169
Warner Bros. Studios: 388
Washington's Fruit Place Visitor Center: 353
Weaver's: *see Affinity*
Wells Fargo: 389
Wendell August Forge: 136
Weyerhaeuser: 344
Wheaton Village: 102
Whetstone Chocolates: 234
White Flower Farm: 59
Wiebe Farms: 390

Wild Turkey: 254
Williamsburg Doll Factory: 141
Williamsburg Pottery Factory: 142
Winnebago Industries: 54–55, 281
Wisconsin Dairy State Cheese: 219
Wolfgang Candy: 137
World of Coca-Cola Atlanta: 237

XYZ

Yankee Candle: 76
Yuengling: 138
Zippo/Case Visitors Center: 139

Product Index

Agriculture, Equipment

Baltimore Museum of Industry: 96
Caterpillar: 148
Henry Ford Museum and Greenfield Village: 175
John Deere: 155, 279
John Deere Pavilion: 32–33, 156

Agriculture, Farms

(see also Coffee)
Amon Orchards: 171
Dole Pineapple Plantation: 397
Gay & Robinson Sugar Plantation: 398
Idaho Potato Expo: 330
Kliebert's Turtle and Alligator Tours: 256
Lane Packing: 236
Musk Ox Farm: 395
Pelindaba Lavender Farm: 349
Purina Farms: 288
Three Chimneys: 252
Washington's Fruit Place Visitor Center: 353
White Flower Farm: 59
Wiebe Farms: 390

Airplanes and Spacecraft

American Airlines C. R. Smith Museum: 299
Aviat Aircraft: 333
Boeing: 285, 346
Jet Propulsion Laboratory: 370
Kennedy Space Center: 231
New Piper Aircraft: 232

Animal Care and Services

Guide Dogs for the Blind: 366
Hoegh Industries: 176
Kliebert's Turtle and Alligator Tours: 256
Magic Wings Butterfly Conservatory & Gardens: 73
Musk Ox Farm: 395
Pipestem Creek: 291
Purina Farms: 288
Three Chimneys: 252

Animated Figures

Blaine Kern's Mardi Gras World: 255
Creegan: 194
Magic of Disney Animation, The: 227
Sally Corporation: 233

Arts and Crafts

(see also China, Cothing and Textiles, Glass, Metal Crafts, Pottery)
Blue Ox Millworks and Historic Park: 358
Byers' Choice Ltd.: 120–121
Churchill Weavers: 242–243
Crayola FACTORY, The: 8–9, 122
Hampshire Pewter: 78
Longaberger: 200
Mrs. Grossman's: 376:
Musk Oxen: 395
Pipestem Creek: 291
Salisbury Pewter: 99
Simplicity Pattern: 180
Wheaton Village: 102

Athletic Equipment

(see Sports and Athletic Equipment)

Automobiles

(see also Motorcycles, Trucks, Recreational Vehicles)
Bill Davis Racing: 264
BMW: 270
Corvette: 244
Ford: 245
Ford Rouge Factory Tour: 174
General Motors: 207
GM Spring Hill Manufacturing: 272
Henry Ford Museum and Greenfield Village: 175
Hyundai Motor Manufacturing Alabama: 26–27, 222
Mercedes-Benz: 224–225
Mitsubishi Motors North America: 159
National Corvette Museum: 249
New United Motor Manufacturing Inc.: 378
Nissan: 275
Shelby Automobiles: 316

Jelly Belly: 211, 369
Kilwin's Chocolates: 178
Liberty Orchards: 347
Long Grove Confectionery Company:
 34–35, 157
Malley's Chocolates: 201
Mauna Loa: 401
Moore's Candies: 98
Old Kentucky Candies: 250
Peanut Patch: 313
Quality Candy/Buddy Squirrel: 215
Rebecca-Ruth Candies: 46–47, 251
Scharffen Berger: 381
Sherm Edwards: 131
Sweet Candy Company: 320
Whetstone Chocolates: 234
Wolfgang Candy: 137

Carousels
Carousel Magic!: 193
New England Carousel Museum: 58

Cheese
Cabot Creamery: 83
Carr Valley Cheese: 206
Crowley Cheese: 84
Grafton Village Cheese: 85
Marin French Cheese: 375
Tillamook Cheese: 343
Wisconsin Dairy State Cheese: 219

China
Byers' Choice Ltd.: 120–121
Homer Laughlin China: 145
Replacements, Ltd.: 267

Chocolates
see Candy and Chocolates

Cigars
Gonzalez y Martínez: 229

Clothing and Textiles
Allen-Edmonds: 205
American Textile History Museum: 65
Baltimore Museum of Industry: 96

Churchill Weavers: 242–243
DeKlomp/Veldheer: 173
Faribault Woolen Mills: 186
Levi Strauss & Co.: 373
Manny Gammage's Texas Hatters: 306
Pendleton Woolen Mills: 341
Simplicity Pattern: 180

Coffee
Green Mountain Coffee Roasters: 86
Holualoa Kona Coffee: 399
Ueshima Coffee: 402
Vashon Island Coffee Roasterie, The: 352

Computers and Electronics
Edison National Historic Site: 100
Intel: 28–29, 368
Microsoft Visitor Center: 248
Peavey Electronics: 262
Sony Wonder Technology Lab: 115

Dolls
Lee Middleton Original Dolls: 139
Williamsburg Doll Factory: 141

Fast Food
Colonel Harland Sanders Museum (KFC):
 239
McDonald's #1 Store Museum: 158

Food
(see also Breads and Baked Goods, Candy
 and Chocolates, Cheese, Fast Food, Fruit
 and Nuts, Ice Cream)
Affinity: 289
Alaska Wild Berry Products: 393
Baltimore Museum of Industry: 96
Cape Cod Potato Chips: 68
Gay & Robinson Sugar Plantation: 398
Graber Olive House: 365
Great American Popcorn Company/Rocky
 Mountain Chocolate Factory: 153
Harry and David: 339
Herr's Snack Factory Tour: 22–25, 124
Honey Acres: 210

Louisville Stoneware: 247
Seagrove Area Potteries: 268
Simon Pearce: 90–91
Sioux Pottery and Crafts: 296
Van Briggle: 328
Williamsburg Pottery Factory: 142

Recreational Vehicles
Airstream: 190
Coachmen: 164
Country Coach: 336
Fleetwood: 362
Jayco: 30–31, 165
Monaco Coach Corporation: 167
Winnebago Industries: 54–55, 281

Retail Stores
JCPenney Museum: 305
Wal-Mart Visitors Center: 278

Snomobiles
Arctic Cat: 184
Polaris: 187

Spacecraft
see Airplanes and Spacecraft

Sports and Athletic Equipment
Bill Davis Racing: 264
Callaway Golf: 361
Cannondale: 119
Christian Brothers: 185
Golden West Billiards: 338
Louisville Slugger Museum: 36–37, 246

Nocona Athletic: 309
Oregon Connection, The / House of Myrtle-wood: 340
Orvis: 88
Ping Golf Equipment: 314
Trek Bicycles: 218
U.S. Olympic Training Center: 327

Teddy Bears
Basic Brown Bear Factory: 6–7, 357
Vermont Teddy Bear: 92

Toys
(see also Dolls, Teddy Bears)
Kazoo Boutique: 110
Legoland: 372
Lionel: 179

Trucks
E-ONE: 228
Ford: 245
General Motors: 207
International: 197
Mack Trucks: 127
New United Motor Manufacturing Inc.: 378
Nissan: 275

U.S. Forest Service
Smokejumper Visitor Center: 332

Wood
see Paper and Wood

Acknowledgments

Special 4th Edition Acknowledgments

The fourth edition would never have happened without Matt Simon. His consistent writing and editorial efforts were invaluable! We appreciate his reliability, high standards, and calmness. Every time effort was needed in the writing, research, editing, or fact checking, Matt willingly took charge and excelled. Tom Mollerus provided computer technical assistance and ideas. Tamar Zaidenweber eagerly pitched in when her schedule permitted. The website www.factorytourusa.com was a resource for discovering new tours.

Our daughter, Hilary, is starting her budding writing career with the new "For Kids by Kids" section in this edition. Our son, Gregory, enjoyed visiting candy tours best and provided other interesting insights.

We thank everyone at Avalon Travel Publishing for facilitating the process of updating this book!

Prior Editions Acknowledgments

First and foremost, we want to thank the companies that provide tours and museums, and also the people at those businesses who met with us, answered our numerous questions, verified the accuracy of our information, and gave us encouragement. The firms that open their doors to the public have stories to tell about their place in America's heritage and in its economic future. Convention and visitors bureaus, state tourism boards, and chambers of commerce gave us information and materials, which we appreciated.

Twenty-five years ago this book wouldn't have been needed, as just about all companies gave public tours. Now many forces, including budget cuts, insurance rates, trade-secret protection, government regulations, and physical security concerns have caused companies to end them. Fortunately, a trend has emerged toward opening new visitors centers and company museums as an alternative to factory tours.

Since this was a very expensive book to research, write, and produce, we also specially thank those companies with photographs in the book. No company paid for its inclusion in *Watch It Made in the U.S.A.* or for the publishing of its logo. Companies did pay a modest fee to include black-and-white or color photos. Without this small amount of funding the book either would not have been published or its purchase price would have been far beyond what the average person spends for a travel book.

We enjoyed the support from our parents, Elaine and Norman Brumberg (actually, Bruce's parents became supportive when we were researching the first edition after we gave his dad a Harley-Davidson T-shirt and his mom T-shirts from Ben & Jerry's and Wild Turkey), and Harriet and David Axelrod (Karen's mother's love of travel inspired us both to do this book; we wish she were alive to see it in print); strength from our grandmother Franziska Hirschhorn (we miss her dearly); and continued guidance and encouragement from our aunt and uncle, Erika and Larry Casler. Elaine Brumberg and Larry Casler set good examples for us, as they have written books of their own.

For the third edition, Kristin Odmark provided pre-game scheduling and ongoing emotional support. Elizabeth Hunt independently pitched the first five innings, working full-time to update the information for most of the existing companies in the book and writing some of the new features. Willa Mueller came in for the last few innings, and diligently coordinated the new companies and the photographs along with the never-ending details. Cheerfully Mariana Agathokolis and Johanna McKenzie pitched in with thorough assistance to complete the manuscript and wrote a few features. Valerie Dumova provided consistent, steady writing support. Other people who helped write a few features are Kathryn Kaplan, Ilyse Kramer, and Mark Malseed.

Other folks who helped us (in alphabetical order) include Harriet Brumberg, Andy Cavatorta, Scott Dimetrosky (who initially developed our website, www.factorytour.com), Sam Donisi, Susan Koffman, Pam Kubbins, Jeanne Lothrop, Amy and Mark Seiden, Judith Woodruff, and Howard Zaharoff.

Unfortunately, we could not list all those friends, relatives, writers, and editorial assistants who helped with research, writing, editing, and word processing and who provided general advice, support, and ideas for all the editions—but we do express our heartfelt appreciation to all of them.